PHP Programming with MySQL

Don Gosselin

THOMSON
COURSE TECHNOLOGY

Australia • Canada • Mexico • Singapore • Spain • United Kingdom • United States

PHP Programming with MySQL

by Don Gosselin

Senior Acquisitions Editor:
Maureen Martin

Product Manager:
Beth Paquin

Development Editor:
Ann Shaffer

Marketing Manager:
Karen Seitz

Associate Product Manager:
Jennifer Smith

Editorial Assistant:
Allison Murphy

Manufacturing Coordinator:
Justin Palmeiro

Production Editor:
Summer Hughes

Copy Editor:
Karen Annett

Proofreader:
Harold Johnson

Indexer:
Sharon Hilgenberg

Cover Design:
Steven Deschene

Compositor:
Gex Publishing Services

Printed in the United States of America

1 2 3 4 5 6 7 8 9 CS 09 08 07 06 05

For more information, contact Thomson Course Technology, 25 Thomson Place, Boston, Massachusetts, 02210.

Or find us on the World Wide Web at: www.course.com

TABLE OF

Contents

CHAPTER TEN
Managing State Information 477

CHAPTER ELEVEN
Developing Object-Oriented PHP 525

APPENDIX C
Processing XML 647

APPENDIX D
Secure Coding with PHP 663

Preface

PHP: Hypertext Preprocessor, or PHP, is an open-source programming language that is used for developing interactive Web sites. More specifically, PHP is a scripting language that is executed from a Web server. First created in 1995, the language is one of today's fastest-growing programming languages. One of the primary reasons for PHP's popularity has to do with its simplicity. The language is relatively easy to learn, allowing non-programmers to quickly incorporate PHP functionality into a Web site. MySQL is an open-source relational database that is often used with PHP. Together, PHP and MySQL are quickly turning into one of the most popular technology combinations for Web site development.

PHP Programming with MySQL teaches Web development with PHP and MySQL for students with little programming or database experience. Although no prior programming or database experience is required, a knowledge of HTML and Web page design is helpful. This book covers the basics of PHP and MySQL along with advanced topics including object-oriented programming and how to build Web sites that incorporate authentication and security. After you complete this course, you will be able to use PHP and MySQL to build professional quality, database-driven Web sites.

The Approach

This book introduces a variety of techniques, focusing on what you need to know to start writing PHP scripts. In each chapter, you perform tasks that let you use a particular technique to build and create PHP scripts. In addition to step-by-step tasks, each chapter includes a Chapter Summary, Review Questions, Hands-on Projects, and Case Projects that highlight major concepts and let you practice the techniques you learn. The Hands-on Projects are guided activities that reinforce the skills you learn in the chapter and build on your learning experience by providing additional ways to apply your knowledge in new situations. At the end of each chapter, you will also complete Case Projects that let you use the skills you learned in the chapter to write PHP scripts on your own.

Overview of This Book

The examples and exercises in this book will help you achieve the following objectives:

- Learn how to use PHP with well-formed Web pages
- Install and configure a Web server, PHP, and MySQL
- Understand PHP variables and data types and the operations that can be performed on them

- Add functions and control structures to your PHP scripts
- Use PHP to manipulate strings
- Access files and directories with PHP
- Use PHP to manipulate data in arrays
- Work with databases and MySQL
- Manipulate MySQL databases with PHP
- Save state information using hidden form fields, query strings, cookies, and sessions
- Include object-oriented programming techniques in your PHP scripts
- Learn techniques and tools that you can use to trace and resolve errors in PHP scripts

PHP Programming with MySQL presents 12 chapters that cover specific aspects of PHP and MySQL Web development. **Chapter 1** discusses basic concepts of the World Wide Web, introduces XHTML documents, and covers the basics of Web development. **Chapter 2** contains detailed instructions on how to install, configure, and test a Web server, the PHP software, and the MySQL relational database management system. Variables, data types, expressions, and operators are discusses in **Chapter 3**. This early introduction of key PHP concepts gives students a framework for better understanding more advanced concepts and techniques later in this book, and allows them to work on more comprehensive projects from the start. **Chapter 4** covers functions and introduces structured logic using control structures and statements. **Chapter 5** discusses techniques for manipulating strings and processing form data with PHP. **Chapter 6** explains how to read and store data in text files on a local computer. **Chapter 7** covers advanced techniques for working with indexed and associative arrays. **Chapter 8** introduces how to work with MySQL databases while **Chapter 9** discusses techniques for manipulating MySQL databases with PHP. **Chapter 10** explains how to save state information using hidden form fields, query strings, cookies, and sessions. **Chapter 11** presents basic object-oriented programming techniques that you can use in your PHP scripts. **Chapter 12** provides a thorough discussion of debugging techniques and tools that you can use to trace and resolve errors in PHP scripts.

Features

PHP is a superior textbook because it also includes the following features:

- **Chapter Objectives**: Each chapter in this book begins with a list of the important concepts to be mastered within the chapter. This list provides you with a quick reference to the contents of the chapter as well as a useful study aid.
- **Illustrations and Tables**: Illustrations help you visualize common components and relationships. Tables list conceptual items and examples in a visual and readable format.
- **Tips**: These helpful asides provide you with practical advice and proven strategies related to the concept being discussed.

- **Notes**: Notes provide additional helpful information on specific techniques and concepts.
- **Cautions**: These short warnings point out troublesome issues that you need to watch out for when writing PHP scripts.
- **Chapter Summaries**: These brief overviews of chapter content provide a helpful way to recap and revisit the ideas covered in each chapter.
- **Review Questions**: This set of 20 review questions reinforces the main ideas introduced in each chapter. These questions help determine whether or not you have mastered the concepts covered in the chapter.
- **Hands-on Projects**: Although it is important to understand the concepts behind PHP programming, no amount of theory can improve on real-world experience. To this end, along with conceptual explanations, each chapter provides Hands-on Projects related to each major topic aimed at providing you with practical experience. Because the Hands-on Projects ask you to go beyond the boundaries of the text itself, they provide you with practice implementing PHP skills in real-world situations.
- **Case Projects**: The Case Projects at the end of each chapter are designed to help you apply what you have learned to business situations much like those you can expect to encounter as a PHP programmer. They give you the opportunity to independently synthesize and evaluate information, examine potential solutions, and make recommendations, much as you would in an actual programming situation.

Teaching Tools

The following supplemental materials are available when this book is used in a classroom setting. All of the teaching tools available with this book are provided to the instructor on a single CD-ROM.

- **Electronic Instructor's Manual**. The Instructor's Manual that accompanies this textbook includes:
  - Additional instructional material to assist in class preparation, including suggestions for lecture topics. It is critical for the instructor to be able to help the students understand how to use the help resources and how to identify problems. The Instructor's Manual will help you identify areas that are more difficult to teach, and provide you with ideas of how to present the material in an easier fashion.
  - Solutions to all end-of-chapter materials, including the Review Questions, and when applicable, Hands-on Projects and Case Projects.
- **ExamView®**. This textbook is accompanied by ExamView, a powerful testing software package that allows instructors to create and administer printed, computer (LAN-based), and Internet exams. ExamView includes hundreds of questions that correspond to the topics covered in this text, enabling students to generate detailed study guides that include page references for further review. The computer-based

and Internet testing components allow students to take exams at their computers, and also save the instructor time by grading each exam automatically.

- **PowerPoint Presentations.** This book comes with Microsoft PowerPoint slides for each chapter. These are included as a teaching aid for classroom presentation, to make available to students on the network for chapter review, or to be printed for classroom distribution. Instructors can add their own slides for additional topics they introduce to the class.
- **Data Files.** Files that contain all of the data necessary for the Hands-on Projects and Case Projects are provided through the Course Technology Web site at www.course.com, and are also available on the Teaching Tools CD-ROM.
- **Solution Files.** Solutions to end-of-chapter Review Questions, Hands-on Projects, and Case Projects are provided on the Teaching Tools CD-ROM and may also be found on the Course Technology Web site at *http://www.course.com*. The solutions are password protected.
- **Distance Learning.** Course Technology is proud to present online test banks in WebCT and Blackboard, as well as MyCourse 2.0, Course Technology's own course enhancement tool, to provide the most complete and dynamic learning experience possible. Instructors are encouraged to make the most of the course, both online and offline. For more information on how to access your online test bank, contact your local Course Technology sales representative.

Acknowledgements

A text such as this represents the hard work of many people, not just the author. I would like to thank all the people who helped make this book a reality. First and foremost, I would like to thank Ann Shaffer, Development Editor, Beth Paquin, Product Manager, and Maureen Martin, Senior Acquisitions Editor, for helping me get the job done. I would also like to thank Summer Hughes, Production Editor, Chris Scriver, QA Manager, Susan Whalen, QA Tester, Danielle Shaw, QA Tester, and Shawn Day, QA Tester.

Many, many thanks to the reviewers who provided plenty of comments and positive direction during the development of this book: Zehai Zhou, Dakota State University; Stu Steiner, Eastern Washington University; Jennifer Rosato, College of St. Scholastica; Lynn Aaron, Rockland Community College; and Karmen Blake, Spokane Community College.

On the personal side, I would like to thank my family and friends for supporting me in my career; I don't see many of you nearly as often as I'd like, but you are always in my thoughts. I would also like to thank Jeremy Chone and Peter Atkins for putting up with my constant and annoying questions about technical issues. My most important thanks always goes to my wonderful wife Kathy for her never ending support and encouragement, and to my dog Noah for helping my lower my blood pressure.

Read This Before You Begin

The following information will help you as you prepare to use this textbook.

To the User of the Data Files

To complete the steps and projects in this book, you will need data files that have been created specifically for this book. The data files are located on the CD-ROM that came with this book. You also can obtain the files electronically from the Course Technology Web site by connecting to *www.course.com* and then searching for this book title. Note that you can use a computer in your school lab or your own computer to complete the steps and Hands-on Projects in this book.

Using Your Own Computer

You can use a computer in your school lab or your own computer to complete the chapters, Hands-on Projects, and Case Projects in this book. To use your own computer, you will need the following:

- **A Web browser**, such as Microsoft Internet Explorer 6.0 or later or Mozilla Firefox 1.0 or later.
- **A code-based HTML editor**, such as Macromedia Dreamweaver, or a text editor such as Notepad on Windows, GNU Emacs on UNIX/Linux, or SimpleText on the Macintosh.
- **A Web server**, such as Apache HTTP Server or Microsoft Internet Information Services.
- **PHP 5 or later**. PHP is a server-side scripting language that is developed by the PHP Group (*http://www.php.net*).
- **MySQL 4.1 or later**. MySQL is an open source database developed by MySQL AB (*http://www.mysql.com/*)

Chapter 2 contains detailed instructions on how to install a Web server, PHP and MySQL.

To the Instructor

To complete all the exercises and chapters in this book, your users must work with a set of user files, called data files, and download software from Web sites. The data files are located on the CD-ROM that came with this book and are also included in the Instructor's Resource Kit. They may also be obtained electronically through the Course Technology Web site at *www.course.com*. Have students follow the instructions in Chapter 1 to install the data files.

Course Technology Data Files

You are granted a license to copy the data files to any computer or computer network used by individuals who have purchased this book.

Visit Our World Wide Web Site

Additional materials designed especially for this book might be available for your course. Periodically search *www.course.com* for more information and materials to accompany this text.

CHAPTER

1

INTRODUCTION TO WEB DEVELOPMENT

In this chapter, you will:

- Study the history of the World Wide Web
- Review the basics of how to create Web pages
- Work with structured Web pages
- Study Web development

The original purpose of the World Wide Web (WWW) was to locate and display information. However, after the Web grew beyond a small academic and scientific community, people began to recognize that greater interactivity would make the Web more useful. As commercial applications of the Web grew, the demand for more interactive and visually appealing Web sites also grew.

But how would Web developers respond to this demand? One solution was the development of JavaScript, which is a client-side scripting language that you, as a programmer, can use to create interactive features within a Web page. However, JavaScript only works within a Web page that runs in a Web browser. Yet, a Web browser is a client in the client/server environment of the Web. Because JavaScript only works within a Web browser, it cannot take advantage of the server side of the Web. To develop fully interactive Web sites that access databases on a server, and perform advanced e-commerce operations such as online transactions, you must use a server-side scripting language such as PHP. Combined with the MySQL database, PHP is one of today's most popular technologies for Web site development.

In this chapter, you learn the basics of Web development. To be successful as a Web developer and in your PHP studies, you should already possess a strong knowledge of HTML and Web page authoring techniques. The first part of this chapter provides a quick refresher on the history of the World Wide Web and the basic aspects of how to create Web pages with HTML and its successor, XHTML. Even if you are highly experienced with HTML, you might not be familiar with the formal terminology that is used in Web page authoring. For this reason, be certain to read the first part of this chapter to ensure that you understand the terminology used in this book.

To learn the most current Web page authoring techniques, refer to Don Gosselin's *XHTML*, also published by Course Technology.

THE WORLD WIDE WEB

The Internet is a vast network that connects computers all over the world. The original plans for the Internet grew out of a series of memos written by J. C. R. Licklider of Massachusetts Institute of Technology (MIT) in August 1962 discussing his concept of a "Galactic Network." Licklider envisioned a global computer network through which users could access data and programs from any site on the network. The Internet was actually developed in the 1960s by the Advanced Research Projects Agency (or ARPA) of the U.S. Department of Defense to connect the main computer systems of various universities and research institutions that were funded by ARPA. This first implementation of the Internet was referred to as the ARPANET. More computers were connected to the ARPANET in the years following its initial development in the 1960s, although access to the ARPANET was still restricted by the U.S. government primarily to academic researchers, scientists, and the military.

Contrary to a persistent false rumor, the ARPANET was not originally designed as a communications network capable of surviving a nuclear attack. That rumor comes from a separate study on communications networks done by the RAND Corporation that did consider the threat of nuclear attack. The RAND study was completed prior to the development of the ARPANET.

The 1980s saw the widespread development of local area networks (LANs) and the personal computer. Although at one time restricted to academia and the military, computers and networks soon became common in business and everyday life. By the end of the 1980s, businesses and individual computer users began to recognize the global communications capabilities and potential of the Internet and convinced the U.S. government to allow commercial access to the Internet.

In 1990 and 1991, Tim Berners-Lee created what would become the **World Wide Web**, or the **Web**, at the European Laboratory for Particle Physics (CERN) in Geneva, Switzerland, as a way to easily access cross-referenced documents that existed on the

CERN computer network. When other academics and scientists saw the usefulness of being able to easily access cross-referenced documents using Berners-Lee's system, the Web as we know it today was born. In fact, this method of accessing cross-referenced documents, known as **hypertext linking**, is probably the most important aspect of the Web because it allows you to quickly open other Web pages. A **hypertext link**, or **hyperlink**, contains a reference to a specific Web page that you can click to open that Web page.

If you want to learn more about the history of the Internet, the Internet Society (ISOC) maintains a list of links to Internet histories at *http://www.isoc.org/internet/history/*.

A common misconception is that the words "Web" and "Internet" are synonymous. However, the Web is only one *part* of the Internet, and is a means of communicating on the Internet. The Internet is also composed of other communication methods such as e-mail systems that send and receive messages. However, due to its enormous influence on computing, communications, and the economy, the World Wide Web is arguably the most important part of the Internet today and is the primary focus of this book.

A document on the Web is called a **Web page** and is identified by a unique address called the **Uniform Resource Locator**, or **URL**. A URL is also commonly referred to as a **Web address**. A URL is a type of **Uniform Resource Identifier** (**URI**), which is a generic term for many types of names and addresses on the World Wide Web. The term **Web site** refers to the location on the Internet of the Web pages and related files (such as graphic files) that belong to a company, organization, or individual. You display a Web page on your computer screen using a program called a **Web browser**. A person can retrieve and open a Web page in a Web browser either by entering a URL in the Web browser's Address box or by clicking a hypertext link. When a user wants to access a Web page, either by entering its URL in a browser's Address box or by clicking a link, the user's Web browser asks a Web server for the Web page in what is referred to as a **request**. A **Web server** is a computer that delivers Web pages. What the Web server returns to the user is called the **response**. You can turn a computer into a Web server by installing Web server software on it. The most popular Web server software used on the Internet is Apache HTTP Server (typically referred to as Apache), which is used by more than half of today's Web sites. The second most popular Web server is Microsoft Internet Information Services (IIS) for Windows operating systems, which is used on about one-third of today's Web sites.

HTML Documents

Originally, people created Web pages using Hypertext Markup Language. **Hypertext Markup Language**, or **HTML**, is a markup language used to create the Web pages that appear on the World Wide Web. Web pages are also commonly referred to as **HTML pages** or **documents**. A **markup language** is a set of characters or symbols that define a document's logical structure—that is, it specifies how a document should be printed or displayed. HTML is based on an older language called **Standard Generalized Markup Language**, or **SGML**, which defines the data in a document independent of how the data will be displayed. In other words, SGML separates the data in a document from the way that data is formatted. Each element in an SGML document is marked according to its type, such as paragraphs, headings, and so on. Like SGML, HTML was originally designed as a way of defining the elements in a document independent of how they would appear. HTML was not intended to be used as a method of designing the actual appearance of the pages in a Web browser. However, HTML has gradually evolved into a language that is capable of defining how elements should appear in a Web browser.

This textbook uses the terms "Web pages" and "HTML documents" interchangeably.

Basic HTML Syntax

HTML documents are text documents that contain formatting instructions, called **tags**, which determine how data is displayed on a Web page. HTML tags range from formatting commands that make text appear in boldface or italic, to controls that allow user input, such as option buttons and check boxes. Other HTML tags allow you to display graphic images and other objects in a document or Web page. Tags are enclosed in brackets (< >), and most consist of an opening tag and a closing tag that surround the text or other items they format or control. The closing tag must include a forward slash (/) immediately after the opening bracket to define it as a closing tag. For example, to make a line of text appear in boldface, you use the opening tag `<b>` and the closing tag `</b>`. Any text contained between this pair of tags appears in boldface when you open the HTML document in a Web browser.

A tag pair and the data it contains are referred to as an **element**. The information contained within an element's opening and closing tags is referred to as its **content**. Some elements do not require a closing tag. Elements that do not require a closing tag are called **empty elements** because you cannot use a tag pair to enclose text or other elements. For instance, the `<hr>` element, which inserts a horizontal rule on a Web page, does not include a closing tag. You simply place the `<hr>` element anywhere in an HTML document where you want the horizontal rule to appear.

HTML documents must have a file extension of .html or .htm.

There are literally hundreds of HTML elements. Table 1-1 lists some of the more common elements.

Table 1-1 Common HTML elements

HTML Element	Description
`<b></b>`	Formats enclosed text in a bold typeface
`<body></body>`	Encloses the body of the HTML document
` `	Inserts a line break
`<center>`	Centers a paragraph in the middle of a Web page
`<head></head>`	Encloses the page header and contains information about the entire page
<h*n*></h*n*>	Indicates heading level elements, where *n* represents a number from 1 to 6
`<hr>`	Inserts a horizontal rule
`<html></html>`	Begins and ends an HTML document; these are required elements
`<i></i>`	Formats enclosed text in an italic typeface
`<img src="...">`	Inserts an image file
`<p></p>`	Identifies enclosed text as a paragraph
`<u></u>`	Formats enclosed text as underlined

All HTML documents must use the `<html>` element as the root element. A **root element** contains all the other elements in a document. This element tells a Web browser to assemble any instructions between the tags into a Web page. The opening and closing `<html>...</html>` tags are required and contain all the text and other elements that make up the HTML document.

Two other important HTML elements are the `<head>` element and the `<body>` element. The `<head>` element contains information that is used by the Web browser, and you place it at the beginning of an HTML document, after the opening `<html>` tag. You place several elements within the `<head>` element to help manage a document's content, including the `<title>` element, which contains text that appears in a browser's title bar. A `<head>` element must contain a `<title>` element. With the exception of the `<title>` element, elements contained in the `<head>` element do not affect the display of the HTML document. The `<head>` element and the elements it contains are referred to as the **document head**.

Following the document head is the `<body>` element, which contains the document body. The `<body>` element and the text and elements it contains are referred to as the **document body**.

When you open an HTML document in a Web browser, the document is assembled and formatted according to the instructions contained in its elements. The process by which a Web browser assembles or formats an HTML document is called **parsing** or **rendering**. The following line is an example of how to make a paragraph appear in boldface in an HTML document:

```
<p><b>This paragraph will appear in boldface in a Web
 browser.</b></p>
```

HTML is not case sensitive, so you can use `<B>` in place of `<b>`. However, the next generation of HTML, a language called XHTML, is case sensitive, and you must use lowercase letters for elements. For this reason, this book uses lowercase letters for all elements. (You learn about XHTML shortly.)

You use various parameters, called **attributes**, to configure many HTML elements. You place an attribute before the closing bracket of the opening tag, and separate it from the tag name or other attributes with a space. You assign a value to an attribute using the syntax `attribute="value"`. For example, you can configure the `<img>` element, which embeds an image in an HTML document, with a number of attributes, including the `src` attribute. The `src` attribute specifies the filename of an image file or video clip. To include the `src` attribute within the `<img>` element, you type `<img src="mygraphic.gif">`.

When a Web browser parses or renders an HTML document, it ignores nonprinting characters such as tabs and line breaks; the final document that appears in the Web browser includes only recognized HTML elements and text. You cannot use line breaks in the body of an HTML document to insert spaces before and after a paragraph; the browser recognizes only paragraph `<p>` and line break `<br>` elements for this purpose. In addition, most Web browsers ignore multiple, contiguous spaces on a Web page and replace them with a single space. The following code shows a simple HTML document, and Figure 1-1 shows how it appears in a Web browser:

```
<html>
<head>
<title>Toner Cartridge Sales</title>
</head>
<body>
<h1>Toner Cartridge Sales</h1>
<hr>
<h2>Lexmark Toner Cartridges</h2>
<img src="lexmark_logo.gif">
<p><b>Model #</b>: LEX 1382100<br>
<b>Compatibility</b>: Optra 4049/3112/3116<br>
<b>Price</b>: $189.99</p>
<p><b>Model #</b>:  LEX 1380520<br>
<b>Compatibility</b>: Lexmark 4019/4028/4029<br>
<b>Price</b>: $209.00</p>
</body>
</html>
```

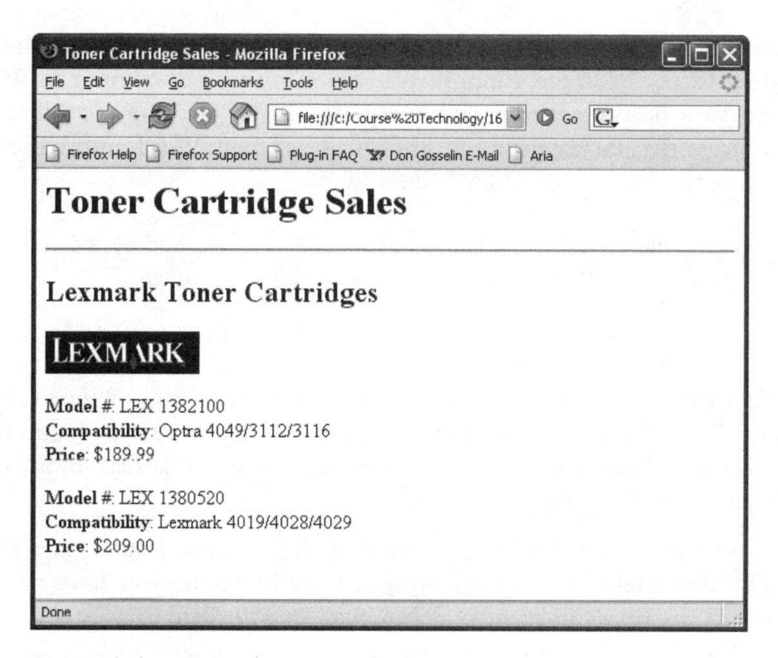

Figure 1-1 A simple HTML document in a Web browser

The majority of the screen captures of Web pages shown in this book were taken in the Mozilla Firefox Web browser, version 1.0, running on the Windows XP operating system. Different Web browsers may render the parts of a Web page slightly differently from other browsers. The appearance of a Web browser itself can also vary across platforms. If you are using a Web browser other than Firefox and an operating system other than Windows XP, your Web pages and Web browser might not match the figures in this book.

Creating an HTML Document

Because HTML documents are text files, you can create them in any text editor, such as Notepad or WordPad, or any word-processing application capable of creating simple text files. If you use a text editor to create an HTML document, you cannot view the final result until you open the document in a Web browser. Instead of a text editor or word processor, you could choose to use an HTML editor, which is an application designed specifically for creating HTML documents. Some popular HTML editors, such as Macromedia Dreamweaver and Microsoft FrontPage, have graphical interfaces that allow you to create Web pages and immediately view the results, similar to the WYSIWYG (what-you-see-is-what-you-get) interface in word-processing programs. In addition, many current word-processing applications, including Microsoft Word and WordPerfect, allow you to save files as HTML documents.

Like text editors, HTML editors create simple text files, but they automate the process of applying elements. For example, suppose you are creating a document in Word. You can add boldface to a heading in the document simply by clicking a toolbar button. Then, when you save the document as an HTML document, Word automatically adds the <b> element to the text in the HTML document.

Many people who are new to creating Web pages are surprised by the fact that you cannot use a Web browser to create an HTML document.

Any HTML editor can greatly simplify the task of creating Web pages. However, HTML editors automatically add many unfamiliar elements and attributes to documents that might confuse you and distract from the learning process. For this reason, in this book you create Web pages using a simple text editor.

Next, you start creating an HTML document that displays the home page for Don's Dessert Shop. The document will contain some of the elements you have seen in this section. You can use any text editor, such as Notepad or WordPad.

Before you begin the first exercise, be certain to extract the data files, located on the CD-ROM that came with this book. Use the 1687-5d.exe file to install the data files on Windows operating systems and the 1687-5d.jar file to install the data files on UNIX/Linux operating systems. You can also download the files from Course Technology's Web site at *http://www.course.com*. The 1687-5d.exe and 1687-5d.jar files automatically create directories where you can store the exercises and projects you create in this book and install any necessary data files that you will need. By default, the directories and data files are installed for Windows platforms in C:\Course Technology\1687-5 and for UNIX/Linux platforms in usr/local/course/1687-5. The 1687-5 directory contains separate directories for each chapter, which, in turn, contain the Chapter, Projects, and Cases directories. Figure 1-2 illustrates the Windows directory structure for Chapter 1.

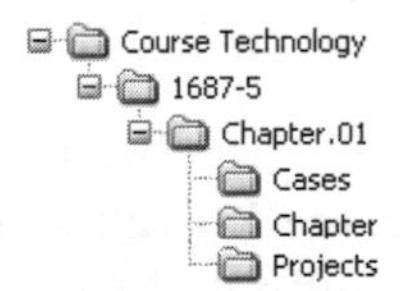

Figure 1-2 Windows directory structure for data files

The Course Technology directory might also contain data files for other books you have used from Course Technology.

Exercises and projects you create in the main body of each chapter should be saved within the Chapter directory. Save the Hands-On Projects and Case Projects you create at the end of each chapter in the Projects and Cases directories, respectively.

To create a simple HTML document:

1. Start your text editor and create a new document, if necessary.
2. Type the following elements to begin the HTML document. Remember that all HTML documents must begin and end with the <html> element.

```
<html>
</html>
```

3. Next add the following <head> and <title> elements between the <html>...</html> tag pair. The title appears in your Web browser's title bar. Remember that the <head> element must include the <title> element. The <title> element cannot exist outside the <head> element.

```
<head>
<title>Don's Dessert Shop</title>
</head>
```

4. Next add the following elements above the closing </html> tag. The <body> element contains all of the elements that are rendered in a Web browser. The <basefont> element defines a base font of Arial for the Web page.

```
<body>
<basefont face="Arial">
</body>
```

5. Add the following elements and text above the closing </body> element. The code contains standard HTML elements along with the text that is displayed in the Web browser.

```
<font color="olive"><h1>Don's Dessert Shop</h1><hr>
<h2>Hours of Operation</h2></font>
<font color="blue"><p>Monday through Thursday, 7:45 a.m.
 - 9:45 p.m.<br>
Friday, 7:45 a.m. - 4:30 p.m.<br>
Saturday, 9:00 a.m. - 4:00 p.m.<br>
Sunday, Noon - 9:00 p.m.</p></font><hr>
<font color="olive"><h2>What's for Dessert?</h2></font>
<font color="blue">
<ul>
  <li>Cookies and pastries</li>
  <li>Cakes and pies</li>
  <li>Gourmet chocolate</li>
</ul></font><hr>
<font color="olive"><h2>Forms of Payment</h2></font>
<font color="blue"><p>Cash, ATM, Visa, American Express,
 Discover Card, and MasterCard.</p></font>
```

6. Save the document as **DessertShop.html** in the Chapter directory for Chapter 1. Some text editors automatically add their own extensions to a document. Notepad, for instance, adds an extension of .txt. Be certain to save your document with an extension of .html. Keep the document open in your text editor.

Some Web servers do not correctly interpret spaces within the names of HTML files. For example, some Web servers might not correctly interpret the filename Dessert Shop.html, which contains a space between Dessert and Shop. For this reason, filenames in this book do not include spaces.

7. Open the **DessertShop.html** document in your Web browser. (You open a local document in most Web browsers by selecting Open or Open File from the File menu.) Figure 1-3 displays the DessertShop.html document as it appears in Firefox.

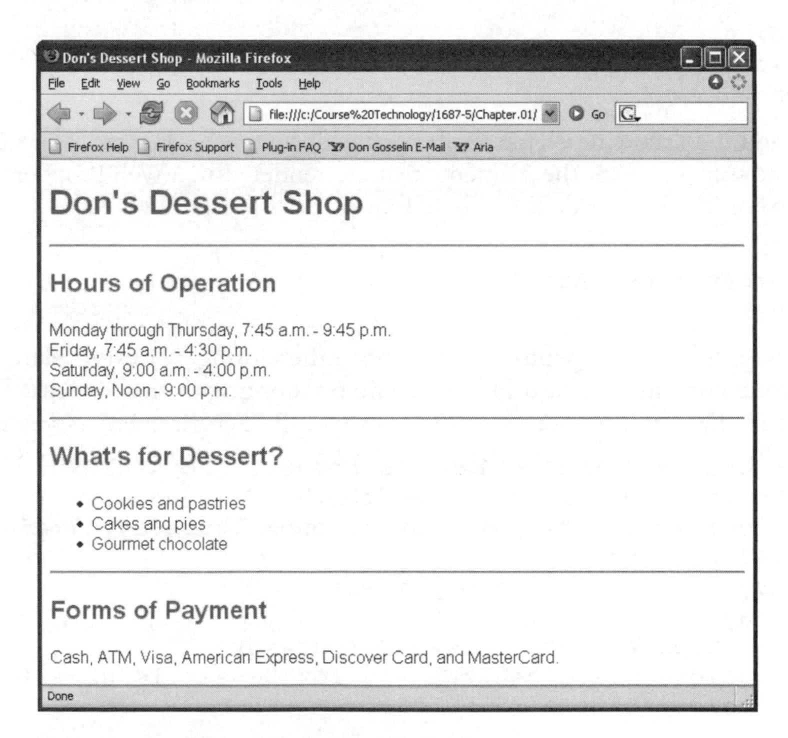

Figure 1-3 DessertShop.html in Firefox

8. Close your Web browser window.

Web Communication Protocols

As you learned earlier, a Web page is identified by a unique address called the URL. A Web page's URL is similar to a telephone number. Each URL consists of two basic parts: a protocol (usually HTTP) and either the domain name for a Web server or a Web server's Internet Protocol address. **Hypertext Transfer Protocol (HTTP)** manages the hypertext links that are used to navigate the Web. HTTP ensures that Web browsers correctly process and display the various types of information contained in Web pages (text, graphics, audio, and so on). The protocol portion of a URL is followed by a colon, two forward slashes, and a host. The term **host** refers to a computer system that is being accessed by a remote computer. In the case of a URL, the host portion of a URL is usually *www* for "World Wide Web." A **domain name** is a unique address used for identifying a computer, often a Web server, on the Internet. The domain name consists of two parts separated by a period. The first part of a domain name is usually text that easily identifies a person or an organization, such as DonGosselin or Course. The last part of a domain name, known as the **domain identifier**, identifies the type of institution or organization. Common domain identifiers include .biz, .com, .edu, .info, .net, .org, .gov, .mil, or .int. Each domain identifier briefly describes the type of business or organization it represents. For instance, com (for *commercial*) represents private companies, gov (for *government*) represents government agencies, and edu (for *educational*) represents educational institutions. Therefore, the domain name consists of descriptive text for the Web site combined with the domain identifier. For example, course.com is the domain name for Course Technology. An example of an entire URL is *http://www.DonGosselin.com* or *http://www.course.com*.

An Internet Protocol, or IP, address is another way to uniquely identify computers or devices connected to the Internet. An IP address consists of a series of four groups of numbers separated by periods. Each Internet domain name is associated with a unique IP address.

In a URL, a specific filename, or a combination of directories and a filename, can follow the domain name or IP address. If the URL does not specify a filename, the requesting Web server looks for a default Web page located in the root or specified directory. Default Web pages usually have names similar to index.html or default.html. For instance, if you want help using Google's Web site and you enter ***`http://www.google.com/help/`*** in your browser's Address box, the Web server automatically opens a file named index.html. Figure 1-4 identifies the parts of the URL that opens the default file in the help directory on Google's Web site.

When a URL does not specify a filename, the index.html file or other file that opens automatically might not appear in your Address box after the document renders.

Figure 1-4 Sample URL

Although HTTP is probably the most widely used protocol on the Internet, it is not the only one. HTTP is a component of **Transmission Control Protocol/Internet Protocol (TCP/IP)**, a large collection of communication protocols used on the Internet. Another common protocol is **Hypertext Transfer Protocol Secure (HTTPS)**, which provides secure Internet connections that are used in Web-based financial transactions and other types of communication that require security and privacy. For instance, to use a Web browser to view your account information through Wells Fargo bank, you need to access the following URL:

```
https://online.wellsfargo.com/
```

Publishing Your Web Site

The question of how to publish Web pages is often a very confusing issue for new Web authors. Before you can publish your Web pages, you need to make a decision about how the Web site will be hosted, create and register a domain name for the site, and FTP the files to the Web server.

Web Hosting

Web hosting refers to the publication of a Web site for public access. You can use your own computer to host your Web site, provided your computer is connected to the Internet. However, using your own computer is not usually a good idea for several reasons. First, hosting a Web site involves many security and maintenance tasks that you might not be able to perform, because you lack either the necessary time or skills. Second, your Internet access might not be fast enough. Although broadband Internet access in the form of cable modems, Digital Subscriber Lines (DSL), and satellite systems is growing, many users still access the Internet through slower, dial-up modems. If you are using a dial-up modem, your Internet connection will have nowhere near enough speed to allow multiple users to access a Web site hosted on your computer. A final consideration is the speed of your computer itself. Although you might have a state-of-the art desktop computer, it will probably still be slower than a professional-strength Web server.

Any computer can act as a Web server, although special types of computers with extremely large hard drives and memory are specifically designed for that purpose.

Most people use an Internet service provider (ISP) to host their Web sites. An ISP provides access to the Internet along with other types of services, including e-mail. Some of the more popular ISPs include America Online, CompuServe, and EarthLink, although many others exist. Almost every ISP also offers Web site hosting. Often, an account with an ISP such as America Online automatically includes a limited amount of Web server space (usually 5–10 megabytes) that you can use to host your Web site. Check with your ISP to find out if your account includes Web hosting.

Five to ten megabytes isn't nearly enough storage space for hosting professional Web sites. However, you might find this amount of storage space sufficient to create a personal Web site with a limited number of pages.

There are many advantages to having an ISP host your Web site. Most ISPs have extremely fast Internet connections using advanced fiber-optic connections that are light years more powerful than a dial-up modem. ISPs also have very large and powerful Web servers, along with the expertise and manpower to maintain and manage them. Using a professional Web hosting service allows you to concentrate solely on developing your Web site without having to worry about the requirements of hosting.

You can find a comprehensive list of ISPs at *http://www.thelist.com*.

Domain Name Registration

One important decision you need to make is what to use for a domain name. You should pick a domain name that is similar to your business name or that describes your Web site. However, you cannot use a domain name that is already in use by someone else. For example, you cannot use microsoft.com or harvard.edu because both of these domain names are already in use. Also, you cannot use a domain name that infringes on another company's trademarked brand name.

To find out the availability of a domain name and register it, you must contact a **domain name registrar**. Domain names are stored in a master database that is maintained by **InterNIC**, the organization that is responsible for the registration of domain names and IP addresses. Any domain name registrar that is accredited by InterNIC is permitted to access and modify the master domain name database. A domain name registrar's Web site helps you search the master database to find out if the domain name you want to use is available. If your desired domain name is available, then for a fee the domain name registrar will assist you in registering the domain name for a specified period of time, usually one to two years.

You can view a list of InterNIC-accredited domain name registrars at *http://www.internic.net/alpha.html*.

A popular domain name registrar is Network Solutions, a division of VeriSign. If you visit the Network Solutions Web site at *http://www.networksolutions.com*, you can search for the availability of a domain name, as shown in Figure 1-5.

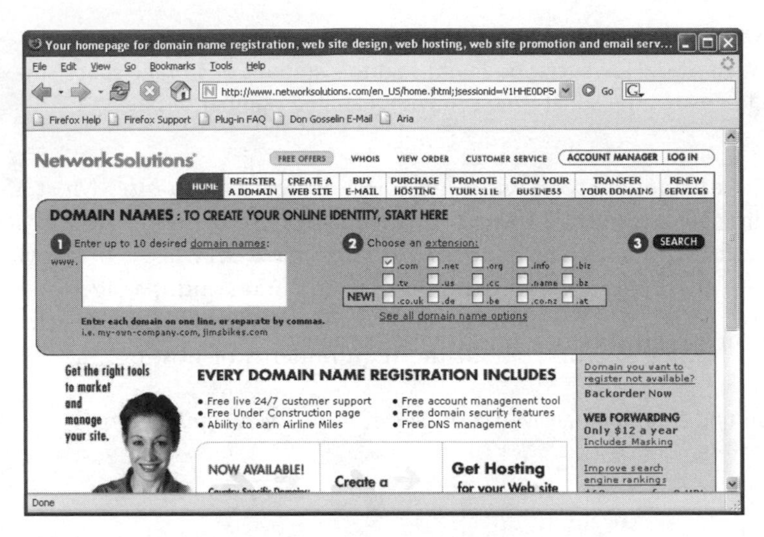

Figure 1-5 Network Solutions Web page

After you register your domain name, you need to notify your ISP of your domain information. Usually, it is easiest to simply register your domain name through the ISP you intend to use (assuming it is a domain name registrar) because the ISP can automatically handle the details of setting up the domain for you. However, if you have already registered a domain name and want to transfer it to another ISP, or if you register your domain name with another domain name registrar, your ISP will probably provide a form or some other procedure to assist you in transferring your domain.

File Transfer Protocol

When you are ready to publish your Web site, you usually use FTP to send the Web pages and other files that make up your Web site to the hosting ISP. **File Transfer Protocol (FTP)** is a TCP/IP protocol used for transferring files across the Internet. It is not the Web browser's job to display files transferred by FTP. Instead, FTP simply transfers files between an FTP client (your computer) and an FTP server (a server capable of running FTP). In the realm of Web page publishing, FTP is simply the vehicle that allows you to get your Web page files to the Web server. The Web server is then responsible for making the Web pages available to Web browsers on the Web.

Your ISP will give you a username and password that you must use to log on to the FTP site. Your username and password should give you permission to upload files to the FTP server. After you log on to an FTP server, you will see a directory structure that looks very similar to Windows Explorer and other types of file management systems. Your ISP will instruct you where to upload your Web site files.

Various types of commercial and shareware software exist that you can use to access an FTP site. In fact, many HTML editors such as FrontPage have built-in commands that you can use to log on to an FTP server and upload your files. However, many current

Web browsers, including Firefox and Internet Explorer, have the capability to act as FTP clients, which means that you can use your browser to log on to an FTP server and upload your files. Figure 1-6 shows how the Project Gutenberg FTP site at the University of North Carolina appears in Firefox.

FTP directory: /pub/docs/books/gutenberg/ - Mozilla Firefox

File Edit View Go Bookmarks Tools Help

ftp://ibiblio.org/pub/docs/books/gutenberg/

Firefox Help Firefox Support Plug-in FAQ Don Gosselin E-Mail Aria

Current directory is /pub/docs/books/gutenberg/

```
[DIRECTORY]  Parent Directory
[DIRECTORY]  1. . . . . . . . . . . . . . . . . . . . .  [Jun 27  2004]
[DIRECTORY]  2. . . . . . . . . . . . . . . . . . . . .  [Sep 27 14:20]
[DIRECTORY]  3. . . . . . . . . . . . . . . . . . . . .  [Nov  6 19:20]
[DIRECTORY]  4. . . . . . . . . . . . . . . . . . . . .  [Dec 17 20:20]
[DIRECTORY]  5. . . . . . . . . . . . . . . . . . . . .  [Jan  4 04:23]
[DIRECTORY]  6. . . . . . . . . . . . . . . . . . . . .  [Jan 25 10:20]
[DIRECTORY]  7. . . . . . . . . . . . . . . . . . . . .  [Dec 18 18:22]
[DIRECTORY]  8. . . . . . . . . . . . . . . . . . . . .  [Dec 18 11:20]
[DIRECTORY]  9. . . . . . . . . . . . . . . . . . . . .  [Jan  2 10:19]
[TEXT]       GUTINDEX-2003.txt. . . . . . . . . . . . .  [Feb 25 17:01]    94K
[TEXT]       GUTINDEX-2004.txt. . . . . . . . . . . . .  [Feb 25 17:01]   477K
[TEXT]       GUTINDEX-2005.txt. . . . . . . . . . . . .  [Feb 25 17:01]    70K
[FILE]       GUTINDEX.00. . . . . . . . . . . . . . . .  [Jan  8 17:22]    55K
[FILE]       GUTINDEX.01. . . . . . . . . . . . . . . .  [Jan  8 17:22]    69K
[FILE]       GUTINDEX.02. . . . . . . . . . . . . . . .  [Jan  8 17:22]    85K
[FILE]       GUTINDEX.03. . . . . . . . . . . . . . . .  [Jan  8 17:22]   131K
[FILE]       GUTINDEX.04. . . . . . . . . . . . . . . .  [Jan  8 17:23]   272K
[FILE]       GUTINDEX.05. . . . . . . . . . . . . . . .  [Jan  8 17:23]   269K
[FILE]       GUTINDEX.06. . . . . . . . . . . . . . . .  [Jan  8 17:23]    55K
[FILE]       GUTINDEX.96. . . . . . . . . . . . . . . .  [Jan  8 18:22]    74K
```

Done

Figure 1-6 Project Gutenberg FTP site at the University of North Carolina

Some of the more popular FTP programs include WS_FTP (*http://www.ipswitch.com*) and Cute FTP (*http://www.globalscape.com*) for Windows, and Fetch (*http://www.fetchsoftworks.com*) for Macintosh.

Project Gutenberg produces free, electronic versions of public domain information, books, and other materials.

If you do not have a logon account, many FTP sites allow you to access the site anonymously. When you access an FTP site anonymously, you can download files from the site, but you cannot upload files. The Project Gutenberg FTP site shown in Figure 1-6 is an example of an anonymous FTP site. Although many anonymous FTP sites exist, the majority of ISPs do not allow anonymous logons to Web hosting FTP sites to protect the privacy of their clients. When you use Firefox to log on to your ISP's Web hosting FTP site, you are presented with a logon dialog box similar to Figure 1-7.

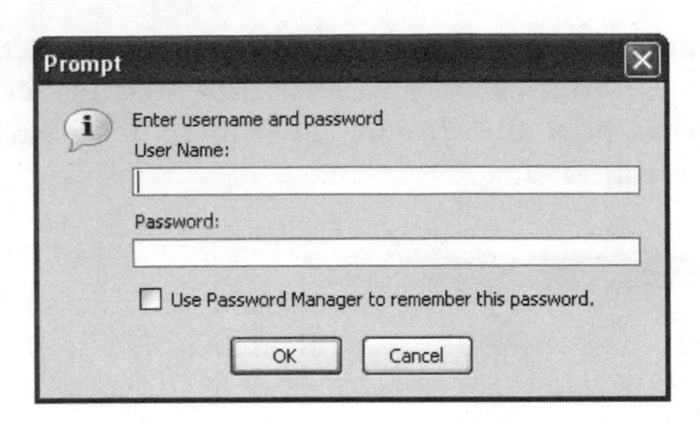

Figure 1-7 FTP logon dialog box

TIP

The process of uploading files is very similar to the process of downloading files.

WORKING WITH WELL-FORMED WEB PAGES

HTML first became an Internet standard in 1993 with the release of version 1.0. The next version of HTML, 2.0, was released in 1994 and included many core HTML features such as forms and the ability to bold and italicize text. However, many of the standard features that are widely used today, such as tables for organizing text and graphics on a page, were not available until the release of HTML 3.2 in 1996. The current version of HTML, 4.01, was released in 1999. HTML 4.01, however, is the last version of the HTML language because it is being replaced with **extensible hypertext markup language**, or **XHTML**.

HTML is being replaced because it is useful only for rendering documents in traditional Web browsers like Firefox or Internet Explorer. The Web, however, is expanding to other media, called **user agents**, which are devices that are capable of retrieving and processing Web Pages. A user agent can be a traditional Web browser or a device such as a mobile phone or PDA, or even an application that simply collects and processes data instead of displaying it.

There are two primary reasons why HTML is not suitable for user agents other than Web browsers. First, even though HTML was originally designed primarily to display data, it has evolved into a markup language that is more concerned with how data appears than with the data itself. (Recall that HTML is based on SGML, which defines the data in a document independently of how it is displayed.) As Web browsers have evolved over the years, they have added extensions (elements and attributes) to HTML to provide functionality for displaying and formatting Web pages. For instance, one extension to the original HTML language is the `<font>` element, which allows you to specify the font for data in an HTML document. The `<font>` element has nothing to do with the type of data in an HTML document. Instead, its sole purpose is to display data in a specific typeface within a Web browser. Remember, however, that HTML is based on SGML and should define data independently of the way it displays. Elements like the `<font>` element violate this rule. There is nothing wrong with continuing to author your Web pages using HTML and design elements such as the `<font>` element—provided your Web pages will be opened only in a Web browser. However, many user agents (such as mobile phones and PDAs) display only black and white or grayscale text and are incapable of processing HTML elements that handle the display and formatting of data. User agents such as these require a language that truly defines data (such as a paragraph or heading) independently of the way it is displayed.

Second, current and older versions of Web browsers allow you to write sloppy HTML code. For instance, earlier you learned that all HTML documents begin with `<html>` and end with `</html>`. To be more precise, all HTML documents *should* begin with `<html>` and end with `</html>`. In addition, all HTML documents *should* also include `<head>` and `<body>` elements. In practice, however, you can omit any of these elements from an HTML document and a Web browser will still render the page correctly. In fact, although elements require a closing tag, you can often omit (either intentionally or accidentally) a closing tag and the Web page will usually be rendered properly.

XHTML is based on extensible markup language, or XML, which is used for creating Web pages and for defining and transmitting data between applications.

The Web page examples and exercises in this book are written in XHTML. Although you need to have a solid understanding of HTML to be successful with this book, you do not necessarily need to be an expert with XHTML. Because XHTML is almost identical to HTML, you can easily adapt any of your existing HTML skills to XHTML, and vice versa.

To ensure backward compatibility with older browsers, you should save XHTML documents with an extension of .html or .htm, just like HTML documents.

XHTML Document Type Definitions (DTDs)

When a document conforms to the rules and requirements of XHTML, it is said to be **well formed**. Among other things, a well-formed document must include a `<!DOCTYPE>` declaration and the `<html>`, `<head>`, and `<body>` elements. The **<!DOCTYPE> declaration** belongs in the first line of an XHTML document and determines the XHTML DTD with which the document complies. A **document type definition**, or **DTD**, defines the elements and attributes that can be used in a document, along with the rules that a document must follow when it includes them. You can use three types of DTDs with XHTML documents: transitional, strict, and frameset.

To understand the differences among the various DTDs, you need to understand the concept of deprecated HTML elements. One of the goals of XHTML is to separate the way the HTML is structured from the way the parsed Web page is displayed in the browser. To accomplish this goal, the W3C decided that several commonly used HTML elements and attributes for display and formatting would not be used in XHTML 1.0. The **World Wide Web Consortium**, or **W3C**, was established in 1994 at MIT to oversee the development of Web technology standards. Instead of using HTML elements and attributes for displaying and formatting Web pages, the W3C recommends you use Cascading Style Sheets (CSS), which are discussed at the end of this section.

The W3C does not actually release a version of a particular technology. Instead, it issues a formal recommendation for a technology, which essentially means that the technology is (or will be) a recognized industry standard.

Elements and attributes that are considered obsolete and that will eventually be eliminated are said to be **deprecated**. Table 1-2 lists the HTML elements that are deprecated in XHTML 1.0.

Table 1-2 HTML elements that are deprecated in XHTML 1.0

Element	Description
`<applet>`	Executes Java applets
`<basefont>`	Specifies the base font size
`<center>`	Centers text
`<dir>`	Defines a directory list
`<font>`	Specifies a font name, size, and color
`<isindex>`	Creates automatic document indexing forms
`<menu>`	Defines a menu list
`<s>` or `<strike>`	Formats strikethrough text
`<u>`	Formats underlined text

The three DTDs are distinguished in part by the degree to which they accept or do not accept deprecated HTML elements. This is explained in more detail in the following sections.

Transitional DTD

The **transitional DTD** allows you to use deprecated style elements in your XHTML documents. The `<!DOCTYPE>` declaration for the transitional DTD is as follows:

```
<!DOCTYPE html PUBLIC
"-//W3C//DTD XHTML 1.0 Transitional//EN"
"http://www.w3.org/TR/xhtml1/DTD/xhtml1-transitional.dtd">
```

You should use the transitional DTD only if you need to create Web pages that use the deprecated elements listed in Table 1-2.

Frameset DTD

The **frameset DTD** is identical to the transitional DTD, except that it includes the `<frameset>` and `<frame>` elements, which allow you to split the browser window into two or more frames. The `<!DOCTYPE>` declaration for the frameset DTD is as follows:

```
<!DOCTYPE html PUBLIC
"-//W3C//DTD XHTML 1.0 Frameset//EN"
"http://www.w3.org/TR/xhtml1/DTD/xhtml1-frameset.dtd">
```

You should understand that frames have been deprecated in favor of tables. However, frameset documents are still widely used, and you need to be able to recognize and work with them in the event that you need to modify an existing Web page that was created with frames.

Strict DTD

The **strict DTD** eliminates the elements that were deprecated in the transitional DTD and frameset DTD. The `<!DOCTYPE>` declaration for the strict DTD is as follows:

```
<!DOCTYPE html PUBLIC
"-//W3C//DTD XHTML 1.0 Strict//EN"
"http://www.w3.org/TR/xhtml1/DTD/xhtml1-strict.dtd">
```

As a rule, you should always try to use the strict DTD. This ensures that your Web pages conform to the most current Web page authoring techniques. Next, you add a `<!DOCTYPE>` declaration for the strict DTD to the Don's Dessert Shop Web page.

To add a `<!DOCTYPE>` declaration for the strict DTD to the Don's Dessert Shop Web page:

1. Return to the **DessertShop.html** document in your text editor.
2. Add the following `<!DOCTYPE>` declaration for the strict DTD as the first line in the document (above the opening `<html>` tag):

   ```
   <!DOCTYPE html PUBLIC
   "-//W3C//DTD XHTML 1.0 Strict//EN"
   "http://www.w3.org/TR/xhtml1/DTD/xhtml1-strict.dtd">
   ```

3. Save your changes to the document.

Writing Well-Formed Documents

As you learned earlier, a well-formed document must include a `<!DOCTYPE>` declaration and the `<html>`, `<head>`, and `<body>` elements. The following list describes some other important components of a well-formed document:

- All XHTML documents must use `<html>` as the root element. The `xmlns` attribute is required in the `<html>` element and must be assigned the *http://www.w3.org/1999/xhtml* URI.
- XHTML is case sensitive.
- All XHTML elements must have a closing tag.
- Attribute values must appear within quotation marks.
- Empty elements must be closed.
- XHTML elements must be properly nested.

Most of the preceding rules are self-explanatory. However, the last rule requires further explanation. **Nesting** refers to how elements are placed inside other elements. For example, in the following code, the `<i>` element is nested within the `<b>` element, while the `<b>` element is nested within a `<p>` element.

```
<p><b><i>This paragraph is bold and italicized.</i></b></p>
```

In an HTML document, it makes no difference how the elements are nested. Examine the following modified version of the preceding statement:

```
<p><b><i>This paragraph is bold and italicized.</b></p></i>
```

In the preceding code, the opening `<i>` element is nested within the `<b>` element, which, in turn, is nested within the `<p>` element. Notice, however, that the closing `</i>` tag is outside the closing `</p>` tag. The `<i>` is the innermost element. In XHTML, each innermost element must be closed before another element is closed. In the preceding statement, the `<b>` and `<p>` elements are closed before the `<i>` element. Although the order in which elements are closed makes no difference in HTML, the preceding code would prevent an XHTML document from being well formed.

The second-to-last rule in the list ("Empty elements must be closed.") also requires further explanation. Three of the most common empty elements in HTML are the `<hr>` element, which inserts a horizontal rule into the document, the `<br>` element, which inserts a line break, and the `<img>` element, which adds an image to the document. You close an empty element in XHTML by adding a space and a slash before the element's closing bracket. For example, the following code shows how to use the `<hr>` and `<br>`

elements in an XHTML document. Figure 1-8 shows how the code appears in a Web browser.

```
<hr />
<p><b>Superman</b>'s alter ego is Clark Kent, <br />
<b>Batman</b>'s alter ego is Bruce Wayne, <br />
and <b>Spiderman</b>'s alter ego is Peter Parker.</p>
<hr />
```

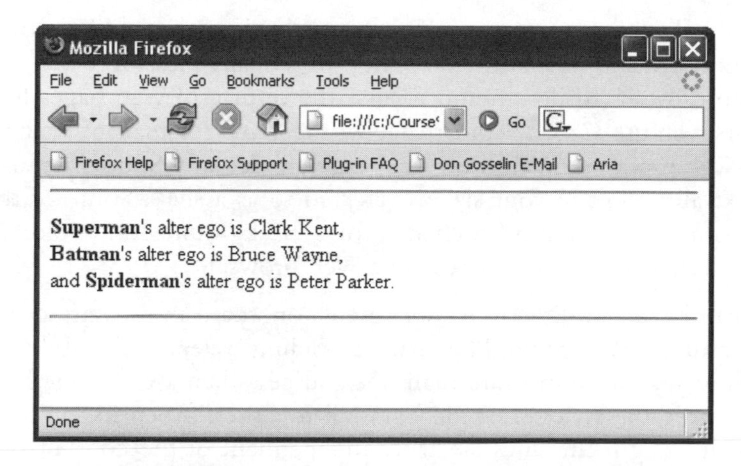

Figure 1-8 XHTML document with closed empty elements

You might be wondering why XHTML documents do not use a root element of `<xhtml>`. The `<html>` element is necessary for backward-compatibility with older browsers that do not recognize the `<!DOCTYPE>` element, which declares the DTD used by an XHTML element.

Next, you modify the Don's Dessert Shop Web page so it is well formed.

To modify the Don's Dessert Shop Web page so it is well formed:

1. Return to the **DessertShop.html** document in your text editor.
2. Modify the opening <html> element so it includes the `xmlns` attribute, as follows:

   ```
   <html xmlns="http://www.w3.org/1999/xhtml">
   ```

3. Delete the `<basefont>` element along with the six `<font>` elements. Be certain also to delete the closing `</font>` tags. (You need to do this because the `<basefont>` and `<font>` elements have been deprecated in XHTML in favor of CSS.)
4. Add a space and a slash before the closing bracket of the three `<hr>` elements. Also add a space and a slash before the closing bracket of the three `<br>` elements beneath the "Hours of Operation" heading.

5. Save the **DessertShop.html** document and open it in your Web browser. The document should appear similar to the way it did before you made it well formed, although it will not contain any formatting. You learn how to add formatting when you study CSS in the next section.

6. Close your Web browser window.

Cascading Style Sheets

Although you should always strive to create Web pages that are compatible with all user agents, you can also design and format them so they are visually pleasing when rendered in a traditional Web browser. To design and format the display of Web pages for traditional Web browsers, you use CSS, a standard set by the W3C for managing the design and formatting of Web pages in a Web browser. A single piece of CSS formatting information, such as text alignment or font size, is referred to as a **style**. Some of the style capabilities of CSS include the ability to change fonts, backgrounds, and colors, and to modify the layout of elements as they appear in a Web browser.

CSS information can be added directly to documents or stored in separate documents and shared among multiple Web pages. The term "cascading" refers to the ability of Web pages to use CSS information from more than one source. When a Web page has access to multiple CSS sources, the styles "cascade," or "fall together." Keep in mind that the CSS design and formatting techniques are truly independent of the content of a Web page, unlike text-formatting elements, such as the `<b>` and `<i>` elements. CSS allows you to provide design and formatting specifications for well-formed documents that are compatible with all user agents.

NOTE

Entire books are devoted to CSS. This chapter provides only enough information to get you started. To learn more about CSS techniques, refer to Don Gosselin's *XHTML*, also published by Course Technology. For other books that cover CSS more fully, search for "css" on the Course Technology Web site at *http://www.course.com*. You can also find the latest information on CSS at the W3C's Web site: *http:/www.w3.org/style/css/*.

CSS Properties

CSS styles are created with two parts separated by a colon: the **property**, which refers to a specific CSS style, and the value assigned to it, which determines the style's visual characteristics. Together, a CSS property and the value assigned to it are referred to as a **declaration** or **style declaration**. Figure 1-9 shows a simple style declaration for the `color` property that changes the color of an element's text to blue.

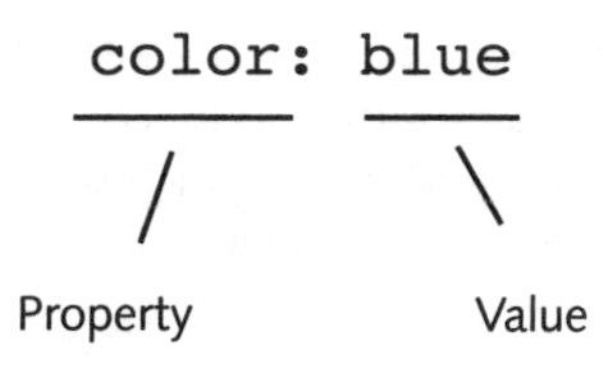

Figure 1-9 Style declaration

Inline Styles

When you design a Web page, you often want the elements on your page to share the same formatting. For example, you might want all of the headings to be formatted in a specific font and color. Later in this section, you learn how to use internal and external style sheets to apply the same formatting to multiple elements on a Web page. However, there might be times you want to change the style of a single element on a Web page. The most basic method of applying styles is to use **inline styles**, which allow you to add style information to a single element in a document. You use the **style attribute** to assign inline style information to an element. You assign to the `style` attribute a property declaration enclosed in quotation marks. Suppose you want to modify a single paragraph in a document so it uses the Verdana font instead of the browser's default font. You can modify the default font using the following statement, which uses an inline style declaration for the `font-family` property. Figure 1-10 shows how the paragraph appears in a Web browser.

```
<p>This paragraph does not use CSS.</p>
<p style="font-family: Verdana">Paragraph formatted with inline
styles.</p>
```

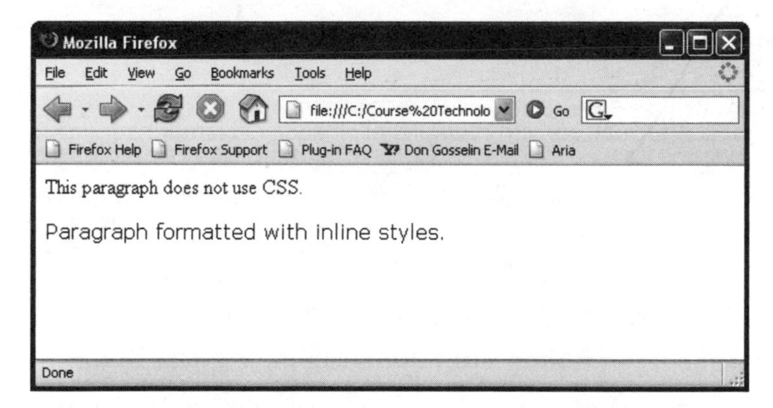

Figure 1-10 Paragraph formatted with an inline style declaration

NOTE

The styles you assign to an element are automatically passed to any nested elements it contains. For example, if you use the `font-family` style to assign a font to a paragraph, that font is automatically assigned to any nested elements the paragraph contains, such as `<strong>` or `<em>` elements.

You can include multiple style declarations in an inline style by separating each declaration with a semicolon. The following statement shows the same paragraph element shown earlier, but this time with two additional style declarations: one for the `color` property, which sets an element's text color to blue, and one for the `text-align` property, which centers the paragraph in the middle of the page. Notice that the `<strong>` element, which is nested in the paragraph element, automatically takes on the paragraph element's style elements. Figure 1-11 shows how the paragraph appears in a Web browser.

```
<p style="font-family: Verdana; color: blue;
text-align: center">Paragraph formatted with <strong>inline
styles</strong>.</p>
```

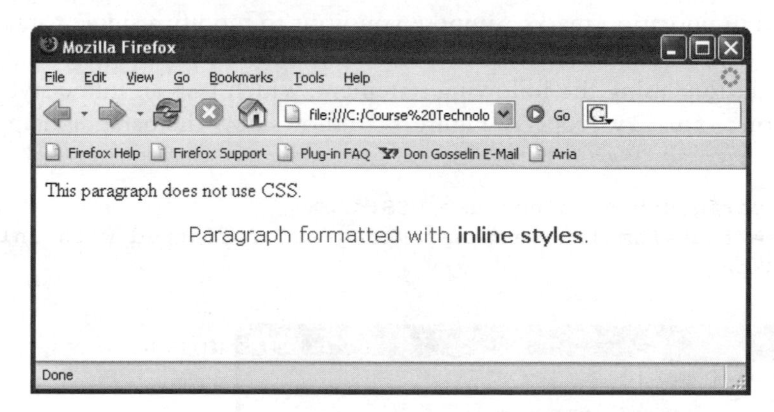

Figure 1-11 Paragraph formatted with multiple inline style declarations

Next, you modify the Don's Dessert Shop Web page so it includes inline styles. You add some simple CSS formatting instructions that format the Web page in the Arial font, the headings in the color olive, and the body text in the color blue.

To modify the Don's Dessert Shop Web page so it includes inline styles:

1. Return to the **DessertShop.html** document in your text editor.
2. Modify the opening `<body>` tag, so it includes inline styles that modify the `font-family`, `color`, and `background-color` properties, as follows:

```
<body style="font-family: Arial; color: blue;
     background-color: transparent">
```

3. Modify the opening `<h1>` tag, so it includes inline styles that modify the `font-family` and `color` properties, as follows:

```
<h1 style="font-family: Arial; color: olive">
```

4. Finally, modify the three opening `<h2>` tags, so they include the same styles as the `<h1>` tag. Each opening `<h2>` tag should appear as follows:

```
<h2 style="font-family: Arial; color: olive">
```

5. Save the **DessertShop.html** document and open it in your Web browser. The Web page should appear the same as the HTML version you created with deprecated formatting elements.

6. Close your Web browser window.

One of the great advantages to using CSS is that you can share styles among multiple Web pages, making it easier to create and maintain a common look and feel for an entire Web site. Inline styles, however, cannot be shared by other Web pages or even by other elements on the same page (except by elements that are nested within other elements). Plus, it is extremely time consuming to add inline styles to each and every element on a Web page. Inline styles are only useful if you need to make a onetime change to a single element on a page. If you want to apply the same formatting to multiple elements on a page or share styles with other Web pages, then you need to use internal or external style sheets.

Internal Style Sheets

Inline styles are useful only if you want to add style information to a single element in a document. You use an **internal style sheet** to create styles that apply to an entire document. You create an internal style sheet within a `<style>` element placed within the document head. The `<style>` element must include a `type` attribute, which is assigned a value of `"text/css"`, as follows:

```
<style type="text/css">
style declarations
</style>
```

You can also use an optional `media` attribute with the `<style>` element, which you use to select the destination medium for the style information. Valid values you can assign to the `media` attribute are `screen`, `tty`, `tv`, `projection`, `handheld`, `print`, `braille`, `aural`, and `all`.

Within the `<style>` element, you create any style instructions for a specific element that are applied to all instances of that element contained in the body of the document. The element to which specific style rules in a style sheet apply is called a **selector**. You create a style declaration for a selector in an internal style sheet by placing a list of declarations within a pair of braces { } following the name of the selector. Figure 1-12 shows some style declarations for the `<p>` element (which is the selector), which change the `color` property to `blue`.

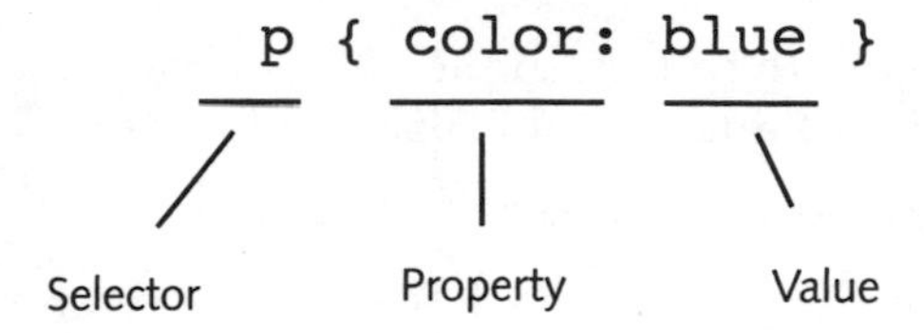

Figure 1-12 Selector style declaration

As with inline styles, you separate multiple properties for a selector by semicolons. The following code shows a portion of the Toner Cartridge Sales Web page you saw earlier, but this time it includes an internal style sheet for the `h1`, `h2`, and `body` selectors. A pair of braces containing style instructions follows each selector. All instances of the associated elements in the body of the document are formatted using these style instructions. Figure 1-13 shows how the document appears in a Web browser.

```
<head>
<title>Toner Cartridge Sales</title>
<style type="text/css">
h1 { color: navy; font-size: 2em; font-family: serif }
h2 { color: red; font-size: 1.5em; font-family: Arial }
body { color: blue; font-family: Arial;
     font-size: .8em; font-weight: normal }
</style>
</head>
<body>
<h1>Toner Cartridge Sales</h1>
<hr />
<h2>Lexmark Toner Cartridges</h2>
...
</body>
</html>
```

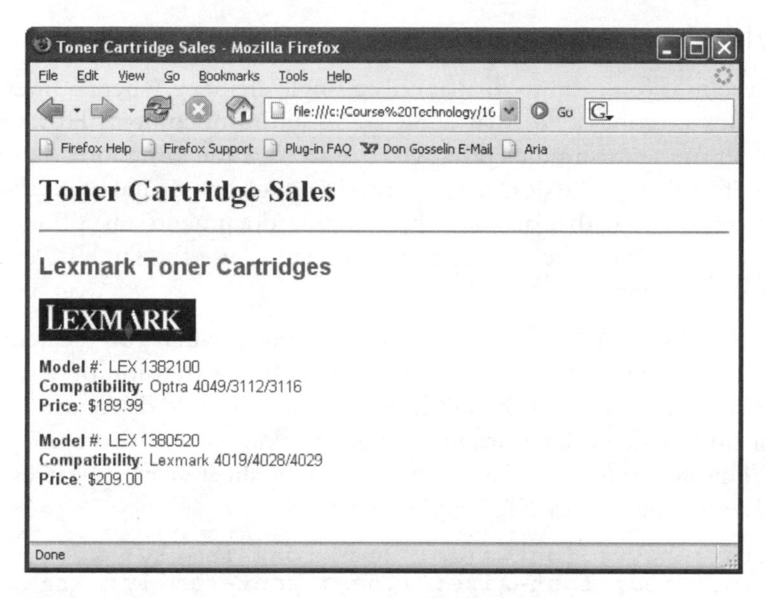

Figure 1-13 Document with an internal style sheet

You can also group selectors so they share the same style declarations by separating each selector with a comma. For example, you use the following single declaration to format all of a document's <h1>, <h2>, and <h3> elements to use the same color:

```
<style type="text/css">
h1, h2, h3 { color: navy }
</style>
```

Next, you modify the Don's Dessert Shop Web page so it contains an internal style sheet.

To modify the Don's Dessert Shop Web page so it contains an internal style sheet:

1. Return to the **DessertShop.html** document in your text editor.
2. Delete the inline styles in the <body>, <h1>, and <h2> tags.
3. Add the following internal style sheet above the closing </head> tag:

   ```
   <style type="text/css">
   body { font-family: Arial; color: blue;
        background-color: transparent }
   h1, h2 { font-family: Arial; color: olive }
   </style>
   ```

4. Save the **DessertShop.html** document and open it in your Web browser. The Web page should format the same as it did with the inline styles.
5. Close your Web browser window.

External Style Sheets

Inline styles are useful if you need to format only a single element, whereas internal style sheets are useful for creating styles that apply to an entire document. However, most companies want all of the documents on a Web site to have the same look and feel. For this reason, it's preferable to use **external style sheets**, which are separate text documents containing style declarations that are used by multiple documents on a Web site. You should create an external style sheet whenever you need to use the same styles on multiple Web pages in the same site.

You create an external style sheet in a text editor, the same as when you create XHTML documents. However, you should save the document with an extension of .css. The style sheet document should not contain XHTML elements, only style declarations. Use the same rules for creating style declarations in an external style sheet as you use in an internal style sheet. The contents of a typical external style sheet may appear as follows. Notice that the code contains no XHTML elements.

```
h1 { color: navy; font-size: 2em; font-family: serif }
h2 { color: red; font-size: 1.5em; font-family: Arial }
body { color: blue; font-family: Arial;
     font-size: .8em; font-weight: normal }
```

The most popular way to access the styles in an external style sheet is to use the empty `<link>` element to link a document to a style sheet. You place the `<link>` element in the document head. You include three attributes in the `<link>` element: an `href` attribute that is assigned the URL of the style sheet, the `rel` attribute that is assigned a value of `"stylesheet"` to specify that the referenced file is a style sheet, and the `type` attribute, which is assigned the same `"text/css"` value as the `type` attribute used in the `<style>` element. For example, to link a document to a style sheet named company_branding.css, you include a link element in the document head, as follows:

```
<head>
...
<link rel="stylesheet" href="company_branding.css"
     type="text/css" />
</head>
```

Next, you modify the Don's Dessert Shop Web page so it is formatted with an external style sheet.

To modify the Don's Dessert Shop Web page so it is formatted with an external style sheet:

1. Return to the **DessertShop.html** document in your text editor.
2. Copy the style declarations within the `<style>` element and create a new document in your text editor. Be certain not to copy the `<style>` tags.
3. Paste the contents into the new file.
4. Save the file as **dessert_shop_styles.css** in your Chapter directory for Chapter 1.

5. Close the **dessert_shop_styles.css** file and return to the **DessertShop.html** file in your text editor.
6. Replace the `<style>` element and the style declarations it contains with the following `<link>` element that links to the dessert_shop_styles.css external style sheet:

```
<link rel="stylesheet" href="dessert_shop_styles.css"
type="text/css" />
```

7. Save the **DessertShop.html** file and open it in your Web browser. The file should appear the same as it did before you linked it to the external style sheet.
8. Close your Web browser window.

The Content-Type <meta> Element

When a user wants to access a Web page, either by entering its URL in a browser's Address box or by clicking a link, the user's Web browser asks the Web server for the Web page. One part of the response from the Web server is the requested Web page. Another important part of the response is the **response header**, which is sent to the Web browser before the Web page is sent to provide information that the browser needs to render the page. One of the most important pieces of information in the response header is the type of data, or content type, that the server is sending. For Web pages, you create a content-type `<meta>` element to specify a content type that the document uses. The term **metadata** means information about information. In a Web page, you use the `<meta>` element to provide information about the information in a Web page. You must place the `<meta>` element within the `<head>` element. You can use three primary attributes with the `<meta>` element: `name`, `content`, and `http-equiv`.

Another important use of the content-type `<meta>` element is to specify a document's character encoding. This allows a Web server to construct a response header in the appropriate character set. To create a content-type `<meta>` element, you assign a value of *content-type* to the `http-equiv` attribute in a `<meta>` element. You then assign to the `<meta>` element's `content` attribute a value of *text/html; charset=iso-8869-1*. This specifies that the document's MIME type is "text/html" and that the document uses the iso-8859-1 character set, which represents English and many western European languages. The following statement shows how to construct the content-type `<meta>` elements:

```
<meta http-equiv="content-type"
    content="text/html; charset=iso-8859-1" />
```

MIME is a protocol that was originally developed to allow different file types to be transmitted as attachments to e-mail messages. Now, MIME has become a standard method of exchanging files over the Internet. You specify MIME types with two-part codes separated by a forward slash (/). The first part specifies the MIME type, and the second part specifies the MIME subtype.

The W3C strongly encourages the use of content-type <meta> elements to specify an XHTML document's character set. However, a content-type <meta> element is not required because most current Web browsers can determine on their own the character set of an XHTML document. For XHTML documents you create in this book, you include the content-type <meta> element in order to comply with the W3C's recommendation.

Next, you add the content-type <meta> element to the Don's Dessert Shop Web page.

To add the content-type <meta> element:

1. Return to the **DessertShop.html** document in your text editor.
2. Add the following content type <meta> element above the closing </head> tag:

```
<meta http-equiv="content-type"
     content="text/html; charset=iso-8859-1" />
```

3. Save the **DessertShop.html** document.

Validating Web Pages

When you open an XHTML document that is not well formed in a Web browser, the browser simply ignores the errors, as it would with an HTML document with errors, and renders the Web page as best it can. The Web browser cannot tell whether the XHTML document is well formed. To ensure that your XHTML document is well formed and that its elements are valid, you need to use a validating parser. A **validating parser** is a program that checks whether an XHTML document is well formed and whether the document conforms to a specific DTD. The term **validation** refers to the process of verifying that your XHTML document is well formed and checking that the elements in your document are correctly written according to the element definitions in a specific DTD. If you do not validate an XHTML document and it contains errors, most Web browsers will probably treat it as an HTML document, ignore the errors, and render the page anyway. However, validation can help you spot errors in your code. Even the most experienced Web page authors frequently introduce typos or some other error into an XHTML document that prevent the document from being well formed.

Various Web development tools, including Macromedia Dreamweaver, offer validation capabilities. In addition, several XHTML validating services can be found online. One of the best available is W3C Markup Validation Service, a free service that validates both HTML and XHTML. The W3C Markup Validation Service is located at *http://validator.w3.org/*. At the time of this writing, the W3C Markup Validation Service did not support validation of PHP files, which you will create extensively in this book. For this reason, you will use another excellent XHTML validating service, the WDG HTML Validator, located at *http://www.htmlhelp.org/tools/validator/*. The WDG HTML Validator is developed by the Web Design Group (WDG), an organization that is dedicated to promoting the creation of Web sites that are accessible by all users worldwide, regardless of physical limitations or the type of user agent. The main Web page for the WDG HTML Validator, shown in Figure 1-14, allows you to validate a Web page by entering its URI.

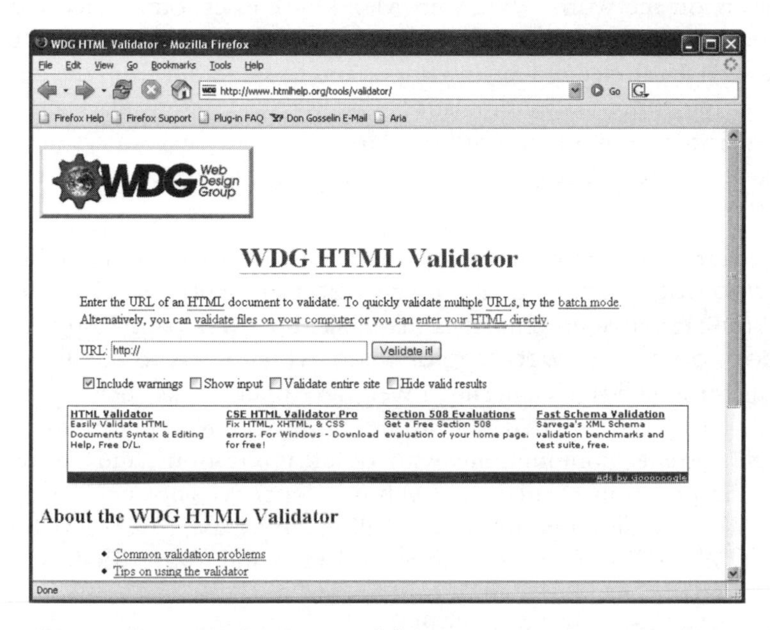

Figure 1-14 WDG HTML Validator

You can also validate files on your local hard drive by clicking the link on the main WDG HTML Validator page or by accessing *http://www.htmlhelp.org/tools/validator/upload.html*.

Next, you validate the Don's Dessert Shop Web page using the upload page of the WDG HTML Validator.

To validate the Don's Dessert Shop Web page using the WDG HTML Validator:

1. Start your Web browser, and enter the Web address of the upload page of the WDG HTML Validator: **http://www.htmlhelp.org/tools/validator/upload.html**.
2. Click the **Browse** button to locate and open the **DessertShop.html** document. The drive, directory path, and filename should appear in the File text box on the upload page.
3. Click the **Validate it!** button. The WDG HTML Validator validates the document. If you receive any errors, fix them, resave the document, and then revalidate the page.
4. Close your Web browser window.

UNDERSTANDING WEB DEVELOPMENT

Web page design, or **Web design**, refers to the visual design and creation of the documents that appear on the World Wide Web. Many businesses today—both prominent and small—have Web sites, and in the future even more businesses are likely to have a presence on the Web. To attract and retain visitors, and to stand out from the crowd, Web sites must be exciting and visually stimulating. Quality Web design plays an important role in attracting first-time and repeat visitors. However, the visual aspect of a Web site is only one part of the story. Equally important is the content of the Web site and how that content is structured.

Web design is an extremely important topic. However, this book is *not* about Web design, nor is it about **Web page authoring** (also called **Web authoring**), which is the creation and assembly of the tags, attributes, and data that make up a Web page. Instead, this book is about **Web development**, or **Web programming**, which refers to the design of software applications for a Web site. Generally, a Web developer works "behind the scenes" with programming languages such as PHP to develop software applications that access databases and file systems, communicate with other applications, and perform other advanced tasks. The programs created by a Web developer will not necessarily be seen by a visitor to a Web site, although the visitor will certainly use a Web developer's programs, particularly if the Web site writes and reads data to and from a database. Although there is certainly some overlap between Web authoring and Web development, this book focuses on how to develop Web sites with PHP.

Another term that you might often see in relation to Web development is a Webmaster. Although there is some dispute over exactly what the term means, a **Webmaster** is a person who is typically responsible for the day-to-day maintenance of a Web site including monitoring Web site traffic and ensuring that the Web site's hardware and software are running properly. The duties of a Webmaster often require knowledge of Web page design, authoring, and development.

Client/Server Architecture

To be successful in Web development, you need to understand the basics of client/server architecture. Many definitions exist of the terms "client" and "server." In traditional client/server architecture, the **server** is usually some sort of database from which a client requests information. A server fulfills a request for information by managing the request or serving the requested information to the client—hence the term, client/server. A system consisting of a client and a server is known as a **two-tier system**.

One of the primary roles of the **client**, or **front end**, in a two-tier system is the presentation of an interface to the user. The user interface gathers information from the user, submits it to a server, or **back end**, then receives, formats, and presents the results returned from the server. The main responsibility of a server is usually data storage and management. On client/server systems, heavy processing, such as calculations, usually takes place on the server. As desktop computers become increasingly powerful, however, many client/server systems have begun placing at least some of the processing responsibilities on the client. In a typical client/server system, a client computer may contain a front end that is used for requesting information from a database on a server. The server locates records that meet the client request, performs some sort of processing, such as calculations on the data, and then returns the information to the client. The client computer can also perform some processing, such as building the queries that are sent to the server or formatting and presenting the returned data. Figure 1-15 illustrates the design of a two-tier client/server system.

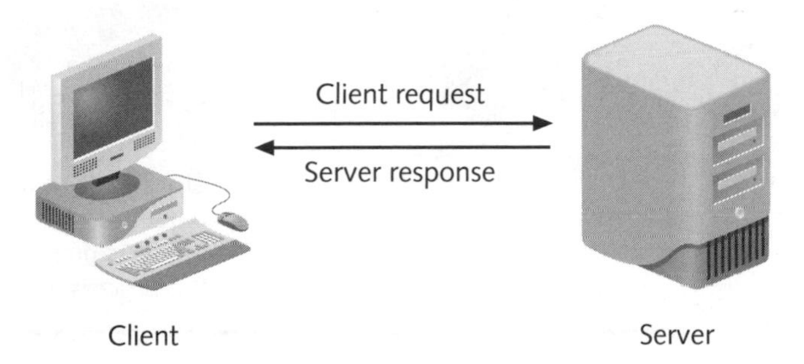

Figure 1-15 The design of a two-tier client/server system

The Web is built on a two-tier client/server system, in which a Web browser (the client) requests documents from a Web server. The Web browser is the client user interface. You can think of the Web server as a database of Web pages. After a Web server returns the requested document, the Web browser (as the client user interface) is responsible for formatting and presenting the document to the user. The requests and responses through which a Web browser and Web server communicate happen with HTTP. For example, if a Web browser requests the URL *http://www.course.com*, the request is made with HTTP because the URL includes the HTTP protocol. The Web server then returns to the Web browser an HTTP response containing the response header and the HTML (or XHTML) for Course Technology's home page.

After you start adding databases and other types of applications to a Web server, the client/server system evolves into what is known as a three-tier client architecture. A **three-tier**, or **multitier, client/server system** consists of three distinct pieces: the client tier, the processing tier, and the data storage tier. The client tier, or user interface tier, is still the Web browser. However, the database portion of the two-tier client/server system is split into a processing tier and the data storage tier. The **processing tier**, or **middle tier**, handles the interaction between the Web browser client and the data storage tier. (The processing tier is also sometimes called the processing bridge.) Essentially, the client tier makes a request of a database on a Web server. The processing tier performs any necessary processing or calculations based on the request from the client tier, and then reads information from or writes information to the data storage tier. The processing tier also handles the return of any information to the client tier. Note that the processing tier is not the only place where processing can occur. The Web browser (client tier) still renders Web page documents (which requires processing), and the database or application in the data storage tier might also perform some processing. Figure 1-16 illustrates the design of a three-tier client/server system.

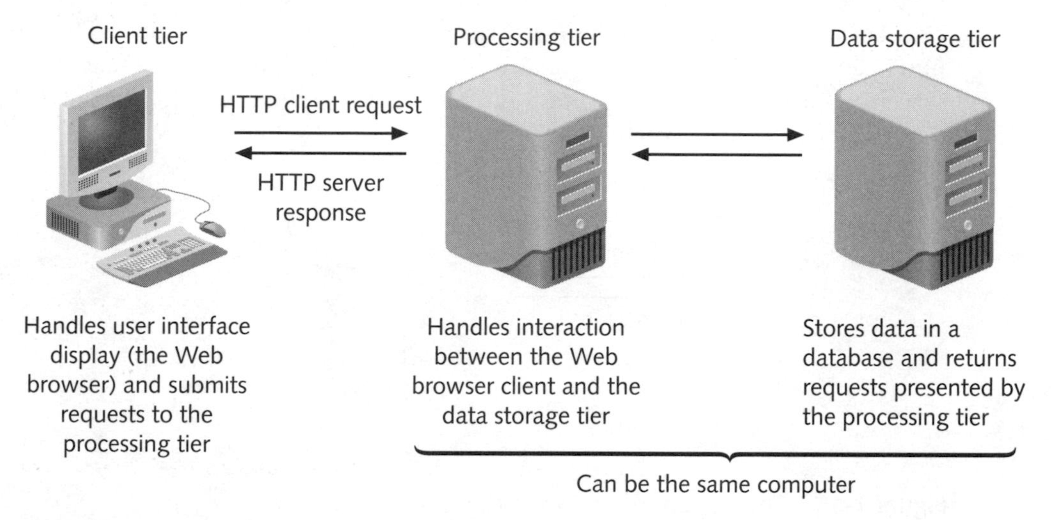

Figure 1-16 The design of a three-tier client/server system

Two-tier client/server architecture is a physical arrangement in which the client and server are two separate computers. Three-tier client/server architecture is more conceptual than physical, because the storage tier can be located on the same server.

Multitier client/server architecture is also referred to as *n*-tier architecture.

JavaScript and Client-Side Scripting

As mentioned earlier, HTML was not intended to control the appearance of pages in a Web browser. When HTML was first developed, Web pages were **static**—that is, they couldn't change after they were rendered by the browser. However, after the Web grew beyond a small academic and scientific community, people began to recognize that greater interactivity and better visual design would make the Web more useful. As commercial applications of the Web grew, the demand for more interactive and visually appealing Web sites also grew.

HTML and XHTML could only be used to produce static documents. You can think of a static Web page written in HTML or XHTML as being approximately equivalent to a document created in a word-processing or desktop publishing program; the only thing you can do with it is view it or print it. Thus, to respond to the demand for greater interactivity, an entirely new Web programming language was needed. Netscape filled this need by developing JavaScript.

JavaScript is a client-side scripting language that allows Web page authors to develop interactive Web pages and sites. **Client-side scripting** refers to a scripting language that runs on a local browser (on the client tier) instead of on a Web server (on the processing tier). Originally designed for use in Navigator Web browsers, JavaScript is now also used in most Web browsers, including Firefox and Internet Explorer.

The term **scripting language** is a general term that originally referred to fairly simple programming languages that did not contain the advanced programming capabilities of languages such as Java or C++. When it comes to Web development, the term scripting language refers to any type of language that is capable of programmatically controlling a Web page or returning some sort of response to a Web browser. It's important to note that although the term scripting language originally referred to simple programming languages, today's Web-based scripting languages are anything but simple.

If you want to learn more about JavaScript, refer to Don Gosselin's *JavaScript*, also published by Course Technology.

The part of a browser that executes scripting language code is called the browser's **scripting engine**. A scripting engine is just one kind of interpreter, with the term **interpreter** referring generally to any program that executes scripting language code. When a scripting engine loads a Web page, it interprets any programs written in scripting languages, such as JavaScript. A Web browser that contains a scripting engine is called a **scripting host**. Firefox and Internet Explorer are examples of scripting hosts that can run JavaScript programs.

Many people think that JavaScript is related to or is a simplified version of the Java programming language. However, the languages are entirely different. Java is an advanced programming language that was created by Sun Microsystems and is considerably more difficult to master than JavaScript. Although Java can be used to create programs that can run from a Web page, Java programs are usually external programs that execute independently of a browser. In contrast, JavaScript programs always run within a Web page and control the browser.

Although JavaScript is considered a programming language, it is also a critical part of Web page design and authoring. This is because the JavaScript language "lives" within a Web page's elements. JavaScript gives you the ability to do the following:

- Turn static Web pages into applications such as games or calculators.
- Change the contents of a Web page after a browser has rendered it.

- Create visual effects such as animation.
- Control the Web browser window itself.

For security reasons, the JavaScript programming language does not include certain types of functionality outside of the Web browser. For example, to prevent mischievous scripts from stealing information, such as your e-mail address or credit card information you use for an online transaction, or from causing damage by changing or deleting files, JavaScript does not allow any file manipulation whatsoever. Similarly, JavaScript does not include any sort of mechanism for creating a network connection or accessing a database. This limitation prevents JavaScript programs from infiltrating a private network or intranet from which information might be stolen or damaged. Another helpful limitation is the fact that JavaScript cannot run system commands or execute programs on a client. The ability to read and write cookies is the only type of access to a client that JavaScript has. Web browsers, however, strictly govern cookies and do not allow access to cookies from outside the domain that created them. This security also means that you cannot use JavaScript to interact directly with Web servers that operate at the processing tier. Although the programmer can employ a few tricks (such as forms and query strings) to allow JavaScript to interact indirectly with a Web server, if you truly want to control what's happening on the server, you need to use a server-side scripting language such as PHP.

Server-Side Scripting and PHP

Server-side scripting refers to a scripting language that is executed from a Web server. One of the primary reasons for using a server-side scripting language is to develop interactive Web sites that communicate with a database. Server-side scripting languages work in the processing tier and have the ability to handle communication between the client tier and the data storage tier. At the processing tier, a server-side scripting language usually prepares and processes the data in some way before submitting it to the data storage tier. Some of the more common uses of server-side scripting language that you have probably already seen on the Web include the following:

- Shopping carts
- Search engines
- Mailing lists and message boards
- Web-based e-mail systems
- Authentication and security mechanisms
- Web logs (blogs)
- Games and entertainment

Although this book focuses on Web development, PHP can also be used for command-line scripting and for developing client-side Graphical User Interface (GUI) applications.

PHP: Hypertext Preprocessor, or **PHP**, is a server-side scripting language that is used for developing interactive Web sites. The language is developed and maintained by the PHP Group (*http://www.php.net*). First created in 1994 by Rasmus Lerdorf for his personal use, PHP originally stood for "Personal Home Page." However, as the language became more powerful and began to be used in professional settings, its name was changed to PHP: Hypertext Preprocessor. PHP has grown into one of today's most popular Web site development tools.

One reason for PHP's popularity has to do with its simplicity. The language is relatively easy to learn, allowing nonprogrammers to quickly incorporate PHP functionality into a Web site. Even though it is easier to learn than other programming languages, PHP is a fast and powerful language that includes object-oriented programming capabilities found in more advanced languages such as C++ and Java. (You study object-oriented programming in Chapter 11.) PHP also makes it surprisingly easy to use databases with your Web sites. Although it's most often used with MySQL databases (which you study in this book), PHP also supports many other types of databases, including Oracle, Sybase, and ODBC-compliant databases.

Do not confuse "relatively easy to learn" with "easy to learn." Although not as involved as an advanced language such as C++ or Java, PHP is nonetheless a programming language and much more complicated than simple HTML.

In addition to PHP, other popular server-side scripting languages used in Web development include Microsoft Active Server Pages (ASP) and Sun Java Server Pages (JSP). An important difference between PHP and its competitors is that PHP is an open source programming language, which is a major factor in PHP's popularity. **Open source** refers to software for which the source code can be freely used and modified. Firefox, Apache, and MySQL are also developed as open source software. Open source software is not developed by commercial software companies such as Microsoft or Sun, but by contributing programmers from around the world who donate their time and skills. One of the main benefits of open source software is that it's free. You do not need to purchase open source software or pay any sort of licensing fee to a commercial software company. The development of open source software takes place outside the business and marketing pressures that drive the development of commercial software. For example, with commercial software, you often need to wait months, or even years, for new features to be added or bugs to be fixed—which you then usually need to pay for by purchasing an upgraded software version. With open source software, new features may be released as soon as they have been developed and tested by the contributing programmer. Similarly, it usually takes commercial software companies several months—or longer—to release fixes for bugs in their software. However, bugs in open source software can often be fixed in a much shorter period, sometimes within days of being reported.

Unlike JavaScript, a server-side scripting language such as PHP can't access or manipulate a Web browser. In fact, PHP cannot run on a client tier at all. Instead, PHP exists and executes solely on a Web server, where it performs various types of processing or accesses databases. When a client requests a PHP script, the script is interpreted and executed by the scripting engine within the Web server software. After the script finishes executing, the Web server software then translates the results of the script (such as the result of a calculation or the records returned from a database) into HTML or XHTML, which it then returns to the client. In other words, a client will never see the PHP code, only the HTML or XHTML that the Web server software returns from the script. Figure 1-17 illustrates how a Web server processes a PHP script.

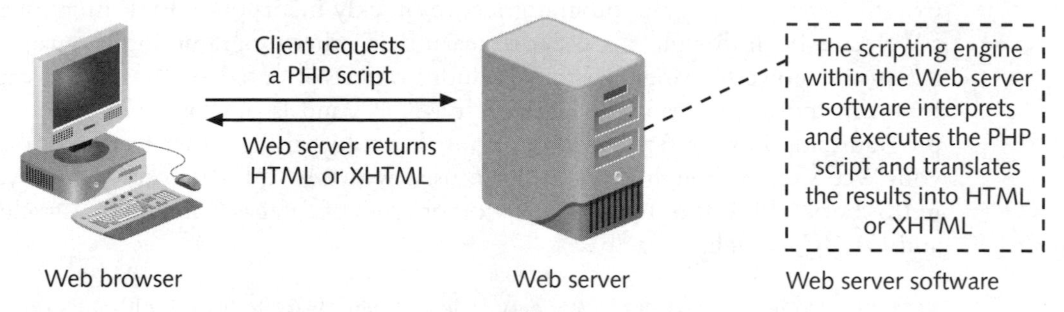

Figure 1-17 How a Web server processes a PHP script

Should You Use Client-Side or Server-Side Scripting?

An important question in the design of any client/server system is deciding how much processing to place on the client or server. In the context of Web site development, you must decide whether to use client-side JavaScript or server-side PHP. This is an important consideration because the choice you make can greatly affect the performance of your program. In some cases, the decision is simple. For example, if you want to control the Web browser, you must use JavaScript. If you want to access a database on a Web server, you must use PHP. However, there are tasks that both languages can accomplish, such as validating forms and manipulating cookies. Further, both languages can perform the same types of calculations and data processing.

A general rule of thumb is to allow the client to handle the user interface processing and light processing, such as data validation, but have the Web server perform intensive calculations and data storage. This division of labor is especially important when dealing with the Web. Unlike with clients on a private network, it's not possible to know in advance the computing capabilities of each client on the Web. You cannot assume that each client (browser) that accesses your client/server application (Web site) has the necessary power to perform the processing required by the application. For this reason, intensive processing should be placed on the server.

Because servers are usually much more powerful than client computers, your first instinct might be to let the server handle all processing and only use the client to display a user interface. Although you do not want to overwhelm clients with processing they cannot handle, it is important to perform as much processing as possible on the client for several reasons:

- Distributing processing among multiple clients creates applications that are more powerful, because the processing power is not limited to the capabilities of a single computer. Client computers become more powerful every day, and advanced capabilities such as JavaScript are now available in local Web browsers. Thus, it makes sense to use a Web application to harness some of this power and capability. A **Web application** is a program that executes on a server but that clients access through a Web page loaded in a browser.
- Local processing on client computers minimizes transfer times across the Internet and creates faster applications. If a client had to wait for all processing to be performed on the server, a Web application could be painfully slow over a busy Internet connection.
- Performing processing on client computers lightens the processing load on the server. If all processing in a three-tier client/server system is on the server, the server for a popular Web site could become overwhelmed trying to process requests from numerous clients.

The term "distributed application" is used to describe multiple computers sharing the computing responsibility for a single application.

Chapter Summary

- In 1990 and 1991, Tim Berners-Lee created what would become the World Wide Web, or the Web, at the European Laboratory for Particle Physics (CERN) in Geneva, Switzerland, as a way to easily access cross-referenced documents that existed on the CERN computer network.
- A Web server is a computer that delivers Web pages.
- A domain name is a unique address used for identifying a computer, often a Web server, on the Internet.
- Transmission Control Protocol/Internet Protocol (TCP/IP) refers to a large collection of communication protocols used on the Internet.
- When a document conforms to the rules and requirements of XHTML, it is said to be well formed.

- A Document Type Definition (DTD) defines the elements and attributes that can be used in a document, along with the rules that a document must follow when it includes them.
- Cascading Style Sheets (CSS) are a standard set by the W3C for managing the design and formatting of Web pages in a Web browser.
- A validating parser is a program that checks whether an XHTML document is well formed and whether the document conforms to a specific DTD.
- A system consisting of a client and a server is known as a two-tier system.
- A three-tier, or multitier, client/server system consists of three distinct pieces: the client tier, the processing tier, and the data storage tier.
- JavaScript is a client-side scripting language that allows Web page authors to develop interactive Web pages and sites.
- PHP: Hypertext Preprocessor (PHP) is a server-side scripting language that is used for developing interactive Web sites.
- Open source refers to software for which the source code can be freely used and modified.

Review Questions

1. Which element is required in the `<head>` element?
   a. `<hr>`
   b. `<meta>`
   c. `<body>`
   d. `<title>`
2. The host portion of a URL is usually ________________.
   a. web
   b. ftp
   c. http
   d. www
3. The final part of a domain name, known as the ________________, identifies the type of institution or organization.
   a. domain
   b. domain identifier
   c. protocol
   d. IP address

4. If a URL does not specify a filename, the requesting Web server looks for a file with which of the following names? (Choose all that apply.)
   a. index.html
   b. index.htm
   c. default.html
   d. default.htm
5. Explain why you should use an ISP to host a Web site.
6. Domain names are stored in a master database that is maintained by ________________.
   a. Microsoft
   b. Mozilla
   c. the W3C
   d. InterNIC
7. You can register a domain name yourself. True or False?
8. Most current Web browsers, including Internet Explorer and Netscape, have the capability to act as FTP clients. True or False?
9. Which of the following belongs in the first line of an XHTML document?
   a. an `<html>` tag
   b. an `<xhtml>` tag
   c. a `<title>` tag
   d. a `<!DOCTYPE>` declaration
10. DTD stands for ________________.
    a. data transfer display
    b. digital technology definition
    c. decimal type determinant
    d. document type definition
11. Which XHTML DTD(s) allow you to use deprecated elements? (Choose all that apply.)
    a. XML
    b. transitional
    c. strict
    d. frameset

12. Which of the following closes the empty `<hr>` element in an XHTML document?
    a. `<hr\>`
    b. `<hr \>`
    c. `<hr/>`
    d. `<hr />`
13. The information contained within an element's opening and closing tags is referred to as its ________.
    a. content
    b. data
    c. attribute
    d. meta information
14. What is the correct syntax for creating an inline style that assigns Arial to the `font-family` property?
    a. `style="font-family, Arial"`
    b. `font-family=Arial`
    c. `style="font-family: Arial"`
    d. `font-family; Arial`
15. You can include multiple style declarations in an inline style by separating each declaration with a ________.
    a. colon
    b. semicolon
    c. comma
    d. forward slash
16. Explain when you should use inline styles, internal style sheets, or external style sheets.
17. Which element do you use to create an internal style sheet?
    a. `<css>`
    b. `<link>`
    c. `<style>`
    d. `<styles>`

18. A system consisting of a client and a server is known as a ______________.
    a. mainframe topology
    b. double-system architecture
    c. two-tier system
    d. wide area network
19. What is usually the primary role of a client?
    a. locating records that match a request
    b. heavy processing, such as calculations
    c. data storage
    d. the presentation of an interface to the user
20. Which of the following functions does the processing tier not handle in a three-tier client/server system?
    a. processing and calculations
    b. reading and writing of information to the data storage tier
    c. the return of any information to the client tier
    d. data storage
21. Which function can a client safely handle?
    a. data validation
    b. data storage
    c. intensive processing
    d. heavy calculations

HANDS-ON PROJECTS

Hands-On Project 1-1

In this project, you create a Web page that displays a birth announcement. The Web page will conform to the transitional DTD.

1. Create a new document in your text editor, and type the `<!DOCTYPE>` declaration, `<html>` element, document head, and `<body>` element. Use the transitional DTD and "Birth Announcement" as the content of the `<title>` element. Your document should appear as follows:

```
<!DOCTYPE html PUBLIC "-//W3C//DTD XHTML 1.0 Transitional//EN"
"http://www.w3.org/TR/xhtml1/DTD/xhtml1-transitional.dtd">
<html xmlns="http://www.w3.org/1999/xhtml">
<head>
<title>Birth Announcement</title>
<meta http-equiv="content-type"
content="text/html; charset=iso-8859-1" />
</head>
<body>
</body>
</html>
```

2. Next add the following text and elements to the document body:

```
<center>
<h1>Birth Announcement</h1>
<p>It's a <b>boy</b>, we're proud to say.<br />
And after nine months, he's ready to <i>play</i>.</p>
<p>Introducing ... </p>
<h2>Noah David Mahoney</h2>
<p><b>Saturday, March 10, 2007<br />
6:20 a.m.<br />
6 pounds, 2 ounces<br />
18 3/4 inches</b></p>
<p><i>The proud parents:</i><br />
Maureen and George</p>
</center>
```

3. Save the document as **BirthAnnouncement.html** in the Projects directory for Chapter 1, then close it in your text editor.
4. Use the WDG HTML Validator to validate the **BirthAnnouncement.html** document, and then open it in your Web browser and examine how the elements are rendered.
5. Close your Web browser window.

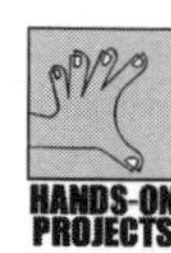

Hands-On Project 1-2

In this project, you create a simple Web page for a shoe company. The Web page will conform to the strict DTD.

1. Create a new document in your text editor, and type the `<!DOCTYPE>` declaration, `<html>` element, document head, and `<body>` element. Use the strict DTD and "Central Valley Shoe Emporium" as the content of the `<title>` element.
2. Next add the following text and elements to the document body:

```
<h1>Central Valley Shoe Emporium</h1>
<h2>Low Sale Prices on Selected Shoes!</h2>
<p><em>Now through August 31, 2007</em></p>
<h3>Men's Specials</h3>
<ul>
<li>Hush Puppies 'Avery' Oxford: $125.00</li>
<li>New Balance Casual Shoes: $37.50</li>
</ul>
<h3>Women's Specials</h3>
<ul>
<li>Designer shoes: 25% off</li>
<li>Athletic shoes: <strong>50% off!</strong></li>
</ul>
```

3. Save the document as **ShoeStore.html** in the Projects directory for Chapter 1, then close it in your text editor.
4. Use the WDG HTML Validator to validate the **ShoeStore.html** document, and then open it in your Web browser and examine how the elements are rendered.
5. Close your Web browser window.

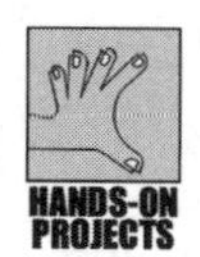

Hands-On Project 1-3

In this project, you fix the errors in a simple Web page for a flooring company. The Web page will conform to the transitional DTD.

1. Create a new document in your text editor, and type the `<!DOCTYPE>` declaration, `<html>` element, document head, and `<body>` element. Use the strict DTD and "Forestville Flooring" as the content of the `<title>` element.
2. Add the following text and elements to the document body:

```
<h1>Forestville Flooring</h1>
<h2>Need New Floors?</h2><hr>
<p>Come to the top flooring specialists in town.
<strong><em>Forestville Flooring</strong></em> has been family
owned and operated for over 35 years. Call for a FREE in-home
estimate.
<p>From now until September 30th, we are offering 0% financing
for the first 90 days.* <br>
* <em>New customers only. Not to be combined with any other
offer.</p>
```

3. Save the document as **ForestvilleFlooring.html** in the Projects directory for Chapter 1, and then open it in your Web browser and examine how the elements are rendered.
4. Although the text and elements you added to the document body will render properly in a Web browser, the code contains several errors that prevent the document from conforming with the strict DTD. Fix the errors and then use the WDG HTML Validator to ensure that the document conforms to the strict DTD.
5. Close your Web browser window and the **ForestvilleFlooring.html** file in your text editor.

Hands-On Project 1-4

In this project, you use inline styles to format a Web page for a property management company. The file to which you will add the style information, PropertyManagement.html, is located in your Projects directory for Chapter 1.

1. In your text editor, open the **PropertyManagement.html** file from your Projects directory for Chapter 1. The document body contains two heading elements and two paragraph elements.
2. Add to the `<body>` element the following inline style declaration that changes the background color of the page to cyan:

```
style="background-color: cyan"
```

3. Next modify the two heading elements so they contain inline style formatting, as follows:

```
<h1 style="font-family: 'Times New Roman', Times, serif; font-
size: 2em; color: navy; background-color: transparent">Central
Valley</h1>
<h2 style="font-family: 'Times New Roman', Times, serif; font-
size: 1.5em; text-spacing: 80%; color: navy; background-color:
transparent">Property Management</h2>
```

4. Now add the following inline style declaration to each of the paragraph elements:

```
style="font-family: 'Times New Roman', Times, serif; font-size:
.8em; color: navy; background-color: transparent"
```

5. Save and close the **PropertyManagement.html** file.
6. Use the WDG HTML Validator to validate the **PropertyManagement.html** file. After the file is valid, open it in your Web browser and see how the new style formatting appears. Your Web page should look similar to Figure 1-18.

Figure 1-18 Property Management Web page

7. Close your Web browser window.

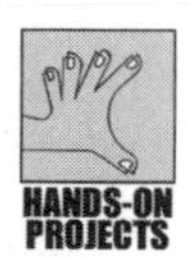

Hands-On Project 1-5

In this project, you use an internal style sheet to add style information to a Web page that contains customer testimonials for a motorcycle accessories business. The file to which you will add the style information, MomsMotorcycles.html, is located in your Projects directory for Chapter 1.

1. In your text editor, open the **MomsMotorcycles.html** file from your Projects directory for Chapter 1. The document body contains three `<blockquote>` elements, each of which includes text and `<em>` elements.
2. Add the following internal style sheet above the document's closing `</head>` element. The style sheet includes declarations for the `h1`, `h2`, and `blockquote` selectors, along with a contextual selector for the `<em>` element when located within a `<blockquote>` element.

```
<style type="text/css">
h1 { font-family: Verdana, Helvetica, sans-serif; font-
size: 1.5em; color: navy }
h2 { font-family: Verdana, Helvetica, sans-serif; font-
size: 1.2em; color: red }
blockquote { font-family: Verdana, Helvetica, sans-
serif; font-size: 1em; color: blue }
blockquote em { font-weight: bold; color: purple }
</style>
```

3. Save the **MomsMotorcycles.html** file, but leave it open in your text editor.
4. Use the WDG HTML Validator to validate the **MomsMotorcycles.html** file. After the file is valid, open it in your Web browser. Figure 1-19 shows how the Web page should appear in a Web browser.

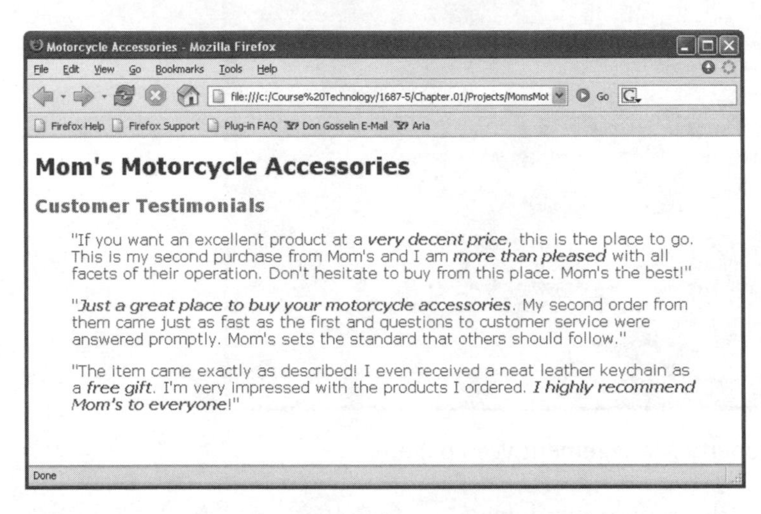

Figure 1-19 Mom's Motorcycle Accessories Web page

5. Close your Web browser window.

Hands-On Project 1-6

In this project, you modify the Mom's Motorcycle Accessories Web page you created in the preceding project so it uses an external style sheet instead of an internal style sheet.

1. Return to the **MomsMotorcycles.html** document in your text editor.
2. Copy the style declarations within the `<style>` element and create a new document in your text editor. Be certain not to copy the `<style>` tags.
3. Paste the contents into the new file.
4. Save the file as **moms.css** in your Projects directory for Chapter 1.
5. Close the **moms.css** file and return to the **MomsMotorcycles.html** file in your text editor.
6. Replace the `<style>` element and style declarations it contains with the following `<link>` element that links to the **moms.css** external style sheet:

```
<link rel="stylesheet" href="moms.css" type="text/css" />
```

7. Save the **MomsMotorcycles.html** file and open it in your Web browser. The file should appear the same as it did before you linked it to the external style sheet.
8. Close your Web browser window and the **MomsMotorcycles.html** file in your text editor.

Case Projects

Save your Case Projects files in the Cases directory for Chapter 1. Be certain to validate the files you create with the WDG HTML Validator.

Case Project 1-1

Create an XHTML document for a charity that accepts vehicle donations. You can use the name of an existing charity or make up any name you like. Include a bulleted list of the benefits both you and the charity will incur if you donate your car to them. Write the document so that it conforms to the transitional DTD. Be certain to use some deprecated elements, such as the `<u>` and `<center>` elements. Save the document as **CarDonation.html**.

Case Project 1-2

Create an XHTML document for a used music CD store. Use an `<h1>` element to contain the store's name. Include an introductory paragraph that describes the music categories the store carries, such as Jazz, Gospel, Hip-Hop, and Country. Use an `<h2>` element for each music category. Beneath each category heading, include artists and titles of CDs that the store currently has in its collection, including the condition (excellent, good, fair, or poor) and price. Write the document so that it conforms to the strict DTD and create an external style sheet that formats the document. Save the HTML document as **CDStore.html**.

Case Project 1-3

In 1994, the Netscape Navigator Web browser controlled 75% of the market. However, at the time of this writing, Microsoft Internet Explorer controls over 90% of the market. This incredible shift in Web browser popularity is a result of the so-called "browser wars." Search the Internet for information on the browser wars and write a paper on why they began—and ended (or did they?). You should also understand that although Netscape browsers are now virtually extinct, they do survive in the form of the Mozilla Firefox browser. Recently, Microsoft has been losing ground to Mozilla. Do you think this signals the start of a new browser war?

Case Project 1-4

In addition to client/server architecture, peer-to-peer architecture is also widely used. Search the Internet for information on peer-to-peer architecture. What are the differences between client/server architecture and peer-to-peer architecture? When should each type of architecture be used? Write a paper summarizing your research and conclusions.

Case Project 1-5

Search the Internet for information on how TCP/IP is used for communication on the Internet. How does TCP/IP work? What are the different protocols available and when should you use them? How is TCP/IP addressing used on the Internet? Write a paper summarizing your research and conclusions.

CHAPTER

2

GETTING STARTED WITH PHP

In this chapter, you will:

- Install and configure a Web server
- Install and configure PHP
- Install and configure MySQL
- Create basic PHP scripts

Understanding how to install and configure the software required for creating and delivering PHP scripts is considered a critical skill for Web developers. Even if you have an Internet service provider (ISP) hosting your Web site, you will still need to develop your PHP scripts on your local computer before uploading them to your ISP. In this chapter, you build a Web development environment consisting of a Web server, PHP, and MySQL. After you have finished installing and testing your Web development environment, you study the basics of how to create PHP scripts.

Even if you already have access to the necessary software for creating and delivering PHP scripts, or if you install the software in some other manner, be certain to follow the instructions in the Configuring Apache or Configuring Internet Information Services sections later in this chapter (depending on which Web server you install). These sections contain procedures you need to perform to configure your Web server to work with the data files you installed in Chapter 1.

Building a Web Development Environment

Before you can write PHP scripts, you need the following:

- A Web browser
- A Web server
- The PHP software
- A database

You should already have a Web browser installed on your computer. Be sure to use a recent Web browser such as Firefox 1.0 or Internet Explorer 6.0. You can use almost any version of the UNIX/Linux operating system to develop PHP scripts, including Red Hat Linux and Mac OS X. To develop PHP scripts with the Windows operating systems, the version of Windows you can use depends primarily on the Web server software you decide to install. Although you can install the Apache Web server on Windows platforms as far back as Windows 95, the Apache Foundation does not recommend installing Apache on Windows 95, Windows 98, or Windows Me. Internet Information Services (IIS) is only available on Windows 2000 and newer versions of Windows. Although not required to run PHP scripts, for PHP to be of much use, you also need install a database. To complete the exercises in this book, you need to install MySQL, an open source database developed by MySQL AB (*http://www.mysql.com/*).

The instructions in this chapter assume that you are familiar with basic commands for your operating system.

If you have an account with an ISP, you may already have access to installations of PHP and MySQL on your ISP's Web server. Check with your ISP for more information. Even if you do not have an account with an ISP, you should install the necessary software on your local computer so that you can develop your PHP scripts before transferring them to your ISP.

Keep in mind that the Web development environment you install in this section should only be used for development and testing purposes, and not for hosting a live Web site. Until you understand the security and maintenance issues involved with hosting a Web site, your best bet is to go through an ISP.

A number of companies offer free and commercial installation kits that automatically install and configure a Web server, PHP, and MySQL. You can find an extensive list of these installation kits at *http://www.hotscripts.com/PHP/Software_and_Servers/Installation_Kits/*. However, the PHP Group (the open source organization that develops PHP) does not endorse any installation kits and recommends that you perform a manual installation for best results.

Understanding Binary and Source Code Installations

You can install open source software from binary format or from source code. **Binary format** (or **binaries**) refer to compiled files, such as executable installation programs. **Source code** is the original programming code in which an application was written. Before you can use source code, it must be **compiled**, or processed and assembled into an executable format. On Windows platforms, your best bet is to install the open source applications discussed in this section using binaries that are available on each application's Web site. Although you can also compile Windows versions of each program, you must have access to an installation of Microsoft Visual Studio, which is a line of development tools for Windows platforms.

The difference between interpreting and compiling is that, while interpreted programs (such as JavaScript and PHP) are processed and assembled into an executable format each time they execute, compiled programs only need to be recompiled when their code changes.

For UNIX and Linux operating systems, you can also install Apache, PHP, and MySQL from either binary or source code format, although the open source organizations that develop these applications do not usually make binary versions available on their Web sites. However, Apache and PHP come preinstalled on many UNIX and Linux-based operating systems. If they are not preinstalled on your system, then you can probably find binaries in the form of "packages" that can be installed with special programs. For example, various Linux platforms allow you to use an application called the Red Hat Package Manager (RPM) to install binary packages (or "RPMs"). You can probably find binary package versions of Apache, PHP, and MySQL with your UNIX/Linux installation files or on your platform vendor's Web site or another third-party Web site. For example, you can download a binary package of PHP for Mac OS X at *http://www.entropy.ch/software/macosx/php/*.

Because of the many UNIX/Linux operating systems that are available, specific instructions cannot be listed here for determining whether an application is installed and for locating and installing binary packages on each platform. You should be able to find detailed instructions on your platform vendor's Web site.

Source code for many UNIX/Linux programs is written in the C programming language. To compile C code on UNIX/Linux systems, you must use the make utility with an ANSI C compiler. Although you may already have an ANSI C compiler installed on your system, it is recommend that you install the most recent version of the GNU C compiler, which is freely available at *http://gcc.gnu.org/*.

Although a binary format can be easier to install, it may not contain the most recent version of an open source application, and you may not be able to customize your installation and configuration. To be successful with this book, you do not necessarily need the latest and greatest version of each application, nor do you need to perform an advanced installations and configurations. However, the ability to install and compile programs from source code is a skill you must possess in order to be a successful Web developer, especially if you work with UNIX/Linux systems for which binary installations do exist. For this reason, the instructions in this chapter describe how to install each open source application from open source format. The instructions use generic steps that are similar for most UNIX-based systems, including Linux platforms and Mac OS X. For detailed instructions on installing each open source application with specific platforms, see the installation documentation on each application's Web site.

Getting Help

You have probably grown to expect a certain level of help and support from vendors of commercial software. For instance, Microsoft provides a great deal of help and support for IIS. The first line of support is the online help that is installed with IIS. Figure 2-1 shows the Web page that should appear in your browser for IIS 5.1.

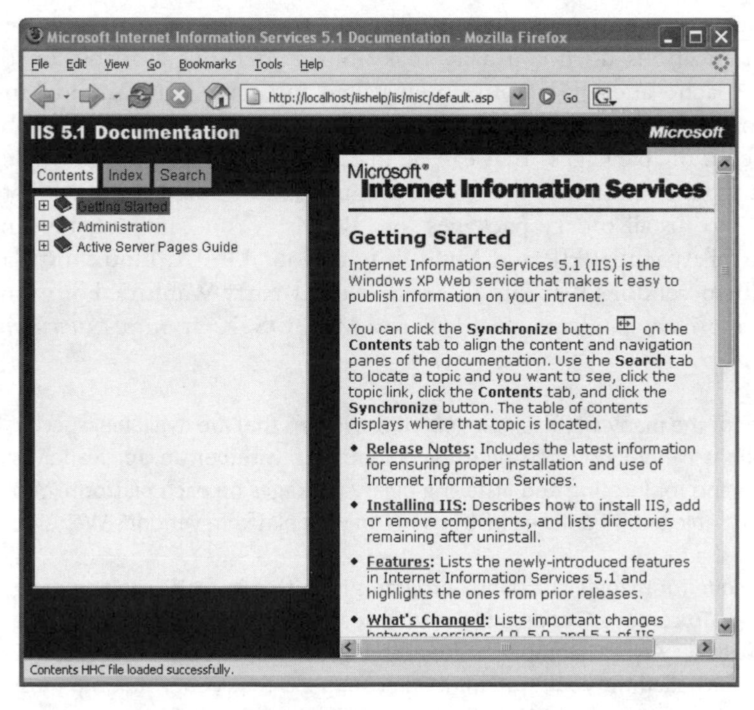

Figure 2-1 Help page for IIS

If you cannot find the answers you need with the online help that is installed with IIS, you can obtain more information as well as professional technical support on Microsoft's Web site at *http://www.microsoft.com*.

However, of the four applications discussed in this section, IIS is the only commercial offering; Apache, PHP, and MySQL are all open source software. One of the downsides to using open-source software is the lack of official support from a commercial software company such as Microsoft to help you through difficulties. Instead, you must rely on online documentation that is maintained by volunteers. You can access the official online documentation for Apache, PHP, and MySQL at the following URLs:

- **Apache documentation:** *http://httpd.apache.org/docs-2.0/*
- **PHP documentation:** *http://www.php.net/docs.php*
- **MySQL documentation:** *http://dev.mysql.com/doc/mysql/en/index.html*

If you cannot find your answers in the online documentation, then you can also post a message to various mailing lists that are available for each application. In most cases, other users who monitor the lists are more than delighted to help you figure out a problem. You can find mailing lists and other support resources for each product at the following URLs:

- **Apache support resources:** *http://httpd.apache.org/lists.html*
- **PHP support resources:** *http://www.php.net/support.php*
- **MySQL support resources:** *http://dev.mysql.com/support*

You can also purchase various technical support packages from MySQL AB, the organization that develops MySQL. For more information, visit *http://www.mysql.com/support/*.

Be warned that if you do send a message to one of the mailing lists, you may receive a response of 'RTFM', which is a commonly used acronym in information technology that stands for *Read the #$%&@#* Manual*. The symbols in the preceding definition represent a colorful word that you can figure out on your own. As impolite as the phrase may be, the acronym RTFM is a standard response to a question that can be easily found in a software manual. So if are certain your answer is not in the manual, then go ahead and send a message to one of the mailing lists. With any luck, you will receive a prompt reply with a solution to your problem. However, if you do receive a response of 'RTFM', try not to take it too personally; at least you will know that somewhere an answer to your question does exist.

Course Technology and the author of this book are more than happy to help with any problems you may have with this book. However, when it comes to installing or running any of the applications discussed in this book, they cannot help you find the answers to your problems as quickly as the open source community can.

INSTALLING AND CONFIGURING A WEB SERVER

As you learned earlier, Apache is the most popular Web server software used on the Internet. Apache is developed as open source software by the Apache Software Foundation (*http://apache.org/*) and runs on most platforms, including the following Windows platforms:

- Windows NT
- Windows 2000 (Professional, Server, and Advanced Server)
- Windows XP Professional
- Windows Server 2003 family for both client and server applications

Microsoft's commercial IIS for Windows operating systems is the second most popular Web server and is used on about a third of today's Web sites. IIS is available as a component of the following Windows platforms:

- Windows 2000 (Professional, Server, and Advanced Server)
- Windows XP Professional
- Windows Server 2003 family for both client and server applications

IIS can only be installed on Windows platforms.

When you install Apache on UNIX and Linux operating systems, you must start and stop the application manually. When you install Apache or IIS on Windows, each Web server is installed as a **service**, which is a term that is used with Windows operating systems to refer to a program that performs a specific function to support other programs. Services are usually launched automatically when Windows first starts, so you do not normally need to start Apache or IIS yourself. However, there will be times when you will need to restart your Web server, especially after you modify your configuration settings. For this reason, instructions for starting and stopping Apache and IIS are listed in the following sections.

PHP scripts are supported by almost every Web server out there. You can use whatever Web server you like with this book, provided it supports PHP. But because Apache and IIS are two of the most popular Web server applications, the installation and configuration instructions in this book focus on Apache and IIS. If you decide to use a Web server other than Apache or IIS, refer to the documentation that came with the Web server for installation and configuration instructions.

NOTE

Other Microsoft Web servers that support PHP are available for older versions of Windows, including Peer Web Services on Windows NT Workstation 4.0 and Personal Web Server for Windows 95/98/ME. However, because these Web servers have been discontinued by Microsoft, this book only includes instructions for IIS.

Installing and Running Apache on UNIX and Linux

This section explains how to install and configure Apache from source code on UNIX and Linux systems. For more detailed installation instructions, refer to the Compiling and Installing Web page at *http://httpd.apache.org/docs-2.0/install.html.*

CAUTION

Before installing Apache on UNIX and Linux systems, you may need to log in as the root user to ensure that you have the necessary permissions to perform administration tasks.

To install Apache from source code on UNIX and Linux systems:

1. Start your Web browser, and enter the Web address for the Apache HTTP Server download page: **http://httpd.apache.org/download.cgi**. Download the compressed UNIX source file containing the Apache version that the Apache Foundation recommends as the best available. At the time of this writing, the best available version is Apache 2.0.52 and the compressed UNIX source file is named httpd-2.0.52.tar.gz. Save the file to a temporary location such as your usr/src directory or another directory of your choice.
2. Run the following `gunzip` command in the directory where you downloaded the compressed file. This command decompresses the httpd-2.0.52.tar.gz file into a tar file named httpd-2.0.52.tar within the same directory.

   ```
   gunzip httpd-2.0.52.tar.gz
   ```

3. Run the following `tar` command, which extracts the files in the httpd-2.0.52.tar to a directory named httpd-2.0.52 within the current directory:

   ```
   tar xvf httpd-2.0.52.tar
   ```

4. Change to the httpd-2.0.52 directory:

   ```
   cd httpd-2.0.52
   ```

5. The httpd-2.0.52 directory contains a `configure` command that prepares your system for installation of Apache. You can specify several parameters when you run the `configure` command. One parameter that you should be aware of is the `--prefix` parameter, which specifies the location to install Apache. By default, Apache is installed in the /usr/local/apache2 directory. Run the `configure` command using default options, including the default installation location, then run the following command:

   ```
   ./configure
   ```

If you want to install Apache in a location other than the default, run the **configure** command as follows:

```
./configure --prefix=installation directory
```

For a complete listing of parameters and syntax for the `configure` command, type `./configure --help`.

6. After the configuration script finishes, compile the Apache source code by running the **make** command in the httpd-2.0.52 directory.
7. Finally, perform the installation by running the **make install** command in the httpd-2.0.52 directory.

You start, stop, and restart Apache using the `apachectl` control script, located in the bin directory beneath the directory where you installed Apache. The following examples assume that Apache is installed in the /usr/local/apache2 directory:

To start Apache, use the `start` option with the `apachectl` control script, as follows:

```
/usr/local/apache2/bin/apachectl start
```

To stop Apache, use the `stop` option of the `apachectl` control script, as follows:

```
/usr/local/apache2/bin/apachectl stop
```

To restart Apache, use the `restart` option of the `apachectl` control script, as follows:

```
/usr/local/apache2/bin/apachectl restart
```

Installing and Running Apache on Windows

This section explains how to install and configure Apache from binary format on Windows operating systems. For more detailed installation instructions, refer to the Using Apache with Microsoft Windows Web page at *http://httpd.apache.org/docs-2.0/platform/windows.html.*

To learn how to compile Apache from source code on Windows, see the Compiling Apache for Microsoft Windows Web page at *http://httpd.apache.org/docs-2.0/platform/win_compiling.html*.

To install Apache from binary format on Windows operating systems:

1. Start your Web browser, and enter the Web address for the Apache HTTP Server download page: **http://httpd.apache.org/download.cgi**. Download the Win32 Binary (MSI Installer) file containing the Apache version that the Apache Foundation recommends as the best available. At the

time of this writing, the best available version is Apache 2.0.52 and the Win32 Binary (MSI Installer) file is named apache_2.0.52-win32-x86-no_ssl.msi. Save the file to a temporary directory on your computer.

2. Open **Windows Explorer** or **My Computer** and navigate to the directory where you downloaded the apache_2.0.52-win32-x86-no_ssl.msi installation file. Double-click the file to start the installation program. The Welcome screen of the installation wizard appears.
3. In the Welcome screen, click the **Next** button to proceed with installation. The License Agreement screen appears.
4. On the License Agreement screen, click the button that accepts the terms of the license agreement, and then click the **Next** button. The Read This First screen appears.
5. Read through the contents of the Read This First screen, and then click the **Next** button. The Server Information screen appears.
6. The Server Information screen asks you for information about your Web server, including the network domain, the server name, and the administrator's e-mail address. If you have registered a domain name and already configured your computer as a Web server, enter this information. However, you are probably only using the current computer to perform the exercises in this book. If that is the case, accept the default values that were entered for your system. If no values are entered, enter *yourname*.net for the network domain, server.*yourname*.net for the server name, and your personal e-mail address for the administrator's e-mail address. In the section of the screen that asks for whom to install Apache, accept the default value of **for All Users, on Port 80, as a Service -- Recommended**. Click the **Next** button to continue. The Setup Type screen appears.
7. The Setup Type screen allows you to select whether to perform a typical or custom installation. Accept the default value of **Typical**, and click the **Next** button. The Destination Folder screen appears.
8. The Destination Folder screen allows you to change the directory where Apache will be installed. Change the destination folder if you need to, although in most cases you should accept the default value of C:\Program Files\Apache Group\. Click the **Next** button to continue. The Ready to Install the Program screen appears.
9. The Ready to Install the Program screen is the final screen that appears before Apache is installed. If you want to change any of the installation options you selected, click the **Back** button. Otherwise, click the **Install** button. When the installation is complete, the Installation Wizard Complete screen appears.
10. Click the **Finish** button to close the Installation Wizard Complete screen.

The preceding steps install Apache as a service, so you do not normally need to start Apache yourself. To control Apache manually, click your Start menu and point to All Programs; you should see an Apache HTTP Server 2.0.52 directory, which in turn contains a Control Apache Server directory. The Control Apache Server directory contains Stop, Start, and Restart commands that you can use if you need to manually control the service. The Control Apache Server directory also contains a Monitor Apache Services command, which places an icon in the notification area to the right of the Windows taskbar. You can also use the Monitor Apache Services icon to stop, start, and restart Apache. The Monitor Apache Services command should start automatically when you first start Windows.

If Apache is running, the Monitor Apache Services icon appears as an arrow. If Apache is not running, the Monitor Apache Services icon appears as a square.

Installing and Running Internet Information Services on Windows

This section explains how to install and configure IIS on Windows operating systems. IIS is available on the installation CD-ROMs for Windows 2000, Windows XP, and Windows Server 2003 operating systems.

To install IIS:

1. Open **Control Panel** from the **Start** menu.
2. If you are using Windows XP, click the **Switch to Classic View** link to display the Control Panel icons, if necessary.
3. Select the **Add or Remove Programs** icon. The Add or Remove Programs window opens.
4. In the Add or Remove Programs window, click **Add/Remove Windows Components**. The Windows Components Wizard window opens. The window lists components that can be installed with the Windows operating system. A selected check box indicates that a component will be installed, whereas a shaded check box indicates that only part of a component will be installed.
5. Scroll down the Components list and click the check box next to Internet Information Services (IIS). By default, IIS is only installed with the most common options, so the check box is shaded. If you want to select additional options for IIS, click the Details button. However, the default IIS installation options are all you need for this book, so click the **Next** button to begin installation.
6. During the installation process, you might be prompted for the location of your original Windows installation CD-ROM. The Windows Components Wizard displays a message when installation is complete. After installation is complete, click the **Finish** button to close the Windows Components Wizard.
7. If prompted, restart Windows.
8. Close Control Panel if you do not need to restart Windows.

The preceding steps install IIS as a service, so you do not normally need to start IIS yourself. To manually control the default Web site that is managed by IIS, you use the Internet Information Services window in Control Panel.

To manually control the default Web site with the Internet Information Services window:

1. Open **Control Panel** from the **Start** menu.
2. Use the **Administrative Tools** icon to open the Administrative Tools window.
3. Select **Internet Information Services**. The Internet Information Services window opens.
4. Click the plus sign next to the icon that represents your computer, and then click the plus sign next to the Web Sites folder, if necessary.
5. Click the **Default Web Site** icon. If the Default Web site is not currently running, the name of the icon changes to Default Web Site (Stopped).
6. Perform one of the following tasks to manually control the default Web site:
   - To start the default Web site, select **Start** from the **Action** menu.
   - To stop the default Web site, select **Stop** from the **Action** menu.
   - To temporarily pause the default Web site, select **Pause** from the **Action** menu.

TIP

You can also use buttons on the IIS toolbar to start, stop, and pause a Web site.

Testing Your Web Server

In Chapter 1, you opened a Web page as a local file in your Web browser. However, when opening a Web page or other type of file from a Web server, you cannot open a file using that method, and instead must open it from the Web server itself. For the typical user, the computer running the Web server and the local computer are two different computers. In that case, you open a file on the Web server by entering the domain name or IP address of a Web site in the local computer's browser. However, when developing a Web site, you need to be able to open your Web pages from a Web server that is running on your local computer. You can do this using *localhost*, which is the name that a local computer uses to refer to itself. Alternatively, you can access a Web server with *127.0.0.1*, which is the IP address that a local computer uses to refer to itself. For example, you can access a default Web page named index.html on your local computer by entering a URL of *http://localhost/*. Similarly, you can access the same Web page by entering a URL of *http://127.0.0.1/*.

By default, Apache serves Web pages from the /usr/local/apache/htdocs directory on UNIX/Linux and from the C:\Program Files\Apache Group\Apache2\htdocs directory on Windows. This directory contains files that generate a default Web page based on your language. You can access Apache's default Web page with either *http://localhost/* or *http://127.0.0.1/*. The default directory from where IIS serves Web pages is C:\Inetpub\wwwroot. IIS does not create a default Web page. However, if you do not create a default Web page yourself, whenever you access *http://localhost/* or *http://127.0.0.1/*, IIS displays one Web page informing you that IIS is running and another Web page opened to the IIS online documentation page.

In the next exercise, you test your Web server with the *http://localhost/* and *http://127.0.0.1/* URLs.

To test your Web server:

1. Open your Web browser.
2. Type **http://localhost/** in the Address box and press **Enter**. If you installed Apache, you should see a Web page similar to Figure 2-2. However, if you installed IIS, you should see a Web page similar to Figure 2-3, along with another Web page opened to the IIS online documentation page.

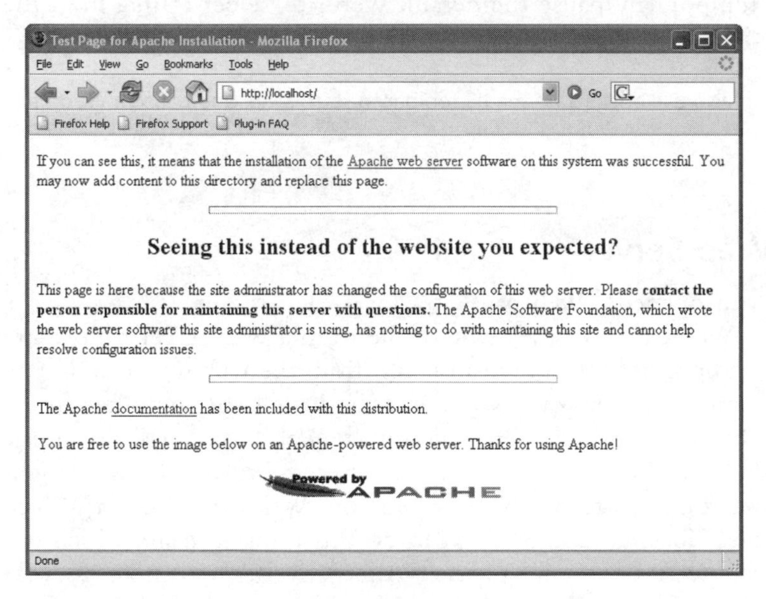

Figure 2-2 Apache's default Web page

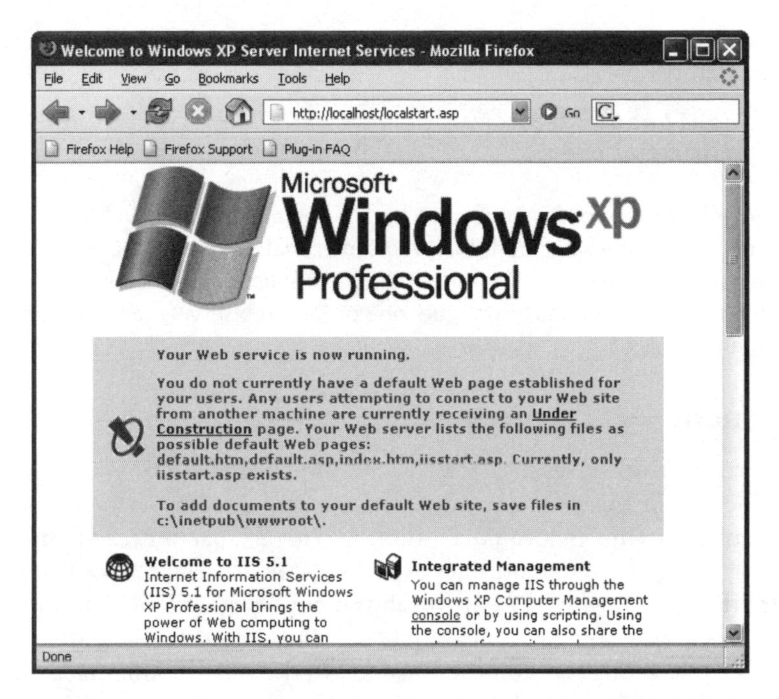

Figure 2-3 Web page informing you that IIS is running

Depending on your operating system and Wev server version, the Web page you receive may appear differently than Figures 2-2 and 2-3.

3. Now type **http://127.0.0.1/** in the Address box, and press **Enter**. You should see the same page you saw in Step 2.

The instructions in this book primarily use *http://localhost/*.

4. Close your Web browser window.

In TCP/IP, a **port** represents the endpoint of a connection between a client and a server. Clients use a port number to identify a specific application on a Web server. Port numbers range from 0 to 65536, with ports 0 to 1024 being reserved for special purposes or well-known protocols. For example, port 80 is reserved for HTTP communications. This means that whenever you access a Web page such as *http://www.yahoo.com/*, you are really accessing it through port 80 on Yahoo's Web server. Although they are assigned by default to port 80, Apache and IIS can be configured to use any nonreserved port. If you do assign a Web server to a different port, you need to specify the port number in the URL by appending the port number with a colon to *localhost* or *127.0.0.1*. For example, to open the default Web page for a Web server that is configured to use port 8083, you can use either of the following URLs:

```
http://localhost:8083/
http://127.0.0.1:8083/
```

Two Web servers cannot share the same port. If you do have two Web servers configured to use the same port, the Web server that starts running first has exclusive access to the port. This means that if you install Apache and IIS on the same computer, you must configure one of the Web servers to use a port other than port 80.

Configuring Apache

To configure ports and other settings for Apache after installation, you must edit the httpd.conf file, located in the conf directory beneath the directory where you installed Apache. By default, this file is located in the /usr/local/apache2/conf directory for UNIX/Linux and in the C:\Program Files\Apache Group\Apache2\conf directory for Windows. In UNIX/Linux, you can edit the httpd.conf file with a text editor such as GNU Emacs. In Windows, you can quickly edit the httpd.conf file in Notepad or your default text editor by selecting the Edit the Apache httpd.config Configuration File command, located in the Configure Apache Server directory in your Apache HTTP Server 2.0.52 directory under All Programs in your Start menu. Figure 2-4 shows a portion of the httpd.conf file. The first lines shown in Figure 2-4 configure Apache for the ports that it will use. Lines that begin with the pound sign (#) are informational comments that do not affect Apache's configuration. The lines without pound signs contain **directives**, which define information about how a program should be configured. The `Listen` directive in Figure 2-4 configures Apache to use port 80.

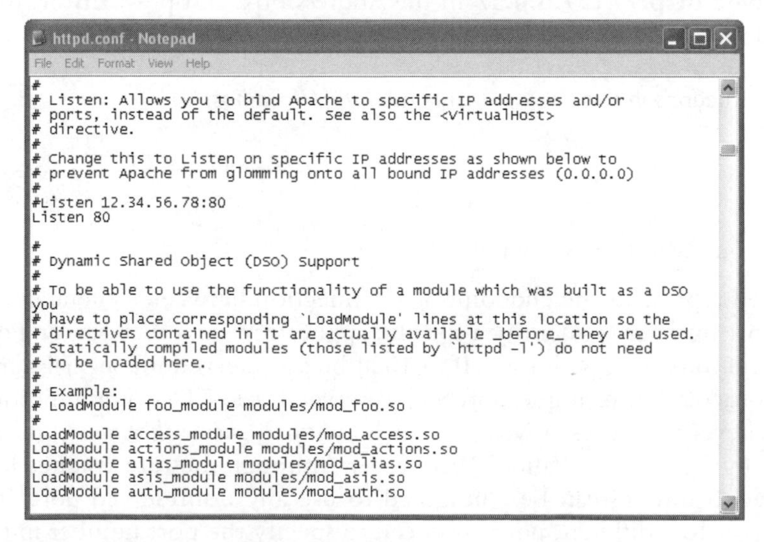

Figure 2-4 httpd.conf

After you edit and save the httpd.conf file, you must restart Apache for the changes to take effect.

Although directives are case insensitive, keep in mind that the values you assign to them might be case sensitive. For example, in UNIX/Linux, directory names are case sensitive. This means that if you assign a directory name to a directive, it must use the correct letter case.

The `DocumentRoot` directive identifies the default directory from where Apache serves Web pages. The default document root is /usr/local/apache2/htdocs on UNIX/Linux systems and C:\Program Files\Apache Group\Apache2\htdocs on Windows systems. You can also use the `Alias` directive to identify other directories that Apache can use to serve Web pages. The syntax for the `Alias` directive is `Alias` ***`URL-path directory-path`***. The URL-path identifies the alias that you will use to access the directory with your Web site's URL. For example, the following UNIX example defines an alias named specials for the /usr/local/WebPages/specials directory:

```
Alias /specials /usr/local/WebPages/specials
```

Here is a Windows example of the preceding `Alias` directive. Notice that the alias and the directory name include an ending forward slash and that the directory name is surrounded by quotation marks. Also notice that, even though this is a Windows example, it uses forward slashes (/). (Windows directories are usually referenced using backslashes.)

```
Alias /specials/ "C:/WebPages/specials/"
```

The preceding `Alias` directives allow you to open files from the specials directory by appending the alias name to *localhost* or *127.0.0.1*. For example, to open a file named sales.html from the specials directory, you can use the URL *http://localhost/specials/sales.html* or *http://127.0.0.1/specials/sales.html*.

Next, you add to the Apache httpd.conf file an `Alias` directive that points to the main directory where you will store the files you create with this book.

To modify the Apache httpd.conf file on UNIX/Linux systems:

1. Open the **httpd.conf** file from the **/usr/local/apache2/conf** directory or other directory where you installed Apache. Use any text editor such as Emacs.
2. Search for the following `Alias` directive:

   ```
   Alias /icons/ "/usr/local/apache2/icons/"
   ```

3. Add the following `Alias` directive immediately after the existing `Alias` directive. The new directive creates an alias for the /usr/local/course/1687-5 directory.

   ```
   Alias /PHP_Projects /usr/local/course/1687-5
   ```

4. Save and close the **httpd.conf** file.

5. Use the following command to restart Apache (you might need to specify a different directory if you installed Apache in a location other than the default):

   ```
   /usr/local/apache2/bin/apachectl restart
   ```

To modify the Apache httpd.conf file on Windows systems:

1. Click **Start** and point to **All Programs**. Select the **Edit the Apache httpd.config Configuration File** command, located in the **Configure Apache Server** directory in the **Apache HTTP Server 2.0.52** directory. The httpd.config file opens in your default text editor, which is usually Notepad.
2. Search for the following `Alias` directive:

   ```
   Alias /icons/ "C:/Program Files/Apache Group/Apache2/icons/"
   ```

3. Add the following `Alias` directive immediately after the existing `Alias` directive. The new directive creates an alias for the C:\Course Technology\1687-5 directory.

   ```
   Alias /PHP_Projects/ "C:/Course Technology/1687-5/"
   ```

4. Save and close the **httpd.conf** file.
5. To restart Apache, click **Start**, point to **All Programs**, point to the **Apache HTTP Server** directory, point to the **Control Apache Server** directory, and then click the **Restart** command.

After you modify the httpd.conf file for your operating system and restart Apache, perform the following steps to test the new alias by opening in your Web server the DessertShop.html file you created in Chapter 1.

To test the `Alias` directive:

1. Open your Web browser.
2. Type the **http://localhost/PHP_Projects/Chapter.01/Chapter/DessertShop.html** in the Address box, and press **Enter**. The Web page should open correctly in your Web browser. Note that the Web page is opening from your Web server and not as a local file.
3. Close your Web browser window.

Configuring Internet Information Services

You configure IIS with the Internet Information Services window. To open the Internet Information Services window, open Control Panel and switch to Classic View, if necessary. Select Administrative Tools, and then select Internet Information Services to display the Internet Information Services window. Within the Internet Information Services window, click the Default Web Site icon, click the Action menu, and then click Properties. The Default Web Site Properties dialog box opens. This dialog box contains several tabs with various configuration options. The Web Site tab, shown in Figure 2-5, allows you to select the default TCP/IP port.

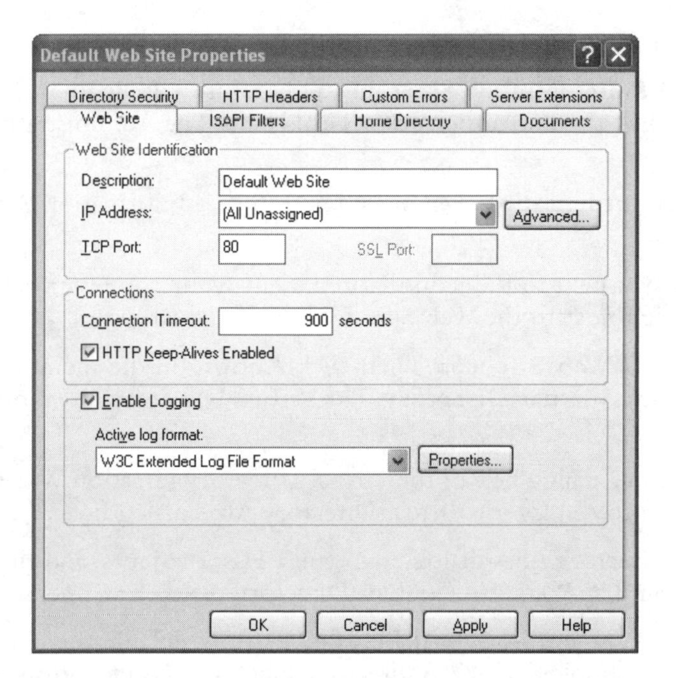

Figure 2-5 Default Web Site Properties dialog box

Depending on the options you selected during installation of IIS, your version of the Default Web Site Properties dialog box may not contain the same tabs and options shown in Figure 2-5.

The Home Directory tab in the Default Web Site Properties dialog box allows you to specify the directory from where IIS serves Web pages. (The default directory is C:\Inetpub\wwwroot.) You can also specify a virtual directory that IIS can use to serve Web pages. After you create a virtual directory in IIS, you can use a Web browser to open any file in the virtual directory. The URL you type in the browser should follow this syntax: `http://`*`localhost/directory/file`* or *`http://`*`127.0.0.1/`*`directory/file`*. For example, if you create a virtual directory named interests, you can open a document named index.html by typing the following URL in a Web browser's Address box: *http://localhost/interests/index.html*.

If you read the previous section on Apache configuration, you should recognize a virtual directory as being the IIS equivalent to an alias in Apache.

Next, you create a virtual directory in IIS that points to the main directory where you will store the files you create with this book.

To create a virtual directory in IIS:

1. Open **Control Panel** from the **Start** menu, switch to Classic View, if necessary, and then click the **Administrative Tools** icon. The Administrative Tools window opens.
2. Select **Internet Information Services**. The Internet Information Services window opens.
3. Click the plus sign next to the icon that represents your computer, and then click the plus sign next to the Web Sites folder, if necessary.
4. Click the **Default Web Site** icon. Then click **Action** on the menu bar, point to **New**, and click **Virtual Directory**. The Virtual Directory Creation Wizard opens.
5. In the introductory dialog box of the Virtual Directory Creation Wizard, click the **Next** button to display the Virtual Directory Alias dialog box.
6. In the Virtual Directory Alias dialog box, type **PHP_Projects**, and then click the **Next** button. The Web Site Content Directory dialog box opens.
7. Type the path where you store your PHP projects. By default, this should be the C:\Course Technology\1687-5 directory. Click the **Next** button when you are finished. The Access Permissions dialog box opens.
8. Leave the options in the Access Permissions dialog box set to their default values, and click the **Next** button to display the final Virtual Direction Wizard Creation dialog box.
9. Click **Finish** to create the virtual directory, and then close Internet Information Services and Control Panel.
10. Open your Web browser to test the virtual directory. Type **http://localhost/PHP_Projects/Chapter.01/Chapter/DessertShop.html** in the Address box, and press **Enter**. The Web page should open correctly in your Web browser. Note that the Web page is opening from your Web server and not as a local file.
11. Close your Web browser window.

INSTALLING PHP

This section explains how to install PHP on UNIX/Linux systems running Apache and Windows systems running either Apache or IIS. Before you install PHP, be certain to install and configure a Web server, as described in the previous section.

For more information on how to install PHP, refer to the installation instructions in the online PHP manual at *http://www.php.net/manual/en/install.php*.

Installing PHP on UNIX and Linux Systems Running Apache

This section explains how to install and configure PHP from source code on UNIX and Linux systems running Apache.

Before installing PHP on UNIX and Linux systems, you might need to log in as the root user to ensure that you have the necessary permissions to perform administration tasks.

To install PHP from source code on UNIX and Linux systems running Apache:

1. Start your Web browser, and enter the Web address for the Apache HTTP Server download page: **http://www.php.net/downloads.php**. Download the compressed UNIX source file containing the most recent version of PHP. At the time of this writing, the most recent version is PHP 5.0.3 and the compressed UNIX source file is named php-5.0.3.tar.gz. Save the file to a temporary location such as your usr/src directory or another directory of your choice.
2. Run the following `gunzip` command in the directory where you downloaded the compressed file. This command decompresses the php-5.0.3.tar.gz file into a tar file named php-5.0.3.tar within the same directory.

   ```
   gunzip php-5.0.3.tar.gz
   ```

3. Run the following `tar` command, which extracts the files in the php-5.0.3.tar to a directory named php-5.0.3 within the current directory:

   ```
   tar xvf php-5.0.3.tar
   ```

4. Change to the php-5.0.3 directory:

   ```
   cd php-5.0.3
   ```

5. The php-5.0.3 directory contains a `configure` command that prepares your system for installation of PHP. You can specify a number of parameters when you run the `configure` command. The two most common parameters are `--with-mysqli` and `with-aspx2=`*`directory`*. The `--with-mysqli` parameter activates PHP's built-in support for MySQL. The `--aspx2=`*`directory`* parameter identifies the location of the Apache Extension Tool, which is necessary to associate PHP with Apache. You assign to the `--aspx2=`*`directory`* parameter the directory path containing the Apache Extension Tool, which is usually /usr/local/apache2/bin/apxs if you installed Apache in the default location. To run the `configure` command with the `--with-mysqli` parameter and the `with-aspx2=`*`directory`* parameter, enter the following, but be certain to enter the correct directory for the Apache Extension Tool if you installed Apache in another location:

   ```
   ./configure --with-mysqli \
   --with-apxs2=/usr/local/apache2/bin/apxs
   ```

For a complete listing of parameters and syntax for the `configure` command, type `./configure --help`.

6. After the configuration script finishes, compile the PHP source code by running the **`make`** command in the php-5.0.3 directory.
7. Perform the installation by running the **`make install`** command in the php-5.0.3 directory.
8. When installation is complete, you need to specify which configuration file you want to use with PHP. The PHP configuration file is named php.ini. The installation process creates two sample configuration files: php.ini-dist and php.ini-recommended. You need to copy one of these files to the usr/local/lib directory and rename it to php.ini. The php.ini-dist file is intended for development environments, whereas the php.ini-recommended file is intended for production environments. Because you are using this book to learn how to develop Web sites with PHP, you will primarily use the php.ini-dist file. Run the following command to copy the php.ini-dist file to your usr/local/lib directory and rename it to php.ini:

```
cp php.ini-dist /usr/local/lib/php.ini
```

Be sure you understand the settings in the php.ini-recommended file before using it as your PHP configuration file in a production environment.

Installing PHP on Windows Running Apache or IIS

This section explains how to install PHP from binary format on Windows systems running either Apache or IIS.

To install PHP from binary format on Windows operating systems:

1. Start your Web browser, and enter the Web address for the PHP download page: **http://www.php.net/downloads.php**. Download the most recent Windows binary installer. At the time of this writing, the most recent version is the PHP 5.0.3 installer; the binary file for this installer is named php-5.0.3-installer.exe. Save the file to a temporary directory on your computer.
2. Open **Windows Explorer** or **My Computer** and navigate to the directory where you downloaded the php-5.0.3-installer.exe installation file. Double-click the file to start the installation program. The Welcome screen of the installation wizard appears.
3. In the Welcome screen, click the **Next** button to proceed with installation. The License Agreement screen appears.

4. In the License Agreement screen, click the **I Agree** button. The Installation Type screen appears.
5. In the Installation Type screen, select **Standard**, and then click the **Next** button. The Choose Destination Location screen appears.
6. The Choose Destination Location screen allows you to change the directory where PHP will be installed. Change the destination directory if you need to, although in most cases you should accept the default value of C:\PHP. Click the **Next** button to continue. The Mail Configuration screen appears.
7. In the Mail Configuration screen, accept the default values of **localhost** as the name of your SMTP server and **me@localhost.com** as the "from" address for the mail function and click the **Next** button. The Server Type screen appears.
8. In the Server Type screen, select the type of Web server that you want to use with PHP. You should select Apache or one of the IIS Web servers. (If you are not sure which version of IIS you are running, open the Internet Information Services application from Control Panel and select **About** from the **Help** menu.) Click the **Next** button to continue. The Start Installation screen appears.
9. In the Start Installation screen, click the **Next** button to begin installation. At the end of the installation process, you see a dialog box that displays the configuration status of the Web server you selected. If you chose Apache in the Server Type screen, a dialog box should open, informing you that you need to configure Apache manually. (The next section explains how to manually configure Apache for PHP.) Click the **OK** button to close whichever dialog box appears. Another dialog box opens, announcing that PHP was successfully installed. Click the last **OK** button to exit installation.

Configuring Apache for PHP

After you install PHP, you need to configure Apache to use it. The necessary configuration steps differ slightly between UNIX/Linux and Windows environments.

To configure Apache for PHP on UNIX/Linux platforms:

1. Open the **httpd.conf** file from the **/usr/local/apache2/conf** directory or other directory where you installed Apache. Use any text editor such as GNU Emacs.
2. Search for the following `LoadModule` directive. If it does not exist, add it to the end of the file.

   ```
   LoadModule php5_module libexec/libphp5.so
   ```
3. Add the following `AddType` directive to the end of the file. This line configures Apache to use PHP to process files with an extension of .php.

   ```
   AddType application/x-httpd-php .php
   ```

4. Save and close the **httpd.conf** file.
5. Use the following command to restart Apache (you might need to specify a different directory if you installed Apache in a location other than the default):

```
/usr/local/apache2/bin/apachectl restart
```

To configure Apache for PHP on Windows systems:

1. Click the **Start** menu and point to **All Programs**. Select the **Edit the Apache httpd.config Configuration File** command, located in the **Configure Apache Server** directory in the **Apache HTTP Server 2.0.52** directory. The httpd.config file opens in your default text editor, which is usually Notepad.
2. Scroll to the end of the file and add the following lines to the end. The `ScriptAlias` directive identifies other directories from which Apache executes server scripts. In this case, the directive identifies the PHP installation directory. The `AddType` directive configures Apache to use PHP to process files with an extension of .php. The `Action` directive defines the php-cgi.exe file as the application to use to process PHP files. For the `ScriptAlias` and `Action` directives, be certain to enter the correct path if you did not install PHP in its default installation location.

```
ScriptAlias /PHP/ "C:/PHP/"
AddType application/x-httpd-php .php
Action application/x-httpd-php "/PHP/php-cgi.exe"
```

3. Save and close the **httpd.conf** file.
4. Restart Apache by clicking your **Start** menu and pointing to **All Programs**. Select the **Restart** command, located in the **Control Apache Server** directory in the **Apache HTTP Server 2.0.52** directory.

Configuring PHP

You configure PHP by modifying the php.ini configuration file. For UNIX/Linux systems, you should have installed this file in the /usr/local/lib directory. On Windows systems, this file is installed automatically in your main Windows directory, which is usually C:\WINDOWS or C:\WINNT. You can edit the php.ini file with a text editor such as GNU Emacs for UNIX/Linux and Notepad in Windows. Figure 2-6 shows a portion of the php.ini file that is used to configure resource limits and error handling and logging. Lines that begin with a semicolon (;) are informational comments that do not affect PHP's configuration. The lines without semicolons contain **directives**, which define information about how a program should be configured.

You will modify some directives in the php.ini configuration file later in this chapter.

PHP reads the php.ini configuration file each time it processes a script. For this reason, you do not need to restart your Web server after modifying the configuration file.

```
php.ini - Notepad
File  Edit  Format  View  Help

;;;;;;;;;;;;;;;;;;;
; Resource Limits ;
;;;;;;;;;;;;;;;;;;;

max_execution_time = 30     ; Maximum execution time of each script, in seconds
max_input_time = 60     ; Maximum amount of time each script may spend parsing request
data
memory_limit = 8M      ; Maximum amount of memory a script may consume (8MB)


;;;;;;;;;;;;;;;;;;;;;;;;;;;;;;
; Error handling and logging ;
;;;;;;;;;;;;;;;;;;;;;;;;;;;;;;

; error_reporting is a bit-field.  Or each number up to get desired error
; reporting level
; E_ALL             - All errors and warnings (doesn't include E_STRICT)
; E_ERROR           - fatal run-time errors
; E_WARNING         - run-time warnings (non-fatal errors)
; E_PARSE           - compile-time parse errors
; E_NOTICE          - run-time notices (these are warnings which often result
;                     from a bug in your code, but it's possible that it was
;                     intentional (e.g., using an uninitialized variable and
;                     relying on the fact it's automatically initialized to an
;                     empty string)
; E_STRICT                    - run-time notices, enable to have PHP suggest changes
;                     to your code which will ensure the best interoperability
;                     and forward compatibility of your code
; E_CORE_ERROR      - fatal errors that occur during PHP's initial startup
; E_CORE_WARNING    - warnings (non-fatal errors) that occur during PHP's
;                     initial startup
```

Figure 2-6 The php.ini configuration file

Installing and Running MySQL

This section explains how to install MySQL on UNIX/Linux and Windows systems. You might be familiar with other types of databases, such as Microsoft Access, that are installed as applications. Unlike other types of databases that are installed as applications, MySQL is installed as a server, similar to the Apache and IIS servers you installed earlier. On UNIX/Linux systems, you must start and stop the MySQL server manually. When you install MySQL on Windows, it is installed as a service. (Recall that services are usually launched automatically when Windows first starts.)

The MySQL installations you create in this chapter will include default user accounts that are not secure. You will learn how to secure the default MySQL user accounts in Chapter 8.

For detailed installation instructions, refer to the online MySQL manual at *http://dev.mysql.com/doc/mysql/en/Installing.html*.

Installing and Running MySQL on UNIX and Linux

Binary installations are available for many UNIX/Linux platforms. In fact, the MySQL AB group recommends that you install MySQL from a binary installation instead of from source code. However, given the numerous binary installations that exist, specific instructions for each platform cannot be included in this book. Therefore, this section lists generic instructions for installing and configuring MySQL from source code on

UNIX and Linux systems. If you prefer a binary installation of MySQL, follow the installation instructions for your platform in the online MySQL manual at *http://dev.mysql.com/doc/mysql/en/Installing.html.*

For detailed information on installing MySQL from source code on UNIX/Linux systems, refer to the MySQL Installation Using a Source Distribution Web page at *http://dev.mysql.com/doc/mysql/en/installing-source.html*.

To install MySQL from source code on UNIX and Linux systems:

1. Log in as the root user.
2. Start your Web browser, and enter the Web address for the MySQL download page: **http://dev.mysql.com/downloads/**. Download the compressed UNIX source file containing the most recent standard version of MySQL. At the time of this writing, the most recent version is MySQL 4.1 and the compressed UNIX source file is named mysql-4.1.9.tar.gz. Save the file to a temporary location such as your usr/src directory or another directory of your choice.
3. By default, MySQL runs as a root process, which can be a security risk because some of the MySQL files are owned by root. For this reason, you should create a separate group and user for running MySQL. Run the following commands to create a group named "mysql" and a user named "mysql." (You can use whichever group and username you want, although most developers prefer to use "mysql.")

```
groupadd mysql
useradd -g mysql mysql
```

Some versions of UNIX/Linux use slightly different commands and syntax for adding groups and users.

4. Run the following `gunzip` command in the directory where you downloaded the compressed file. This command decompresses the mysql-4.1.9.tar.gz file into a tar file within the same directory.

```
gunzip mysql-4.1.9.tar.gz
```

5. Run the following `tar` command, which extracts the files in the mysql-4.1.9.tar to a directory named mysql-4.1.9 within the current directory:

```
tar xvf mysql-4.1.9.tar
```

6. Change to the mysql-4.1.9 directory:

```
cd mysql-4.1.9
```

7. The mysql-4.1.9 directory contains a **configure** command that prepares your system for installation of MySQL. You can specify a number of parameters when you run the **configure** command. One parameter that you should be aware of is the **--prefix** parameter, which specifies the location to install MySQL. By default, MySQL is installed in the /usr/local/mysql directory. Run the **configure** command using default options, including the default installation location, and then run the following command:

   ```
   ./configure
   ```

   If you want to install MySQL in a location other than the default, run the **configure** command as follows:

   ```
   ./configure --prefix=installation directory
   ```

For a complete listing of parameters and syntax for the `configure` command, type `./configure --help`.

8. After the configuration script finishes, compile the MySQL source code by running the **make** command in the mysql-4.1.9 directory.
9. Now perform the installation by running the **make install** command in the mysql-4.1.9 directory.
10. Change to the scripts directory within the mysql-4.1.9 directory:

    ```
    cd scripts
    ```

11. Run the following **mysql_install_db** script to create the MySQL grant tables, which determine a user's privileges in a database.

    ```
    mysql_install_db --user=mysql
    ```

12. Run the following commands. The first command changes ownership of the MySQL files to root. The second and third commands change the ownership of the MySQL data directory to the mysql user and group.

    ```
    chown -R root /usr/local/mysql
    chown -R mysql /usr/local/mysql/var
    chgrp -R mysql /usr/local/mysql
    ```

You can administer MySQL with a number of different programs, most of which are located in the bin directory beneath the directory where you installed MySQL. The following examples assume that MySQL is installed in the /usr/local/mysql directory.

To start the MySQL server, use the **mysql_safe** startup script along with the **--user** argument assigned the name of the user you created in the previous steps. For example, the following command starts the MySQL server with the "mysql" user (be certain to include the ampersand [&] at the end of the statement):

```
/usr/local/mysql/bin/mysqld_safe --user=mysql &
```

Versions of MySQL older than 4.0 used the `safe_mysqld` command to start the MySQL server.

The `mysqladmin` command includes numerous options for administering MySQL. To stop the MySQL server, use the `mysqladmin` command with the `shutdown` argument, as follows:

```
/usr/local/mysql/bin/mysqladmin shutdown
```

Installing MySQL on Windows

This section explains how to install and configure MySQL from binary format on Windows operating systems. For more detailed installation instructions, refer to the Installing MySQL on Windows Web page at *http://dev.mysql.com/doc/mysql/en/windows-installation.html.*

To install MySQL from binary format on Windows operating systems:

1. Start your Web browser, and enter the Web address for the MySQL Downloads page: **http://dev.mysql.com/downloads/**. On the MySQL Downloads page, click the link for the recommended MySQL database server. At the time of this writing, the recommended version is MySQL 4.1. Download the Windows Essentials version of MySQL. Save the installation file to a temporary directory on your computer.
2. Open **Windows Explorer** or **My Computer** and navigate to the directory where you downloaded the MySQL installation file. Double-click the file to start the installation program. The Welcome screen of the installation wizard appears.
3. In the Welcome screen, click the **Next** button to proceed with installation. The Setup Type screen appears.
4. In the Setup Type screen, accept the default setup type of **Typical** and click the **Next** button. The Ready to Install the Program screen appears.
5. The Ready to Install the Program screen is the final screen that appears before MySQL is installed. If you want to change any of the installation options you selected, click the **Back** button. Otherwise, click the **Install** button. When installation is completed, the MySQL.com Sign-Up screen appears.
6. The MySQL.com Sign-Up screen appears, prompting you to create an account that you can use to receive technical support. You can create a new account, log in with an existing account, or skip sign-up. Select whichever option you want, and click the **Next** button. If you choose to create a new MySQL.com account, you will see three additional screens prompting you for your new account information. After you are finished creating a new account, or if you log in with an existing account or skip sign-up, the Wizard Completed screen appears.

7. In the Wizard Completed screen, leave the **Configure the MySQL Server now** check box selected, and click the **Finish** button. The first screen in the MySQL Server Instance Configuration Wizard appears.
8. In the first screen of the MySQL Server Instance Configuration Wizard, click the **Next** button to proceed with configuration. The Configuration Type screen appears.
9. In the Configuration Type screen, select **Standard Configuration**, and click the **Next** button. The Windows Options screen appears.
10. In the Windows Options screen, accept the default values, which install MySQL as a Windows service. Leave the **Launch the MySQL Server Automatically** check box selected, but do not select the **Include Bin Directory in Windows PATH** check box. Click the **Next** button to continue. The Security Options screen appears.
11. In the Security Options screen, deselect the **Modify Security Settings** check box and click the **Next** button. The final screen in the MySQL Server Instance Configuration Wizard appears.

You should not create an anonymous account, which results in an insecure system. Although you are creating an anonymous account in this exercise, you correct this security problem when you learn how to make MySQL secure in Chapter 8.

12. If you want to change any of the configuration options you selected, click the **Back** button. Otherwise, click the **Execute** button. When configuration is completed, click the **Finish** button to exit the MySQL Server Instance Configuration Wizard.

The preceding steps install the MySQL server as a service, so you do not normally need to start the server yourself. To control the MySQL server manually, you use the Services application in Control Panel.

To manually control the MySQL service:

1. Open **Control Panel** from the **Start** menu.
2. Use the **Administrative Tools** icon to open the Administrative Tools window.
3. Select **Services**. The Services window opens.
4. Locate MySQL in the list of services. The status column tells you whether the service is started. If you click the name of a service, you can perform the following tasks:
   - To start a service, select **Start** from the **Action** menu.
   - To stop a service, select **Stop** from the **Action** menu.
   - To temporarily pause the default Web site, select **Pause** from the **Action** menu.

- To restart a paused service, select **Resume** from the **Action** menu.
- To restart a service, select **Restart** from the **Action** menu.

You can also use the links in the Services window to control a service.

You can also manually administer the MySQL server from the command line using the various programs located in the \bin directory beneath the directory where you installed MySQL.

Testing the MySQL Server

Although you do not actually start using MySQL until Chapter 8, you can at least test your MySQL server to make sure it is running. The **mysqladmin** command includes several options for testing your MySQL server, including the **version** argument, which you use next to test your server. The **version** argument lists the server version and other information about your SQL server. The following exercise assumes that you have installed MySQL in the default directory of /usr/local/mysql on UNIX/Linux systems and in the C:\Program Files\MySQL\MySQL Server 4.1 directory on Windows platforms.

To test your installation of MySQL server:

1. First, you need to ensure that you have started your instance of MySQL server. For UNIX/Linux systems, enter the following command:

   ```
   /usr/local/mysql/bin/mysqld_safe --user=mysql &
   ```

   For Windows operating systems, use the Services window to determine whether the MySQL service is running, as described in the preceding section.

2. Run the **mysqladmin version** command to display version information for your installation of MySQL server. For UNIX/Linux systems, run the following command:

   ```
   /usr/local/mysql/bin/mysqladmin version
   ```

   For Windows operating systems, change to the **C:\Program Files\MySQL\MySQL Server 4.1\bin** directory and run the following command:

   ```
   mysqladmin version
   ```

   If your MySQL server is running properly, you should see output similar to Figure 2-7. If the server is not running properly, you should see output similar to Figure 2-8.

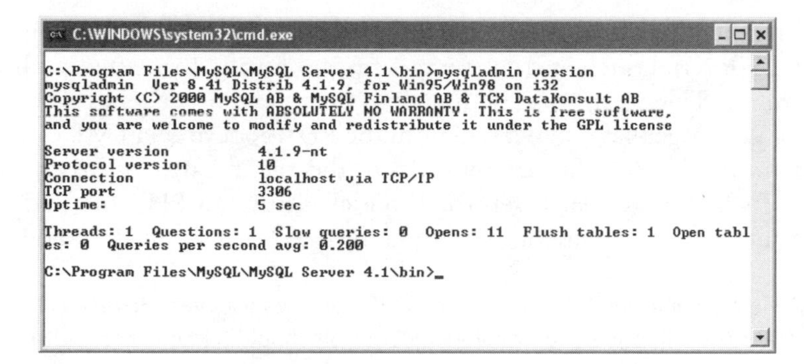

Figure 2-7 Output of the `mysqladmin version` command when the MySQL server is running properly

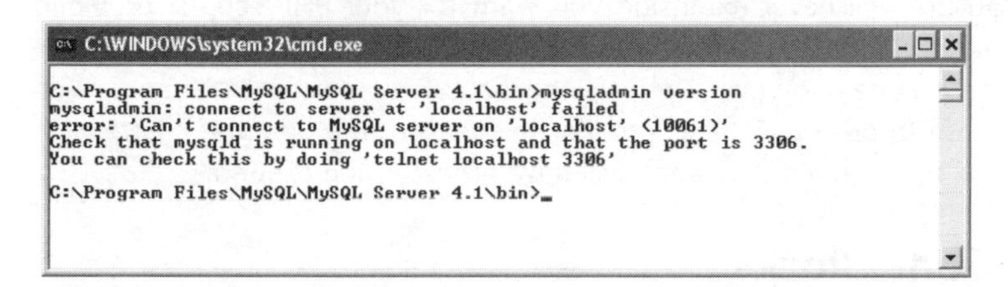

Figure 2-8 Output of the `mysqladmin version` command when the MySQL server is not running properly

For help with troubleshooting your MySQL installation, refer to the Starting and Troubleshooting the MySQL Server Web page at *http://dev.mysql.com/doc/mysql/en/starting-server.html* and the Troubleshooting a MySQL Installation Under Windows Web page at *http://dev.mysql.com/doc/mysql/en/windows-troubleshooting.html*.

Creating Basic PHP Scripts

JavaScript and PHP are both referred to as **embedded scripting languages** because code for both languages is embedded within a Web page (either an HTML or XHTML document). You type this code directly into a Web page as a separate section. Although JavaScript code can be added to standard Web page documents that have an extension of .html, a Web page document containing PHP code must have an extension of .php. Whenever a request is made for a document with an extension of .php, the Web server sends the file to the scripting engine for processing. The scripting engine then processes any PHP code it encounters. Although PHP files use an extension of .php, they can contain the same HTML or XHTML elements you would find in a static Web page. The scripting engine ignores any non-PHP code and only processes any PHP code it finds within PHP code blocks (which you study next). The Web server then returns the results of the PHP script along with any HTML or XHTML elements found in the PHP file to the client, where it is rendered by the client's Web browser. In most cases, the results returned from a PHP script, such as database records, are usually formatted with HTML or XHTML elements. This means that PHP code is never sent to a client's Web browser; only the resulting Web page that is generated from the PHP code and HTML or XHTML elements found within the PHP file are returned to the client. Later in this chapter, you see an example of a Web page that is returned to a client from a PHP file that contains both PHP code and XHTML elements. First, you need to learn about PHP code blocks.

A PHP file does not need to contain any PHP code whatsoever. However, if this is the case with a file you are working on, you should name the file with an extension of .html to avoid the extra step of having the file processed by the scripting engine.

You can use whichever extension you want for your PHP scripts, provided that your Web server is configured to process the extensions you use with the scripting engine. However, .php is the default extension that most Web servers use to process PHP scripts. For this reason, the files you create with this book that contain PHP code will have an extension of .php.

Creating PHP Code Blocks

You write PHP scripts within **code declaration blocks**, which are separate sections within a Web page that are interpreted by the scripting engine. You can include as many code declaration blocks as you want within a document. This section discusses the following four types of code declaration blocks you can use to write PHP:

- Standard PHP script delimiters
- The `<script>` element
- Short PHP script delimiters
- ASP-style script delimiters

Standard PHP Script Delimiters

The standard method of writing PHP code declaration blocks is to use the `<?php` and `?>` script delimiters. A **delimiter** is a character or sequence of characters used to mark the beginning and end of a code segment. When the scripting engine encounters the `<?php` and `?>` script delimiters, it processes any code between the delimiters as PHP. The individual lines of code that make up a PHP script are called **statements**. You need to use the following syntax in a document to tell the Web server that the statements that follow must be interpreted by the scripting engine:

```
<?php
statements;
?>
```

The following script contains a single statement that writes the text "Explore Africa!" to a Web browser window, using an `echo()` statement, which you will study shortly:

```
<?php
echo "Explore Africa!";
?>
```

Notice that the preceding statement ends in a semicolon. PHP, along with other programming languages including C++ and Java, requires you to end all statements with a semicolon. Note that the primary purpose of a semicolon is to identify the end of a statement, not the end of a line. Just as Web browsers ignore white space in an HTML or XHTML document, the scripting engine ignores white space within code blocks. For this reason, semicolons are critical to identify the end of a statement. This also means that you do not need to place each statement on its own line. For example, the following script contains two `echo()` statements on the same line, with each statement ending in a semicolon:

```
<?php
echo "Explore "; echo "Africa!";
?>
```

Further, statements can be placed on the same line with the `<?php` and `?>` script delimiters, as follows:

```
<?php echo "Explore "; echo "Africa!"; ?>
```

Although the preceding syntax is legal, for better readability you should usually place the `<?php` and `?>` script delimiters and each statement within a code block on separate lines. However, many of the examples in this book show delimiters and statements on the same line to conserve space.

The PHP Group officially recommends that you use the standard PHP script delimiters to write PHP code declaration blocks. One reason for this is that the standard PHP script delimiters are guaranteed to be available on any Web server that supports PHP. (As you will learn shortly, both the short PHP script delimiters and the ASP-style script delimiters can be disabled.) However, the primary reason is that using the standard PHP script delimiters is the only method that is completely compliant with XML. (Recall from Chapter 1 that the Web page examples and exercises in this book are written in XHTML, which is based on XML.) XML is the way of the future in Web development, not only because it is the basis of XHTML documents, but also because it has become the standard for transmitting data on the Internet. For this reason, you should always ensure that any Web pages you create or scripts that you write are compliant with XML.

Even though the PHP Group officially recommends that you use the standard PHP script delimiters to write PHP, some Web developers prefer the other types of code declaration blocks, so you should be able to recognize them when you see them.

Next, you create a PHP script that contains standard PHP script delimiters.

To create a PHP script with standard PHP script delimiters:

1. Create a new document in your text editor.
2. Type the `<!DOCTYPE>` declaration, `<html>` element, header information, and `<body>` element. Use the strict DTD and "PHP Code Blocks" as the content of the `<title>` element. Your document should appear as follows:

```
<!DOCTYPE html PUBLIC "-//W3C//DTD XHTML 1.0 Strict//EN"
"http://www.w3.org/TR/xhtml1/DTD/xhtml1-strict.dtd">
<html xmlns="http://www.w3.org/1999/xhtml">
<head>
<title>PHP Code Blocks</title>
<meta http-equiv="content-type"
     content="text/html; charset=iso-8859-1" />
</head>
<body>
</body>
</html>
```

3. Add the following paragraph element and standard PHP script delimiters to the document body. Be sure to nest the script delimiters within the paragraph element. The paragraph element forces the output from the script delimiters to render on a separate line.

```
<p>
<?php
?>
</p>
```

4. Add the following bolded `echo()` statement between the script delimiters:

```
<p>
<?php
echo "This text is printed using standard PHP script
delimiters.";
?>
</p>
```

5. Save the document as **PHPCodeBlocks.php** in the Chapter directory for Chapter 2. Be sure to use an extension of .php, which is required for your Web server to recognize the file as a PHP script. After you save the document, validate it with the WDG HTML Validator at **http://www.htmlhelp.org/tools/validator/upload.html**.
6. Open the **PHPCodeBlocks.php** file in your Web browser by entering the following URL: **http://localhost/PHP_Projects/Chapter.02/Chapter/PHPCodeBlocks.php**. You should see the Web page shown in Figure 2.9.

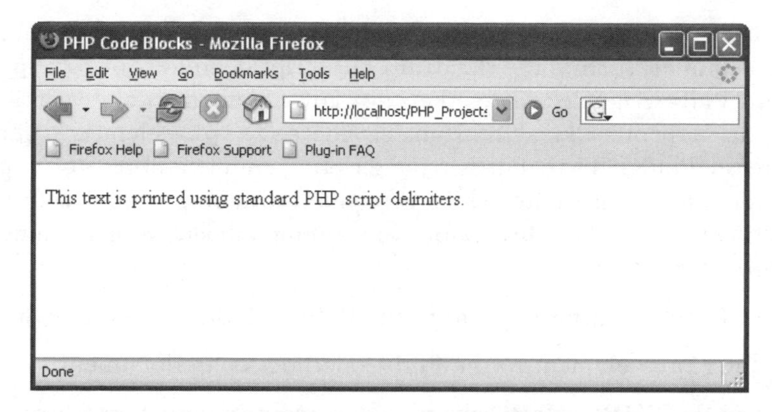

Figure 2-9 Output of a PHP script with standard PHP script delimiters

7. Close your Web browser window.

The <script> Element

If you have worked with JavaScript or another client-side scripting language, you should be familiar with the `<script>` **element**, which identifies a script section in a Web page document. With client-side scripting, the `type` attribute of the `<script>` element tells the browser which client-side scripting language and which version of the scripting language is being used. You assign a value of "text/javascript" to the `type` attribute to indicate that the script is written with JavaScript. You need to include the following syntax in a document to tell the Web browser that the statements that follow must be interpreted by the JavaScript scripting engine:

```
<script type="text/javascript">
statements;
</script>
```

When the `<script>` element is used with PHP, you do not include the `type` attribute. Instead, you must assign a value of "php" to the `language` attribute of the `<script>` element to identify the code block as PHP. When the scripting engine encounters a `<script>` element with "php" assigned to its `language` attribute, it processes any code within the element as PHP. The syntax for using PHP with the `<script>` element is as follows:

```
<script language="php">
statements;
</script>
```

The following example contains the same `echo()` statement you saw with the standard PHP script delimiters, but this time the statement is contained within a PHP `<script>` element:

```
<script language="php">
echo "Explore Africa!";
</script>
```

One reason for using the `<script>` element with PHP is because some HTML editors don't recognize delimiters such as the standard PHP script delimiters of `<?php` and `?>`. Like the standard PHP script delimiters, the `<script>` element is always available on any Web server that supports PHP. Unfortunately, the `<script>` element's `language` attribute is deprecated in XHTML. Further, the scripting engine ignores `<script>` elements that include the type attribute, which is required for compatibility with both the strict and transitional DTDs. For this reason, you cannot validate your documents that include PHP `<script>` elements.

Next, you add a PHP `<script>` element to the PHPCodeBlocks.php document.

To add a PHP `<script>` element to the PHPCodeBlocks.php document:

1. Return to the **PHPCodeBlocks.php** document in your text editor.
2. Add the following paragraph element and `<script>` element to the end of the document body:

```
<p>
<script language="php">
</script>
</p>
```

3. Add the following bolded `echo()` statement between the script delimiters:

```
<p>
<script language="php">
echo "This text is printed using a PHP script section.";
</script>
</p>
```

4. Save the **PHPCodeBlocks.php** document and then open it from your Web server. Your Web browser should appear similar to Figure 2-10.

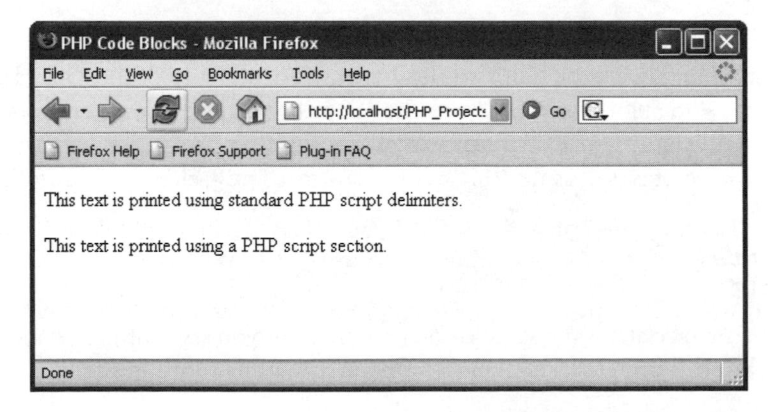

Figure 2-10 Output of a PHP script after adding a PHP script section

5. Close your Web browser window.

Short PHP Script Delimiters

A more simplified method of writing PHP code declaration blocks is to use the short `<?` and `?>` script delimiters. Short PHP script delimiters are similar to standard PHP script delimiters, except they do not include 'php' in the opening delimiter. The syntax for the short PHP script delimiters is as follows:

```
<? statements; ?>
```

The following example shows how to use short delimiters with the `echo()` statement you saw earlier:

```
<? echo "Explore Africa!"; ?>
```

Unlike the `<?php` and `?>` script delimiters and the `<script>` element, which are always available on any Web server that supports PHP, the short `<?` and `?>` delimiters can be disabled in a Web server's php.ini configuration file. Because a Web server on which your PHP script will run might not always be under your control, the PHP Group discourages the use of short delimiters, especially when developing scripts that will be redistributed and used by other Web developers. Although you can use the short PHP script delimiters if you prefer, your PHP scripts will not work if your Web site is hosted by an ISP that does not support short PHP script delimiters. Another reason to avoid the use of the short `<?` and `?>` delimiters is that although you can use them in XHTML documents, including documents that conform to the strict DTD, you cannot use them in XML documents. With XML documents, you must use the `<?php` and `?>` script delimiters. Appendix C explains how to use PHP with XML documents.

The php.ini configuration file contains a `short_open_tag` directive that can be assigned a value of "On" or "Off." A value of "On" enables short PHP script delimiters, whereas a value of "Off" disables them. When you first install PHP, the `short_open_tag` directive is assigned a value of "On," which allows you to immediately begin using short delimiters with your PHP scripts.

Next, you add short PHP script delimiters to the PHPCodeBlocks.php document.

To add short PHP script delimiters to the PHPCodeBlocks.php document:

1. Open your php.ini configuration file in your text editor. For UNIX/Linux systems, you should have installed this file in the /usr/local/lib directory. On Windows systems, this file is installed automatically in your main Windows directory, which is usually C:\WINDOWS or C:\WINNT.
2. In the php.ini file, locate the `short_open_tag` directive. If the directive is assigned a value of "Off," change it to "On," so the statement reads as follows:

   ```
   short_open_tag = On
   ```

3. Save the **php.ini** file.
4. Return to the **PHPCodeBlocks.php** document in your text editor.

5. Add the following paragraph element and short PHP script delimiters to the end of the document body:

```
<p>
<?
?>
</p>
```

6. Add the following bolded `echo()` statement between the script delimiters:

```
<p>
<?
echo "This text is printed using short PHP script delimiters.";
?>
</p>
```

7. Save the **PHPCodeBlocks.php** document and open it from your Web server. Your Web browser should appear similar to Figure 2-11.

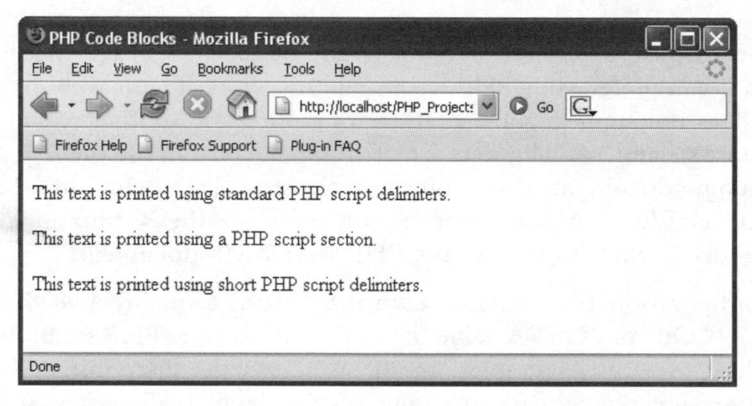

Figure 2-11 Output of a PHP script after adding short PHP script delimiters

8. Close your Web browser window.

ASP-Style Script Delimiters

Some Web developers prefer to use the ASP-style script delimiters of `<%` and `%>` to develop PHP scripts. The syntax for ASP-style script delimiters is similar to short PHP script delimiters, as follows:

```
<% statements; %>
```

The following example shows how to use ASP-style script delimiters with the `echo()` statement you saw earlier:

```
<% echo "Explore Africa!"; %>
```

Like the short PHP script delimiters, ASP-style script delimiters are compliant with XHTML, including the strict DTD, but not with XML. ASP-style script delimiters can also be enabled or disabled in the php.ini configuration file, so you should not use them unless you are sure that they are enabled on any Web servers on which you anticipate your PHP scripts will run. However, unless you are a hard-core ASP developer who only uses PHP occasionally, or if you are using an HTML editor that does not support PHP script delimiters, there is little reason to use ASP-style scripts delimiters.

To enable or disable ASP-style script delimiters, you assign a value of "On" or "Off" to the `asp_tags` directive in the php.ini configuration file. When you first install PHP, the `asp_tags` directive is assigned a value of "Off," so you cannot use ASP-style script delimiters with a default installation.

Next, you add ASP-style script delimiters to the PHPCodeBlocks.php document.

To add ASP-style script delimiters to the PHPCodeBlocks.php document:

1. Return to the php.ini configuration file in your text editor.
2. In the php.ini file, locate the `asp_tags` directive. The directive should be assigned a value of "Off." Modify the statement so it is assigned a value of "On," so the statement reads as follows:

   ```
   asp_tags = On
   ```

3. Save the **php.ini** file and close it in your text editor.
4. Return to the **PHPCodeBlocks.php** document in your text editor.
5. Add the following paragraph element and ASP-style script delimiters to the end of the document body:

   ```
   <p>
   <%
   %>
   </p>
   ```

6. Add the following bolded `echo()` statement between the script delimiters:

   ```
   <p>
   <%
   echo "This text is printed using ASP-style script delimiters.";
   %>
   </p>
   ```

7. Save the **PHPCodeBlocks.php** document and open it from your Web server. Your Web browser should appear similar to Figure 2-12.

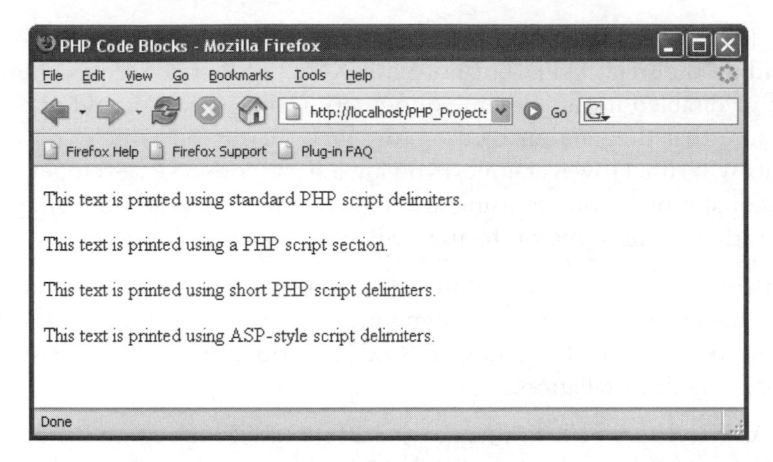

Figure 2-12 Output of a PHP script after adding ASP-style script delimiters

8. Close your Web browser window.

Understanding Functions

Before you start writing PHP scripts, you need to understand a little about functions. The term **function** refers to a procedure (or individual statements grouped into a logical unit) that performs a specific task. PHP includes numerous built-in functions that perform various types of tasks. You will work with many built-in PHP functions throughout this book. To execute a function, you must invoke, or **call**, it from somewhere in your script. The statement that calls a function is referred to as a **function call** and consists of the function name followed by any data that the function needs. The data (which you place in parentheses following the function name) are called **arguments** or **actual parameters**. Sending data to a called function is called **passing arguments**. Many functions generate, or return, some sort of a value that you can use in your script. For example, PHP includes a `round()` function that rounds a decimal to the nearest whole number. You pass a number as an argument to the `round()` function, which calculates and returns the nearest whole number. The following statement calls the `round()` function, and passes to it a value of 3.556. The `round()` function calculates and returns a value of 4, which is then printed with an `echo()` statement.

```
<?php echo round(3.556); ?>
```

Many functions can accept multiple arguments, which you separate with commas. For example, the second argument you pass to the `round()` function determines the number of digits after the decimal point that it should use to round the number. The following statement calls the `round()` function, passes to it a first argument of 3.556 and a second argument of 2. The `round()` function calculates and returns a value of 3.56 (rounded to two decimal places), which is then printed with an `echo()` statement.

```
<?php echo round(3.556, 2); ?>
```

You learn more about functions, including how to create your own, in Chapter 4.

Next, you create a PHP script that uses the `phpinfo()` function, which creates a Web page that lists diagnostic information for PHP.

To create a Web page that displays diagnostic information:

1. Create a new document in your text editor.
2. Type the `<!DOCTYPE>` declaration, `<html>` element, header information, and `<body>` element. Use the strict DTD and "PHP Diagnostic Information" as the content of the `<title>` element.
3. Add the following standard PHP script delimiters and `phpinfo()` function to the document body. Be certain to include the parentheses and semicolon in the statement containing the `phpinfo()` function.

```
<?php
phpinfo();
?>
```

4. Save the document as **PHPTest.php** in the Chapter directory for Chapter 2. After you save the document, close it in your text editor and validate it with the WDG HTML Validator.
5. Open the **PHPTest.php** file in your Web browser by entering the following URL: **http://localhost/PHP_Projects/Chapter.02/Chapter/PHPTest.php**. You should see the Web page in Figure 2-13 that lists diagnostic information for PHP.
6. Close your Web browser window.

Displaying Script Results

When you write a PHP script, you will often want to display the results of the script in the Web page that is returned as a response to a client. For example, you might want the Web page to display database records that the client requested or the result of a calculation that was processed by the PHP script. Recall that the scripting engine ignores any non-PHP code and only processes any PHP code it finds within PHP code blocks. The Web server then returns the results of the PHP script along with any HTML or XHTML elements found in the PHP file to the client, where it is rendered by the client's Web browser. To return to the client the results of any processing that occurs within a PHP code block, you must use an `echo()` statement, which you've already seen, or the `print()` statement. The **`echo()`** and **`print()` statements** create new text on a Web page that is returned as a response to a client.

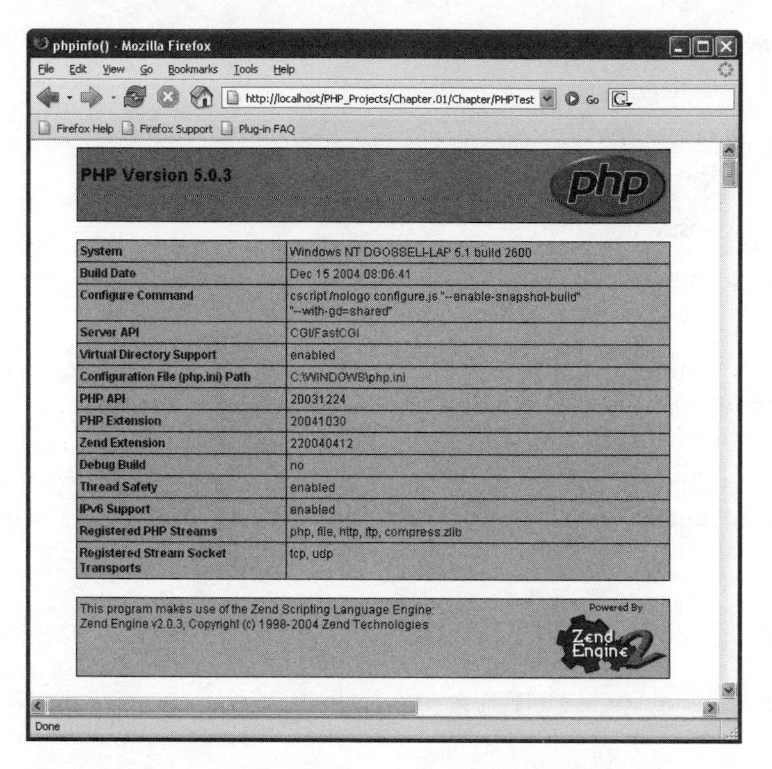

Figure 2-13 PHP Diagnostic Information Web page

You might be thinking that the `echo()` and `print()` statements resemble functions because function names are usually followed by a set of parentheses. Actually, they are not functions, but language constructs of the PHP programming language. A **programming language construct** refers to a built-in feature of a programming language. Both the `echo()` and `print()` statements are virtually identical, although the `print()` statement returns a value of 1 if it was successful or a value of 0 if it was not successful. You need to learn a little more about functions before you can understand why the `print()` statement returns a value. However, keep in mind that you can use the exact same syntax with the `print()` statement that you use with the `echo()` statement. Next, you modify the PHPCodeBlocks.php document so it uses `print()` statements instead of `echo()` statements.

To modify the PHPCodeBlocks.php document so it uses `print()` statements instead of `echo()` statements:

1. Return to the **PHPCodeBlocks.php** document in your text editor.

2. Replace each of the echo() statements with print() statements. For example, the statement within the standard PHP script delimiters should read as follows:

   ```
   <?php
   print "This text is printed using standard PHP script
   delimiters.";
   ?>
   ```

3. Save the **PHPCodeBlocks.php** document, close it in your text editor, and then open it from your Web server. The document should render the same as it did with the echo() statements.

4. Close your Web browser window.

You should understand that the only reason to use the echo() and print() statements is to include the results of a PHP script within a Web page that is returned to a client. For example, you might want to return a new Web page based on information a user enters into a form for an online transaction and submits to a Web server. You can use a PHP script to process the submitted information and return a new Web page to the client that displays the sales total, order confirmation, and so on. If you simply want to display text in a Web page that is returned to the client, there is no need to use anything but standard XHTML elements. The procedures for submitting and processing data are a little too complicated for this introductory chapter. In this chapter, you use the echo() and print() statements to return the results of a script to a client to learn the basics of PHP.

For both the echo() and print() statements, you need to include a text string that contains the text that will display in the Web browser. A **text string**, or **literal string**, is text that is contained within double or single quotation marks. As you saw earlier, the following echo() statement uses double quotation marks to print the text "Explore Africa!" to the Web browser window:

```
<?php echo "Explore Africa!"; ?>
```

Programmers often talk about code that "writes to" or "prints to" a Web browser window. For example, you might say that a piece of code writes a text string to the Web browser window. This is just another way of saying that the code displays the text string in the Web browser window.

You can also use single quotation marks with the preceding echo() statement, as follows:

```
<?php echo 'Explore Africa!'; ?>
```

If you want to pass multiple arguments to the echo() and print() statements, separate them with commas, just as with arguments passed to a function. In the following example, three text string arguments are passed to the echo() statement:

```
<?php echo "Explore Africa, ", "South America, ",
    " and Australia!"; ?>
```

Next, you create a script that passes multiple arguments to an `echo()` statement.

To create a script that passes multiple arguments to an `echo()` statement:

1. Create a new document in your text editor.
2. Type the `<!DOCTYPE>` declaration, `<html>` element, header information, and `<body>` element. Use the strict DTD and "How to Talk Like a Pirate" as the content of the `<title>` element.
3. Add the following heading element to the document body:

   ```
   <h1>How to Talk Like a Pirate</h1>
   ```

4. Next, add a standard PHP script delimiter to the end of document body:

   ```
   <?php
   ?>
   ```

5. Now add the following `echo()` statement to the PHP code block:

   ```
   echo "Avast me hearties! ", "Return handsomely with some fine
   swag, ye scurvy dogs! ", "Else, we be keehaulin' ye' next morn
   ...";
   ```

6. Save the document as **PirateTalk.php** in the Chapter directory for Chapter 2. After you save the document, validate it with the WDG HTML Validator.
7. Open the **PirateTalk.php** file from your Web server by entering the following URL: **http://localhost/PHP_Projects/Chapter.02/Chapter/PirateTalk.php**. Your Web browser should appear similar to Figure 2-14.

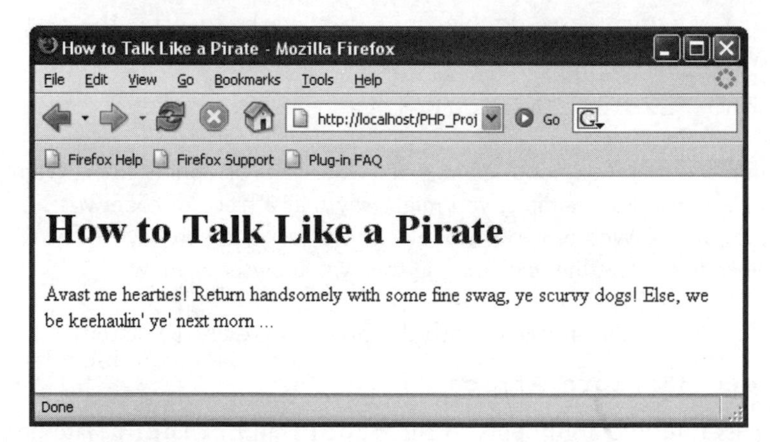

Figure 2-14 How to Talk Like a Pirate Web page

8. Close your Web browser window.

You can also use parentheses with the `echo()` and `print()` statements, in the same manner that you use them with functions, as follows:

```
<?php echo("Explore Africa, ", "South America, ",
     " and Australia!";); ?>
```

NOTE

You will not use parentheses with most of the `echo()` statements you write in this book. However, you should be able to recognize the parenthesized version as just another form of the `echo()` statement, not a separate type of function.

So far, the arguments you have seen and used with the `echo()` statements have consisted of raw text that is rendered in the Web browser's default font. To format the output of text that is printed with `echo()` and `print()` statements, you can use whichever elements you want as part of the text string arguments. The following code shows a modified version of the previous script, but this time the `echo()` statement includes several XHTML elements to format the appearance of the text string in a Web browser. Figure 2-15 shows how the script renders in a Web browser.

```
<?php echo "<p>Explore <strong>Africa</strong>, <br />",
     "<strong>South America</strong>, <br />",
     " and <strong>Australia</strong>!</p>"; ?>
```

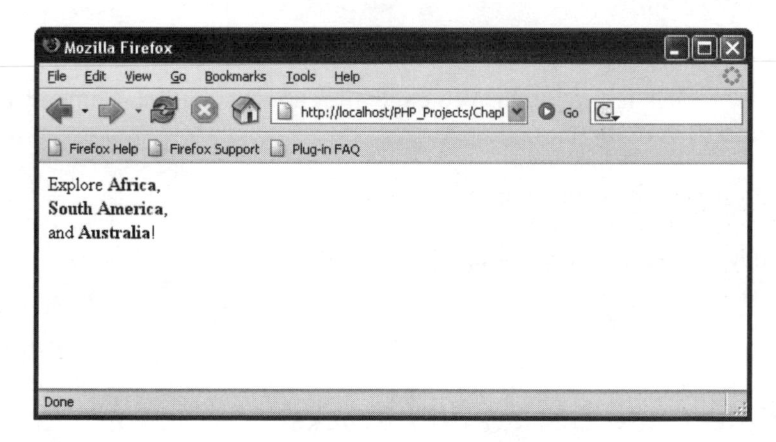

Figure 2-15 Output of an `echo()` statement with XHTML elements

Next, you modify the PirateTalk.php script so the `echo()` statement includes XHTML elements.

To modify the PirateTalk.php script so the `echo()` statement includes XHTML elements:

1. Return to the **PirateTalk.php** script in your text editor.
2. Modify the values passed to the `echo()` statement so they include paragraph and line break elements, as follows:

```
echo "<p>Avast me hearties!<br />", "Return handsomely with some
fine swag,<br />ye scurvy dogs!<br />", "Else, we be keehaulin'
ye' next morn ...</p>";
```

3. Save the **PirateTalk.php** file and close it in your text editor. Validate the document with the WDG HTML Validator, and then open it from your Web server. The document should appear similar to Figure 2-16.

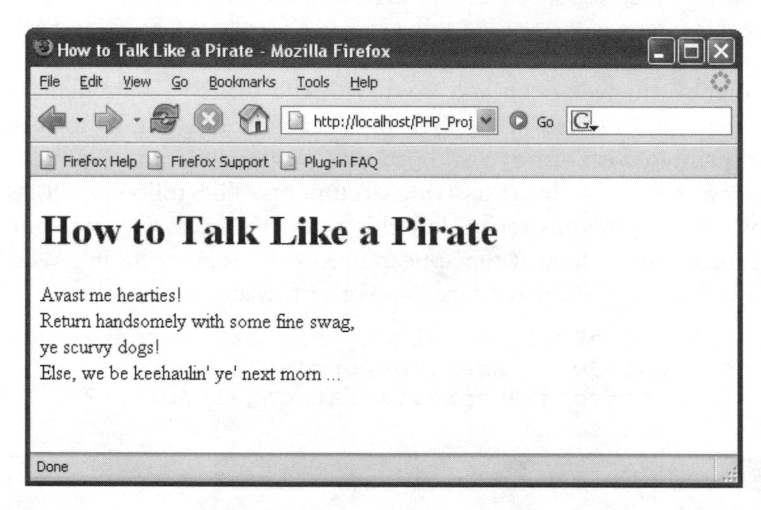

Figure 2-16 How to Talk Like a Pirate Web page after adding XHTML elements to the `echo()` statement

4. Close your Web browser window.

You study additional techniques for working with text strings in Chapter 5.

Creating Multiple Code Declaration Blocks

You can include as many PHP script sections as you want within a document. However, when you include multiple script sections in a document, you must include a separate code declaration block for each section. The following document includes two separate script sections. The script sections create the information that is displayed beneath the `<h2>` heading elements.

```
...
</head>
<body>
<h1>Multiple Script Sections</h1>
<h2>First Script Section</h2>
```

```
<?php echo "<p>Output from the first script section.</p>";
 ?>
<h2>Second Script Section</h2>
<?php echo "<p>Output from the second script section.</p>"
; ?>
</body>
</html>
```

Remember that PHP code declaration blocks execute on a Web server before a Web page is sent to a client. If a client were to view the source document after they receive the PHP document, they would not see any PHP code declaration blocks. Instead, the client will only see the results returned from the PHP code. The following example shows how the preceding document appears after a client receives it. Notice that the PHP code declaration blocks have been converted to elements and text. Figure 2-17 shows how the text and elements appear in a Web browser.

```
...
</head>
<body>
<h1>Multiple Script Sections</h1>
<h2>First Script Section</h2>
<p>Output from the first script section.</p>
<h2>Second Script Section</h2>
<p>Output from the second script section.</p>
</body>
</html>
```

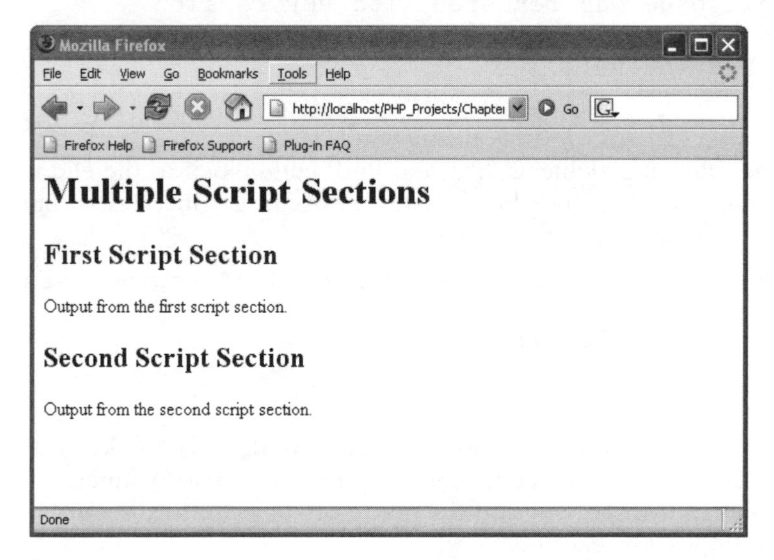

Figure 2-17 Output of a document with two PHP script sections

Even though everyone enjoys talking like a pirate, the PirateTalk.html document is of limited use in demonstrating how to write PHP scripts. Therefore, in the next exercise, you write a PHP script that prints the results of several built-in PHP functions using multiple script sections. You use the `phpversion()`, `zend_version()`, and `ini_get()` functions. The `phpversion()` function returns the version of PHP that processed the current page. The `zend_version()` function returns the version number of the Zend Engine, which is PHP's scripting engine. The `ini_get()` function returns the value assigned to a directive in the php.ini configuration file. You need to pass the name of a directive to the `ini_get()` function, surrounded by quotations.

Next, you create a script with multiple script sections.

To create a script with multiple script sections:

1. Create a new document in your text editor.
2. Type the `<!DOCTYPE>` declaration, `<html>` element, header information, and `<body>` element. Use the strict DTD and "PHP Environment Info" as the content of the `<title>` element.
3. Add the following heading element to the document body:

```
<h1>PHP Environment Info</h1>
```

4. Add the following elements, text, and PHP code block to the document body. The code block prints the PHP version number using the `phpversion()` function.

```
<p>This page was rendered with PHP version
<?php
echo phpversion();
?>
.</p>
```

5. Add the following elements, text, and PHP code block to the end of the document body. The code block prints the Zend Engine version number using the `zend_version()` function.

```
<p>The PHP code was rendered with Zend Engine version
<?php
echo zend_version();
?>
.</p>
```

6. Finally, add the following elements, text, and PHP code blocks to the end of the document body. The code blocks use the `ini_get()` function to print PHP's default MIME type and the maximum amount of time that a PHP script is allowed to execute.

```
<p>PHP's default MIME type is
<?php
echo ini_get("default_mimetype");
?>
```

```
.</p>
<p>The maximum allowed execution time of a PHP script is
<?php
echo ini_get("max_execution_time");
?>
 seconds.</p>
```

7. Save the document as **MultipleScripts.php** in the Chapter directory for Chapter 2. After you save the document, validate it with the WDG HTML Validator.

8. Open the **MultipleScripts.php** file from your Web server by entering the following URL: **http://localhost/PHP_Projects/Chapter.02/Chapter/MultipleScripts.php**. Your Web browser should appear similar to Figure 2-18.

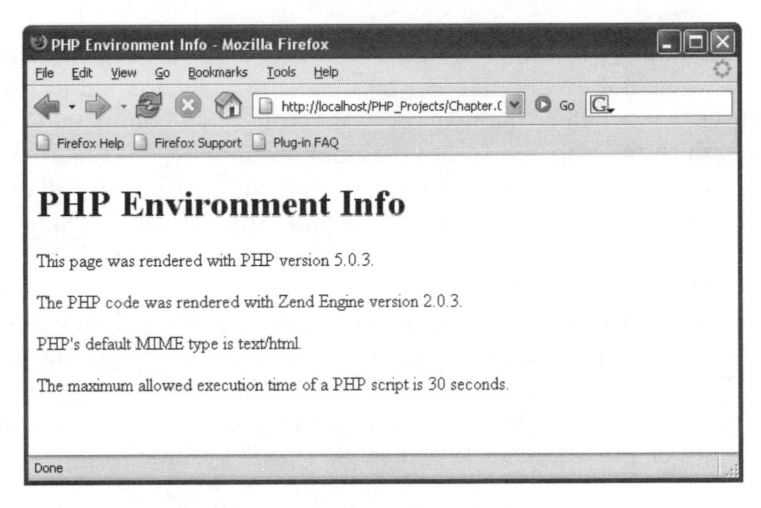

Figure 2-18 Web page with multiple PHP scripts

9. Close your Web browser window.

Case Sensitivity in PHP

Unlike XHTML and JavaScript, programming language constructs in PHP are mostly case insensitive, although there are some exceptions. This means that you can use any of the following versions of the `echo()` statement without receiving an error message:

```
<?php
echo "<p>Explore <strong>Africa</strong>, <br />";
Echo "<strong>South America</strong>, <br />";
ECHO " and <strong>Australia</strong>!</p>";
?>
```

Even though you can use whatever case you want, be certain to use the letter cases presented in this book for consistency and to make it easier to locate any problems in your scripts.

Exceptions to PHP's case insensitivity include variable and constant names, which *are* case sensitive. You study variables and constants in Chapter 3.

Adding Comments to a PHP Script

When you write a script, whether in PHP or any other programming language, it is considered good programming practice to add comments to your code. **Comments** are nonprinting lines that you place in your code to contain various types of remarks, including the name of the script, your name and the date you created the program, notes to yourself, or instructions to future programmers who might need to modify your work. When you are working with long scripts, comments make it easier to decipher how a program is structured.

PHP supports two kinds of comments: line comments and block comments. A **line comment** hides a single line of code. To create a line comment, add either two slashes // or the pound symbol # before the text you want to use as a comment. (You do not need to include both the two slashes // and the pound symbol # to create a single-line comment.) The // or # characters instruct the scripting engine to ignore all text immediately following the characters to the end of the line. You can place a line comment either at the end of a line of code or on its own line. **Block comments** hide multiple lines of code. You create a block comment by adding /* to the first line that you want included in the block and typing */ after the last character in the block. Any text or lines between the opening /* characters and the closing */ characters are ignored by the PHP engine. The following code shows a PHP code block containing line and block comments. If a client requests a Web page containing the following script in a Web browser, the scripting engine ignores the text marked with comments.

```
<?php
/*
This line is part of the block comment.
This line is also part of the block comment.
*/
echo "<h1>Comments Example</h1>";  // Line comments can follow
code statements
// This line comment takes up an entire line.
# This is another way of creating a line comment.
/* This is another way of creating
a block comment. */
?>
```

Comments created with two slashes // or the /* and */ characters are also used in C++, Java, and JavaScript. Comments created with the pound symbol # are used in Perl and shell script programming.

Next, you add comments to the PHP Environment Info Web page.

To add comments to the PHP Environment Info Web page:

1. Return to the **MultipleScripts.php** document in your text editor.
2. Add the following block comment immediately after the first opening PHP script delimiter:

```
/*
PHP code for Chapter 2.
The purpose of this code is to demonstrate how to add multiple
PHP code blocks to a Web page.
*/
```

3. Next, add the following line comments immediately after the block comment, taking care to replace "your name" with your first and last name and "today's date" with the current date:

```
// your name
# today's date
```

4. Save the **MultipleScripts.php** document, close it in your text editor, and validate it with the WDG HTML Validator. Open the document from your Web server to ensure that the comments are not displayed.
5. Close your Web browser window.

Chapter Summary

- Binary format (or "binaries") refers to files that can be in the form of executable installation programs.
- Source code is the original programming code in which an application was written.
- Directives define information about how a program should be configured.
- JavaScript and PHP are both referred to as embedded scripting languages because code for both languages is embedded within a Web page (either an HTML or XHTML document).
- You write PHP scripts within code declaration blocks, which are separate sections within a Web page that are interpreted by the scripting engine.
- The individual lines of code that make up a PHP script are called statements.
- The term function refers to a procedure (or individual statements grouped into a logical unit) that perform a specific task.
- The term programming language construct refers to a built-in feature of a programming language. Programming language constructs in PHP are mostly case insensitive, although there are some exceptions.

- Comments are nonprinting lines that you place in code to contain various types of remarks, including the name of the script, your name and the date you created the program, notes to yourself, or instructions to future programmers who might need to modify your work.

Review Questions

1. Which of the following are required to run PHP scripts? (Choose all that apply.)
   a. a Web browser
   b. a Web server
   c. the PHP software
   d. a database
2. The Web development environment you install in this section should only be used for development and testing purposes, and not for hosting a live Web site. True or False?
3. Explain the difference between compiling and interpreting.
4. Explain how you should go about finding help with Apache, PHP, and MySQL.
5. Apache only runs on UNIX/Linux operating systems. True or False?
6. IIS only runs on Windows platforms. True or False?
7. A computer can refer to itself using *localhost* or ________________.
   a. *self*
   b. *this*
   c. *127.0.0.1*
   d. *index.html*
8. What port number is reserved for HTTP communications?
   a. 0
   b. 80
   c. 256
   d. 1024
9. What is the name of the file used for configuring PHP?
   a. php.conf
   b. php.ini
   c. httpd.conf
   d. httpd.ini
10. MySQL is installed as an application. True or False?

11. What is the default extension that most Web servers use to process PHP scripts?
    a. .php
    b. .html
    c. .xhtml
    d. .ini
12. Which of the following types of code declaration blocks are always available on any Web server that supports PHP? (Choose all that apply.)
    a. `<?php ... ?>`
    b. `<script> ... </script>`
    c. `<? ... ?>`
    d. `<% ... %>`
13. What do you use to separate multiple arguments that are passed to a function?
    a. a period (.)
    b. a comma (,)
    c. a forward slash (/)
    d. a backwards slash (\)
14. What is the difference between `echo()` and `print()`?
15. The `echo()` and `print()` statements are functions. True or False?
16. How many PHP script sections can you include within a document?
    a. 1
    b. 2
    c. 10
    d. There is no limit.
17. Which of the following versions of the `print()` statement can you use in a PHP script? (Choose all that apply.)
    a. `print "Welcome to Hawaii!";`
    b. `Print "Welcome to Hawaii!";`
    c. `PRINT "Welcome to Hawaii!";`
    d. `Print("Welcome to Hawaii!");`
18. You create line comments in PHP code by adding ______________ to a line you want to use as a comment. (Choose all that apply.)
    a. `||`
    b. `**`
    c. `#`
    d. `//`

19. Block comments begin with /* and end with ________.
    a. */
    b. /*
    c. //
    d. **
20. PHP code cannot include both line comments and block comments. True or False?

Hands-On Projects

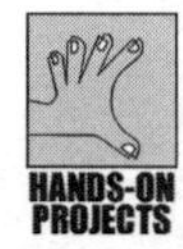

Hands-On Project 2-1

In this project, you create a Web page that uses `echo()` statements to print a short biography of NASCAR drive Jeff Burton.

1. Create a new document in your text editor.
2. Type the `<!DOCTYPE>` declaration, `<html>` element, header information, and `<body>` element. Use the strict DTD and "NASCAR Drivers" as the content of the `<title>` element.
3. Add standard PHP script delimiters to the document body. Add a comment block to the code section that contains your name and today's date.
4. Use `echo()` statements to create the text shown in Figure 2-19. Be certain to include the same formatting that is shown in the figure.

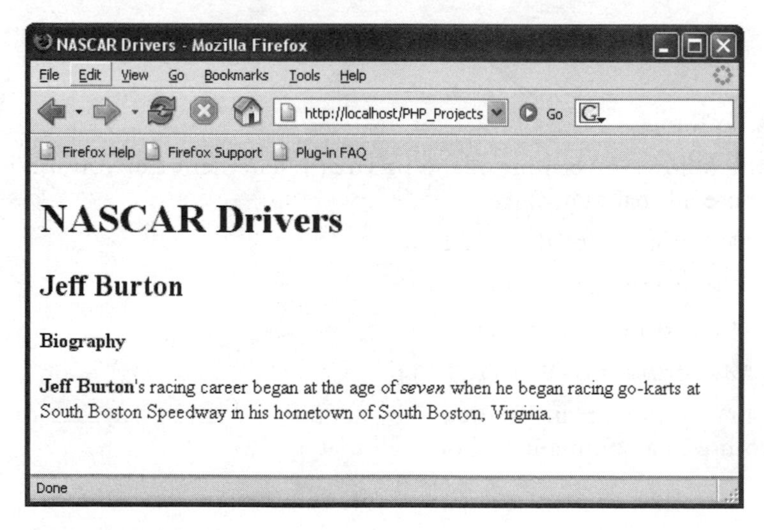

Figure 2-19 NASCAR.php

5. Save the document as **NASCAR.php** in the Projects directory for Chapter 2. After you save the document, validate it with the WDG HTML Validator.
6. Open the **NASCAR.php** file from your Web server by entering the following URL: **http://localhost/PHP_Projects/Chapter.02/Projects/NASCAR.php**.
7. Close your Web browser window.

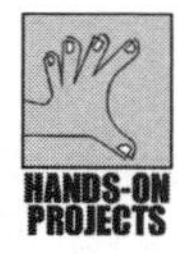

Hands-On Project 2-2

In this project, you create a Web page that contains two PHP code blocks. Both code blocks have multiple errors that you need to track down and fix.

1. Create a new document in your text editor.
2. Type the <!DOCTYPE> declaration, <html> element, header information, and <body> element. Use the strict DTD and "Locksmiths" as the content of the <title> element.
3. Add the following PHP code block to the document body exactly as shown:

```
<?php
*/
your name
today's date
*/
echo <h1>California Occupational Guide</h2>";
echo ("<h2>Locksmiths</h2>
echo "<p>A locksmith installs, services, and repairs various
types of locks and security devices. Locksmiths also install and
repair door hardware and pneumatic closing fixtures. Some
additional responsibilities of a locksmith may include cutting
new or duplicate keys and stamps with identification and
troubleshooting, repairing, and maintaining electronic keycard
systems."
>
```

4. Save the document as **Locksmiths.php** in the Projects directory for Chapter 2. The PHP code block contains multiple errors that will prevent the script from rendering properly. Locate and fix each error.
5. After you have fixed the errors, validate the Locksmiths.php document with the WDG HTML Validator, then open the document from your Web server by entering the following URL: **http://localhost/PHP_Projects/Chapter.02/Projects/Locksmiths.php**. Figure 2-20 shows how the document should appear.
6. Close your Web browser window.

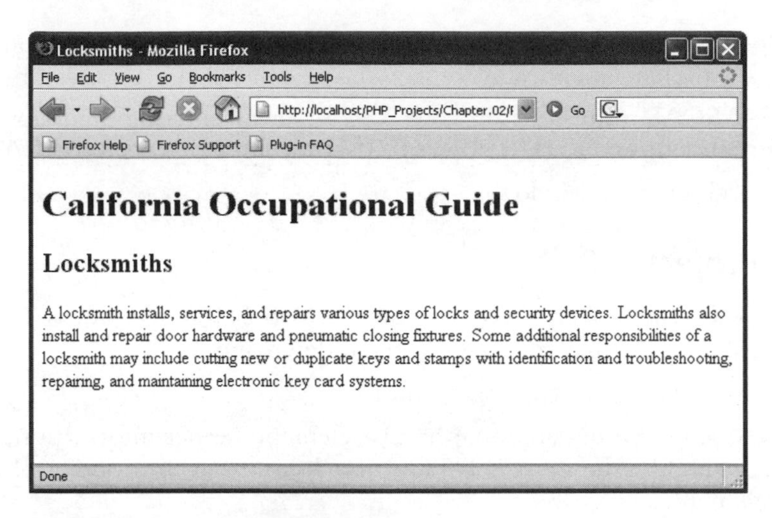

Figure 2-20 Locksmiths.php

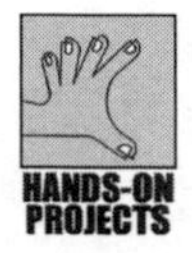

Hands-On Project 2-3

In addition to using the `echo()` and `print()` statements to print text to a Web browser, you can also use the "here document" syntax, as follows:

```
echo <<<terminator
text
terminator;
```

The *terminator* identifies the beginning and end of the "here document" block. You can use whatever text you want for the *terminator* portion of a "here document" block, provided you use the same at the start and the end. You must also use the same case with both references to the terminator.

In this project, you create a Web page that contains a "here document" block.

1. Create a new document in your text editor.
2. Type the `<!DOCTYPE>` declaration, `<html>` element, header information, and `<body>` element. Use the strict DTD and "Aquaculture" as the content of the `<title>` element.
3. Add the following text and element to the document body:

   ```
   <h1>Aquaculture</h1>
   ```

4. Add the following PHP code block to the end of document body:

   ```
   <?php
   ?>
   ```

5. Add to the PHP code block the following "here document" block. Be certain to use the same case for the terminator. Also, be sure not to include any white space in the last statement that contains the terminator and semicolon.

```
echo <<<HERE
<p>According to the online edition of the Columbia Encyclopedia,
<strong>aquaculture</strong> is the raising and harvesting of
fresh and saltwater plants and animals. The most economically
important form of aquaculture is fish farming, an industry that
accounts for nearly 20% of world fisheries production, and is
steadily increasing its share.</p>
HERE;
```

6. Save the document as **Aquaculture.php** in the Projects directory for Chapter 2. After you save the document, validate it with the WDG HTML Validator.
7. Open the **Aquaculture.php** file from your Web server by entering the following URL: **http://localhost/PHP_Projects/Chapter.02/Projects/Aquaculture.php**. Figure 2-21 shows how the document should appear.

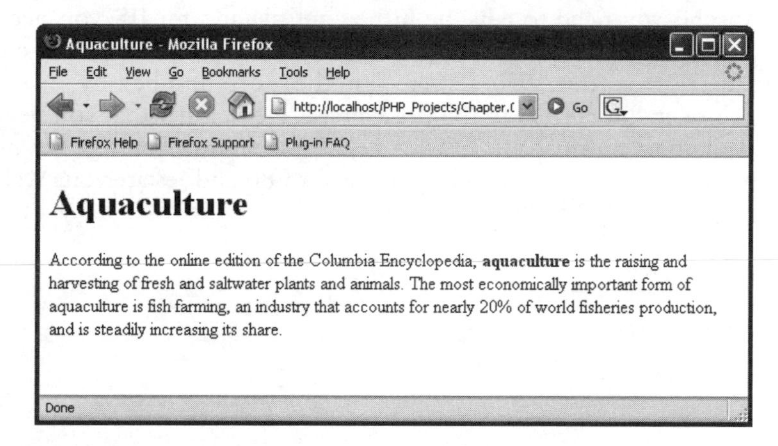

Figure 2-21 Aquaculture.php

8. Close your Web browser window.

Case Projects

Save your Case Projects files in the Cases directory for Chapter 2. Be certain to validate the files you create with the WDG HTML Validator. Also, be sure to open the documents you create from your Web server and not as a local file.

Case Project 2-1

Create a document with a PHP code block that uses `echo()` statements to print your name, address, and date of birth to the screen. Also, add PHP comments with your name and today's date. Write the document so that it conforms to the strict DTD. Save the document as **PersonalInfo.php**.

Case Project 2-2

Create a document with an <h1> element containing the text "Forestville Credit Union" and an `<h2>` element containing the text "CD Rates." Add a PHP code block in the document body. Within the code block, use `echo()` statements to print the following CD rate information: 4.35% (36-Month Term CD), 3.85% (12-Month Term CD), and 2.65% (6-Month Term CD). Use another `echo()` statement to print a paragraph element after the unordered list that contains the text "$1,000 minimum deposit." Add comments with your name and today's date. Write the document so that it conforms to the strict DTD. Save the document as **CDRates.php**.

Case Project 2-3

Practice changing the port that your Web server uses to listen for Web page requests from 80 to 8083. For Apache, you need to edit the httpd.conf file and for IIS, you need to use the Internet Information Services application in Control Panel. After you change the port number, be sure to restart your Web server. Test the port number by opening the CDRates.html document you created in the last exercise. Remember that you need to use a colon to append the port number to *localhost* or *127.0.0.1*. After you test the new port number, be sure to change your Web server's port back to 80 and restart your Web server.

CHAPTER

3

WORKING WITH DATA TYPES AND OPERATORS

In this chapter, you will:

- Work with variables and constants
- Study data types
- Use expressions and operators
- Cast the data types of variables
- Learn about operator precedence

One of the most important aspects of programming is the ability to store values in computer memory and to manipulate those values. The values stored in computer memory are called variables. The values, or data, contained in variables are classified into categories known as data types. In this chapter, you learn about PHP variables and data types, and the operations that can be performed on them.

USING VARIABLES AND CONSTANTS

The values a program stores in computer memory are commonly called **variables**. Technically speaking, though, a variable is actually a specific location in the computer's memory. Data stored in a specific variable often changes. You can think of a variable as similar to a storage locker—a program can put any value into it, and then retrieve the value later for use in calculations. To use a variable in a program, you first have to write a statement that creates the variable and assigns it a name. For example, you can have a program that creates a variable that stores the current time in that variable. Each time the program runs, the current time is different, so the value varies.

Programmers often talk about "assigning a value to a variable," which is the same as storing a value in a variable. For example, a shopping cart program might include variables that store customer names and purchase totals. Each variable will contain different values at different times, depending on the name of the customer and the items they are purchasing.

Naming Variables

The name you assign to a variable is called an **identifier**. You must observe the following rules and conventions when naming a variable:

- Identifiers must begin with a dollar sign ($).
- You can use numbers or an underscore (_) in an identifier, but not as the first character after the dollar sign.
- You cannot include spaces in an identifier.
- Identifiers are case sensitive.

It's common practice to use an underscore (_) character to separate individual words within a variable name, as in `$my_variable_name`. Another option is to use initial caps for each word in a variable name, as in `$MyVariableName`.

Unlike other types of PHP code, variable names are case sensitive. Therefore, the variable name `$MyVariable` is a completely different variable than one named `$Myvariable`, `$myVariable`, or `$MYVARIABLE`. If you receive an error when running a script, be sure that you are using the correct case when referring to any variables in your code.

Declaring and Initializing Variables

Before you can use a variable in your code, you have to create it. The process of specifying and creating a variable name is called **declaring** the variable. The process of assigning a first value to a variable is called **initializing** the variable. Some programming languages allow you to first declare a variable without initializing it. However, in PHP, you must declare and initialize a variable in the same statement, using the following syntax:

```
$variable_name = value;
```

The equal sign in the preceding statement assigns an initial value to (or initializes) the variable you created (or declared) with the name *$variable_name*.

If you attempt to declare a variable without initializing it, you will receive an error.

The value you assign to a variable can be a literal string or a numeric value. For example, the following statement assigns the literal string "Don" to the variable `$MyName`:

```
$MyName = "Don";
```

When you assign a literal string value to a variable, you must enclose the text in single or double quotation marks (as shown in the preceding statement), the same as when you use a literal string with the `echo()` statement. However, when you assign a numeric value to a variable, do not enclose the value in quotation marks or PHP will treat the value as a string instead of a number. The following statement assigns the numeric value 59 to the variable `$RetirementAge`:

```
$RetirementAge = 59;
```

In addition to assigning literal strings and numeric values to a variable, you can also assign the value of one variable to another. For instance, in the following code, the first statement declares a variable named `$SalesTotal` and assigns it an initial value of 0 (remember that in PHP you must initialize a variable when you first declare it). The second statement creates another variable named `$CurOrder` and assigns to it a numeric value of 40. The third statement then assigns the value of the `$CurOrder` variable (40) to the `$SalesTotal` variable.

```
$SalesTotal = 0;
$CurOrder = 40;
$SalesTotal = $CurOrder;
```

Displaying Variables

To print a variable with the `echo()` statement, you simply pass the variable name to the `echo()` statement, but without enclosing it in quotation marks, as follows:

```
$VotingAge = 18;
echo $VotingAge;
```

If you want to print both text strings and variables, you can send them to the `echo()` statement as individual arguments, separated by commas. For example, the following code prints the text shown in Figure 3-1. Notice that the text and elements are contained within quotation marks, but the `$VotingAge` variable is not.

```
echo "<p>The legal voting age is ", $VotingAge, ".</p>";
```

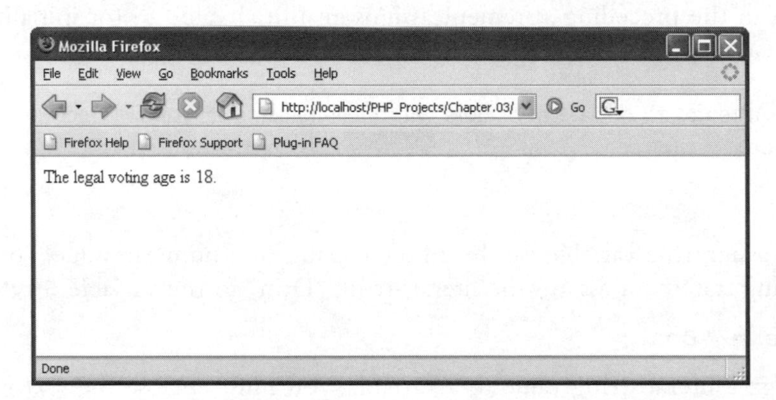

Figure 3-1 Output from an `echo()` statement that is passed text and a variable

You can also include variable names inside a text string, although the results you see printed on the screen depend on whether you use double quotation marks or single quotation marks. If you surround a variable name inside a text string with double quotation marks, the value assigned to the variable will print. For example, the following statement prints the same output that is shown in Figure 3-1:

```
echo "<p>The legal voting age is $VotingAge.</p>";
```

By contrast, if you surround a variable name inside a text string with single quotation marks, the name of the variable will print. For example, the following statement prints the output shown in Figure 3-2:

```
echo '<p>The legal voting age is $VotingAge.</p>';
```

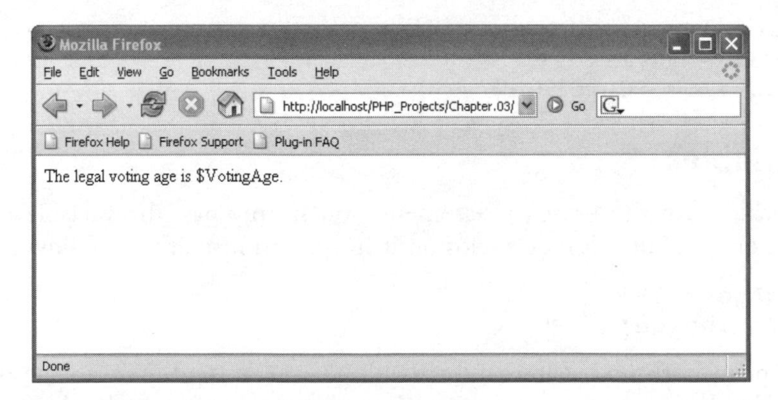

Figure 3-2 Output of an `echo()` statement that includes text and a variable surrounded by single quotation marks

Modifying Variables

You can change the variable's value at any point in a script. The following code declares a variable named `$SalesTotal`, assigns it an initial value of 40, and prints it using an `echo()` statement. The third statement changes the value of the `$SalesTotal` variable and the fourth statement prints the new value. Figure 3-3 shows the output in a Web browser.

```
$SalesTotal = 40;
echo "<p>Your sales total is $$SalesTotal</p>";
$SalesTotal = 50;
echo "<p>Your new sales total is $$SalesTotal</p>";
```

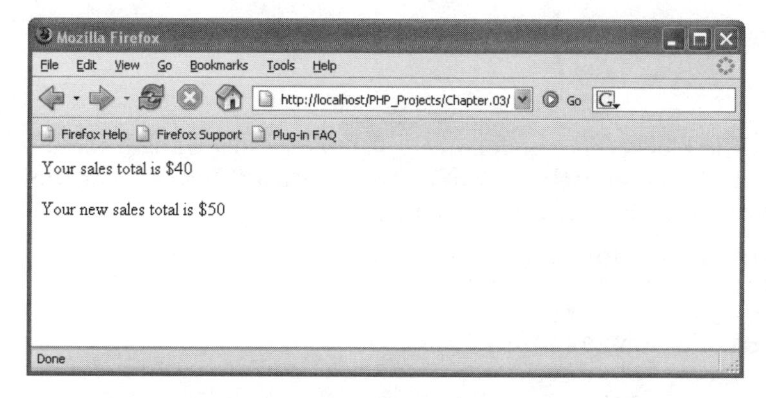

Figure 3-3 Results of a script that includes a changing variable

It's an old tradition among programmers to practice a new language by writing a script that prints or displays the text "Hello World!". The tradition of creating a Hello World program is surprisingly addictive. If you are an experienced programmer, you have undoubtedly created Hello World programs in the past. If you are new to programming, you will probably find yourself creating Hello World programs when you learn new programming languages in the future. Next, you create your own Hello World program in PHP. You create a simple script that prints the text "Hello World!" and that also says hello to the sun and the moon, as well as printing a line of scientific information about each celestial body. You use variables to store and print each piece of information.

To create the Hello World program:

1. Create a new document in your text editor.

2. Type the <!DOCTYPE> declaration, <html> element, header information, and <body> element. Use the strict DTD and "Hello World" as the content of the <title> element. Your document should appear as follows:

```
<!DOCTYPE html PUBLIC "-//W3C//DTD XHTML 1.0 Strict//EN"
"http://www.w3.org/TR/xhtml1/DTD/xhtml1-strict.dtd">
<html>
<head>
<title>Hello World</title>
</head>
<body>
</body>
</html>
```

3. Add the following standard PHP script delimiters to the document body:

```
<?php
?>
```

4. In the code block, type the following statements that declare variables containing the name of each celestial body along with variables containing scientific information about each celestial body:

```
$WorldVar = "World";
$SunVar = "Sun";
$MoonVar = "Moon";
$WorldInfo = 92897000;
$SunInfo = 72000000;
$MoonInfo = 3456;
```

5. Add the following statements to the end of the script section that print the values stored in each of the variables you declared and initialized in the last step:

```
echo "<p>Hello $WorldVar!<br />";
echo "The $WorldVar is $WorldInfo miles from the $SunVar.<br />";
echo "Hello ", $SunVar, "!<br />";
echo "The $SunVar's core temperature is approximately $SunInfo
degrees Fahrenheit.<br />";
echo "Hello ", $MoonVar, "!<br />";
echo "The $MoonVar is $MoonInfo miles in diameter.</p>";
```

6. Save the document as **HelloWorld.php** in the Chapter directory for Chapter 3. After you save the document, validate it with the WDG HTML Validator at **http://www.htmlhelp.org/tools/validator/upload.html**.

7. Open the **HelloWorld.php** file in your Web browser by entering the following URL: **http://localhost/PHP_Projects/Chapter.03/Chapter/HelloWorld.php**. You should see the Web page in Figure 3-4.

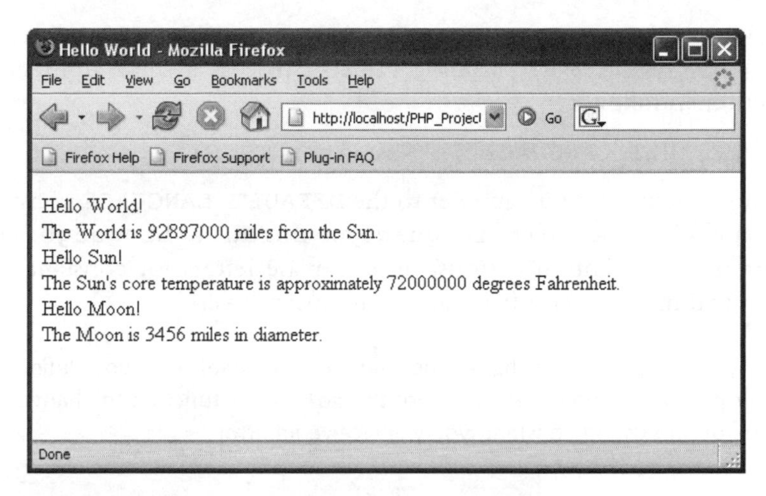

Figure 3-4 Output of HelloWorld.php

If you receive error messages, make sure that you typed all the variables in the correct case. (Remember that variables in PHP are case sensitive.)

8. Close your Web browser window.

Defining Constants

A **constant** contains information that does not change during the course of program execution. You can think of a constant as a variable with a *constant* value. A common example of a constant is the value of pi (π), which represents the ratio of the circumference of a circle to its diameter. The value of pi never changes from the constant value 3.141592.

Unlike variable names, constant names do not begin with a dollar sign ($). In addition, it is common practice to use all uppercase letters for constant names. When you create a constant, you do not declare and initialize it the way you declare a variable. Instead, you use the **`define()` function** to create a constant. The syntax for the `define()` function is as follows:

```
define("CONSTANT_NAME", value);
```

The value you pass to the `define()` function can be a text string, number, or Boolean value. In the following example, the first constant definition passes a text string to the `define()` function while the second constant definition passes a number:

```
define("DEFAULT_LANGUAGE", "Navajo");
define("VOTING_AGE", 18);
```

By default, constant names are case sensitive, the same as variables. However, you make constant names case insensitive by passing a value of true as a third argument to the `define()` function, as follows:

```
define("DEFAULT_LANGUAGE", "Navajo", TRUE);
```

With the preceding statement, you can refer to the `DEFAULT_LANGUAGE` constant using any letter case, including `default_language` or `Default_Language`. However, standard programming convention is to use all uppercase letters for constant names, so you should avoid making your constant names case insensitive.

Remember that you cannot change the value of a constant after you define it in your program. If you attempt to use the `define()` function to change the value of an existing constant, you will receive an error.

When you refer to a constant in code, remember *not* to include a dollar sign, as you would with variable names. You can pass a constant name to the `echo()` statement the same as you pass a variable name (but without the dollar sign), as follows:

```
echo "<p>The legal voting age is ", VOTING_AGE, ".</p>";
```

The preceding statements print the text "The legal voting age is 18." to the Web browser. Unlike variables, you cannot include the constant name within the quotations that surround a text string. If you do, PHP treats the constant name as text that is part of the text string. For example, consider the following statement, which includes the constant name within the quotations that surround the text string:

```
echo "<p>The legal voting age is VOTING_AGE.</p>";
```

Instead of printing the value of the constant (18), the preceding statement prints "The legal voting age is VOTING_AGE." to the Web browser.

PHP includes numerous predefined constants that you can use in your scripts.

Next, you replace the `$WorldInfo`, `$SunInfo`, and `$MoonInfo` variables in the HelloWorld.php script with constants.

To replace the `$WorldInfo`, `$SunInfo`, and `$MoonInfo` variables in the HelloWorld.php script with constants:

1. Return to the **HelloWorld.php** document in your text editor.
2. Replace the `$WorldInfo`, `$SunInfo`, and `$MoonInfo` variable declarations with the following constant definitions:

```
define("WORLD_INFO", 92897000);
define("SUN_INFO", 72000000);
define("MOON_INFO", 3456);
```

3. Replace the the `$WorldInfo`, `$SunInfo`, and `$MoonInfo` variable references in the `echo()` statements with the new constants. The modified `echo()` statements should appear as follows:

```
echo "<p>Hello ", $WorldVar, "!<br />";
echo "The $WorldVar is ", WORLD_INFO, " miles from the
$SunVar.<br />";
echo "Hello ", $SunVar, "!<br />";
echo "The $SunVar's core temperature is approximately ",
SUN_INFO, " degrees Fahrenheit.<br />";
echo "Hello ", $MoonVar, "!<br />";
echo "The $MoonVar is ", MOON_INFO, " miles in diameter.</p>";
```

4. Save the **HelloWorld.php** document, and then validate it with the WDG HTML Validator. After the file is valid, close it in your text editor.
5. Open the **HelloWorld.php** document from your Web server. The Web page should appear the same as it did before you added the constant declarations.
6. Close your Web browser window.

3

Working with Data Types

Variables can contain many different kinds of values—for example, the time of day, a dollar amount, or a person's name. A **data type** is the specific category of information that a variable contains. The concept of data types is often difficult for beginning programmers to grasp because in real life you don't often distinguish among different types of information. If someone asks you for your name, your age, or the current time, you don't usually stop to consider that your name is a text string and that your age and the current time are numbers. However, a variable's specific data type is very important in programming because the data type helps determine how much memory the computer allocates for the data stored in the variable. The data type also governs the kinds of operations that can be performed on a variable.

Data types that can be assigned only a single value are called **primitive types**. PHP supports the five primitive data types described in Table 3-1.

Table 3-1 Primitive PHP data types

Data Type	Description
Integer numbers	Positive or negative numbers with no decimal places
Floating-point numbers	Positive or negative numbers with decimal places or numbers written using exponential notation
Boolean	A logical value of true or false
String	Text such as "Hello World"
NULL	An empty value, also referred to as a `NULL` value

PHP also supports a "resource" data type, which is a special variable that holds a reference to an external resource, such as a database or XML file.

The term NULL refers to a data type as well as a value that can be assigned to a variable. Assigning the value `NULL` to a variable indicates the variable does not contain a usable value. A variable with a value of `NULL` has a value assigned to it—null is really the value "no value." You assign the `NULL` value to a variable when you want to ensure that the variable does not contain any data. For instance, with the `$SalesTotal` variable you saw earlier, you may want to ensure that the variable does not contain any data before you use it to create another purchase order.

The PHP language also supports **reference**, or **composite**, data types, which can contain multiple values or complex types of information, as opposed to the single values stored in primitive data types. The two reference data types supported by the PHP language are arrays and objects. In this chapter, you study basic array techniques. You learn about advanced arrays and objects in later chapters.

Many programming languages require that you declare the type of data that a variable contains. Programming languages that require you to declare the data types of variables are called **strongly typed programming languages**. Strong typing is also known as **static typing** because data types do not change after they have been declared. Programming languages that do not require you to declare the data types of variables are called **loosely typed programming languages**. Loose typing is also known as **dynamic typing** because data types can change after they have been declared. PHP is a loosely typed programming language. In PHP, you are not required to declare the data type of variables, and, in fact, are not allowed to do so. Instead, the PHP Scripting engine automatically determines what type of data is stored in a variable and assigns the variable's data type accordingly. The following code demonstrates how a variable's data type changes automatically each time the variable is assigned a new literal value.

```
$ChangingVariable = "Hello World";  // String
$ChangingVariable = 8;              // Integer number
$ChangingVariable = 5.367;          // Floating-point number
$ChangingVariable = TRUE;           // Boolean
$ChangingVariable = NULL;           // NULL
```

Although you cannot declare a data type when you first create a variable, you can force a variable to be converted to a specific type. You learn how to force a variable to be a specific type at the end of this section.

The next two sections focus on two especially important data types: numeric and Boolean data types.

Numeric Data Types

Numeric data types are an important part of any programming language, and are particularly useful for arithmetic calculations. PHP supports two numeric data types: integers and floating-point numbers. An **integer** is a positive or negative number with no decimal places. The numbers -250, -13, 0, 2, 6, 10, 100, and 10,000 are examples of integers. The numbers -6.16, -4.4, 3.17, .52, 10.5, and 2.7541 are not integers; they are floating-point numbers because they contain decimal places. A **floating-point number** is a number that contains decimal places or that is written in exponential notation. **Exponential notation**, or **scientific notation**, is a shortened format for writing very large numbers or numbers with many decimal places. Numbers written in exponential notation are represented by a value between 1 and 10 multiplied by 10 raised to some power. The value of 10 is written with an uppercase or lowercase *E*. For example, the number 200,000,000,000 can be written in exponential notation as 2.0e11, which means "two times ten to the eleventh power."

Next, you create a script that assigns integers and exponential numbers to variables and prints the values.

To create a script that assigns integers and exponential numbers to variables and prints the values:

1. Create a new document in your text editor.
2. Type the `<!DOCTYPE>` declaration, `<html>` element, header information, and `<body>` element. Use the strict DTD and "Print Numbers" as the content of the `<title>` element.
3. Add the following standard PHP script delimiters to the document body:

```
<?php
?>
```

4. Add the following lines to the script section that declare an integer variable and a floating-point variable:

```
$IntegerVar = 150;
$FloatingPointVar = 3.0e7; // floating-point number 30000000
```

5. Finally, to print the variables, add the following statements to the end of the script section:

```
echo "<p>Integer variable: $IntegerVar<br />";
echo "Floating-point variable: $FloatingPointVar</p>";
```

6. Save the document as **PrintNumbers.php** in the Chapter directory for Chapter 3, and then validate it with the WDG HTML Validator. After the file is valid, close it in your text editor.
7. Open the **PrintNumbers.php** file in your Web browser by entering the following URL: **http://localhost/PHP_Projects/Chapter.03/Chapter/PrintNumbers.php**. The integer 150 and the number 30000000 (for the exponential expression 3.0e7) should appear in your Web browser window, as shown in Figure 3-5.

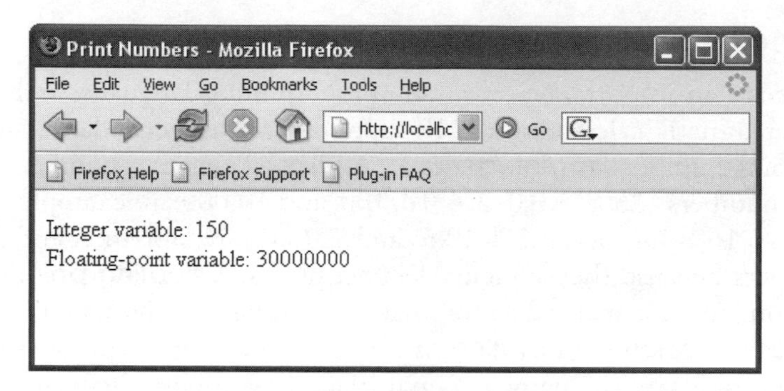

Figure 3-5 Output of PrintNumbers.php

8. Close your Web browser window.

Boolean Values

A **Boolean value** is a value of true or false. (You can also think of a Boolean value as either yes or no, or on or off.) Boolean values are most often used for deciding which parts of a program should execute and for comparing data. In programming languages other than PHP, you can use the integer value 1 to indicate a Boolean value of true and 0 to indicate a Boolean value of false. In PHP programming, however, you can only use the words "true" or "false" to indicate Boolean values. PHP then converts the values true and false to the integers 1 and 0. For example, when you attempt to use a Boolean variable of true in a mathematical operation, PHP converts the variable to an integer value of 1. The following shows a simple example of a variable that is assigned a Boolean value of true. Figure 3-6 shows the output in a Web browser. Notice that the Boolean value of true is printed as the integer 1.

```
$RepeatCustomer = TRUE;
echo "<p>Repeat customer: $RepeatCustomer</p>";
```

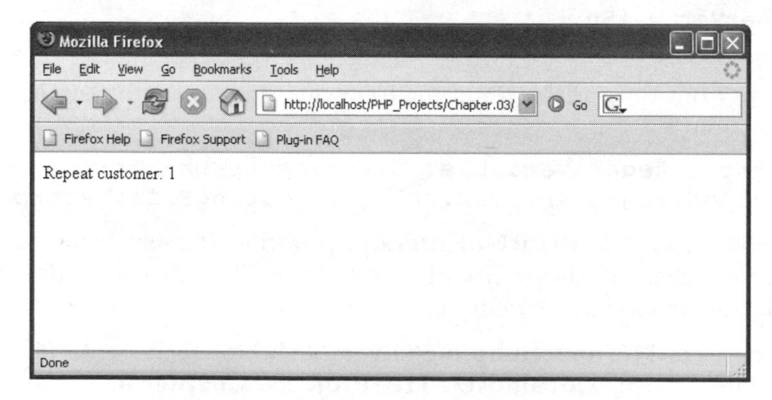

Figure 3-6 Boolean values

Arrays

An **array** contains a set of data represented by a single variable name. You can think of an array as a collection of variables contained within a single variable. You use arrays when you want to store groups or lists of related information in a single, easily managed location. Lists of names, courses, test scores, and prices are typically stored in arrays. Figure 3-7 conceptually shows how you can store the names of each Canadian province (but not territories) using a single array named `$Provinces[]`. Array names are often referred to with the array operators ([ ]) at the end of the name to clearly define them as arrays. You can use the array to refer to each province without having to retype the names and possibly introduce syntax errors through misspellings.

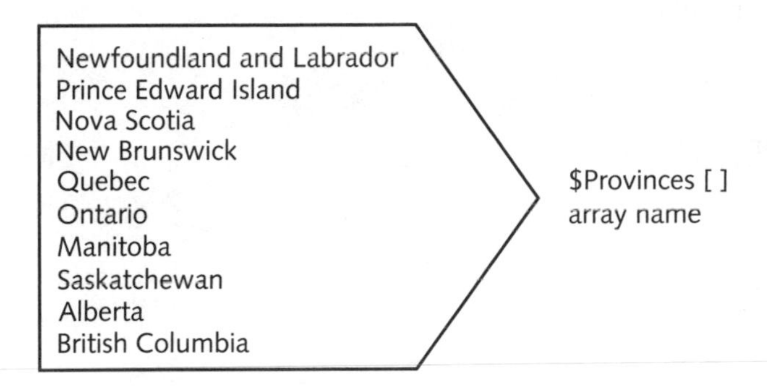

Figure 3-7 Conceptual example of an array

The identifiers you use for an array name must follow the same rules as identifiers for variables: They must begin with a dollar sign, can include numbers or an underscore (but not as the first character after the dollar sign), cannot include spaces, and are case sensitive.

Declaring and Initializing Indexed Arrays

In PHP, you can create numerically indexed arrays and associative arrays. In this chapter, you study numerically indexed arrays. You learn how to use associate arrays in Chapter 7.

An **element** refers to each piece of data that is stored within an array. By default, the numbering of elements within a PHP array starts with an index number of zero (0). (This numbering scheme can be very confusing for beginners.) An **index** is an element's numeric position within the array. You refer to a specific element by enclosing its index in brackets at the end of the array name. For example, the first element in the `$Provinces[]` array is `$Provinces[0]`, the second element is `$Provinces[1]`, the third element is `$Provinces[2]`, and so on. This also means that if you have an array consisting of 10 elements, the 10th element in the array is referred to using an index of 9.

You create an array using the `array()` construct or by using the array name and brackets. The `array()` construct uses the following syntax:

```
$array_name = array(values);
```

The following code uses the `array()` construct to create the `$Provinces[]` array:

```
$Provinces = array("Newfoundland and Labrador", "Prince Edward
Island", "Nova Scotia", "New Brunswick", "Quebec", "Ontario",
"Manitoba", "Saskatchewan", "Alberta", "British Columbia");
```

The following code shows another example of the preceding array declaration, but this time with line breaks to make it easier to work with:

```
$Provinces = array(
     "Newfoundland and Labrador",
     "Prince Edward Island",
     "Nova Scotia",
     "New Brunswick",
     "Quebec",
     "Ontario",
     "Manitoba",
     "Saskatchewan",
     "Alberta",
     "British Columbia"
     );
```

Next, you create a script that declares and initializes an array using the `array()` construct.

To create a script that declares and initializes an array using the `array()` construct:

1. Create a new document in your text editor.
2. Type the `<!DOCTYPE>` declaration, `<html>` element, header information, and `<body>` element. Use the strict DTD and "Central Valley Civic Center" as the content of the `<title>` element.
3. Add the following elements, text, and standard PHP script delimiters to the document body:

   ```
   <h1>Central Valley Civic Center</h1>
   <h2>Summer Concert Season</h2>
   <?php
   ?>
   ```

4. Add the following lines to the script section that declare and initialize an array named `$Concerts[]`:

   ```
   $Concerts = array("Jimmy Buffet", "Chris Isaak", "Bonnie Raitt",
   "James Taylor", "Alicia Keys");
   ```

5. Save the document as **Concerts.php** in the Chapter directory for Chapter 3.

You can also use the following syntax to assign values to an array by using the array name and brackets:

```
$Provinces[] = "Newfoundland and Labrador";
$Provinces[] = "Prince Edward Island";
$Provinces[] = "Nova Scotia";
$Provinces[] = "New Brunswick";
$Provinces[] = "Quebec";
$Provinces[] = "Ontario";
$Provinces[] = "Manitoba";
$Provinces[] = "Saskatchewan";
$Provinces[] = "Alberta";
$Provinces[] = "British Columbia";
```

Unlike with variables, the preceding statements do not overwrite the existing values in the `$Provinces[]` array. Instead, each value is assigned to the array as a new element using the next available index number.

Next, you add statements to the Concerts.php document that use the array name and brackets to add additional elements to the `$Concerts[]` array.

To add statements to the Concerts.php document that use the array name and brackets to add additional elements to the `$Concerts[]` array:

1. Return to the **Concerts.php** document in your text editor.
2. Add the following statements immediately after the statement containing the `array()` construct:

   ```
   $Concerts[] = "Bob Dylan";
   $Concerts[] = "Ryan Cabrera";
   ```

3. Save the **Concerts.php** document.

Most programming languages require that all elements in an array be of the exact same data type. However, in PHP the values assigned to array elements can be of different data types. For example, the following code uses the `array()` construct to create an array named `$HotelReservation` that stores values with different data types in the array elements:

```
$HotelReservation = array(
     "Don Gosselin", // guest name (string)
     2,              // # of nights (integer)
     89.95,          // price per night (floating-point)
     true);          // nonsmoking room (Boolean)
```

Accessing Element Information

You access an element's value the same as any variable, except you include brackets and the element index. For example, the following code prints the value of the second element

("Prince Edward Island") and fifth element ("Quebec") in the `$Provinces[]` array. Figure 3-8 shows the output.

```
echo "<p>Canada's smallest province is $Provinces[1].<br />";
echo "Canada's largest province is $Provinces[4].</p>";
```

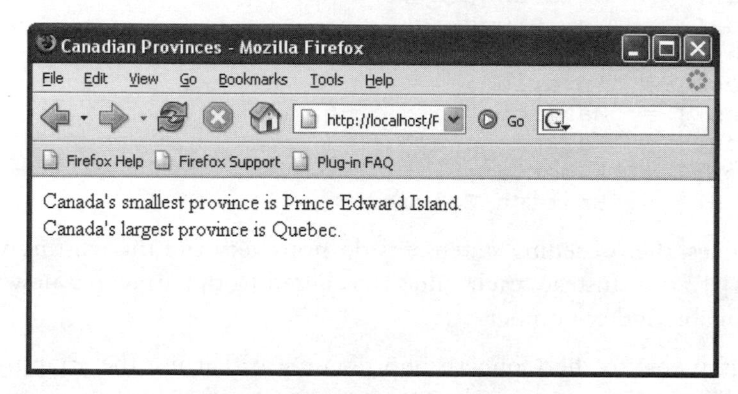

Figure 3-8 Output of elements in the `$Provinces[]` array

To find the total number of elements in an array, use the `count()` function. You pass to the `count()` function the name of the array whose elements you want to count. The following code uses the `count()` function to print the number of elements in the `$Provinces[]` array and the `$Territories[]` array. Figure 3-9 shows the output.

```
$Provinces = array("Newfoundland and Labrador", "Prince Edward
Island", "Nova Scotia", "New Brunswick", "Quebec", "Ontario", "
Manitoba", "Saskatchewan", "Alberta", "British Columbia");
$Territories = array("Nunavut", "Northwest Territories", "Yukon
Territory");
echo "<p>Canada has ", count($Provinces), " provinces and ",
     count($Territories), " territories.</p>";
```

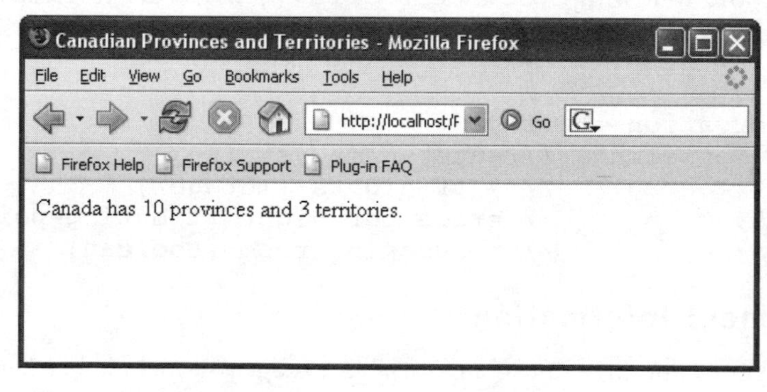

Figure 3-9 Output of the `count()` function

Next, you add statements to the Concerts.php document that use the `count()` function to print the number of scheduled concerts and the names of each performer.

To add output statements to the Concerts.php document:

1. Return to the **Concerts.php** document in your text editor.
2. Add the following output statements to the end of the code block, but above the closing `?>` delimiter:

```
echo "<p>The following ", count($Concerts), " concerts are
scheduled:</p><p>";
echo "$Concerts[0]<br />";
echo "$Concerts[1]<br />";
echo "$Concerts[2]<br />";
echo "$Concerts[3]<br />";
echo "$Concerts[4]<br />";
echo "$Concerts[5]<br />";
echo "$Concerts[6]</p>";
```

3. Save the **Concerts.php** document and then validate it with the WDG HTML Validator.
4. Open the **Concerts.php** file in your Web browser by entering the following URL: **http://localhost/PHP_Projects/Chapter.03/Chapter/Concerts.php**. Your Web browser should appear similar to Figure 3-10.

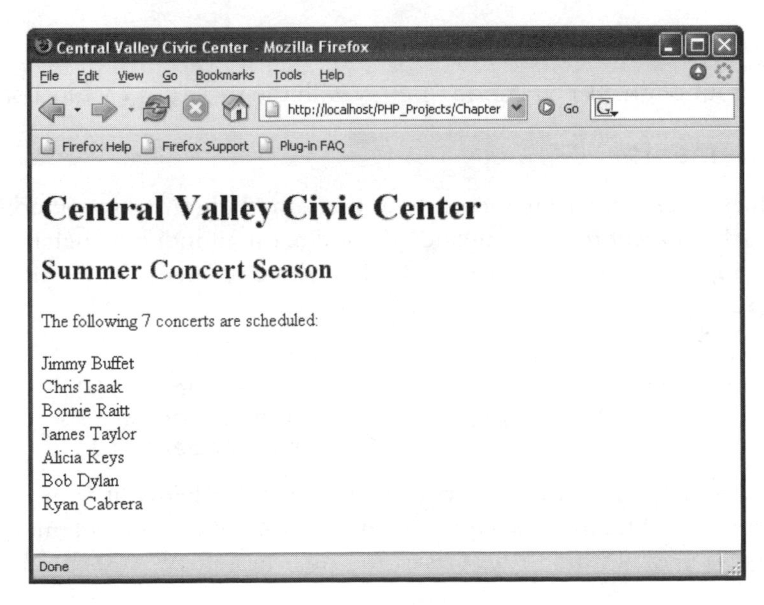

Figure 3-10 Output of Concerts.php

5. Close your Web browser window.

A looping statement provides a more efficient method for printing all the elements of an array. You learn about looping statements in Chapter 4.

PHP includes the `print_r()`, `var_export()`, and `var_dump()` functions that you can use to print or return information about variables. These functions are most useful with arrays because they print the index and value of each element. You pass to each function the name of an array (or other type of variable). The following `print_r()` function prints the index and values of each element in the `$Provinces[]` array. Figure 3-11 shows the output. Notice in the figure that the 10 Canadian provinces are assigned to elements 0 through 9 in the `$Provinces[]` array.

```
print_r($Provinces);
```

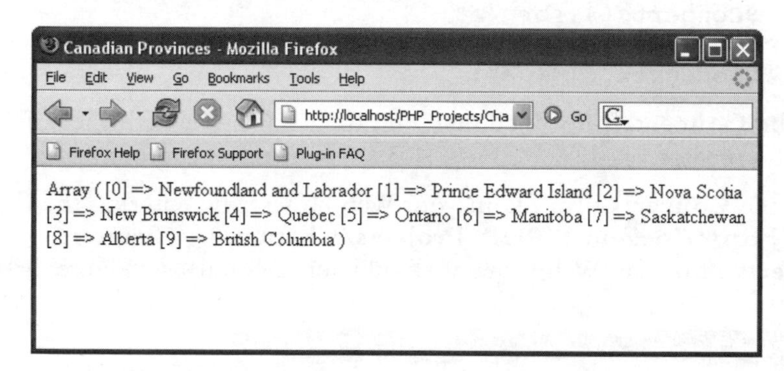

Figure 3-11 Output of the `$Provinces[]` array with the `print_r()` function

Modifying Elements

You modify values in existing array elements in the same fashion as you modify values in a standard variable, except that you include the index for an individual element of the array. The following code assigns values to the first three elements in an array named `$HospitalDepts[]`:

```
$HospitalDepts = array(
     "Anesthesia",              // first element (0)
     "Molecular Biology",       // second element (1)
     "Neurology");              // third element (2)
```

After you have assigned a value to an array element, you can change it later, just as you can change other variables in a script. To change the first array element in the `$HospitalDepts[]` array from "Anesthesia" to "Anesthesiology," you use the following statement:

```
$HospitalDepts[0] = "Anesthesiology";
```

Next, you modify the second and third elements in the `$Concerts[]` array from Bonnie Raitt and James Taylor to Joe Cocker and Van Morrison.

To add output statements to the Concerts.php document:

1. Return to the **Concerts.php** document in your text editor.
2. Add the following statements above the first `echo()` statement:

```
$Concerts[2] = "Joe Cocker";
$Concerts[3] = "Van Morrison";
```

3. Save the **Concerts.php** document, validate it with the WDG HTML Validator, and then close it in your text editor.
4. Open the **Concerts.php** file in your Web browser by entering the following URL: **http://localhost/PHP_Projects/Chapter.03/Chapter/Concerts.php**. The concert list should include Joe Cocker and Van Morrison instead of Bonnie Raitt and James Taylor.
5. Close your Web browser window.

BUILDING EXPRESSIONS

Variables and data become most useful when you use them in an expression. An **expression** is a literal value or variable (or a combination of literal values, variables, operators, and other expressions) that can be evaluated by the PHP scripting engine to produce a result. You use operands and operators to create expressions in PHP. **Operands** are variables and literals contained in an expression. A **literal** is a value such as a literal string or a number. **Operators** are symbols, such as the addition operator (+) and multiplication operator (*), that are used in expressions to manipulate operands. You have worked with several simple expressions so far that combine operators and operands. Consider the following statement:

```
$MyNumber = 100;
```

This statement is an expression that results in the value 100 being assigned to `$MyNumber`. The operands in the expression are the `$MyNumber` variable name and the integer value 100. The operator is the equal sign (=). The equal sign operator is a special kind of operator, called an assignment operator, because it assigns the value 100 on the right side of the expression to the variable (`$MyNumber`) on the left side of the expression. Table 3-2 lists the main types of PHP operators. You learn more about specific operators in the following sections.

Table 3-2 PHP operator types

Operator Type	Description
Array	Performs operations on arrays
Arithmetic	Performs mathematical calculations
Assignment	Assigns values to variables
Comparison	Compares operands and returns a Boolean value
Logical	Performs Boolean operations on Boolean operands
Special	Performs various tasks; these operators do not fit within other operator categories
String	Performs operations on strings

Other types of PHP operators include bitwise operators, which operate on integer values and are a fairly complex topic. Bitwise operators and other complex operators are beyond the scope of this book.

You study string operators in Chapter 5 and arrays in Chapter 7.

PHP operators are binary or unary. A **binary operator** requires an operand before and after the operator. The equal sign in the statement `$MyNumber = 100;` is an example of a binary operator. A **unary operator** requires a single operand either before or after the operator. For example, the increment operator (++), an arithmetic operator, is used for increasing an operand by a value of one. The statement `$MyNumber++;` changes the value of the `$MyNumber` variable to 101.

The operand to the left of an operator is known as the left operand, and the operand to the right of an operator is known as the right operand.

Next, you learn more about the different types of PHP operators.

Arithmetic Operators

Arithmetic operators are used in PHP to perform mathematical calculations, such as addition, subtraction, multiplication, and division. You can also use an arithmetic operator to return the modulus of a calculation, which is the remainder left when you divide one number by another number.

Arithmetic Binary Operators

Table 3-3 lists the PHP binary arithmetic operators and their descriptions.

Table 3-3 PHP arithmetic binary operators

Operator	Name	Description
+	Addition	Adds two operands
-	Subtraction	Subtracts one operand from another operand
*	Multiplication	Multiplies one operand by another operand
/	Division	Divides one operand by another operand
%	Modulus	Divides one operand by another operand and returns the remainder

The following code shows examples of expressions that include arithmetic binary operators. Figure 3-12 shows how the expressions appear in a Web browser.

```
// ADDITION
$x = 100;
$y = 200;
$ReturnValue = $x + $y;  // $ReturnValue changes to 300
echo '<p>$ReturnValue after addition expression: ',
     $ReturnValue, "</p>";
// SUBTRACTION
$x = 10;
$y = 7;
$ReturnValue = $x - $y;  // $ReturnValue changes to 3
echo '<p>$ReturnValue after subtraction expression: ',
     $ReturnValue, "</p>";
// MULTIPLICATION
$x = 2;
$y = 6;
$ReturnValue = $x * $y;  // $ReturnValue changes to 12
echo '<p>$ReturnValue after multiplication expression: ',
     $ReturnValue, "</p>";
// DIVISION
$x = 24;
$y = 3;
$ReturnValue = $x / $y;  // $ReturnValue changes to 8
echo '<p>$ReturnValue after division expression: ',
     $ReturnValue, "</p>";
// MODULUS
$x = 3;
$y = 2;
$ReturnValue = $x % $y;  // $ReturnValue changes to 1
echo '<p>$ReturnValue after modulus expression: ',
     $ReturnValue, "</p>";
```

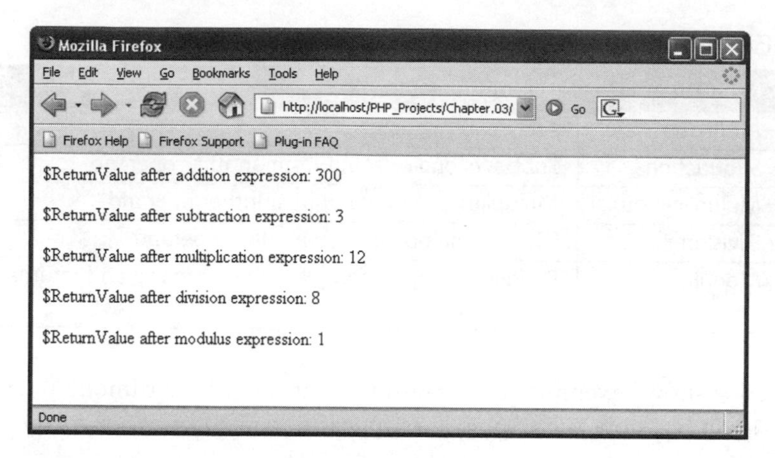

Figure 3-12 Results of arithmetic expressions

Notice in the preceding code that when PHP performs an arithmetic calculation, it performs the operation on the right side of the assignment operator, and then assigns the value to a variable on the left side of the assignment operator. For example, in the statement `$ReturnValue = $x + $y;`, the operands `$x` and `$y` are added, and then the result is assigned to the `$ReturnValue` variable on the left side of the assignment operator.

You might be confused by the difference between the division (`/`) operator and the modulus (`%`) operator. The division operator performs a standard mathematical division operation. For example, dividing 15 by 6 results in a value of 2.5. In comparison, the modulus operator returns the remainder that results from the division of two integers. The following code, for instance, uses the division and modulus operators to return the result of dividing 15 by 6. The division of 15 by 6 results in a value of 2.5, because 6 goes into 15 exactly 2.5 times. But if you express this in whole numbers, 6 goes into 15 only 2 times, with a remainder of 3 left over. Thus, the modulus of 15 divided by 6 is 3 because 3 is the remainder left over following the division. Figure 3-13 shows the output.

```
$DivisionResult = 15 / 6;
$ModulusResult = 15 % 6;
echo "<p>15 divided by 6 is
     $DivisionResult.</p>"; // prints '2.5'
echo "The whole number 6 goes into 15 twice, with a
     remainder of $ModulusResult.</p>"; // prints '3'
```

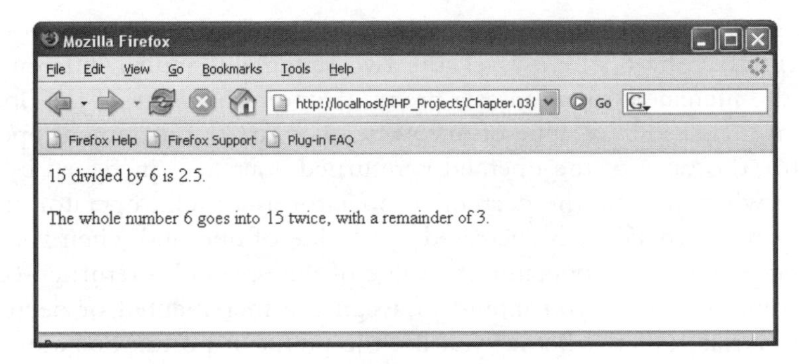

Figure 3-13 Division and modulus expressions

You can include a combination of variables and literal values on the right side of an assignment statement. For example, any of the following addition statements are correct:

```
$ReturnValue = 100 + $y;
$ReturnValue = $x + 200;
$ReturnValue = 100 + 200;
```

However, you cannot include a literal value as the left operand because the PHP Scripting engine must have a variable to which to assign the returned value. Therefore, the statement `100 = $x + $y;` causes an error.

When performing arithmetic operations on string values, the PHP Scripting engine attempts to convert the string values to numbers. The variables in the following example are assigned as string values instead of numbers because they are contained within quotation marks. Nevertheless, the PHP scripting engine correctly performs the multiplication operation and returns a value of 6.

```
$x = "2";
$y = "3";
$ReturnValue = $x * $y; // the value returned is 6
```

Arithmetic Unary Operators

Arithmetic operations can also be performed on a single variable using unary operators. Table 3-4 lists the unary arithmetic operators available in PHP.

Table 3-4 PHP arithmetic unary operators

Operator	Name	Description
++	Increment	Increases an operand by a value of one
--	Decrement	Decreases an operand by a value of one

The increment (++) and decrement (--) unary operators can be used as prefix or postfix operators. A **prefix operator** is placed before a variable. A **postfix operator** is placed after a variable. The statements `++$MyVariable;` and `$MyVariable++;` both increase `$MyVariable` by one. However, the two statements return different values. When you use the increment operator as a prefix operator, the value of the operand is returned *after* it is increased by a value of one. When you use the increment operator as a postfix operator, the value of the operand is returned *before* it is increased by a value of one. Similarly, when you use the decrement operator as a prefix operator, the value of the operand is returned *after* it is decreased by a value of one, and when you use the decrement operator as a postfix operator, the value of the operand is returned *before* it is decreased by a value of one. If you intend to assign the incremented or decremented value to another variable, then whether you use the prefix or postfix operator makes a difference.

You use arithmetic unary operators in any situation in which you prefer a simplified expression for increasing or decreasing a value by 1. For example, the statement `$Count = $Count + 1;` is identical to the statement `++$Count;`. As you can see, if your goal is only to increase a variable by 1, it is easier to use the unary increment operator. But remember that with the prefix operator the value of the operand is returned *after* it is increased or decreased by a value of 1, whereas with the postfix operator, the value of the operand is returned *before* it is increased or decreased by a value of 1.

For an example of when you would use the prefix operator or the postfix operator, consider an integer variable named `$StudentID` that is used for assigning student IDs in a class registration script. One way of creating a new student ID number is to store the last assigned student ID in the `$StudentID` variable. When it's time to assign a new student ID, the script could retrieve the last value stored in the `$StudentID` variable and then increase its value by 1. In other words, the last value stored in the `$StudentID` variable will be the next number used for a student ID number. In this case, you would use the postfix operator to return the value of the expression *before* it is incremented by using a statement similar to `$CurStudentID = $StudentID++;`. If you are storing the last assigned student ID in the `$CurStudentID` variable, you would want to increment the value by 1 and use the result as the next student ID. In this scenario, you would use the prefix operator, which returns the value of the expression after it is incremented using a statement similar to `$CurStudentID = ++$StudentID;`.

Figure 3-14 shows a simple script that uses the prefix increment operator to assign three student IDs to a variable named `$CurStudentID`. The initial student ID is stored in the `$StudentID` variable and initialized to a starting value of 100. Figure 3-15 shows the output.

```
$StudentID = 100;
$CurStudentID = ++$StudentID; // assigns '101'
echo "<p>The first student ID is ",
     $CurStudentID, "</p>";
$CurStudentID = ++$StudentID; // assigns '102'
echo "<p>The second student ID is ",
     $CurStudentID, "</p>";
$CurStudentID = ++$StudentID; // assigns '103'
echo "<p>The third student ID is ",
     $CurStudentID, "</p>";
```

prefix increment operator

Figure 3-14 Script that uses the prefix increment operator

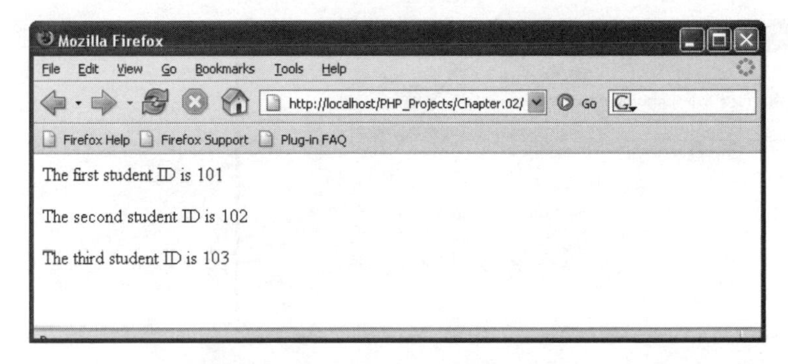

Figure 3-15 Output of the prefix version of the student ID script

The script in Figure 3-16 performs the same tasks, but using a postfix increment operator. Notice that the output in Figure 3-17 differs from the output in Figure 3-15. Because the first example of the script uses the prefix increment operator, which increments the `$StudentID` variable *before* it is assigned to `$CurStudentID`, the script does not use the starting value of 100. Rather, it first increments the `$StudentID` variable and uses 101 as the first student ID. In comparison, the second example of the script does use the initial value of 100 because the postfix increment operator increments the `$StudentID` variable *after* it is assigned to the `$CurStudentID` variable.

```
$StudentID = 100;
$CurStudentID = $StudentID++; // assigns '101'
echo "<p>The first student ID is ",
     $CurStudentID, "</p>";
$CurStudentID = $StudentID++; // assigns '102'
echo "<p>The second student ID is ",
     $CurStudentID, "</p>";
$CurStudentID = $StudentID++; // assigns '103'
echo "<p>The third student ID is ",
     $CurStudentID, "</p>";
```

postfix increment operator

Figure 3-16 Script that uses the postfix increment operator

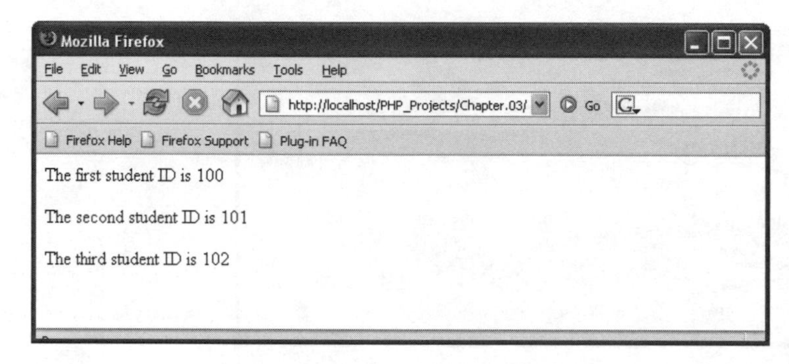

Figure 3-17 Output of the postfix version of the student ID script

Next, you create a script that performs arithmetic calculations.

To create a script that performs arithmetic calculations:

1. Create a new document in your text editor.
2. Type the `<!DOCTYPE>` declaration, `<html>` element, header information, and `<body>` element. Use the strict DTD and "Arithmetic Examples" as the content of the `<title>` element.
3. Add the following standard PHP script delimiters to the document body:

```
<?php
?>
```

4. Add the following statements to the script section to declare two variables. These statements include a number variable to contain a number, which you will use in several arithmetic operations, and a result variable to contain the value of each arithmetic operation.

```
$Number = 100;
$Result = 0;
```

5. Now add the following statements that perform addition, subtraction, multiplication, and division operations on the `$Number` variable and assign each value to the `$Result` variable. The `$Result` variable is printed each time it changes.

```
$Result = $Number + 50;
echo '<p>$Result after addition = ', $Result, "<br />";
$Result = $Number / 4;
echo '$Result after division = ', $Result, "<br />";
$Result = $Number - 25;
echo '$Result after subtraction = ', $Result, "<br />";
$Result = $Number * 2;
echo '$Result after multiplication = ', $Result, "<br />";
```

6. Next, add the following two statements. The first statement uses the increment operator to increase the value of the `$Number` variable by one and assigns the new value to the `$Result` variable. The second statement prints the `$Result` variable. Notice that the increment operator is used as a prefix, so the new value is assigned to the `$Result` variable. If you used the postfix increment operator, you would assign the old value of the `$Number` variable to the `$Result` variable, before the `$Number` variable is incremented by one.

```
$Result = ++$Number;
echo '$Result after increment = ', $Result, "</p>";
```

7. Save the document as **ArithmeticExamples.php** in the Chapter directory for Chapter 3, and then validate it with the WDG HTML Validator. After the file is valid, close it in your text editor.

8. Open the **ArithmeticExamples.php** file in your Web browser by entering the following URL: **http://localhost/PHP_Projects/Chapter.03/Chapter/ArithmeticExamples.php**. Figure 3-18 shows the output.

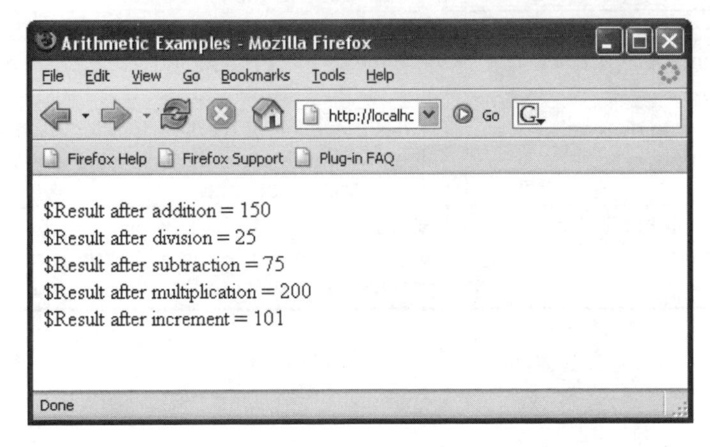

Figure 3-18 Output of ArithmeticExamples.php

9. Close your Web browser window.

Assignment Operators

Assignment operators are used for assigning a value to a variable. You have already used the most common assignment operator, the equal sign (=), to assign values to variables you declared. The equal sign assigns an initial value to a new variable or assigns a new value to an existing variable. For example, the following code creates a variable named `$MyFavoriteSuperHero`, uses the equal sign to assign it an initial value, and then uses the equal sign again to assign it a new value.

```
$MyFavoriteSuperHero = "Superman";
$MyFavoriteSuperHero = "Batman";
```

PHP includes other assignment operators in addition to the equal sign. These additional assignment operators, called **compound assignment operators**, perform mathematical calculations on variables and literal values in an expression, and then assign a new value to the left operand. Table 3-5 displays a list of the common PHP assignment operators.

Table 3-5 PHP assignment operators

Operator	Name	Description
=	Assignment	Assigns the value of the right operand to the left operand
+=	Compound addition assignment	Combines the value of the right operand with the value of the left operand or adds the value of the right operand to the value of the left operand and assigns the new value to the left operand
-=	Compound subtraction assignment	Subtracts the value of the right operand from the value of the left operand and assigns the new value to the left operand
*=	Compound multiplication assignment	Multiplies the value of the right operand by the value of the left operand and assigns the new value to the left operand
/=	Compound division assignment	Divides the value of the left operand by the value of the right operand and assigns the new value to the left operand
%=	Compound modulus assignment	Divides the value of the left operand by the value of the right operand and assigns the remainder (modulus) to the left operand

The following code shows examples of the different assignment operators. Figure 3-19 shows the output.

```
echo "<p>";
$x = 100;
$y = 200;
$x += $y;              // $x changes to 300
echo $x, "<br />";
$x = 10;
$y = 7;
$x -= $y;              // $x changes to 3
echo $x, "<br />";
$x = 2;
$y = 6;
$x *= $y;              // $x changes to 12
echo $x, "<br />";
$x = 24;
$y = 3;
$x /= $y;              // $x changes to 8
echo $x, "<br />";
$x = 3;
$y = 2;
$x %= $y;              // $x changes to 1
echo $x, "<br />";
$x = "100";
$y = 5;
$x *= $y;              // $x changes to 500
echo $x, "</p>";
```

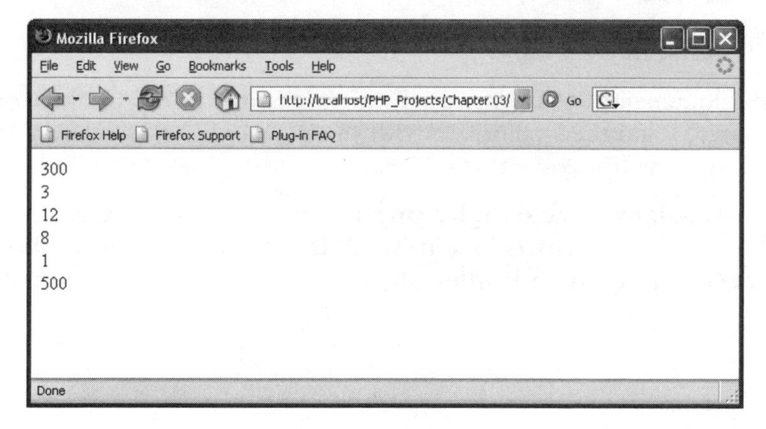

Figure 3-19 Assignment expressions

Next, you create a script that uses assignment operators.

To create a script that uses assignment operators:

1. Create a new document in your text editor.
2. Type the `<!DOCTYPE>` declaration, `<html>` element, header information, and `<body>` element. Use the strict DTD and "Assignment Examples" as the content of the `<title>` element.
3. Add the following standard PHP script delimiters to the document body:

```
<?php
?>
```

4. Type the following statements in the script section. These statements perform several compound assignment operations on a variable named `$ChangingVar`. After each assignment operation, the result is printed.

```
$ChangingVar = 100;
$ChangingVar += 50;
echo "Variable after addition assignment =
     $ChangingVar<br />";
$ChangingVar -= 30;
echo "Variable after subtraction assignment =
     $ChangingVar<br />";
$ChangingVar /= 3;
echo "Variable after division assignment =
     $ChangingVar<br />";
$ChangingVar *= 8;
echo "Variable after multiplication assignment =
     $ChangingVar<br />";
$ChangingVar %= 300;
echo "Variable after modulus assignment =
     $ChangingVar</p>";
```

5. Save the document as **AssignmentExamples.php** in the Chapter directory for Chapter 3, and then validate it with the WDG HTML Validator. After the file is valid, close it in your text editor.
6. Open the **AssignmentExamples.php** file in your Web browser by entering the following URL: **http://localhost/PHP_Projects/Chapter.03/Chapter/AssignmentExamples.php**. Figure 3-20 shows the output.

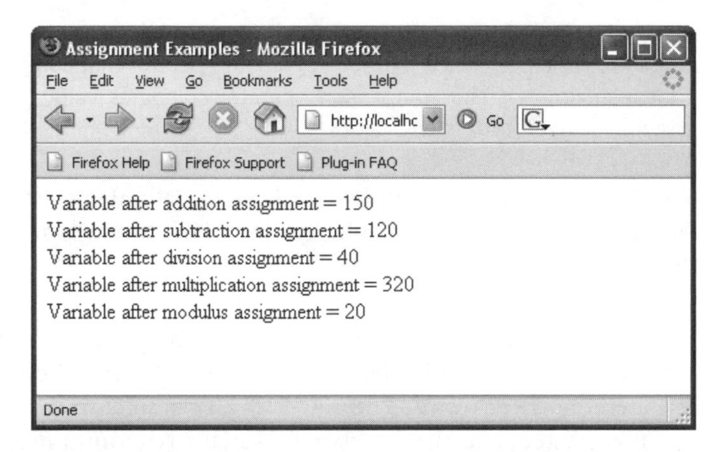

Figure 3-20 Output of AssignmentExamples.php

7. Close the Web browser window.

Comparison and Conditional Operators

Comparison operators are used to compare two operands and determine how one operand compares to another. A Boolean value of true or false is returned after two operands are compared. For example, the statement `5 < 3` returns a Boolean value of false because 5 is not less than 3. Table 3-6 lists the PHP comparison operators.

Table 3-6 PHP comparison operators

Operator	Name	Description
==	Equal	Returns true if the operands are equal
===	Strict equal	Returns true if the operands are equal and of the same type
!= or <>	Not equal	Returns true if the operands are not equal
!==	Strict not equal	Returns true if the operands are not equal or not of the same type
>	Greater than	Returns true if the left operand is greater than the right operand
<	Less than	Returns true if the left operand is less than the right operand
>=	Greater than or equal to	Returns true if the left operand is greater than or equal to the right operand
<=	Less than or equal to	Returns true if the left operand is less than or equal to the right operand

The comparison operator (==) consists of two equal signs and performs a different function than the one performed by the assignment operator that consists of a single equal sign (=). The comparison operator *compares* values, whereas the assignment operator *assigns* values.

Comparison operators are often used with two kinds of special statements: conditional statements and looping statements. You learn how to use comparison operators in such statements in Chapter 4.

You can use number or string values as operands with comparison operators. When two numeric values are used as operands, the PHP Scripting engine compares them numerically. For example, the statement `$ReturnValue = 5 > 4;` results in true because the number 5 is numerically greater than the number 4. When two nonnumeric values are used as operands, the PHP Scripting engine compares them in alphabetical order. The statement `$ReturnValue = "b" > "a";` returns true because the letter *b* is alphabetically greater than the letter *a*. When one operand is a number and the other is a string, the PHP Scripting engine attempts to convert the string value to a number. If the string value cannot be converted to a number, a value of false is returned. For example, the statement `$ReturnValue = 10 == "ten";` returns a value of false because the PHP Scripting engine cannot convert the string "ten" to a number. However, the statement `$ReturnValue = 10 == "10";` returns a value of false because the PHP Scripting engine cannot convert the string "10" to a number.

The comparison operator is often used with another kind of operator, the conditional operator. The **conditional operator** executes one of two expressions, based on the results of a conditional expression. The syntax for the conditional operator is ***`conditional expression ? expression1 : expression2;`***. If the conditional expression evaluates to true, ***`expression1`*** executes. If the conditional expression evaluates to false, ***`expression2`*** executes.

The following code shows an example of the conditional operator. In the example, the conditional expression checks to see if the `$BlackjackPlayer1` variable is less than or equal to 21. If `$BlackjackPlayer1` is less than or equal to 21, the text "Player 1 is still in the game" is assigned to the `$Result` variable. If `$BlackjackPlayer1` is greater than 21, the text "Player 1 is out of the action" is assigned to the `$Result` variable. Because `$BlackjackPlayer1` is equal to 20, the conditional statement returns a value of true, the first expression executes, and "Player 1 is still in the game" prints to the screen. Figure 3-21 shows the output.

```
$BlackjackPlayer1 = 20;
 ($BlackjackPlayer1 <= 21) ? $Result =
      "Player 1 is still in the game." : $Result =
      "Player 1 is out of the action.";
echo "<p>", $Result, "</p>";
```

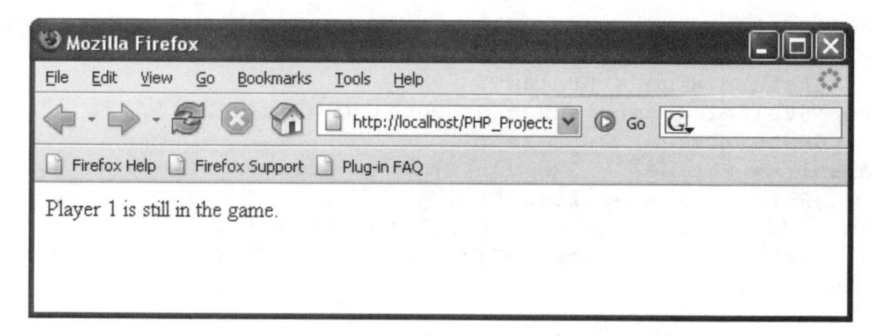

Figure 3-21 Output of a script with a conditional operator

Next, you create a script that uses comparison and conditional operators.

To create a script that uses comparison and conditional operators:

1. Create a new document in your text editor.
2. Type the `<!DOCTYPE>` declaration, `<html>` element, header information, and `<body>` element. Use the strict DTD and "Comparison Examples" as the content of the `<title>` element.
3. Add the following standard PHP script delimiters to the document body:

```
<?php
?>
```

4. Add the following statements to the script section that perform various comparison operations on two variables. Notice that the comparison statements use the conditional operator to assign a text value of "true" or "false" to the `$ReturnValue` variable.

```
$Value1 = "first text string";
$Value2 = "second text string";
$Value1 == $Value2 ? $ReturnValue = "true" :
     $ReturnValue = "false";
echo '<p>$Value1 equal to $Value2: ', $ReturnValue, "<br />";
$Value1 = 50;
$Value2 = 75;
$Value1 == $Value2 ? $ReturnValue = "true" :
     $ReturnValue = "false";
echo '$Value1 equal to $Value2: ', $ReturnValue, "<br />";
$Value1 != $Value2 ? $ReturnValue = "true" :
     $ReturnValue = "false";
echo '$Value1 not equal to $Value2: ', $ReturnValue, "<br />";
$Value1 <> $Value2 ? $ReturnValue = "true" :
     $ReturnValue = "false";
echo '$Value1 not equal to $Value2: ', $ReturnValue, "<br />";
$Value1 > $Value2 ? $ReturnValue = "true" :
     $ReturnValue = "false";
echo '$Value1 greater than $Value2: ', $ReturnValue, "<br />";
$Value1 < $Value2 ? $ReturnValue = "true" :
     $ReturnValue = "false";
```

```
echo '$Value1 less than $Value2: ', $ReturnValue, "<br />";
$Value1 >= $Value2 ? $ReturnValue = "true" :
     $ReturnValue = "false";
echo '$Value1 greater than or equal to $Value2: ',
     $ReturnValue, "<br />";
$Value1 <= $Value2 ? $ReturnValue = "true" :
     $ReturnValue = "false";
echo '$Value1 less than or equal to $Value2 : ',
     $ReturnValue, "<br />";
$Value1 = 25;
$Value2 = 25;
$Value1 === $Value2 ? $ReturnValue = "true" :
     $ReturnValue = "false";
echo '$Value1 equal to $Value2 AND the same data type: ',
     $ReturnValue, "<br />";
$Value1 !== $Value2 ? $ReturnValue = "true" :
     $ReturnValue = "false";
echo '$Value1 not equal to $Value2 AND not the same data type: ',
     $ReturnValue, "</p>";
```

5. Save the document as **ComparisonExamples.php** in the Chapter directory for Chapter 3, and then validate it with the WDG HTML Validator. After the file is valid, close it in your text editor.

6. Open the **ComparisonExamples.php** file in your Web browser by entering the following URL: **http://localhost/PHP_Projects/Chapter.03/Chapter/ComparisonExamples.php**. Figure 3-22 shows the output.

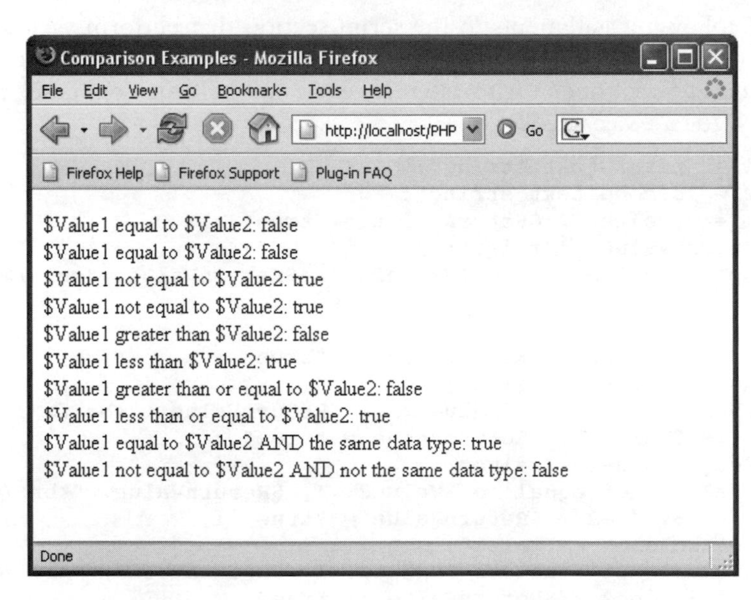

Figure 3-22 Output of ComparisonExamples.php

7. Close your Web browser window.

Logical Operators

Logical operators are used for comparing two Boolean operands for equality. For example, a script for an automobile insurance company might need to determine whether a customer is male *and* under 21 to determine the correct insurance quote. As with comparison operators, a Boolean value of true or false is returned after two operands are compared. Table 3-7 lists the PHP logical operators.

3

Table 3-7 PHP logical operators

Operator	Name	Description
`&&`, `and`	And	Returns true if both the left operand and right operand return a value of true; otherwise, it returns a value of false
`||`, `or`	Or	Returns true if either the left operand or right operand returns a value of true; if neither operand returns a value of true the expression containing the Or (`||`) operator returns a value of false
`!`	Not	Returns true if an expression is false and returns false if an expression is true

For the Or operator, you can use either || or "or". For the And operator, you can use either && or "and". The Or and the And operators are binary operators (requiring two operands), whereas the Not (`!`) operator is a unary operator (requiring a single operand). Logical operators are often used with comparison operators to evaluate expressions, allowing you to combine the results of several expressions into a single statement. For example, the And operator is used to determine whether two operands return an equivalent value. The operands themselves are often expressions. The following code uses the And (`&&`) operator to compare two separate expressions:

```
$Gender = "male";
$Age = 17;
$RiskFactor = $Gender=="male" && $Age<=21;     // returns true
```

In the preceding example, the `$Gender` variable expression evaluates to true because it is equal to "male" and the `$Age` variable expression evaluates to true because its value is less than or equal to 21. Because both expressions are true, `$RiskFactor` is assigned a value of true. The statement containing the And operator (`&&`) essentially says, "If variable `$Gender` is equal to 'male' *and* variable `$Age` is less than or equal to 21, then assign a value of true to `$RiskFactor`. Otherwise, assign a value of false to `$RiskFactor`." In the following code, however, `$RiskFactor` is assigned a value of false because the `$Age` variable expression does not evaluate to true. Notice that the following code uses the "and" version of the And operator.

```
$Gender = "male";
$Age = 28;
$RiskFactor = $Gender=="male" and $Age<=21; // returns false
```

The logical Or operator checks to see if either expression evaluates to true. For example, the statement containing the Or operator (`||`) in the following code says, "If variable `$SpeedingTicket` is equal to true *or* variable `$Age` is less than or equal to 21, then assign a value of true to `$RiskFactor`. Otherwise, assign a value of false to `$RiskFactor`."

```
$SpeedingTicket = 2;
$Age = 28;
$RiskFactor = $SpeedingTicket > 0 || $Age <= 21; // returns true
```

The `$RiskFactor` variable in the preceding example is assigned a value of true because the `$SpeedingTicket` variable expression evaluates to true, even though the `$Age` variable expression evaluates to false. This result occurs because the Or operator returns true if *either* the left *or* right operand evaluates to true. The following example shows another version of the preceding code, but this time using the "or" version of the Or operator:

```
$SpeedingTicket = 2;
$Age = 28;
$RiskFactor = $SpeedingTicket > 0 or $Age <= 21; // returns true
```

The following code is an example of the Not (`!`) operator, which returns true if an operand evaluates to false and returns false if an operand evaluates to true. Notice that because the Not (`!`) operator is unary, it requires only a single operand.

```
$TrafficViolations = true;
$SafeDriverDiscount = !$TrafficViolations;     // returns false
```

Logical operators are often used within conditional and looping statements such as the `if...else`, `for`, and `while` statements. You learn about conditional and looping statements in Chapter 4.

Next, you create a script that uses logical operators.

To create a script that uses logical operators:

1. Create a new document in your text editor.
2. Type the `<!DOCTYPE>` declaration, `<html>` element, header information, and `<body>` element. Use the strict DTD and "Logical Examples" as the content of the `<title>` element.
3. Add the following standard PHP script delimiters to the document body:

```
<?php
?>
```

4. Add the following statements to the script section that use logical operators on two variables. The conditional expressions evaluate the logical expressions and then assign a text value of "true" or "false" to the `$ReturnValue` variable.

```
$TrueValue = true;
$FalseValue = false;
!$TrueValue ? $ReturnValue = "true" :
     $ReturnValue = "false";
echo "<p>$ReturnValue<br />";
!$FalseValue ? $ReturnValue = "true" :
     $ReturnValue = "false";
echo "$ReturnValue<br />";
$TrueValue || $FalseValue ? $ReturnValue = "true" :
     $ReturnValue = "false";
echo "$ReturnValue<br />";
$TrueValue && $FalseValue ? $ReturnValue = "true" :
     $ReturnValue = "false";
echo "$ReturnValue<br />";
```

5. Save the document as **LogicalExamples.php** in the Chapter directory for Chapter 3, and then validate it with the WDG HTML Validator. After the file is valid, close it in your text editor.

6. Open the **LogicalExamples.php** file from your Web server by entering the following URL: **http://localhost/PHP_Projects/Chapter.03/Chapter/LogicalExamples.php**. Figure 3-23 shows the output.

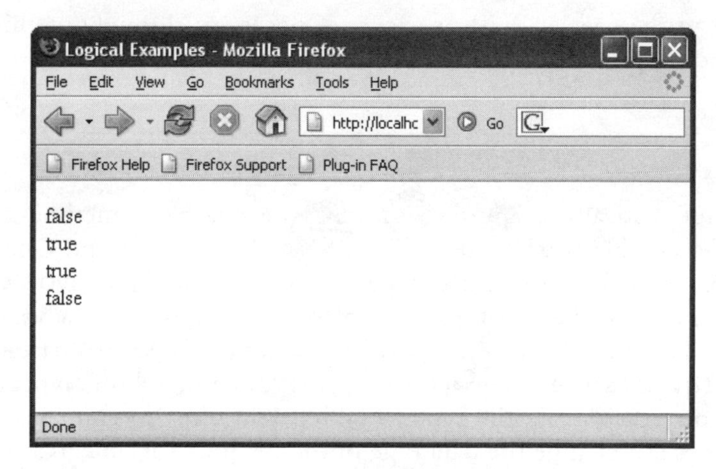

Figure 3-23 Output of LogicalExamples.php

7. Close the Web browser window.

Special Operators

PHP also includes the special operators that are listed in Table 3-8. These operators are used for various purposes and do not fit within any other category.

Table 3-8 PHP special operators

Operator	Description
`new`	Creates a new instance of a user-defined object type or a predefined PHP object type
`[]`	Accesses an element of an array
`=>`	Specifies the index or key of an array element
`,`	Separates arguments in a list
`?:`	Executes one of two expressions based on the results of a conditional expression
`instanceof`	Returns true if an object is of a specified object type
`@`	Suppresses any errors that might be generated by an expression to which it is prepended (or "placed before")
`(int)`, `(integer)`, `(bool)`, `(boolean)`, `(double)`, `(string)`, `(array)`, `(object)`	Casts (or transforms) a variable of one data type into a variable of another data type

You are introduced to the special PHP operators as necessary throughout this book, beginning with the casting operators in the following section.

TYPE CASTING

Even though PHP automatically assigns the data type of a variable, sometimes you will want to ensure that a variable is of the data type expected by your script. One way to ensure that a variable is of the correct data type is through **casting**, or **type casting**, which copies the value contained in a variable of one data type into a variable of another data type. The PHP syntax for casting variables is `$NewVariable = (new_type) $OldVariable;`. The `(new_type)` portion of the syntax is the type-casting operator representing the type to which you want to cast the variable. Note that casting does not change the data type of the original variable. Rather, casting copies the data from the old variable, converts it to the data type of the target variable, and then assigns the value to the new variable.

Type-casting operators are useful because the data type of variables can change during the course of program execution. This can cause problems if you attempt to perform an arithmetic operation on a variable that happens to contain a string or the NULL value. For example, the first statement in the following code assigns a string value of "55 mph" to a variable named `$SpeedLimitMiles`. The second statement then multiplies the `$SpeedLimitMiles` variable by 1.6 to convert the value to kilometers. Notice that the second statement also includes the `(int)` operator, which converts the string value in the `$SpeedLimitMiles` variable to an integer.

```
$SpeedLimitMiles = "55 mph";
$SpeedLimitKilometers = (int) $SpeedLimitMiles * 1.6;
echo "$SpeedLimitMiles is equal to
     $SpeedLimitKilometers kph";
```

The third statement in the preceding code prints the text "55 mph is equal to 88 kph" to the Web browser. The `(int)` operator converted the string value of "55 mph" to an integer value of 55, which was multiplied by 1.6 to calculate the kilometers. To be honest, the PHP scripting engine would have performed the type cast automatically, without the `(int)` operator. However, it doesn't hurt to use type casting to ensure that your variables are of the data type you expect them to be. This is especially true if you need to perform operations on data that is entered by users. As you learn in Chapter 5, one of the most common uses of PHP (and other server-side scripting languages) is to process form data that is submitted from a client. Only heaven knows what characters a user might enter into a form, so it's a good idea for you to ensure that the data entered is of the type that is expected by your script.

You can also perform a type cast with the `settype()` function.

Instead of just guessing data types, you can view a variable's type by using the `gettype()` function, which returns one of the following strings, depending on the data type:

- Boolean
- Integer
- Double
- String
- Array
- Object
- Resource
- NULL
- Unknown type

You pass to the `gettype()` function the name of a variable as a parameter using the syntax `gettype($variable_name);`. For example, the first statement in the following code declares a double variable named `$MortgageRate`. The second statement passes the name of the `$MortgageRate` variable to the `gettype()` function. The value returned from the `gettype()` function is then printed by an `echo()` statement. The following code prints the text string "double" to the screen.

```
$MortgageRate = .0575;
echo gettype($MortgageRate);
```

Although you can use the `gettype()` function to view a variable's data type, you should not use the function to determine whether a variable is of a specified data type because the PHP Group may change the value returned from the `gettype()` function in a future edition of PHP. To test whether a variable is of a given data type, you should instead use an `is_*()` function. There are 15 `is_*()` functions that test for various kinds of data types. Each function returns a Boolean value to indicate whether the variable is of a given data type. For instance, the `is_numeric()` function tests whether a variable contains a numeric data type, whereas the `is_string()` function tests whether a variable contains a string data type. There are also more specific `is_*()` functions, such as the `is_int()` function, which tests whether a variable is an integer data type and the `is_double()` function, which tests whether a variable is a double data type. To use an `is_*()` function, you pass a variable name as an argument to the function you want to use. The following example uses the `is_double()` function along with the conditional operator to test the data type of the `$MortgageRate` variable. The conditional expression passes the `$MortgageRate` variable to the `is_double()` function, and then determines whether the returned result is true. Because the `$MortgageRate` variable is a double data type, a value of true is returned with the text "The variable contains a decimal number."

```
$MortgageRate = .0575;
(is_double($MortgageRate)) ? $Result =
     "The variable contains a decimal number." :
     $Result = "The variable does not contain a decimal number.";
echo $Result;
```

The following example contains a modified version of the miles-to-kilometers script. This time, a conditional operator uses the `is_int()` function to determine whether the `$SpeedLimitMiles` variable is an integer. If the variable is an integer, its value is simply multiplied by 1.6 and assigned to the `$SpeedLimitKilometers` variable. However, if the variable is not an integer (and it's not), its value is cast to an integer data type before being multiplied by 1.6 and assigned to the `$SpeedLimitKilometers` variable.

```
$SpeedLimitMiles = "55 mph";
(is_int($SpeedLimitMiles)) ? $Result =
     $SpeedLimitKilometers = $SpeedLimitMiles * 1.6 :
     $SpeedLimitKilometers = (int) $SpeedLimitMiles * 1.6;
echo "$SpeedLimitMiles is equal to
     $SpeedLimitKilometers kph";
```

Understanding Operator Precedence

When using operators to create expressions in PHP, you need to be aware of the precedence of an operator. The term **operator precedence** refers to the order in which operations in an expression are evaluated. Table 3-9 shows the order of precedence for PHP operators. Operators in the same grouping in Table 3-9 have the same order of precedence. When performing operations with operators in the same precedence group, the order of precedence is determined by the operator's **associativity**—that is, the order in which operators of equal precedence execute. Associativity is evaluated on a left-to-right or a right-to-left basis.

Table 3-9 Operator precedence in PHP

<table>
<tr><th>Operators</th><th>Description</th><th>Associativity</th></tr>
<tr><td>new</td><td>New object—highest precedence</td><td>None</td></tr>
<tr><td>[]</td><td>Array elements</td><td>Right to left</td></tr>
<tr><td>!</td><td>Logical Not</td><td>Right to left</td></tr>
<tr><td>++</td><td>Increment</td><td>Right to left</td></tr>
<tr><td>--</td><td>Decrement</td><td>Right to left</td></tr>
<tr><td>(int), (double), (string), (array), (object)</td><td>Cast</td><td>Right to left</td></tr>
<tr><td>@</td><td>Suppress errors</td><td>Right to left</td></tr>
<tr><td>* / %</td><td>Multiplication/division/modulus</td><td>Left to right</td></tr>
<tr><td>+ - .</td><td>Addition/subtraction/string concatenation</td><td>Left to right</td></tr>
<tr><td>< <= > >=</td><td>Comparison</td><td>None</td></tr>
<tr><td>== != <> === !==</td><td>Equality</td><td>None</td></tr>
<tr><td>&&</td><td>Logical And</td><td>Left to right</td></tr>
<tr><td>||</td><td>Logical Or</td><td>Left to right</td></tr>
<tr><td>?:</td><td>Conditional</td><td>Left to right</td></tr>
<tr><td>= += -= *= /= %=</td><td>Assignment</td><td>Right to left</td></tr>
<tr><td>and</td><td>Logical And</td><td>Left to right</td></tr>
<tr><td>or</td><td>Logical Or</td><td>Left to right</td></tr>
<tr><td>,</td><td>List separator—lowest precedence</td><td>Left to right</td></tr>
</table>

The preceding list in Table 3-9 does not include bitwise operators.

Operators in a higher grouping have precedence over operators in a lower grouping. For example, the multiplication operator (*) has a higher precedence than the addition operator (+). Therefore, the statement 5 + 2 * 8 evaluates as follows: The numbers 2 and 8 are multiplied first for a total of 16, then the number 5 is added, resulting in a total of 21. If the addition operator had a higher precedence than the multiplication operator, the statement would evaluate to 56 because 5 would be added to 2 for a total of 7, which would then be multiplied by 8.

As an example of how associativity is evaluated, consider the multiplication and division operators, which have an associativity of left to right. This means that the statement 30 / 5 * 2 results in a value of 12 because, although the multiplication and division operators have equal precedence, the division operation executes first due to the left-to-right associativity of both operators. If the multiplication operator had higher precedence than the division operator, the statement 30 / 5 * 2 would result in a value of 3 because the multiplication operation (5 * 2) would execute first. By comparison, the assignment operator and compound assignment operators such as the compound multiplication assignment operator (*=) have an associativity of right to left. Therefore, in the following code, the assignment operations take place from right to left. The variable **$x** is incremented by one *before* it is assigned to the **$y** variable using the compound multiplication assignment operator (*=). Then, the value of variable **$y** is assigned to variable **$x**. The result assigned to both the **$x** and **$y** variables is 8.

```
$x = 3;
$y = 2;
$x = $y *= ++$x;
```

You can use parentheses with expressions to change the associativity with which individual operations in an expression are evaluated. For example, the statement 5 + 2 * 8, which evaluates to 21, can be rewritten to (5 + 2) * 8, which evaluates to 56. The parentheses tell the PHP Scripting engine to add the numbers 5 and 2 before multiplying by the number 8. Using parentheses forces the statement to evaluate to 56 instead of 21.

Chapter Summary

- The values a program stores in computer memory are commonly called variables.
- The name you assign to a variable is called an identifier.
- A constant contains information that does not change during the course of program execution.
- A data type is the specific category of information that a variable contains.
- PHP is a loosely typed programming language.
- An integer is a positive or negative number with no decimal places.
- A floating-point number is a number that contains decimal places or that is written in exponential notation.
- A Boolean value is a logical value of true or false.

- An array contains a set of data represented by a single variable name.
- An expression is a single literal value or variable or a combination of literal values, variables, operators, and other expressions that can be evaluated by the PHP scripting engine interpreter to produce a result.
- Operands are variables and literals contained in an expression. A literal is a value such as a literal string or a number.
- Operators are symbols used in expressions to manipulate operands, such as the addition operator (+) and multiplication operator (*).
- A binary operator requires an operand before and after the operator.
- A unary operator requires a single operand either before or after the operator.
- Arithmetic operators are used in the PHP scripting engine to perform mathematical calculations, such as addition, subtraction, multiplication, and division.
- Assignment operators are used for assigning a value to a variable.
- Comparison operators are used to compare two operands and determine how one operand compares with another.
- The conditional operator executes one of two expressions, based on the results of a conditional expression.
- Logical operators are used for comparing two Boolean operands for equality.
- Casting or type casting copies the value contained in a variable of one data type into a variable of another data type.
- Operator precedence is the order in which operations in an expression are evaluated.

Review Questions

1. Which of the following is a valid variable name?
   a. `SalesOrder`
   b. `salesOrder`
   c. `$SalesOrder`
   d. `$1SalesOrder`
2. You are not required to initialize a variable when you first declare it. True or False?
3. Which is the correct syntax for declaring a variable and assigning it a string?
   a. `$MyVariable = "Hello";`
   b. `$MyVariable = "Hello"`
   c. `"Hello" = $MyVariable;`
   d. `$MyVariable = Hello;`

4. Explain the concept of data types.
5. Explain the purpose of the `NULL` data type.
6. A loosely typed programming language ________________.
   a. does not require data types of variables to be declared
   b. requires data types of variables to be declared
   c. does not have different data types
   d. does not have variables
7. How many decimal places does an integer store?
   a. zero
   b. one
   c. two
   d. as many as necessary
8. Which of the following is not a floating-point number?
   a. -439.35
   b. 3.17
   c. 10
   d. -7e11
9. Which of the following values can be assigned to a Boolean variable? (Choose all that apply.)
   a. true
   b. false
   c. 1
   d. yes
10. In PHP, the values assigned to array elements can be of different data types. True or False?
11. Which of the following refers to the first element in an indexed array named `$Employees[]`?
    a. `$Employees[0]`
    b. `$Employees[1]`
    c. `$Employees[first]`
    d. `$Employees[a]`
12. Explain the difference between binary and unary operators.

13. The modulus operator (`%`) ______________.
    a. converts an operand to base 16 (hexadecimal) format
    b. returns the absolute value of an operand
    c. calculates the percentage of one operand compared to another
    d. divides two operands and returns the remainder
14. What value is assigned to the `$ReturnValue` variable in the statement `$ReturnValue = 100 != 200;`?
    a. true
    b. false
    c. 100
    d. 200
15. Which arithmetic operators can be used as both prefix and postfix operators? (Choose all that apply.)
    a. ++
    b. --
    c. +
    d. –
16. The And (`&&`) operator returns true if ______________.
    a. the left operand returns a value of true
    b. the right operand returns a value of true
    c. the left operand and right operand both return a value of true
    d. the left operand and right operand both return a value of false
17. What value is assigned to the `$ReturnValue` variable in the statement `$ReturnValue = !$x;`, assuming that $x has a value of true?
    a. true
    b. false
    c. null
    d. undefined
18. Explain how to use the conditional operator.
19. The order of priority in which operations in an expression are evaluated is known as ______________.
    a. prerogative precedence
    b. operator precedence
    c. expression evaluation
    d. priority evaluation

20. What is the value of the expression `4 * (2 + 3)`?
    a. 11
    b. -11
    c. 20
    d. 14

HANDS-ON PROJECTS

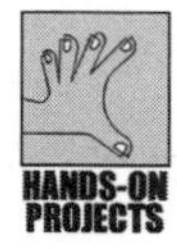

Hands-On Project 3-1

When you use short PHP script delimiters (`<?` and `?>`), you can use an output directive to send the result of an expression to a user's Web browser. The syntax for the output directive is `<?= expression ?>`. For example, if your script includes a variable named `$SalesTotal` that has been assigned a value of $24.95, the output directive `<?= $SalesTotal ?>` sends the value $24.95 to the Web browser. In this project, you create a script that uses an output directive and the `phpversion()` function to print the PHP version.

1. Create a new document in your text editor.
2. Type the `<!DOCTYPE>` declaration, `<html>` element, header information, and `<body>` element. Use the strict DTD and "Output Directive" as the content of the `<title>` element.
3. Add the following elements, text, and output directive to the document body:

```
<p>This Web page was generated with PHP version
<?= phpversion() ?>
.</p>
```

4. Save the document as **OutputDirective.php** in the Projects directory for Chapter 3, close it in your text editor, and then open it in your Web browser to see how it renders.
5. Close your Web browser window.

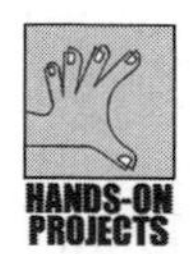

Hands-On Project 3-2

Identify the data types assigned to the result variable in each of the following statements:

1. `$Result = "Hello World";`
2. `$Result = 3e10;`
3. `$Result = 10;`
4. `$Result = NULL;`
5. `$Result = 874.0;`
6. `$Result = true;`

Hands-On Project 3-3

In this project, you create and modify a script that stores interest rates in an array.

1. Create a new document in your text editor.
2. Type the `<!DOCTYPE>` declaration, `<html>` element, header information, and `<body>` element. Use the strict DTD and "Interest Array" as the content of the `<title>` element.
3. Add the following standard PHP script delimiters to the document body:

```
<?php
?>
```

4. Add the following statements to the script section:

```
$InterestRate1 = .0725;
$InterestRate2 = .0750;
$InterestRate3 = .0775;
$InterestRate4 = .0800;
$InterestRate5 = .0825;
$InterestRate6 = .0850;
$InterestRate7 = .0875;
```

5. Modify the statements you added in the preceding step so the variables are saved in an array named `$RatesArray` by using the `array()` construct. Also, add statements to the program that print the contents of each array element.
6. Save the document as **InterestArray.php** in the Projects directory for Chapter 3, and then validate it with the WDG HTML Validator. After the document is valid, close it in your text editor, and then open it in your Web browser to see how it renders.
7. Close your Web browser window.

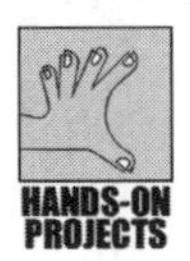

Hands-On Project 3-4

What value is assigned to `$ReturnValue` for each of the following expressions?

1. `$ReturnValue = 2 == 3;`
2. `$ReturnValue = "2" + "3";`
3. `$ReturnValue = 2 >= 3;`
4. `$ReturnValue = 2 <= 3;`
5. `$ReturnValue = 2 + 3;`
6. `$ReturnValue = (2 >= 3) && (2 > 3);`
7. `$ReturnValue = (2 >= 3) || (2 > 3);`

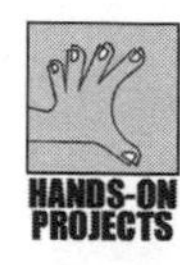

Hands-On Project 3-5

You use the `number_format()` function when you want to format the appearance of a number. The `number_format()` function adds commas that separate thousands and determines the number of decimal places to display. You can pass two arguments to the `number_format()` function: The first argument represents the literal number or variable you want to format, and the second argument determines the number of decimal places to display. If you exclude the second argument, the number is formatted without decimal places.

In this project, you create a script that demonstrates how to use the `number_format()` function.

1. Create a new document in your text editor.
2. Type the `<!DOCTYPE>` declaration, `<html>` element, header information, and `<body>` element. Use the strict DTD and "Single Family Home" as the content of the `<title>` element.
3. Add the following standard PHP script delimiters to the document body:

```
<?php
?>
```

4. Add the following statements to the script section. The first statement assigns an integer value to a variable named `$SingleFamilyHome`. The second statement then formats the value in the `$SingleFamilyHome` variable and assigns the formatted number to the `$SingleFamilyHome_Print` variable. The number in the `$SingleFamilyHome_Print` variable will include a comma that separates the thousands and will include two decimal places. The final statement prints the formatted number to the screen.

```
$SingleFamilyHome = 399500;
$SingleFamilyHome_Print = number_format($SingleFamilyHome, 2);
echo "<p>The current median price of a single family home in
Pleasanton, CA is $$SingleFamilyHome_Print.</p>";
```

4. Save the document as **SingleFamilyHome.php** in the Projects directory for Chapter 3, and then validate it with the WDG HTML Validator. After the document is valid, close it in your text editor, and then open it in your Web browser to see how it renders. You should see the text "The current median price of a single family home in Pleasanton, CA is $399,500.00." printed to the screen.
5. Close your Web browser window.

Hands-On Project 3-6

In this project, you create a script that demonstrates how to modify the order of precedence in an expression.

1. Create a new document in your text editor.
2. Type the `<!DOCTYPE>` declaration, `<html>` element, header information, and `<body>` element. Use the strict DTD and "Order of Precedence" as the content of the `<title>` element.
3. Add the following standard PHP script delimiters to the document body:

```
<?php
?>
```

4. Add the following statements to the script section:

```
$x  =  75;
$x =  $x + 30 * $x / 4;
echo '<p>The value of $x is ", $x, ".</p>";
```

5. Use parentheses to modify the order of precedence of the statements you added in the preceding step so that the final value of `$x` is `581.25`. (The value of `$x` using the current syntax is `637.5`.)
6. Save the document as **OrderOfPrecedence.php** in the Projects directory for Chapter 3, and then open it in your Web browser to see if the correct value of 581.25 is printed to the screen. After you get the order of precedence correct, validate the **OrderOfPrecedence.php** document with the WDG HTML Validator. After the document is valid, close it in your text editor.
7. Close your Web browser window.

CASE PROJECTS

Save your Case Projects document in the Cases directory for Chapter 3. Create the documents so they are well formed according to the strict DTD. Be certain to validate each document with the WDG HTML Validator.

Case Project 3-1

Write a script that declares and assigns three integer variables: one for your house number or apartment number (not your street name), one for your zip code, and another for your area code. Use `echo()` statements to print each variable, along with the `gettype()` function to make sure each variable is of the integer data type. Save the document as **IntVariables.php**.

Case Project 3-2

Write a script that assigns the days of the week to an array named `$Days[]`. Use output statements to print "The days of the week in English are: " along with the values in the `$Days[]` array. Following the output statements, reassign the values in the `$Days[]` array with the days of the week in French. Sunday is *Dimanche*, Monday is *Lundi*, Tuesday is *Mardi*, Wednesday is *Mercredi*, Thursday is *Jeudi*, Friday is *Vendredi*, and Saturday is *Samedi*. Then use output statements to print "The days of the week in French are: " along with the French values in the `$Days[]` array. Save the document as **DaysArray.php**.

Case Project 3-3

Write a script that declares and assigns floating-point variables for the interest rate you are paying on your car, credit card, mortgage, student loan, or some other type of loan. Create floating-point variables for at least three types of loans. If you do not have any type of loan with an interest rate, look in your local newspaper or on the Internet for current interest rates for mortgages and autos. Use `echo()` statements to print each variable, along with a description of the loan, and the `gettype()` function to make sure each variable is of the double data type. Save the document as **DecimalVariables.php**.

Case Project 3-4

You can use the `round()`, `ceil()`, and `floor()` functions to round a fraction up or down to the nearest whole number. The `round()` function rounds a fraction to the nearest whole number, the `ceil()` function rounds a fraction up to the nearest whole number, and the `floor()` function rounds a fraction down to the nearest whole number. Write a script that demonstrates the use of these functions. Save the document as **RoundedValues.php**.

Case Project 3-5

Write a script that uses a conditional operator to determine whether a variable contains a number and whether the number is even. You need to use the `is_numeric()` function and the conditional operator. For floating-point numbers, you need to use the `round()` function to convert the value to the nearest whole number. Save the document as **IsEven.php**.

CHAPTER

4

FUNCTIONS AND CONTROL STRUCTURES

In this chapter, you will:

- Study how to use functions to organize your PHP code
- Learn about variable scope and autoglobal variables
- Use `if` statements, `if...else` statements, and `switch` statements to make decisions
- Use nested control structures
- Use `while` statements, `do...while` statements, `for`, and `foreach` statements to repeatedly execute code

So far, the code you have written has consisted of simple statements placed within script sections. However, almost all programming languages, including PHP, allow you to group programming statements in logical units. In PHP, groups of statements that you can execute as a single unit are called **functions**. You learn how to create your own custom functions in this chapter. The code you have written so far has also been linear in nature. In other words, your programs start at the beginning and end when the last statement in the program executes. Decision-making and looping statements allow you to determine the order in which statements execute in a program. Controlling the flow of code and making decisions during program execution are two of the most fundamental skills required in programming. In this chapter, you learn about both decision-making statements and flow-control statements.

WORKING WITH FUNCTIONS

In Chapter 2, you learned that PHP includes numerous built-in functions that you can use in your scripts. Functions are useful because they make it possible to treat a related group of PHP statements as a single unit. In this section, you learn how to write custom functions. Then, you learn how to use these functions in your scripts.

Defining Functions

Before you can use a function in a PHP program, you must first create, or define, it. The lines of code that make up a function are called the **function definition**. The syntax for defining a function is as follows:

```
<?php
function name_of_function(parameters) {
     statements;
}
?>
```

NOTE

As shown in the preceding example, functions, like all PHP code, must be contained within `<?php ... ?>` tags.

Parameters are placed within the parentheses that follow the function name. A **parameter** is a variable that is used within a function. Unlike with other variables, to declare a parameter, you only need to place the parameter name within the parentheses of a function definition. In other words, you do not need to explicitly declare and initialize a parameter as you do a regular variable. For example, suppose you want to write a function named `calculateSalesTotal()` that calculates the sales total of a number contained in a parameter named `$Subtotal` for an online transaction. The function name would then be written as: `calculateSalesTotal($Subtotal)`. In this case, the function declaration is declaring a new parameter (which is a variable) named `$Subtotal`. Functions can contain multiple parameters separated by commas. To declare three separate number parameters in the `calculateSalesTotal()` function, you write the function name as `calculateSalesTotal($Subtotal, $SalesTax, $Shipping)`. Note that parameters (such as the `$Subtotal`, `$SalesTax`, and `$Shipping` parameters) receive their values when you call the function from elsewhere in your program. You can also assign default values to a parameter as follows:

```
function sampleFunction($Num1="100", $Num2="200", $Num3="300") {
     echo ("<p>$Num1</p>");
     echo ("<p>$Num2</p>");
     echo ("<p>$Num3</p>");
}
```

Functions do not have to contain parameters. Many functions only perform a task and do not require external data. For example, you might create a function that displays the same message each time a user visits your Web site; this type of function only needs to be executed and does not require any other information.

Following the parentheses that contain the function parameters is a set of curly braces (called function braces) that contain the function statements. Function statements are the statements that do the actual work of the function (such as calculating the sales total) and must be contained within the function braces. The following is an example of a function that prints the names of multiple companies:

```
function printCompanyName($Company1, $Company2, $Company3) {
     echo "<p>$Company1</p>";
     echo "<p>$Company2</p>";
     echo "<p>$Company3</p>";
}
```

Notice how the preceding function is structured. The opening curly brace is on the same line as the function name, and the closing curly brace is on its own line following the function statements. Each statement between the curly braces is indented five character spaces. This structure is the preferred format among many PHP programmers. However, for simple functions it is sometimes easier to include the function name, curly braces, and statements on the same line. (Recall that PHP ignores line breaks, spaces, and tabs.) For example, the following simplified version of the `printCompanyName()` function is declared on a single line:

```
function printCompanyName($Company1) { echo "<p>$Company1</p>"; }
```

Calling Functions

A function definition does not execute automatically. Creating a function definition only names the function, specifies its parameters, and organizes the statements it will execute. As you learned in Chapter 2, you must use a function call to execute a function from elsewhere in your program. When you pass arguments to a function, the value of each argument is then assigned to the value of the corresponding parameter in the function definition. (Again, remember that parameters are simply variables that are declared within a function definition.)

In PHP 3 and earlier, it was necessary to put a function definition above any calling statements to ensure that the function was created before it was actually called. If you did not follow this convention, you received an error. This convention is no longer necessary in PHP 4 and higher. However, other scripting languages, including JavaScript, still require you to follow this convention. Even though this convention is no longer required in PHP, you should continue to place your function definitions above any calling statements for good programming practice and to keep your programming skills portable to other languages. The following code shows a script that prints the name of a company. Figure 4-1 shows the output. Notice that the function is defined above the calling statement.

```
function printCompanyName($CompanyName) {
    echo "<p>$CompanyName</p>";
}
printCompanyName("Course Technology");
```

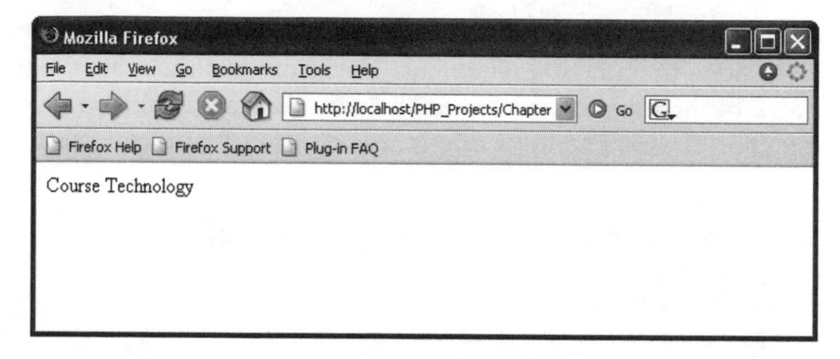

Figure 4-1 Output of a call to a custom function

The script that appears in Figure 4-1 contains a statement that calls the function and passes the literal string "Course Technology" to the function. When the `printCompanyName()` function receives the literal string, it assigns it to the `$CompanyName` variable.

Unlike variables, function names are case insensitive. This means that you can call the `printCompanyName()` function with any of the following statements:

```
printcompanyname("Course Technology");
PrintCompanyName("Course Technology");
PRINTCOMPANYNAME("Course Technology");
```

However, it is good practice to always call a function using the same case that was used to define the function name.

Returning Values

In many instances, you might want your program to receive the results from a called function and then use those results in other code. For instance, consider a function that calculates the average of a series of numbers that are passed to it as arguments. Such a function is useless if your program cannot print or use the result elsewhere. As another example, suppose you have created a function that simply prints the name of a company. Now suppose that you want to alter the program so that it uses the company name in another section of code. You can return a value from a function to a calling statement by assigning the calling statement to a variable. The following statement calls a function named `averageNumbers()` and assigns the return value to a variable named `$ReturnValue`. The statement also passes three literal values to the function.

```
$ReturnValue = averageNumbers(1, 2, 3);
```

To actually return a value to a `$ReturnValue` variable, the code must include a return statement within the `averageNumbers()` function. A **return statement** is a statement that returns a value to the statement that called the function. The following script contains the `averageNumbers()` function, which calculates the average of three numbers. The script also includes a return statement that returns the value (contained in the result variable) to the calling statement.

```
function averageNumbers($a, $b, $c) {
     $SumOfNumbers = $a + $b + $c;
     $Result = $SumOfNumbers / 3;
     return $Result;
}
```

A function does not necessarily have to return a value.

Next, you create a script that contains two functions. The first function prints a message when it is called, and the second function returns a value that is printed after the calling statement.

To create a script that contains two functions:

1. Open your text editor and create a new document.
2. Type the `<!DOCTYPE>` declaration, `<html>` element, header information, and `<body>` element. Use the strict DTD and "Two Functions" as the content of the `<title>` element.
3. Add the following script section to the document body:

```
<?php
?>
```

4. Add the first function to the script section as follows. This function writes a message to the screen using an argument that will ultimately be passed to it from the calling statement.

```
function printMessage($FirstMessage) {
     echo "<p>$FirstMessage</p>";
}
```

5. Add the second function, which displays a second message, to the end of the script section. In this case, the message ("This message was returned from a function.") is defined within the function itself. The only purpose of this function is to return the literal string "This message was returned from a function." to the calling statement.

```
function returnMessage() {
     return "<p>This message was returned from a function.</p>";
}
```

6. Add the following three statements to the end of the script section. The first statement sends the text string "This message was printed from a function." This statement does not receive a return value. The second statement assigns the function call to a variable named `$ReturnValue`, but does not send any arguments to the function. The third statement writes the value of the `$ReturnValue` variable to the screen.

```
printMessage("This message was printed from a function.");
$ReturnValue = returnMessage();
echo $ReturnValue;
```

7. Save the document as **TwoFunctions.php** in the Chapter directory for Chapter 4, and then close it in your text editor.
8. Open the **TwoFunctions.php** file in your Web browser by entering the following URL: **http://localhost/PHP_Projects/Chapter.04/Chapter/TwoFunctions.php**. You should see the Web page shown in Figure 4-2.

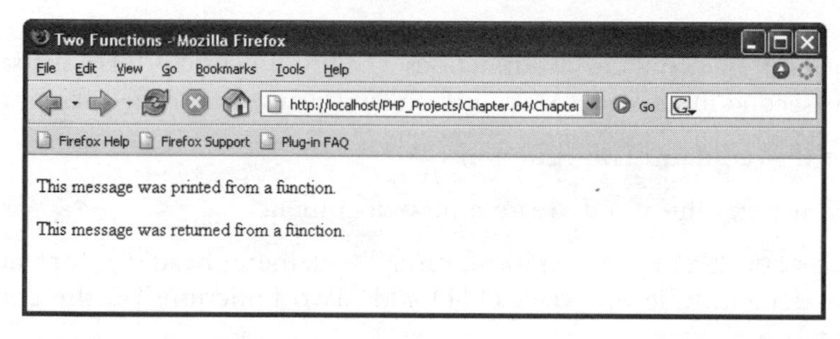

Figure 4-2 Output of TwoFunctions.php

9. Close your Web browser window.

In scripts that include functions, where and how you declare variables is very important. In the following section, you study variable scope, a topic that will help you understand how to use variables in scripts that include functions.

UNDERSTANDING VARIABLE SCOPE

When you use a variable in a PHP program, particularly a complex PHP program, you need to be aware of the **variable's scope**—that is, you need to think about where in your program a declared variable can be used. A variable's scope can be either global or local. A **global variable** is one that is declared outside a function and is available to all parts of your program. A **local variable** is declared inside a function and is only available within the function in which it is declared. Local variables cease to exist when the function ends. If you attempt to use a local variable outside the function in which it is declared, you receive an error message.

NOTE

The parameters within the parentheses of a function declaration are local variables.

The following script includes a function containing a local variable. When the function is called, the local variable prints successfully from within the function. However, when the script tries to print the local variable from outside the function definition, an error message is generated because the local variable ceases to exist when the function ends.

```
<?php
$GlobalVariable = "Global variable";
function scopeExample() {
     $LocalVariable = "<p>Local variable</p>";
     echo "<p>$LocalVariable</p>"; // prints successfully
}
scopeExample();
echo "<p>$GlobalVariable</p>";
echo "<p>$LocalVariable</p>"; // error message
?>
```

The `global` Keyword

With many programming languages, global variables are automatically available to all parts of your program, including functions. However, this is not the case in PHP. As an example, the output statement in the following script generates an error because `$GlobalVariable` is not recognized within the scope of the `scopeExample()` function:

```
<?php
$GlobalVariable = "Global variable";
function scopeExample() {
     echo "<p>$GlobalVariable</p>"; // error message
}
scopeExample();
?>
```

In PHP, you must declare a global variable with the `global` keyword inside of a function definition for the variable to be available within the scope of that function. When you declare a global variable with the `global` keyword, you do not need to assign the variable a value, as you do when you declare a standard variable. Instead, within the declaration statement you only need to include the `global` keyword along with the name of the variable. The correct syntax for this is: `global $variable_name;`. The following code shows a modified version of the preceding script. This time, the code declares the global variable within the function, which allows the output message to print successfully.

```
<?php
$GlobalVariable = "Global variable";
function scopeExample() {
    global $GlobalVariable;
    echo "<p>$GlobalVariable</p>";
}
scopeExample();
?>
```

Using Autoglobals

PHP includes various predefined global arrays, called **autoglobals** or **superglobals**, which contain client, server, and environment information that you can use in your scripts. Table 4-1 lists the PHP autoglobals.

Table 4-1 PHP autoglobals

Array	Description
$_COOKIE	An array of values passed to the current script as HTTP cookies
$_ENV	An array of environment information
$_FILES	An array of information about uploaded files
$_GET	An array of values from a form submitted with the GET method
$_POST	An array of values from a form submitted with the POST method
$_REQUEST	An array of all the elements found in the $_COOKIE, $_GET, and $_POST arrays
$_SERVER	An array of information about the Web server that served the current script
$_SESSION	An array of session variables that are available to the current script
$GLOBALS	An array of references to all variables that are defined with global scope

You work with most of the autoglobals in later chapters.

Autoglobals are **associative arrays**, which are arrays whose elements are referred to with an alphanumeric key instead of an index number. For example, with associative arrays you can create an array of a company's payroll information that uses each employee's last name instead of an index number to refer to elements in the array. To refer to an element in an associative array, you place an element's key in single or double quotation marks inside the array brackets. For example, the following statements print three elements of the `$_SERVER` autoglobal. The `$_SERVER["PHP_SELF"]` element prints the path and name of the current script, the `$_SERVER["SERVER_SOFTWARE"]` element prints the name of the server software that executed the script, and the `$_SERVER["SERVER_PROTOCOL"]` element prints the server protocol that was used to request the script. Figure 4-3 shows the output.

```
echo "<p>The name of the current script is ",
$_SERVER["PHP_SELF"], "<br />";
echo "This script was executed with the following server
software: ", $_SERVER["SERVER_SOFTWARE"], "<br />";
echo "This script was requested with the following server
protocol: ", $_SERVER["SERVER_PROTOCOL"], "</p>";
```

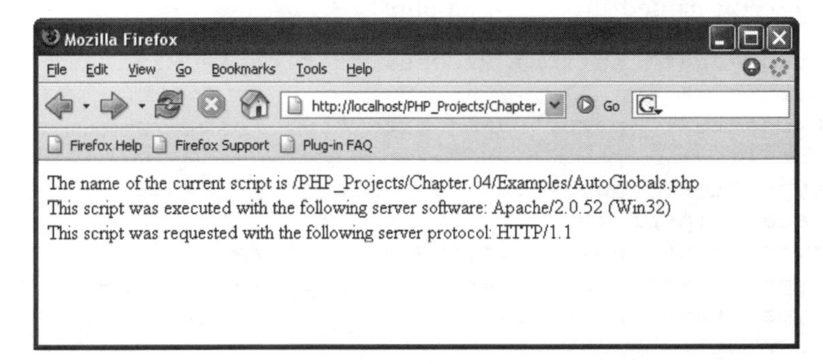

Figure 4-3 Output of a script that references the `$_SERVER` autoglobal

The elements that are available with the `$_SERVER` autoglobal depend on the Web server that executes the PHP script. For more information on the `$_SERVER` autoglobal, see the online PHP documentation at *http://www.php.net/docs.php*.

You learn how to create associative arrays in Chapter 7.

As mentioned in the previous section, you must use the `global` keyword to declare a global variable within the scope of a function. You can also use the `$GLOBALS` autoglobal to refer to the global version of a variable from inside a function. To refer to a global variable with the `$GLOBALS` autoglobal, you use the variable's name as the key in single or double quotation marks inside the array brackets. The following example shows a modified version of the script containing the `scopeExample()` function you saw earlier. In this example, the script references `$GlobalVariable` using the `$GLOBALS` autoglobal instead of the `global` keyword.

```
<?php
$GlobalVariable = "Global variable";
function scopeExample() {
     echo "<p>", $GLOBALS["GlobalVariable"], "</p>";
}
scopeExample();
?>
```

Two of the most commonly used autoglobals are `$_GET` and `$_POST`, which allow you to access the values of forms that are submitted to a PHP script. The `$_GET` autoglobal contains values of forms that are submitted with the "get" method while the `$_POST` autoglobal contains values of forms that are submitted with the "post" method. Which autoglobal you use depends on the value you assign to a **`form`** element's `method` attribute. The following code contains a typical form that uses the "get" method to submit the form to a script named ProcessOrder.php:

```
<form method="get" action="ProcessOrder.php">
<p>Name<br />
<input type="text" name="name" size="50" /><br />
Address<br />
<input type="text" name="address" size="50" /><br />
City, State, Zip<br />
<input type="text" name="city" size="38" />
<input type="text" name="state" size="2" maxlength="2" />
<input type="text" name="zip" size="5" maxlength="5" /><br />
E-Mail<br />
<input type="text" name="email" size="50" /></p>
<p><input type="reset" />
<input type="submit" /></p>
</form>
```

The default method for submitting a form is "get", which appends form data as one long string to the URL specified by the `action` attribute. The "post" option sends form data as a transmission separate from the URL specified by the `action` attribute.

When you click a form's Submit button, each field on the form is submitted to the server as a name=value pair. When the "get" method is specified, the name portion of the name=value pair becomes the key of an element in the `$_GET` autoglobal and the value portion is assigned as the value of the element. Similarly, when the "post" method is specified, the name portion of the name=value pair becomes the key of an element in the `$_POST` autoglobal and the value portion is assigned as the value of the element. Upon submitting the preceding form to the ProcessOrder.php script, you can access the form fields with the following statements:

```
$_GET["name"]
$_GET["address"]
$_GET["city"]
$_GET["state"]
$_GET["zip"]
$_GET["email"]
```

Before PHP version 4.2.0, client, server, and environment information were automatically available as global variables that you could access directly in your scripts. For example, instead of using `$_SERVER["SERVER_SOFTWARE"]` to obtain information about your server software, you could simply use `$SERVER_SOFTWARE`. Similarly, a field named "email" in a submitted form could be accessed with `$email` instead of `$_GET["email"]`. However, making all client, server, and environment information automatically available as variables in a script exposes security issues that an unscrupulous hacker can take advantage of. You can still use the old global variables by changing the value assigned to the `register_globals` directive in your php.ini configuration file to "on". However, for your code to be secure, the PHP Group strongly recommends that you leave the `register_globals` directive turned off and instead use autoglobal arrays to access client, server, and environment information in your scripts.

Next, you start creating a Great Explorers quiz that you will submit to a PHP script for processing. The quiz will be set up in a form that allows users to select answers by means of radio buttons created with the `<input>` tag. To save you from too much typing, you can open the ExplorersQuiz.html document in the Chapter directory for Chapter 4. If you do not have access to the Data Disk files, complete the following set of steps to create the ExplorersQuiz.html document. Even if you do have a Data Disk, read the following steps to understand how the ExplorersQuiz.html document is set up.

To create the Great Explorers quiz and its form section:

1. Create a new document in your text editor.
2. Type the `<!DOCTYPE>` declaration, `<html>` element, header information, and `<body>` element. Use the strict DTD and "Great Explorers Quiz" as the content of the `<title>` element. Add a `<link>` element that gives the Web page access to the php_styles.css style sheet located in your Chapter directory for Chapter 4. Add the following elements to the document body. The form will be submitted to a PHP script named ScoreQuiz.php using the "get" method.

```
<h1>Great Explorers Quiz</h1>
<p>Answer all of the questions on the quiz, then select the
     Score button to grade the quiz. </p>
<form action="ScoreQuiz.php" method="get">
</form>
```

3. Add the following lines for the first question to the `<form>` element. The four radio buttons represent the answers. Because each button within a radio button group requires the same `name` attribute, these four radio buttons have the same name of "question1". Each radio button is also assigned a value corresponding to its answer letter: *a*, *b*, *c*, or *d*. The correct answer is identified by the HTML comment.

```
<p><b>1. Which desert did David Livingston cross to reach
     Lake Ngami?</b></p>
<p><input type="radio" name="question1" value="a" />Gobi<br />
<input type="radio" name="question1" value="b" />
     Kalahari<br /> <!-- correct answer -->
<input type="radio" name="question1" value="c" />Sahara<br />
<input type="radio" name="question1" value="d" />Negev</p>
```

TIP

You can build the program quickly by copying the input button code for the first question, pasting it into a new document, and then editing it to create questions two through five. If you use copy and paste to create the input buttons in the following steps, make sure you change the question number for each input button name and the function it calls.

4. Add the lines for the second question. If you prefer, copy and paste the code you typed earlier, taking care to make the necessary edits.

```
<p><b>2. In what year did Sir Edmund Hillary and Tenzing Norgay
     become the first climbers to reach the summit of
     Mt. Everest?</b></p>
<p><input type="radio" name="question2" value="a" />1927<br />
<input type="radio" name="question2" value="b" />1936<br />
<input type="radio" name="question2" value="c" />1949<br />
<input type="radio" name="question2" value="d" />
     1953</p><!-- correct answer -->
```

5. Add the lines for the third question, using copy and paste if you prefer:

```
<p><b>3. What African-American explorer reached the North Pole
with Robert Peary in 1909?</b></p>
<p><input type="radio" name="question3" value="a" />
     Matthew Henson<br /><!-- correct answer -->
<input type="radio" name="question3" value="b" />
     Jim Beckwourth<br />
<input type="radio" name="question3" value="c" />
     Jesse Owens<br />
<input type="radio" name="question3" value="d" />
     Booker T. Washington</p>
```

6. Add the lines for the fourth question:

```
<p><b>4. What was the name of Jacques Cousteau's research
vessel?</b></p>
<p><input type="radio" name="question4" value="a" />
     Sea Witch<br />
<input type="radio" name="question4" value="b" />
     Calypso<br /><!-- correct answer -->
<input type="radio" name="question4" value="c" />
     New Frontier<br />
<input type="radio" name="question4" value="d" />Avignon</p>
```

7. Add the lines for the fifth question:

```
<p><b>5. Who was the first European to explore Florida?</b></p>
<p><input type="radio" name="question5" value="a" />
     Hernando De Soto<br />
<input type="radio" name="question5" value="b" />
     Sir Francis Drake<br />
<input type="radio" name="question5" value="c" />
     Ponce De Leon<br /><!-- correct answer -->
<input type="radio" name="question5" value="d" />James Cook</p>
```

8. Add the following Submit button to the end of the form:

```
<p><input type="submit" value="Score" /></p>
```

9. Save the document as **ExplorersQuiz.html** in the Chapter directory for Chapter 4 and close it in your text editor.

Next, you create a PHP script that displays form values submitted with the Great Explorers quiz.

To create the Great Explorers quiz and its form section:

1. Create a new document in your text editor.
2. Type the `<!DOCTYPE>` declaration, `<html>` element, header information, and `<body>` element. Use the strict DTD and "Great Explorers Quiz" as the content of the `<title>` element. Add a `<link>` element that gives the Web page access to the php_styles.css style sheet located in your Chapter directory for Chapter 4.
3. Add the following text, elements, and script section to the document body:

```
<h1>Quiz Results</h1>
<?php
?>
```

4. Add to the script section the following `echo()` statements, which print the values assigned to the selected radio button within each group of questions:

```
echo "<p>Question 1: ", $_GET["question1"], "</p>";
echo "<p>Question 2: ", $_GET["question2"], "</p>";
echo "<p>Question 3: ", $_GET["question3"], "</p>";
echo "<p>Question 4: ", $_GET["question4"], "</p>";
echo "<p>Question 5: ", $_GET["question5"], "</p>";
```

Remember to use brackets ([ ]) when referring to array elements and not parentheses as you do with functions.

5. Save the document as **ScoreQuiz.php** in the Chapter directory for Chapter 4.
6. Open the **ExplorersQuiz.html** file in your Web browser by entering the following URL: **http://localhost/PHP_Projects/Chapter.04/Chapter/ExplorersQuiz.html**. You should see the Web page shown in Figure 4-4.

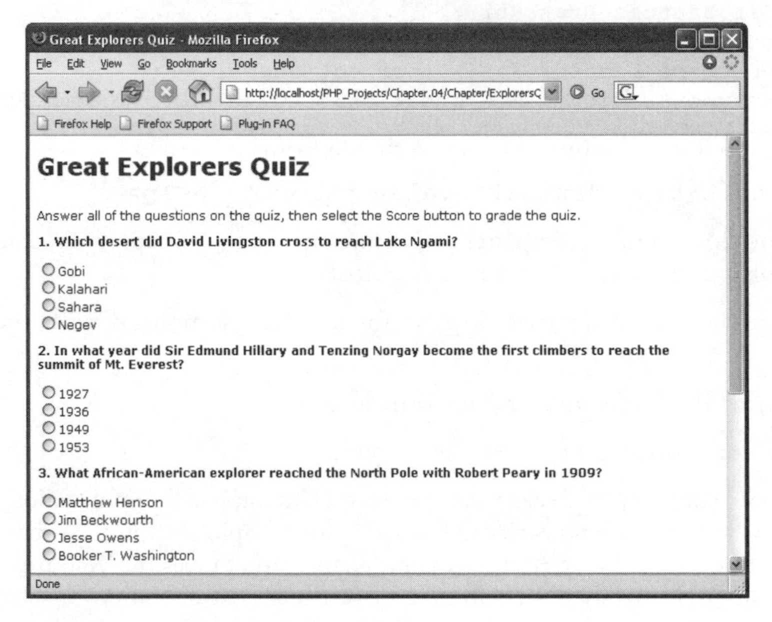

Figure 4-4 ExplorersQuiz.php

7. Select an answer for each question and click the **Score** button. The ScoreQuiz.php file should open and display the answers you selected.

Be sure to select answers for each question before clicking the Submit button or you will receive errors from the ScoreQuiz.php file. Later in this chapter, you learn how to check whether users have answered all of the questions in the quiz.

8. Close your Web browser window.

MAKING DECISIONS

When you write a computer program, regardless of the programming language, you often need to execute different sets of statements, depending on some predetermined criteria. For example, you might create a program that needs to execute one set of code in the morning and another set of code at night. Or, you might create a program that depends on user input to determine exactly what code to run. For instance, suppose you create a Web page through which users place online orders. If a user clicks an Add to Shopping Cart button, a set of statements that builds a list of items to be purchased must execute. However, if the user clicks a Checkout button, an entirely different set of statements, which completes the transaction, must execute. The process of determining the order in which statements execute in a program is called **decision making** or **flow control**. The special types of PHP statements used for making decisions are called decision-making statements or decision-making structures. The most common type of decision-making statement is the `if` statement, which you study in the following section.

`if` Statements

The **`if` statement** is used to execute specific programming code if the evaluation of a conditional expression returns a value of true. The syntax for a simple `if` statement is as follows:

```
if (conditional expression)
    statement;
```

The `if` statement contains three parts: the keyword `if`, a conditional expression enclosed within parentheses, and the executable statements. Note that the conditional expression must be enclosed within parentheses.

If the condition being evaluated returns a value of true, the statement immediately following the conditional expression executes. After the `if` statement executes, any subsequent code executes normally. Consider the following code. The `if` statement uses the equal (==) comparison operator to determine whether the variable `$ExampleVar` is equal to 5. (You learned about operators in Chapter 3.) Because the condition returns a value of true, two `echo()` statements execute. The first `echo()` statement is generated by the `if` statement when the condition returns a value of true, and the second `echo()` statement executes after the `if` statement is completed.

```
$ExampleVar = 5;
if ($ExampleVar == 5)      // CONDITION EVALUATES TO 'TRUE'
     echo "<p>The variable is equal to $ExampleVar.</p>";
echo "<p>This text is generated after the if statement.</p>";
```

The statement immediately following the `if` statement in the preceding code can be written on the same line as the `if` statement itself. However, using a line break and indentation makes the code easier for the programmer to read.

In contrast, the following code displays only the second `echo()` statement. The condition evaluates to false because `$ExampleVar` is assigned the value 4 instead of 5.

```
$ExampleVar = 4;
if ($ExampleVar == 5)      // CONDITION EVALUATES TO 'FALSE'
     echo "<p> This text will not appear.</p>";
echo "<p> This is the only text that appears.</p>";
```

You can use a command block to construct a decision-making structure using multiple `if` statements. A **command block** is a group of statements contained within a set of braces, similar to the way function statements are contained within a set of braces. Each command block must have an opening brace ({) and a closing brace (}). If a command block is missing either the opening or closing brace, an error occurs. The following code shows a script that runs a command block if the conditional expression within the `if` statement evaluates to true:

```
$ExampleVar = 5;
if ($ExampleVar == 5) {     // CONDITION EVALUATES TO 'TRUE'
     echo "<p>The condition evaluates to true.</p>";
     echo '<p>$ExampleVar is equal to ', "$ExampleVar.</p>";
     echo "<p>Each of these lines will be printed.</p>";
}
echo "<p>This statement always executes after the if
statement.</p>";
```

When an `if` statement contains a command block, the statements in the command block execute when the `if` statement condition evaluates to true. After the command block executes, the code that follows executes normally. When the condition evaluates to false, the command block is skipped, and the statements that follow execute. If the conditional expression within the `if` statement in the preceding code evaluates to false, only the `echo()` statement following the command block executes.

Next, you add the functions to score each of the questions in the Great Explorers quiz. The functions contain `if` statements that evaluate each answer.

To add PHP code to score each of the questions:

1. Return to the **ScoreQuiz.php** document in your text editor.
2. Replace the `echo()` statements in the script section with the following function that scores the first question. The first statement in the function prints the question number and the selected answer. The `if` statement then prints a response of "Correct!" if the user provides the correct answer and "Incorrect" if the user provides an incorrect answer.

```
function scoreQuestion1() {
     echo "<p>Question 1: ", $_GET["question1"];
     if ($_GET["question1"] == "a")
          echo " (Incorrect)</p>";
     if ($_GET["question1"] == "b")
          echo " (Correct!)</p>";
     if ($_GET["question1"] == "c")
          echo " (Incorrect)</p>";
     if ($_GET["question1"] == "d")
          echo " (Incorrect)</p>";
}
```

3. Add the `scoreQuestion2()` function after the `scoreQuestion1()` function:

```
function scoreQuestion2() {
     echo "<p>Question 2: ", $_GET["question2"];
     if ($_GET["question2"] == "a")
          echo " (Incorrect)</p>";
     if ($_GET["question2"] == "b")
          echo " (Incorrect)</p>";
     if ($_GET["question2"] == "c")
          echo " (Incorrect)</p>";
     if ($_GET["question2"] == "d")
         echo " (Correct!)</p>";
}
```

4. Add the `scoreQuestion3()` function after the `scoreQuestion2()` function:

```
function scoreQuestion3() {
     echo "<p>Question 3: ", $_GET["question3"];
     if ($_GET["question3"] == "a")
         echo " (Correct!)</p>";
     if ($_GET["question3"] == "b")
          echo " (Incorrect)</p>";
     if ($_GET["question3"] == "c")
          echo " (Incorrect)</p>";
     if ($_GET["question3"] == "d")
          echo " (Incorrect)</p>";
}
```

5. Add the `scoreQuestion4()` function after the `scoreQuestion3()` function:

```
function scoreQuestion4() {
     echo "<p>Question 4: ", $_GET["question4"];
     if ($_GET["question4"] == "a")
          echo " (Incorrect)</p>";
     if ($_GET["question4"] == "b")
         echo " (Correct!)</p>";
     if ($_GET["question4"] == "c")
          echo " (Incorrect)</p>";
     if ($_GET["question4"] == "d")
          echo " (Incorrect)</p>";
}
```

6. Add the `scoreQuestion5()` function after the `scoreQuestion4()` function:

```
function scoreQuestion5() {
     echo "<p>Question 5: ", $_GET["question5"];
     if ($_GET["question5"] == "a")
          echo " (Incorrect)</p>";
     if ($_GET["question5"] == "b")
```

```
            echo " (Incorrect)</p>";
        if ($_GET["question5"] == "c")
            echo " (Correct!)</p>";
        if ($_GET["question5"] == "d")
            echo " (Incorrect)</p>";
}
```

7. Finally, add the following statements at the end of the script section to call each function:

```
scoreQuestion1();
scoreQuestion2();
scoreQuestion3();
scoreQuestion4();
scoreQuestion5();
```

8. Save the **ScoreQuiz.php** document.
9. Open the **ExplorersQuiz.html** file in your Web browser by entering the following URL: **http://localhost/PHP_Projects/Chapter.04/Chapter/ExplorersQuiz.html**. Select an answer for each question and click the **Score** button. Again, be sure to answer each question before clicking the Score button or you will receive errors. The ScoreQuiz.php file should open and score your quiz, as shown in Figure 4-5.

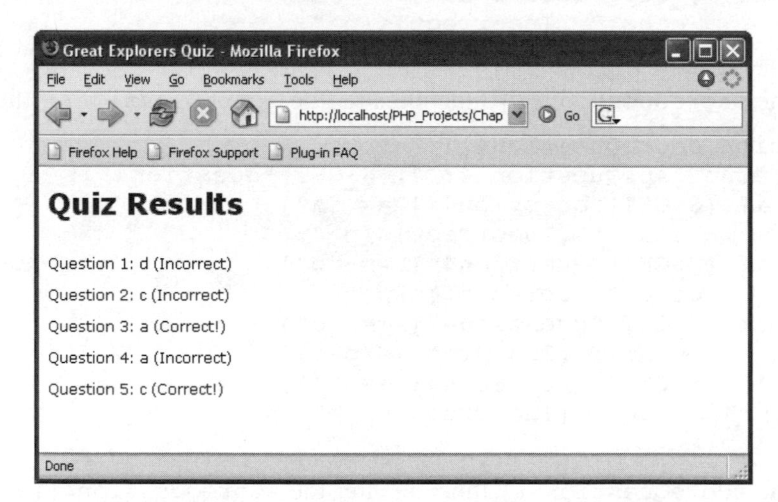

Figure 4-5 Output of a ScoreQuiz.php after adding `if` statements

10. Close your Web browser window.

`if...else` Statements

So far, you've learned how to use an `if` statement to execute a statement (or statements) if a condition evaluates to true. In some situations, however, you might want to execute one set of statements when the condition evaluates to false, and another set of statements when the condition evaluates to true. In that case, you need to add an `else` clause to your `if` statement. For instance, suppose you create a form that includes a check box that users click to indicate whether they want to invest in the stock market. When the user submits the form to a PHP script, an `if` statement in the script might contain a conditional expression that evaluates the user's input. If the condition evaluates to true (the user clicked the check box), the `if` statement displays a Web page on recommended stocks. If the condition evaluates to false (the user did not click the check box), the statements in an `else` clause display a Web page on other types of investment opportunities.

4

An `if` statement that includes an `else` clause is called an **`if...else` statement**. You can think of an `else` clause as being a backup plan that is implemented when the condition returns a value of false. The syntax for an `if...else` statement is as follows:

```
if (conditional expression)
     statement;
else
     statement;
```

You can use command blocks to construct an `if...else` statement as follows:

```
if (conditional expression) {
     statements;
}
else {
     statements;
}
```

An `if` statement can be constructed without the `else` clause. However, the `else` clause can only be used with an `if` statement.

The following code shows an example of an `if...else` statement:

```
$Today = "Tuesday";
if ($Today == "Monday")
     echo "<p>Today is Monday</p>";
else
     echo "<p>Today is not Monday</p>";
```

In the preceding code, the `$Today` variable is assigned a value of "Tuesday." If the condition `($Today == "Monday")` evaluates to false, control of the program passes to the `else` clause, the statement `echo "<p>Today is not Monday</p>";` executes, and the string "Today is not Monday" prints. If the `$Today` variable had been assigned a value of "Monday," the condition `($Today == "Monday")` would have evaluated to true, and the statement `echo "<p>Today is Monday</p>";` would have executed. Only one set of statements executes: either the statements following the `if` statement or the statements following the `else` clause. When either set of statements executes, any code following the `if...else` statements executes normally.

The PHP code for the ScoreQuiz.php document you created earlier uses multiple `if` statements to evaluate the results of the quiz. Although the multiple `if` statements function properly, they can be simplified using an `if...else` statement. Next, you simplify the ScoreQuiz.php script by replacing multiple `if` statements with one `if...else` statement.

To add `if...else` statements to ScoreQuiz.php:

1. Return to the **ScoreQuiz.php** document in your text editor.
2. Because you only need the `if` statement to test for the correct answer, you can group all the incorrect answers in the `else` clause. Modify each of the functions that scores a question so that the multiple `if` statements are replaced with an `if...else` statement. The following code shows how the statements for the `scoreQuestion1()` function should look:

```
echo "<p>Question 1: ", $_GET["question1"];
if ($_GET["question1"] == "b")
     echo " (Correct!)</p>";
else
     echo " (Incorrect)</p>";
```

TIP

Keep in mind that the correct answer for Question 2 is *d*, the correct answer for Question 3 is *a*, the correct answer for Question 4 is *b*, and the correct answer for Question 5 is *c*. You need to modify the preceding code accordingly for each question. Copy and paste code and then edit it to save on typing time.

3. Save the **ScoreQuiz.php** document.
4. Open the **ExplorersQuiz.html** file in your Web browser by entering the following URL: **http://localhost/PHP_Projects/Chapter.04/Chapter/ExplorersQuiz.html**. Select an answer for each question and click the **Score** button. The ScoreQuiz.php file should open and score your quiz, the same as when it contained only `if` statements.
5. Close your Web browser window.

Nested `if` and `if...else` Statements

As you have seen, you can use a control structure such as an `if` or `if...else` statement to allow a program to make decisions about what statements to execute. In some cases, however, you might want the statements executed by the control structure to make other decisions. For instance, you might have a program that uses an `if` statement to ask users if they like sports. If users answer yes, you might want to run another `if` statement that asks users whether they like team sports or individual sports. You can include any code you want within the code block for an `if` statement or an `if...else` statement, and that includes other `if` or `if...else` statements.

When one decision-making statement is contained within another decision-making statement, they are referred to as **nested decision-making structures**. An `if` statement contained within an `if` statement or within an `if...else` statement is called a nested `if` statement. Similarly, an `if...else` statement contained within an `if` or `if...else` statement is called a nested `if...else` statement. You use nested `if` and `if...else` statements to perform conditional evaluations that must be executed after the original conditional evaluation. For example, the following code evaluates two conditional expressions before the `echo()` statement executes:


```
if ($_GET["SalesTotal"] > 50)
    if ($_GET["SalesTotal"] < 100)
        echo "<p>The sales total is between 50 and 100.</p>";
```

The `echo()` statement in the preceding example only executes if the conditional expressions in both `if` statements evaluate to true.

The PHP code in the ScoreQuiz.php document is somewhat inefficient because it contains multiple functions that perform essentially the same task of scoring the quiz. A more efficient method of scoring the quiz is to include the scoring statements within a single function. Another problem with the ExplorersQuiz.html document is that if a user does not select answers to all of the questions, the ScoreQuiz.php script generates errors when it attempts to access elements in the `$_GET` autoglobal array that might not be there. To check whether users have answered all the questions, you create an `if...else` statement that uses the `count()` function to count the number of elements in `$_GET` autoglobal array; there should be five, one for each question. If the count is equal to five, the `if` portion of the statement executes the code that scores the questions. However, if the count is not equal to five, the `else` portion of the statement prints a message instructing the user to answer all of the questions.

To modify the Great Explorers program so it contains a single function and nested `if...else` statements:

1. Return to the **ScoreQuiz.php** document in your text editor.
2. Delete the five functions within the script section, but be sure to leave the PHP script section.
3. Add to the script section the following function that will check all the answers:

   ```
   function scoreQuestions() {
   }
   ```

4. Add the following `if...else` statement to the `scoreQuestions()` function. In the next few steps, you add code to the `if` statement that scores the questions; this code only executes if the `$_GET` autoglobal array contains a value of 5. If the `$_GET` autoglobal array does not contain a value of 5, the `else` statement executes and prints a message instructing the user to answer all of the questions.

   ```
   if (count($_GET) == 5) {
   }
   else
        echo "You did not answer all the questions! Click your
        browser's Back button to return to the quiz.";
   ```

5. Add to the first `if` statement the following `echo()` statement and nested `if...else` statement, which scores Question 1:

```
echo "<p>Question 1: ", $_GET["question1"];
if ($_GET["question1"] == "b")
     echo " (Correct!)</p>";
else
     echo " (Incorrect)</p>";
```

6. Add to the end of the first `if` statement the following `echo()` statement and nested `if...else` statement, which scores Question 2:

```
echo "<p>Question 2: ", $_GET["question2"];
if ($_GET["question2"] == "d")
     echo " (Correct!)</p>";
else
     echo " (Incorrect)</p>";
```

7. Add to the end of the `if` statement the following `echo()` statement and nested `if...else` statement, which scores Question 3:

```
echo "<p>Question 3: ", $_GET["question3"];
if ($_GET["question3"] == "a")
     echo " (Correct!)</p>";
else
     echo " (Incorrect)</p>";
```

8. Add to the end of the `if` statement the following `echo()` statement and nested `if...else` statement, which scores Question 4:

```
echo "<p>Question 4: ", $_GET["question4"];
if ($_GET["question4"] == "b")
     echo " (Correct!)</p>";
else
     echo " (Incorrect)</p>";
```

9. Add to the end of the `if` statement the following `echo()` statement and nested `if...else` statement, which scores Question 5:

```
echo "<p>Question 5: ", $_GET["question5"];
if ($_GET["question5"] == "c")
     echo " (Correct!)</p>";
else
     echo " (Incorrect)</p>";
```

10. Replace the five function calls at the end of the script section with a single call to the `scoreQuestions()` function:

```
scoreQuestions();
```

11. Save the **ScoreQuiz.php** document.
12. Open the **ExplorersQuiz.html** file in your Web browser by entering the following URL: **http://localhost/PHP_Projects/Chapter.04/Chapter/ExplorersQuiz.html**. Select an answer for some of the questions, but leave

at least one of the questions unanswered. When you click the **Score** button, you should see the Web page shown in Figure 4-6 (assuming you did not answer all of the questions).

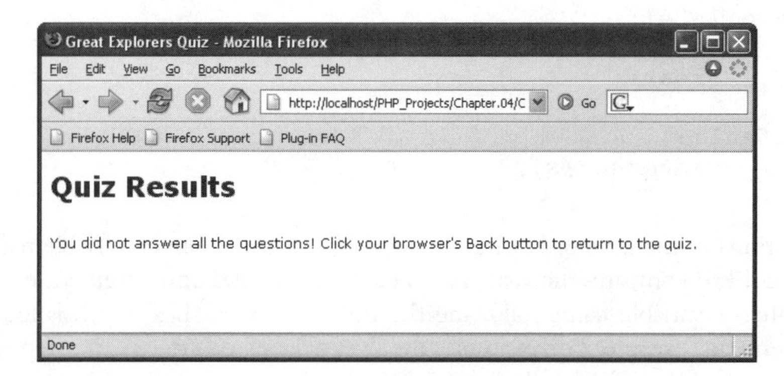

Figure 4-6 Output of ScoreQuiz.php after adding nested `if...else` statements

13. Close your Web browser window.

`switch` Statements

Another PHP statement that is used for controlling program flow is the `switch` statement. The **`switch` statement** controls program flow by executing a specific set of statements, depending on the value of an expression. The `switch` statement compares the value of an expression to a value contained within a special statement called a `case` label. A **`case` label** in a `switch` statement represents a specific value and contains one or more statements that execute if the value of the `case` label matches the value of the `switch` statement's expression. For example, your script for an insurance company might include a variable named `$CustomerAge`. A `switch` statement can evaluate the variable and compare it to a `case` label within the `switch` construct. The `switch` statement might contain several `case` labels for different age groups that calculate insurance rates based on a customer's age. If the `$CustomerAge` variable is equal to 25, the statements that are part of the `"25" case` label execute and calculate insurance rates for customers who are 25 or older. Although you could accomplish the same task using `if` or `if...else` statements, a `switch` statement makes it easier to organize the different branches of code that can be executed.

A `switch` statement consists of the following components: the keyword `switch`, an expression, an opening brace, a `case` label, the executable statements, the keyword `break`, a default label, and a closing brace. The syntax for the `switch` statement is as follows:

```
switch (expression) {
     case label:
          statement(s);
          break;
     case label:
          statement(s);
          break;
     ...
     default:
          statement(s);
}
```

A **case** label consists of the keyword **case**, followed by a literal value or variable name, followed by a colon. PHP compares the value returned from the **switch** statement expression to the literal value or variable name following the **case** keyword. If a match is found, the **case** label statements execute. For example, the **case** label **case 3.17:** represents a floating-point integer value of 3.17. If the value of a **switch** statement expression equals 3.17, the **case 3.17:** label statements execute. You can use a variety of data types as **case** labels within the same **switch** statement. The following code shows examples of four **case** labels:

```
case $ExampleVar:          // variable name
     statement(s);
case "text string":        // string literal
     statement(s);
case 75:                   // integer literal
     statement(s);
case -273.4:               // floating-point literal
     statement(s);
```

A `case` label can be followed by a single statement or multiple statements. However, unlike with `if` statements, multiple statements for a `case` label do not need to be enclosed within a command block.

Other programming languages, such as Java and C++, require all `case` labels within a `switch` statement to be of the same data type.

Another type of label used within **switch** statements is the **default** label. The **default label** contains statements that execute when the value returned by the **switch** statement expression does not match a **case** label. A **default** label consists of the keyword **default** followed by a colon.

When a **switch** statement executes, the value returned by the expression is compared to each **case** label in the order in which it is encountered. After a matching label is found, its statements execute. Unlike the **if...else** statement, execution of a **switch** statement does not automatically stop after particular **case** label statements execute. Instead, the

switch statement continues evaluating the rest of the **case** labels in the list. After a matching **case** label is found, evaluation of additional **case** labels is unnecessary. If you are working with a large **switch** statement with many **case** labels, evaluation of additional **case** labels can potentially slow down your program.

To avoid slow performance, you need to give some thought to how and when to end a **switch** statement. A **switch** statement ends automatically after the PHP interpreter encounters its closing brace (}). You can, however, use a special kind of statement, called a **break** statement, to end a **switch** statement after it has performed its required task. A **break statement** is used to exit control structures.

A **break** statement is also used to exit other types of control statements, such as the while, do...while, and for looping statements. You learn about these statements later in this chapter.

The following code shows a **switch** statement contained within a function. When the function is called, it is passed an argument named **$AmericanCity**. The **switch** statement compares the contents of the **$AmericanCity** argument to the **case** labels. If a match is found, the city's state is returned and a **break** statement ends the **switch** statement. If a match is not found, the value "United States" is returned from the default label.

```
function city_location($AmericanCity) {
     switch ($AmericanCity) {
          case "Boston":
               return "Massachusetts";
               break;
          case "Chicago":
               return "Illinois";
               break;
          case "Los Angeles":
               return "California";
               break;
          case "Miami":
               return "Florida";
               break;
          case "New York":
               return "New York";
               break;
          default:
               return "United States";
     }
}
echo "<p>", city_location("Boston"), "</p>";
```

Next, you add a new function to the Great Explorers quiz that contains a `switch` statement that checks each answer.

To add a new function to the Great Explorers quiz that contains a switch statement to check each answer:

1. Return to the **ScoreQuiz.php** document in your text editor.
2. Add the following new function named `checkAnswer()` above the `scoreQuestions()` function. The parameter you pass to the `checkAnswer()` function will contain the name of the current question (question1, question2, and so on).

```
function checkAnswer($CurQuestion) {
}
```

3. Add the following `switch` statement to the `checkAnswer()` function:

```
switch ($CurQuestion) {
  case "question1":
  case "question2":
  case "question3":
  case "question4":
  case "question5":
  default:
    echo "You did not pass a valid question number!";
}
```

4. Move the statements that check the answer to each question from the `scoreQuestions()` function to the appropriate `case` label in the `checkAnswer()` function. Also, add a `break` statement to the end of each `case` label. The `case` label for "question1" should appear as follows:

```
case "question1":
  echo "<p>Question 1: ", $_GET["question1"];
  if ($_GET["question1"] == "b")
    echo " (Correct!)</p>";
  else
    echo " (Incorrect)</p>";
  break;
```

5. Add the following call statements to the `if` statement in the `scoreQuestions()` function. Each statement calls the `checkAnswer()` function and passes to it the name of each question.

```
checkAnswer("question1");
checkAnswer("question2");
checkAnswer("question3");
checkAnswer("question4");
checkAnswer("question5");
```

6. Save the **ScoreQuiz.php** document.

7. Open the **ExplorersQuiz.html** file in your Web browser by entering the following URL: **http://localhost/PHP_Projects/Chapter.04/Chapter/ExplorersQuiz.html**. Test the program by answering all five questions and clicking the **Score** button. The program should function just as it did with the single function.
8. Close your Web browser window.

REPEATING CODE

The statements you have worked with so far execute one after the other in a linear fashion. The `if`, `if...else`, and `switch` statements select only a single branch of code to execute, then continue to the statement that follows. But what if you want to repeat the same statement, function, or code section 5 times, 10 times, or 100 times? For example, you might want to perform the same calculation until a specific number is found. In this case, you need to use a **loop statement**, a control structure that repeatedly executes a statement or a series of statements while a specific condition is true or until a specific condition becomes true. In this chapter, you learn about four types of loop statements: `while` statements, `do...while` statements, `for` statements, and `foreach` statements.

`while` Statements

One of the simplest types of loop statements is the **`while` statement**, which repeats a statement or series of statements as long as a given conditional expression evaluates to true. The syntax for the `while` statement is as follows:

```
while (conditional expression) {
     statement(s);
}
```

The conditional expression in the `while` statement is enclosed within parentheses following the keyword `while`. As long as the conditional expression evaluates to true, the statement or command block that follows executes repeatedly. Each repetition of a looping statement is called an **iteration**. When the conditional expression evaluates to false, the loop ends and the next statement following the `while` statement executes.

A `while` statement keeps repeating until its conditional expression evaluates to false. To ensure that the `while` statement ends after the desired tasks have been performed, you must include code that tracks the progress of the loop and changes the value produced by the conditional expression. You track the progress of a `while` statement, or any other loop, with a counter. A **counter** is a variable that increments or decrements with each iteration of a loop statement.

Many programmers often name counter variables `$Count`, `$Counter`, or something similar. The letters *i*, *j*, *k*, *l*, *x*, *y*, *z* are also commonly used as counter names. Using a name such as count, or the letter *i* (for increment) helps you remember (and lets other programmers know) that the variable is being used as a counter.

The following code shows a simple script that includes a `while` statement. The script declares a variable named `$Count` and assigns it an initial value of 1. The `$Count` variable is then used in the `while` statement conditional expression (`$Count <= 5`). As long as the `$Count` variable is less than or equal to 5, the `while` statement loops. Within the body of the `while` statement, the `echo()` statement prints the value of the `$Count` variable, then the `$Count` variable increments by a value of 1. The `while` statement loops until the `$Count` variable increments to a value of 6.

```
$Count = 1;
while ($Count <= 5) {
     echo "$Count<br />";
     ++$Count;
}
echo "<p>You have printed 5 numbers.</p>";
```

The preceding code prints the numbers 1 to 5, with each number representing one iteration of the loop. When the counter reaches 6, the message "You have printed 5 numbers" prints, thus demonstrating that the loop has ended. Figure 4-7 shows the output of this simple script.

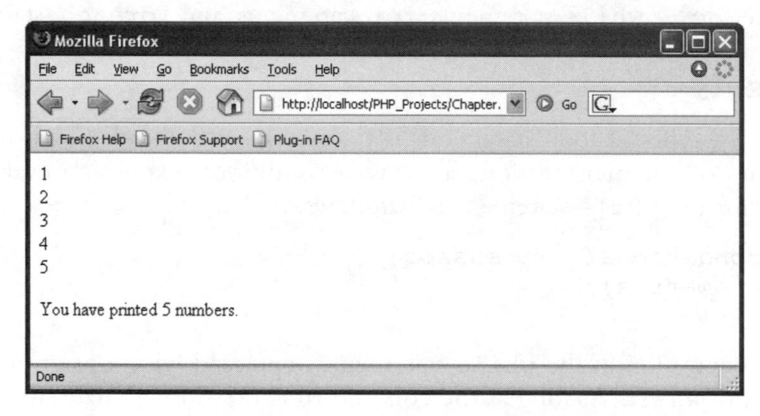

Figure 4-7 Output of a `while` statement using an increment operator

You can also control the repetitions in a `while` loop by decrementing (decreasing the value of) counter variables. Consider the following script:

```
$Count = 10;
while ($Count > 0) {
     echo "$Count<br />";
     --$Count;
}
echo "<p>We have liftoff.</p>";
```

In this example, the initial value of the `$Count` variable is 10, and the decrement operator (--) is used to decrease `count` by one. When the `$Count` variable is greater than zero, the statement within the `while` loop prints the value of the `$Count` variable. When the value of `$Count` is equal to zero, the `while` loop ends, and the statement immediately following it prints. Figure 4-8 shows the script output.

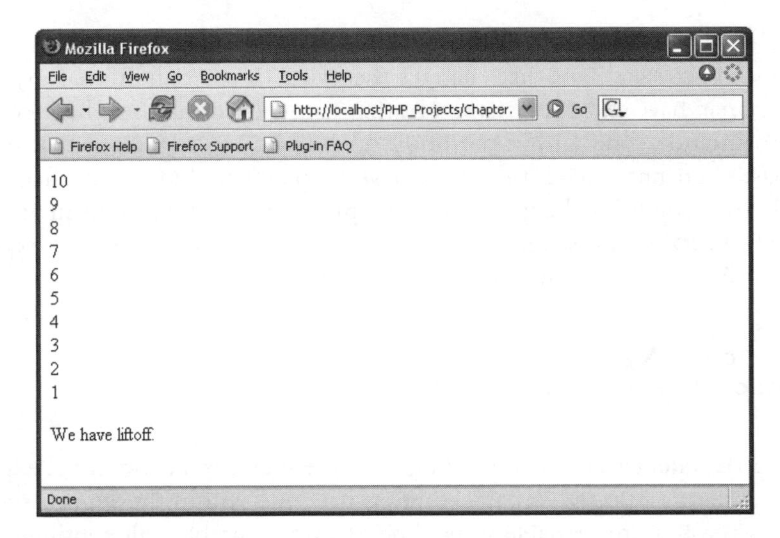

Figure 4-8 Output of a `while` statement using a decrement operator

There are many ways to change the value of a counter variable and to use a counter variable to control the repetitions of a `while` loop. The following example uses the `*=` assignment operator to multiply the value of the `$Count` variable by two. When the `$Count` variable reaches a value of 128, the `while` statement ends. Figure 4-9 shows the script output.

```
$Count = 1;
while ($Count <= 100) {
     echo "$Count<br />";
     $Count *= 2;
}
```

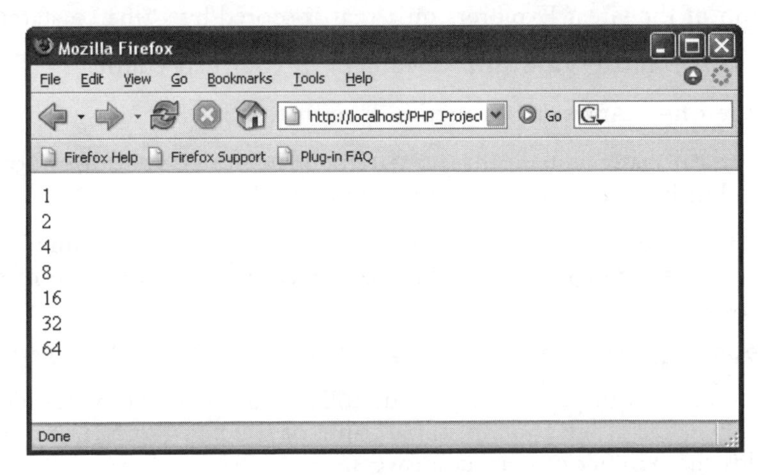

Figure 4-9 Output of a `while` statement using the assignment operator `*=`

To ensure that the **while** statement will eventually end, you must include code within the body of the **while** statement that changes the value of the conditional expression. For example, you may have a **while** statement that prints even numbers between 0 and 100. You need to include code within the body of the **while** statement that ends the loop after the last even number (100) prints. If you do not include code that changes the value used by the conditional expression, your program will be caught in an infinite loop. In an **infinite loop**, a loop statement never ends because its conditional expression is never false. Consider the following **while** statement:

```
$Count = 1;
while ($Count <= 10) {
     echo "The number is $Count";
}
```

Although the **while** statement in the preceding example includes a conditional expression that checks the value of a **$Count** variable, there is no code within the **while** statement body that changes the **$Count** variable value. The **$Count** variable will continue to have a value of 1 through each iteration of the loop. This means that the text string "The number is 1" will print over and over again, until the user closes the Web browser window.

You can use the `continue` statement to halt a looping statement and restart the loop with a new iteration.

Next, you create a new version of the Great Explorers quiz that will be scored by a single **while** statement containing a nested **if** statement. Although this **while** statement is somewhat more complicated than the statements you created previously, it requires many fewer lines of code, which helps make the script run faster and more efficiently.

To create a version of the Great Explorers quiz that is scored by a **while** statement:

1. Return to the **ScoreQuiz.php** document in your text editor.
2. Delete the `checkAnswer()` function from the script.
3. Delete the call statements in the `if` statement in the `scoreQuestions()` function, but be sure to leave the `if` statement's braces.
4. Add the following line to the `if` statement to create an array named `$CorrectAnswers[]`, which holds the correct response for each of the questions:

   ```
   $CorrectAnswers = array("b", "d", "a", "b", "c");
   ```

5. Add to the end of the `if` statement the following statement, which declares a new variable, and assign to it an initial value of 0. The `$TotalCorrect` variable holds the number of correct answers.

   ```
   $TotalCorrect = 0;
   ```

6. Add the following variable declaration and `while` statement at the end of the `if` statement. In this code, a counter named `$Count` is declared and initialized to a value of 0. The conditional expression within the `while` statement checks to see if `count` is less than or equal to 5, which is the number of questions in the quiz. With each iteration of the loop, the statement in the `while` loop increments the `count` variable by one.

```
$Count = 1;
while ($Count <= 5) {
    ++$Count;
}
```


7. Add the following `if...else` statement to the beginning of the `while` loop, above the statement that increments the `$Count` variable. This `if` statement compares each element within the form values in the `$_GET` autoglobal array to each corresponding element within the `$CorrectAnswers[]` array. If the elements match, the `$TotalCorrect` variable increments by one. Notice how the statements reference the `$Count` variable. In the first `echo()` statement and in the conditional expression, the `$_GET` autoglobal uses the `$Count` variable inside the quotations to build the key that represents the current question. The conditional expression also uses the `$Count` variable to reference the correct element index by subtracting a value of 1 from the variable to account for indexed elements beginning with an index of 0.

```
echo "<p>Question $Count: ", $_GET["question$Count"];
if ($_GET["question$Count"] == $CorrectAnswers[$Count-1]) {
     echo " (Correct!)</p>";
     ++$TotalCorrect;
}
else
     echo " (Incorrect)</p>";
```

8. Add the following statement after the `while` loop's closing brace to print the number of questions that were answered correctly:

```
echo "<p><strong>You scored $TotalCorrect out of 5 answers
correctly!</strong></p>";
```

9. Save the **ScoreQuiz.php** document.

10. Open the **ExplorersQuiz.html** file in your Web browser by entering the following URL: **http://localhost/PHP_Projects/Chapter.04/Chapter/ExplorersQuiz.html**. Test the program by answering all five questions and clicking the **Score** button. Figure 4-10 shows how the program appears in a Web browser.

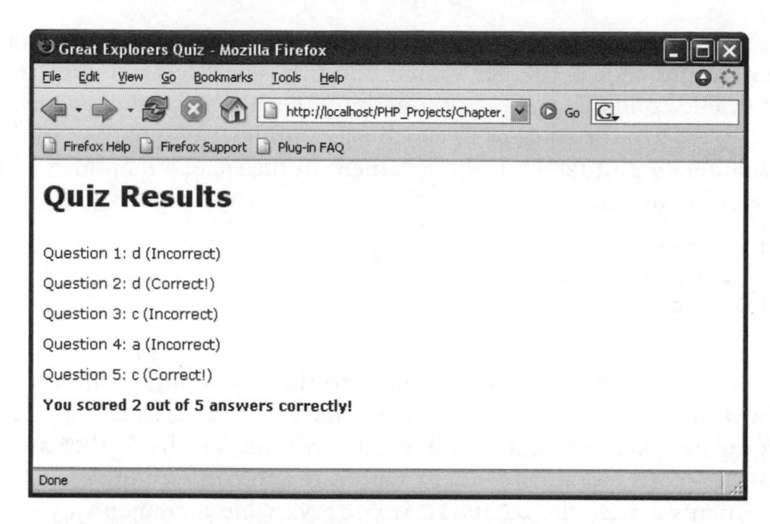

Figure 4-10 Output of ScoreQuiz.php after adding a `while` statement

11. Close your Web browser window.

`do...while` Statements

Another PHP looping statement, similar to the `while` statement, is the `do...while` statement. The **`do...while` statement** executes a statement or statements once, then repeats the execution as long as a given conditional expression evaluates to true. The syntax for the `do...while` statement is as follows:

```
do {
     statement(s);
} while (conditional expression);
```

As you can see in the syntax description, the statements execute before a conditional expression is evaluated. Unlike the simpler `while` statement, the statements in a `do...while` statement always execute once, before a conditional expression is evaluated.

The following `do...while` statement executes once before the conditional expression evaluates the `count` variable. Therefore, a single line that reads "The count is equal to 2" prints. After the conditional expression (`$Count < 2`) executes, the `$Count` variable is equal to 2. This causes the conditional expression to return a value of false, and the `do...while` statement ends.

```
$Count = 2;
do {
     echo "<p>The count is equal to $Count</p>";
     ++$Count;
} while ($Count < 2);
```

Note that this `do...while` example includes a counter within the body of the `do...while` statement. As with the `while` statement, you need to include code that changes the conditional expression to prevent an infinite loop.

In the following example, the `while` statement never executes because the `count` variable does not fall within the range of the conditional expression:

```
$Count = 2;
while ($Count > 2) {
     echo "<p>The count is equal to $Count</p>";
     ++$Count;
}
```

The following script shows an example of a `do...while` statement that prints the days of the week, using an array:

```
$DaysOfWeek = array("Monday", "Tuesday", "Wednesday", "Thursday",
"Friday", "Saturday", "Sunday");
$Count = 0;
do {
     echo $DaysOfWeek[$Count], "<br />";
     ++$Count;
} while ($Count < 7);
```

In the preceding example, an array is created containing the days of the week. A variable named `$Count` is declared and initialized to zero. (Remember, the first subscript or index in an array is zero.) Therefore, in the example, the statement `$DaysOfWeek[0];` refers to Monday. The first iteration of the `do...while` statement prints "Monday" and then increments the `count` variable by one. The conditional expression in the `while` statement then checks to determine when the last element of the array has been printed. As long as the count is less than seven (which is one number higher than the largest element in the `$DaysOfWeek[] array`), the loop continues. Figure 4-11 shows the output of the script in a Web browser.

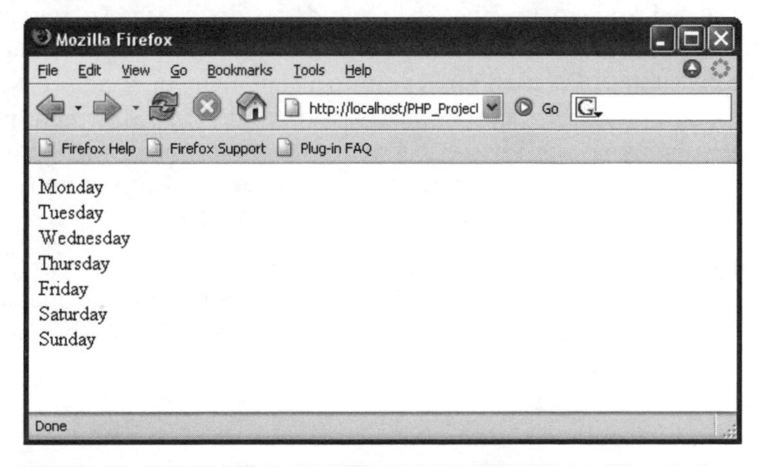

Figure 4-11 Output of days of week script in Web browser

Next, you replace the `while` statement in the Great Explorers quiz with a `do...while` statement. Because the `do...while` statement is very similar to the `while` statement, there is little benefit in replacing the `while` statement in the Great Explorers quiz. You add a `do...while` statement to the script for practice.

To replace the `while` statement in the Great Explorers quiz with a `do...while` statement:

1. Return to the **ScoreQuiz.php** document in your text editor.
2. Change the `while` statement within the `scoreQuestions()` function to a `do...while` statement, as follows:

```
do {
    echo "<p>Question $Count: ", $_GET["question$Count"];
    if ($_GET["question$Count"] == $CorrectAnswers[$Count-1]) {
        echo " (Correct!)</p>";
        ++$TotalCorrect;
    }
    else
        echo " (Incorrect)</p>";
    ++$Count;
} while ($Count <= 5);
```

3. Save the **ScoreQuiz.php** document.
4. Open the **ExplorersQuiz.html** file in your Web browser by entering the following URL: **http://localhost/PHP_Projects/Chapter.04/Chapter/ExplorersQuiz.html**. Test the program by answering all five questions and clicking the **Score** button. The program should function just as it did with the `while` statement.
5. Close your Web browser window.

for Statements

So far, you have learned how to use the `while` and the `do...while` statements to repeat, or loop through, code. You can also use the `for` statement to loop through code. Specifically, the **`for` statement** is used for repeating a statement or series of statements as long as a given conditional expression evaluates to true. The `for` statement performs essentially the same function as the `while` statement: If a conditional expression within the `for` statement evaluates to true, the `for` statement executes and continues to execute repeatedly until the conditional expression evaluates to false.

One of the primary differences between the `while` statement and the `for` statement is that in addition to a conditional expression, the `for` statement can also include code that initializes a counter and changes its value with each iteration. This is useful because it provides a specific place for you to declare and initialize a counter, and to update its value, which helps prevent infinite loops. The syntax of the `for` statement is as follows:

```
for (counter declaration and initialization; condition;
    update statement) {
     statement(s);
   }
```


When the PHP interpreter encounters a `for` loop, the following steps occur:

1. The counter variable is declared and initialized. For example, if the initialization expression in a `for` loop is `$Count = 1;`, a variable named `$Count` is declared and assigned an initial value of 1. The initialization expression is only started once, when the `for` loop is first encountered.
2. The `for` loop condition is evaluated.
3. If the condition evaluation in Step 2 returns a value of true, the `for` loop statements execute, Step 4 occurs, and the process starts over again with Step 2. If the condition evaluation in Step 2 returns a value of false, the `for` statement ends and the next statement following the `for` statement executes.
4. The `update` statement in the `for` statement is executed. For example, the `$Count` variable may increment by one.

You can omit any of the three parts of the `for` statement, but you must include the semicolons that separate each section. If you omit a section, be sure you include code within the body that will end the `for` statement or your program might get caught in an infinite loop.

The following script shows a `for` statement that prints the contents of an array:

```
$FastFoods = array("pizza", "burgers", "french fries", "tacos",
"fried chicken");
for ($Count = 0; $Count < 5; ++$Count) {
     echo $FastFoods[$Count], "<br />";
}
```

As you can see in this example, the counter is initialized, evaluated, and incremented within the parentheses. You do not need to include a declaration for the `$Count` variable before the `for` statement, nor do you need to increment the `$Count` variable within the body of the `for` statement. Figure 4-12 shows the output of the fast-foods script.

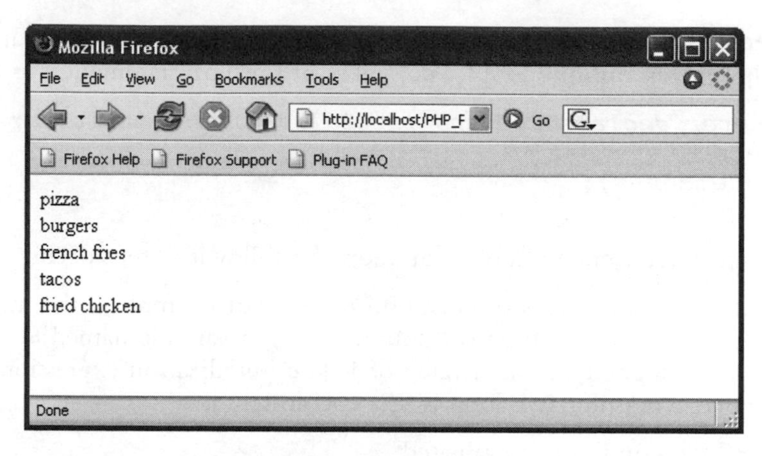

Figure 4-12 Output of fast-foods script

Using a `for` statement is more efficient because you do not need as many lines of code. Consider the following `while` statement:

```
$Count = 1;
while ($Count <= 5) {
        echo "$Count<br />";
        ++$Count;
}
```

You could achieve the same flow control more efficiently by using a `for` statement as follows:

```
for ($Count = 1; $Count <= 5; ++$Count) {
        echo "$Count<br />";
}
```

The following code shows an example of the days of week script you saw earlier. This time, however, the script includes a `for` statement instead of a `do...while` statement. Notice that the declaration of the `$Count` variable, the conditional expression, and the statement that increments the `$Count` variable are now all contained within the `for` statement. Using a `for` statement instead of a `do...while` statement simplifies the script somewhat because you do not need as many lines of code.

```
$DaysOfWeek = array("Monday", "Tuesday", "Wednesday", "Thursday",
"Friday", "Saturday", "Sunday");
for ($Count = 0; $Count < 7; ++$Count) {
       echo $DaysOfWeek[$Count], "<br />";
}
```

Next, you modify the Great Explorers quiz so it is scored with a `for` statement instead of a `do...while` statement.

To replace the `do...while` statement in the Great Explorers quiz with a `for` statement:

1. Return to the **ScoreQuiz.php** document in your text editor.

2. Delete the declaration for the `$Count` variable within the `scoreQuestions()` function.

3. Replace the `do...while` statement within the `scoreQuestions()` function with the following `for` statement:

```
for ($Count=1; $Count<=5; ++$Count) {
     echo "<p>Question $Count: ", $_GET["question$Count"];
     if ($_GET["question$Count"] == $CorrectAnswers[$Count-1]) {
          echo " (Correct!)</p>";
          ++$TotalCorrect;
     }
     else
          echo " (Incorrect)</p>";
}
```

4. Save the **ScoreQuiz.php** document.

5. Open the **ExplorersQuiz.html** file in your Web browser by entering the following URL: **http://localhost/PHP_Projects/Chapter.04/Chapter/ExplorersQuiz.html**. Test the program by answering all five questions and clicking the **Score** button. The program should function just as it did with the `do...while` statement.

6. Close your Web browser window.

foreach Statements

The **`foreach` statement** is used to iterate or loop through the elements in an array. With each loop, a `foreach` statement moves to the next element in an array. Unlike other types of looping statements, you do not need to include any sort of counter within a `foreach` statement. Instead, you specify an array expression within a set of parentheses following the `foreach` keyword. The basic syntax for the `foreach` statement is as follows:

```
foreach ($array_name as $variable_name) {
statements;
}
```

During each iteration, a `foreach` statement assigns the value of the current array element to the *`$variable_name`* argument specified in the array expression. You use the *`$variable_name`* argument to access the value of the element that is available in an iteration. For example, the following code declares the same `$DaysOfWeek[]` array you've seen a few times in this chapter. During each iteration, the expression in the `foreach` statement assigns the value of each array element to the `$Day` variable. An `echo()` statement within the `foreach` statement's braces prints the value of the current element.

```
$DaysOfWeek = array("Monday", "Tuesday", "Wednesday", "Thursday",
"Friday", "Saturday", "Sunday");
```

```
foreach ($DaysOfWeek as $Day) {
     echo "<p>$Day</p>";
}
```

The **foreach** statement in the preceding code simply prints the days of the week to the Web browser.

You will receive an error if you attempt to use a `foreach` statement with any variable types other than arrays.

Next, you create a final version of the Great Explorers quiz that is scored with a `foreach` statement instead of a `for` statement. Note that a `foreach` statement is not necessarily more efficient than a `for` statement. In fact, for this next exercise, the `foreach` statement is more complex than the `for` statement version because it uses a `$Count` variable to keep track of the current question number. However, `foreach` statements are very useful when working with arrays, so you should understand how they work.

To replace the `for` statement in the Great Explorers quiz with a `foreach` statement:

1. Return to the **ScoreQuiz.php** document in your text editor.
2. Re-add the `$Count` variable declaration, initialized to a value of 1, after the statement that declares the `$TotalCorrect` variable. You need the `$Count` variable to keep track of the current question number.

   ```
   $Count=1;
   ```

3. Change the `for` statement within the `scoreQuestions()` function to the following `foreach` statement, which uses a variable named `$Answer` to refer to each element in the `$_GET` array. Notice that the first `echo()` statement and the `if` statement use the `$Answer` variable to obtain the submitted answer to each question.

   ```
   foreach ($_GET as $Answer) {
     echo "<p>Question $Count: $Answer";
      if ($Answer == $CorrectAnswers[$Count-1]) {
         echo "  (Correct!)</p>";
         ++$TotalCorrect;
      }
      else
         echo "  (Incorrect)</p>";
      ++$Count;
   }
   ```

4. Save the **ScoreQuiz.php** document.
5. Open the **ExplorersQuiz.html** file in your Web browser by entering the following URL: **http://localhost/PHP_Projects/Chapter.04/Chapter/ExplorersQuiz.html**. Test the program by answering all five questions and

clicking the **Score** button. The program should function just as it did with the `for` statement.

6. Close your Web browser window and text editor.

Chapter Summary

- The lines that make up a function are called the function definition.
- A global variable is one that is declared outside a function and is available to all parts of your program.
- A local variable is declared inside a function and is only available within the function in which it is declared.
- PHP includes various predefined global arrays, called autoglobals or superglobals, which contain client, server, and environment information that you can use in your scripts.
- The process of determining the order in which statements execute in a program is called decision making or flow control.
- The `if` statement is used to execute specific programming code if the evaluation of a conditional expression returns a value of true.
- An `if` statement that includes an `else` clause is called an `if...else` statement. An `else` clause executes when the condition in an `if...else` statement evaluates to false.
- When one decision-making statement is contained within another decision-making statement, they are referred to as nested decision-making structures.
- The `switch` statement controls program flow by executing a specific set of statements, depending on the value of an expression.
- A loop statement is a control structure that repeatedly executes a statement or a series of statements while a specific condition is true or until a specific condition becomes true.
- A `while` statement repeats a statement or series of statements as long as a given conditional expression evaluates to true.
- The `do...while` statement executes a statement or statements once, then repeats the execution as long as a given conditional expression evaluates to true.
- The `for` statement is used for repeating a statement or series of statements as long as a given conditional expression evaluates to true.
- The `foreach` statement is used to iterate or loop through the elements in an array.

REVIEW QUESTIONS

1. A(n) ________________ allows you to treat a related group of PHP commands as a single unit.
    a. statement
    b. variable
    c. function
    d. event
2. Functions must contain parameters. True or False?
3. Explain how to use a return statement to return a value to a statement that calls a function.
4. A variable that is declared outside a function is called a(n) ________________ variable.
    a. local
    b. class
    c. program
    d. global
5. A local variable must be declared ________________.
    a. before a function
    b. after a function
    c. within the braces of a function definition
    d. with the local keyword
6. Which of the following autoglobals can you use to access submitted form values? (Choose all that apply.)
    a. `$_GET`
    b. `$_POST`
    c. `$_SERVER`
    d. `$_REQUEST`
7. Which of the following is the correct syntax for an `if` statement?
    a.
    ```
    if ($MyVariable == 10);
        echo "Your variable is equal to 10.";
    ```
    b.
    ```
    if $MyVariable == 10
        echo "Your variable is equal to 10.";
    ```
    c.
    ```
    if ($MyVariable == 10)
        echo "Your variable is equal to 10.";
    ```
    d.
    ```
    if ($MyVariable == 10),
        echo "Your variable is equal to 10.";
    ```

8. An `if` statement can include multiple statements provided that they ________.
   a. execute after the `if` statement's closing semicolon
   b. are not contained within a command block
   c. do not include other `if` statements
   d. are contained within a command block

9. Explain how to construct an `if` statement that executes multiple statements.
10. Which is the correct syntax for an `else` clause?
    a. `else (echo "Printed from an else clause.";`
    b. `else echo "Printed from an else clause.";`
    c. `else "echo 'Printed from an else clause.'";`
    d. `else; echo "Printed from an else clause.";`
11. The `switch` statement controls program flow by executing a specific set of statements, depending on ________.
    a. the result of an `if...else` statement
    b. the version of PHP being executed
    c. whether an `if` statement executes from within a function
    d. the value returned by a conditional expression
12. Decision-making structures cannot be nested. True or False?
13. When the value returned by a `switch` statement expression does not match a `case` label, the statements within the ________ label execute.
    a. `exception`
    b. `else`
    c. `error`
    d. `default`
14. You can exit a `switch` statement using a(n) ________ statement.
    a. `break`
    b. `end`
    c. `quit`
    d. `complete`

15. Each repetition of a looping statement is called a(n) ________________.
    a. recurrence
    b. iteration
    c. duplication
    d. reexecution
16. Which of the following is the correct syntax for a `while` statement?
    a.
    ```
    while ($i <= 5, ++$i) {
         $echo "<p>$i</p>";
    }
    ```
    b.
    ```
    while ($i <= 5) {
         $echo "<p>$i</p>";
         ++$i;
    }
    ```
    c.
    ```
    while ($i <= 5);
         $echo "<p>$i</p>";
         ++$i;
    ```
    d.
    ```
    while ($i <= 5; $echo "<p>$i</p>") {
         ++$i;
    }
    ```
17. Counter variables ________________. (Choose all that apply.)
    a. can only be incremented
    b. can only be decremented
    c. can be changed using any conditional expression
    d. do not change
18. Explain how an infinite loop is caused.
19. Which of the following is the correct syntax for a `for` statement?
    a.
    ```
    for (var $i = 0; $i < 10; ++$i)
         echo "Printed from a for statement.";
    ```
    b.
    ```
    for (var $i = 0, $i < 10, ++$i)
         echo "Printed from a for statement.");
    ```
    c.
    ```
    for {
         echo "Printed from a for statement.");
    } while (var $i = 0; $i < 10; ++$i)
    ```

d. `for (var $i = 0; $i < 10);`

```
echo "Printed from a for statement.");
++$i;
```

20. When is a `for` statement initialization expression executed?
    a. when the `for` statement begins executing
    b. with each repetition of the `for` statement
    c. when the counter variable increments
    d. when the `for` statement ends
21. The `foreach` statement can only be used with arrays. True or False?

HANDS-ON PROJECTS

Hands-On Project 4-1

In this project, you create a script with a function that returns a string value.

1. Create a new document in your text editor.
2. Type the `<!DOCTYPE>` declaration, `<html>` element, document head, and `<body>` element. Use the strict DTD and "Company Name" as the content of the `<title>` element.
3. Create a script section in the document body that contains the following `getCompanyName()` function:

```
<?php
function getCompanyName() {
     $CompanyName = "Course Technology";
}
?>
```

4. Modify the `getCompanyName()` function so that it returns the company name to a calling function.
5. Add statements after the `getCompanyName()` function definition that call the `getCompanyName()` function and assign the return value to a variable named `$RetValue`.
6. Finally, write code that prints the contents of the `$RetValue` variable.
7. Save the document as **CompanyName.php** in the Projects directory for Chapter 4, and then close it in your text editor.
8. Open the **CompanyName.php** file in your Web browser by entering the following URL: **http://localhost/PHP_Projects/Chapter.04/Projects/CompanyName.php**.
9. Close your Web browser window.

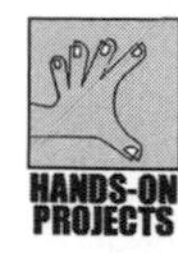

Hands-On Project 4-2

In this project, you create a simple document containing a conditional operator that you rewrite into an `if...else` statement.

1. Create a new document in your text editor.
2. Type the `<!DOCTYPE>` declaration, `<html>` element, document head, and `<body>` element. Use the strict DTD and "Conditional Script" as the content of the `<title>` element.
3. Create a script section in the document body that includes the following code, but replace the conditional expression statement with an `if...else` statement:

```
<?php
$IntVariable = 75;
($IntVariable > 100) ?
     $Result = '$IntVariable is greater than 100'
     : $Result = '$IntVariable is less than or equal to 100';
echo "<p>$Result</p>";
?>
```

4. Save the document as **ConditionalScript.php** in the Projects directory for Chapter 4, and then close it in your text editor.
5. Open the **ConditionalScript.php** file in your Web browser by entering the following URL: **http://localhost/PHP_Projects/Chapter.04/Projects/ConditionalScript.php**.
6. Close your Web browser window.

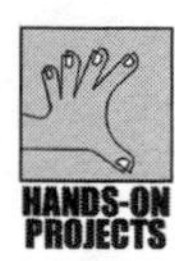

Hands-On Project 4-3

In this project, you write a `while` statement that prints all odd numbers between 1 and 100 to the screen.

1. Create a new document in your text editor.
2. Type the `<!DOCTYPE>` declaration, `<html>` element, document head, and `<body>` element. Use the strict DTD and "Odd Numbers" as the content of the `<title>` element.
3. Create a script section in the body section with a `while` statement that prints all odd numbers between 1 and 100 to the screen.
4. Save the document as **OddNumbers.php** in the Projects directory for Chapter 4, and then close it in your text editor.
5. Open the **OddNumbers.php** file in your Web browser by entering the following URL: **http://localhost/PHP_Projects/Chapter.04/Projects/OddNumbers.php**.
6. Close your Web browser window.

Hands-On Project 4-4

In this project, you identify and fix the logic flaws in a `while` statement.

1. Create a new document in your text editor.
2. Type the `<!DOCTYPE>` declaration, `<html>` element, document head, and `<body>` element. Use the strict DTD and "While Logic" as the content of the `<title>` element.
3. Create a script section in the document body that includes the following code:

```
<?php
$Count = 0;
while ($Count > 100) {
      $Numbers[] = $Count;
      ++$Count;
foreach ($Count as $CurNum)
      echo "<p>$CurNum</p>";
}
?>
```

4. The code you typed in the preceding step should fill the array with the numbers 1 through 100, and then print them to the screen. However, the code contains several logic flaws that prevent it from running correctly. Identify and fix the logic flaws.
5. Save the document as **WhileLogic.php** in the Projects directory for Chapter 4, and then close it in your text editor.
6. Open the **WhileLogic.php** file in your Web browser by entering the following URL: **http://localhost/PHP_Projects/Chapter.04/Projects/WhileLogic.php**.
7. Close your Web browser window.

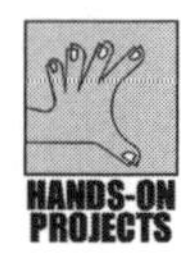

Hands-On Project 4-5

In this project, you create a document with a simple form that displays the value of a letter grade.

1. Create a new document in your text editor.
2. Type the `<!DOCTYPE>` declaration, `<html>` element, document head, and `<body>` element. Use the strict DTD and "Letter Grades" as the content of the `<title>` element.

3. Create a script section in the document body that includes the following `checkGrade()` function and `switch` statement:

```
<?php
function checkGrade($Grade) {
     switch ($Grade) {
          case "A":
               echo "Your grade is excellent.";
          case "B":
               echo "Your grade is good.";
          case "C":
               echo "Your grade is fair.";
          case "D":
               echo "You are barely passing.";
          case "F":
               echo "You failed.";
     }
?>
```

4. Add code to the `switch` statement you created in the previous step so that after the statements in a `case` label execute, the `switch` statement ends.
5. Modify the `switch` statement so that a default value of "You did not enter a valid letter grade." is printed if none of the `case` labels match the `grade` variable.
6. Save the document as **LetterGrades.php** in the Projects directory for Chapter 4.
7. Create a new document in your text editor.
8. Type the `<!DOCTYPE>` declaration, `<html>` element, document head, and `<body>` element. Use the strict DTD and "Letter Grades" as the content of the `<title>` element.
9. Add the following form to the document body that is submitted to the LetterGrades.php document with a method of "get". The form contains a single text box that you will use to enter a letter grade.

```
<form action="LetterGrades.php" method="get" >
<p>Grade: <input type="text" name="grade" />
<input type="submit" /></p>
</form>
```

10. Save the document as **LetterGrades.html** in the Projects directory for Chapter 4, and then close it in your text editor.
11. Return to the **LetterGrades.php** document in your text editor and add a call statement to the end of the script that calls the `checkGrade()` function and passes to it the value from the `grade` form variable.
12. Save **LetterGrades.php** and close it in your text editor.
13. Open the **LetterGrades.html** file in your Web browser by entering the following URL: **http://localhost/PHP_Projects/Chapter.04/Projects/ LetterGrades.html**. Enter a letter grade and click the **Submit** button.
14. Close your Web browser window.

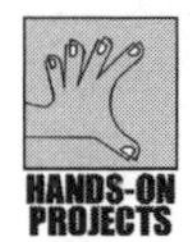

Hands-On Project 4-6

In this project, you modify a nested `if` statement so it instead uses a compound conditional expression. You use logical operators such as the `||` (or) and `&&` (and) operators to execute a conditional or looping statement based on multiple criteria.

1. Create a new document in your text editor.
2. Type the `<!DOCTYPE>` declaration, `<html>` element, document head, and `<body>` element. Use the strict DTD and "Gas Prices" as the content of the `<title>` element.
3. Create a script section in the document body that includes the following variable declaration and nested `if` statement:

```
<?php
$GasPrice = 1.57;
if ($GasPrice > 1) {
     if ($GasPrice < 2)
           echo "<p>Gas prices are between
                $1.00 and $2.00.</p>";
}
?>
```

4. Modify the nested `if` statement you created in the previous step so it uses a single `if` statement with a compound conditional expression. You need to use the `&&` (and) logical operator.
5. Add an `else` clause to the `if` statement that prints "Gas prices are not between $1.00 and $2.00" if the compound conditional expression returns false.
6. Save the document as **GasPrices.php** in the Projects directory for Chapter 4.
7. Create a new document in your text editor.
8. Type the `<!DOCTYPE>` declaration, `<html>` element, document head, and `<body>` element. Use the strict DTD and "Gas Prices" as the content of the `<title>` element.
9. Add to the document body a form contain a single text box and a Submit button. Use the text box to enter a gasoline price that you can submit to the GasPrices.php script. Add the appropriate code to the form that allows you to submit the form to the GasPrices.php document with a method of "get".
10. Save the document as **GasPrices.html** in the Projects directory for Chapter 4, and then close it in your text editor.
11. Return to the **GasPrices.php** document in your text editor and modify the script so it uses the `$_GET` autoglobal to refer to the form variable.
12. Save GasPrices.php and then close them in your text editor.
13. Open the **GasPrices.html** file in your Web browser by entering the following URL: **http://localhost/PHP_Projects/Chapter.04/Projects/GasPrices.html**. Test the script by entering a price in the text box and click the **Submit** button.
14. Close your Web browser window.

Case Projects

Save the documents you create for the following projects in the Cases directory for Chapter 4.

Case Project 4-1

Write a script that calculates a 15% return on an investment of $10,000. Calculate the number of years required for a single $10,000 investment to reach $1,000,000 at an average annual return of 15%. Use a looping statement and assume that each iteration is equivalent to one year. Save the document as **Investment.php**.

Case Project 4-2

Use an appropriate looping statement to write a script that prints a list of the Celsius equivalents of zero degrees Fahrenheit through 100 degrees Fahrenheit. To convert Fahrenheit to Celsius, subtract 32 from the Fahrenheit temperature, and then multiply the remainder by .55. To convert Celsius to Fahrenheit, multiply the Celsius temperature by 1.8, and then add 32. Save the document as **TempConversion.php**.

Case Project 4-3

Create a script that calculates an employee's weekly gross salary, based on the number of hours worked and an hourly wage that you choose. Use a PHP document and an HTML document containing a form with two text boxes—one for the number of hours worked and the other for the hourly wage. Compute any hours over 40 as time-and-a-half. Use the appropriate decision structure to create the program. Save the documents as **Paycheck.php** and **Paycheck.html**, respectively.

Case Project 4-4

Create a script that calculates the square feet of carpet required to carpet a room. Use a PHP document and an HTML document containing a form with three text boxes. Create one text box for the width of the room in linear feet and another for the length of the room in linear feet. Also, create a text box for the cost per square foot of carpeting. When you calculate the cost, add 25% to the total number of square feet to account for closets and other features of the room. Save the documents as **CarpetCost.php** and **CarpetCost.html**, respectively.

Case Project 4-5

Write a script that allows users to enter a number of cents into a text box. Use a PHP document and an HTML document containing a form with a single text box to enter the number of cents. Determine how many dollars the cents make up and print the number of dollars and remaining cents. Save the documents as **CentsToDollars.php** and **CentsToDollars.html**, respectively.

Case Project 4-6

You can determine whether a year is a leap year by testing if it is divisible by 4. However, years that are also divisible by 100 are not leap years, unless they are also divisible by 400, in which case they are leap years. Write a script that allows a user to enter a year and then determines whether the year entered is a leap year. Use a PHP document and an HTML document containing a form with a single text box to enter the year. Print a message to the user stating whether the year they entered is a standard year or a leap year. Save the documents as **LeapYear.php** and **LeapYear.html**, respectively.

Case Project 4-7

The combined length of any two sides of a triangle must be greater than the length of the third side for the segments to form a triangle. For example, 8, 6, and 12 can form a triangle because the sum of any two of the three segments is greater than the third segment. However, 25, 5, and 15 cannot form a triangle because the sum of segments 5 and 15 are not greater than the length of segment 25. Using this logic, write a script that allows a user to enter three integers, one for each side of a triangle. Test whether the three sides can form a triangle. Use a PHP document and an HTML document containing a form with three text boxes to gather the segment lengths from the user. Print a message to the user that states whether their segments can form a triangle. Save the documents as **Triangle.php** and **Triangle.html**, respectively.

Case Project 4-8

Write a script that allows a user to enter a number between 1 and 999. Determine whether the number is a prime number and display your results with an `echo()` statement. A prime number is a number that can only be divided by itself or by one. Examples of prime numbers include 1, 3, 5, 13, and 17. Use a PHP document and an HTML document containing a form with a single text box in which users can enter a number. You need to use a looping statement to test all division possibilities. Save the document as **PrimeNumber.php** and **PrimeNumber.html**, respectively.

CHAPTER

5

MANIPULATING STRINGS

In this chapter, you will:

- Manipulate strings
- Parse strings
- Compare strings
- Handle form submissions

One of the most common uses of PHP is for processing form data submitted by users. Because form data is submitted as strings, a good PHP programmer must be adept at dealing with strings. This chapter discusses techniques for manipulating strings and processing form data with PHP.

Constructing Text Strings

As you learned in Chapter 2, a text string contains zero or more characters surrounded by double or single quotation marks. You can use text strings as literal values or assign them to a variable. For example, the first statement in the following code prints a literal text string, whereas the second statement assigns a text string to a variable. The third statement then uses the **echo()** statement to print the text string assigned to the variable.

```
echo "<p>Dr. Livingstone, I presume?</p>";
$Explorer = "Henry M. Stanley";
echo $Explorer;
```

You can also surround a text string with single quotation marks. Whichever method you use, a string must begin and end with the same type of quotation mark. For example, **echo "<p>This is a text string.</p>";** is valid because it starts and ends with double quotation marks. Likewise, **'echo <p>This is a text string.</p>';** is valid because it begins and ends with single quotation marks. By contrast, the statement **echo "<p>This is a text string.</p>';** is invalid because it starts with a double quotation mark and ends with a single quotation mark. In this case, you would receive an error message because the PHP interpreter cannot tell where the literal string begins and ends.

Unlike other programming languages, PHP has no special data type for a single character, such as the char data type in the C, C++, and Java programming languages.

When you want to include a quoted string within a literal string surrounded by double quotation marks, you surround the quoted string with single quotation marks. When you want to include a quoted string within a literal string surrounded by single quotation marks, you surround the quoted string with double quotation marks. For example, the following statement assigns a text string surrounded by double quotation marks to the **$ExplorerQuote** variable. Figure 5-1 shows the output of the **echo()** statement.

```
$ExplorerQuote = '<p>"Dr. Livingstone, I presume?"</p>';
echo $ExplorerQuote;
```

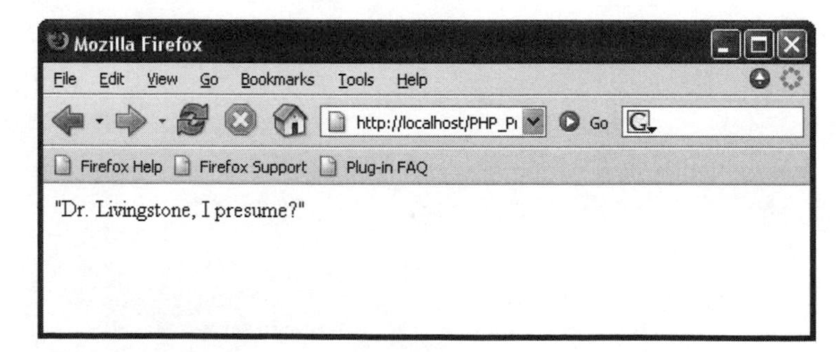

Figure 5-1 Output of a text string containing double quotation marks

Later in this chapter, you learn how to include other special characters in text strings.

In this chapter, you create a PHP script that sends e-mail messages using the `mail()` function. The basic syntax for the function is `mail(`***`recipient(s), subject, message`***`[,additional_headers])`. The value you assign to the ***`recipient(s)`*** argument must be an e-mail address in the format *name@domain.com*. The optional ***`additional_headers`*** argument can include additional headers that are typically found in e-mail messages, such as To, From, CC, BCC, and Date headers. For the To, From, CC, and BCC headers, you can include the recipient's display name and e-mail address in the format ***`display_name`*** *`<name@domain.com>`*. For the sake of simplicity, the To, CC, and BCC e-mail addresses you work with in this chapter's projects do not include fields for display names. The `mail()` function returns a value of true if a message was delivered successfully or false if it was not. The following example demonstrates how to send a simple message:

```
$To = "bill@centralvalleyhardware.com";
$Subject = "This is the subject";
$Message = "This is the message.";
$Headers="From: Don Gosselin <don@coastcitysoftware.com>";
mail($To, $Subject, $Message, $Headers);
```

See Appendix B for information on formatting text strings for output.

On Windows platforms, before you can use the `mail()` function, you must edit your php.ini configuration file and assign an e-mail address to the `sendmail_from` directive and the name of your SMTP server to the `SMTP` directive. Simple Mail Transfer Protocol (SMTP) is a protocol that most e-mail systems use to send messages over the Internet. Contact your ISP for the name of your SMTP server. On UNIX/Linux systems, you must install sendmail, which is an open source application for routing and delivering e-mail messages. Sendmail comes preinstalled on most UNIX/Linux systems, although you can also download the most recent version from *http://www.sendmail.org*. Edit your php.ini configuration file and assign the path where sendmail is installed to the `sendmail_path` directive.

The main purpose of the e-mail project in this chapter is to demonstrate how to manipulate strings and validate form data in PHP. Even if you do not have access to an SMTP e-mail system, you can perform the exercises in this chapter by commenting out the `mail()` function statement in your scripts.

Your Chapter directory for Chapter 5 includes a Web page named PHPEmail.html that you will use to submit data to a PHP script that submits the e-mail message. Figure 5-2 shows how the Web page appears in a browser.

Figure 5-2 PHPEmail.html in a Web browser

Before you use the PHPEmail.html Web page, you create and work with a PHP script named PHPEmail.php that will contain the code that processes and submits e-mail messages.

To start creating the PHPEmail.php script:

1. Open your text editor and create a new document.
2. Type the `<!DOCTYPE>` declaration, `<html>` element, header information, and `<body>` element. Use the strict DTD and "PHP E-Mail" as the content of the `<title>` element.
3. Add the following `<link>` element above the closing `</head>` tag to link to the php_styles.css style sheet in your Chapter directory:

   ```
   <link rel="stylesheet" href="php_styles.css" type="text/css" />
   ```

4. Add the following script section to the document body:

   ```
   <?php
   ?>
   ```

5. Add the following variable declarations to the script section. Be sure to replace the e-mail addresses assigned to the `$From` and `$To` variables with your own e-mail address, or with an e-mail address assigned by your instructor.

```
$From = "Don Gosselin <don@coastcitysoftware.com>";
$To = "sales@coastcitysoftware.com";
$Subject = "Agenda for tomorrow's meeting";
$Message = "In tomorrow's meeting, we will discuss our new
marketing campaign and third-quarter sales results.";
$Headers = "From: $From";
```


6. Add the following statements to the end of the script section. The `mail()` function sends a message using the data you assigned to the variables in the previous step. The `mail()` function assigns a value of true or false to the `$MessageSent` variable, depending on whether the message was sent successfully.

```
$MessageSent = mail($To, $Subject, $Message, $Headers);
```

If you do not have access to an SMTP e-mail system, add two slashes (//) before the preceding statement to comment it out and add another statement immediately after the preceding statement that assigns a value of true to the `$MessageSent` variable.

7. Add to the end of the script section the following `if...else` statement, which prints the contents of the e-mail message to the Web browser, as well as a text string stating whether the message transmission was successful:

```
if ($MessageSent) {
     echo "<p>The following message was sent
         successfully:</p><hr />";
     echo "<p><strong>From</strong>: $From</p>";
     echo "<p><strong>To</strong>: $To</p>";
     echo "<p><strong>Subject</strong>: $Subject</p>";
     echo "<p><strong>Message</strong>: $Message</p>";
}
else
     echo "<p>The message was not sent successfully!</p>";
```

8. Add the following text and elements to the end of the document body, after the closing `?>` delimiter:

```
<hr /><p><a href="PHPEmail.html">Return to E-Mail Form</a></p>
```

9. Save the document as **PHPEmail.php** in the Chapter directory for Chapter 5.

10. Open the **PHPEmail.php** file in your Web browser by entering the following URL: **http://localhost/PHP_Projects/Chapter.05/Chapter/PHPEmail.php**. In your Web browser, you should see "The following message was sent successfully:" The Web browser should also display the contents of the message itself.

11. Check your e-mail account to ensure that the message was sent successfully, and then delete the message.

Most SMTP servers can be configured to prevent relaying, or forwarding, of spam. (The term spam generally refers to unsolicited or unwanted junk e-mail. To prevent relaying, many SMTP servers require users to regularly send and receive e-mail at the same time. This allows the SMTP server to identify the user based on his IP address. Because your Web server is probably not part of your ISP's domain, you might receive a "relaying denied" error message when you attempt to send a message with the PHPEmail.php file. If you do receive a "relaying denied" error message, try sending and receiving your e-mail with commercial software such as Microsoft Outlook before attempting to use PHP to send e-mail messages.

12. Close your Web browser window.

Working with String Operators

Up to this point, to print values from multiple literal strings and variables, you have passed them to the `echo()` and `print()` statements as multiple arguments separated by commas. For example, the following passes two literal strings and a variable to the `echo()` statement:

```
$Explorer = "Henry M. Stanley";
echo '<p>"Dr. Livingstone, I presume?", asked ', $Explorer, ".</p>";
```

In PHP, you can also use two operators to combine strings. The first of these operators is the **concatenation operator** (.). The following code uses the concatenation operator to combine several string variables and literal strings, and assigns the new value to another variable:

```
$Destination = "Paris";
$Location = "France";
$Destination = "<p>" . $Destination . " is in "
    . $Location . ".</p>";
echo $Destination;
```

The combined value of the `$Location` variable and the literal strings that are assigned to the `$Destination` variable is "<p>Paris is in France.</p>".

You can also combine strings using the **concatenation assignment operator** (.=) to combine two strings. The following code combines two text strings, but without using the `$Location` variable:

```
$Destination = "<p>Paris";
$Destination .= " is in France.</p>";
echo $Destination;
```

With the `mail()` function, you can specify multiple recipients by separating e-mail addresses in the recipients argument with a comma. Next, you modify the e-mail script so it sends a message to multiple recipients.

To modify the e-mail script so it sends a message to multiple recipients:

1. Return to the **PHPEmail.php** script in your text editor.
2. Use the concatenation operator to modify the statement that declares the `$To` variable so it includes two recipients separated by a comma. Use the e-mail address of one of your classmates for the second recipient. (If you do not have access to another e-mail address, you can just use the same e-mail address twice, although your e-mail server will probably only deliver a single copy to your e-mail account.) Your `$To` variable declaration statement should appear similar to the following:

```
$To = "sales@coastcitysoftware.com" . ","
      . "marketing@coastcitysoftware.com";
```

3. Save the **PHPEmail.php** file and then open it in your Web browser by entering the following URL: **http://localhost/PHP_Projects/Chapter.05/Chapter/PHPEmail.php**. You should see "The following message was sent successfully:", along with the contents of the message, printed to your Web browser window.
4. Check both e-mail accounts to ensure that the message was sent successfully to both addresses, and then delete the message.
5. Close your Web browser window.

Adding Escape Characters and Sequences

You need to use extra care when using single quotation marks with possessives and contractions in strings surrounded by single quotation marks because the PHP interpreter always looks for the first closing single quotation mark to match an opening single quotation mark. For example, consider the following statement:

```
echo '<p>Marilyn Monroe's real name was Norma Jeane Baker.</p>';
```

This statement causes an error because the PHP interpreter assumes that the literal string ends with the apostrophe following "Monroe." To get around this problem, you include an escape character before the apostrophe in "Monroe's". An **escape character** tells the compiler or interpreter that the character that follows it has a special purpose. In PHP, the escape character is the backslash \. Placing a backslash in front of an apostrophe tells the PHP interpreter that the apostrophe is to be treated as a regular keyboard character, such as "a," "b," "1," or "2," and not as part of a single quotation mark pair that encloses a text string. The backslash in the following statement tells the PHP interpreter to print the apostrophe following the word "Monroe" as an apostrophe.

```
echo '<p>Marilyn Monroe\'s real name was Norma Jeane Baker.</p>';
```

There's no need for a backslash before an apostrophe if you surround the text string with double quotation marks, as follows:

```
echo "<p>Marilyn Monroe's real name was Norma Jeane Baker.</p>";
```

Although the apostrophe in the preceding statement prints correctly, there are other escape characters that you must use within a string surrounded by double quotation marks. The escape character combined with one or more other characters is called an **escape sequence**. The backslash followed by an apostrophe `\'` is an example of an escape sequence. Most escape sequences carry out special functions. For example, the escape sequence `\t` inserts a tab into a string. Table 5-1 describes the escape sequences that can be added to a double-quoted string in PHP.

Table 5-1 PHP escape sequences within double quotation marks

Escape Sequence	Description
`\\`	Inserts a backslash
`\$`	Inserts a dollar sign
`\r`	Inserts a carriage return
`\"`	Inserts a double quotation mark
`\t`	Inserts a horizontal tab
`\n`	Inserts a new line
`\regular expression`	Inserts a character in hexadecimal notation that matches the regular expression

Within a literal string surrounded by double quotation marks, if you place a backslash before any character other than those listed in Table 5-1, the backslash is also printed.

You study regular expressions (mentioned in Table 5-1) later in this chapter.

Notice that one of the characters inserted into a string by an escape sequence is the backslash. Because the escape character itself is a backslash, you must use the escape sequence `\\` to include a backslash as a character in a string. For example, to include the path "C:\Course Technology\1687-5" in a string, you must include two backslashes for every single backslash you want to appear in the string, as in the following statement:

```
echo "<p>My PHP files are located in
C:\\Course Technology\\1687-5\\.</p>";
```

The following code shows another example of an escape character, this time with the double quotation escape sequence (\"). Figure 5-3 shows the output.

```
$Explorer = "Henry M. Stanley";
echo "<p>\"Dr. Livingstone, I presume?\" asked $Explorer.</p>";
```

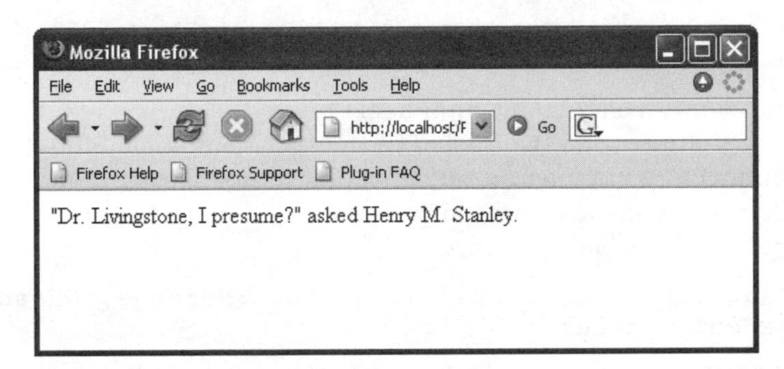

Figure 5-3 Output of literal text containing double quotation escape sequences

Although you could enclose the preceding `echo()` statement within single quotation marks, the name of the `$Explorer` variable would then print instead of its value. An alternative to using the double quotation escape sequence is to use single quotation marks for the starting text portion of the literal string, and then combine the `$Explorer` variable with the concatenation operator, as follows:

```
$Explorer = "Henry M. Stanley";
echo '<p>"Dr. Livingstone, I presume?" asked '
     . $Explorer . ".</p>";
```

Next, you add escape sequences to the e-mail script.

To add escape sequences to the e-mail script:

1. Return to the **PHPEmail.php** script in your text editor.
2. Remove the code that adds the second recipient to the `$To` variable.
3. Add a sentence to the string assigned to the `$Message` variable as follows. The sentence includes double quotation mark escape sequences around "100% Club".

   ```
   $Message = "In tomorrow's meeting, we will discuss our new
   marketing campaign and third-quarter sales results. We will also
   introduce the sales associates who made this quarter's \"100%
   Club\".";
   ```

4. To include multiple headers in the fourth argument you pass to the `mail()` function, you must separate each header with carriage return and newline escape sequences (\r\n). Modify the statement that declares the `$Headers` variable so it includes carriage return and newline escape sequences, as follows:

   ```
   $Headers="From: $From\r\n";
   ```

5. Add the following statements after the statement that declares the `$Headers` variable. The statements use the concatenation assignment operator to append some additional headers to the `$Headers` variable. Notice that each header ends with carriage return and newline escape sequences.

```
$Headers .= "MIME-Version: 1.0\r\n";
$Headers .= "Content-Type: text/plain; charset=\"iso-8859-1\"\r\n";
$Headers .= "Content-Transfer-Encoding: 8bit\r\n";
```

6. To prevent your e-mail account from being glutted with messages that you submit in this chapter, add two slashes to the statement containing the `mail()` function to comment it out (if you have not already done so) and add an additional statement that assigns a value of true to the `$MessageSent` variable, as follows:

```
// $MessageSent = mail($To, $Subject, $Message, $Headers);
$MessageSent = true;
```

7. Save the **PHPEmail.php** file and then open it in your Web browser by entering the following URL: **http://localhost/PHP_Projects/Chapter.05/Chapter/PHPEmail.php**. You should see "The following message was sent successfully:", along with the contents of the message, printed to your Web browser window. Notice that the double quotation marks in the message body print correctly.
8. Close your Web browser window.

Simple and Complex String Syntax

Values and variables can be combined in a literal string using simple or complex syntax. **Simple string syntax** allows you to use the value of a variable within a string by including the variable name inside a text string with double quotation marks. For example, the following code prints the text "Do you have any broccoli?" to the Web browser.

```
$Vegetable = "broccoli";
echo "<p>Do you have any $Vegetable?</p>";
```

Also recall that if you surround a variable name inside a text string with single quotation marks, the name of the variable prints.

When the PHP interpreter encounters a dollar sign with a text string, it attempts to evaluate any characters that follow the dollar sign as part of the variable name until it comes to a character that is not allowed in an identifier, such as a space. With the preceding example, the `$Vegetable` variable is interpreted correctly because the question mark is not a legal character for an identifier. However, consider the following version of the preceding code:

```
$Vegetable = "tomato";
echo "<p>Do you have any $Vegetables?</p>";
```

Because an 's' is appended to the `$Vegetable` variable name, the preceding `echo()` statement causes an error. This is because the PHP interpreter is attempting to locate a variable named `$Vegetables` (plural), which has not been declared. To make the preceding code work, you need to surround the variable name with curly braces { }, as shown in the following example. This type of structure, in which variables are placed within curly braces inside of a string, is called **complex string syntax**.

```
$Vegetable = "carrot";
echo "<p>Do you have any {$Vegetable}s?</p>";
```


The preceding `echo()` statement prints the text string "Do you have any carrots?" Complex string syntax is only recognized if the opening brace is immediately before or after a variable's dollar sign. The following version of the preceding code also works:

```
$Vegetable = "carrot";
echo "<p>Do you have any ${Vegetable}s?</p>";
```

However, if you place any characters between the opening brace and the dollar sign, the contents of the string are interpreted as literal values. For example, because the following code includes a space between the dollar sign and the opening brace, the `echo()` statement prints the text string "Do you have any { $Vegetable}s?":

```
$Vegetable = "carrot";
echo "<p>Do you have any { $Vegetable}s?</p>";
```

Next, you start working with the e-mail form you saw at the beginning of this chapter. You need to modify the statements that assign values to the variables in the e-mail script so the values of the `$_GET` autoglobal are assigned instead. To include the `$_GET` autoglobal inside of a string, you must use complex string syntax.

To start using the e-mail form:

1. Return to the **PHPEmail.php** script in your text editor.
2. Modify the `$From`, `$To`, `$Subject`, and `$Message` variable declarations so they are assigned values from the `$_GET` autoglobal, as follows. Notice that the value assigned to the `$From` variable uses complex string syntax.

```
$From="{$_GET['sender_name']} <{$_GET['sender_email']}>";
$To = $_GET['to'];
$Subject = $_GET['subject'];
$Message = $_GET['message'];
```

3. Save the **PHPEmail.php** file and then open the **PHPEmail.html** file in your Web browser by entering the following URL: **http://localhost/PHP_Projects/Chapter.05/Chapter/PHPEmail.html**. Enter values in the Name, E-Mail Address, To, Subject, and Message fields. For now, only enter a single e-mail address in the To field and do not enter any e-mail addresses in the CC or BCC fields; you still need to add additional functionality for these fields. Click the **Send** button and you should see

"The following message was sent successfully:", along with the contents of the message, printed to your Web browser window.

4. Close your Web browser window.

PARSING STRINGS

When applied to text strings, the term **parsing** refers to the act of extracting characters or substrings from a larger string. This is essentially the same as the parsing (rendering) that occurs in a Web browser when the Web browser extracts the necessary formatting information from a Web page before displaying it on the screen. In the case of a Web page, the document itself is one large text string from which formatting and other information needs to be extracted. However, when working on a programming level, parsing usually refers to the extraction of information from string literals and variables.

In this section, you study basic techniques for parsing strings, including how to count characters and words, and how to find, extract, and replace characters and substrings.

Counting Characters and Words in a String

You will often find it necessary to count characters and words in strings, particularly with strings from form submissions. For example, you might need to count the number of characters in a password to ensure that a user selects a password with a minimum number of characters. Or, you might have a Web page that allows users to submit classified ads that cannot exceed a maximum number of words. Table 5-2 lists the functions you can use to count characters and words in a string.

Table 5-2 PHP string counting functions

Function	Description
`str_word_count(`*string* [, *format*]`)`	Returns the number of words in a string
`strcspn(`*string1*, *string2*`)`	Returns the initial number of characters in one string that do not have matching values in another string
`strlen(`*string*`)`	Returns the number of characters in a string
`strspn(`*string1*, *string2*`)`	Returns the initial number of characters in one string that have matching values in another string
`substr_count(`*string*, *search_string*`)`	Returns the number of occurrences of a substring

The most commonly used string counting function is the `strlen()` function, which returns the total number of characters in a string. You pass to the `strlen()` function a literal string or the name of a string variable whose characters you want to count. For example, the following code uses the `strlen()` function to count the number of characters in a variable named `$BookTitle`. The `echo()` statement prints "The book title contains 23 characters."

```
$BookTitle = "The Cask of Amontillado";
echo "<p>The book title contains " . strlen($BookTitle)
     . " characters.</p>";
```

The `strlen()` function counts escape sequences such as \n as one character.

Another commonly used string counting function is the `str_word_count()` function, which returns the number of words in a string. You pass to the `str_word_count()` function a literal string or the name of a string variable whose words you want to count. The following example shows a modified version of the preceding code, but this time with the `str_word_count()` function. The `echo()` statement prints "The book title contains 4 words."

```
$BookTitle = "The Cask of Amontillado";
echo "<p>The book title contains " . str_word_count($BookTitle)
     . " words.</p>";
```

The form includes a Subject field in which users can enter the subject of a message. Next, you modify the e-mail script so it uses the `strlen()` function to prevent users from entering a subject of more than 40 characters.

To modify the e-mail script so it uses the `strlen()` function to prevent users from entering a subject of more than 40 characters:

1. Return to the **PHPEmail.php** script in your text editor.
2. Modify the `mail()` function and the nested `if...else` statements so they are contained within another `if...else` statement that checks the length of the Subject field, as follows. If the length of the subject field is greater than 40 characters, a message displays to the user that she has exceeded the maximum number of characters. However, if the length of the Subject field is less than or equal to 40 characters, the `mail()` function and the nested `if...else` statements execute.

```
if (strlen($Subject) > 40)
     echo "<p>The subject must be 40 characters or less! Click
     your browser's Back button to return to the message.</p>";
else {
     // $MessageSent = mail($To, $Subject,
          $Message, $Headers);
     if ($MessageSent) {
          echo "<p>The following message was sent
               successfully:</p>";
```

```
            echo "<p><strong>From</strong>: $From</p>";
            echo "<p><strong>To</strong>: $To</p>";
            echo "<p><strong>Subject</strong>: $Subject</p>";
            echo "<p><strong>Message</strong>: $Message</p>";
        }
        else
            echo "<p>The message was not sent successfully!</p>";
}
```

3. Save the **PHPEmail.php** file and then open the **PHPEmail.html** file in your Web browser by entering the following URL: **http://localhost/PHP_Projects/Chapter.05/Chapter/PHPEmail.html**. Enter values in the Name, E-Mail Address, To, and Message fields. For the Subject field, enter more than 40 characters and click the **Send** button. You should see the message informing you that the subject contains more than 40 characters.
4. Close your Web browser window.

Finding and Extracting Characters and Substrings

In some situations, you will need to find and extract characters and substrings from a string. For example, if your script receives an e-mail address, you may need to extract the name portion of the e-mail address or domain name. To search for and extract characters and substrings in PHP, you use the functions listed in Table 5-3.

Table 5-3 PHP string search and extraction functions

Function	Description
`stripos(string, search_string [, start_position])`	Performs a case-insensitive search and returns the position of the first occurrence of one string in another string
`stristr(string, search_string)`	Performs a case-insensitive search for specified characters in a string and returns a substring from the first occurrence of the specified characters to the end of the string
`strpos(string, search_string [, start_position])`	Performs a case-sensitive search and returns the position of the first occurrence of one string in another string
`strrchr(string, character)`	Performs a case-sensitive search for specified characters in a string and returns a substring from the last occurrence of the specified characters to the end of the string
`strripos(string, search_string [, start_position])`	Performs a case-insensitive search and returns the position of the last occurrence of one string in another string

Table 5-3 PHP string search and extraction functions (continued)

Function	Description
`strrpos(string, search_string [, start_position])`	Performs a case-sensitive search and returns the position of the last occurrence of one string in another string
`strstr(string, search_string)` or `strchr(string, search_string)`	Performs a case-sensitive search for specified characters in a string and returns a substring from the first occurrence of the specified characters to the end of the string
`substr(string, start_position [, length])`	Returns a portion of a string

There are two types of string search and extraction functions: functions that return a numeric position in a text string and functions that return a character or substring. With the exception of the `substr()` function, all of the functions in Table 5-3 return a value of false if the search string is not found. To use functions that return the numeric position in a text string, you need to understand that the position of characters in a text string begins with a value of 0, the same as with indexed array elements. For example, the `strpos()` function performs a case-sensitive search and returns the position of the first occurrence of one string in another string. You pass two arguments to the `strpos()` function: The first argument is the string you want to search, and the second argument contains the characters for which you want to search. If the search string is not found, the `strpos()` function returns a Boolean value of false. The following code uses the `strpos()` function to determine whether the `$Email` variable contains an @ character. Because the position of text strings begin with 0, the `echo()` statement returns a value of 9, even though the @ character is the tenth character in the string.

```
$Email = "president@whitehouse.gov";
echo strpos($Email, '@'); // returns 9
```

If you simply want to determine whether a character exists in a string, you need to keep in mind that PHP converts the Boolean values true and false to 1 and 0, respectively. However, these values are character positions within a string. For example, the following statement returns a value of 0 because "p" is the first character in the string:

```
$Email = "president@whitehouse.gov";
echo strpos($Email, 'p'); // returns 0
```

To determine whether the `strpos()` function (and other string functions) actually returns a Boolean false value and not a 0 representing the first character in a string, you must use the strict not equal operator (`!==`). The following example uses the `strpos()`

function and the strict not equal operator to determine whether the `$Email` variable contains an @ character:

```
$Email = "president@whitehouse.gov";
if (strpos($Email, '@') !== FALSE)
     echo "<p>The e-mail address contains an @ character.</p>";
else
     echo "<p>The e-mail address does not contain an @
character.</p>";
```

You first encountered the strict not equal operator in Table 3-6, in Chapter 3.

To return the last portion of a string, starting with a specified character, you use `strchr()` or `strrchr()`. You pass to both functions the string and the character for which you want to search. Both functions return a substring from the specified characters to the end of the string. The only difference between the two functions is that the `strchr()` function starts searching at the beginning of a string, whereas the `strrchr()` function starts searching at the end of a string. The following code uses the `strchr()` function to return the domain identifier of the e-mail address in the `$Email` variable:

```
$Email = "president@whitehouse.gov";
echo "<p>The domain identifier of the e-mail address is "
    . strchr($Email, ".") . ".</p>";
```

Because the e-mail address in the `$Email` variable in the preceding code only contains a single period, you can use either the `strchr()` or `strrchr()` function.

To extract characters from the beginning or middle of a string, you must combine the `substr()` function with other functions. You pass to the `substr()` function a text string along with the starting and ending positions of the substring you want to extract. For example, the second statement in the following code uses the `strpos()` function to identify the position of the @ character in the `$Email` variable. The `substr()` function then returns the name portion of the e-mail address by using a starting position of 0 (the first character in the string) to the position assigned to the `$NameEnd` variable.

```
$Email = "president@whitehouse.gov";
$NameEnd = strpos($Email, "@");
echo "<p>The name portion of the e-mail address is '" .
substr($Email, 0, $NameEnd) . "'.</p>";
```

If the *string* argument you pass to the `substr()` function is shorter than the value passed to the *start_position* argument, the function returns a value of false.

The following code contains another example of the `substr()` function. In this version, the code uses two `strpos()` functions to return the domain name of the e-mail address. Notice that the second statement increments the position returned from the `strpos()` function by one. This prevents the @ character from being included in the substring returned from the `substr()` function. Also notice that the third statement, which assigns the ending position to the `$DomainEnd` variable, subtracts the value assigned to the `$DomainBegin` variable from the value returned from the `strpos()` function. This is necessary to assign the correct number of characters to the `$DomainEnd` variable, which is used by the `substr()` function to determine how many characters to extract from the string.

```
$Email = "president@whitehouse.gov";
$DomainBegin = strpos($Email, "@") + 1;
$DomainEnd = strpos($Email, ".") - $DomainBegin;
echo "<p>The domain name portion of the e-mail address is '"
     . substr($Email, $DomainBegin, $DomainEnd) . "'.</p>";
```

Later in this chapter, you learn how to use regular expressions to validate strings, including e-mail addresses. For now, you use the `strpos()` function to simply check whether the e-mail addresses entered into the form contain ampersands and a period to separate the domain and identifier.

To use the `strpos()` function to check whether the e-mail addresses entered into the form contain ampersands and a period to separate the domain and identifier:

1. Return to the **PHPEmail.php** script in your text editor.
2. Add the following function to the beginning of the script section, immediately above the declaration statement for the `$From` variable. The function uses two `strpos()` functions to determine whether the string passed to it contains an ampersand and a period. If the string does contain both characters, a value of true is returned. If not, a value of false is returned.

   ```
   function validateSender($Address) {
   if (strpos($Address, '@') !== FALSE && strpos($Address, '.') !== FALSE)
        return true;
   else
        return false;
   }
   ```

3. Add the following `else...if` statement immediately above the `else` clause in the main `if...else` statement that sends the message. The `if` conditional expression passes the `$_GET['sender_email']` autoglobal to the

`validateSender()` function. If the function returns a value of false, the `echo()` statement executes.

```
else if (validateSender($_GET['sender_email']) == false)
     echo "The sender's e-mail address does not appear to be
     valid.  Click your browser's Back button to return to the
     message.";
```

4. Save the **PHPEmail.php** file and then open the **PHPEmail.html** file in your Web browser by entering the following URL: **http://localhost/PHP_Projects/Chapter.05/Chapter/PHPEmail.html**. Enter values in the Name, To, Subject, and Message fields. In the **E-Mail Address** field, enter an invalid e-mail address that is missing either an ampersand or a period. Click the **Send** button and you should see the message about the e-mail address being invalid.
5. Click your browser's **Back** button, enter a valid e-mail address in the **E-Mail Address** field, and then click the **Send** button. You should see "The following message was sent successfully.", along with the contents of the message, printed to your Web browser window.
6. Close your Web browser window.

Replacing Characters and Substrings

In addition to finding and extracting characters in a string, you might also need to replace them. You can use the functions listed in Table 5-4 to replace characters and substrings in PHP.

Table 5-4 PHP string replacement functions

Function	Description
`str_ireplace(`*`search_string, replacement_string, string`*`)`	Performs a case-insensitive replacement of all occurrences of specified characters in a string
`str_replace(`*`search_string, replacement_string, string`*`)`	Performs a case-sensitive replacement of all occurrences of specified characters in a string
`substr_replace(`*`string, replacement_string, start_position`*`[, `*`length`*`])`	Replaces characters within a specified portion of a string

The `str_replace()` and `str_ireplace()` functions both accept three arguments: the string you want to search for, a replacement string, and the string in which you want to replace characters. The replacement functions do not modify the contents of an existing string. Instead, they return a new string, which you can assign to a variable, use in an `echo()` statement, or use in your script some other way. The following example demonstrates how to use the `str_replace()` function to replace "president" in the `$Email` variable with "vice.president."

```
$Email = "president@whitehouse.gov";
$NewEmail = str_replace("president", "vice.president", $Email);
echo $NewEmail; // prints 'vice.president@whitehouse.gov'
```

Instead of replacing all occurrences of characters within a string, the `substr_replace()` function allows you to replace characters within a specified portion of a string. You pass to the `substr_replace()` function the string you want to search, the replacement text, and the starting and ending positions of the characters you want to replace. If you do not include the last argument, the `substr_replace()` function replaces all the characters from the starting position to the end of the string. For example, the following code uses the `strpos()` and `substr_replace()` functions to replace "president" in the `$Email` variable with "vice.president."


```
$Email = "president@whitehouse.gov";
$NameEnd = strpos($Email, "@");
$NewEmail = substr_replace($Email, "vice.president", 0,
$NameEnd);
echo $NewEmail; // prints 'vice.president@whitehouse.gov'
```

The following code demonstrates how to use the `substr_replace()` function to replace text within a string. The code uses the `strpos()` and `strrpos()` functions to locate the starting and ending positions of President George W. Bush's middle name. The `substr_replace()` function then replaces the middle name with "Herbert Walker," the middle names of President Bush's father, former president George H.W. Bush.

```
$President43 = "George Walker Bush";
$MiddleNameStart = strpos($President43, " ") + 1;
$MiddleNameEnd = strrpos($President43, " ") - $MiddleNameStart;
$President41 = substr_replace($President43, "Herbert Walker",
     $MiddleNameStart, $MiddleNameEnd);
echo "<p>$President41 was the 41st president of the
     United States.</p>";
echo "<p>$President43 is the 43rd president of the
     United States.</p>";
```

Recall that multiple e-mail addresses that are sent to the `mail()` function must be separated by commas. However, the fact that the e-mail form instructs users to place multiple e-mail addresses in the To, CC, and BCC fields on separate lines results in carriage return and newline escape sequences (\r\n) between each address. Next, you use the `str_replace()` function to replace the carriage return and newline escape sequences with commas. You also add functionality that sends CC and BCC headers to the `mail()` function.

To use the `str_replace()` function to replace the carriage return escape sequences with commas in the e-mail form:

1. Return to the **PHPEmail.php** script in your text editor.

2. Modify the statement that declares the `$To` variable so it includes an `str_replace()` function that replaces the carriage return and newline escape sequences with commas, as follows:

```
$To = str_replace("\r\n", ",", $_GET['to']);
```

3. Add the following variable declarations for the CC and BCC e-mail addresses:

```
$CC = str_replace("\r\n", ",", $_GET['cc']);
$BCC = str_replace("\r\n", ",", $_GET['bcc']);
```

4. Immediately after the statement that first declares the `$Headers` variable, add the following statements, which add the CC and BCC headers to the `$Headers` variable:

```
$Headers .= "CC: $CC\r\n";
$Headers .= "BCC: $BCC\r\n";
```

5. Modify the nested `if` statement so it also includes the following statements that print the CC and BCC e-mail addresses:

```
if ($MessageSent) {
     echo "<p>The following message was sent successfully:</p>";
     echo "<p><strong>From</strong>: $From</p>";
     echo "<p><strong>To</strong>: $To</p>";
     echo "<p><strong>CC</strong>: $CC</p>";
     echo "<p><strong>BCC</strong>: $BCC</p>";
...
```

6. Save the **PHPEmail.php** file and then open the **PHPEmail.html** file in your Web browser by entering the following URL: **http://localhost/PHP_Projects/Chapter.05/Chapter/PHPEmail.html**. Enter values in each of the fields. Be sure to enter multiple e-mail addresses in the To, CC, and BCC fields. Click the **Send** button and you should see "The following message was sent successfully:", along with the contents of the message, printed to your Web browser window.

7. Close your Web browser window.

Dividing Strings into Smaller Pieces

If you receive a text string that contains multiple data separated by the same character, you will probably want to split the string into smaller pieces that are easier to work with. For example, you may receive a list of names, separated by commas. Although you could use some of the string functions you've seen so far to manually parse such a string into smaller pieces, you can save yourself a lot of work by using the `strtok()` function to break a string into smaller strings, called **tokens**. When it is first called, the syntax for the `strtok()` function is `$variable = strtok(string, separators);`. The `strtok()` function assigns to `$variable` the token (substring) from the beginning of the string to the first separator. To assign the next token to *$variable*, you call the `strtok()` function again, but only pass to it a single argument containing the separator. The PHP scripting engine keeps track of the current token and assigns the next token to *$variable* each time the *strtok()* function is called until the end of the string is reached.

If you specify an empty string as the second argument of the `strtok()` function, or if the string does not contain any of the separators you specify, the `strtok()` function returns the entire string.

The first statement in the following code assigns the names of the past five American presidents to the `$Presidents` variable, separated by semicolons. The first `strtok()` function assigns the first token ("George W. Bush") to the `$President` variable. The `while` statement then prints the token and assigns the next token to the `$President` variable. The `while` loop iterates through the tokens until the `$President` variable is equal to NULL. Figure 5-4 shows the output.

```
$Presidents = "George W. Bush;William Clinton;George H.W.
Bush;Ronald Reagan;Jimmy Carter";
$President = strtok($Presidents, ";");
while ($President != NULL) {
     echo "$President<br />";
     $President = strtok(";");
}
```

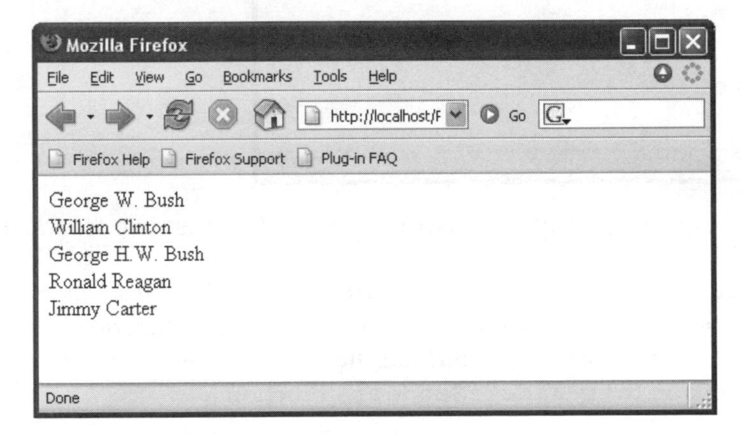

Figure 5-4 Output of a script that uses the `strtok()` function

The `strtok()` function does not divide a string into tokens by using a substring that is passed as its second argument. Instead, it divides a string into tokens using any of the characters that are passed. For example, if you include a semicolon and a space ("; ") in the second argument for the `strtok()` function, the string is split into tokens at each semicolon and space in the string. The following example contains a modified version of the preceding code. In this version, the *separator* arguments passed to the `strtok()` functions contain a semicolon and a space. For this reason, the string is split into tokens at each semicolon and individual space in the `$Presidents` variable, as shown in Figure 5-5.

```
$Presidents = "George W. Bush;William Clinton;George H.W.
Bush;Ronald Reagan;Jimmy Carter";
$President = strtok($Presidents, "; ");
while ($President != NULL) {
     echo "$President<br />";
     $President = strtok("; ");
}
```

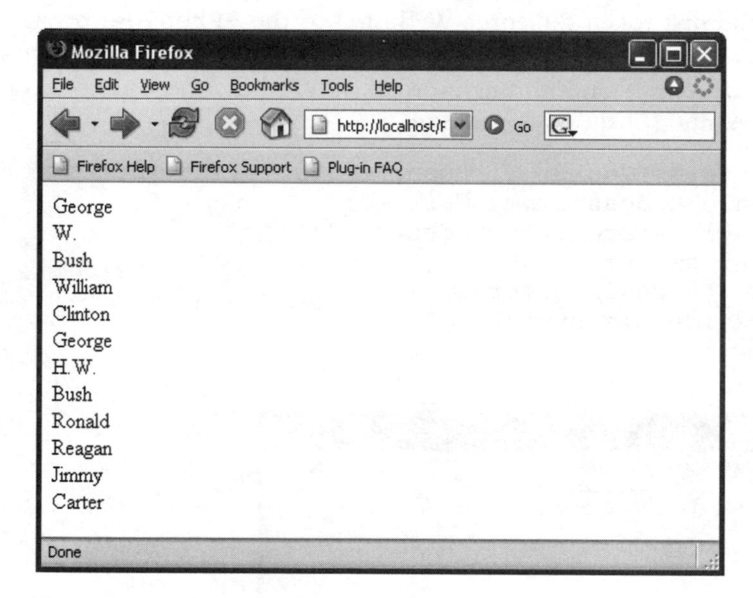

Figure 5-5 Output of a script with a `strtok()` function that uses two separators

Next, you add code to the e-mail script that validates each of the e-mail addresses in the To, CC, and BCC fields. The value from each field is passed to a function where it will be tokenized with the `strtok()` function, and then validated with code that is similar to the validation code in the `validateSender()` function.

To validate the e-mail addresses in the To, CC, and BCC fields:

1. Return to the **PHPEmail.php** script in your text editor.
2. Immediately after the `validateSender()` function, add the following function, which validates the values passed to the `$Addresses` variable. The function contains similar code to the validation code in the `validateSender()` function. However, this version tokenizes each string before performing the validation.

```
function validateRecipients($Addresses) {
     $Address = strtok($Addresses, ",");
     while ($Address != NULL) {
          $RetValue = true;
          if (strpos($Address, '@') !== FALSE
               && strpos($Address, '.') !== FALSE)
               $RetValue = true;
          else {
               $RetValue = false;
               break;
          }
          $Address = strtok(",");
     }
     return $RetValue;
}
```

3. Add the following `else...if` clauses immediately above the `else` statement in the main `if...else` statement. Each clause calls the `validateRecipients()` function and passes to the function the variable containing the To, CC, or BCC e-mail addresses.

```
else if (validateRecipients($To) == false)
     echo "<p>One or more of the \"To\" e-mail addresses does not
appear to be valid.  Click your browser's Back button to return
to the message.</p>";
else if (validateRecipients($CC) == false)
     echo "<p>One or more of the \"CC\" e-mail addresses does not
appear to be valid.  Click your browser's Back button to return
to the message.</p>";
else if (validateRecipients($BCC) == false)
     echo "<p>One or more of the \"BCC\" e-mail addresses does not
appear to be valid.  Click your browser's Back button to return
to the message.</p>";
```

4. Save the **PHPEmail.php** file and then open the **PHPEmail.html** file in your Web browser by entering the following URL: **http://localhost/PHP_Projects/Chapter.05/Chapter/PHPEmail.html**. Enter multiple e-mail addresses in the To, CC, and BCC fields, but be sure to enter some invalid e-mail addresses. Click the **Send** button. You should see a message informing you that the e-mail addresses are invalid.

5. Click your browser's **Back** button, fix the invalid e-mail addresses, and then click the **Send** button. The Web browser displays "The following message was sent successfully." You should also see the contents of the message.

6. Close your Web browser window.

Converting Between Strings and Arrays

In addition to splitting a string into tokens, you can also split a string into an array, in which each array element contains a portion of the string. In most cases, you will probably find it more useful to split a string into an array instead of tokens because you have more control over each array element. With strings that are split with the `strtok()` function, you can only work with a substring if it is the current token. Although tokenizing a string is useful if you want to quickly print or iterate through the tokens in a string, if you want to modify the tokens in any way, you need to assign them to another variable or array. By contrast, when you split a string into an array, portions of the string are automatically assigned to elements.

You use the `str_split()` or `explode()` function to split a string into an indexed array. The `str_split()` function splits each character in a string into an array element, using the syntax `$array = str_split(string[, length]);`. The *`length`* argument represents the number of characters you want assigned to each array element. The `explode()` function splits a string into an indexed array at a specified separator. The syntax for the `explode()` function is `$array = explode(separators, string);`. Be sure to notice that the order of the arguments for the `explode()` function is the reverse of the arguments for the `strtok()` function. The following code demonstrates how to split the `$Presidents` string into an array named `$PresidentArray`:

```
$Presidents = "George W. Bush;William Clinton;George H.W.
Bush;Ronald Reagan;Jimmy Carter";
$PresidentArray = explode(";", $Presidents);
foreach ($PresidentArray as $President) {
     echo "$President<br />";
}
```

If the string does not contain the specified separators, the entire string is assigned to the first element of the array. Also, unlike the `strtok()` function, the `explode()` function does not separate a string at each character that is included in the *separator* argument. Instead, the `explode()` function evaluates the characters in the *separator* argument as a substring. For example, a semicolon and a space separate each president's name in the following example. Therefore, the `explode()` function includes a semicolon and a space as the *separator* argument.

```
$Presidents = "George W. Bush; William Clinton; George H.W.
 Bush; Ronald Reagan; Jimmy Carter";
$PresidentArray = explode("; ", $Presidents);
foreach ($PresidentArray as $President) {
     echo "$President<br />";
}
```

If you pass to the `explode()` function an empty string as the *separator* argument, the function returns a value of false.

The opposite of the `explode()` function is the `implode()` function, which combines an array's elements into a single string, separated by specified characters. The syntax for the `implode()` function is `$variable = implode(separators, array);`. The following example first creates an array named `$PresidentsArray`, then uses the `implode()` function to combine the array elements into the `$Presidents` variable, separated by a comma and a space. Figure 5-6 shows the output.

```
$PresidentsArray = array("George W. Bush", "William Clinton",
"George H.W. Bush", "Ronald Reagan", "Jimmy Carter");
$Presidents = implode(", ", $PresidentsArray);
echo $Presidents;
```


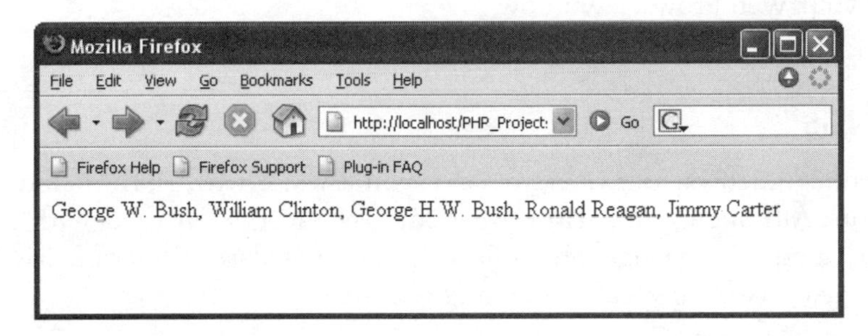

Figure 5-6 Output of a string created with the `implode()` function

Next, you modify the `validateRecipients()` function so the strings are split into arrays instead of tokens.

To modify the `validateRecipients()` function so the strings are split into arrays instead of tokens:

1. Return to the **PHPEmail.php** script in your text editor.
2. Modify the `validateRecipients()` function as follows:

```
function validateRecipients($Addresses) {
     $Address = explode(",", $Addresses);
     $RetValue = true;
     foreach ($Address as $Email) {
          if (strpos($Email, '@') !== FALSE && strpos($Email,
               '.') !== FALSE)
               $RetValue = true;
          else {
               $RetValue = false;
               break;
          }
     }
     return $RetValue;
}
```

3. Save the **PHPEmail.php** file and then open the **PHPEmail.html** file in your Web browser by entering the following URL: **http://localhost/PHP_Projects/Chapter.05/Chapter/PHPEmail.html**. Enter multiple e-mail addresses in the To, CC, and BCC fields, but be sure to enter some invalid e-mail addresses. Click the **Send** button. You see a message explaining that the e-mail addresses are invalid.
4. Click your browser's **Back** button, fix the invalid e-mail addresses, and then click the **Send** button. Your browser displays "The following message was sent successfully:" You should also see the contents of the message printed to your Web browser window.
5. Close your Web browser window.

COMPARING STRINGS

In Chapter 3, you studied various operators that you can use with PHP, including comparison operators. Although comparison operators are most often used with numbers, they can also be used with strings. The following statement uses the comparison operator (==) to compare two variables containing text strings:

```
$Florida = "Miami is in Florida.";
$Cuba = "Havana is in Cuba.";
if ($Florida == $Cuba)
     echo "<p>Same location.</p>";
else
     echo "<p>Different location.</p>";
```

Because the text strings are not the same, the `else` clause prints the text "Different locations." You can also use comparison operators to determine whether one letter is higher in the alphabet than another letter. In the following code, the first `echo()` statement executes because the letter "B" is higher in the alphabet than the letter "A":

```
$FirstLetter = "A";
$SecondLetter = "B";
if ($SecondLetter > $FirstLetter)
     echo "<p>The second letter is higher in the alphabet than
the first letter.</p>";
else
     echo "<p>The second letter is lower in the alphabet than
the first letter.</p>";
```

The comparison operators actually compare individual characters according to their position in **American Standard Code for Information Interchange**, or **ASCII**, which are numeric representations of English characters. ASCII values range from 0 to 256. Lowercase letters are represented by the values 97 ("a") to 122 ("z"). Uppercase letters are represented by the values 65 ("A") to 90 ("Z"). Because lowercase letters have higher values than uppercase letters, the lowercase letters are evaluated as being "greater" than the uppercase letters. For example, an uppercase letter "A" is represented by ASCII value 65, whereas a lowercase letter "a" is represented by ASCII value 96. For this reason, the statement `"a" > "A"` returns a value of true because the uppercase letter "A" has a lower ASCII value than the lowercase letter "a."

Next, you modify the e-mail script so it uses comparison operators to determine if the To, CC, and BCC fields contain duplicate e-mail addresses.

To modify the e-mail script so it uses comparison operators to determine if the To, CC, and BCC fields contain duplicate e-mail addresses:

5

1. Return to the **PHPEmail.php** script in your text editor.
2. Add the following function immediately after the `validateRecipients()` function. The function uses a nested `while` statement to check whether each element in the `$Address[]` array is a duplicate of another element. The conditional expression in the `if` statement uses the comparison operator to compare each array element. Notice that the conditional expression also checks to ensure that the `$i` variable is not equal to the `$j` variable. This prevents each array element from being compared to itself.

```
function checkForDuplicates($Addresses) {
     $Address = explode(",", $Addresses);
     $Count = count($Address);
     $RetValue = false;
     $i = 0;
     while ($i<$Count) {
          $j = 0;
          while ($j<$Count) {
               if ($Address[$i] == $Address[$j] && $i != $j)
                    $RetValue = true;
               ++$j;
          }
          ++$i;
     }
     return $RetValue;
}
```

3. Add the following `else...if` clauses immediately above the `else` statement in the main `if...else` statement. Each clause calls the `checkForDuplicates()` function and passes to the function the variable containing the To, CC, or BCC e-mail addresses.

```
else if (checkForDuplicates($To) == true)
     echo "<p>The \"To\" e-mail addresses contain duplicates.  Click
your browser's Back button to return to the message.</p>";
else if (checkForDuplicates($CC) == true)
     echo "<p>The \"CC\" e-mail addresses contain duplicates.  Click
your browser's Back button to return to the message.</p>";
else if (checkForDuplicates($BCC) == true)
     echo "<p>The \"BCC\" e-mail addresses contain duplicates.
Click your browser's Back button to return to the message</p>.";
```

4. Save the **PHPEmail.php** file and then open the **PHPEmail.html** file in your Web browser by entering the following URL: **http://localhost/PHP_Projects/Chapter.05/Chapter/PHPEmail.html**. Enter multiple e-mail addresses in the To, CC, and BCC fields, and be sure to duplicate some addresses. Click the **Send** button. You see a message explaining that the e-mail addresses contain duplicates.

Be sure to separate multiple e-mail addresses in the To, CC, and BCC fields with line breaks.

5. Click your browser's **Back** button, remove the duplicate e-mail addresses, and then click the **Send** button. You should see "The following message was sent successfully:", along with the contents of the message, printed to your Web browser window.
6. Close your Web browser window.

In Chapter 7, you learn how to use the `array_unique()` function to remove duplicate elements from an array.

In the next few sections, you study additional functions that you can use to compare strings in PHP.

String Comparison Functions

In addition to the comparison operators, you can also use the functions listed in Table 5-5 to compare strings in PHP.

Table 5-5 PHP string comparison functions

Function	Description
`strcasecmp(string1, string2)`	Performs a case-insensitive comparison of two strings
`strcmp(string1, string2)`	Performs a case-sensitive comparison of two strings
`strnatcasecmp(string1, string2)`	Performs a case-insensitive natural order comparison of two strings, so that, for example, a set a strings would be ordered as Purchase1, Purchase2, Purchase3, Purchase4, Purchase5, Purchase6, Purchase7, Purchase8, Purchase9, Purchase10, Purchase11 (the way a human would naturally sort them), and not as Purchase1, Purchase10, Purchase11, Purchase2, Purchase3, Purchase4, Purchase5, Purchase6, Purchase7, Purchase8, Purchase9 (the way a computer would otherwise normally sort them)

Table 5-5 PHP string comparison functions (continued)

Function	Description
`strnatcmp(string1, string2)`	Performs a case-sensitive natural order comparison of two strings
`strncasecmp(string1, string2, length)`	Performs a case-insensitive comparison of a specified number of characters within two strings
`strncmp(string1, string2, length)`	Performs a case-sensitive comparison of a specified number of characters within two strings
`levenshtein(string1, string2,)`	Returns the number of characters you need to change to make two strings the same
`metaphone(string)`	Determines a string's value as calculated by metaphone, which is an algorithm for indexing words by their sound, when pronounced in English
`similar_text(string1, string2[, float_percent])`	Returns the number of characters that two strings have in common
`soundex()`	Determines a string's value as calculated by soundex, which is an algorithm for indexing words by their sound, when pronounced in English

The comparison functions you will probably use the most are **`strcasecmp()`** and **`strcmp()`**. The only difference between these two functions is that the **`strcasecmp()`** function performs a case-insensitive comparison of strings, whereas the **`strcmp()`** function performs a case-sensitive comparison of strings. Both functions accept two arguments representing the strings you want to compare. It's important to understand that most of the string comparison functions compare strings based on their ASCII values. If the combined ASCII values in the first string argument are less than the combined ASCII values in the second string argument, the functions return a value less than 0, usually -1. However, if the combined ASCII values in the second string argument are greater than the combined ASCII values in the first string argument, the functions return a value greater than 0, usually 1. For example, consider the following **`strcmp()`** function, which compares the strings "Dan" and "Don." Because the "a" in "Dan" has a lower ASCII value than the "o" in "Don," the function returns a value of -1.

```
strcmp("Dan", "Don"); // returns -1
```

In comparison, the following statement, which switches the "Dan" and "Don" arguments, returns a value of 1:

```
strcmp("Don", "Dan"); // returns 1
```

If both string values are equal, the **`strcmp()`** function returns a value of 0, as in the following example:

```
strcmp("Don", "Don"); // returns 0
```

Keep in mind that the `strcmp()` function performs a case-sensitive comparison of two strings. The following statement returns a value of -1 because the uppercase "D" in the first string has a lower ASCII value than the lowercase "d" in the second string:

```
strcmp("Don", "don"); // returns -1
```

To perform a case-insensitive comparison of two strings, use the `strcasecmp()` function, which converts the text in both strings to lowercase before they are compared. The following statement returns a value of 0 because it uses the case-insensitive `strcasecmp()` function:

```
strcasecmp("Don", "don"); // returns 0
```

The `strncmp()` and `strncasecmp()` functions are very similar to the `strcmp()` and `strcasecmp()` functions, except you can pass a third integer argument representing the number of characters you want to compare in the strings. The following code uses the `strncmp()` function to compare the first three letters in two text strings:

```
$FirstCity = "San Diego";
$SecondCity = "San Jose";
if (strncmp($FirstCity, $SecondCity, 3) == 0)
    echo "<p>Both cities begin with 'San'.</p>";
```

Next, you modify the `checkForDuplicates()` function so it uses the `strcasecmp()` function instead of comparison operators to check for duplicate e-mail addresses in the e-mail script.

To modify the `checkForDuplicates()` function so it uses the `strcasecmp()` function instead of comparison operators to check for duplicate e-mail addresses in the e-mail script:

1. Return to the **PHPEmail.php** script in your text editor.
2. Modify the conditional expression in the `if` statement within the `checkForDuplicates()` function so it uses the `strcasecmp()` function instead of the comparison operator, as follows:

   ```
   if (strcasecmp($Address[$i], $Address[$j]) == 0 && $i != $j)
   ```

3. Save the **PHPEmail.php** file and then open the **PHPEmail.html** file in your Web browser by entering the following URL: **http://localhost/PHP_Projects/Chapter.05/Chapter/PHPEmail.html**. Enter multiple e-mail addresses in the To, CC, and BCC fields, and be sure to duplicate some addresses. Click the **Send** button. You see a message explaining that the e-mail addresses contain duplicates.
4. Click your browser's **Back** button, remove the duplicate e-mail addresses, and then click the **Send** button. Your Web browser displays "The following message was sent successfully:" You also see the contents of the message printed to your Web browser window.
5. Close your Web browser window.

Determining the Similarity of Two Strings

The `similar_text()` and `levenshtein()` functions are used to determine the similarity between two strings. The `similar_text()` function returns the number of characters that two strings have in common, whereas the `levenshtein()` function returns the number of characters you need to change for two strings to be the same. Both functions accept two string arguments representing the values you want to compare. The following code demonstrates how to use the `similar_text()` and `levenshtein()` functions with the names "Don" and "Dan." Figure 5-7 shows the output.


```
$FirstName = "Don";
$SecondName = "Dan";
echo "<p>The names \"$FirstName\" and \"$SecondName\" have " .
similar_text($FirstName, $SecondName) . " characters in
common.</p>";
echo "<p>You must change " . levenshtein($FirstName, $SecondName)
. " character(s) to make the names \"$FirstName\" and
\"$SecondName\" the same.</p>";
```

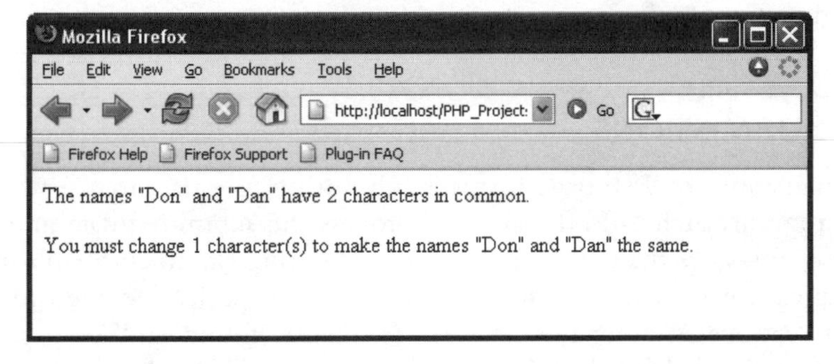

Figure 5-7 Output of a script with the `similar_text()` and `levenshtein()` functions

Determining if Words Are Pronounced Similarly

You can use the `soundex()` and `metaphone()` functions to determine whether two strings are pronounced similarly. Both functions return a value representing how words sound. The `soundex()` function returns a value representing a name's phonetic equivalent, whereas the `metaphone()` function returns a code representing an English word's approximate sound. For example, consider the last name of the author of this book, Gosselin. The `soundex()` function returns a value of "G245" for this string, whereas the `metaphone()` function returns a value of "KSLN." The following code uses the `metaphone()` function to compare the name with an alternative spelling, "Gauselin":

```
$FirstName = "Gosselin";
$SecondName = "Gauselin";
$FirstNameSoundsLike = metaphone($FirstName);
$SecondNameSoundsLike = metaphone($SecondName);
```

```
if ($FirstNameSoundsLike == $SecondNameSoundsLike)
     echo "<p>The names are pronounced the same.</p>";
else
     echo "<p>The names are not pronounced the same.</p>";
```

Because both versions of the name are pronounced the same way, the preceding code prints "The names are pronounced the same."

Although they perform the same type of function, the `soundex()` and `metaphone()` functions cannot be used with each other because they represent words with different kinds of values. To compare the name with the alternative spelling of "Gauselin," you must compare the values returned from two `soundex()` functions, as follows:

```
$FirstName = "Gosselin";
$SecondName = "Gauselin";
$FirstNameSoundsLike = soundex($FirstName);
$SecondNameSoundsLike = soundex($SecondName);
if ($FirstNameSoundsLike == $SecondNameSoundsLike)
     echo "<p>The names are pronounced the same.</p>";
else
     echo "<p>The names are not pronounced the same.</p>";
```

Handling Form Submissions

One of the primary jobs of Web page forms is submitting user data to a server. Server-side scripting programs such as PHP can then process the submitted data and return a response to the client, store the data in a database, or use the data to perform some other type of task. Typical forms that you submit to a server-side script include order forms, surveys, and applications. Another type of form frequently found on Web pages gathers search criteria from a user. After the user enters search criteria, the data is sent to a database on a Web server. The server then queries the database, using the data gathered in the search form, and returns the results to a Web browser. The data that a PHP script receives from a form submission usually takes the form of a text string assigned to the `$_GET` and `$_POST` autoglobals, which you can process with PHP string functions and manipulation techniques.

JavaScript is often used with forms to validate or process form data before the data is submitted to a server-side script. For example, customers may use an online order form to order merchandise from your Web site. When a customer clicks the form's Submit button, you can use JavaScript to ensure that the customer has entered important information, such as his name, shipping address, and so on. The problem with using JavaScript to validate form data is that you cannot always ensure that the data submitted to your PHP script was submitted from the Web page containing the JavaScript validation code. Every self-respecting hacker knows how to bypass JavaScript validation code in an HTML form by appending a query string directly to the URL of the PHP script that processes the form. To understand how this works, you need to understand the concept of a **query string**, which is a set of name=value pairs appended to a target URL. When you submit a form to a Web server, the form data is submitted in name=value pairs, based on the `name` and `value` attributes of each element. A question mark (`?`) and a query string are automatically appended to the URL of a server-side script for any forms that are submitted with the `GET` method. Each name=value pair within the query string is separated with ampersands (`&`). For example, consider the following simple form containing two text `<input>` fields:

```
<form method="get" action="ProcessOrder.php">
<input type="text" name="favorite_books" value="technical" />
<input type="text" name="favorite_author" value="Gosselin" />
</form>
```


For the preceding form, a query string is appended to the ProcessOrder.php URL as follows:

```
ProcessOrder.php?favorite_books=technical&favorite_author=Gosselin
```

As you can see then, instead of submitting data through a form, any user can simply type the ProcessOrder.php URL and a query string in the Address box of a Web browser. If a user does bypass the form and type the ProcessOrder.php URL and a query string in the Address box of a Web browser, any JavaScript validation code in the Web page containing the form does not execute. Because JavaScript validation code can be bypassed in this way, you should always include PHP code to validate any submitted data. If your PHP script lacks such code, you cannot be sure that all of the necessary data was submitted (such as a shipping address for an online order) nor can you tell if an unscrupulous hacker is attempting to submit malicious data that may cause problems in your script or on your Web site.

Recall that the `POST` method sends form data as a transmission separate from the URL specified by the `action` attribute. However, don't think that you can force users to submit form data from a Web page by specifying the `POST` method. Anyone who has a strong understanding of HTTP headers can construct a separate transmission containing the form data required by your script.

In the next section, you learn how to use a single script to display and process a form. This technique helps force users to submit data from a form instead of trying to call a PHP script directly.

Using a Single Script to Display and Process a Form

If you have a large form with many fields, or if your form requires intensive processing, you are usually better off using a separate HTML document and PHP script. However, for simple forms that require only a minimal amount of processing, it's often easier to use a single script to display the form and process its data. When the user clicks the Submit button, the script submits the form data to itself. You then use validation code to ensure that the data exists when the form first opens and to ensure that the data was submitted correctly. For example, the following code contains a simple script and form that calculates body mass index with the formula `weight ÷ (height x height) x 703`:

```
<h1>Body Mass Index</h1><hr />
<?php
$BodyMass = $_GET['weight'] / ($_GET['height']
     * $_GET['height']) * 703;
printf("<p>Your body mass index is %d.</p>", $BodyMass);
?>
<form action="BodyMassIndex.php" method="get"
enctype="application/x-www-form-urlencoded">
<p>Height: <input type="text" name="height" size="30"
value="<?php echo $_GET['height'] ?>" /> (Enter a height in
inches)</p>
<p>Weight: <input type="text" name="weight" size="30"
value="<?php echo $_GET['weight'] ?>" />  (Enter a weight in
pounds)</p>
<p><input type="submit" value="Calculate" />
<input type="reset" value="Reset Form" /></p>
</form><hr />
```

Notice that the PHP code in the preceding example refers to the `$_GET['height']` and `$_GET['weight']` autoglobals. However, when you first open the document, it generates errors because values have not been assigned to either variable. In the next section, you learn how to validate variables to ensure they contain data.

Validating Submitted Data

You can validate data that is submitted from a form to a PHP script in essentially two ways:

- Use the `isset()` or `empty()` functions to ensure that a variable contains a value.
- Use the `is_numeric()` function to test whether a variable contains a numeric string.

Determining if Form Variables Contain Values

Both the `isset()` function and the `empty()` function can be used to determine if form variables contain values, but they do this in different ways. The `isset()` function determines whether a variable has been declared and initialized (or "set"), whereas the `empty()` function determines whether a variable is empty. You pass to both functions the name of the variable you want to check.

The following example contains a modified version of the script you saw in the previous section. The first script section uses the `isset()` function to determine whether the `$_GET['height']` and `$_GET['weight']` variables are set. If both variables are set, the script performs the body mass index calculation. In the form section of the example, `if` statements use the `empty()` function to determine whether the variables are empty. If they are not empty, their values are displayed in the text boxes. If the variables are empty, only the form displays.

```
<h1>Body Mass Index</h1><hr />
<?php
if (isset($_GET['height']) && isset($_GET['weight'])) {
     $BodyMass = $_GET['weight'] / ($_GET['height']
          * $_GET['height']) * 703;
     printf("<p>Your body mass index is %d.</p>", $BodyMass);
}
?>
<form action="BodyMassIndex.php" method="get"
enctype="application/x-www-form-urlencoded">
<p>Height: <input type="text" name="height" size="30"
value="<?php if (!empty($_GET['height'])) echo $_GET['height']
?>" /> (Enter a height in inches)</p>
<p>Weight: <input type="text" name="weight" size="30"
value="<?php if (!empty($_GET['weight'])) echo $_GET['weight']
?>" /> (Enter a weight in pounds)</p>
<p><input type="submit" value="Calculate" />
<input type="reset" value="Reset Form" /></p>
</form><hr />
```

Next, you add `empty()` functions to the e-mail script to prevent the form from being submitted if the Sender Name, Sender E-Mail, To, Subject, or Message fields are empty. You also add `isset()` functions to the statements that validate the CC and BCC fields to prevent them from being validated if they do not contain data.

To add `empty()` and `isset()` functions to the e-mail script:

1. Return to the **PHPEmail.php** script in your text editor.
2. Replace the `if` statement that checks whether the subject line is greater than 40 characters with the following:

   ```
   if (empty($_GET['sender_name']) || empty($_GET['sender_email'])
   || empty($_GET['to']) || empty($_GET['subject']) ||
   empty($_GET['message']))
        echo "<p>You must enter values in the Sender Name, Sender
   E-Mail, To, Subject, and Message fields.</p>";
   ```

3. Now, you need to modify the statements that validate the CC and BCC fields so they are not called unless they are set. To accomplish this, add `isset()` functions to the `else...if` statements, as follows:

   ```
   else if (isset($GET['cc']) && validateRecipients($CC) == false)
   echo "<p>One or more of the \"CC\" e-mail addresses does not
   appear to be valid.  Click your browser's Back button to return
   to the message.</p>";
   ```

```
else if (isset($GET['bcc']) && validateRecipients($BCC) == false)
echo "<p>One or more of the \"BCC\" e-mail addresses does not
appear to be valid.  Click your browser's Back button to return
to the message.</p>";
```

4. Save the **PHPEmail.php** file and then open the **PHPEmail.html** file in your Web browser by entering the following URL: **http://localhost/PHP_Projects/Chapter.05/Chapter/PHPEmail.html**. Test the new code to see if it prevents you from submitting the form if you do not fill in the required fields.
5. Close your Web browser window and text editor.

Testing if Form Variables Contain Numeric Values

Even though the data that a PHP script receives from a form submission is usually in the form of a text string, the PHP scripting engine can usually perform the necessary type casting. This means that you do not need to explicitly convert form data to a specific data type. This is especially important when your script expects a numeric value that will be used in a calculation. For example, with the Body Mass Index script, PHP converts any numbers that are submitted from the form to a numeric format. However, you cannot be sure that a user will always enter a number into each text box. If a submitted form value must be numeric data, you should use an `is_numeric()` function to test the variable. The following example contains a modified version of the first script section from the previous example. This version contains a nested `if` statement that tests whether the `$_GET['height']` and `$_GET['weight']` variables are numeric after the first `if` statement checks to see whether they are set.

```
if (isset($_GET['height']) && isset($_GET['weight'])) {
     if (is_numeric($_GET['weight']) && is_numeric($_GET['height'])) {
          $BodyMass = $_GET['weight'] / ($_GET['height']
               * $_GET['height']) * 703;
          printf("<p>Your body mass index is %d.</p>",
                    $BodyMass);
     }
     else
          echo "<p>You must enter numeric values!</p>";
}
```

You cannot use any other `is_*()` functions to test the data type of a form variable. If you want to ensure that a form variable is of a specific numeric data type, such as an integer, you should first use the `is_numeric()` function to test whether the variable is numeric, then cast the variable to the required data type.

Chapter Summary

- The concatenation operator (`.`) and the concatenation assignment operator (`.=`) can be used to combine two strings.
- An escape character tells the compiler or interpreter that the character following the escape character has a special purpose. An escape character combined with one or more other characters is called an escape sequence.
- Simple string syntax allows you to use the value of a variable within a string by including the variable name inside a text string with double quotation marks.
- The type of structure in which variables are placed within curly braces inside of a string is called complex string syntax.
- When applied to text strings, the term "parsing" refers to the act of extracting characters or substrings from a larger string.
- The most commonly used string counting function is the `strlen()` function, which returns the total number of characters in a string.
- There are two types of string search and extraction functions: functions that return a numeric position in a text string and functions that return a character or substring.
- You use the `str_replace()`, `str_ireplace()`, and `substr_replace()` functions to replace text in strings.
- The `strtok()` function breaks a string into smaller strings, called tokens.
- You use the `str_split()` or `explode()` function to split a string into an indexed array, in which each character in the string becomes a separate element in the array.
- The `implode()` function combines an array's elements into a single string, separated by specified characters.
- The `strcasecmp()` function performs a case-insensitive comparison of strings, whereas the `strcmp()` function performs a case-sensitive comparison of strings.
- The `similar_text()` and `levenshtein()` functions are used to determine the similarity of two strings.
- You can use the `soundex()` and `metaphone()` functions to determine whether two strings are pronounced similarly.
- You should always include PHP code to validate any submitted data.
- Use the `isset()` or `empty()` functions to ensure that a variable contains a value.
- Use the `is_numeric()` function to test whether a variable contains a numeric string.
- If a submitted form value must be numeric data, use an `is_numeric()` function to test the variable.

REVIEW QUESTIONS

1. Which of the following function statements is invalid?
   a. echo "<p>Welcome to the *combat zone*!</p>";
   b. echo '<p>Welcome to the "combat zone"!</p>';
   c. echo "<p>Welcome to the 'combat zone'!</p>";
   d. echo '<p>Welcome to the 'combat zone'!</p>';
2. Which of the following operators can be used with strings? (Choose all that apply.)
   a. .
   b. ==
   c. .=
   d. +=
3. Explain why you need to use escape characters in strings.
4. What is the escape sequence for a single quotation mark?
   a. \\
   b. \'
   c. \~
   d. There is no escape sequence for a single quotation mark.
5. Which of the following character sets do you use for complex string syntax?
   a. {}
   b. []
   c. ()
   d. // //
6. Explain why you need to use complex string syntax. Be sure to include an example.
7. If you include an autoglobal variable within a text string, you need to use complex string syntax. True or False?
8. Which of the following functions returns the number of occurrences of a substring?
   a. strlen()
   b. strspn()
   c. substr_count()
   d. strcspn()

9. Which of the following functions performs a case-sensitive search for specified characters in a string and returns a substring from the first occurrence of the specified characters to the end of the string? (Choose all that apply.)
   a. `substr()`
   b. `strstr()`
   c. `strrchr()`
   d. `strpos()`
10. Explain the difference between the two types of extraction functions.

11. Explain how to determine whether the `strpos()` function (and other string functions) actually returns a Boolean value false and not a 0 representing the first character in a string.
12. Which of the following functions allows you to replace characters within a specified portion of a string?
    a. `str_ireplace()`
    b. `str_replace()`
    c. `substr_replace()`
    d. `strstr()`
13. Explain how to use the `strok()` function to break a string into tokens, and then navigate through each token.
14. If you specify an empty string as the second argument of the `strtok()` function, or if the string does not contain any of the separators you specify, the `strtok()` function returns a value of false. True or False?
15. Which of the following functions splits each character in a string into an array element?
    a. `str_split()`
    b. `split()`
    c. `explode()`
    d. `implode()`
16. String comparison operators and most string comparison functions compare individual characters according to their ASCII position. True or False?
17. Which of the following functions returns the number of characters you need to change for two strings to be the same?
    a. `similar_text()`
    b. `levenshtein()`
    c. `soundex()`
    d. `metaphone()`

18. You should always rely on JavaScript code to perform data validation. True or False?
19. Explain how to use a single script to display and process a form.
20. If you want to ensure that a form variable is of a specific numeric data type, such as an integer, you should first use the `is_numeric()` function to test whether the variable is numeric, then cast the variable to the required data type. True or False?

HANDS-ON PROJECTS

Hands-On Project 5-1

In this project, you create a script that converts cardinal numbers to ordinal numbers. For example, the script should be able to convert the cardinal number 23 to the ordinal number 23rd.

1. Create a new document in your text editor.
2. Type the `<!DOCTYPE>` declaration, `<html>` element, document head, and `<body>` element. Use the strict DTD and "Ordinal Numbers" as the content of the `<title>` element.
3. Add the following text and elements to the document body:

```
<h1>Ordinal Numbers</h1><hr />
```

4. Add the following script section to the document body:

```
<?php
?>
```

5. Add the following form to the end of the document body. Notice that the `<input>` element includes PHP code that fills in the value from the `$_GET['number']` autoglobal, if it exists.

```
<form action="OrdinalNumbers.php" method="get"
enctype="application/x-www-form-urlencoded">
<p><input type="text" name="number" size="20" value="<?php if
(!empty($_GET['number'])) echo $_GET['number'] ?>" /></p>
<p><input type="submit" value="Get Ordinal" />
</form><hr />
```

6. Add the following `if` and `if...else` statements to the script section. This code ensures that the user enters an integer and that it's not equal to 0.

```
if (!isset($_GET['number']))
     echo "<p>Enter an integer.</p>";
else if (!is_numeric($_GET['number']))
     echo "<p>You must enter an integer!</p>";
else if ($_GET['number'] == 0)
     echo "<p>0 is not an ordinal number!</p>";
```

7. Add the following `else` clause, which converts the cardinal number to an ordinal. The first nested `if` statement checks whether the number contains more than two digits. If it does, the first statement uses the `substr()` and `strlen()` functions to retrieve just the last two digits in the variable. The nested `if` prints the ordinal form for just the numbers 11 through 13 because numbers that end with these values use "th" in their ordinal form. The `else` clause then prints the ordinal form for all other numbers. The last `else...if` clause prints the ordinal form for the numbers 1 through 9. Notice that the `echo()` statements use complex string syntax to print the ordinal numbers.

```
else {
     if (strlen($_GET['number']) > 1) {
          $LastCharacters = substr($_GET['number'],
               strlen($_GET['number'])-2, 2);
          if ($LastCharacters > 10 && $LastCharacters < 14)
               echo "<p>{$_GET['number']}th</p>";
          else {
               $LastCharacter = substr($LastCharacters,
                    strlen($LastCharacters)-1, 1);
               if ($LastCharacter == 1)
                    echo "<p>{$_GET['number']}st</p>";
               else if ($LastCharacter == 2)
                    echo "<p>{$_GET['number']}nd</p>";
               else if ($LastCharacter ==3)
                    echo "<p>{$_GET['number']}rd</p>";
               else
                    echo "<p>{$_GET['number']}th</p>";
          }
     }
     else if (strlen($_GET['number']) == 1) {
          if ($_GET['number'] ==1)
               echo "<p>{$_GET['number']}st</p>";
          else if ($_GET['number'] ==2)
               echo "<p>{$_GET['number']}nd</p>";
          else if ($_GET['number'] ==3)
               echo "<p>{$_GET['number']}rd</p>";
          else
               echo "<p>{$_GET['number']}th</p>";
     }
}
```

8. Save the document as **OrdinalNumbers.php** in the Projects directory for Chapter 5.
9. Open **OrdinalNumbers.php** in your Web browser by entering the following URL: **http://localhost/PHP_Projects/Chapter.05/Projects/OrdinalNumbers.php**. Test the form to see if the correct ordinal number prints.
10. Close your Web browser window.

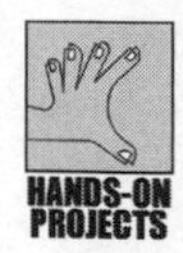

Hands-On Project 5-2

In this project, you create a script that validates whether a credit card number contains only integers. The script will remove dashes and spaces from the string. After the dashes and spaces are removed, the script should reject the credit card number if it contains any other nonnumeric characters.

1. Create a new document in your text editor.
2. Type the `<!DOCTYPE>` declaration, `<html>` element, document head, and `<body>` element. Use the strict DTD and "Validate Credit Card" as the content of the `<title>` element.
3. Add the following text and elements to the document body:

```
<h1>Validate Credit Card</h1><hr />
```

4. Add the following script section to the document body:

```
<?php
?>
```

5. Add the following form to the end of the document body. The `<input>` element includes PHP code that fills in the value from the `$_GET['ccnumber']` autoglobal, if it exists.

```
<form action="ValidateCreditCard.php" method="get"
enctype="application/x-www-form-urlencoded">
<p><input type="text" name="ccnumber" size="20" value="<?php if
(!empty($_GET['ccnumber'])) echo $_GET['ccnumber'] ?>" /></p>
<p><input type="submit" value="Validate Credit Card" />
</form><hr />
```

6. Add the following `if` statement to the script section to determine whether a value is assigned to the `$_GET['ccnumber']` autoglobal:

```
if (!isset($_GET['ccnumber']))
     echo "<p>Enter your credit card number.</p>";
```

7. Add the following `else` clause to validate the credit card number. The code uses `str_replace()` functions to remove any dashes and spaces in the number. Then, a nested `if...else` statement checks whether the new value is numeric. If the number is not numeric, a warning is printed. If the number is numeric, the modified credit card number is printed to the browser.

```
else {
     $Payment = $_GET['ccnumber'];
     $ValidPayment = str_replace("-", "", $Payment);
     $ValidPayment = str_replace(" ", "", $ValidPayment);
     if (!is_numeric($ValidPayment))
          echo "<p>You did not enter a valid credit card
               number!</p>";
     else
          echo "<p>Your credit card number is
               $ValidPayment.</p>";
}
```

8. Save the document as **ValidateCreditCard.php** in the Projects directory for Chapter 5.
9. Open **ValidateCreditCard.php** in your Web browser by entering the following URL: **http://localhost/PHP_Projects/Chapter.05/Projects/ValidateCreditCard.php**. Test the form to see if it correctly strips dashes and spaces from the numbers you enter. Also check whether the form only allows you to enter numeric values.
10. Close your Web browser window.

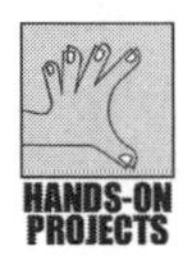

Hands-On Project 5-3

In this project, you create a script that takes a string entered by a user and prints it backward using the strrev() function. You pass to the strrev() function a single argument containing the string you want to reverse. The function then returns the reverse string value, which you can print or use in your code.

1. Create a new document in your text editor.
2. Type the <!DOCTYPE> declaration, <html> element, document head, and <body> element. Use the strict DTD and "Reverse String" as the content of the <title> element.
3. Add the following text and elements to the document body:

```
<h1>Reverse String</h1><hr />
```

4. Add the following script section to the document body:

```
<?php
?>
```

5. Add the following form to the end of the document body. The <input> element includes PHP code that fills in the value from the $_GET['input_text'] autoglobal, if it exists.

```
<form action="ReverseString.php" method="get"
enctype="application/x-www-form-urlencoded">
<p><input type="text" name="input_text" size="20" value="<?php if
(!empty($_GET['input_text'])) echo $_GET['input_text'] ?>" /></p>
<p><input type="submit" value="Reverse String" />
</form><hr />
```

6. Add the following if statement to the script section to determine whether a value is assigned to the $_GET['input_string] autoglobal:

```
if (!isset($_GET['input_text']))
     echo "<p>Enter the string you want to reverse.</p>";
```

7. Add to the end of the script section the following else clause, which uses the strrev() function to reverse the string entered by the user:

```
else {
     $ForwardString = $_GET['input_text'];
     $ReverseString = strrev($ForwardString);
     echo "<p>'$ForwardString' spelled backwards is
          '$ReverseString'.</p>";
}
```

8. Save the document as **ReverseString.php** in the Projects directory for Chapter 5.
9. Open **ReverseString.php** in your Web browser by entering the following URL: **http://localhost/PHP_Projects/Chapter.05/Projects/ReverseString.php**. Test the form to see if it correctly reverses strings.
10. Close your Web browser window.

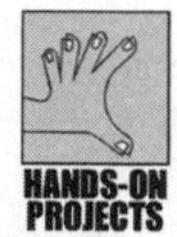

Hands-On Project 5-4

In this project, you create a script that uses comparison operators and functions to compare two strings entered by a user.

1. Create a new document in your text editor.
2. Type the <!DOCTYPE> declaration, <html> element, document head, and <body> element. Use the strict DTD and "Compare Strings" as the content of the <title> element.
3. Add the following text and elements to the document body:

```
<h1>Compare Strings</h1><hr />
```

4. Add the following script section to the document body:

```
<?php
?>
```

5. Add the following form to the end of the document body. The <input> elements include PHP code that fills in the values from the $_GET[first_string'] and $_GET[second_string'] autoglobals, if they exist.

```
<form action="CompareStrings.php" method="get"
enctype="application/x-www-form-urlencoded">
<p>First String <input type="text" name="first_string" size="20"
value="<?php if (!empty($_GET['first_string'])) echo
$_GET['first_string'] ?>" /></p>
<p>Second String <input type="text" name="second_string"
size="20" value="<?php if (!empty($_GET['second_string'])) echo
$_GET['second_string'] ?>" /></p>
<p><input type="submit" value="Compare Strings" />
</form><hr />
```

6. Add the following `if` statement to the script section. If both the `$_GET['first_string']` and `$_GET['second_string']` autoglobals are set, the statements in the `if` statement execute. The nested `if` statement uses the comparison operator (==) to determine if both strings are the same. If the strings are not the same, the `else` clause uses the `similar_text()` and `levenshtein()` functions to compare the strings.

```
if (isset($_GET['first_string']) && isset($_GET['second_string'])) {
     $FirstString = $_GET['first_string'];
     $SecondString = $_GET['second_string'];
     if ($FirstString == $SecondString)
          echo "<p>Both strings are the same.</p>";
     else {
          echo "<p>Both strings have "
             . similar_text($FirstString, $SecondString)
             . " character(s) in common.<br />";
          echo "<p>You must change " . levenshtein($FirstString,
              $SecondString) . " character(s) to make the strings
              the same.<br />";
     }
}
```


7. Add to the end of the script section the following `else` clause, which executes if values are not assigned to both the `$_GET['first_string']` and `$_GET['second_string']` autoglobals:

```
else
     echo "<p>Enter two strings you want to compare.</p>";
```

8. Save the document as **CompareStrings.php** in the Projects directory for Chapter 5.
9. Open **CompareStrings.php** in your Web browser by entering the following URL: **http://localhost/PHP_Projects/Chapter.05/Projects/CompareStrings.php**. Test the form to see if it correctly compares strings.
10. Close your Web browser window.

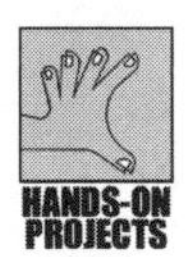

Hands-On Project 5-5

In this project, you create a script that uses the `soundex()` function to determine whether two words entered by a user sound alike.

1. Create a new document in your text editor.
2. Type the `<!DOCTYPE>` declaration, `<html>` element, document head, and `<body>` element. Use the strict DTD and "Compare Words" as the content of the `<title>` element.
3. Add the following text and elements to the document body:

```
<h1>Compare Words</h1><hr />
```

4. Add the following script section to the document body:

```
<?php
?>
```

5. Add the following form to the end of the document body. The `<input>` elements include PHP code that fills in the value from the `$_GET['first_word']` and `$_GET['second_word']` autoglobals, if they exist.

```
<form action="CompareWords.php" method="get"
enctype="application/x-www-form-urlencoded">
<p>First Word <input type="text" name="first_word" size="20"
value="<?php if (!empty($_GET['first_word'])) echo
$_GET['first_word'] ?>" /></p>
<p>Second Word <input type="text" name="second_word" size="20"
value="<?php if (!empty($_GET['second_word'])) echo
$_GET['second_word'] ?>" /></p>
<p><input type="submit" value="Compare Words" />
</form><hr />
```

6. Add the following `if` statement to the script section. If both the `$_GET['first_word']` and `$_GET['second_word']` autoglobals are set, the statements in the `if` statement execute. The nested `if` statement uses the `str_word_count()` function to confirm that the user entered a single word in each text box. If each string does contain a single word, the `else` clause uses the `soundex()` function to compare them.

```
if (isset($_GET['first_word']) && isset($_GET['second_word'])) {
     $FirstWord = $_GET['first_word'];
     $SecondWord = $_GET['second_word'];
     if (str_word_count($FirstWord) > 1
          || str_word_count($SecondWord) > 1)
          echo "<p>You can only enter a single word in each
               text box!</p>";
     else {
          $FirstWordSoundsLike = soundex($FirstWord);
          $SecondWordSoundsLike = soundex($SecondWord);
          if ($FirstWordSoundsLike == $SecondWordSoundsLike)
               echo "<p>Both words are pronounced the same.</p>";
          else
               echo "<p>Both words are not pronounced the same.</p>";
     }
}
```

7. Add to the end of the script section the following `else` clause, which executes if values are not assigned to both the `$_GET['first_word']` and `$_GET['second_word']` autoglobals:

```
else
     echo "<p>Enter two words you want to compare.</p>";
```

8. Save the document as **CompareWords.php** in the Projects directory for Chapter 5.
9. Open **CompareWords.php** in your Web browser by entering the following URL: **http://localhost/PHP_Projects/Chapter.05/Projects/CompareWords.php**. Test the form to see if it correctly compares the word pronunciations.
10. Close your Web browser window.

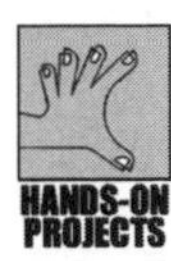

Hands-On Project 5-6

Some form elements, such as selection lists created with the `<select>` element, allow users to select multiple values. When multiple values are selected in a single element, you can only access the values in PHP if they are assigned to an array. (This is also true for multiple elements that share the same `name` attribute.) To create an array containing multiple values from a single element, or from multiple elements that share the same `name` attribute, you append two brackets (`[ ]`) to the value you assign to an element's `name` attribute. For example, if you have a group of check boxes that allow users to select their favorite book genre, you assign a value of "books[]" to each check box's `name` attribute. When you submit the form, the values of each selected check box are assigned to a global array in PHP named `$books[ ]`. In this project, you create a form with a `<select>` element containing education levels. Users will be able to select each of their education levels and submit them to PHP.

1. Create a new document in your text editor.
2. Type the `<!DOCTYPE>` declaration, `<html>` element, document head, and `<body>` element. Use the strict DTD and "Educational Achievements" as the content of the `<title>` element.
3. Add the following text and elements to the document body:

```
<h1>Educational Achievements</h1><hr />
```

4. Add the following script section to the document body:

```
<?php
?>
```

5. Add the following form to the end of the document body. The form contains a `<select>` element with a value of "education[]" assigned to its `name` attribute. Notice that each of the `<option>` elements calls a function named `checkEducation()`, which verifies if the option was selected when the form was submitted.

```
<form action="Education.php" method="get" enctype="application/
x-www-form-urlencoded">
<p><select name="education[]" multiple="multiple" size="8">
<option value="High School Diploma" <?= checkEducation("High
School Diploma"); ?> >High School Diploma</option>
```

```
<option value="Associate's Degree" <?= checkEducation("Associate's
Degree"); ?> >Associate's Degree</option>
<option value="Bachelor's Degree" <?= checkEducation("Bachelor's
Degree"); ?> >Bachelor's Degree</option>
<option value="Master's Degree" <?= checkEducation("Master's
Degree"); ?> >Master's Degree</option>
<option value="Doctorate Degree" <?= checkEducation("Doctorate
Degree"); ?> >Doctorate Degree</option>
<option value="Undergraduate Certificate" <?=
checkEducation("Undergraduate Certificate"); ?> >Undergraduate
Certificate</option>
<option value="Postbaccalaureate Certificate" <?=
checkEducation("Postbaccalaureate Certificate"); ?>
>Postbaccalaureate Certificate</option>
</select></p>
<p><input type="submit" value="Submit Education" />
</form><hr />
```

6. Add the following `checkEducation()` function to the script section. This function is called from within each of the `<option>` elements in the form and is passed a single argument named `$Level` that contains the education level to check. Notice that the first statement uses the `global` keyword to make the `$education[]` array available within the function. The `if` statement then checks to see if the `$education[]` array is set. If it is, code within the `if` function uses the `implode()` function to convert the array elements to a string. Then, the `strpos()` function determines whether the function contains the value assigned to the `$Level` argument. If the value of `$Level` is contained within the array, "selected=selected" is returned to the `<option>` element, which selects the item in the selection list when the Web page renders.

```
function checkEducation($Level) {
     global $education;
     if (isset($education)) {
          $FindLevel = implode(",", $education);
          if (strpos($FindLevel, $Level) !== FALSE)
          return " selected='selected'";
     }
     return "";
}
```

7. Add the following `if` statement to the end of the script section. If the `$education[]` array contains values, the `foreach` statement prints the values of each element.

```
if (isset($education)) {
     echo "<p>You selected the following:</p>";
     foreach ($education as $degree) {
          echo "$degree<br />";
     }
}
```

8. Add to the end of the script section the following **else** clause, which first executes when the page opens. This clause also executes if the user submits the form without selecting any values in the selection list.

```
else
     echo "<p>Select all your education achievements.
  (Hold your Ctrl key to select multiple items.)</p>";
```

9. Save the document as **Education.php** in the Projects directory for Chapter 5.
10. Open **Education.php** in your Web browser by entering the following URL: **http://localhost/PHP_Projects/Chapter.05/Projects/Education.php**. Test the form to see if you can select and submit multiple values in the selection list.
11. Close your Web browser window.

CASE PROJECTS

Save the documents you create for the following projects in the Cases directory for Chapter 5.

Case Project 5-1

Create a script that presents a word guessing game. Allow users to guess the word letter-by-letter by entering a character in a form. Start by assigning a secret word to a variable. After each guess, print the word using asterisks for each remaining letter, but fill in the letters that the user guessed correctly. You need to store the user's guess in a hidden form field. For example, if the word you want users to guess is "suspicious" and the user has successfully guessed the letters "s" and "i," then store s*s*i*i**s in the hidden form field. Use a single script named **GuessingGame.php** to display and process the form.

Case Project 5-2

A palindrome is a word or phrase that is identical forward or backward, such as the word "racecar." A standard palindrome is similar to a perfect palindrome except that spaces and punctuation are ignored. For example, "Madam, I'm Adam" is a standard palindrome because the characters are identical forward or backward, provided you remove the spaces and punctuation marks. Write a script that checks whether a word or phrase entered by a user is a palindrome. Start with a program that checks for perfect palindromes. If you feel ambitious, see if you can modify the program to check for standard palindromes. Use a single script to display and process the form. Save the perfect palindrome script as **PerfectPalindrome.php** and the standard palindrome script as **StandardPalindrome.php**.

Case Project 5-3

A passenger train averages a speed of 50 mph. However, each stop of the train adds an additional five minutes to the train's schedule. In addition, during bad weather the train can only average a speed of 40 mph. Write a script that allows a traveler to calculate how long it will take to travel a specified number of miles, based on speed, number of stops, and weather conditions. Include code that requires the user to enter numeric values for miles and number of stops. Also, use a radio button that allows users to select good or bad weather. Use a single script named **PassengerTrain.php** to display and process the form.

Case Project 5-4

Write a script that calculates the correct amount of change to return when performing a cash transaction. Allow the user (a cashier) to enter the cost of a transaction and the exact amount of money that the customer hands over to pay for the transaction. Determine the largest amount of each denomination to return to the customer. Assume that the largest denomination a customer will use is a $100 bill. Therefore, you will need to calculate the correct amount of change to return for $50, $20, $10, $5, and $1 bills, along with quarters, dimes, nickels, and pennies. For example, if the price of a transaction is $5.65 and the customer hands the cashier $10, the cashier should return $4.35 to the customer. Include code that requires the user to enter a numeric value for the cash transaction. Use a single script named **CashRegister.php** to display and process the form.

CHAPTER

6

WORKING WITH FILES AND DIRECTORIES

In this chapter, you will:

- Open and close files
- Write data to files
- Read data from files
- Manage files and directories

So far, all of the projects you have created performed some sort of calculation or task that was applicable only to the current Web browser session. For example, the Great Explorers quiz from Chapter 4 only gathered information from the user and returned a response with the number of correct answers. Similarly, the e-mail submission script from Chapter 5 only validated user form data before sending the data as an e-mail message. A very important missing piece of the application puzzle is the ability to store data that you can retrieve later. The Great Explorers quiz, for instance, would be much more useful if you could store each student's test results. The e-mail submission script would be much more valuable if you could save information from each submitted message, such as recipient e-mail addresses. With the current version of the e-mail script, you could fill in the form for each message, write each e-mail address down on a piece of paper, and then reenter each address when you want to send the recipient a new message. But this is the Information Age—you should not need to manually write information on a piece of paper. Instead, you should be able to save that information to a computer's hard drive. As another example, consider the invoice script you will create in this chapter. What good is an invoice script if you cannot save the data you entered? Your only alternative is to print a hard copy of each invoice that you then store in a filing cabinet. If you have to store a hard copy, you might as well use a typewriter to fill in a preprinted form, or even write your invoice information onto the preprinted form by hand. In this chapter, you study how to read and store data in text files on your local computer.

As you work through this chapter, keep in mind that your ability to access files on a local computer or network depends on the security permissions you have been granted to the files and to the directories where they are stored. Who grants these permissions? On some networks, the owner of a resource (typically the person who created the resource, such as a file or directory) can grant permission to access his resources. On other networks, the network administrator is in charge of granting permissions to resources.

Typical permissions include the abilities to read, write, modify, and execute. For example, you might have permission to read a file, but not to write to it. Because the procedures for granting permissions to resources such as files and directories are platform specific, this book does not explain the process of updating file and directory permissions. However, later in this chapter, you learn how to verify whether you have security access to any files and directories to which you want to write or read data.

See your operating system's documentation for information on how to set permissions for resources such as files and directories.

Opening and Closing File Streams

PHP includes several functions for reading data from a file. You learn how to use these functions later in this chapter. But before any of these functions can do their jobs, you must create a stream. A **stream** is a channel that is used for accessing a resource that you can read from and write to. For example, you might use a stream to access a file. The **input stream** reads data from a resource (such as a file), whereas the **output stream** writes data to a resource (again, such as a file). You have already used an output stream with the `echo()` and `print()` functions. Both functions send data to an output stream, which writes the data to a Web browser window. Using a file stream involves the following steps:

1. Open the file stream with the `fopen()` function.
2. Write data to or read data from the file stream.
3. Close the file stream with the `fclose()` function.

In the following sections, you first learn how to open and close file streams, and then you learn how to write and read data.

Opening a File Stream

When you use the `echo()` or `print()` functions to send data to an output stream, you only need to call each function for the data to be sent to the stream. With external files, such as text files, you must write code that opens and closes a handle to a file. A **handle** is a special type of variable that PHP uses to represent a resource such as a file. You use the `fopen()` function to open a handle to a file stream. The syntax for the `fopen()` function is *`open_file`* `= fopen("`*`text file`*`", "`*`mode`*`");`. The *`open_file`* variable is the handle that you can use to read and write data from and to the file. The *`mode`* argument can be one of several values that determine what you can do with the file after you open it.

Table 6-1 lists the *`mode`* arguments that you can use with the `fopen()` function. Among other things, these arguments control the position of the file pointer. A **file pointer** is a special type of variable that refers to the currently selected line or character in a file. The file pointer is a way of keeping track of where you are in a file. Later in this chapter, you work with functions that change the position of the file pointer.

6

Table 6-1 Mode arguments of the `fopen()` function

Argument	Description
`a`	Opens the specified file for writing only and places the file pointer at the end of the file; attempts to create the file if it doesn't exist
`a+`	Opens the specified file for reading and writing and places the file pointer at the end of the file; attempts to create the file if it doesn't exist
`r`	Opens the specified file for reading only and places the file pointer at the beginning of the file
`r+`	Opens the specified file for reading and writing and places the file pointer at the beginning of the file
`w`	Opens the specified file for writing only and deletes any existing content in the file; attempts to create the file if it doesn't exist
`w+`	Opens the specified file for reading and writing and deletes any existing content in the file; attempts to create the file if it doesn't exist
`x`	Creates and opens the specified file for writing only; returns false if the file already exists
`x+`	Creates and opens the specified file for reading and writing; returns false if the file already exists

The following statement shows how to use the `fopen()` function to open a handle to a file stream:

```
$BowlersFile = fopen("bowlers.txt", "r+");
```

Assume that the preceding statement opens a file that contains a list of people who have signed up for a bowling tournament. The `fopen()` function assigns the file to a handle named `$BowlersFile`. Notice that the function uses a *`mode`* argument of "r+", which opens the specified file for reading and writing and places the file pointer at the beginning of the file, before the first record. This allows you to add new data to the beginning of the file, as conceptually illustrated in Figure 6-1.

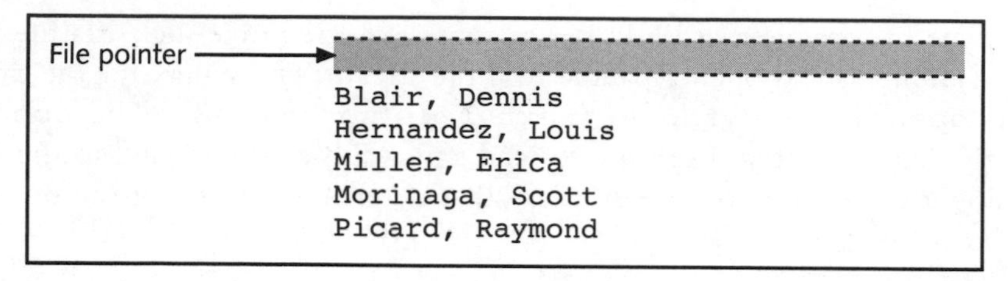

Figure 6-1 Location of the file pointer when the `fopen()` function uses a *mode* argument of "r+"

If you want to open a file and place the file pointer at the end of the file, you use a ***mode*** argument of "a+", as shown in the following statement:

```
$BowlersFile = fopen("bowlers.txt", "a+");
```

The preceding statement places the file pointer at the end of the file, after the last record, as conceptually illustrated in Figure 6-2.

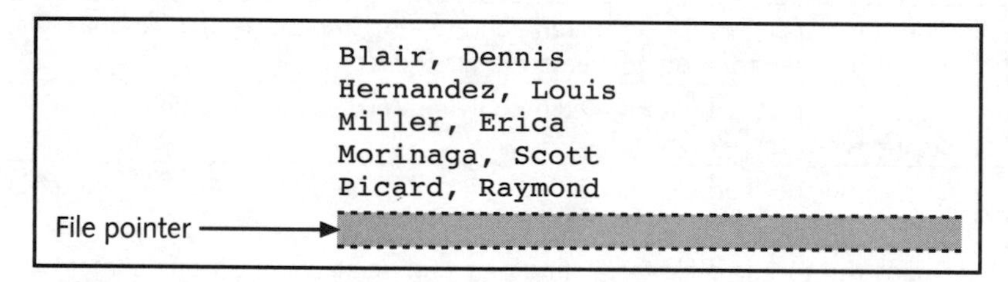

Figure 6-2 Location of the file pointer when the `fopen()` function uses a *mode* argument of "a+"

In this chapter, you work on an invoice script that allows you to save individual invoices to a text file. The script will be fairly simple and will only allow you to save up to three lines of billing information. However, it will help you learn how to write to and read from data files. Your Chapter directory for Chapter 6 contains two files to get you started: CreateInvoice.html and SaveInvoice.php. You will use the CreateInvoice.html file to enter invoice information, which you will then submit to the SaveInvoice.php script. The CreateInvoice.html file has some simple JavaScript code that calculates the invoice total, based on values you enter in the form. The version of the SaveInvoice.php script in your Chapter directory currently only displays the information that is submitted from the CreateInvoice.html file. Next, you begin modifying the SaveInvoice.php file so it saves the invoice data to a text file.

To begin modifying the SaveInvoice.php file so it saves the invoice data to a text file:

1. Open the **SaveInvoice.php** file in your text editor.
2. The script section in the SaveInvoice.php file only contains statements that assign the values of the autoglobals from the CreateInvoice.html file to variables, along with `echo()` statements that print the values in the variables in a table. Modify the statements so they are contained within `if...else` statements that validate the submitted data, as follows. To keep things simple, the validation code simply requires that all fields in the form contain values, and that the Quantity, Rate, Amount, and Total fields contain numeric values. Be sure to add the statements below the statement that declares and initializes the `$Total` variable.

```
if (empty($BillTo) ||
    empty($Date) ||
    empty($Terms) ||
    empty($Description1) ||
    empty($Description2) ||
    empty($Description3))
    echo "<hr/><p>You must enter a value in each field.
          Click your browser's Back button to return to
          the invoice.</p><hr />";
else if (!is_numeric($InvoiceNum) ||
    !is_numeric($Quantity1) ||
    !is_numeric($Quantity2) ||
    !is_numeric($Quantity3) ||
    !is_numeric($Rate1) ||
    !is_numeric($Rate2) ||
    !is_numeric($Rate3) ||
    !is_numeric($Amount1) ||
    !is_numeric($Amount2) ||
    !is_numeric($Amount3) ||
    !is_numeric($Total))
    echo "<p>The Invoice #, Quantity, Rate, Amount, and Total fields
          must contain numeric values! Click your browser's Back button
          to return to the invoice.</p>";
```

3. Enclose the `echo()` statements at the end of the script section within an `else` clause, as follows (only the first few `echo()` statements are shown here to save space):

```
else {
     echo "<h1>Invoice Saved</h1>";
     echo "<hr /><br /><table frame='border' rules='rows'>";
     echo "<tr><td><strong>Bill To</strong>";
```

6

```
        echo "<pre>$BillTo</pre></td>";
        echo "<td style='text-align: right' colspan='3'>";
...
}
```

4. Add the following `fopen()` statement as the first statement in the `else` clause you created in Step 3. The invoices you save will use the invoice number as the filename. For this reason, the following statement passes the `$InvoiceNum` variable and an extension of .txt as the first argument of the `fopen()` function. The mode argument uses a value of "w," which opens the specified file for writing only, or attempts to create the file if it doesn't exist, and deletes any existing content in the file.

```
$InvoiceFile = fopen($InvoiceNum . ".txt", "w");
```

5. Save the **SaveInvoice.php** file.
6. Open the **CreateInvoice.html** file in your Web browser by entering the following URL: **http://localhost/PHP_Projects/Chapter.06/Chapter/CreateInvoice.html**. Enter values in each of the fields. Note that you do not need to enter values in the Amount or TOTAL fields because their values are calculated automatically with some JavaScript code. Figure 6-3 shows how the form looks after some data had been entered.

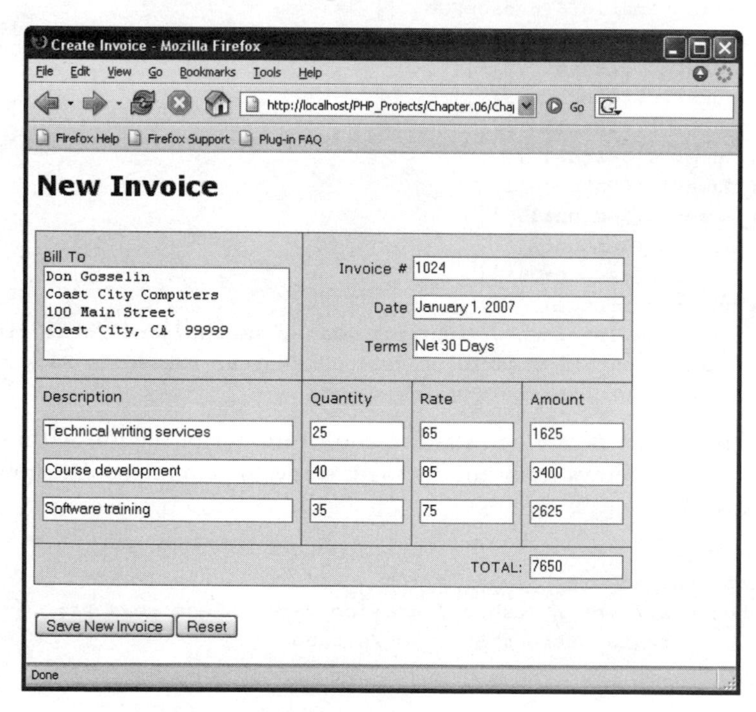

Figure 6-3 New Invoice Web page

7. After you fill in the form, click the **Save New Invoice** button. You should see the Invoice Saved Web page shown in Figure 6-4.

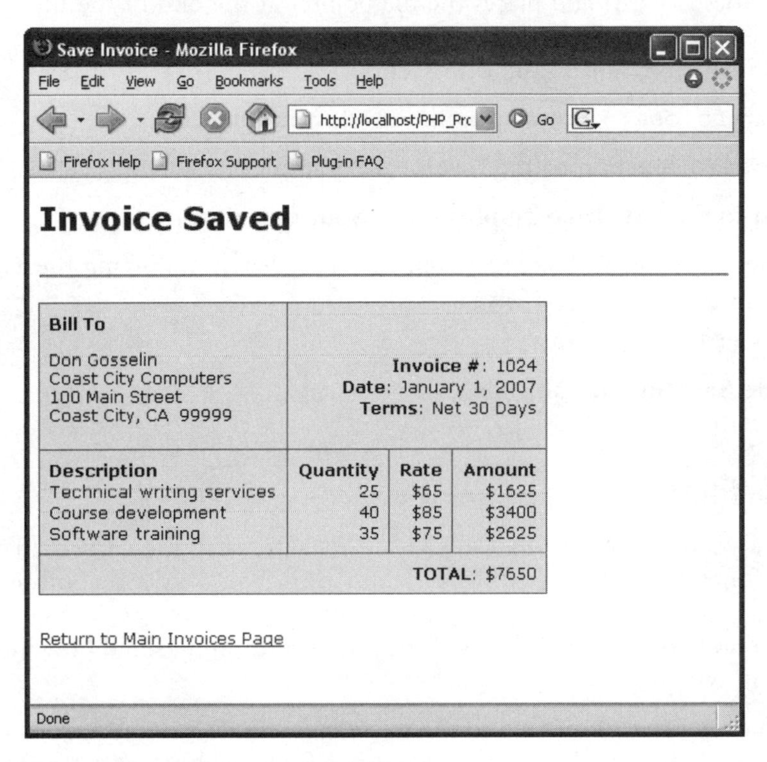

Figure 6-4 Invoice Saved Web page

8. Close your Web browser window, then look in your Chapter directory for Chapter 6. You should see a text file that is the same name as the number you assigned to the invoice. However, the file will be empty because you still need to learn how to write data to it.

Closing a File Stream

When you are finished working with a file stream, you use the statement `fclose($handle);` to ensure that the file doesn't keep taking up space in your computer's memory. The following code includes an `fclose()` statement:

```
$BowlersFile = fopen("bowlers.txt", "a");
$NewBowler = "Gosselin, Don\n";
fwrite($BowlersFile, $NewBowler);
fclose($BowlersFile);
```

Notice that the `fopen()` function in the preceding statement uses "a" as the *mode* argument. The *mode* argument of "a" opens the bowlers.txt file for writing only (or attempts to create it if it doesn't exist) and places the file pointer at the end of the file. The code also includes the `fwrite()` function, which writes a line to the open file. You learn about the `fwrite()` function in the next section.

Next, you add an `fclose()` function to the SaveInvoice.php file.

To add an `fclose()` function to the SaveInvoice.php file:

1. Return to the **SaveInvoice.php** file in your text editor.
2. Add the following `fclose()` statement immediately following the `fopen()` statement:

   ```
   fclose($InvoiceFile);
   ```

3. Save the **SaveInvoice.php** file.

Writing Data to Files

PHP supports two basic functions for writing data to text files: the `file_put_contents()` function and the `fwrite()` function. You study the more limited `file_put_contents()` function shortly, followed by the `fwrite()` function. But before you learn how to write data to text files, you need to understand how line breaks vary by operating systems.

Recall from Chapter 5 that you need to use an escape sequence to add special characters to a string, including the `\n` escape sequence for new lines and the `\r` escape sequence for carriage returns. Different operating systems use different escape sequences to identify the end of a line. UNIX/Linux platforms use the `\n` carriage return escape sequence to identify the end of a line, Macintosh platforms use `\r` to identify the end of a line, and Windows operating systems use both the `\r` carriage return escape sequence and the `\n` newline escape sequence to identify the end of a line. For example, to identify the end of a line on UNIX/Linux platforms, you append the `\n` carriage return escape sequence to the end of a line, as follows:

```
This is how you end a line on UNIX/Linux platforms.\n
```

The following statement demonstrates how to use both the `\r` carriage return escape sequence and the `\n` newline escape sequence to identify the end of a line on Windows operating systems:

```
This is how you end a line on Windows operating systems.\r\n
```

If you do not use the correct end-of-line escape sequence, you may experience problems when working with text files on different platforms. For example, the following names of people registered for the bowling tournament end with the `\n` newline escape sequence, as required for UNIX/Linux operating systems:

```
Blair, Dennis\n
Hernandez, Louis\n
Miller, Erica\n
Morinaga, Scott\n
Picard, Raymond\n
```

If you attempt to open a text file containing the preceding lines in the Notepad text editor on Windows operating systems, the `\n` characters are replaced by rectangle characters, as shown in Figure 6-5.

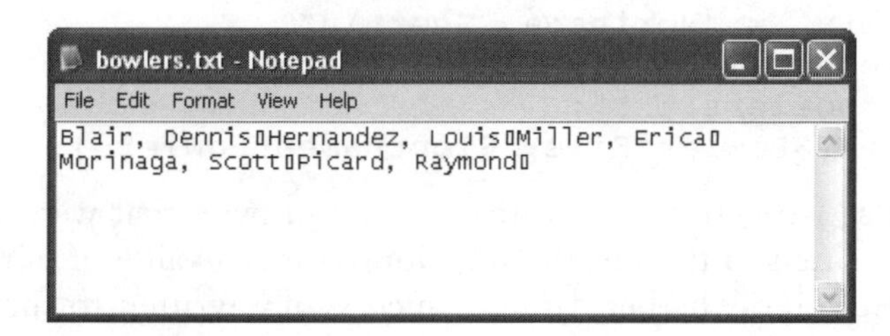

Figure 6-5 Notepad with a file opened containing UNIX/Linux end-of-line characters

For the names to display correctly on Windows, they must end with the `\r\n` escape sequences, as follows:

```
Blair, Dennis\r\n
Hernandez, Louis\r\n
Miller, Erica\r\n
Morinaga, Scott\r\n
Picard, Raymond\r\n
```

The PHP file functions that you study in this chapter can usually accommodate any of these escape sequences and end lines in a text file appropriately, regardless of the operating system. For this reason, although the examples in this book use the `\n` newline escape sequence that is supported by UNIX/Linux operating systems, the PHP scripts you write will function correctly on any platform. However, keep in mind that if you attempt to open a text file that does not contain the required characters for the current operating system, the line breaks may not appear correctly in your text editor.

Writing an Entire File

The `file_put_contents()` function writes or appends a text string to a file. The syntax for the `file_put_contents()` function is `file_put_contents(`*`filename`*`, `*`string`*`[, `*`options`*`])`. If the specified filename does not exist, it is created. However, if the specified filename does exist, any data it contains is overwritten. With the `file_put_contents()` function, you do not need to use the `fopen()` and `fclose()` functions. Instead, you simply call the `file_put_contents()` function and pass to it the name of the file to which you want to write data along with a text string containing the data you want to write. For example, the following code builds a variable named `$TournamentBowlers` that contains the names of bowlers in the tournament separated by line breaks, along with a variable named `$BowlersFile` that contains the filename where the bowler names will be stored. The last statement passes the `$BowlersFile` and the `$TournamentBowlers` variables to the `file_put_contents()` function.

```
$TournamentBowlers = "Blair, Dennis\n";
$TournamentBowlers .= "Hernandez, Louis\n";
$TournamentBowlers .= "Miller, Erica\n";
$TournamentBowlers .= "Morinaga, Scott\n";
$TournamentBowlers .= "Picard, Raymond\n";
$BowlersFile = "bowlers.txt";
file_put_contents($BowlersFile, $TournamentBowlers);
```

The `file_put_contents()` function returns the number of bytes that were written to the file. If no data was written to the file, the function returns a value of 0. You can use the return value to determine whether data was successfully written to the file, as follows:

```
if (file_put_contents($BowlersFile, $TournamentBowlers) > 0)
      echo "<p>Data was successfully written to the
           $BowlersFile file.</p>";
else
      echo "<p>No data was written to the $BowlersFile file.</p>";
```

You can use an absolute or relative path with the filename you pass to the `file_put_contents()` function. However, even though the function will create a filename that does not exist, it will not create any directories that do not exist. If you specify a nonexistent directory, you receive an error. For this reason, you should use the `is_dir()` function to test whether a directory exists before you attempt to write to it. You study the `is_dir()` function later in this chapter.

Next, you add statements to the SaveInvoice.php file that use the `file_put_contents()` function to save the invoice data to a text file.

To add statements to the SaveInvoice.php file that use the `file_put_contents()` function to save the invoice data to a text file:

1. Return to the **SaveInvoice.php** file in your text editor.
2. Recall that the new invoice form includes a `<textarea>` element. Any line breaks that are included in the value assigned to this element will throw off the order in which data is saved to the text file. Therefore, add the following

statements above the `fopen()` statement. The first statement uses the `explode()` function to convert the value in the `$BillTo` variable to an array by splitting the text at the line break. The second statement then uses the `implode()` function to assign the values back to the `$BillTo` variable, but this time separated by a tilde (~) character.

```
$FixBillTo = explode("\n", $BillTo);
$BillTo = implode("~", $FixBillTo);
```

On Windows platforms, you need to specify the `\r\n` escape sequence.

3. Add the following statements above the `fopen()` statement to build a variable named `$Invoice` using the submitted form data. Each value is separated by a line break.

```
$Invoice = $BillTo . "\n";
$Invoice .= $InvoiceNum . "\n";
$Invoice .= $Date . "\n";
$Invoice .= $Terms . "\n";
$Invoice .= $Description1 . "\n";
$Invoice .= $Description2 . "\n";
$Invoice .= $Description3 . "\n";
$Invoice .= $Quantity1 . "\n";
$Invoice .= $Quantity2 . "\n";
$Invoice .= $Quantity3 . "\n";
$Invoice .= $Rate1 . "\n";
$Invoice .= $Rate2 . "\n";
$Invoice .= $Rate3 . "\n";
$Invoice .= $Amount1 . "\n";
$Invoice .= $Amount2 . "\n";
$Invoice .= $Amount3 . "\n";
$Invoice .= $Total . "\n";
```

4. Add line comments before the `fopen()` and `fclose()` statements; you will use these statements again later:

```
// $InvoiceFile = fopen($InvoiceNum . ".txt", "w");
// fclose($InvoiceFile);
```

5. Place the `echo()` statements at the end of the script section into the following `if...else` statement, which executes the `file_put_contents()` function:

```
if (file_put_contents($InvoiceNum . ".txt", $Invoice) > 0) {
    echo "<h1>Invoice Saved</h1>";
```

```
            echo "<hr /><br /><table frame='border' rules='rows'>";
            echo "<tr><td><strong>Bill To</strong>";
            echo "<pre>$BillTo</pre></td>";
            echo "<td style='text-align: right' colspan='3'>";
            echo "<br /><strong>Invoice #</strong>: $InvoiceNum<br />";
            echo "<strong>Date</strong>: $Date<br />";
            echo "<strong>Terms</strong>: $Terms</td></tr>";
            echo "<tr>";
            echo "<td><strong>Description</strong><br />$Description1
                  <br />$Description2<br />$Description3</td>";
            echo "<td style='text-align: right'><strong>Quantity</strong>
                  <br />$Quantity1<br />$Quantity2<br />$Quantity3</td>";
            echo "<td style='text-align: right'><strong>Rate</strong>
                  <br />$$Rate1<br />$$Rate2<br />$$Rate3</td>";
            echo "<td style='text-align: right'><strong>Amount</strong>
                  <br />$$Amount1<br />$$Amount2<br />$$Amount3</td></tr>";
            echo "<tr><td colspan='4' style='text-align: right'>
                  <strong>TOTAL</strong>: $$Total</td></tr>";
            echo "</table>";
      }
      else
            echo "<p>The invoice could not be saved!</p>";
```

6. Save the **SaveInvoice.php** file.
7. Open the **CreateInvoice.html** file in your Web browser by entering the following URL: **http://localhost/PHP_Projects/Chapter.06/Chapter/CreateInvoice.html**. Enter values in each of the fields and click the **Save New Invoice** button. You should see the Invoice Saved Web page.
8. Close your Web browser window, then look in your Chapter directory for Chapter 6. Open the invoice file you just created in your text editor. You should see the invoice data saved on individual lines of the file.
9. Close the invoice file in your text editor.

In addition to the filename and text string arguments, you can pass a third argument to the `file_put_contents()` function that contains the `FILE_USE_INCLUDE_PATH` or the `FILE_APPEND` constant. The `FILE_USE_INCLUDE_PATH` constant instructs PHP to search for the specified filename in the path that is assigned to the `include_path` directive in your php.ini configuration file. The `FILE_APPEND` constant instructs PHP to append data to any existing contents in the specified filename instead of overwriting it.

The following example demonstrates how to use the `file_put_contents()` function with the `FILE_APPEND` constant to add the names of bowlers to the bowlers.txt file. The example consists of a single script that displays and processes a form that bowlers can use to register. Because the `file_put_contents()` function includes the

FILE_APPEND constant, any new names that are entered in the form are appended to the bowlers.txt file. Figure 6-6 shows the form in a Web browser.

```
<h1>Coast City Bowling Tournament</h1>
<?php
if (isset($_GET['first_name']) && isset($_GET['last_name'])) {
      $BowlerFirst = $_GET['first_name'];
      $BowlerLast = $_GET['last_name'];
      $NewBowler = $BowlerLast . ", " . "$BowlerFirst" . "\n";
      $BowlersFile = "bowlers.txt";
      if (file_put_contents($BowlersFile, $NewBowler, FILE_APPEND) > 0)
            echo "<p>{$_GET['first_name']} {$_GET['last_name']} has
                 been registered for the bowling tournament!</p>";
      else
            echo "<p>Registration error!</p>";
}
else
      echo "<p>To sign up for the bowling tournament, enter your first
           and last name and click the Register button.</p>";
?>
<form action="BowlingTournament.php" method="get"
enctype="application/x-www-form-urlencoded">
<p>First Name: <input type="text" name="first_name" size="30" /></p>
<p>Last Name: <input type="text" name="last_name" size="30" /></p>
<p><input type="submit" value="Register" /></p>
</form>
```


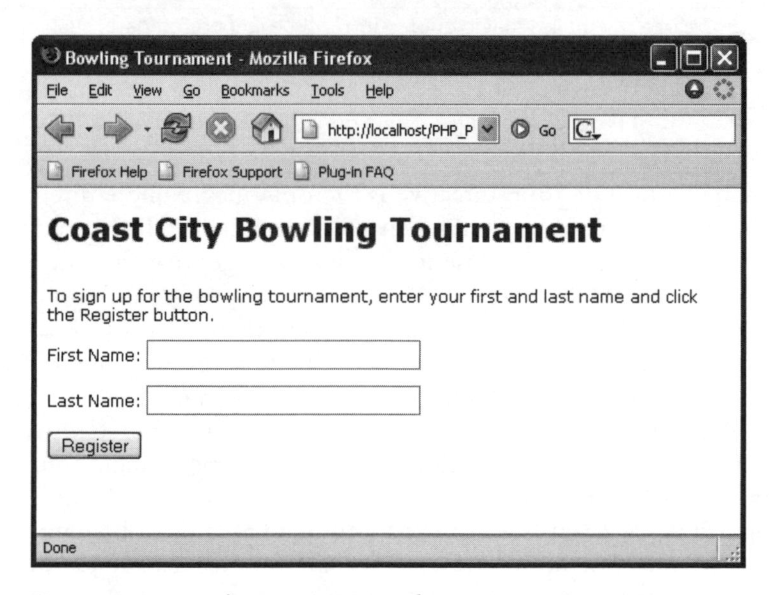

Figure 6-6 Bowling registration form

Handling Magic Quotes

Recall from Chapter 5 that you should use escape sequences for special characters in text strings, especially single or double quotes because they may cause problems when the PHP interpreter attempts to identify the beginning and ending of a string. Because the data a user submits to a PHP script may also contain single or double quotes, you should also use escape sequences for any user data your script receives, especially before you write it to a data source, such as a text file or database. PHP includes a feature called **magic quotes**, which automatically adds a backslash (\) to any single quote ('), double quote ("), or NULL character contained in data that a user submits to a PHP script. For example, consider the following text:

```
My best friend's nickname is "Bubba"
```

If a user enters the preceding text into a form field, and then submits the form to a PHP script, magic quotes automatically escape the single and double quotes, as follows:

```
My best friend\'s nickname is \"Bubba\"
```

Magic quotes are enabled within your php.ini configuration file with the directives listed in Table 6-2.

Table 6-2 Magic quote directives

Directive	Description
`magic_quotes_gpc`	Applies magic quotes to any user-submitted data
`magic_quotes_runtime`	Applies magic quotes to runtime-generated data, such as data received from a database
`magic_quotes_sybase`	Applies Sybase-style magic quotes, which escape special characters with a single quote (') instead of a backslash (\)

By default, the `magic_quotes_gpc` directive is the only magic quote directive that is enabled in your php.ini configuration file when you first install PHP. Magic quotes are very unpopular with programmers because it's so easy to forget that they are enabled in a php.ini configuration file. Many PHP programmers have spent countless hours trying to determine why backslashes were being added to data their scripts received, only to discover that the culprit was one of the magic quote directives in the php.ini file. Rather than relying on magic quotes to escape text strings, you should disable magic quotes in your php.ini configuration file and instead manually escape the strings with the `addslashes()` function. The `addslashes()` function accepts a single argument representing the text string you want to escape and returns a string containing the escaped string. For example, if the `$_GET['nickname']` autoglobal in the following code contains the "My best friend ..." string you saw earlier, the following code escapes the single and double quotes contained in the string:

```
$Nickname = addslashes($_GET['nickname']);
echo $Nickname; // My best friend\'s nickname is \"Bubba\".
```

The existence of the **addslashes()** function is actually another reason why magic quotes are unpopular. If you execute the **addslashes()** function on user-submitted data when magic quotes are turned on, the data is escaped twice. For example, if you execute the preceding code when magic quotes are enabled, the text string appears as follows:

```
My best friend\\\'s nickname is \\\"Bubba\\\"
```

Because of the problems they can cause, you should turn off magic quotes on your server and rely on the **addslashes()** function to escape user-submitted text strings.

If you want to display an escaped text string that contains escape characters, you can use the **stripslashes()** function to remove the slashes that were added with the **addslashes()** function. For example, the following code is a modified version of the script you saw in the previous section that adds the names of bowlers to the file bowlers.txt. The script now includes **addslashes()** functions that escape the first and last names submitted by the user. (The script also assumes that magic quotes are disabled.) If you attempt to print the values assigned to the **$BowlerFirst** and **$BowlerLast** variables, any escaped characters contained in the variables also print. Figure 6-7 shows the output if the first name field contains a value of Don "The Rocket," which is the bowler's true first name, plus a nickname, and if the last name field contains a value of "Gosselin."

```
if (isset($_GET['first_name']) && isset($_GET['last_name'])) {
      $BowlerFirst = addslashes($_GET['first_name']);
      $BowlerLast = addslashes($_GET['last_name']);
      $NewBowler = $BowlerLast . ", " . "$BowlerFirst" . "\n";
      $BowlersFile = "bowlers.txt";
      if (file_put_contents($BowlersFile, $NewBowler, FILE_APPEND) > 0)
            echo "<p>{$_GET['first_name']} {$_GET['last_name']}
                   has been registered for the bowling tournament!</p>";
      else
            echo "<p>Registration error!</p>";
}
else
      echo "<p>To sign up for the bowling tournament, enter your first
           and last name and click the Register button.</p>";
```

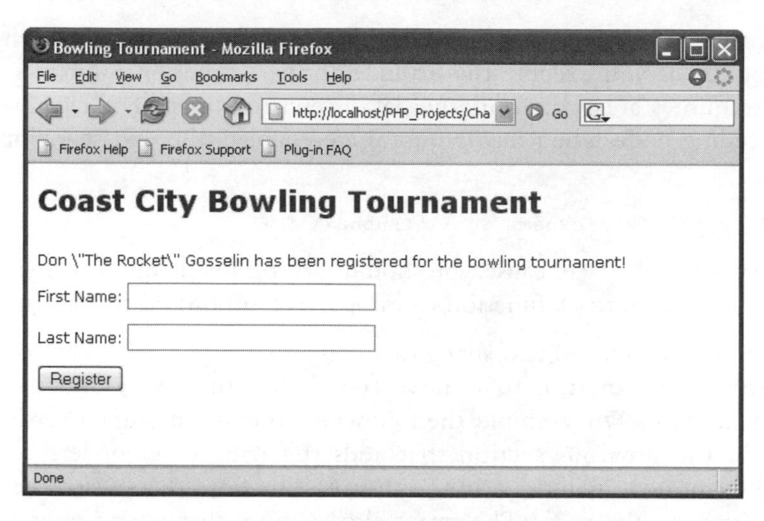

Figure 6-7 Output of text with escaped characters

To prevent the display of escaped characters, use the `stripslashes()` function with the text you want to print. The following example shows a modified version of the output statements from the preceding code, but this time containing `stripslashes()` functions:

```
if (file_put_contents($BowlersFile, $NewBowler, FILE_APPEND) > 0)
      echo "<p>" . stripslashes($_GET['first_name']) . " "
             . stripslashes($_GET['last_name'])
             . " has been registered for the bowling tournament!</p>";
else
      echo "<p>Registration error!</p>";
```

Next, you disable magic quotes and add the `addslashes()` and `stripslashes()` functions to the SaveInvoice.php script.

1. Open your **php.ini** configuration file in your text editor. For UNIX/Linux systems, you should have installed this file in the /usr/local/lib directory. On Windows systems, this file is installed automatically in your main Windows directory, which is usually C:\WINDOWS or C:\WINNT.
2. In the **php.ini** file, locate the magic quotes section, which contains three directives: `magic_quotes_gpc`, `magic_quotes_runtime`, and `magic_quotes_sybase`. If any of these directives are assigned a value of "On," change them to "Off," so the statements read as follows:

   ```
   magic_quotes_gpc = Off
   magic_quotes_runtime = Off
   magic_quotes_sybase = Off
   ```

3. Save and close the **php.ini** file.
4. Return to the **SaveInvoice.php** file in your text editor.

5. Add `addslashes()` functions to the statements that assign the values from the Bill To, Date, Terms, and Description fields to variables, as follows. Note that you do not need to use the `addslashes()` function with the Invoice #, Quantity, Rate, Amount, and TOTAL fields because you already added validation that ensures the fields only contain numeric values.

```
$BillTo = addslashes($_POST["billto"]);
$Date = addslashes($_POST["date"]);
$Terms = addslashes($_POST["terms"]);
$Description1 = addslashes($_POST["description1"]);
$Description2 = addslashes($_POST["description2"]);
$Description3 = addslashes($_POST["description3"]);
```

6. Add the following statements above the `echo()` statements at the end of the script. These statements use the `stripslashes()` function to strip the slashes that were added with the `addslashes()` functions in the preceding step.

```
$BillTo = stripslashes($_POST["billto"]);
$Date = stripslashes($_POST["date"]);
$Terms = stripslashes($_POST["terms"]);
$Description1 = stripslashes($_POST["description1"]);
$Description2 = stripslashes($_POST["description2"]);
$Description3 = stripslashes($_POST["description3"]);
```

7. Save the **SaveInvoice.php** file.
8. Open the **CreateInvoice.html** file in your Web browser by entering the following URL: **http://localhost/PHP_Projects/Chapter.06/Chapter/CreateInvoice.html**. Enter values in each of the fields, and be certain to enter some double quotation marks in either the Bill To or Description field. After you click the **Save New Invoice** button, you should see the quotation marks in the Invoice Saved Web page, but not magic quotes.
9. Close your Web browser window, and then open the invoice file from your Chapter directory for Chapter 6 in your text editor. The quotations you entered in the form should appear as magic quotes in the text file.
10. Close the invoice file in your text editor.

Writing Data Incrementally

The `file_put_contents()` function is useful if you want to quickly replace the contents of a file or append data to the end of an existing file. In addition to the `file_put_contents()` function, you can also use the `fwrite()` function to incrementally write data to a text file. To write data to the text file with the `fwrite()` function, you use the following syntax: `fwrite($handle, data[, length]);`. As with the `file_put_contents()` function, the `fwrite()` function returns the number of bytes that were written to the file. If no data was written to the file, the function returns a value of 0. You can use the return value to determine whether data was successfully written to the file. Before you can use the `fwrite()` function, you must first open a handle to the text file with the `fopen()` function. Because you use the `fopen()` function with `fwrite()`, you can specify what type of operations can be performed on the file and where and how the data will be written. For example, with the `file_put_contents()` function, you can only replace the contents of a file or append data to the end of a file. By comparison, the *`mode`* arguments of the `fopen()` function allow you to specify whether to open a file for reading or writing, whether to create a file if it doesn't exist, and whether to place the file pointer at the beginning or end of the text file.

The `fputs()` function is an alias for the `fwrite()` function.

The following code demonstrates how to use the `fopen()` and `fclose()` functions with multiple `fwrite()` statements to add names to the bowlers.txt file:

```
$BowlersFile = fopen("bowlers.txt", "a");
fwrite($BowlersFile, "Blair, Dennis\n");
fwrite($BowlersFile, "Hernandez, Louis\n");
fwrite($BowlersFile, "Miller, Erica\n");
fwrite($BowlersFile, "Morinaga, Scott\n");
fwrite($BowlersFile, "Picard, Raymond\n");
fclose($BowlersFile);
```

The following contains a modified version of the single script that displays and processes a form that bowlers can use to register. This time, the script uses `fopen()`, `fwrite()`, and `fclose()` functions instead of the `file_put_contents()` function.

```
if (isset($_GET['first_name']) && isset($_GET['last_name'])) {
      $BowlerFirst = addslashes($_GET['first_name']);
      $BowlerLast = addslashes($_GET['last_name']);
      $NewBowler = $BowlerLast . ", " . "$BowlerFirst" . "\n";
      $BowlersFile = fopen("bowlers.txt", "a");
      if (fwrite($BowlersFile, $NewBowler) > 0)
            echo "<p>" . stripslashes($_GET['first_name']) . " "
                  . stripslashes($_GET['last_name']) . " has been registered
                  for the bowling tournament!</p>";
      else
            echo "<p>Registration error!</p>";
      fclose($BowlersFile);
}
else
      echo "<p>To sign up for the bowling tournament, enter your first
            and last name and click the Register button.</p>";
```

The *length* argument of the `fwrite()` function allows you to specify the maximum number of bytes that should be written. If the *data* argument you pass to the `fwrite()` function is greater than the value of the *length* argument, the data is truncated.

Next, you modify the SaveInvoice.php file so it saves the invoice data with `fwrite()` functions instead of the `file_put_contents()` function.

To modify the SaveInvoice.php file so it saves the invoice data with `fwrite()` functions instead of the `file_put_contents()` function:

1. Return to the **SaveInvoice.php** file in your text editor.
2. Remove the comments from before the `fopen()` and `fclose()` statements, and then move the `fclose()` statement to immediately after the `else` clause, as follows:

```
...
else
     echo "<p>The invoice could not be saved!</p>";
fclose($InvoiceFile);
```

3. Modify the `file_put_contents()` function into an `fwrite()` function, as follows:

```
if (fwrite($InvoiceFile, $Invoice) > 0) {
```

4. Save the **SaveInvoice.php** file.
5. Open the **CreateInvoice.html** file in your Web browser by entering the following URL: **http://localhost/PHP_Projects/Chapter.06/Chapter/CreateInvoice.html**. Enter values in each of the fields and click the **Save New Invoice** button. The script should function the same as it did with the `file_put_contents()` function.
6. Close your Web browser window.

Locking Files

When your program opens a text file via the `fopen()` method, there is a chance that another program will attempt to open the same file. If both programs are simply reading data from the file, there should be no problem. However, if more than one program attempts to write data to a text file at the same time, data corruption could occur. To prevent multiple users from modifying a file simultaneously, you need to use the `flock()` function. The basic syntax for the `flock()` function is `flock($handle, operation)`. The first argument you pass to the `flock()` function is the handle that represents the open file. The second argument you pass to the `flock()` function is one of the operational constants listed in Table 6-3.

Table 6-3 Operational constants of the `flock()` function

Constant	Description
`LOCK_EX`	Opens the file with an exclusive lock for writing
`LOCK_NB`	Prevents the `flock()` function from waiting, or "blocking," until a file is unlocked
`LOCK_SH`	Opens the file with a shared lock for reading
`LOCK_UN`	Releases a file lock

You use the **`LOCK_SH`** constant to create a shared lock for reading, which allows other users to also read the file while you have it locked. The **`LOCK_EX`** constant creates an exclusive lock to write data to the file. An exclusive lock prevents other users from accessing the file until you are finished with it. After you are through with either lock type, you should call the **`flock()`** function with the **`LOCK_UN`** constant, which releases the lock. If you call the **`flock()`** function with either the **`LOCK_SH`** or **`LOCK_EX`** constants, and the file you want to lock is already locked by another user, your script waits until the other user releases the lock. If you don't want your script to wait until a file is unlocked, you can include the **`LOCK_NB`** constant in the ***`operation`*** argument. As a general rule, you should only use the **`LOCK_NB`** constant when your script needs to write an exceptionally large amount of data to a file. However, it's important to note that if you need to store a large amount of data, you should store it in a database and *not* in a text file. If you do find some reason to use the **`LOCK_NB`** constant, separate it from the **`LOCK_SH`** or **`LOCK_EX`** constants with the **`&&`** (and) operator, as shown in the following example:

```
flock($BowlersFile, LOCK_EX && LOCK_NB);
```

It's important to understand that the PHP file locking mechanism is simply "advisory." This means that PHP does not actually shut out other programs from accessing the file, as other programming languages do. Instead, PHP only prevents other PHP scripts that use `flock()` from accessing a file that was locked by another PHP script. In other words, a PHP script that does not use `flock()` to open a file can go ahead and modify the file, even if it is exclusively locked by another PHP script. For PHP file locking to be effective, it's up to you (and your ISP) to ensure that any scripts that open a file on your server use the `flock()` function.

The **`flock()`** function returns a value of true if it successfully locks a file and false if it fails. You can use this return value to determine whether the lock was successful, as shown in the following code, which contains a modified example of the script that adds new names to the bowlers.txt file. In this example, a single name is assigned to the **`$NewBowler`** variable. The **`flock()`** function uses the **`LOCK_EX`** constant to lock the bowlers.txt file for writing. If the lock is successful, a nested **`if...else`** statement attempts to write the name to the file and prints a message stating whether the `fwrite()` function was successful. The last statement in the main `if` statement then uses the `LOCK_UN` constant with the `flock()` function to unlock the bowlers.txt file.

```
$BowlersFile = fopen("bowlers.txt", "a");
$FirstName = "Don \"The Rocket\"";
$LastName = "Gosselin";
$NewBowler = addslashes("$LastName, $FirstName\n");
if (flock($BowlersFile, LOCK_EX)) {
      if (fwrite($BowlersFile, $NewBowler) > 0)
            echo "<p>" . stripslashes($FirstName) . " "
                  . stripslashes($LastName) . " has been registered
                  for the bowling tournament!</p>";
      else
            echo "<p>Registration error!</p>";
      flock($BowlersFile, LOCK_UN);
}
else
      echo "<p>Cannot write to the file. Please try again later</p>";
fclose($BowlersFile);
```


Next, you modify the SaveInvoice.php file so it uses the `flock()` function when writing data to a text file.

To modify the SaveInvoice.php file so it uses the `flock()` function when writing data to a text file:

1. Return to the **SaveInvoice.php** file in your text editor.

2. Modify the `if` statement that executes the `fwrite()` statement so it is contained within another `if` statement that executes an `flock()` statement to lock the file. Also, add another `flock()` statement to the end of the nested `if` statement that unlocks the file and move the `fclose()` statement to beneath the `flock()` statement. The end of your script should appear as follows. (To save space, some statements within the nested `if` statement are not shown.)

```
...
$InvoiceFile = fopen($InvoiceNum . ".txt", "w");
if (flock($InvoiceFile, LOCK_EX)) {
      if (fwrite($InvoiceFile, $Invoice) > 0) {
            $BillTo = stripslashes($_POST["billto"]);
            $Date = stripslashes($_POST["date"]);
            ...
            echo "</table>";
            flock($InvoiceFile, LOCK_UN);
            fclose($InvoiceFile);
      }
      else
            echo "<p>The invoice could not be saved!</p>";
}
else
```

```
        echo "<p>The invoice could not be saved!</p>";
}
?>
```

3. Save the **SaveInvoice.php** file.
4. Open the **CreateInvoice.html** file in your Web browser by entering the following URL: **http://localhost/PHP_Projects/Chapter.06/Chapter/CreateInvoice.html**. Enter values in each of the fields and click the **Save New Invoice** button. The script should function the same as it did before you added the `flock()` statements.
5. Close your Web browser window.

Reading Data from Files

PHP includes a number of different functions for reading data from text files. These functions can be generally classified as functions that read an entire file or functions that read the contents of a file incrementally. You study the functions that read an entire file first.

Reading an Entire File

Table 6-4 lists the PHP functions that you can use to read the entire contents of a text file.

Table 6-4 PHP functions that read the entire contents of a text file

Function	Description
`file(`*`filename`*`[, `*`use_include_path`*`])`	Reads the contents of a file into an indexed array
`file_get_contents(`*`filename`*`[, `*`use_include_path`*`])`	Reads the contents of a file into a string
`fread(`*`$handle, length`*`)`	Reads the contents of a file into a string up to a maximum number of bytes
`readfile(`*`filename`*`[, `*`use_include_path`*`])`	Prints the contents of a file

NOTE

You do not need to use the `fopen()` and `fclose()` functions with the functions listed in Table 6-4.

The `file_get_contents()` function reads the entire contents of a file into a string. If you have a text file containing a single block of data (that is not a collection of individual records), the `file_get_contents()` function can be useful. For example, assume a weather service uses a text file to store daily weather forecasts. The following code uses the `file_put_contents()` function to write the daily forecast for San Francisco to a text file named sfweather.txt:

```
$DailyForecast = "<p><strong>San Francisco daily weather
forecast</strong>: Today: Partly cloudy. Highs from the 60s to
mid 70s. West winds 5 to 15 mph. Tonight: Increasing clouds. Lows
in the mid 40s to lower 50s. West winds 5 to 10 mph.</p>";
file_put_contents("sfweather.txt", $DailyForecast);
```

The following example uses the `file_get_contents()` function to read the contents of the sfweather.txt file into a string variable, which is then printed with an `echo()` statement:

```
$SFWeather = file_get_contents("sfweather.txt");
echo $SFWeather;
```


Next, you create new files that allow you to view the contents of an existing invoice.

To create new files that allow you to view the contents of an existing invoice:

1. Create a new document in your text editor.
2. Type the `<!DOCTYPE>` declaration, `<html>` element, header information, and `<body>` element. Use the strict DTD and "Invoices" as the content of the `<title>` element.
3. Add the following `<link>` element above the closing `</head>` tag to link to the php_styles.css style sheet in your Chapter directory:

   ```
   <link rel="stylesheet" href="php_styles.css" type="text/css" />
   ```

4. Add the following heading element and forms to the document body. The first form opens the CreateInvoice.html file, and the second form opens the ViewInvoice.php file, which you create next.

   ```
   <h1>Invoices</h1><hr />
   <form action="CreateInvoice.html" method="get"
   enctype="application/x-www-form-urlencoded">
   <p><input type="submit" value="Create Invoice" /></p>
   </form>
   <form action="ViewInvoice.php" method="get"
   enctype="application/x-www-form-urlencoded">
   <p><input type="submit" value="  View Invoice #  " /> 
   <input type="text" name="invoicenum" /></p>
   <p>(Enter an existing invoice number.)</p>
   </form>
   ```

5. Save the document as **Invoices.html** in the Chapter directory for Chapter 6.
6. Open **CreateInvoice.html** in your text editor and add the following text and elements to the end of the document body:

   ```
   <p><a href="Invoices.html">Return to Main Invoices Page</a></p>
   ```

7. Save and close the **CreateInvoice.html** file.

8. Return to the **SaveInvoice.php** file in your text editor and add the following text and elements to the end of the document body:

```
<p><a href="Invoices.html">Return to Main Invoices Page</a></p>
```

9. Save the **SaveInvoice.php** file.

Next, you create a document that allows you to view invoices.

To create a document that allows you to view invoices:

1. Create a new document in your text editor.

2. Type the `<!DOCTYPE>` declaration, `<html>` element, header information, and `<body>` element. Use the strict DTD and "View Invoice" as the content of the `<title>` element.

3. Add the following script section to the document body:

```
<?php
?>
```

4. Add the following `if` statement to the script section. The conditional expression uses the `empty()` function to confirm whether the user entered an invoice number in the Invoices Web page.

```
if (empty($_GET['invoicenum']))
   echo "<hr /><p>You must enter an existing invoice number.
        Click your browser's Back button to return to the
        Invoices page.</p><hr />";
```

5. Add the following `else` clause after the `if` statement. The first statement uses the `file_get_contents()` function to read the contents of the specified invoice file into a variable named `$Invoice`. The second statement uses the `explode()` function to split the lines in the `$Invoice` variable into an array named `$InvoiceFields`.

```
else {
     $Invoice = file_get_contents($_GET['invoicenum'] . ".txt");
     $InvoiceFields = explode("\n", $Invoice);
}
```

6. Add the following lines to the end of the `else` clause to convert the tilde characters in the Bill To line to line breaks:

```
$FixBillTo = explode("~", $InvoiceFields[0]);
$BillTo = implode("\n", $FixBillTo);
```

7. Add the following lines to the end of the `else` clause to strip the slashes from each field and to copy the values from each array element into a variable:

```
$BillTo = stripslashes($BillTo);
$InvoiceNum = stripslashes($InvoiceFields[1]);
```

```
$Date = stripslashes($InvoiceFields[2]);
$Terms = stripslashes($InvoiceFields[3]);
$Description1 = stripslashes($InvoiceFields[4]);
$Description2 = stripslashes($InvoiceFields[5]);
$Description3 = stripslashes($InvoiceFields[6]);
$Quantity1 = stripslashes($InvoiceFields[7]);
$Quantity2 = stripslashes($InvoiceFields[8]);
$Quantity3 = stripslashes($InvoiceFields[9]);
$Rate1 = stripslashes($InvoiceFields[10]);
$Rate2 = stripslashes($InvoiceFields[11]);
$Rate3 = stripslashes($InvoiceFields[12]);
$Amount1 = stripslashes($InvoiceFields[13]);
$Amount2 = stripslashes($InvoiceFields[14]);
$Amount3 = stripslashes($InvoiceFields[15]);
$Total = stripslashes($InvoiceFields[16]);
```


8. Finally, add the following `echo()` statements to the end of the `else` clause to print the invoice information:

```
echo "<h1>View Invoice</h1>";
echo "<hr /><br /><table frame='border' rules='rows'>";
echo "<tr><td><strong>Bill To</strong>";
echo "<pre>$BillTo</pre></td>";
echo "<td style='text-align: right' colspan='3'>";
echo "<br /><strong>Invoice #</strong>: $InvoiceNum<br />";
echo "<strong>Date</strong>: $Date<br />";
echo "<strong>Terms</strong>: $Terms</td></tr>";
echo "<tr>";
echo "<td><strong>Description</strong><br />$Description1
     <br />$Description2<br />$Description3</td>";
echo "<td style='text-align: right'><strong>Quantity</strong>
     <br />$Quantity1<br />$Quantity2<br />$Quantity3</td>";
echo "<td style='text-align: right'><strong>Rate</strong>
     <br />$$Rate1<br />$$Rate2<br />$$Rate3</td>";
echo "<td style='text-align: right'><strong>Amount</strong>
     <br />$$Amount1<br />$$Amount2<br />$$Amount3</td></tr>";
echo "<tr><td colspan='4' style='text-align: right'><strong>TOTAL
     </strong>: $$Total</td></tr>";
echo "</table>";
```

9. Save the document as **ViewInvoice.php** in the Chapter directory for Chapter 6.

10. Open the **Invoices.html** file in your Web browser by entering the following URL: **http://localhost/PHP_Projects/Chapter.06/Chapter/Invoices.html**. Enter an existing invoice number and click the **View Invoice #** button. Be certain to enter an invoice number you have already saved or you will receive an error message. Later in this chapter, you learn how to verify whether a file exists before opening it.

11. Close your Web browser window.

If you only want to print the contents of a text file, you do not need to use the `file_get_contents()` function to assign the contents of a file. Instead, use the `readfile()` function, which prints the contents of a text file along with the file size to a Web browser. For example, the following `readfile()` function accomplishes the same task as the `file_get_contents()` version you saw earlier:

```
readfile("sfweather.txt");
```

Text files are most often used to store records on individual lines. The easiest way to read the contents of a text file that stores records on individual lines is to use the `file()` function, which reads the entire contents of a file into an indexed array. The `file()` function automatically recognizes whether the lines in a text file end in `\n`, `\r`, or `\r\n`. Each individual line in the text file is assigned as the value of an element. You pass to the `file()` function the name of the text file enclosed in quotation marks. For example, the weather service that stores daily weather reports may also store average daily high, low, and mean temperatures, separated by commas, on individual lines in a single text file. The following code uses the `file_put_contents()` function to write the temperatures for the first week in January to a text file named sfjanaverages.txt:

```
$January = "48, 42, 68\n";
$January .= "48, 42, 69\n";
$January .= "49, 42, 69\n";
$January .= "49, 42, 61\n";
$January .= "49, 42, 65\n";
$January .= "49, 42, 62\n";
$January .= "49, 42, 62\n";
file_put_contents("sfjanaverages.txt", $January);
```

The first statement in the following code uses the `file()` function to read the contents of the sfjanaverages.txt file into an indexed array named `$JanuaryTemps[]`. The `for` statement then loops through each element in the `$JanuaryTemps[]` and calls the `explode()` function to split each element at the comma into another array named `$CurDay`. The high, low, and mean averages in the `$CurDay` array are then printed with `echo()` statements. Figure 6-8 show the output.

```
$JanuaryTemps = file("sfjanaverages.txt");
for ($i=0; $i<count($JanuaryTemps); ++$i) {
     $CurDay = explode(", ", $JanuaryTemps[$i]);
     echo "<p><strong>Day " . ($i + 1) . "</strong><br />";
     echo "High: {$CurDay[0]}<br />";
     echo "Low: {$CurDay[1]}<br />";
     echo "Mean: {$CurDay[2]}</p>";
}
```

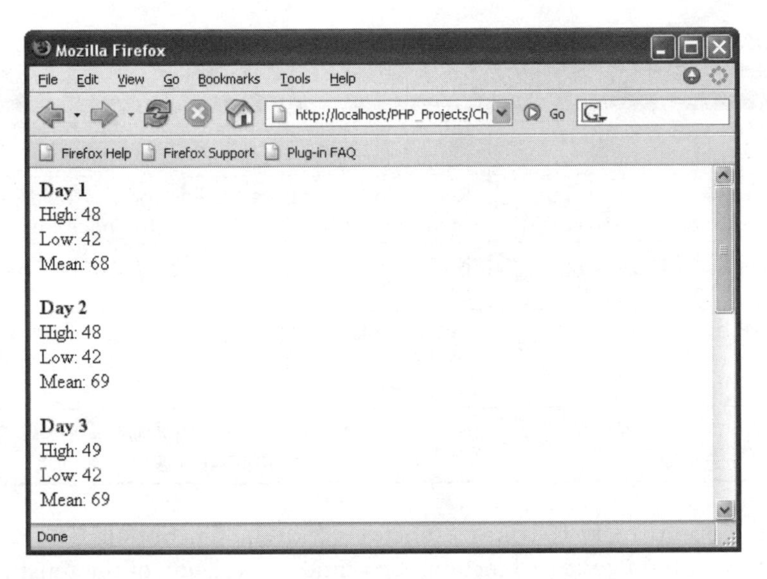

Figure 6-8 Output of individual lines in a text file

Next, you modify the ViewInvoice.php file so it opens the invoice text files with the `file()` function instead of the `file_get_contents()` function.

To modify the ViewInvoice.php file so it opens the invoice text files with the `file()` function instead of the `file_get_contents()` function:

1. Return to the **ViewInvoice.php** file in your text editor.
2. Replace the `file_get_contents()` and the `explode()` statements in the `else` clause with the following `file()` statement:

   ```
   $InvoiceFields = file($_GET['invoicenum'] . '.txt');
   ```
3. Save the **ViewInvoice.php** file.
4. Open the **Invoices.html** file in your Web browser by entering the following URL: **http://localhost/PHP_Projects/Chapter.06/Chapter/Invoices.html**. Enter an existing invoice number and click the **View Invoice #** button. The script should function the same as it did before you replaced the `file_get_contents()` function with the `file()` function.
5. Close your Web browser window.

Reading Data Incrementally

For large text files, reading the entire contents of the file into PHP can take up a lot of memory on your server and affect the performance of your script. Instead of reading an entire file into PHP, you can use the file pointer to iterate through a text file. As mentioned earlier, a file pointer is a special type of variable that refers to the currently selected line or character in a file. The functions listed in Table 6-5 allow you to use the file pointer to iterate through a text file.

Table 6-5 PHP functions that iterate through a text file

Function	Description
`fgetc($handle)`	Returns a single character and moves the file pointer to the next character
`fgetcsv($handle, length[, delimiter, string_enclosure])`	Returns a line, parses the line for CSV fields, and then moves the file pointer to the next line
`fgets($handle[, length])`	Returns a line and moves the file pointer to the next line
`fgetss($handle, length[, allowed_tags])`	Returns a line, strips any HTML tags the line contains, and then moves the file pointer to the next line
`stream_get_line($handle, length, delimiter)`	Returns a line that ends with a specified delimiter and moves the file pointer to the next line

You must use the `fopen()` and `fclose()` functions with the functions listed in Table 6-5. With the exception of the `fgetc()` function, each time you call any of the functions listed in Table 6-5, the file pointer automatically moves to the next line in the text file. Each time you call the `fgetc()` function, the file pointer moves to the next character in the file.

The functions listed in Table 6-5 are often combined with the `feof()` function, which returns a value of true when a file pointer reaches the end of a file. The `feof()` function accepts a single argument containing the name of the handle that represents the open file. The following code demonstrates how to use the `feof()` function along with the `fgets()` function, which returns a line and moves the file pointer to the next line. The code reads and parses each line in the sfjanaverages.txt text file, similar to the previous example you saw that parsed the data by using the `file()` function. In this version, a `while` statement uses the value returned from the `feof()` function as the conditional expression. The lines in the `while` statement then parse and print the contents of each line, and the last statement calls the `fgets()` function, which reads the current line and moves the file pointer to the next line.

```
$JanuaryTemps = fopen("sfjanaverages.txt", "r");
$Count = 1;
$CurAverages = fgets($JanuaryTemps);
while (!feof($JanuaryTemps)) {
     $CurDay = explode(", ", $CurAverages);
     echo "<p><strong>Day $Count</strong><br />";
     echo "High: {$CurDay[0]}<br />";
     echo "Low: {$CurDay[1]}<br />";
     echo "Mean: {$CurDay[2]}</p>";
     $CurAverages = fgets($JanuaryTemps);
     ++$Count;
}
fclose($JanuaryTemps);
```

Next, you modify the ViewInvoice.php file so it accesses the lines in the invoice text files with `fgets()` functions instead of the `file_get_contents()` function.

To modify the ViewInvoice.php file so it accesses the lines in the invoice text files with `fgets()` functions instead of the `file_get_contents()` function:

1. Return to the **ViewInvoice.php** file in your text editor.
2. Replace the `file()` statement in the `else` clause with the following `fopen()` statement:

   ```
   $InvoiceFields = fopen($_GET['invoicenum'] . ".txt", "r");
   ```

3. Modify the statements that fix the line breaks in the Bill To field so they use the `fgets()` function, as follows:

   ```
   $BillTo = fgets($InvoiceFields);
   $FixBillTo = explode("~", $BillTo);
   ```

4. Modify the following statements so the variables are assigned their values with the `fgets()` function instead of by referring to the array variables. Notice the `fgets()` function is nested within the `stripslashes()` function.

   ```
   $InvoiceNum = stripslashes(fgets($InvoiceFields));
   $Date = stripslashes(fgets($InvoiceFields));
   $Terms = stripslashes(fgets($InvoiceFields));
   $Description1 = stripslashes(fgets($InvoiceFields));
   $Description2 = stripslashes(fgets($InvoiceFields));
   $Description3 = stripslashes(fgets($InvoiceFields));
   $Quantity1 = stripslashes(fgets($InvoiceFields));
   $Quantity2 = stripslashes(fgets($InvoiceFields));
   $Quantity3 = stripslashes(fgets($InvoiceFields));
   $Rate1 = stripslashes(fgets($InvoiceFields));
   $Rate2 = stripslashes(fgets($InvoiceFields));
   $Rate3 = stripslashes(fgets($InvoiceFields));
   $Amount1 = stripslashes(fgets($InvoiceFields));
   $Amount2 = stripslashes(fgets($InvoiceFields));
   $Amount3 = stripslashes(fgets($InvoiceFields));
   $Total = stripslashes(fgets($InvoiceFields));
   ```

5. Add the following statement after the statement that declares the `$Total` variable:

   ```
   fclose($InvoiceFields);
   ```

6. Save the **ViewInvoice.php** file.
7. Open the **Invoices.html** file in your Web browser by entering the following URL: **http://localhost/PHP_Projects/Chapter.06/Chapter/Invoices.html**. Enter an existing invoice number and click the **View Invoice #** button. The script should function the same as it did before you replaced the `file()` function with the `fgets()` functions.
8. Close your Web browser window.

Managing Files and Directories

In addition to creating and accessing files, you can also use PHP to manage files and the directories that store them. In fact, you can use PHP to perform many of the same file and directory management tasks that are available on most operating systems, including copying, moving, renaming, and deleting files and directories. In this section, you study various techniques for managing files and directories with PHP. First, you learn how to work with directories.

Working with Directories

So far, you have only used PHP to read from and write to text files. You have also learned that several of the mode arguments of the `fopen()` function will create a text file if it doesn't exist. PHP also includes functions for reading the contents of a directory and for creating new directories.

Reading Directories

In addition to using PHP to read the individual lines in a text file, you can also read the names of files and directories that exist within a specified directory. To read the contents of a directory, you use the PHP functions listed in Table 6-6.

Table 6-6 PHP directory functions

Function	Description
`chdir(`*`directory`*`)`	Changes to the specified directory
`chroot(`*`directory`*`)`	Changes to the root directory
`closedir(`*`$handle`*`)`	Closes a directory handle
`getcwd()`	Gets the current working directory
`opendir(`*`directory`*`)`	Opens a handle to the specified directory
`readdir(`*`$handle`*`)`	Reads a file or directory name from the specified directory handle
`rewinddir(`*`$handle`*`)`	Resets the directory pointer to the beginning of the directory
`scandir(`*`directory`*`[, `*`sort`*`])`	Returns an indexed array containing the names of files and directories in the specified directory

To iterate through the entries in a directory, you open a handle to the directory with the `opendir()` function. You can then use the `readdir()` function to return the file and directory names from the open directory. Each time you call the `readdir()` function, it moves a directory pointer to the next entry in the directory. After the directory pointer reaches the end of the directory, the `readdir()` function returns a value of false. The following code demonstrates how to use the `readdir()` function to print the names of the files in the PHP program directory. Notice that the `readdir()` function is included as the conditional expression for the `while` statement. As long as the `readdir()` function does not return a value of false, the `while` loop continues printing the names of the directory entries. Also notice at the end of the code that the directory handle is closed with the `closedir()` function.

```
$Dir = "C:\\PHP";
$DirOpen = opendir($Dir);
while ($CurFile = readdir($DirOpen)) {
     echo $CurFile . "<br />";
}
closedir($DirOpen);
```

6

Next, you create a new Web page that displays a listing of the invoices you have created.

To create a new Web page that displays open invoices:

1. Create a new document in your text editor.
2. Type the `<!DOCTYPE>` declaration, `<html>` element, header information, and `<body>` element. Use the strict DTD and "View Open Invoices" as the content of the `<title>` element.
3. Add the following script section to the document body:

   ```
   <?php
   ?>
   ```

4. Add the following code to the script section to read the text files in the current directory. Notice that the first statement refers to the current directory by using a single period. Also notice that the `while` statement uses the `strpos()` function to display only files that end with .txt. This way, the "`.`" and "`..`" entries and any other entries in the directory will not display in the list of invoices.

   ```
   $Dir = ".";
   $DirOpen = opendir($Dir);
   while ($CurFile = readdir($DirOpen)) {
        if (strpos($CurFile, '.txt') !== FALSE)
              echo $CurFile . "<br />";
   }
   closedir($DirOpen);
   ```

5. Add the following text and elements to the end of the document body:

   ```
   <hr /><p><a href="Invoices.html">Return to Main Invoices
   Page</a></p>
   ```

6. Save the document as **ViewOpenInvoices.php** in the Chapter directory for Chapter 6.
7. Return to the **Invoices.html** document in your text editor.

8. Add the following new form between the two existing forms. This form opens the ViewOpenInvoices.php file.

```
<form action="ViewOpenInvoices.php" method="get"
enctype="application/x-www-form-urlencoded">
<p><input type="submit" value="View Open Invoices" /></p>
</form>
```

9. Save the **Invoices.html** file, and then open it in your Web browser by entering the following URL: **http://localhost/PHP_Projects/Chapter.06/Chapter/Invoices.html**. Click the **View Open Invoices** button. You should see a list of the invoices you have created so far.
10. Close your Web browser window.

Instead of using the `opendir()`, `readdir()`, and `closedir()` functions, you can also use the `scandir()` function, which returns an indexed array containing the names of files and directories in the specified directory. The following code shows how to print the names of the files and directories in the PHP program directory. Notice that this version does not use the `opendir()` or `closedir()` functions. Instead, it just uses the `scandir()` function to return the names of the entries in the PHP program directory to an array named `$DirEntries`, which are then printed with a `foreach` loop.

```
$Dir = "C:\\PHP";
$DirEntries = scandir($Dir);
foreach ($DirEntries as $Entry) {
     echo $Entry . "<br />";
}
```

When you use the `readdir()` function to return the entries in a directory, the entries are not sorted, but are instead returned in the order in which they are stored by your operating system. One benefit to using the `scandir()` function instead of the `readdir()` function is that the `scandir()` function sorts the returned entries in ascending alphabetical order. If you pass a value of 1 as a second argument to the `scandir()` function, as shown in the following example, the entries are sorted in descending alphabetical order:

```
$Dir = "C:\\PHP";
$DirEntries = scandir($Dir, 1);
foreach ($DirEntries as $Entry) {
     echo $Entry . "<br />";
}
```

Next, you modify the ViewOpenInvoices.php script so it uses the `scandir()` function.

To modify the ViewOpenInvoices.php script so it uses the `scandir()` function:

1. Return to the **ViewOpenInvoices.php** file in your text editor.
2. Replace the existing statements in the script section with the following statements that use the `scandir()` function:

```
$Dir = ".";
$DirEntries = scandir($Dir);
```

```
foreach ($DirEntries as $Entry) {
     if (strpos($Entry, '.txt') !== FALSE)
          echo $Entry . "<br />";
}
```

3. Save the **ViewOpenInvoices.php** file.
4. Open the **Invoices.html** file in your Web browser by entering the following URL: **http://localhost/PHP_Projects/Chapter.06/Chapter/Invoices.html**. Click the **View Open Invoices** button. You should see a listing of the invoices you have created so far.
5. Close your Web browser window.

Creating Directories

You can use the `mkdir()` function to create a new directory. To create a new directory within the current directory, you pass just the name of the directory you want to create to the `mkdir()` function. The following statement creates a new directory named "bowlers" within the current directory:

```
mkdir("bowlers");
```

To create a new directory in a location other than the current directory, you can use a relative or an absolute path. For example, the first statement in the following code uses a relative path to create a new directory named "tournament" at the same level as the current directory. The second statement uses an absolute path to create a new directory named "utilities" in the PHP program directory.

```
mkdir("..\\tournament");
mkdir("C:\\PHP\\utilities");
```

If you attempt to create a directory that already exists, you receive an error, similar to the one shown in Figure 6-9.

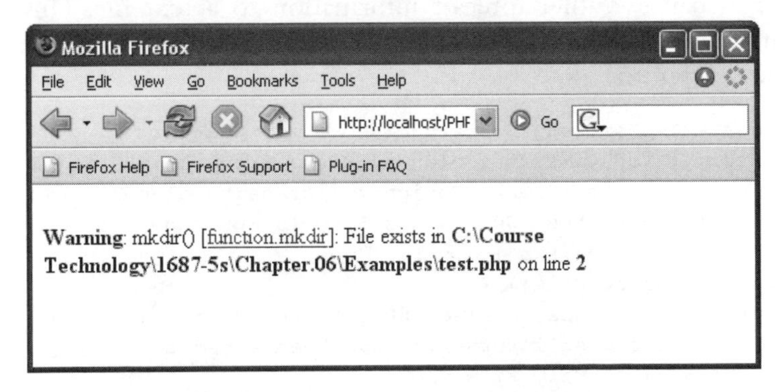

Figure 6-9 Warning that appears if a directory already exists

You also receive a warning if you attempt to use an absolute or relative path to create a new directory within a directory that doesn't exist. In the next section, you learn how to check whether a directory exists before attempting to access it or create a new directory within it.

Obtaining File and Directory Information

To successfully work with files and directories, you need to be able to obtain information about them. Some of the most important pieces of information you need to obtain about files and directories include whether they exist and whether you have the necessary permissions to work with them. Table 6-7 lists the common PHP file and directory status functions.

Table 6-7 PHP file and directory status functions

Function	Description
`file_exists(filename)`	Determines whether a file or directory exists
`is_dir(filename)`	Determines whether a filename is a directory
`is_executable(filename)`	Determines whether a file is executable
`is_file(filename)`	Determines whether a file is a regular file
`is_readable(filename)`	Determines whether a file is readable
`is_writable(filename)`	Determines whether a file is writable

Each of the functions listed in Table 6-7 returns a value of true if the file exists and if the given status is true. Two of the most commonly used file and directory status functions are the `is_writable()` and `is_readable()` functions. It is common practice to use these functions when you want to read from or write to a text file. Because both functions return a value of true, you can use them in a conditional expression to determine a file's status. The following example shows a modified version of the code you saw earlier that saves daily weather forecast information to a text file. This example includes an `if` statement that uses the `is_writable()` function to determine whether the text file can be written to.

```
$DailyForecast = "<p><strong>San Francisco daily weather
forecast</strong>: Today: Partly cloudy. Highs from the 60s to
mid 70s. West winds 5 to 15 mph. Tonight: Increasing clouds. Lows
in the mid 40s to lower 50s. West winds 5 to 10 mph.</p>";
$WeatherFile = "sfweather.txt";
if (is_writable($WeatherFile)) {
     file_put_contents($WeatherFile, $DailyForecast);
     echo "<p>The forecast information has been saved to
            the $WeatherFile file.</p>";
}
else
     echo "<p>The forecast information cannot be saved to
            the $WeatherFile file.</p>";
```

The following example uses the `file_get_contents()` function to read the contents of the sfweather.txt file into a string variable, which is then printed with an `echo()` statement. This example includes an `if` statement that uses the `is_readable()` function to determine whether the text file can be read.

```
$WeatherFile = "sfweather.txt";
if (is_readable($WeatherFile)) {
     $SFWeather = file_get_contents("sfweather.txt");
     echo $SFWeather;
}
else
     echo "<p>The $WeatherFile file cannot be read.</p>";
```


You can also use the `is_dir()` function to check whether a directory exists before attempting to access it. The following example demonstrates how to use the `is_dir()` function before using the `scandir()` function:

```
$Dir = "C:\\PHP";
if (is_dir($Dir)) {
     $DirEntries = scandir($Dir, 1);
     foreach ($DirEntries as $Entry) {
           echo $Entry . "<br />";
     }
}
else
     echo "<p>The directory does not exist.</p>";
```

PHP includes other types of functions that return additional information about files and directories. Table 6-8 lists common file and directory information functions.

Table 6-8 Common file and directory information functions

Function	Description
`fileatime(`*`filename`*`)`	Returns the last time the file was accessed
`filectime(`*`filename`*`)`	Returns the last time the file was modified
`fileowner(`*`filename`*`)`	Returns the name of the file's owner
`filetype(`*`filename`*`)`	Returns the file type

The following code demonstrates how to use two of the functions listed in Table 6-8: `filesize()` and `filetype()`. The script builds a table that contains the filename, file size, and file type. Figure 6-10 shows the output.

```
$Dir = "C:\\PHP";
if (is_dir($Dir)) {
     echo "<table border='1' width='100%'>";
     echo "<tr><th>Filename</th><th>File Size</th>
           <th>File Type</th></tr>";
     $DirEntries = scandir($Dir);
```

```
        foreach ($DirEntries as $Entry) {
              echo "<tr><td>$Entry</td><td>" . filesize($Dir . "\\"
                    . $Entry) . "</td><td>" . filetype($Dir . "\\"
                    . $Entry) . "</td></tr>";
        }
        echo "</table>";
}
else
        echo "<p>The directory does not exist.</p>";
```

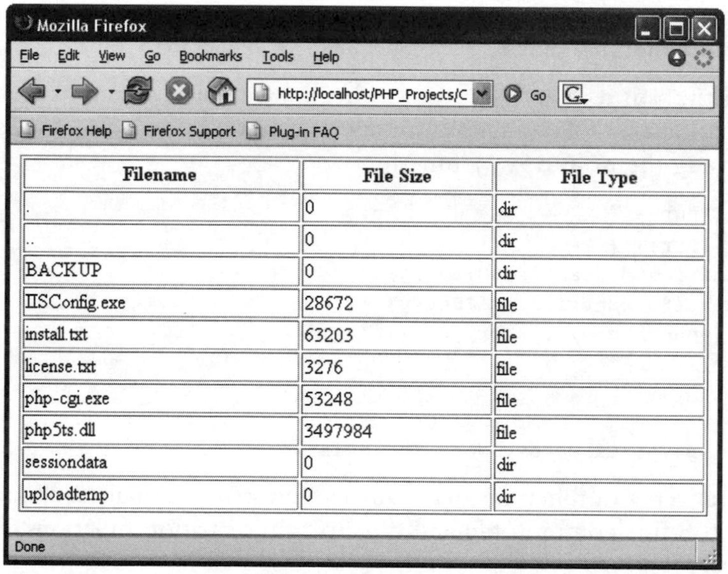

Filename	File Size	File Type
.	0	dir
..	0	dir
BACKUP	0	dir
IISConfig.exe	28672	file
install.txt	63203	file
license.txt	3276	file
php-cgi.exe	53248	file
php5ts.dll	3497984	file
sessiondata	0	dir
uploadtemp	0	dir

Figure 6-10 Output of script with file and directory information functions

Next, you modify the files in the invoices program so they use PHP file and directory status functions. You also modify the files so that invoices are stored within a directory named Open within your Chapter directory.

To modify the SaveInvoice.php file so it saves invoices to a directory named Open:

1. Return to the **SaveInvoice.php** file in your text editor.
2. Add the following statements above the `fopen()` statement. The conditional expression in the `if` statement determines whether the Open directory exists. If the directory doesn't exist, it is created by the `mkdir()` function.

   ```
   if (!file_exists("Open"))
        mkdir("Open");
   ```

3. Modify the `fopen()` function so it saves invoices in the Open directory, as follows:

   ```
   $InvoiceFile = fopen("Open\\" . $InvoiceNum . ".txt", "w");
   ```

4. Save the **SaveInvoice.php** file.

To modify the ViewInvoice.php file so it uses the `is_readable()` function:

1. Return to the **ViewInvoice.php** file in your text editor.
2. Modify the `else` clause into an `else...if` clause that uses the `is_readable()` function as its conditional expression, as follows:

```
else if (is_readable("Open\\" . $_GET['invoicenum'] . ".txt")) {
```

3. Modify the statement that declares and initializes the $InvoiceFields variable so it references the Open directory, as follows:

```
$InvoiceFields = fopen("Open\\" . $_GET['invoicenum'] . ".txt", "r");
```

4. Add an `else` clause to the end of the script, as follows:

```
else
     echo "<p>Could not read the invoice!</p>";
```

5. Save the **ViewInvoice.php** file.

To modify the ViewOpenInvoices.php file so it uses the `is_dir()` function:

1. Return to the **ViewOpenInvoices.php** file in your text editor.
2. Modify the script section so the Open directory is assigned to the `$Dir` variable. Also, create an `if...else` statement that uses the `is_dir()` function to determine whether the directory exists. Your script section should appear as follows:

```
$Dir = "open";
if (is_dir($Dir)) {
     $DirEntries = scandir($Dir);
     foreach ($DirEntries as $Entry) {
          if (strpos($Entry, '.txt') !== FALSE)
               echo $Entry . "<br />";
     }
}
else
     echo "<p>The Open directory does not exist! You must first
save an invoice to create the Open directory.</p>";
```

3. Save the **ViewOpenInvoices.php** file.
4. Open **Invoices.html** in your Web browser by entering the following URL: **http://localhost/PHP_Projects/Chapter.06/Chapter/Invoices.html**. Enter some new invoices, and then test the View Invoice and View Open Invoices scripts.
5. Close your Web browser window.

Copying and Moving Files

You use the **copy()** function to copy a file with PHP. The function returns a value of true if it is successful or false if it is not. The syntax for the **copy()** function is **copy(*source, destination*)**. For the *source* and *destination* arguments, you can include just the name of a file to make a copy in the current directory or you can specify the entire path for each argument. The following example demonstrates how to use the **copy()** function to copy the sfweather.txt file to a file named sfweather01-27-2006.txt in a directory named "history." The first **if** statement checks whether the sfweather.txt file exists, whereas the first nested **if** statement checks whether the history directory exists within the current directory. If both **if** statements are true, the **copy()** function attempts to copy the file.

```
if (file_exists("sfweather.txt")) {
        if(is_dir("history")) {
            if (copy("sfweather.txt",
                  "history\\sfweather01-27-2006.txt"))
                  echo "<p>File copied successfully.</p>";
            else
                  echo "<p>Unable to copy the file!</p>";
      }
      else
            echo ("<p>The directory does not exist!</p>");
}
else
      echo ("<p>The file does not exist!</p>");
```

PHP does not contain a separate command for moving files. Instead, you can rename the file with the **rename()** function and specify a new directory in which you want to store the renamed file. Or, you must copy the file with the **copy()** function, and then delete the original file with the **unlink()** function.

Next, you use the **copy()** function to copy your open invoices to a backup directory.

To use the **copy()** function to copy your open invoices to a backup directory:

1. Create a new document in your text editor.
2. Type the **<!DOCTYPE>** declaration, **<html>** element, header information, and **<body>** element. Use the strict DTD and "Backup Invoices" as the content of the **<title>** element.
3. Add the following **<link>** element above the closing **</head>** tag to link to the php_styles.css style sheet in your Chapter directory:

   ```
   <link rel="stylesheet" href="php_styles.css" type="text/css" />
   ```

4. Add the following script section to the document body:

   ```
   <?php
   ?>
   ```

5. Declare the following two variables in the script section. The `$Source` variable contains the name of the Open directory, and the `$Destination` variable contains the name of the directory, "Backups," where you will back up your files.

```
$Source = "Open";
$Destination = "Backups";
```

6. Add the following `if` statement to the end of the script section. The `if` statement creates the Backups directory if it does not exist.

```
if (!file_exists($Destination))
     mkdir($Destination);
```

7. Finally, add the following `if...else` statement, which executes the `copy()` function:

```
if (is_dir($Source)) {
        $DirEntries = scandir($Source);
        foreach ($DirEntries as $Entry) {
              if (strpos($Entry, '.txt') !== FALSE)
                      copy("$Source\\" . $Entry, "$Destination\\"
                           .$Entry);
        }
        echo "<p>Invoices successfully backed up.</p>";
}
else
        echo "<p>The Open directory does not exist! You must first
              save an invoice to create the Open directory.</p>";
```

8. Save the document as **BackupInvoices.php** in the Chapter directory for Chapter 6.
9. Return to the **Invoices.html** document in your text editor.
10. Add the following new form to the end of the document body. This form opens the BackupInvoices.php file.

```
<form action="BackupInvoices.php" method="get"
enctype="application/x-www-form-urlencoded">
<p><input type="submit" value="Backup Invoices" /></p>
</form>
```

11. Save the **Invoices.html** file, and then open it in your Web browser by entering the following URL: **http://localhost/PHP_Projects/Chapter.06/Chapter/Invoices.html**. Click the **Backup Invoices** button. You should see the message that the invoices were successfully backed up. Look in your Chapter directory for Chapter 6 and see if the Backups directory was created, and that it contains copies of the invoices in your Open directory.
12. Close your Web browser window.

Renaming Files and Directories

You use the `rename()` function to rename a file or directory with PHP. As with the `copy()` function, the `rename()` function returns a value of true if it is successful or false if it is not. The syntax for the `rename()` function is `rename(old_name, new_name)`. For the *`old_name`* and *`new_name`* arguments, you can include just the name of a file to make a copy in the current directory or you can specify the entire path for each argument. If you specify a different path for the *`new_name`* argument when renaming a file, the file is effectively moved from the old directory to the specified directory.

The following example demonstrates how to rename and move a file. Notice that the script contains three levels of nested `if` statements to check the file and directory names, and a fourth nested `if` statement that verifies whether the `rename()` function was successful. The first `if` statement checks to see whether the original file exists, the second `if` statement determines whether the destination directory exists, and the third `if` statement confirms that a file of the same name does not exist in the target directory.

```
$OldName = "sfweather.txt";
$NewName = "sfweather01-28-2006.txt";
$NewDirectory = "history";
if (file_exists($OldName)) {
      if(is_dir($NewDirectory)) {
            if (!file_exists($NewDirectory . "\\" . $NewName)) {
                  if (rename($OldName, $NewDirectory . "\\"
                        . $NewName))
                        echo "<p>File renamed successfully.</p>";
                  else
                        echo "<p>Unable to rename the file!</p>";
            }
}
else
      echo ("<p>The directory does not exist!</p>");
}
else
      echo ("<p>The file does not exist!</p>");
```

Removing Files and Directories

You use the `unlink()` function to delete files and the `rmdir()` function to delete directories. You pass the name of a file to the `unlink()` function and the name of a directory to the `rmdir()` function. Both functions return a value of true if successful or false if not. With both functions, you can use the `file_exists()` function to determine whether a file or directory name exists before you attempt to delete it. For example, the following code uses the `file_exists()` and `unlink()` functions to delete a file:

```
$FileName = "sfweather.txt";
if (file_exists($FileName)) {
```

```
        if(unlink($FileName))
              echo "<p>File deleted successfully.</p>";
        else
              echo "<p>Unable to delete the file!</p>";
  }
  else
        echo ("<p>The file does not exist!</p>");
```

The `rmdir()` function takes a little more developmental effort because it does not work unless a directory is empty. To check whether a directory is empty, you first use the `file_exists()` function to determine whether the directory exists. Then, you use the `scandir()` function to copy the names of the files in the directory to an array. Some operating systems always list two directory entries named "`.`" and "`..`" within another directory. The "`.`" directory is a reference to the current directory, whereas the "`..`" directory is a reference to the directory that contains the current directory. The `rmdir()` function only works when these are the only two entries present, indicating that the directory is empty. For this reason, you need to write code that verifies that the directory you want to delete contains only the "`.`" and "`..`" entries. The following example uses the `file_exists()` function to see whether the history directory exists, then uses the `scandir()` function and a `foreach()` loop to determine whether the directory contains any entries other than the "`.`" and "`..`" entries.


```
$DirName = "history";
if (file_exists($DirName)) {
      $DirEntries = scandir($DirName);
      $EmptyDir = FALSE;
      foreach ($DirEntries as $Dir) {
            if ($Dir != "." && $Dir != "..")
                  $EmptyDir = "TRUE";
      }
      if ($EmptyDir == FALSE) {
                  if(rmdir($DirName))
                        echo "<p>Directory deleted successfully.</p>";
                  else
                        echo "<p>Unable to delete the directory!</p>";
            }
      else
            echo "<p>The directory is not empty!</p>";
}
else
      echo ("<p>The directory does not exist!</p>");
```

Chapter Summary

- The stream is used for accessing a resource, such as a file, that you can read from and write to. The input stream reads data from a resource (such as a file), whereas the output stream writes data to a resource (again, such as a file).
- A handle is a special type of variable that PHP uses to represent a resource such as a file.
- The `fopen()` function opens a stream to a text file.
- A file pointer is a special type of variable that refers to the currently selected line or character in a file.
- When you are finished working with a file stream, you use the `fclose` function to ensure that the file doesn't keep taking up space in your computer's memory.
- PHP supports two basic methods for writing data to text files: the `file_put_contents()` function, which writes or appends a text string to a file, and the `fwrite()` function, which incrementally writes data to a text file.
- Magic quotes automatically add backslashes (\) to any single quote ('), double quote ("), or NULL character contained in data that a user submits to a PHP script. Rather than relying on magic quotes to escape text strings, you should disable magic quotes in your php.ini configuration file and instead manually escape the strings with the `addslashes()` function.
- The `stripslashes()` function removes slashes that were added with the `addslashes()` function.
- The `flock()` function prevents multiple users from modifying a file simultaneously.
- The `file_get_contents()` function reads the entire contents of a file into a string.
- The `readfile()` function prints the contents of a text file to a Web browser.
- The `file()` function reads the entire contents of a file into an indexed array.
- PHP includes various functions, such as the `fgets()` function, that allow you to use the file pointer to iterate through a text file.
- To iterate through the entries in a directory, you open a handle to the directory with the `opendir()` function. You can then use the `readdir()` function to return the file and directory names from the open directory. You use the `closedir()` function to close a directory handle.
- The `scandir()` function returns an indexed array containing the names of files and directories in the specified directory.
- The `mkdir()` function creates a new directory.
- PHP includes various file and directory status functions, such as the `file_exists()` function, which determines whether a file or directory exists.

- PHP includes other types of functions that return additional information about files and directories, such as the `file_size()` function, which returns the size of a file.
- The `copy()` function copies a file.
- PHP does not contain a separate command for moving files. Instead, you can rename the file with the `rename()` function and specify a new directory where you want to store the renamed file. Or, you must copy the file with the `copy()` function, and then delete the original file with the `unlink()` function.
- The `rename()` function renames a file or directory.
- The `unlink()` function deletes files, and the `rmdir()` function deletes directories.

REVIEW QUESTIONS

1. Which of the following reads data from a resource such as a file?
   a. an input stream
   b. an output stream
   c. a pointer
   d. a reference
2. Which of the following is the correct syntax for opening a handle for reading only to a text file named prospects.txt?
   a. `$SalesProspects= fopen("prospects.txt", "r+");`
   b. `$SalesProspects= open("prospects.txt", "w");`
   c. `$SalesProspects= fopen("prospects.txt", "r");`
   d. `$SalesProspects= fileopen("prospects.txt", "a");`
3. Which of the following best describes the "w+" *mode* argument?
   a. creates and opens the specified file for reading and writing; returns false if the file already exists
   b. opens the specified file for reading and writing and places the file pointer at the end of the file; attempts to create the file if it doesn't exist
   c. opens the specified file for writing only and deletes any existing content in the file; attempts to create the file if it doesn't exist
   d. opens the specified file for reading and writing and deletes any existing content in the file; attempts to create the file if it doesn't exist
4. A ________________ is a special type of variable that refers to the currently selected line or character in a file.
   a. character pointer
   b. line pointer

   c. file pointer
   d. directory pointer

5. Explain why you should call the `fclose()` function when you are finished working with a file.
6. Which of the following escape sequences is used on Macintosh platforms?
   a. `\n`
   b. `\r`
   c. `\n\r`
   d. `\r\n`
7. You must open and close a file stream when you use the `file_put_contents()` function. True or False?
8. Which of the following constants can you use with the `file_put_contents()` function to append data to the end of a file?
   a. `INCLUDE_FILE`
   b. `FILE_USE_INCLUDE_PATH`
   c. `APPEND`
   d. `FILE_APPEND`
9. Explain what magic quotes are and how you should handle them in your scripts.
10. What is the correct syntax for using the `fwrite()` function to assign a value of "Forestville Foods" to a handle named `$SalesProspects`?
    a. `$SalesProspects = fwrite("Forestville Foods\n");`
    b. `fwrite($SalesProspects, "Forestville Foods\n");`
    c. `fwrite("Forestville Foods\n", $SalesProspects);`
    d. `fwrite("$SalesProspectsForestville Foods\n");`
11. Explain why you should lock files before writing data to them.
12. Which of the following operational constants can you use with the `flock()` function? (Choose all that apply.)
    a. `LOCK_EX`
    b. `LOCK_NB`
    c. `LOCK_SH`
    d. `LOCK_UN`
13. Which of the following functions reads the contents of a file into a string?
    a. `file()`
    b. `file_get_contents()`

c. `fread()`

d. `readfile()`

14. The `file()` function automatically recognizes whether the lines in a text file end in `\n`, `\r`, or `\r\n`. True or False?
15. Which of the following functions can you use to iterate through a text file? (Choose all that apply.)

a. `stream_get_line()`

b. `fgets()`

c. `fread()`

d. `readfile()`

16. Which of the following functions returns a value of true when a file pointer reaches the end of a file?

a. `is_end()`

b. `end()`

c. `eof()`

d. `feof()`

17. Which of the following functions sorts directory entries?

a. `scandir()`

b. `readdir()`

c. `opendir()`

d. `sortdir()`

18. Which of the following statements creates a directory named "students" at the same level as the current directory?

a. `mkdir("\\students");`

b. `mkdir("students");`

c. `mkdir("\\students\\");`

d. `mkdir("..\\students");`

19. Explain when you should use file and directory status functions such as the `file_exists()` and the `is_dir()` functions.
20. Explain the two ways in which you can move a file with PHP.

HANDS-ON PROJECTS

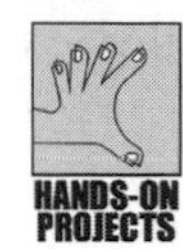

Hands-On Project 6-1

In this project, you create a hit counter script that keeps track of the number of hits a Web page receives.

1. Create a new document in your text editor and type the `<!DOCTYPE>` declaration, `<html>` element, document head, and `<body>` element. Use the strict DTD and "Hit Counter" as the content of the `<title>` element.
2. Add the following script section to the document body:

```
<?php
?>
```

3. Add the following statement to the script section to declare a variable named `$CounterFile` that contains the name of the file where the hits will be stored:

```
$CounterFile = "hitcount.txt";
```

4. Add the following `if` statement to the end of the script section. The `if` statement determines whether the hitcount.txt file already exists. If it does, the `file_get_contents()` function retrieves the value from the file and increments it by one.

```
if (file_exists($CounterFile)) {
     $Hits = file_get_contents($CounterFile);
     ++$Hits;
}
```

5. Add the following else statement to the end of the script section. The else statement contains a single statement that assigns a value of 1 to the $Hits variable in the event that the hitcount.txt file has not yet been created.

```
else
     $Hits = 1;
```

6. Finally, add the following statements to the end of the script section. The echo() statement prints the number of hits and the *if* statement updates the value in the hitcount.txt file. Remember that the file_put_contents() function opens the file if it already exists or creates it if it doesn't.

```
echo "<h1>There have been $Hits hits to this page!</h1>";
if (file_put_contents($CounterFile, $Hits))
     echo "<p>The counter file has been updated.</p>";
```

7. Save the document as **HitCounter.php** in the Projects directory for Chapter 6.
8. Open **HitCounter.php** file in your Web browser by entering the following URL: **http://localhost/PHP_Projects/Chapter.06/Projects/HitCounter.php**. The first time you open the Web page, you should see a hit count of 1. Reload the Web page a few times to see if the count increases.
9. Close your Web browser window.

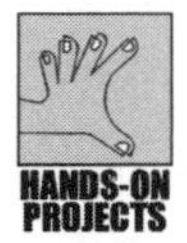

Hands-On Project 6-2

In this project, you create an RSVP form for a party you are hosting. A PHP script will save respondents to two separate text files: one file will contain the names of people who will be attending and another file will contain the names of people who will not be attending. The form will also contain links that display the contents of each file.

1. Create a new document in your text editor and type the `<!DOCTYPE>` declaration, `<html>` element, document head, and `<body>` element. Use the strict DTD and "RSVP" as the content of the `<title>` element.
2. Add the following text and elements to the document body:

```
<h1>Invitation</h1>
<p>You are cordially invited to attend the celebration of the
Anderson's 50th wedding anniversary on October 15 at 8:00 p.m.</p>
<form action="SendRSVP.php" method="get">
<h2>RSVP</h2>
<p>Name   <input type="text" name="name" size="50" /></p>
<p><input type="radio" name="attendance" value="yes" />I will
attend   <input type="radio" name="attendance" value="no" />I
will NOT attend  </p>
<p>Number of guests besides myself   <input type="text" name=
"guests" /></p>
<p><input type="submit" value=" Send RSVP" /><input type="reset" />
</p></form>
<p><a href="attending.php">See Who's Attending</a><br />
<a href="notattending.php">See Who's Not Attending</a></p>
```

3. Save the document as **RSVP.html** in the Projects directory for Chapter 6.
4. Create a new document in your text editor and type the `<!DOCTYPE>` declaration, `<html>` element, document head, and `<body>` element. Use the strict DTD and "RSVP" as the content of the `<title>` element.
5. Add the following script section to the document body:

```
<?php
?>
```

6. Add the following `if` and `else...if` statements to the script section. The `if` statement determines whether the user entered a value in the name field and selected a radio button that specifies whether they will attend. The `else...if` statement determines whether a user who is attending entered a number in the guests field.

```
if (empty($_GET['name']) || !isset($_GET['attendance']))
     echo "<p>You must enter your name and specify whether you
          will attend! Click your browser's Back button to
          return to the RSVP form.</p>";
```

```
else if ($_GET['attendance'] == "yes"
     && !is_numeric($_GET['guests']))
     echo "<p>Please specify the number of guests who will
          accompany you! Click your browser's Back button to
          return to the RSVP form.</p>";
```

7. Add the following else clause to the end of the script section. The first if statement in the else clause adds attendee names and their number of guests to a text file named attending.txt. The second if statement just adds the names of people who aren't attending to the notattending.txt file.

```
else {
     if ($_GET['attendance'] == "yes") {
          $YesFile = "attending.txt";
          if (file_put_contents($YesFile, addslashes($_GET['name'])
                    . ", " . $_GET['guests'] . "\n", FILE_APPEND))
               echo "<p>Thanks for RSVP'ing! We're looking forward
                    to seeing you!</p>";
          else
               echo "<p>Cannot save to the $YesFile file.</p>";
     }
     if ($_GET['attendance'] == "no") {
          $NoFile = "notattending.txt";
          if (file_put_contents($NoFile, addslashes($_GET['name'])
                    . "\n", FILE_APPEND))
               echo "<p>Thanks for RSVP'ing! Sorry you can't
                    make it!</p>";
          else
               echo "<p>Cannot save to the $NoFile file.</p>";
     }
}
```

8. Save the document as **SendRSVP.php** in the Projects directory for Chapter 6.
9. Create a document named **attending.php** that displays the list of attendees and their guests when a user clicks the See Who's Attending link on the RSVP form.
10. Create a document named **notattending.php** that displays the names of people who will not be attending when a user clicks the See Who's Not Attending link on the RSVP form.
11. Open the **RSVP.html** file in your Web browser by entering the following URL: **http://localhost/PHP_Projects/Chapter.06/Projects/RSVP.html**. Test the form to see if you can write data to and read data from the text files.
12. Close your Web browser window.

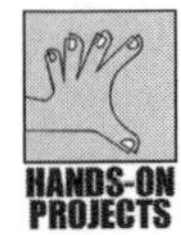

Hands-On Project 6-3

In this project, you create a Web page that allows visitors to your site to sign a guest book that is saved to a text file.

1. Create a new document in your text editor and type the `<!DOCTYPE>` declaration, `<html>` element, document head, and `<body>` element. Use the strict DTD and "Guest Book" as the content of the `<title>` element.
2. Add the following text and elements to the document body:

```
<h2>Enter your name to sign our guest book</h2>
<form method="get" action="SignGuestBook.php">
<p>First Name <input type="text" name="first_name" /></p>
<p>Last Name <input type="text" name="last_name" /></p>
<p><input type="submit" value=" Submit" /></p>
</form>
<p><a href="ShowGuestBook.php">Show Guest Book</a></p>
```

3. Save the document as **GuestBook.html** in the Projects directory for Chapter 6.
4. Create a new document in your text editor and type the `<!DOCTYPE>` declaration, `<html>` element, document head, and `<body>` element. Use the strict DTD and "Guest Book" as the content of the `<title>` element.
5. Add the following script section to the document body:

```
<?php
?>
```

6. Add the following `if` statement to the script section to check whether the user filled in the first name and last name fields:

```
if (empty($_GET['first_name']) || empty($_GET['last_name']))
     echo "<p>You must enter your first and last name! Click
          your browser's Back button to return to the RSVP
          form.</p>";
```

7. Add the following `else` clause to the end of the script section. The statements in the `else` clause use the `fwrite()` function to add visitor names to a text file named guestbook.txt.

```
else {
     $FirstName = addslashes($_GET['first_name']);
     $LastName = addslashes($_GET['last_name']);
     $GuestBook = fopen("guestbook.txt", "a");
     if (is_writable("guestbook.txt")) {
          if (fwrite($GuestBook, $LastName . ", "
               . $FirstName . "\n"))
               echo "<p>Thank you for signing our guest book!</p>";
          else
               echo "<p>Cannot add your name to the guest
                    book.</p>";
     }
```

```
        else
             echo "<p>Cannot write to the file.</p>";
        fclose($GuestBook);
   }
```

8. Save the document as **SignGuestBook.php** in the Projects directory for Chapter 6.
9. Create a document named **ShowGuestBook.php** that displays the visitors who have signed the guest book. Use the `readfile()` function to print the contents of the guestbook.txt. Note that you will need to use the `<pre>` element for Web browsers to recognize the line breaks.
10. Open **GuestBook.html** file in your Web browser by entering the following URL: **http://localhost/PHP_Projects/Chapter.06/Projects/GuestBook.html**. Test the form to see if you can write data to and read data from the guestbook.txt file.
11. Close your Web browser window.

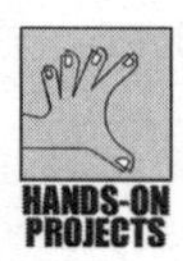

Hands-On Project 6-4

PHP provides the following functions, which allow you to use external files in your PHP scripts: `include()`, `require()`, `include_once()`, and `require_once()`. You pass to each function the name and path of the external file you want to use. The `include()` and `require()` functions both insert the contents of an external file, called an include file, into a PHP script. The difference between the two functions is that the `include()` function only generates a warning if the file isn't available, whereas the `require()` function halts the processing of the Web page if the file isn't available. The `include_once()` and `require_once()` functions are similar to the `include()` and `require()` functions, except they only include an external file once during the processing of a script. The external files you call with these statements usually contain PHP code or HTML code. Any PHP code must be contained within a PHP script section (`<?php ... ?>`) in an external file. You will find include files very useful for organizing your PHP and HTML code, or for reusing PHP or HTML code on multiple Web pages.

One common use of include files is to store a Web site's header and footer information in external files. This helps maintain a common look and feel for all the pages on the Web site. It is also easier to update header and footer information in one place instead of updating all the pages in a Web site. In this project, you create header and footer pages that you will add to a Web page with the `include()` function.

1. Create a new document in your text editor and type the `<!DOCTYPE>` declaration, `<html>` element, document head, and `<body>` element. Use the strict DTD and "Coast City Computers" as the content of the `<title>` element.
2. Add the following text and elements to the document body:

```
<h2>Memorial Day Sale</h2>
<ul>
<li>Compaq Presario m2007us Notebook:
```

```
<strong>$799.99</strong></li>
<li>Epson Stylus CX6600 Color All-In One Printer,
Print/Copy/Scan: <strong>$699.99</strong></li>
<li>Proview Technology Inc. KDS K715s 17-inch LCD Monitor,
Silver/Black: <strong>$199.99</strong></li>
<li>Hawking Technology Hi-Speed Wireless-G Cardbus Card:
<strong>$9.99</strong></li>
</ul>
```

3. Add the following PHP code section and `include()` statement to the beginning of the document body. This statement includes an external file named header.html at the start of the Web page.

```
<?php include("header.html"); ?>
```


4. Add the following PHP code section and `include()` statement to the end of the document body. This statement includes an external file named footer.html at the end of the Web page.

```
<?php include("footer.html"); ?>
```

5. Save the document as **CoastCityComputers.php** in the Projects directory for Chapter 6.
6. Create a new document in your text editor and add the following text and elements:

```
<table width="100%" border="0">
<tr><td><h1>Coast City Computers</h1></td>
<td align="right"><strong>Buy Online or Call 1-800-555-
1212</strong></td></tr></table><hr />
```

7. Save the document as **header.html** in the Projects directory for Chapter 6.
8. Create a new document in your text editor and add the following text and elements:

```
<hr />
<table width="100%" border="0">
<tr><td><strong>Updated</strong> 06 January, 2007</td>
<td align="right">&copy; 2003 by Coast City Computers.</td>
</tr>
<tr><td>
    <a href="http://validator.w3.org/check/referer"><img
        src="http://www.w3.org/Icons/valid-xhtml10"
        alt="Valid XHTML 1.0!" height="31" width="88" /></a>
</td>
<td align="right" valign="top">All Rights Reserved.</td></tr>
</table>
```

9. Save the document as **footer.html** in the Projects directory for Chapter 6.

10. Open the **CoastCityComputers.php** file in your Web browser by entering the following URL: **http://localhost/PHP_Projects/Chapter.06/Projects/CoastCityComputers.php**. The contents of the header and footer documents should appear on the Web page.
11. Close your Web browser window and text editor.

CASE PROJECTS

Save the documents you create for the following projects in the Cases directory for Chapter 6.

Case Project 6-1

Create a document with a form that registers users for a professional conference. Use a single text file that saves information for each registrant on a single line, separated by commas.

Case Project 6-2

Create a telephone directory application that saves entries to a single text file. You should include standard telephone directory fields in the database, such as first name, last name, address, city, state, zip, telephone number, and so on. Create a document as a main "directory," where you can select and retrieve records. Also, create one document that you can use to add new entries to your text file and another document that you can use to edit entries.

Case Project 6-3

Create a Web page to be used for storing software development bug reports in text files. Include fields such as product name and version, type of hardware, operating system, frequency of occurrence, and proposed solutions. Include links on the main page that allow you to create a new bug report and update an existing bug report.

Case Project 6-4

Create a Web site for tracking, documenting, and managing the process of interviewing candidates for professional positions. On the main page, include a form with fields for the interviewer's name, position, and date of interview. Also include fields such as candidate's name, communication abilities, professional appearance, computer skills, business knowledge, and interviewer's comments. Clicking the Submit button should save the data in a text file. Include a link for opening a document that displays each candidate's interview information.

Case Project 6-5

Create a Web page that stores airline surveys in text files. Include fields for the date and time of the flight, flight number, and so on. Also, include radio buttons for the following questions:

- Friendliness of customer staff?
- Space for luggage storage?
- Comfort of seating?
- Cleanliness of aircraft?
- Noise level of aircraft?

Each radio button group should include the following buttons, to allow users to select a rating for each question: No Opinion, Poor, Fair, Good, or Excellent. Separate text files should store the results of a single survey. Include a View Past Survey Results button on the main survey page that displays a list of past survey results.

Case Project 6-[illegible]

[illegible] with [illegible] [illegible] [illegible] field [illegible] [illegible] of the [illegible] [illegible] and [illegible]. Also include [illegible] [illegible] [illegible]

[illegible]

[illegible] the [illegible]

[illegible]

[illegible]

[illegible]

[illegible] should include the following [illegible] [illegible] [illegible] [illegible] [illegible] [illegible] [illegible] results of [illegible] [illegible] [illegible] [illegible]

CHAPTER

7

MANIPULATING ARRAYS

In this chapter, you will:

- Manipulate array elements
- Declare and initialize associative arrays
- Use iteration functions
- Find and extract elements and values
- Sort, combine, and compare arrays
- Work with multidimensional arrays

Earlier in this book, you learned that an array contains a set of data represented by a single variable name. You also learned that PHP includes two types of arrays: indexed and associative. You refer to the elements in an indexed array by their numeric position, whereas you refer to the elements in an associative array with an alphanumeric key. Although you have already learned how to create and work with basic indexed arrays, you have only worked with PHP's predefined autoglobal arrays. In this chapter, you learn how to use advanced techniques on both indexed and associative arrays.

Manipulating Elements

As you use arrays in your scripts, you will undoubtedly need to add and remove elements. For example, suppose you have a shopping cart program that uses an array to store the names of products that a customer plans to purchase. As the customer selects additional products to purchase, or changes her mind about an item, you will need to manipulate the elements in the array of products.

In this chapter, you work on a Discussion Forum script that allows users to post and read messages to and from a text file. If you are not familiar with them, discussion forums are online discussion groups in which users with similar interests can exchange messages. The Discussion Forum script you work with in this chapter is fairly simple and doesn't have the advanced capabilities of some of the real discussion forums you have probably seen and used yourself. However, the script gives you a chance to practice the advanced array techniques presented in this chapter. Your Chapter directory for Chapter 7 contains the following files to get you started with the Discussion Forum script:

- DiscussionForum.html
- PostMessage.php
- ViewDiscussion.php
- php_styles.css
- messages.txt

The DiscussionForum.html file is the main entry point to the script. The PostMessage.php script uses the following PHP code to write and read data to and from the messages.txt file:

```
$Topic = $_POST['topic'];
$Name = $_POST['name'];
$Message = $_POST['message'];
$PostMessage = addslashes("$Topic~$Name~$Message\n");
$MessageStore = fopen("messages.txt", "a");
fwrite($MessageStore, "$PostMessage");
fclose($MessageStore);
echo "<p><strong>Topic</strong>: $Topic<br />";
echo "<strong>Name</strong>: $Name<br />";
echo "<strong>Message</strong>: $Message</p>";
```

The first few statements use the `$_POST['name']`, `$_POST['topic']`, and `$_POST['message']` form variables to create a string that is assigned to the `$PostMessages` variable. Notice that each form variable value is separated by a tilde character (~) and that the string ends with the new line escape character (`\n`). This allows the name, topic, and message for each posting to be stored on a single line in the messages.txt file. For the *mode* argument, the `fopen()` function uses "a", which opens the specified file for writing (or creates the file if it doesn't exist) and places the file pointer at the end of the file. Because the **fopen()** function's "a" *mode* parameter places the file pointer at the end of the file, each new posting is appended to the end of the file.

The ViewDiscussion.php file contains the following PHP code, which reads and prints the messages in the messages.txt file:

```
if (!file_exists("messages.txt") || filesize("messages.txt") == 0)
     echo "<p>There are no messages posted.</p>";
else {
     $MessageArray = file("messages.txt");
      for ($i=0; $i<count($MessageArray); ++$i) {
           $CurMessage = explode("~", $MessageArray[$i]);
           echo "<tr>";
           echo "<td><strong>" . ($i + 1) . "</strong>.</td>";
           echo "<td><strong>Topic</strong>: "
                . stripslashes($CurMessage[0]) . "<br />";
           echo "<strong>Name</strong>: "
                . stripslashes($CurMessage[1]) . "<br />";
           echo "<strong>Message</strong>: "
                . stripslashes($CurMessage[2]);
          echo "</td></tr>";
     }
}
```

The first statement in the **else** clause in the preceding code uses the **file()** function to read the contents of the messages.txt file into an indexed array named **$MessageArray[]**. The **for** statement then loops through each element in the **$MessageArray[]** array and calls the **explode()** function to split each element at the tilde character into an another array named **$CurMessage**. The topic, name, and message values in the **$CurMessage** array are then printed with **echo()** statements.

Next, you practice using the Discussion Forum script.

To practice using the Discussion Forum script:

1. Open the **Post New Message** page in your Web browser by entering the following URL: **http://localhost/PHP_Projects/Chapter.07/Chapter/DiscussionForum.html**. You should see a Web page similar to the one shown in Figure 7-1.

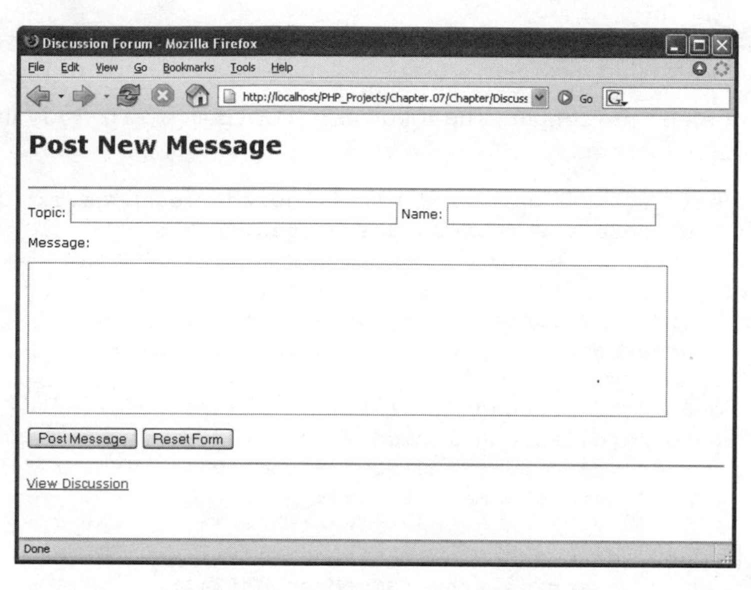

Figure 7-1 Post New Message page of the Discussion Forum script

2. Type some data in the **Topic**, **Name**, and **Message** boxes and click the **Post Message** button. The data you entered appears on the Message Posted page.
3. Use the **Post Another Message** link to enter some more messages. After you have entered a few more messages, click the **View Discussion** link to view the messages you have entered. You should see the Web page shown in Figure 7-2.

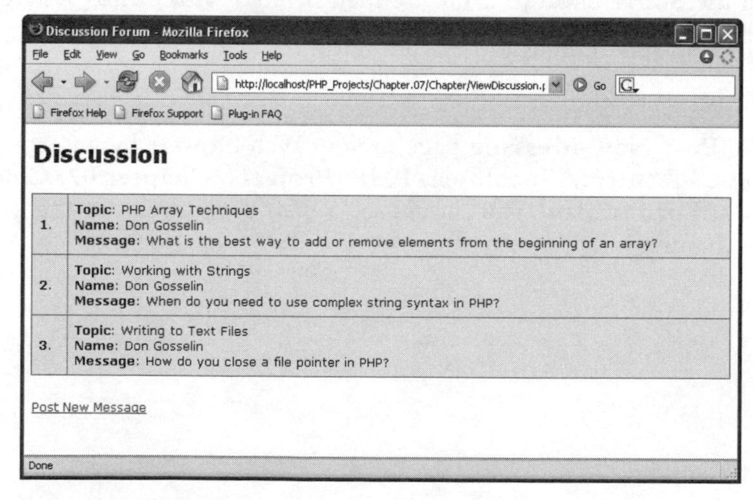

Figure 7-2 Message Posted page of the Discussion Forum script

4. Close your Web browser window.

Adding and Removing Elements from the Beginning of an Array

To add or remove elements from the beginning of an array, you need to use the `array_shift()` and `array_unshift()` functions. The `array_shift()` function removes the first element from the beginning of an array, whereas the `array_unshift()` function adds one or more elements to the beginning of an array. You pass to the `array_shift()` function the name of the array whose first element you want to remove. You pass to the `array_unshift()` function the name of an array followed by comma-separated values for each element you want to add. For example, the following code declares and initializes an array containing the names of the world's top-ranked golfers in 2005. The `array_shift()` function removes the first golfer, Ernie Els, from the top of the array, and the `array_unshift()` function adds the two highest-ranked players, Tiger Woods and Vijay Singh, to the top of the array. Figure 7-3 shows the output of the `print_r()` function.


```
$TopGolfers = array(
     "Ernie Els",
     "Phil Mickelson",
     "Retief Goosen",
     "Padraig Harrington",
     "David Toms",
     "Sergio Garcia",
     "Adam Scott",
     "Stewart Cink");
array_shift($TopGolfers);
array_unshift($TopGolfers, "Tiger Woods", "Vijay Singh");
print_r($TopGolfers);
```

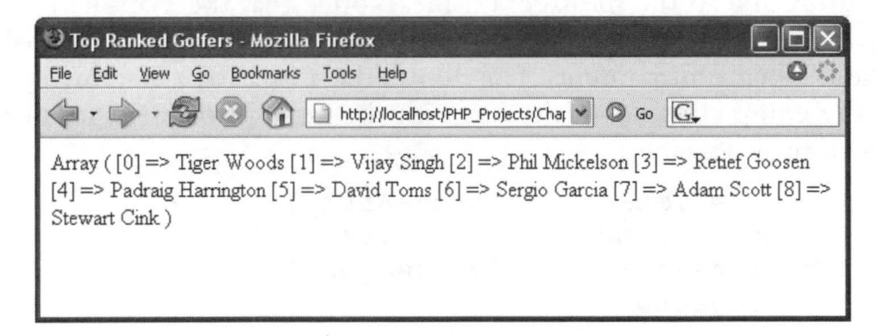

Figure 7-3 Output of an array modified with the `array_shift()` and `array_unshift()` functions

Next, you add a new PHP file that uses the `array_shift()` function to remove the first message in the Discussion Forum script.

To create a new PHP file that uses the `array_shift()` function to remove the first message in the Discussion Forum script:

1. Open your text editor and create a new document.
2. Add the following script section to the document. You do not need to add any HTML elements to the document because it will not display in a Web browser.

```
<?php
?>
```

3. Add the following `if` statement to the script section. The conditional expression checks that the messages.txt file exists and that it contains messages.

```
if (file_exists("messages.txt")
        && filesize("messages.txt") != 0) {
}
```

4. Add the following two statements to the body of the `if` statement. The first statement uses the `file()` function to read the contents of the file into an array named `$MessageArray[]`. The second statement then uses the `array_shift()` function to remove the first element in the array.

```
$MessageArray = file("messages.txt");
array_shift($MessageArray);
```

5. Add the following four statements to the end of the `if` statement. The first statement uses the `implode()` function to convert `$MessageArray[]` into a text string, which is assigned to the `$NewMessage` variable. The second statement then uses the `fopen()` function to open a handle named `$MessageStore` to the messages.txt file. Notice that the `fopen()` function uses the "w" *mode* parameter, which opens a file for writing only and deletes all of the file's current contents. This allows the `fwrite()` statement to replace the entire contents of the file with the new list of messages in the `$NewMessages` variable.

```
$NewMessages = implode($MessageArray);
$MessageStore = fopen("messages.txt", "w");
fwrite($MessageStore, "$NewMessages");
fclose($MessageStore);
```

6. Finally, add the following redirection statement to the end of the script section, after the `if` statement's closing brace. The redirection statement opens the ViewDiscussion.php file.

```
header("location:ViewDiscussion.php");
```

The script should appear as follows:

```
<?php
if (file_exists("messages.txt") && filesize("messages.txt") == 0) {
      $MessageArray = file("messages.txt");
      array_shift($MessageArray);
      $NewMessages = implode($MessageArray);
      $MessageStore = fopen("messages.txt", "w");
      fwrite($MessageStore, "$NewMessages");
      fclose($MessageStore);
}
header("location:ViewDiscussion.php");
?>
```

7. Save the document as **DeleteFirstMessage.php** in the Chapter directory for Chapter 7.
8. Open the **ViewDiscussion.php** file in your text editor.
9. Modify the paragraph element at the end of the file so it contains an anchor element that calls the DeleteFirstMessage.php file, as follows:

```
<p><a href="DiscussionForum.html">Post New Message</a><br />
<a href="DeleteFirstMessage.php">Delete First Message</a></p>
```

10. Save the **ViewDiscussion.php** file.
11. Open the **View Discussion** page in your Web browser by entering the following URL: **http://localhost/PHP_Projects/Chapter.07/Chapter/ViewDiscussion.php**. Click the **Delete First Message** link to test the new code. The first message in your list should be deleted.
12. Close your Web browser window.

Adding and Removing Elements from the End of an Array

The easiest way to add additional elements to the end of an array is to simply use the array name and brackets syntax that you first saw in Chapter 3. For example, the first statement in the following code uses the `array()` construct to create the initial `$HospitalDepts[]` array. The second statement then adds a new value, "Pediatrics," as the fourth element of the array.

```
$HospitalDepts = array(
      "Anesthesia",
      "Molecular Biology",
      "Neurology");
$HospitalDepts[] = "Pediatrics";
```

You can also add and remove elements from the end of an array by using the `array_pop()` and `array_push()` functions. The `array_pop()` function removes the last element from the end of an array, whereas the `array_push()` function adds one or more elements to the end of an array. You pass to the `array_pop()` function the name of the array whose last element you want to remove. You pass to the `array_push()` function the name of an array followed by comma-separated values for each element you want to add. In the following example, the `array_pop()` function removes the last department, "Pediatrics," from the end of the array and the `array_push()` function adds the two additional departments, "Psychiatry" and "Pulmonary Diseases," to the end of the array.

```
$HospitalDepts = array(
     "Anesthesia",
     "Molecular Biology",
     "Neurology",
     "Pediatrics");
array_pop($HospitalDepts);
array_push($HospitalDepts, "Psychiatry", "Pulmonary Diseases");
```

Next, you add a new PHP file that uses the `array_pop()` function to remove the last message in the Discussion Forum script.

To create a new PHP file that uses the `array_pop()` function to remove the last message in the Discussion Forum script:

1. Return to the **DeleteFirstMessage.php** file in your text editor and immediately save it as **DeleteLastMessage.php** in your Chapter directory for Chapter 7.
2. Modify the `array_shift()` function in the `if` statement into an `array_pop()` function. The modified statement reads as follows:

   ```
   array_pop($MessageArray);
   ```

3. Save the **DeleteLastMessage.php** file.
4. Return to the **ViewDiscussion.php** file in your text editor.
5. Modify the paragraph element at the end of the file so it contains an anchor element that calls the DeleteLastMessage.php file, as follows:

   ```
   <p><a href="DiscussionForum.html">Post New Message</a><br />
   <a href="DeleteFirstMessage.php">Delete First Message</a><br />
   <a href="DeleteLastMessage.php">Delete Last Message</a></p>
   ```

6. Save the **ViewDiscussion.php** file.
7. Open the View Discussion page in your Web browser by entering the following URL: **http://localhost/PHP_Projects/Chapter.07/Chapter/ViewDiscussion.html**. Click the **Delete Last Message** link to test the new code. The last message in your list should be deleted.
8. Close your Web browser window.

Adding and Removing Elements Within an Array

So far, you have learned to add and remove elements from the beginning and end of an array. To add or remove elements anywhere else in an array, you need to use an array function. PHP includes numerous functions for working with arrays, including the `array_splice()` function, which adds or removes array elements. After adding or removing array elements, the `array_splice()` function also renumbers the indexes in the array. The syntax for the `array_splice()` function is `array_splice(array_name, start, characters_to_delete, values_to_insert);`. The *array_name* argument indicates the name of the array you want to modify. The *start* argument indicates the element within the array at which point elements should be added or removed. The *characters_to_delete* argument is an integer value that indicates the number of elements to remove from the array, starting with the element indicated by the *start* argument. The *values_to_insert* argument represents the values you want to add as new elements to an array.

7

To add an element within an array, include a value of 0 as the third argument to the `array_splice()` function. The `array_splice()` function in the following code adds a new element with a value of "Ophthalmology" between the "Neurology" and "Pediatrics" elements, and renumbers the elements.

```
$HospitalDepts = array(
     "Anesthesia",            // first element (0)
     "Molecular Biology",     // second element (1)
     "Neurology",             // third element (2)
     "Pediatrics");           // fourth element (3)
array_splice($HospitalDepts, 3, 0, "Ophthalmology");
```

To add more than one element within an array, pass the `array()` construct as the fourth argument to the `array_splice()` function. Include within the `array()` construct the new element values separated by commas, just as if you were creating a new array. The following example shows how to add two new elements, "Opthalmology" and "Otolaryngology," between the "Neurology" and "Pediatrics" elements.

```
$HospitalDepts = array(
     "Anesthesia",            // first element (0)
     "Molecular Biology",     // second element (1)
     "Neurology",             // third element (2)
     "Pediatrics");           // fourth element (3)
array_splice($HospitalDepts, 3, 0, array("Opthalmology",
     "Otolaryngology"));
```

You can also delete array elements by omitting the fourth argument from the `array_splice()` function. After you delete array elements with the `array_splice()` function, the remaining indexes are renumbered, just as when you add new elements. For example, to delete the second and third elements in the `$HospitalDepts[]` array, you use the following statement:

```
$HospitalDepts = array(
     "Anesthesia",              // first element (0)
     "Molecular Biology",       // second element (1)
     "Neurology",               // third element (2)
     "Pediatrics");             // fourth element (3)
array_splice($HospitalDepts, 1, 2);
```

If you do not include the third argument (*characters_to_delete*), the `array_splice()` function deletes all the elements from the second argument (*start*) to the end of the array.

If the `$HospitalDepts[]` array contains four elements with the values "Anesthesia," "Molecular Biology," "Neurology," and "Pediatrics" (in that order), then executing the preceding statement removes the elements containing "Molecular Biology" and "Neurology" from the array.

Next, you add a new PHP file that uses the `array_splice()` function to remove a specified message in the Discussion Forum script.

To create a new PHP file that uses the `array_splice()` function to remove a specified message in the Discussion Forum script:

1. Return to the **DeleteLastMessage.php** file in your text editor and immediately save it as **DeleteMessage.php** in your Chapter directory for Chapter 7.
2. Add the following statement immediately after the statement that declares and instantiates the `$MessageArray` variable. Because indexed arrays begin with an index of 0, a value of 1 is subtracted from the value submitted by the user to assign the correct index number to the `$Message` variable.

   ```
   $Message = $_POST["message"] - 1;
   ```

3. Modify the remaining statements in the `if` statement so they are enclosed within a nested `if` statement, as follows. Be sure to replace the `array_pop()` function with the `array_splice()` function. The conditional expression checks whether the element number specified in the `$Message` variable exists in `$MessageArray[]`. If it does, the `array_splice()` function deletes the specified element from `$MessageArray[]` and the remaining statements write the new list of messages to the messages.txt file.

   ```
   if (isset($MessageArray[$Message])) {
        array_splice($MessageArray, $Message, 1);
        $NewMessages = implode($MessageArray);
        $MessageStore = fopen("messages.txt", "w");
        fwrite($MessageStore, "$NewMessages");
        fclose($MessageStore);
   }
   ```

The completed script should appear as follows:

```
<?php
if (file_exists("messages.txt") && filesize("messages.txt") != 0) {
     $MessageArray = file("messages.txt");
     $MessageArray = stripslashes($MessageArray);
     $Message = $_POST["message"] - 1;
     if (isset($MessageArray[$Message])) {
          array_splice($MessageArray, $Message, 1);
          $NewMessages = implode($MessageArray);
          $MessageStore = fopen("messages.txt", "w");
          fwrite($MessageStore, "$NewMessages");
          fclose($MessageStore);
     }
}
header("location:ViewDiscussion.php");
?>
```

4. Save the **DeleteMessage.php** file.
5. Return to the **ViewDiscussion.php** file in your text editor.
6. Add the following form to the end of the document body. The form allows users to enter a message number to delete, which is submitted to the DeleteMessage.php script.

```
<form action="DeleteMessage.php" method="post"
enctype="application/x-www-form-urlencoded">
<p>Delete message number: <input type="text" name="message"
size="5" />
<input type="submit" value="Delete" /></p>
</form>
```

7. Save the **ViewDiscussion.php** file.
8. Open the **View Discussion** page in your Web browser by entering the following URL: **http://localhost/PHP_Projects/Chapter.07/Chapter/ViewDiscussion.php**. Enter a message number and click the **Delete** button to test the new code. The specified message in your list should be deleted.
9. Close your Web browser window.

You can also use the `unset()` function to remove array elements and other variables. You pass to the `unset()` function the array name and index number of the element you want to remove. To remove multiple elements, separate each index name and element number with commas. For example, the following `unset()` function also removes the elements containing "Molecular Biology" and "Neurology" from the `$HospitalDepts[]` array:

```
unset($HospitalDepts[1], $HospitalDepts[2]);
```

One problem with the `unset()` function is that it does not renumber the remaining elements in the array. If the `$HospitalDepts[]` array contains four elements with the values "Anesthesia," "Molecular Biology," "Neurology," and "Pediatrics" (in that order), then executing the preceding statement removes the elements containing "Molecular Biology" and "Neurology" from the array. However, if you run the `print_r()` function with the `$HospitalDepts[]` array after executing the preceding `unset()` function, you would see that the "Anesthesia" element has an index of 1 and the "Pediatrics" still has an index of 3.

To renumber an indexed array's element, you need to run the `array_values()` function. You pass to the `array_values()` function the name of the array whose index you want to renumber. The `array_values()` function does not operate directly on an array. Instead, it returns a new array with the renumbered indexes. For this reason, you need to write a statement that assigns the array that is returned from the `array_values()` function to a new variable name or to the original array. The following statement demonstrates how to use the `array_values()` function to renumber the element indexes in the `$HospitalDepts[]` array, and then assign the renumbered array back to the `$HospitalDepts[]` array:

```
$HospitalDepts = array_values($HospitalDepts);
```

Next, you modify the DeleteMessage.php file so it uses the `unset()` function instead of the `array_splice()` function to delete messages.

To modify the DeleteMessage.php file so it uses the `unset()` function instead of the `array_splice()` function to delete messages:

1. Return to the **DeleteMessage.php** file in your text editor.
2. Replace the `array_splice()` statement with the following two `unset()` and `array_values()` statements:

   ```
   unset($MessageArray[$Message]);
   $MessageArray = array_values($MessageArray);
   ```

3. Save the **DeleteMessage.php** file.
4. Open the **View Discussion** page in your Web browser by entering the following URL: **http://localhost/PHP_Projects/Chapter.07/Chapter/ViewDiscussion.php**. Enter a message number and click the **Delete** button to test the new code.
5. Close your Web browser window.

Removing Duplicate Elements

You might find it necessary to ensure that an array in a script does not contain duplicate values. For example, your script may use arrays of e-mail addresses, customer names, or sales items, each of which should contain unique elements. You can use the `array_unique()` function to remove duplicate elements from an array. You pass to the `array_unique()` function the name of the array from which you want to remove duplicate elements. As with the `array_values()` function, the `array_unique()` function does not operate directly on an array. Instead, it returns a new array with the renumbered indexes. For this reason, you need to write a statement that assigns the array that is returned from the the `array_unique()` function to a new variable name or to the original array.

The following code shows an example of the array containing the world's top-ranked golfers. The array should only contain unique values, but several of the names are duplicated. The `array_unique()` function removes the duplicate elements and then assigns the renumbered array back to the `$TopGolfers[]` array. Figure 7-4 shows the output.


```
$TopGolfers = array(
     "Tiger Woods", "Tiger Woods", "Vijay Singh", "Vijay Singh",
     "Ernie Els", "Phil Mickelson", "Retief Goosen",
     "Retief Goosen", "Padraig Harrington", "David Toms",
     "Sergio Garcia", "Adam Scott", "Stewart Cink");
echo "<p>The world's top golfers are:</p><p>";
$TopGolfers = array_unique($TopGolfers);
$TopGolfers = array_values($TopGolfers);
for ($i=0; $i<count($TopGolfers); ++$i) {
     echo "{$TopGolfers[$i]}<br />";
}
echo "</p>";
```

The `array_unique()` function does renumber the indexes after removing duplicate values in an array. For this reason, the preceding code includes a statement that uses the `array_values()` function to renumber the indexes in the `$TopGolfers[]` array.

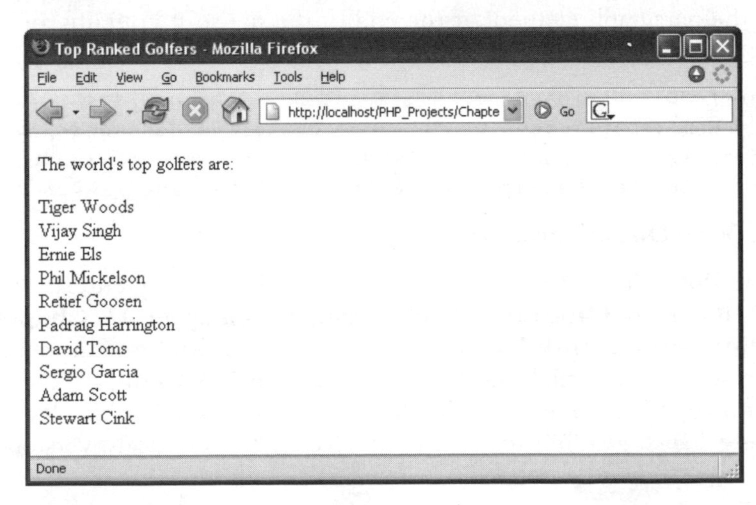

Figure 7-4 Output of an array after removing duplicate values with the `array_unique()` function

Next, you add a new PHP file that uses the `array_unique()` function to remove duplicate messages in the Discussion Forum script.

To add a new PHP file that uses the `array_unique()` function to remove duplicate messages in the Discussion Forum script:

1. Return to the **DeleteMessage.php** file in your text editor and immediately save it as **RemoveDuplicates.php** in your Chapter directory for Chapter 7.
2. Replace the second statement in the `if` statement that declares and initializes the `$Message` variable with the following `array_unique()` statement, which removes duplicate elements from `$MessageArray[]`:

   ```
   $MessageArray = array_unique($MessageArray);
   ```

3. Remove the nested `if` statement and the `unset()` statement. The completed script should appear as follows:

   ```
   <?php
   if (file_exists("messages.txt") && filesize("messages.txt") != 0) {
        $MessageArray = file("messages.txt");
        $MessageArray = array_unique($MessageArray);
        $MessageArray = array_values($MessageArray);
        $NewMessages = implode($MessageArray);
        $MessageStore = fopen("messages.txt", "w");
        fwrite($MessageStore, "$NewMessages");
        fclose($MessageStore);
   }
   header("location:ViewDiscussion.php");
   ?>
   ```

4. Save the **RemoveDuplicates.php** file.
5. Return to the **ViewDiscussion.php** file in your text editor.
6. Modify the paragraph element at the end of the file so it contains an anchor element that calls the RemoveDuplicates.php file, as follows:

   ```
   <p><a href="DiscussionForum.html">Post New Message</a><br />
   <a href="RemoveDuplicates.php">Remove Duplicate Messages</a><br />
   <a href="DeleteFirstMessage.php">Delete First Message</a><br />
   <a href="DeleteLastMessage.php">Delete Last Message</a><br /></p>
   ```

7. Save the **ViewDiscussion.php** file.
8. Open the **Post New Message** file in your Web browser by entering the following URL: **http://localhost/PHP_Projects/Chapter.07/Chapter/DiscussionForum.html**. Add several new messages that contain identical information, and then click the **View Discussion** link to display the View Discussion page. You should see the duplicate messages. Click the **Remove Duplicate Messages** link to test the new code. Any duplicate versions of the same message should be deleted.
9. Close your Web browser window.

DECLARING AND INITIALIZING ASSOCIATIVE ARRAYS

As you know, PHP creates indexed arrays by default with a starting element of 0. For example, the following code uses the `array()` construct to create the indexed `$Provinces[]` array that you saw in Chapter 3:

```
$Provinces = array("Newfoundland and Labrador", "Prince Edward
Island", "Nova Scotia", "New Brunswick", "Quebec", "Ontario",
"Manitoba", "Saskatchewan", "Alberta", "British Columbia");
```

With associative arrays, you can use any alphanumeric keys that you want for the array elements. You specify an element's key by using the array operator (=>) in the `array()` construct. The syntax for declaring and initializing an associative array is as follows:

```
$array_name = array(key=>value, ...);
```

7

For example, the following code creates an array named `$ProvincialCapitals[]`, which contains the Canadian provinces and their capitals. The name of each province is used as the element key, and the name of each capital city is assigned as the element's value.

```
$ProvincialCapitals = array("Newfoundland and Labrador"=>"St.
John's", "Prince Edward Island"=>"Charlottetown", "Nova
Scotia"=>"Halifax", "New Brunswick"=>"Fredericton",
"Quebec"=>"Quebec City", "Ontario"=>"Toronto",
"Manitoba"=>"Winnipeg", "Saskatchewan"=>"Regina",
"Alberta"=>"Edmonton", "British Columbia"=>"Victoria");
```

You can also use the following syntax to assign key values to an associative array by using array names and brackets. Note that when using this syntax, you use the standard assignment operator (=) and not the array operator (=>).

```
$ProvincialCapitals["Newfoundland and Labrador"] = "St. John's";
$ProvincialCapitals["Prince Edward Island"] = "Charlottetown";
$ProvincialCapitals["Nova Scotia"] = "Halifax";
...
```

The preceding syntax creates the array if it doesn't exist. If the array does exist, each assignment statement overwrites any existing elements that already use the same key or appends any new keys and values to the end of the array.

To refer to an element in an associative array, you place an element's key in single or double quotation marks inside the array brackets. The following code prints the capitals of Quebec and British Columbia:

```
echo "<p>The capital of Quebec is
    {$ProvincialCapitals['Quebec']}.</p>";
echo "<p>The capital of British Columbia is
    {$ProvincialCapitals['British Columbia']}.</p>";
```

If you create an associative array and then add a new element without specifying a key, PHP automatically assumes that the array is indexed and assigns the new element an index of 0 or the next available integer. The following example declares and initializes an array named `$TerritorialCapitals[]`, which contains the capitals of the Canadian territories. The first two statements assign keys to the first two elements in the array. However, because the third statement does not declare a key, the element is assigned a value of 0. Figure 7-5 shows the output of the `print_r()` function.

```
$TerritorialCapitals["Nunavut"] = "Iqaluit";
$TerritorialCapitals["Northwest Territories"] = "Yellowknife";
$TerritorialCapitals[] = "Whitehorse";
print_r($TerritorialCapitals);
```

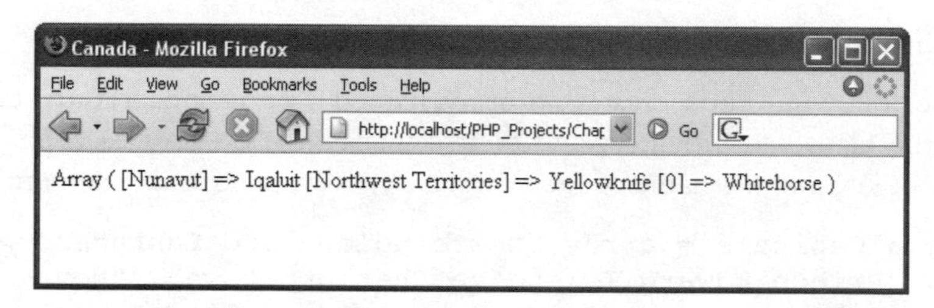

Figure 7-5 Output of array with associative and indexed elements

The functionality of associative arrays also allows you to start the numbering of indexed arrays at any integer you want. For example, the following code uses the `array()` construct to declare and initialize an array named `$Territories[]` containing just the names of the Canadian territories. Notice that only the first element uses the array operator (=>) to begin numbering at 1 instead of 0. The subsequent elements are automatically assigned the next available integer.

```
$Territories = array(1=>"Nunavut", "Northwest Territories",
"Yukon Territory");
```

For the `$Territories[]` array created with the preceding statement, the first element is `$Territories[1]` ("Nunavut"), the second element is `$Territories[2]` ("Northwest Territories"), and the third element is `$Territories[3]` ("Yukon Territory"). You can also specify index values by using the array name and brackets as follows:

```
$Territories[1] = "Nunavut";
$Territories[2] = "Northwest Territories";
$Territories[3] = "Yukon Territory";
```

In many programming languages, if you declare an array and use a starting index other than 0, empty elements are created for each index between 0 and the index value you specify. For example, in JavaScript, if you use an index of 10, 11 elements are automatically created for indexes 0 through 10. In PHP, elements are only created with the indexes or keys you specify, or that you append to the beginning or end of an existing array. The following code shows another example of the `$Territories[]` array, but this time the starting index is 100. Because the second and third statements do not declare an index or key, the starting index of 100 is incremented by one and used as the index for the next two elements. However, as the `count()` function shows in Figure 7-6, the index consists of just three elements.

```
$Territories[100] = "Nunavut";
$Territories[] = "Northwest Territories";
$Territories[] = "Yukon Territory";
print_r($Territories);
echo '<p>The $Territories array consists of ',
     count($Territories), " elements.</p>";
```


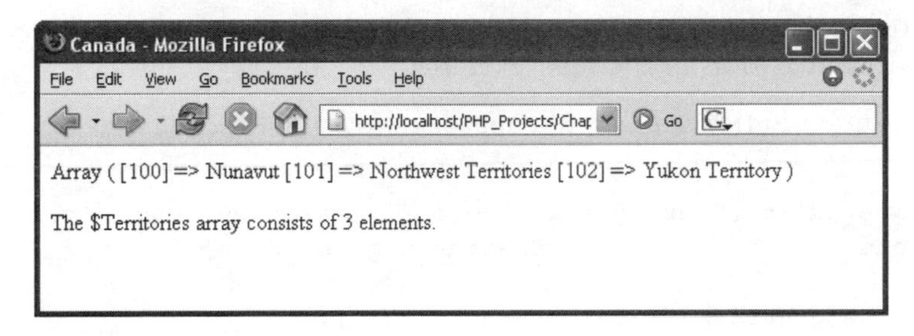

Figure 7-6 Output of an array with a starting index of 100

Use the `array_values()` function to renumber an indexed array with a starting element of 0.

Next, you modify the ViewDiscussion.php file so the array returned with the `file()` function is converted to an associative array that uses the message topic as the key. Although the array will still be stored in the messages.txt file as an indexed array, you will use the associative version of the array later in this chapter to find and sort data in the messages.

To modify the ViewDiscussion.php file so the array returned with the `file()` function is converted to an associative array:

1. Return to the **ViewDiscussion.php** file in your text editor.
2. Add the following `for` loop immediately after the `$MessageArray[]` declaration statement in the `else` clause. The `for` loop uses `$MessageArray[]` to build a new associative array named `$KeyMessageArray[]`. Notice that

`$KeyMessageArray[]` uses the second element (the topic name) in `$MessageArray[]`as the key name.

```
for ($i=0; $i<count($MessageArray); ++$i) {
     $CurMessage = explode("~", $MessageArray[$i]);
     $KeyMessageArray[$CurMessage[0]] = $CurMessage[1]
     . "~" . $CurMessage[2];
}
```

3. Add the following `print_r()` statement immediately after the new `for` loop's closing brace. The `print_r()` function is only a temporary way of printing the contents of `$KeyMessageArray[]` until you learn how to iterate through arrays in the next section.

```
print_r($KeyMessageArray);
```

4. Add block comments around the second `for` loop in the `else` clause. You modify this `for` loop in the next exercise.

Your modified PHP script should appear as follows:

```
<?php
if (!file_exists("messages.txt") || filesize("messages.txt") == 0)
     echo "<p>There are no messages posted.</p>";
else {
     $MessageArray = file("messages.txt");
     $MessageArray = stripslashes($MessageArray);
     for ($i=0; $i<count($MessageArray); ++$i) {
          $CurMessage = explode("~", $MessageArray[$i]);
          $KeyMessageArray[$CurMessage[0]] = $CurMessage[1]
                . "~" . $CurMessage[2];
     }
print_r($KeyMessageArray);
/*
     for ($i=0; $i<count($MessageArray); ++$i) {
          $CurMessage = explode("~", $MessageArray[$i]);
          echo "<tr>";
          echo "<td><strong>" . ($i + 1) . "</strong>.</td>";
          echo "<td><strong>Topic</strong>: "
                . stripslashes($CurMessage[0]) . "<br />";
          echo "<strong>Name</strong>: "
                . stripslashes($CurMessage[1]) . "<br />";
          echo "<strong>Message</strong>: "
                . stripslashes($CurMessage[2]);
          echo "</td></tr>";
     }
*/
}
?>
```

5. Save the **ViewDiscussion.php** file.

6. Open the **View Discussion** page in your Web browser by entering the following URL: **http://localhost/PHP_Projects/Chapter.07/Chapter/ViewDiscussion.php**. The `print_r()` function should output an associative version of the messages array.
7. Close your Web browser window.

ITERATING THROUGH AN ARRAY

7

In Chapter 4, you learned how to use a `foreach` statement to iterate through the elements in an array. As a refresher, the following example declares and initializes an indexed array named `$DaysOfWeek[]` and uses a `foreach` statement to iterate through it:

```
$DaysOfWeek = array("Monday", "Tuesday", "Wednesday", "Thursday",
     "Friday", "Saturday", "Sunday");
foreach ($DaysOfWeek as $Day) {
     echo "<p>$Day</p>";
}
```

Even though a `foreach` statement allows you to loop through the elements of an array, it does not change the position of the **internal array pointer**, which is a special type of variable that refers to the currently selected element in an array. The internal array pointer is a way of keeping track of which element you are working with in an array. You use the functions listed in Table 7-1 to iterate through an array with the internal array pointer.

Table 7-1 Array pointer iteration functions

Function	Description
`current(array)`	Returns the current array element
`each(array)`	Returns the key and value of the current array element and moves the internal array pointer to the next element
`end(array)`	Moves the internal array pointer to the last element
`key(array)`	Returns the key of the current array element
`next(array)`	Moves the internal array pointer to the next element
`prev(array)`	Moves the internal array pointer to the previous element
`reset(array)`	Resets the internal array pointer to the first element

As a simple example of how to use the iteration functions, the `next()` function in the following code moves the internal array pointer in the `$DaysOfWeek[]` array to the second array element ("Tuesday"), whereas the `end()` function moves the internal array pointer to the final array element ("Sunday"). The `echo()` statements use the `current()` function to print the value of the element in the `$DaysOfWeek[]` array where the internal array pointer is located.

```
next($DaysOfWeek);
echo current($DaysOfWeek);
end ($DaysOfWeek);
echo current($DaysOfWeek);
```

You might be wondering why you need iteration functions at all. Why not just use a `foreach` statement or other type of looping statement to iterate through an array? For indexed arrays, a looping statement is usually all you need to work with the elements in an array. However, because the keys in an associative array might not be in a predictable sequence, you can't always use a looping statement to determine which element you are currently working with in associative arrays. For example, consider the following code, in which a `foreach` statement prints the values in the `$ProvincialCapitals[]` array. To print an element key (which, in this case, contains the name of each province), you must use the `key()` function. However, the `key()` function only returns the key in an array in which the internal array pointer is located. Because the internal array pointer points to the first element by default, the following code prints the first element value ("Newfoundland and Labrador"), as shown in Figure 7-7:

```
$ProvincialCapitals = array("Newfoundland and Labrador"=>"St.
John's", "Prince Edward Island"=>"Charlottetown", "Nova
Scotia"=>"Halifax", "New Brunswick"=>"Fredericton",
"Quebec"=>"Quebec City", "Ontario"=>"Toronto",
"Manitoba"=>"Winnipeg", "Saskatchewan"=>"Regina",
"Alberta"=>"Edmonton", "British Columbia"=>"Victoria");
echo "<p>";
foreach ($ProvincialCapitals as $Capital) {
     echo "The capital of ", key($ProvincialCapitals), "
     is $Capital<br />";
}
```

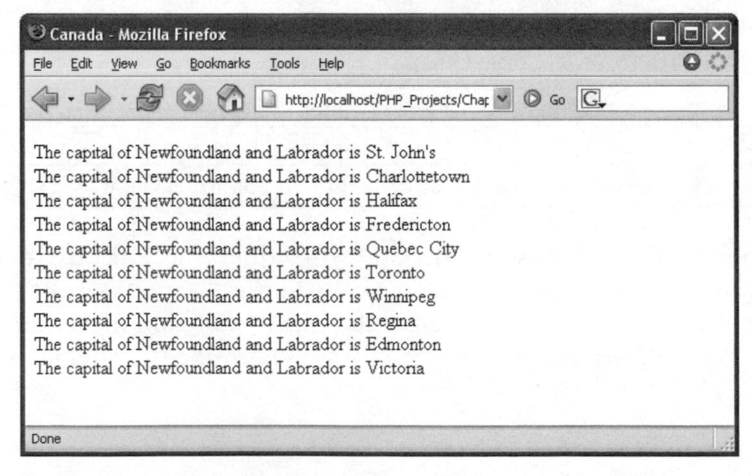

Figure 7-7 Output of an array without advancing the internal array pointer

To print the correct key for each element, you need to add the `next()` function, as follows:

```
foreach ($ProvincialCapitals as $Capital) {
     echo "The capital of ", key($ProvincialCapitals), "
     is $Capital<br />";
     next($ProvincialCapitals);
}
```

If you use an iteration function to move the internal array pointer either before the first element or after the last element in an array, the only way to move the array pointer back to a valid element in the array is to use the `reset()` or `end()` functions.

Next, you modify the ViewDiscussion.php file so it includes code that iterates through `$KeyMessageArray[]`.

To modify the ViewDiscussion.php file so it includes code that iterates through `$KeyMessageArray[]`:

1. Return to the **ViewDiscussion.php** file in your text editor.
2. Remove the `print_r()` function and the block comments from the `else` clause.
3. Between the two `for` loops, add the following statement to declare and initialize a variable named `$Count`. You will use the `$Count` variable to numerate the associative elements in `$KeyMessageArray[]`.

   ```
   $Count = 1;
   ```

4. Modify the second `for` loop into the following `foreach` loop. Be sure to modify the portions of the code that are highlighted in bold and to add the `next()` statement to the end of the loop.

   ```
   foreach($KeyMessageArray as $Message) {
        $CurMessage = explode("~", $Message);
        echo "<tr>";
        echo "<td><strong>" . $Count++ . "</strong>.</td>";
        echo "<td><strong>Topic</strong>: "
              . stripslashes(key($KeyMessageArray)) . "<br />";
        echo "<strong>Name</strong>: ". stripslashes($CurMessage[0])
              . "<br />";
        echo "<strong>Message</strong>: " . stripslashes($CurMessage[1]);
        echo "</td></tr>";
        next($KeyMessageArray);
   }
   ```

5. Save the **ViewDiscussion.php** file.

6. Open the **View Discussion** page in your Web browser by entering the following URL: **http://localhost/PHP_Projects/Chapter.07/Chapter/ViewDiscussion.php**. The messages should print normally.
7. Close your Web browser window.

Finding and Extracting Elements and Values

This section discusses methods for finding and extracting elements and values in an array. One of the most basic methods for finding a value in an array is to use a looping statement to iterate through the array until you find a particular value. For example, the `for` statement in the following code loops through the `$HospitalDepts[]` array to see if it contains "Neurology." If it does, a message prints and the `break` statement ends the `for` loop.

```
$HospitalDepts = array("Anesthesia", "Molecular Biology",
     "Neurology", "Pediatrics");
for ($i=0; $i<=count($HospitalDepts); ++$i) {
     if ($HospitalDepts[$i] == "Neurology") {
          echo "<p>The hospital has a Neurology
               department.</p>";
          break;
     }
}
```

Rather than writing custom code that is similar to the preceding example, you can use various functions that PHP provides for finding and extracting elements and values in an array.

Determining if a Value Exists

You can use the `in_array()` and `array_search()` functions to determine whether a value exists in an array. The `in_array()` function returns a Boolean value of true if a given value exists in an array. The `array_search()` function determines whether a given value exists in an array and returns the index or key of the first matching element if it exists or false if it does not exist. Both functions accept two arguments: The first argument represents the value to search for, whereas the second argument represents the name of the array in which to search. For example, the following code uses the `in_array()` function to search for "Neurology" in the `$HospitalDepts[]` array. In this example, the `in_array()` function is used in an `if` statement's conditional expression to determine whether "Neurology" exists in the array.

```
if (in_array("Neurology", $HospitalDepts))
     echo "<p>The hospital has a Neurology department.</p>";
```

The following example demonstrates how to use the `array_search()` function with the `$TopGolfers[]` array:

```
$TopGolfers = array("Tiger Woods", "Vijay Singh", "Ernie Els",
"Phil Mickelson", "Retief Goosen", "Padraig Harrington", "David
Toms", "Sergio Garcia", "Adam Scott", "Stewart Cink");
$Ranking = array_search("Tiger Woods", $TopGolfers);
if ($Ranking !== FALSE) {
     ++$Ranking;
     echo "<p>Tiger Woods is one of the top ten golfers in the
          Official World Golf Ranking.</p>";
}
else
     echo "<p>Tiger Woods is not one of the top ten golfers in
          the Official World Golf Ranking.</p>";
```


In the preceding code, the comparison statement in the `if` statement uses the strict not equal operator (`!==`). This operator is necessary because PHP equates a Boolean value of false with 0, which is the same value that identifies the first element in an indexed array. The strict not equal operator determines whether the 0 value assigned to the `$Ranking` variable is really a Boolean value of false or whether it is the index value of 0. Because "Tiger Woods" is in the first element of the array (which is identified with an index of 0), a numeric value of 0 (not a Boolean value of 0) is assigned to the `$Ranking` variable.

When you work with arrays, you should always ensure that your indexes or keys are unique. If you do not use unique values, you will have trouble determining what each array element contains. Because the Discussion Forum script uses message topics as element keys in the associative array that is displayed with the ViewDiscussion.php script, you need to ensure that each topic is unique. Remember that although the ViewDiscussion.php script displays the message data using an associative array, the data is stored as individual lines in messages.txt that you convert to an indexed array using the `file()` function. Because the message topic is stored in an element in the array that is returned with the `file()` function, you use the `array_values()` function to check whether the topic exists as a value in the array.

To modify the Discussion Forum script so users can only enter unique topics:

1. Open the **PostMessage.php** file in your text editor.
2. Add the following statements after the statement that declares and initializes the **$PostMessage** variable. The first statement declares a Boolean variable named `$TopicExists` that you will use to determine whether a topic already exists. The `if` statement is very similar to the code in the ViewDiscussion.php file. First, the conditional expression checks whether the messages.txt file exists and if it is larger than 0 KB. If the condition evaluates to true, the `file()` function assigns the text in messages.txt to `$MessageArray[]`. The `for` loop then explodes each element in `$MessageArray[]` into the `$CurMessage[]`

array. Finally, an `if` statement uses the `in_array()` function to check whether the topic exists in the `$CurMessage[]` array.

```
$TopicExists = FALSE;
if (file_exists("messages.txt") && filesize("messages.txt") > 0) {
     $MessageArray = file("messages.txt");
     for ($i=0; $i<count($MessageArray); ++$i) {
          $CurMessage = explode("~", $MessageArray[$i]);
          if (in_array(addslashes($Topic), $CurMessage)) {
               $TopicExists = TRUE;
               break;
          }
     }
}
```

3. Modify the last six statements in the script so they are contained the following `if...else` statement. The conditional expression uses the `$TopicExists` variable to determine whether the topic already exists in the messages.txt file. If the topic exists, a message is displayed to the user and the new message data is not written to the messages.txt file. If the topic does not yet exist, the new message data is written to the file.

```
if ($TopicExists)
     echo "<p>The topic you entered already exists!</p>";
else {
     $MessageStore = fopen("messages.txt", "a");
     fwrite($MessageStore, "$PostMessage");
     fclose($MessageStore);
     echo "<p><strong>Topic</strong>: " . stripslashes($Topic)
          . "<br />";
     echo "<strong>Name</strong>: " . stripslashes($Name)
          . "<br />";
     echo "<strong>Message</strong>: " . stripslashes($Message)
          . "</p>";
}
```

4. Save the **PostMessage.php** file and close it in your text editor.

5. Open the **Post New Message** page in your Web browser by entering the following URL: **http://localhost/PHP_Projects/Chapter.07/Chapter/DiscussionForum.html**. Add a new message, and then click the **Post Another Message** link to return to the Post New Message page. Try adding another message with exactly the same topic as the message you just entered. You should see a message in the Message Posted page informing you that the topic already exists.

6. Close your Web browser window.

Determining if a Key Exists

In addition to determining whether a specific value exists in an array, you can also use the **array_key_exists()** function to determine whether a given index or key exists. You pass two arguments to the **array_key_exists()** function: The first argument represents the key to search for, whereas the second argument represents the name of the array in which to search. As an example, suppose you write an online, multiplayer game that includes a finite number of characters or "game pieces." A player selects a game piece for each new game. Now suppose that the name of each game piece is an element's key in an associative array, whereas the name of the player who has selected that game piece is the element's value. Before assigning a player's name to a particular game piece in the array, you could use the **array_key_exists()** function to determine whether another player has already selected that game piece. The following code shows some imaginary game pieces that are assigned to an array named **$GamePieces[]**. Before assigning a new name to "The Fat Man," the **if** statement uses the **array_key_exists()** function to determine whether the array element already exists.

```
$GamePieces["Dancer"] = "Daryl";
$GamePieces["Fat Man"] = "Dennis";
$GamePieces["Assassin"] = "Jennifer";
if (array_key_exists("Fat Man", $GamePieces))
     echo "<p>{$GamePieces["Fat Man"]} is already
     'Fat Man'.</p>";
else {
     $GamePieces["Fat Man"] = "Don";
     echo "<p>{$GamePieces["Fat Man"]} is now
     'Fat Man'.</p>";
}
```

7

You can use the **array_keys()** function to return an indexed array containing all the keys in an associative array, as shown in the following example. In the example, a new indexed array named **$UsedGamePieces[]** containing the keys from the **$GamePieces[]** array is created with the **array_keys()** function. A **for** loop then prints the values in the **$UsedGamePieces[]** array.

```
$GamePieces["Dancer"] = "Daryl ";
$GamePieces["The Fat Man"] = "Dennis ";
$GamePieces["Assassin"] = "Jennifer ";
$UsedGamePieces = array_keys($GamePieces);
for ($i=0; $i<count($UsedGamePieces); ++$i) {
     echo "<p>{$UsedGamePieces[$i]}</p>";
}
```

You can also pass a second argument to the **array_keys()** function that specifies an element value to search for. These keys are returned for any elements that match the specified value.

Returning a Portion of an Array

You use the `array_slice()` function to return (copy) a portion of an array and assign it to another array. The syntax for the `array_slice()` function is `array_slice(array_name, start, characters_to_return);`. The *array_name* argument indicates the name of the array from which you want to extract elements. The *start* argument indicates the start position within the array to begin extracting elements. The *characters_to_return* argument is an integer value that indicates the number of elements to return from the array, starting with the element indicated by the *start* argument. The syntax for returning a portion of an array with the `array_slice()` function is very similar to the syntax for deleting a portion of an array with the `array_splice()` function. The main difference is that, whereas the `array_splice()` function removes elements, the `array_slice()` function only copies elements to another array.

The following example demonstrates how to use the `array_slice()` function to return the first five elements in the `$TopGolfers[]` array. The elements are assigned to a new element named `$TopFiveGolfers[]`. Figure 7-8 shows the output.

```
$TopGolfers = array("Tiger Woods", "Vijay Singh", "Ernie Els",
"Phil Mickelson", "Retief Goosen", "Padraig Harrington", "David
Toms", "Sergio Garcia", "Adam Scott", "Stewart Cink");
$TopFiveGolfers = array_slice($TopGolfers, 0, 5);
echo "<p>The top five golfers in the world are:</p><p>";
for ($i=0; $i<count($TopFiveGolfers); ++$i) {
     echo "{$TopFiveGolfers[$i]}<br />";
}
echo "</p>";
```

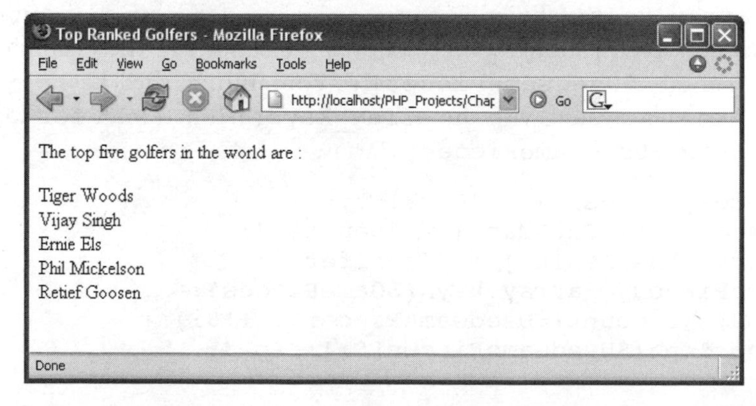

Figure 7-8 Output of an array returned with the `array_slice()` function

MANIPULATING ARRAYS

In the preceding section, you studied techniques for working with the individual elements in an array. In this section, you study techniques for manipulating entire arrays. More specifically, this section discusses how to sort, combine, and compare arrays. First, you learn how to sort arrays.

Sorting Arrays

You sort arrays using the functions listed in Table 7-2.

Table 7-2 Array sorting functions

Function	Description
`array_multisort(array[, array, ...])`	Sorts multiple arrays or multidimensional arrays
`arsort(array[, SORT_REGULAR | SORT_NUMERIC | SORT_STRING])`	Performs a reverse sort of values in an associative array and maintains the existing keys
`asort(array[, SORT_REGULAR | SORT_NUMERIC | SORT_STRING])`	Sorts an associative array by value and maintains the existing keys
`krsort(array[, SORT_REGULAR | SORT_NUMERIC | SORT_STRING])`	Performs a reverse sort of an associative array by key
`ksort(array[, SORT_REGULAR | SORT_NUMERIC | SORT_STRING])`	Sorts an associative array by key
`natcasesort(array)`	Performs a case-sensitive natural order sort by value and maintains the existing indexes or keys
`natsort(array)`	Performs a natural order sort by value and maintains the existing indexes or keys
`rsort(array[, SORT_REGULAR | SORT_NUMERIC | SORT_STRING])`	Performs a reverse sort of values in an indexed array and renumbers the indexes
`sort(array[, SORT_REGULAR | SORT_NUMERIC | SORT_STRING])`	Sorts an indexed array by value and renumbers the indexes

Table 7-2 Array sorting functions (continued)

Function	Description
uk_sort(*array*[, *comparison_function*])	Uses a comparison expression to sort an associative array by keys, maintaining the existing keys
usort(*array*[, *comparison_function*])	Uses a comparison expression to sort an indexed array by values, renumbering the indexes

The most commonly used array sorting functions are **sort()** and **rsort()** for indexed arrays, and **ksort()** and **krsort()** for associative arrays. These functions operate directly on an array, not on a new copy of an array, as occurs with the **array_values()** function. This means that you can execute each function simply by passing the name of an array to it. Keep in mind that the sort function you use depends on whether you need to sort an indexed or associative array. For example, the **sort()** and **rsort()** functions sort indexed arrays and renumber the element indexes. The following code demonstrates how to sort and reverse sort the indexed **$TopFiveGolfers[]** array. In this example, the golfer names are assigned to the array in the format "*last name, first name*" so the elements are sorted by last name. Figure 7-9 shows the output.

```
$TopGolfers = array("Woods, Tiger", "Singh, Vijay", "Els, Ernie",
"Mickelson, Phil", "Goosen, Retief", "Harrington, Padraig",
"Toms, David", "Garcia, Sergio", "Scott, Adam", "Cink, Stewart");
     echo "<p>The top five golfers in the world by ranking
are:</p><p>";
$TopFiveGolfers = array_slice($TopGolfers, 0, 5);
for ($i=0; $i<count($TopFiveGolfers); ++$i) {
     echo "{$TopFiveGolfers[$i]}<br />";
}
echo "</p>";
sort($TopFiveGolfers);
echo "<p>The top five golfers in the world in alphabetical order
     are:</p><p>";
for ($i=0; $i<count($TopFiveGolfers); ++$i) {
     echo "{$TopFiveGolfers[$i]}<br />";
}
echo "</p>";
rsort($TopFiveGolfers);
     echo "<p>The top five golfers in the world in reverse
alphabetical order are:</p><p>";
for ($i=0; $i<count($TopFiveGolfers); ++$i) {
     echo "{$TopFiveGolfers[$i]}<br />";
}
echo "</p>";
```

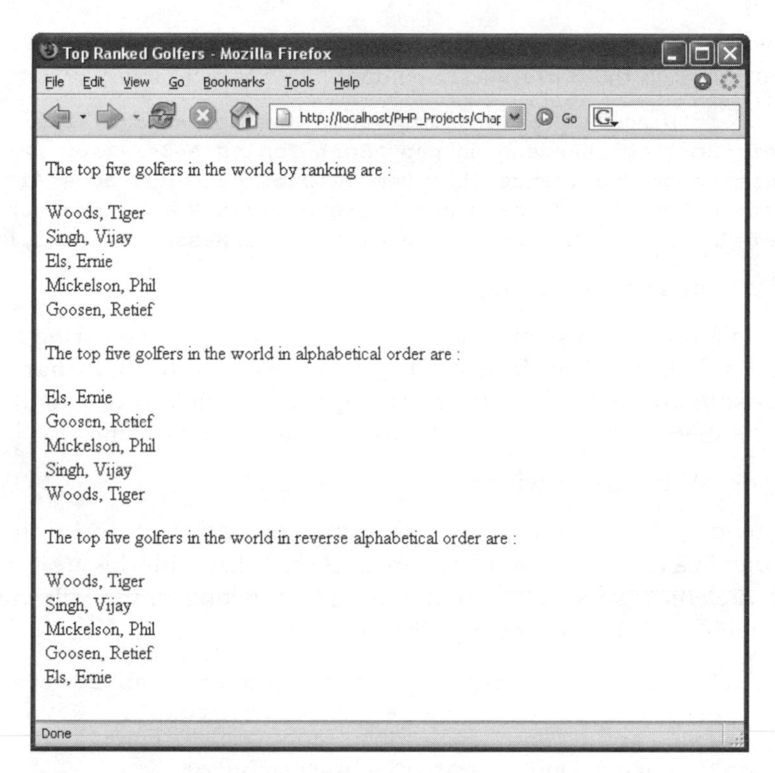

Figure 7-9 Output of an array after applying the `sort()` and `rsort()` functions

CAUTION

If you use the `sort()` and `rsort()` functions on an associative array, the keys are replaced with indexes.

Next, you add a new PHP file that uses the `sort()` function to sort the messages in the Discussion Forum script by topic in ascending order.

To add a new PHP file that uses the `sort()` function to sort the messages in the Discussion Forum script by topic in ascending order:

1. Return to the **RemoveDuplicates.php** file in your text editor and immediately save it as **SortTopicsAscending.php** in your Chapter directory for Chapter 7.
2. Replace the `array_unique()` and `array_values()` functions in the `if` statement with the following `sort()` function:

   ```
   sort($MessageArray);
   ```

3. Save the **SortTopicsAscending.php** file.
4. Return to the **ViewDiscussion.php** file in your text editor.

5. Modify the paragraph element at the end of the file so it contains an anchor element that calls the SortTopicsAscending.php file, as follows:

```
<p><a href="DiscussionForum.html">Post New Message</a><br />
<a href="SortTopicsAscending.php">Sort Topics A-Z</a><br />
<a href="RemoveDuplicates.php">Remove Duplicate Messages</a><br />
<a href="DeleteFirstMessage.php">Delete First Message</a><br />
<a href="DeleteLastMessage.php">Delete Last Message</a><br /></p>
```

6. Save the **ViewDiscussion.php** file.
7. Open the **View Discussion** page in your Web browser by entering the following URL: **http://localhost/PHP_Projects/Chapter.07/Chapter/ViewDiscussion.php**. Click the **Sort Topics A-Z** link to test the new code. The message list should sort by topic in ascending order.
8. Close your Web browser window.

The following code includes a statement that uses the `sort()` function on the `$ProvincialCapitals[]` array you saw earlier. Recall that with this array, province names are used as element keys. However, the `sort()` function in the following code replaces the keys with indexes, as shown in Figure 7-10.

```
$ProvincialCapitals = array("Newfoundland and Labrador"=>"St.
John's", "Prince Edward Island"=>"Charlottetown", "Nova
Scotia"=>"Halifax", "New Brunswick"=>"Fredericton",
"Quebec"=>"Quebec City", "Ontario"=>"Toronto",
"Manitoba"=>"Winnipeg", "Saskatchewan"=>"Regina",
"Alberta"=>"Edmonton", "British Columbia"=>"Victoria");
sort($ProvincialCapitals);
print_r($ProvincialCapitals);
```

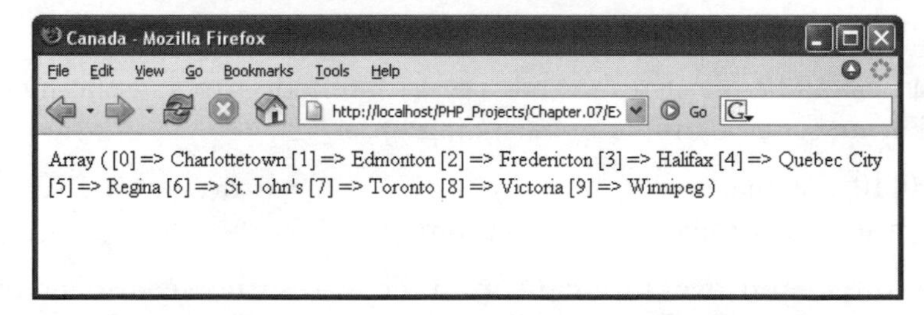

Figure 7-10 Output of an associative array after executing the `sort()` function

To sort an associative array and maintain the existing keys, you use the `ksort()` function, as follows:

```
ksort($ProvincialCapitals);
print_r($ProvincialCapitals);
```

The `ksort()` function in the preceding code sorts and maintains the existing keys, as shown in Figure 7-11.

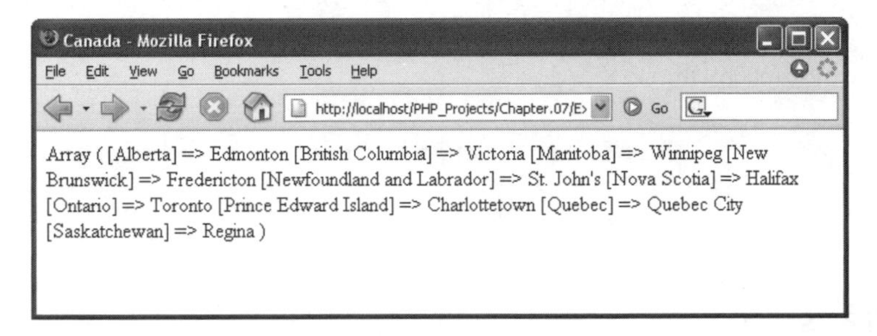

Figure 7-11 Output of an associative array after executing the `ksort()` function

To perform a reverse sort on an associative array and maintain the existing keys, be sure to use the `krsort()` function, not the `rsort()` function. The following statement demonstrates how to perform a reverse sort on the `$ProvincialCapitals[]` array:

```
krsort($ProvincialCapitals);
```

Next, you add a new PHP file that uses the `rsort()` function to sort the messages in the Discussion Forum script by topic in descending order.

To add a new PHP file that uses the `rsort()` function to sort the messages in the Discussion Forum script by topic in descending order:

1. Return to the **SortTopicsAscending.php** file in your text editor and immediately save it as **SortTopicsDescending.php** in your Chapter directory for Chapter 7.
2. Replace the `sort()`function in the `if` statement with the following `rsort()` function:

   ```
   rsort($MessageArray);
   ```

3. Save the **SortTopicsDescending.php** file and close it in your text editor.
4. Return to the **ViewDiscussion.php** file in your text editor.
5. Modify the paragraph element at the end of the file so it contains an anchor element that calls the SortTopicsDescending.php file, as follows:

   ```
   <p><a href="DiscussionForum.html">Post New Message</a><br />
   <a href="SortTopicsAscending.php">Sort Topics A-Z</a><br />
   <a href="SortTopicsDescending.php">Sort Topics Z-A</a><br />
   <a href="RemoveDuplicates.php">Remove Duplicate Messages</a><br />
   <a href="DeleteFirstMessage.php">Delete First Message</a><br />
   <a href="DeleteLastMessage.php">Delete Last Message</a><br /></p>
   ```

6. Save the **ViewDiscussion.php** file.

7. Open the **View Discussion** page in your Web browser by entering the following URL: **http://localhost/PHP_Projects/Chapter.07/Chapter/ViewDiscussion.php**. Click the **Sort Topics Z-A** link to test the new code. The message list should sort by topic in descending order.
8. Close your Web browser window.

You can also use the `shuffle()` function to randomize the order of array elements.

Combining Arrays

If you want to combine arrays, you have two options. You can either append one array to another or merge the two arrays. To append one array to another, you use the addition (+) or the compound assignment operator (+=). When you use either operator, any duplicate indexes or keys in an array you are appending to another array are ignored. For example, consider the following code, which declares and initializes indexed `$Provinces[]` and `$Territories[]` arrays. The `$Territories[]` array is appended to the `$Provinces[]` array with the addition (+) operator, and the resulting array is assigned to an array named `$Canada[]`. However, notice in the output shown in Figure 7-12 that the `$Canada[]` array only contains the elements that were assigned to the `$Provinces[]` array. This occurs because the first three indexes in the `$Territories[]` array already exist in the `$Provinces[]` array and are, therefore, ignored.

```
$Provinces = array("Newfoundland and Labrador", "Prince Edward
Island", "Nova Scotia", "New Brunswick", "Quebec", "Ontario",
"Manitoba", "Saskatchewan", "Alberta", "British Columbia");
$Territories = array("Nunavut", "Northwest Territories", "Yukon
Territory");
$Canada = $Provinces + $Territories;
print_r($Canada);
```

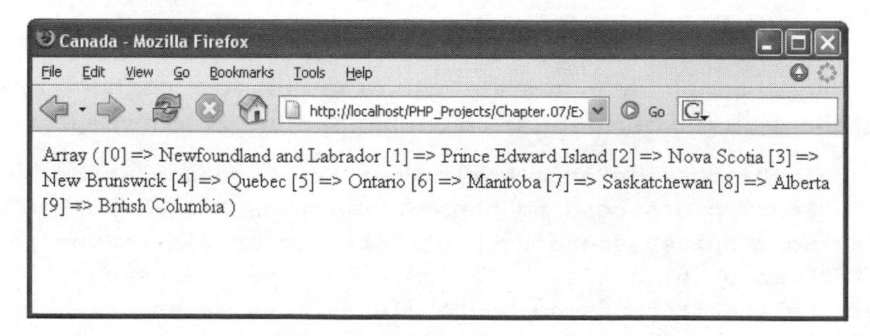

Figure 7-12 Output of two combined indexed arrays

In comparison, the following code declares and initializes the associative `$ProvincialCapitals[]` and `$TerritorialCapitals[]` arrays. The `$TerritorialCapitals[]` array is appended to the `$ProvincialCapitals[]` array with the addition (+) operator, and the resulting array is assigned to an array named `$CanadianCapitals[]`. Because the keys in the `$TerritorialCapitals[]` array do not exist in the `$ProvincialCapitals[]` array, the elements in the `$TerritorialCapitals[]` array are successfully appended to the elements in the `$ProvincialCapitals[]` array.

```
$ProvincialCapitals = array("Newfoundland and Labrador"=>"St.
John's", "Prince Edward Island"=>"Charlottetown", "Nova
Scotia"=>"Halifax", "New Brunswick"=>"Fredericton",
"Quebec"=>"Quebec City", "Ontario"=>"Toronto",
"Manitoba"=>"Winnipeg", "Saskatchewan"=>"Regina",
"Alberta"=>"Edmonton", "British Columbia"=>"Victoria");
$TerritorialCapitals = array("Nunavut"=>"Iqaluit", "Northwest
Territories"=>"Yellowknife", "Yukon Territory"=>"Whitehorse");
$CanadianCapitals = $ProvincialCapitals + $TerritorialCapitals;
```


You can also combine two arrays with the compound assignment operator (+=), as follows:

```
$CanadianCapitals = $ProvincialCapitals;
$CanadianCapitals += $TerritorialCapitals;
```

Instead of appending one array to another, you can merge two or more arrays with the `array_merge()` function. The syntax for the `array_merge()` function is `new_array = array_merge($array1, $array2, $array3, ...);`. The `$array2` array is appended to the `$array1` array, the `$array3` array is appended to the `$array2` array, and so on. If you use the `array_merge()` function with associative arrays, the keys in the array you are appending overwrite any duplicate keys in the array to which you are appending. With indexed arrays, all elements in one array are appended to another array and renumbered. The following statement demonstrates how to combine the associative `$ProvincialCapitals[]` and `$TerritorialCapitals[]` arrays:

```
$CanadianCapitals = array_merge($ProvincialCapitals,
$TerritorialCapitals);
```

The following code demonstrates how to combine the indexed `$Provinces[]` and `$Territories[]` arrays. Unlike with the example that used the addition (+) and compound assignment (+=) operators, this version successfully combines both arrays, renumbers the indexes, and assigns the new array to the `$Canada[]` array.

```
$Provinces = array("Newfoundland and Labrador", "Prince Edward
Island", "Nova Scotia", "New Brunswick", "Quebec", "Ontario",
"Manitoba", "Saskatchewan", "Alberta", "British Columbia");
$Territories = array("Nunavut", "Northwest Territories", "Yukon
Territory");
$Canada = array_merge($Provinces, $Territories);
```

In addition to appending and merging the elements in two arrays, you can create a new associative array that uses the values from one array as keys and values from another array as element values. To do this, you use the `array_combine()` function. For example, the following code declares a `$Territories[]` array and a `TerritorialCapitals[]` array and then combines the two arrays into a new array named `$CanadianTerritories[]`.

```
$Territories = array("Nunavut", "Northwest Territories", "Yukon
Territory");
$TerritorialCapitals = array("Iqaluit", "Yellowknife",
"Whitehorse");
$CanadianTerritories = array_combine($Territories,
$TerritorialCapitals);
```

Next, you add the `array_combine()` function to the ViewDiscussion.php to create a new associative array.

To add the `array_combine()` function to the ViewDiscussion.php file to create a new associative array:

1. Return to the **ViewDiscussion.php** file in your text editor.
2. Modify the `for` loop in the `else` clause as follows. The second and third statements in the loop create two separate arrays: `$KeyArray[]` and `$ValueArray[]`. The third statement then uses the `array_combine()` function to create `$KeyMessageArray[]`.

```
for ($i=0; $i<count($MessageArray); ++$i) {
	$CurMessage = explode("~", $MessageArray[$i]);
	$KeyArray[] = $CurMessage[0];
	$ValueArray[] = $CurMessage[1]. "~" . $CurMessage[2];
	$KeyMessageArray = array_combine($KeyArray, $ValueArray);
}
```

3. Save the **ViewDiscussion.php** file.
4. Open the **View Discussion** page in your Web browser by entering the following URL: **http://localhost/PHP_Projects/Chapter.07/Chapter/ViewDiscussion.php**. The message list should display the same as it did before you added the `array_combine()` function.
5. Close your Web browser window.

Comparing Arrays

PHP includes several functions for comparing the contents of two or more arrays. Two of the most basic comparison functions are `array_diff()` and `array_intersect()`. The The `array_diff()` function returns an array of elements that exist in one array but not in any other arrays to which it is compared. The syntax for the `array_diff()` function is *`new_array`* `= array_diff(`*`$array1`*`, `*`$array2`*`, `*`$array3`*`, ...);`.

A new array is returned containing elements that occur in *$array1* but not in any of the other array arguments. Keys and indexes are not renumbered in the new array. As an example, consider the following code, which declares and initializes an array named **$NATO[ ]** containing the names of NATO member countries, and another array named **$G7[ ]** containing the names of countries that are members of the G7 group of industrialized nations. The **array_diff()** determines which countries are not members of NATO by comparing the values in the **$G7[ ]** array with the values in the **$NATO[ ]** array and assigns the difference to the **$Result[ ]** array. The **array_values()** statement then renumbers the indexes in the **$Result[ ]** array. The **$Result[ ]** array is assigned a single element containing the value "Japan," which is a member of the G7 group of industrialized nations but not NATO.

```
$NATO = array("Belgium", "Bulgaria", "Canada", "Czech Rep",
"Denmark", "Estonia", "France", "Germany", "Greece", "Hungary",
"Iceland", "Italy", "Latvia", "Lithuania", "Luxembourg",
"Netherlands", "Norway", "Poland", "Portugal", "Romania",
"Slovakia", "Slovenia", "Spain", "Turkey", "United Kingdom",
"United States");
$G7 = array("Canada", "France", "Germany", "Japan", "Italy",
"United Kingdom", "United States");
$Result = array_diff($G7, $NATO);
$Result = array_values($Result);
echo "<p>The following countries are not members of
NATO:</p><p>";
for ($i=0; $i<count($Result); ++$i) {
     echo "{$Result[$i]}<br />";
}
```

The **array_intersect()** function returns an array of elements that exist in all of the arrays that are compared. The syntax for the **array_intersect()** function is `new_array = array_intersect($array1, $array2, $array3, ...);`. As with the **array_diff()** function, keys and indexes are not renumbered in the new array, so you must use the **array_values()** function to renumber an indexed array. The following code uses the **array_intersect()** function on the same **$NATO[ ]** and **$G7[ ]** arrays. The output shown in Figure 7-13 shows the names of the six countries that are members of both NATO and G7.

```
$Result = array_intersect($G7, $NATO);
$Result = array_values($Result);
echo "</p><p>The following countries are members of both G7 and
NATO:</p>";
for ($i=0; $i<count($Result); ++$i) {
     echo "{$Result[$i]}<br />";
}
echo "</p>";
```

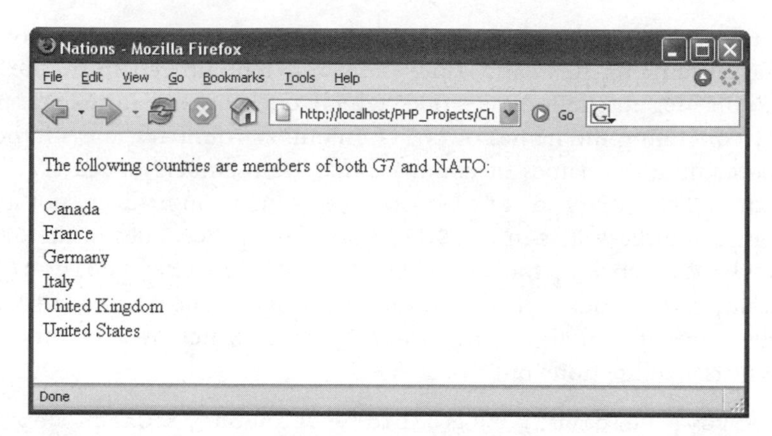

Figure 7-13 Output of an array created with the `array_intersect()` function

UNDERSTANDING MULTIDIMENSIONAL ARRAYS

The arrays you have created so far are known as one-dimensional arrays because they have consisted of a single index or key. You can also create **multidimensional arrays** that consist of multiple indexes or keys. The procedures for creating multidimensional arrays are essentially the same for indexed and associative arrays. However, to avoid confusion, you first learn how to create indexed multidimensional arrays.

Creating Two-Dimensional Indexed Arrays

The most common type of multidimensional array is a **two-dimensional** array, which has two sets of indexes or keys. To understand how a two-dimensional array works, first consider the following one-dimensional indexed array named `$USDollars[]` that converts the U.S. dollar to various world currencies:

```
$USDollars = array(
     104.6100, // Yen
     0.7476, // Euro
     0.5198, // UK Pound
     1.2013, // Canadian Dollar
     1.1573 // Swiss Francs
);
```

This single-dimensional array works fine if you only need to store a single currency conversion. However, what if you want to store additional currency conversions, such as Yen to Euros? Table 7-3 contains a table that lists conversion rates for each of the currencies in the preceding example.

Table 7-3 Currency conversion table

	U.S. $	Yen	Euro	U.K. Pound	Canadian $	Swiss Franc
U.S. $	1	104.61	0.7476	0.5198	1.2013	1.1573
Yen	0.009559	1	0.007146	0.004969	0.011484	0.011063
Euro	1.3377	139.9368	1	0.6953	1.6070	1.5481
U.K. Pound	1.9239	201.2592	1.4382	1	2.3112	2.2265
Canadian $	0.8324	87.0807	0.6223	0.4327	1	0.9634
Swiss Franc	0.8641	90.3914	0.6459	0.4491	1.0380	1

The first set of indexes (or keys) in a two-dimensional array determines the number of rows in the array, and the second set of indexes (or keys) determines the number of columns. The easiest way to create a two-dimensional array is to first create individual arrays for each of the rows the array will include. The following statements declare and initialize individual indexed arrays for each of the rows in Table 7-3:

```
$USDollars = array(1, 104.61, 0.7476, 0.5198, 1.2013, 1.1573);
$Yen = array(0.009559, 1, 0.007146, 0.004969, 0.011484, 0.011063);
$Euro = array(1.3377, 139.9368, 1, 0.6953, 1.6070, 1.5481);
$UKPound = array(1.9239, 201.2592, 1.4382, 1, 2.3112, 2.2265);
$CanadianDollar = array(0.8324, 87.0807, 0.6223, 0.4327, 1, 0.9634);
$SwissFranc = array(0.8641, 90.3914, 0.6459, 0.4491, 1.0380, 1);
```

A multidimensional array in PHP is essentially "an array of arrays." To declare and initialize a multidimensional array with the preceding data, you include each of the array names as an element value in a new declaration. For example, the following statement uses each of the preceding array names to declare and initialize a two-dimensional indexed array named `$ExchangeRates[]`:

```
$ExchangeRates = array($USDollars, $Yen, $Euro, $UKPound,
$CanadianDollar, $SwissFranc);
```

You refer to the values in a multidimensional indexed array by including two sets of brackets following the array name with the syntax `$array_name[index][index]`. The first set of brackets refers to the row, and the second set of brackets refers to the column. Table 7-4 conceptually illustrates the elements and index numbers in the `$ExchangeRates[]` array.

Table 7-4 Elements and indexes in the `$ExchangeRates[]` array

	0 (U.S. $)	1 (Yen)	2 (Euro)	3 (U.K. Pound)	4 (Canadian $)	5 (Swiss Franc)
0 (U.S. $)	1	104.61	0.7476	0.5198	1.2013	1.1573
1 (Yen)	0.009559	1	0.007146	0.004969	0.011484	0.011063
2 (Euro)	1.3377	139.9368	1	0.6953	1.6070	1.5481
3 (U.K. Pound)	1.9239	201.2592	1.4382	1	2.3112	2.2265
4 (Canadian $)	0.8324	87.0807	0.6223	0.4327	1	0.9634
5 (Swiss Franc)	0.8641	90.3914	0.6459	0.4491	1.0380	1

To access the exchange rate from Yen to Euros, you refer to the second row (index 1) and third column (index 2) of the `$ExchangeRates[]` array as follows: `$ExchangeRates[1][2]`. The following statement prints the exchange rate from Yen to Euros.

```
echo "<p>At today's exchange rate, 1 Japanese Yen converts to
{$ExchangeRates[1][2]} Euros.</p>";
```

Use the same format to modify an element value in a two-dimensional indexed array. The following statement demonstrates how to modify the exchange rate from Canadian dollars to Swiss Francs:

```
$ExchangeRates[4][5] = 0.9254;
```

Next, you add an indexed two-dimensional array to the ViewDiscussion.php file for displaying the contents of the messages.txt file.

To add an indexed two-dimensional array to the ViewDiscussion.php file for displaying the contents of the messages.txt file:

1. Return to the **ViewDiscussion.php** file in your text editor.
2. Replace the first `for` loop in the `else` clause with the following `foreach` loop. This construct loops through `$MessageArray[]` and explodes each element into the `$CurElement[]` array. Notice that the last statement in the loop assigns the `$CurElement[]` array to `$KeyMessageArray[]`, which creates a two-dimensional array. Because the `$KeyMessageArray[]` statement includes two array brackets at the end of the array name, each subsequent value in `$CurMessage[]` is appended to `$KeyMessageArray[]`.

   ```
   foreach ($MessageArray as $Message) {
        $CurMessage = explode("~", $Message);
        $KeyMessageArray[] = $CurMessage;
   }
   ```

3. Delete the following statement:

   ```
   $Count = 1;
   ```

4. Modify the second `foreach` loop at the end of the `else` clause into the following `for` loop. The `$i` variable is used for looping through the elements in the first dimension of the array. However, because each "row" in the `$KeyMessageArray[]` two-dimensional array only contains three elements (topic, name, and message), the second dimension is referred to using literal values.

```
for ($i=0; $i<count($KeyMessageArray); ++$i) {
     echo "<tr>";
     echo "<td><strong>" . ($i + 1) . "</strong>.</td>";
     echo "<td><strong>Topic</strong>: " .
          stripslashes($KeyMessageArray[$i][0]) . "<br />";
     echo "<strong>Name</strong>: "
          . stripslashes($KeyMessageArray[$i][1]) . "<br />";
     echo "<strong>Message</strong>: "
          . stripslashes($KeyMessageArray[$i][2]);
     echo "</td></tr>";
}
```

The completed script should appear as follows:

```
<?php
if (!file_exists("messages.txt") || filesize("messages.txt") == 0)
     echo "<p>There are no messages posted.</p>";
else {
     $MessageArray = file("messages.txt");
     foreach ($MessageArray as $Message) {
          $CurMessage = explode("~", $Message);
          $KeyMessageArray[] = $CurMessage;
     }
     for ($i=0; $i<count($KeyMessageArray); ++$i) {
          echo "<tr>";
          echo "<td><strong>" . ($i + 1) . "</strong>.</td>";
          echo "<td><strong>Topic</strong>: "
               . stripslashes($KeyMessageArray[$i][0]) . "<br />";
          echo "<strong>Name</strong>: "
               . stripslashes($KeyMessageArray[$i][1]) . "<br />";
          echo "<strong>Message</strong>: "
               . stripslashes($KeyMessageArray[$i][2]);
          echo "</td></tr>";
     }
}
```

5. Save the **ViewDiscussion.php** file and close it in your text editor.

6. Open the **View Discussion** page in your Web browser by entering the following URL: **http://localhost/PHP_Projects/Chapter.07/Chapter/ViewDiscussion.php**. The message list should display the same as it did before you added the two-dimensional array.
7. Close your Web browser window.

Creating Two-Dimensional Associative Arrays

The primary difference in creating two-dimensional associative arrays is that you need to specify the key for each element. The following statements declare the same exchange rate arrays you saw earlier, but this time as associative arrays:

```
$USDollars = array("U.S. $"=>1, "Yen"=>104.61, "Euro"=>0.7476,
"U.K. Pound"=>0.5198, "Canadian $"=>1.2013, "Swiss
Franc"=>1.1573);
$Yen = array("U.S. $"=>0.009559, "Yen"=>1, "Euro"=>0.007146,
"U.K. Pound"=>0.004969, "Canadian $"=>0.011484, "Swiss
Franc"=>0.011063);
$Euro = array("U.S. $"=>1.3377, "Yen"=>139.9368, "Euro"=>1, "U.K.
Pound"=>0.6953, "Canadian $"=>1.6070, "Swiss Franc"=>1.5481);
$UKPound = array("U.S. $"=>1.9239, "Yen"=>201.2592,
"Euro"=>1.4382, "U.K. Pound"=>1, "Canadian $"=>2.3112, "Swiss
Franc"=>2.2265);
$CanadianDollar = array("U.S. $"=>0.8324, "Yen"=>87.0807,
"Euro"=>0.6223, "U.K. Pound"=>0.4327, "Canadian $"=>1, "Swiss
Franc"=>0.9634);
$SwissFranc = array("U.S. $"=>0.8641, "Yen"=>90.3914,
"Euro"=>0.6459, "U.K. Pound"=>0.4491, "Canadian $"=>1.0380,
"Swiss Franc"=>1);
```

You can access elements in the preceding arrays by specifying an element's key. For example, you can access the exchange rate for Swiss Francs to Canadian dollars with `$SwissFranc["Canadian $"]`. Things get a little confusing when you use the preceding array names to declare and initialize an associative version of the two-dimensional `$ExchangeRates[]` array. For example, the following statement is the same statement you saw earlier to declare and initialize the indexed version of the two-dimensional `$ExchangeRates[]` array:

```
$ExchangeRates = array($USDollars, $Yen, $Euro, $UKPound,
$CanadianDollar, $SwissFranc);
```

Because the preceding statement does not declare keys for the elements represented by each of the individual arrays, the first dimension in the resulting `$ExchangeRates[]` array is indexed and the second dimension is associative. To access the exchange rate from Yen to Euros, you refer to the second row (index 1) and third column (associative key "Euro") of the `$ExchangeRates[]` function as follows: `$ExchangeRates[1]["Euro"]`. Although this syntax is legal, it can be confusing. To make both dimensions associative, assign keys to each of the array names in the statement that declares and initializes the `$ExchangeRates[ ]` array, as follows:

```
$ExchangeRates = array("U.S. $"=>$USDollars,"Yen"=>$Yen,
"Euro"=>$Euro, "U.K. Pound"=>$UKPound, "Canadian
$"=>$CanadianDollar, "Swiss Franc"=>$SwissFranc);
```

Figure 7-14 conceptually illustrates the elements and keys in the `$ExchangeRates[ ]` array.

Keys

	"U.S. $"	"Yen"	"Euro"	"U.K. Pound"	"Canadian $"	"Swiss Franc"
"U.S. $"	1	104.61	0.7476	0.5198	1.2013	1.1573
"Yen"	0.009559	1	0.007146	0.004969	0.0114484	0.011063
"Euro"	1.3377	139.9368	1	0.6953	1.6070	1.5481
"U.K. Pound"	1.9239	201.2592	1.4382	1	2.3112	2.2265
"Canadian $"	0.8324	87.0807	0.6223	0.4327	1	0.9634
"Swiss Franc"	0.8641	90.3914	0.6459	0.4491	1.0380	1

Keys

Elements

Elements

Figure 7-14 Elements and keys in the `$ExchangeRates[ ]` array

Assigning keys to each of the array names in the declaration statement for the `$ExchangeRates[ ]` array allows you to access the exchange rate from Yen to Euros by using keys for both array dimensions. The following statement prints the exchange rate from Yen to Euros.

```
echo "<p>At today's exchange rate, 1 Japanese Yen converts to
{$ExchangeRates["Yen"]["Euro"]} Euros.</p>";
```

Use the same format to modify an element value in a two-dimensional associative array. The following statement demonstrates how to modify the exchange rate from Canadian Dollars to Swiss Francs:

```
$ExchangeRates["Canadian $"]["Swiss Francs"] = 0.9254;
```

Creating Multidimensional Arrays with a Single Statement

In the preceding two sections, you created multidimensional arrays using a series of statements. First, you created the individual arrays, then you created the multidimensional array itself. You can also create a multidimensional array with a single statement. Instead of writing separate declaration statements, you can include the array construct for each individual array as the value for each element within the declaration statement for the multidimensional array. The following example demonstrates how to declare an indexed version of the multidimensional `$ExchangeRates[]` array with a single declaration statement:

```
$ExchangeRates = array(
    array(1, 104.61, 0.7476, 0.5198, 1.2013, 1.1573),   // U.S. $
    array(0.009559, 1, 0.007146, 0.004969, 0.011484, 0.011063), // Yen
    array(1.3377, 139.9368, 1, 0.6953, 1.6070, 1.5481),   // Euro
    array(1.9239, 201.2592, 1.4382, 1, 2.3112, 2.2265),   // U.K. Pound
    array(0.8324, 87.0807, 0.6223, 0.4327, 1, 0.9634),   // Canadian $
    array(0.8641, 90.3914, 0.6459, 0.4491, 1.0380, 1)   // Swiss Franc
);
```

The following example demonstrates how to declare an associative version of the multidimensional `$ExchangeRates[]` array with a single declaration statement:

```
$ExchangeRates = array(
     "U.S. $"=>array("U.S. $"=>1, "Yen"=>104.61, "Euro"=>0.7476,
     "U.K. Pound"=>0.5198, "Canadian $"=>1.2013,
     "Swiss Franc"=>1.1573), "Yen"=>array("U.S. $"=>0.009559, "Yen"=>1,
     "Euro"=>0.007146, "U.K. Pound"=>0.004969, "Canadian $"=>0.011484,
     "Swiss Franc"=>0.011063), "Euro"=>array("U.S. $"=>1.3377,
     "Yen"=>139.9368, "Euro"=>1, "U.K. Pound"=>0.6953,
     "Canadian $"=>1.6070, "Swiss Franc"=>1.5481),
     "U.K. Pound"=>array("U.S. $"=>1.9239, "Yen"=>201.2592,
     "Euro"=>1.4382, "U.K. Pound"=>1, "Canadian $"=>2.3112,
     "Swiss Franc"=>2.2265), "Canadian $"=>array("U.S. $"=>0.8324,
     "Yen"=>87.0807, "Euro"=>0.6223, "U.K. Pound"=>0.4327,
    "Canadian $"=>1, "Swiss Franc"=>0.9634),
     "Swiss Franc"=>array("U.S. $"=>0.8641, "Yen"=>90.3914,
     "Euro"=>0.6459, "U.K. Pound"=>0.4491, "Canadian $"=>1.0380,
     "Swiss Franc"=>1)
);
```

Although you can declare and initialize multidimensional arrays with a single statement, as you can see from the preceding examples, the statements are considerably more difficult to decipher than arrays created using a series of statements.

Working with Additional Dimensions

Multidimensional arrays are not limited to two dimensions. You can include as many dimensions as you need when you declare the array. However, the more dimensions you use, the more complex the array becomes. Beginning programmers rarely need to use arrays larger than two dimensions, so this book does not spend much time discussing how to create them. Nevertheless, you should understand that the concepts underlying arrays of three or more dimensions are similar to concepts underlying two-dimensional arrays. As an example of an array of more than two dimensions, consider an array that stores quarterly sales figures by state for a company's five-person sales force. For this type of multidimensional array, you would need three indexes. The first index would consist of 50 elements, one for each state. The second index would consist of five elements, one for each salesperson. The third index would consist of four elements, one for each quarter in the year. You can think of such an array as containing fifty tables, with each table containing a row for each salesperson and a column for each quarter. Table 7-5 shows how the Alaska table might appear for the first year in an associative version of the array.

Table 7-5 The Alaska table of a three-dimensional array

Salesperson	Quarters of the year: Q1	Q2	Q3	Q4
Sam	874	76	98	890
Jane	656	133	64	354
Lisa	465	668	897	64
Hiroshi	31	132	651	46
Jose	654	124	126	456

To create the three-dimensional array, you first declare individual arrays for each of the rows in Table 7-5. Then, you create two-dimensional arrays for each state consisting of the individual arrays containing each salesperson's figures for that particular state. Finally, you create the three-dimensional array by assigning each of the two-dimensional state arrays as elements in the three-dimensional array. The following statements demonstrate how to build a three-dimensional array named `$AnnualSales[]` for just the state of Alaska. The first five statements declare individual arrays for each salesperson's quarterly figures for the state of Alaska. The sixth statement creates a two-dimensional array named `$Alaska[]` containing the quarterly sales figures for each salesperson. The last statement creates a three-dimensional array named `$AnnualSales[]` by assigning the two-dimensional `$Alaska[]` array as an element.

```
$Sam = array("Q1"=>874, "Q2"=>76, "Q3"=>98, "Q4"=>890);
$Jane = array("Q1"=>656, "Q2"=>133, "Q3"=>64, "Q4"=>354);
$Lisa = array("Q1"=>465, "Q2"=>668, "Q3"=>897, "Q4"=>64);
$Hiroshi = array("Q1"=>31, "Q2"=>132, "Q3"=>651, "Q4"=>46);
$Jose = array("Q1"=>654, "Q2"=>124, "Q3"=>126, "Q4"=>456);
$Alaska = array("Sam"=>$Sam, "Jane"=>$Jane, "Lisa"=>$Lisa,
"Hiroshi"=>$Hiroshi, "Jose"=>$Jose);
$AnnualSales = array("Alaska"=>$Alaska);
```

To access or modify a value in a three-dimensional array, you must specify all dimensions. For example, the following statement prints Hiroshi's third-quarter sales figures for Alaska:

```
echo "</p>Hiroshi's third-quarter sales figure for Alaska is
{$AnnualSales['Alaska']['Hiroshi']['Q3']}.</p>";
```

CHAPTER SUMMARY

- The `array_shift()` function removes the first element from the beginning of an array, whereas the `array_unshift()` function adds one or more elements to the beginning of an array.
- The `array_pop()` function removes the last element from the end of an array, whereas the `array_push()` function adds one or more elements to the end of an array.
- The `array_splice()` function adds or removes array elements.
- The `unset()` function removes array elements and other variables.
- The `array_values()` function renumbers an indexed array's elements.
- The `array_unique()` function removes duplicate elements from an array.
- With associative arrays, you specify an element's key by using the array operator (=>).
- The internal array pointer refers to the currently selected element in an array.
- The `in_array()` function returns a Boolean value of true if a given value exists in an array.
- The `array_search()` function determines whether a given value exists in an array and 1) returns the index or key of the first matching element if the value exists, or 2) returns false if the value does not exist.
- The `array_key_exists()` function determines whether a given index or key exists.
- The `array_slice()` function returns a portion of an array and assigns it to another array.
- The most commonly used array sorting functions are `sort()` and `rsort()` for indexed arrays, and `ksort()`and `krsort()` for associative arrays.
- To append one array to another, you use the addition (+) or the compound assignment (+=) operator.
- The `array_merge()` function merges two or more arrays.
- The `array_diff()` function returns an array of elements that exist in one array but not in any other arrays to which it is compared.
- The `array_intersect()` function returns an array of elements that exist in all of the arrays that are compared.
- A multidimensional array consists of multiple indexes or keys.

Review Questions

1. Which of the following functions removes the first element from the beginning of an array?
   a. `array_shift()`
   b. `array_unshift()`
   c. `array_push()`
   d. `array_pop()`
2. Explain the easiest way to add elements to the end of an array.
3. Which of the following functions removes the last element from the end of an array? (Choose all that apply.)
   a. `array_shift()`
   b. `array_unshift()`
   c. `array_push()`
   d. `array_pop()`
4. Explain how to use the `array_splice()` function to add and remove elements to and from an array.
5. After removing elements from an array, the `unset()` function automatically renumbers the remaining elements. True or False?
6. Which of the following functions removes duplicate elements from an array?
   a. `array_duplicates()`
   b. `array_unique()`
   c. `remove_duplicates()`
   d. `unique()`
7. What is the correct syntax for declaring and initializing an associative array?
   a. `$AutoMakers = array("Ford" . "Mustang", "Chevrolet" . "Corvette");`
   b. `$AutoMakers = array("Ford"="Mustang", "Chevrolet"="Corvette");`
   c. `$AutoMakers = array("Ford">"Mustang", "Chevrolet">"Corvette");`
   d. `$AutoMakers = array("Ford"=>"Mustang", "Chevrolet"=>"Corvette");`
8. If an array contains a mixture of indexes and keys, what value or key is used if you do not specify one when adding a new element to the array?
9. If you declare an array in PHP and use a starting index other than 0, empty elements are created for each index between 0 and the index value you specify. True or False?

10. Which of the following functions moves an array's internal pointer to the first element?

    a. `first()`

    b. `top()`

    c. `start()`

    d. `reset()`

11. Which of the following functions returns the value of an element where an array's internal pointer is positioned?

    a. `current()`

    b. `key()`

    c. `array()`

    d. `array_values()`

12. Explain the difference between the `in_array()` and `array_search()` functions.

13. Which of the following locates a key named "Ford" in an array named `$AutoMakers[]`?

    a. `array_key_exists($AutoMakers=>"Ford");`

    b. `$AutoMakers = array_key_exists("Ford");`

    c. `array_key_exists($AutoMakers, "Ford");`

    d. `array_key_exists("Ford", $AutoMakers);`

14. Explain how to use the `array_slice()` function to return a portion of an array and assign it to another array.

15. Which of the following functions perform a reverse sort on an array? (Choose all that apply.)

    a. `asort()`

    b. `usort()`

    c. `rsort()`

    d. `krsort()`

16. Which of the following operators can you use to append one array to another? (Choose all that apply.)

    a. `.`

    b. `+`

    c. `+=`

    d. `=>`

17. If you use the `array_merge()` function with indexed arrays, all elements in one array are appended to another array and renumbered. True or False?

18. Which of the following returns an array of elements that exist in all of the arrays that are compared?
    a. `usort()`
    b. `array_common()`
    c. `array_diff()`
    d. `array_intersect()`
19. Explain how to create an associative two-dimensional array using separate statements to build the array and how to create the same array with a single statement.
20. Suppose you are working with an indexed two-dimensional array named `$InterestRates[]` that begins with an index of 0. Which of the following refers to the second element in the first dimension and the third element in the second dimension?
    a. `$InterestRates[1],[2]`
    b. `$InterestRates[1][2]`
    c. `$InterestRates[1, 2]`
    d. `$InterestRates[1].[2]`

HANDS-ON PROJECTS

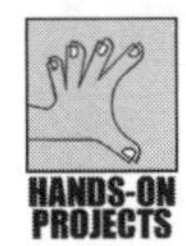

Hands-On Project 7-1

In this project, you create an associative array that contains a list of a car dealer's top five salespeople and the number of cars sold by each. You use each person's name as the key for the associative array and the numbers of cars sold as the element value.

1. Create a new document in your text editor.
2. Type the `<!DOCTYPE>` declaration, `<html>` element, document head, and `<body>` element. Use the strict DTD and "Top Five Salespeople" as the content of the `<title>` element.
3. Add the following text and elements to the document body:

```
<h1>Gosselin Automotive</h1>
<h2>Top Five Salespeople in January</h2>
<hr />
```

4. Create a script section in the document body that contains the following associative array declaration:

```
<?php
$Salespeople = array(
     "Hiroshi Morinaga"=>57,
     "Judith Stein"=>44,
     "Jose Martinez"=>26,
     "Tyrone Winters"=>22,
     "Raja Singh"=>21);
?>
```

5. Now add the following `foreach` loop to the end of the script section. The `foreach` loop prints the key and value of each element and then moves the internal pointer to the next element.

```
foreach ($Salespeople as $Salesperson) {
     echo key($Salespeople) . ": $Salesperson cars<br />";
     next($Salespeople);
}
```

6. Save the document as **TopSales.php** in the Projects directory for Chapter 7, and then close it in your text editor.
7. Open the **TopSales.php** file in your Web browser by entering the following URL: **http://localhost/PHP_Projects/Chapter.07/Projects/TopSales.php**.
8. Close your Web browser window.

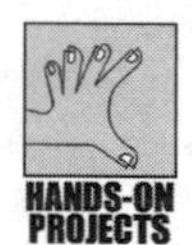

Hands-On Project 7-2

In this project, you create a script that fills an indexed array with the numbers 1 through 100. Then, you use the `shuffle()` function to randomize the order of the array elements to return five "winning numbers" in a simple lottery game. You pass the name of an element to the `shuffle()` function to randomize its elements.

1. Create a new document in your text editor.
2. Type the `<!DOCTYPE>` declaration, `<html>` element, document head, and `<body>` element. Use the strict DTD and "Winning Numbers" as the content of the `<title>` element.
3. Create a script section in the document body that contains the following array declaration:

```
<?php
$PossibleNumbers = array();
?>
```

4. Add the following `for` loop to the end of the script section, which fills the `$PossibleNumbers[]` array with the values 1 through 99:

```
for ($i=1; $i<100; ++$i) {
     $PossibleNumbers[] = $i;
}
```

5. Add the following two statements to the end of the script section. The first statement uses the `shuffle()` function to randomize the array. The second statement then uses the `array_slice()` function to return the first five elements in the `$PossibleNumbers[]` array, which are then assigned to an array named `$WinningNumbers[]`.

```
shuffle($PossibleNumbers);
$WinningNumbers = array_slice($PossibleNumbers, 0, 5);
```

6. Finally, add the following `foreach` statement to print the numbers in the `$WinningNumbers[]` array:

```
foreach ($WinningNumbers as $Number) {
     echo "$Number<br />";
}
```

7. Save the document as **WinningNumbers.php** in the Projects directory for Chapter 7, and then close it in your text editor.
8. Open the **WinningNumbers.php** file in your Web browser by entering the following URL: **http://localhost/PHP_Projects/Chapter.07/Projects/WinningNumbers.php**.
9. Close your Web browser window.

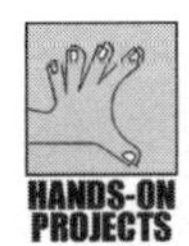

Hands-On Project 7-3

The `array_walk()` function allows you to send every element in an array to a custom function. You pass two arguments to the `array_walk()` function: The first argument is the name of the array, and the second argument is the name of the custom function, enclosed in quotation marks. You cannot use the `array_walk()` function to modify the elements in an array. However, it is useful for iterating through an array's elements. In this project, you create a script with an indexed array containing five floating-point values. You send each element in the array to the `array_walk()` function to apply a 10% discount to each value.

1. Create a new document in your text editor.
2. Type the `<!DOCTYPE>` declaration, `<html>` element, document head, and `<body>` element. Use the strict DTD and "Retail Discount" as the content of the `<title>` element.
3. Create a script section in the document body that contains the following array declaration:

```
<?php
$RetailPrices = array(99.5, 78.65, 32.4, 59.95, 12.75);
?>
```

4. Add the following `echo()` and `foreach` statements to the end of the script section to print the values in the `$RetailPrices[]` array:

```
echo "<p><strong>Standard Prices</strong></p><p>";
foreach ($RetailPrices as $Price) {
     printf("$%01.2f<br />", $Price);
     next($RetailPrices);
}
echo "</p>";
```

5. Next, add the following statements to the end of the script section to print the values in the `$RetailPrices[]` array with a discount of 10%. The second statement uses the `array_walk()` function to pass each array element to a function named `discount()`, which you add next.

```
echo "<p><strong>10% Discount</strong></p><p>";
array_walk($RetailPrices, "discount");
echo "</p>";
```

6. Finally, add the following function declaration named `discount()` to the beginning of the script section. The function accepts a single parameter, which represents each array element that is passed to it. The first statement in the function increases the value of each element by 10%, and the second statement prints the modified value. (Keep in mind that the function does not change the original array; it only operates on the value assigned to the `$Price` parameter.)

```
function discount($Price) {
     $Price = $Price / 1.1;
     printf("$%01.2f<br />", $Price);
}
```

7. Save the document as **RetailDiscount.php** in the Projects directory for Chapter 7, and then close it in your text editor.
8. Open the **RetailDiscount.php** file in your Web browser by entering the following URL: **http://localhost/PHP_Projects/Chapter.07/Projects/RetailDiscount.php**.
9. Close your Web browser window.

Hands-On Project 7-4

In this project, you create a multidimensional array containing the measurements in inches for several boxes that a shipping company might use to determine the volume of a box.

1. Create a new document in your text editor.
2. Type the `<!DOCTYPE>` declaration, `<html>` element, document head, and `<body>` element. Use the strict DTD and "Box Array" as the content of the `<title>` element.

3. Create a script section in the document body:

```
<?php
?>
```

4. Declare and initialize an associative multidimensional array using the information shown in the following table:

	Length	Width	Depth
Small box	12	10	2.5
Medium box	30	20	4
Large box	60	40	11.5

5. Add statements to the end of the script section that print the volume (length * width * depth) of each box.
6. Save the document as **BoxArray.php** in the Projects directory for Chapter 7, and then close it in your text editor.
7. Open the **BoxArray.php** file in your Web browser by entering the following URL: **http://localhost/PHP_Projects/Chapter.07/Projects/BoxArray.php**.
8. Close your Web browser window.

Case Projects

Save the documents you create for the following projects in the Cases directory for Chapter 7.

Case Project 7-1

Use the techniques that you learned in this chapter to create a Guest Book script that stores visitor names and e-mail addresses in a text file. Include functionality that allows users to view the guest book and that prevents the same username from being entered twice. Also, include code that sorts the guest book by name and deletes duplicate entries.

Case Project 7-2

Create a Song Organizer script that stores songs in a text file. Include functionality that allows users to view the song list and prevents the same song name from being entered twice. Also, include code that sorts the songs by name, deletes duplicate entries, and randomizes the song list with the `shuffle()` function.

Case Project 7-3

You can calculate body mass index (BMI) with the formula `weight ÷ (height x height) x 703`. This is a fairly simple calculation that you can use to create a PHP script that calculates body mass index based on a user's height and weight. However, instead of creating a script that uses the formula to calculate a person's body mass index, you create a two-dimensional array containing BMI values. The first dimension should represent height, and the second dimension should represent weight. (Use the BMI formula to determine the value for each dimension.) To keep things simple, only include in the array body mass indexes for heights between 58 and 76 inches and for weights between 100 and 200 pounds in 10-pound increments. Include code to validate whether users have entered the correct values in the height and weight fields.

Case Project 7-4

The goal of the game of Blackjack is to obtain a hand that totals a value of 21 ("blackjack") or that is higher than the total value of the dealer's hand. Use PHP to design your own Blackjack program. For the sake of simplicity, write a simplified version of the program that does not include a dealer, but in which the user wins if he hits 21 or loses if he exceeds 21. Create a form with a "Deal" link and a "Hit Me" link. The Deal link should build an array containing all the cards in a deck of cards. After you build the array, use the `shuffle()` function to randomize the array elements. Then store the array as the first line of a text file. The Hit Me link should open the text file, remove the first "card" from the line in the text file that contains the deck, and then present it to the user along with the other cards they have been dealt. Store the cards that have been dealt to the user on the second line of the text file. Allow the user to keep selecting the Hit Me link until he either hits blackjack or exceeds 21. Cards 2 through 10 have a value equal to the card's value, and face cards (Jack, Queen, King) have a value of 10. Keep in mind that in Blackjack, an Ace can have a value of either 1 or 11, depending on which combination of cards is most beneficial to the player. For example, a King and an Ace automatically results in Blackjack, whereas a Nine, a Five, and an Ace results in a value of 15. You need to write the appropriate programming logic to score each hand.

CHAPTER

8

WORKING WITH DATABASES AND MYSQL

In this chapter, you will:

- Study the basics of databases and MySQL
- Work with MySQL databases
- Manage user accounts
- Define database tables
- Work with database records

A common use of Web pages is to gather information that is stored in a database on a Web server. Most server-side scripting languages, including PHP, allow you to create Web pages that can read and write data to and from databases. In this chapter, you take a break from PHP to learn how to work with MySQL databases. Your goal is to learn the basics of database manipulation. Then, in Chapter 9, you apply many of the techniques from this chapter to PHP scripts that manipulate MySQL databases.

As you learned in Chapter 2, MySQL is an open source database developed by MySQL AB (*http://www.mysql.com/*). Many people mistakenly believe that MySQL is part of PHP. Even though MySQL is probably the database that is used most often with PHP, it is just one of many databases that PHP can manipulate directly or through ODBC. As its name implies, MySQL uses SQL as its data manipulation language. MySQL is primarily used for Web applications and is extremely popular for several reasons, first and foremost is that it's open source and free.

INTRODUCTION TO DATABASES

Formally defined, a **database** is an ordered collection of information from which a computer program can quickly access information. You can probably think of many databases that you work with in your everyday life. For example, your address book is a database. So is the card file containing recipes in a kitchen. Other examples of databases include a company's employee directory and a file cabinet containing client information. Essentially, any information that can be organized into ordered sets of data, then quickly retrieved, can be considered a database. A collection of hundreds of baseball cards thrown into a shoebox is not a database because an individual card cannot be quickly or easily retrieved (except by luck). However, if the baseball card collection was organized in binders by team, and then further organized according to each player's field position or batting average, it could be considered a database because you could quickly locate a specific card.

The information stored in computer databases is actually stored in tables similar to spreadsheets. Each row in a database table is called a record. A **record** in a database is a single complete set of related information. Each recipe in a recipe database, for instance, is a single database record. Each column in a database table is called a field. **Fields** are the individual categories of information stored in a record. Examples of fields that might exist in a recipe database include ingredients, cooking time, cooking temperature, and so on.

To summarize, you can think of databases as consisting of tables, which consist of records, which consist of fields. Figure 8-1 shows an example of an employee directory for programmers at an application development company. The database consists of five records, one for each employee. Each record consists of six fields: `last_name`, `first_name`, `address`, `city`, `state`, and `zip`.

last_name	first_name	address	city	state	zip
Blair	Dennis	204 Spruce Lane	Brookfield	MA	01506
Hernandez	Louis	68 Boston Post Road	Spencer	MA	01562
Miller	Erica	271 Baker Hill Road	Brookfield	MA	01515
Morinaga	Scott	17 Ashley Road	Brookfield	MA	01515
Picard	Raymond	1113 Oakham Road	Barre	MA	01531

Figure 8-1 Employee directory database

The database in Figure 8-1 is an example of a flat-file database, one of the simplest types of databases. A **flat-file database** stores information in a single table. For simple collections of information, flat-file databases are usually adequate. With large and complex collections of information, flat-file databases can become unwieldy. A better solution for large and complex databases is a relational database. A **relational database** stores information across multiple related tables. Although you will not actually work with a relational database in this chapter, understanding how they work is helpful because relational databases are among the most common in use today.

Two other types of database systems you might encounter are hierarchical databases and network databases.

Understanding Relational Databases

Relational databases consist of one or more related tables. In fact, large relational databases can consist of dozens or hundreds of related tables. Although relational databases can consist of many tables, you create relationships within the database by working with two tables at a time. One table in a relationship is always considered to be the primary table, whereas the other table is considered to be the related table. A **primary table** is the main table in a relationship that is referenced by another table. A **related table** (also called a **child table**) references a primary table in a relational database. Tables in a relationship are connected using primary and foreign keys. A **primary key** is a field that contains a unique identifier for each record in a primary table. A primary key is a type of **index**, which identifies records in a database to make retrievals and sorting faster. An index can consist of just a primary key, or it can be a combination of multiple fields. A **foreign key** is a field in a related table that refers to the primary key in a primary table. Primary and foreign keys link records across multiple tables in a relational database.

There are three basic types of relationships within a relational database: one-to-one, one-to-many, and many-to-many. A **one-to-one relationship** exists between two tables when a related table contains exactly one record for each record in the primary table. You create one-to-one relationships when you want to break information into multiple, logical sets. It is important to understand that information in the tables in a one-to-one relationship can usually be placed within a single table. However, you might want to break the information into multiple tables to better organize the information into logical sets. Another reason for using one-to-one relationships is that they allow you to make the information in one of the tables confidential and accessible only by certain individuals. For example, you might want to create a personnel table that contains basic information about an employee, similar to the information in the table in Figure 8-1. Yet, you might also want to create a payroll table that contains confidential information about each employee's salary, benefits, and other types of compensation, and that can be accessed only by the Human Resources and Accounting departments. Figure 8-2 shows two tables, `Employees` and `Payroll`, with a one-to-one relationship. The primary table is the employee information table from Figure 8-1. The related table is a payroll table that contains confidential salary and compensation information. Notice that each table contains an identical number of records; one record in the primary table corresponds to one record in the related table. The relationship is achieved by adding a primary key to the `Employees` table and a foreign key to the `Payroll` table.

Primary key

Employees table

employee_id	last_name	first_name	address	city	state	zip
101	Blair	Dennis	204 Spruce Lane	Brookfield	MA	01506
102	Hernandez	Louis	68 Boston Post Road	Spencer	MA	01562
103	Miller	Erica	271 Baker Hill Road	Brookfield	MA	01515
104	Morinaga	Scott	17 Ashley Road	Brookfield	MA	01515
105	Picard	Raymond	1113 Oakham Road	Barre	MA	01531

Foreign key

Payroll table

employee_id	start_date	pay_rate	health_coverage	year_vested	401k
101	2002	$21.25	none	na	no
102	1999	$28.00	Family Plan	2001	yes
103	1997	$24.50	Individual	na	yes
104	1994	$36.00	Family Plan	1996	yes
105	1995	$31.00	Individual	1997	yes

Figure 8-2 One-to-one relationship

A **one-to-many relationship** exists in a relational database when one record in a primary table has many related records in a related table. You create a one-to-many relationship to eliminate redundant information in a single table. Primary and foreign keys are the only pieces of information in a relational database table that should be duplicated. Breaking tables into multiple related tables to reduce redundant and duplicate information is called **normalization**. The elimination of redundant information (normalization) reduces the size of a database and makes the data easier to work with. For example, consider the table in Figure 8-3. The table lists every programming language in which the programmer is proficient. Notice that each programmer's name is repeated for each programming language with which he or she is most familiar. This repetition is an example of redundant information that can occur in a single table.

employee_id	last_name	first_name	language
101	Blair	Dennis	JavaScript
101	Blair	Dennis	ASP.NET
102	Hernandez	Louis	JavaScript
102	Hernandez	Louis	ASP.NET
102	Hernandez	Louis	Java
103	Miller	Erica	JavaScript
103	Miller	Erica	ASP.NET
103	Miller	Erica	Java
103	Miller	Erica	C++
104	Morinaga	Scott	JavaScript
104	Morinaga	Scott	ASP.NET
104	Morinaga	Scott	Java
105	Picard	Raymond	JavaScript
105	Picard	Raymond	ASP.NET

Figure 8-3 Table with redundant information

A one-to-many relationship provides a more efficient and less redundant method of storing this information in a database. Figure 8-4 shows the same information organized into a one-to-many relationship.

`Employees` table

employee_id	last_name	first_name	address	city	state	zip
101	Blair	Dennis	204 Spruce Lane	Brookfield	MA	01506
102	Hernandez	Louis	68 Boston Post Road	Spencer	MA	01562
103	Miller	Erica	271 Baker Hill Road	Brookfield	MA	01515
104	Morinaga	Scott	17 Ashley Road	Brookfield	MA	01515
105	Picard	Raymond	1113 Oakham Road	Barre	MA	01531

`Languages` table ("many" side)

employee_id	language
101	JavaScript
101	ASP.NET
102	JavaScript
102	ASP.NET
102	Java
103	JavaScript
103	ASP.NET
103	Java
103	C++
104	JavaScript
104	ASP.NET
104	Java
105	JavaScript
105	ASP.NET

One record on the top table is linked to many records in the bottom table

Figure 8-4 One-to-many relationship

In some databases, the table containing multiple records for one entity (for example, the programming language table in Figure 8-4) is the primary table. In these cases, the relationship is often referred to as a many-to-one relationship.

Although Figure 8-4 is an example of a one-to-many relationship, the tables are not normalized because the language field contains duplicate values. Recall that primary and foreign keys are the only pieces of information in a relational database that should be duplicated. To further reduce repetition, you could organize the `Languages` table in Figure 8-4 into another one-to-many relationship. However, a better choice is to create a many-to-many relationship. A **many-to-many relationship** exists in a relational database when many records in one table are related to many records in another table.

Consider the relationship between programmers and programming languages. Each programmer can work with many programming languages, and each programming language can be used by many programmers. To create a many-to-many relationship, you must use a junction table because most relational database systems cannot work directly with many-to-many relationships. A **junction table** creates a one-to-many relationship for each of the two tables in a many-to-many relationship. A junction table contains foreign keys from the two tables in a many-to-many relationship, along with any other fields that correspond to a many-to-many relationship. Figure 8-5 contains an example of a many-to-many relationship between the `Employees` table and a `Languages` table. The `Employees` table contains a primary key named `employee_id`, and the `Languages` table contains a primary key named `language_id`. A junction table named `Experience` contains two foreign keys, one corresponding to the `employee_id` primary key in the `Employees` table and one corresponding to the `language_id` primary key in the `Languages` table. The `Experience` junction table also contains a field named `years`. You add records to the `Experience` junction table to build a list of the years that each programmer has been working with a particular programming language.

Working with Database Management Systems

With a grasp of basic database design, you can now begin to consider how to create and manipulate databases. An application or collection of applications used to access and manage a database is called a **database management system**, or **DBMS**. A DBMS is also used to define a database's **schema**, which is the the structure of a database, including its tables, fields, and relationships. Database management systems run on many different platforms, ranging from personal computers, to client/server systems, to mainframes. Different database management systems exist for different types of database formats. A database management system that stores data in a flat-file format is called a **flat-file database management system**. A database management system that stores data in a relational format is called a **relational database management system**, or **RDBMS**. Other types of database management systems include hierarchical and network database management systems. In addition to the open source MySQL database, some of the more popular relational database management systems you might have heard of include Oracle, Sybase, and Informix for high-end computers such as UNIX systems, dBase on mainframes, and Microsoft Access, FoxPro, and Paradox for PCs.

`Employees` table

employee_id	last_name	first_name	address	city	state	zip
101	Blair	Dennis	204 Spruce Lane	Brookfield	MA	01506
102	Hernandez	Louis	68 Boston Post Road	Spencer	MA	01562
103	Miller	Erica	271 Baker Hill Road	Brookfield	MA	01515
104	Morinaga	Scott	17 Ashley Road	Brookfield	MA	01515
105	Picard	Raymond	1113 Oakham Road	Barre	MA	01531

`Languages` table

language_id	language
10	JavaScript
11	ASP.NET
12	Java
13	C++

`Experience` junction table

employee_id	language_id	years
101	10	5
101	11	4
102	10	3
102	11	2
102	12	3
103	10	2
103	11	3
103	12	6
103	13	3
104	10	7
104	11	5
104	12	8
105	10	4
105	11	2

Figure 8-5 Many-to-many relationship

PostgreSQL is another open source relational database management system that is becoming a popular alternative to MySQL. You can find more information on PostgreSQL at *http://www.postgresql.org/*.

Database management systems perform many of the same functions as other types of applications you might have encountered, such as word-processing and spreadsheet programs. For example, database management systems create new database files and contain interfaces that allow users to enter and manipulate data. One of the most important functions of a database management system is the structuring and preservation of the database file. In addition, a database management system must ensure that data is stored correctly in a database's tables, regardless of the database format (flat-file, relational, hierarchical, or network). In relational databases, the database management system ensures that the appropriate information is entered according to the relationship structure in the database tables. Many DBMS systems also have security features that can be used to restrict user access to specific types of data.

Another important aspect of a database management system is its querying capability. A **query** is a structured set of instructions and criteria for retrieving, adding, modifying, and deleting database information. Most database management systems use a **data manipulation language**, or **DML**, for creating queries. Different database management systems support different data manipulation languages. However, **structured query language**, or **SQL** (pronounced sequel), has become somewhat of a standard data manipulation language among many database management systems.

Many database management systems include tools that make it easier to build queries. Figure 8-6 shows an example of the MySQL Query Browser, which is a graphic tool from MySQL AB that allows you to work with MySQL queries in a graphical environment. You can use the MySQL Query Browser to create queries by typing SQL commands into the query area at the top of the screen or by dragging tables and fields from the Schemata area to the query area.

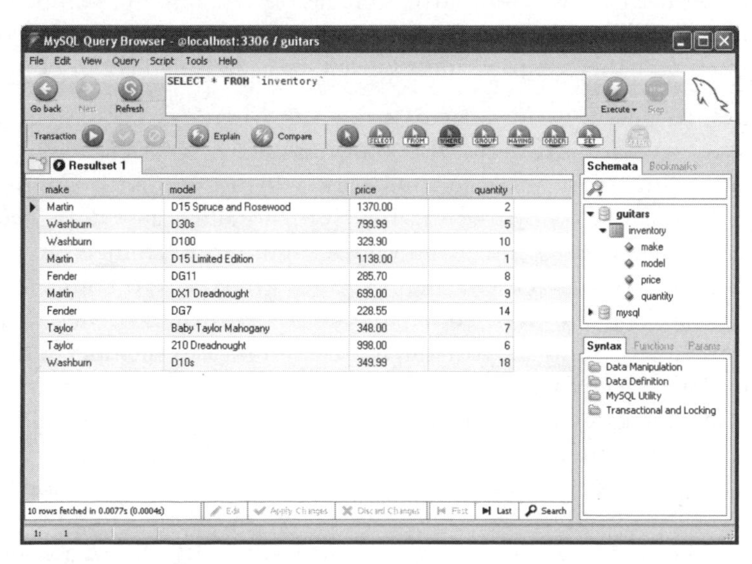

Figure 8-6 MySQL Query Browser

Although working with an interface to design queries is helpful, you must still learn the database management system's data manipulation language. For example, when accessing databases with PHP, you must use a data manipulation language. Because SQL is the underlying data manipulation language for many database management systems, including MySQL, you learn more about the language as you progress through this chapter.

Many database management systems also use a data definition language, or DDL, for creating databases, tables, fields, and other components of a database.

It is important to understand that even though many database management systems support the same database formats (flat-file, relational, hierarchical, or network), each database management system is an individual application that creates its own proprietary file types. For example, even though Access and Paradox are both relational database management systems, Access creates its database files in a proprietary format with an extension of .mdb, whereas Paradox creates its database files in a proprietary format with an extension of .db. Although both Paradox and Access contain filters that allow you to import each other's file formats, the database files are not completely interchangeable between the two programs. The same is true for most database management systems; they can import each other's file formats, but they cannot directly read each other's files.

In today's ever-evolving technology environment, it is often necessary for an application to access multiple databases created in different database management systems. For example, a company might need a PHP script that simultaneously accesses a large legacy database written in dBase and a newer database written in Oracle. Converting the large dBase database to Oracle would be cost prohibitive. On the other hand, the company cannot continue using the older dBase database because its needs have grown beyond the older database's capabilities. Still, the company must be able to access the data in both systems.

To allow easy access to data in various database formats, Microsoft established the open database connectivity standard. **Open database connectivity**, or **ODBC**, allows ODBC-compliant applications to access any data source for which there is an ODBC driver. ODBC uses SQL commands (known as ODBC SQL) to allow an ODBC-compliant application to access a database. Essentially, an ODBC application connects to a database for which there is an ODBC driver and then executes ODBC SQL commands. Then, the ODBC driver translates the SQL commands into a format that the database can understand. PHP includes strong support for ODBC. PHP also includes functionality that allows you to work directly with different types of databases, without going through ODBC. Some of the databases that you can access directly from PHP include Oracle, Informix, MySQL, and PostgresSQL. By eliminating the ODBC layer, your PHP scripts will be faster. Further, PHP code that directly accesses a database is also easier to write than code that goes through ODBC. Therefore, your rule of thumb should be to always use direct database access functionality if it is available in PHP. Otherwise, use PHP's ODBC functionality to access ODBC-compliant databases.

NOTE

In Chapter 9, you learn how to use PHP to access MySQL databases directly.

Querying Databases with Structured Query Language

Programmers at IBM invented SQL in the 1970s as a way to query databases for specific criteria. Since then, SQL has been adopted by numerous database management systems running on mainframes, minicomputers, and PCs. In 1986, the American National Standards Institute (ANSI) approved an official standard for the SQL language. In 1991, the X/Open and SQL Access Group created a standardized version of SQL known as the Common Applications Environment (CAE) SQL draft specification. Even with two major standards available, however, most database management systems use their own version of the SQL language. MySQL corresponds primarily to the ANSI SQL standard, although it includes a few of its own extensions to the language.

CAUTION

If you ever work directly with another database management system, keep in mind that the SQL you learn in this chapter might not correspond directly to that database management system's version of SQL.

SQL uses fairly easy-to-understand statements to execute database commands. SQL statements are composed of keywords that perform actions on a database. Table 8-1 lists several SQL keywords that are common to most versions of SQL.

Table 8-1 Common SQL keywords

Keyword	Description
`DELETE`	Deletes a row from a table
`FROM`	Specifies the tables from which to retrieve or delete records
`INSERT`	Inserts a new row into a table
`INTO`	Determines the table into which records should be inserted
`ORDER BY`	Sorts the records returned from a table
`SELECT`	Returns information from a table
`UPDATE`	Saves changes to fields in a record
`WHERE`	Specifies the conditions that must be met for records to be returned from a query

The simple SQL statement `SELECT * FROM Employees` returns all fields (using the asterisk `*` wildcard) from the `Employees` table. The following code shows a more complex SQL statement that selects the `last_name` and `first_name` fields from the `Employees` table if the record's city field is equal to "Spencer." The results are then sorted by the `last_name` and `first_name` fields using the `ORDER BY` keyword. Notice that commas separate multiple field names.

```
SELECT last_name, first_name FROM Employees
WHERE city = "Spencer" ORDER BY last_name, first_name
```

You study many of the basic SQL keywords in this chapter. For in-depth information on SQL statements supported in MySQL, refer to the MySQL Reference Manual at *http://dev.mysql.com/doc/mysql/en/index.html*.

GETTING STARTED WITH MYSQL

As open source software, MySQL is a logical fit with Apache and PHP, both of which are also developed as open source software. But being open source is not reason enough for MySQL's popularity: It is also fast and reliable, and supports other programming languages besides PHP, including C, C++, and Java. MySQL is also fairly easy to use and install and is available on a number of different platforms.

Be sure that you have followed the instructions in Chapter 2 for installing and testing MySQL, or that you have access to a MySQL installation, before continuing with this chapter.

MySQL includes various programs that you can use to access and manage your databases and the MySQL database server. You already used the **`mysqladmin`** program in Chapter 2 to test your installation of MySQL. The MySQL program you will primarily use in this chapter is the MySQL Monitor, which is a command-line program that you use to manipulate MySQL databases. You execute the MySQL Monitor program with the **`mysql`** command. The programs that are installed with MySQL, such as **`mysqladmin`** and **`mysql`**, are command-line programs that you run in a console window. The MySQL AB group also offers several Graphical User Interface (GUI) utilities for working with MySQL, including the MySQL Query Browser that you saw in the preceding section and the MySQL Administrator, which you can use to administer your MySQL server installation. The MySQL Administrator is shown in Figure 8-7.

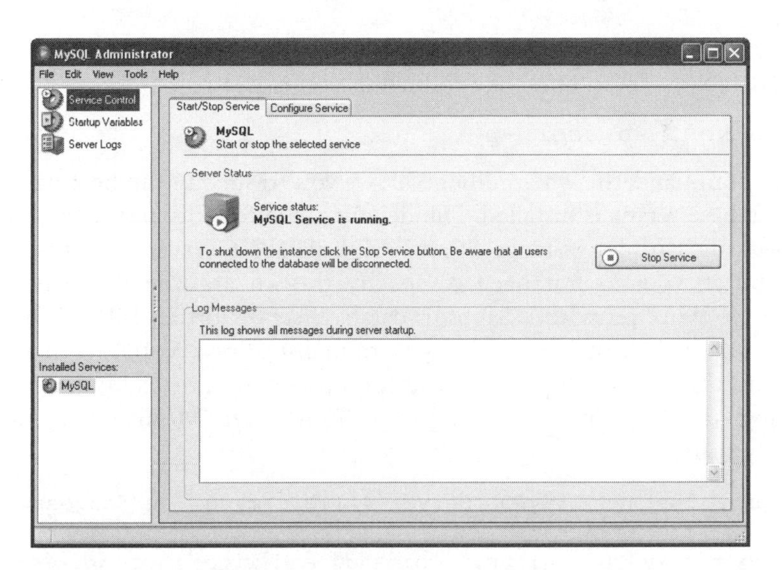

Figure 8-7 MySQL Administrator

You can download the MySQL Query Browser and the MySQL Administrator from *http://dev.mysql.com/downloads/index.html*.

Many of the SQL commands you study in this chapter can be more easily executed from the MySQL Query Browser. Nevertheless, to successfully execute SQL commands, you must first understand how to write them manually. You also need to know how to write SQL commands manually to access MySQL databases from PHP scripts, as you do in the next chapter. For these reasons, you use the MySQL Monitor in this chapter to learn how to execute SQL commands. Feel free to experiment with the MySQL Query Browser on your own, but be certain to use the MySQL Monitor to perform the exercises in this chapter.

In the next section, you learn how to log in to MySQL.

Logging in to MySQL

In Chapter 2, you learned that, unlike other types of databases that are installed as applications, MySQL is installed as a server. On UNIX/Linux systems, you must start and stop the MySQL server manually. When you install MySQL on Windows, it is installed as a service. (Recall that services are usually launched automatically when Windows first starts.) After your instance of the MySQL database server is started, you can execute the programs that are installed with MySQL, such as the `mysqladmin` and `mysql` programs.

Even though your instance of the MySQL database server might be started, you need to log in to the server to access or manipulate databases with MySQL programs such as `mysqladmin` or the MySQL Monitor (`mysql`). To use the MySQL Monitor to log in to the MySQL database server, enter the following command:

```
mysql -h host -u user -p
```

In the preceding command, the `-h` argument allows you to specify the host name where your MySQL database server is installed. The default value for this argument is *localhost*, so if you are working with an instance of a MySQL database server that is installed on your local computer, you do not need to specify the `-h` argument and host name. However, if you are working with a MySQL database server on an ISP's Web site, you need to enter your ISP's host name. The `-u` argument allows you to specify a user account name, and the `-p` switch prompts you for a password. For example, the following command logs the username *dongosselin* into the MySQL Monitor on a Windows installation of MySQL:

```
C:\Program Files\MySQL\MySQL Server 4.1\bin>mysql -u dongosselin -p
Enter password: **********
Welcome to the MySQL monitor.  Commands end with ; or \g.
Your MySQL connection id is 6611 to server version: 4.1.9-nt

Type 'help;' or '\h' for help. Type '\c' to clear the buffer.

mysql>
```

You know you are successfully logged in when you see the `mysql>` prompt.

When you first install MySQL, two accounts are created: an anonymous user account and a `root` account. The anonymous user account allows anyone to log in to MySQL without specifying a username or password. For example, the anonymous user account allows you to log in to a local installation of MySQL simply by typing `mysql`. Similarly, you can execute the `mysqladmin` command and any other MySQL program without specifying an account. The `root` account is the primary administrative account for MySQL. It is initially created without a password, so you can log in to the MySQL Monitor with the following command:

```
mysql -u root
```

Unless you are working with a local instance of MySQL that will not be available on a network or the Internet, you should remove the anonymous user account because it represents a major security hole in your Web site. The `root` account with no password represents another major security hole because anyone who has access to your Web server can use the `root` account to modify or delete your databases and tamper with your installation of MySQL. Later in this chapter, you remove the anonymous user account and assign a password to the `root` account.

Next, you log in to the MySQL Monitor.

To log in to the MySQL Monitor:

1. Open a new console window.
2. Change to the bin directory in the location where you installed MySQL. On UNIX/Linux systems, the bin directory is installed by default in the following location:

   ```
   /usr/local/mysql/bin
   ```

   On Windows operating systems, the bin directory is installed by default in the following location:

   ```
   C:\Program Files\MySQL\MySQL Server 4.1\bin
   ```

3. If you are working with your own installation of MySQL, verify that you have started your instance of MySQL server by entering the following command:

   ```
   /usr/local/mysql/bin/mysqld_safe --user=mysql &
   ```

   For Windows operating systems, use the Services application in Control Panel to determine whether the MySQL service is running, as described in Chapter 2.

If you are working a MySQL instance that is hosted by an ISP, you do not need to perform this step.

4. If you followed the instructions in Chapter 2 to install MySQL on your own computer, log in with the `root` account by entering the following command:

   ```
   mysql -u root
   ```

   If you are working with a MySQL instance that is hosted by an ISP or your school, log in with the following command. Be sure to replace *host* and *user* with the host name and username provided by your ISP or instructor.

   ```
   mysql -h host -u user -p
   ```

   When prompted, enter the password provided by your ISP or instructor. If you are working on a Windows platform, your screen should appear similar to Figure 8-8.

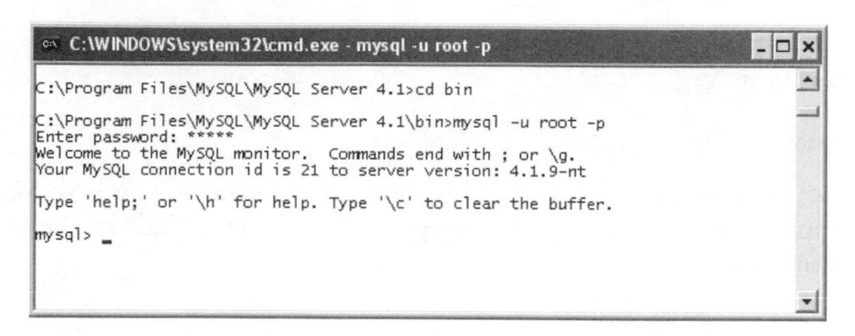

Figure 8-8 MySQL Monitor on a Windows platform

Although the screen captures in this chapter are taken on a Windows operating system, the MySQL Monitor portion of your window should appear the same regardless of which operating system you use.

When you are finished working with the MySQL Monitor, you can log out by entering either the `exit` or `quit` commands. Both commands log you out and then exit the MySQL Monitor. You are successfully logged out when you see "Bye" and your command prompt is restored to the command line for your operating system. The following example shows how the command line appears on a Windows installation of MySQL:

```
mysql> exit
Bye

C:\Program Files\MySQL\MySQL Server 4.1\bin>
```

Next, you log out of the MySQL Monitor.

To log out of the MySQL Monitor:

1. Return to the MySQL Monitor.
2. Type **exit** or **quit** and press **Enter** to log out of the MySQL Monitor. You should see "Bye" printed to the screen and the command prompt restored to the command line for your operating system.

Working with the MySQL Monitor

The `mysql>` command prompt in the MySQL Monitor is where most of the action occurs when you create or manipulate databases in MySQL. If you are familiar with graphical database management systems, such as Access, the `mysql>` command prompt might take some getting used to. However, keep in mind that most database management systems, including Access, use SQL to manipulate databases. MySQL just removes the graphical "front end" and allows you to enter SQL commands directly. After you become familiar with working in the MySQL Monitor, you may find that you prefer manipulating databases with the `mysql>` command prompt over using a graphical database management system because you have more exact control over what is happening with your database. It's also worth repeating that you must understand how to write SQL commands manually to access MySQL databases from PHP scripts, as you do in the next chapter.

When you enter a SQL command at the `mysql>` command prompt, you must terminate the command with a semicolon. For example, the following SQL statement selects all fields from a table named `inventory` that contains the guitar inventory for a music store:

```
mysql> SELECT * FROM inventory;
```

The preceding statement prints all the records in the `inventory` table to the screen as follows:

```
+----------+-------------------------+---------+----------+
| make     | model                   | price   | quantity |
+----------+-------------------------+---------+----------+
| Martin   | D15 Spruce and Rosewood | 1370.00 |        2 |
| Washburn | D30s                    |  799.99 |        5 |
| Washburn | D100                    |  329.90 |       10 |
| Martin   | D15 Limited Edition     | 1138.00 |        1 |
| Fender   | DG11                    |  285.70 |        8 |
| Martin   | DX1 Dreadnought         |  699.00 |        9 |
| Fender   | DG7                     |  228.55 |       14 |
| Taylor   | Baby Taylor Mahogany    |  348.00 |        7 |
| Taylor   | 210 Dreadnought         |  998.00 |        6 |
| Washburn | D10s                    |  349.99 |       18 |
+----------+-------------------------+---------+----------+
10 rows in set (0.00 sec)
```

If you leave off the ending semicolon when you enter a SQL statement, the MySQL Monitor assumes that you want to enter a multiple-line command and changes the prompt to `->`. For example, the following version of the preceding `SELECT` command does not include the terminating semicolon. For this reason, the command prompt changes to `->` so you can enter more statements.

```
mysql> SELECT * FROM inventory
    ->
```

To finish executing the preceding statement, just type a semicolon by itself at the `->` command prompt and press Enter.

As you learn more about SQL, you will find the multiple-line command prompt to be helpful when entering more complex SQL statements. The following example shows a multiple-line SQL command that selects all records from the `inventory` table in which the make is equal to "Washburn," and sorts the returned records by price. Notice that the terminating semicolon is entered on the third line.

```
mysql> SELECT * FROM inventory
    -> WHERE make = "Washburn"
    -> ORDER BY price;
```

```
+----------+-------+--------+----------+
| make     | model | price  | quantity |
+----------+-------+--------+----------+
| Washburn | D100  | 329.90 |       10 |
| Washburn | D10s  | 349.99 |       18 |
| Washburn | D30s  | 799.99 |        5 |
+----------+-------+--------+----------+
3 rows in set (0.27 sec)
```

The SQL keywords you enter in the MySQL Monitor are not case sensitive, so you can enter any of the following statements to retrieve all fields in the `inventory` table:

```
mysql> SELECT * FROM inventory;
mysql> select * from inventory;
mysql> Select * From inventory;
```

Although you can use any case for SQL keywords, most programmers follow the convention of using uppercase letters to clearly distinguish SQL keywords from the names of databases, tables, and fields.

Understanding MySQL Identifiers

In MySQL, you must define identifiers (names) for databases, tables, fields, indexes, and aliases. An **alias** is an alternate name that you can use to refer to a table or field in SQL statements. For database and table names, you can include any characters that your operating system allows in directory and filenames, with the exception of forward slashes (/), backslashes (\), and periods (.). Fields, indexes, and aliases can consist of any characters, including forward slashes (/), backslashes (\), and periods (.). However, if you include any of the following characters within an identifier name, you must enclose the identifier in backtick characters (`) when you refer to it in the MySQL Monitor:

- A SQL reserved word
- An underscore (_)
- A dollar sign ($)
- A space
- Any special characters that are not part of the alphanumeric characters in the current character set

For example, if the `first name` and `last name` fields in the `Employees` table include spaces, you must use backticks to refer to the fields. The following statement demonstrates how to return the `first name` and `last name` fields from the `Employees` table:

```
mysql> SELECT * `first name`, `last name` FROM Employees
    -> WHERE city = "Spencer" ORDER BY `last name`, `first name`;
```

Remember that directory and file identifiers are not case sensitive on Windows platforms, but are case sensitive on UNIX/Linux systems.

Even though SQL keywords are not case sensitive, the case sensitivity of database and table identifiers depends on your operating system. MySQL stores each database in a directory of the same name as the database identifier. Tables are stored in the database directory in files of the same name as the table identifier. Directory and filenames are not case sensitive on Windows platforms, but are case sensitive on UNIX/Linux systems. This means although you do not need to worry about case sensitivity in database and table names on Windows platforms, you do need to observe letter case when referring to database and table names on UNIX/Linux systems.

Field and index identifiers are case insensitive on all platforms.

Getting Help with MySQL Commands

Most of the commands you enter in the MySQL Monitor are SQL commands. However, the MySQL Monitor includes additional commands, such as the **exit** and **quit** commands, which are not part of the SQL language. If you type **help;** or **?** at the MySQL command prompt, you should see several support URLs along with the following command descriptions:

List of all MySQL commands:

```
Note that all text commands must be first on line and end with ';'

?          (\?) Synonym for 'help'.
clear      (\c) Clear command.
connect    (\r) Reconnect to the server. Optional arguments are db and host.
delimiter  (\d) Set query delimiter.
edit       (\e) Edit command with $EDITOR.
ego        (\G) Send command to mysql server, display result vertically.
exit       (\q) Exit mysql. Same as quit.
go         (\g) Send command to mysql server.
nopager    (\n) Disable pager, print to stdout.
help       (\h) Display this help.
notee      (\t) Don't write into outfile.
pager      (\P) Set PAGER [to_pager].
                Print the query results via PAGER.
print      (\p) Print current command.
prompt     (\R) Change your mysql prompt.
quit       (\q) Quit mysql.
rehash     (\#) Rebuild completion hash.
```

```
source    (\.) Execute a SQL script file. Takes a filename as an argument.
status    (\s) Get status information from the server.
system    (\!) Execute a system shell command.
tee       (\T) Set outfile [to_outfile]. Append everything into given outfile.
use       (\u) Use another database. Takes database name as argument.
```

NOTE

The `edit`, `nopager`, `pager`, and `system` commands are only available on UNIX/Linux systems.

Each of the preceding commands has a long and a short form. The long form of each command is not case sensitive, so you can use any case you want. (For example, `QUIT` and `Quit` are both acceptable.) However, for the sake of consistency, you should stick with the letter cases that are presented in this book for each command. The short form of each command allows you to type a backslash and a character to execute the command. Unlike each command's long form, the short form is case sensitive. This means to enter the short form of the `quit` command, you must use `\q`, not `\Q`. With both the long and short forms of each command, you can optionally include a semicolon to terminate the line, although it is not required.

Next, you log back in to the MySQL Monitor and display help for the MySQL Monitor commands.

To log back in to the MySQL Monitor and display help for the MySQL Monitor commands:

1. Return to your console window and log back in to MySQL with the `root` account or with the username and password supplied by your ISP or instructor.
2. Type **help;** or **?** at the MySQL command prompt and press **Enter**. You should see a list of MySQL commands, as shown in Figure 8-9.
3. Log out by typing **\q** at the MySQL command prompt and pressing **Enter**. You should see "Bye" printed to the screen and the command prompt restored to the command line for your operating system.

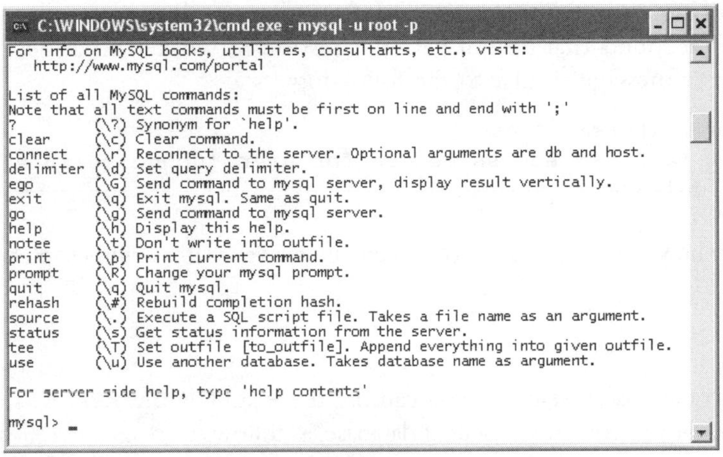

```
C:\WINDOWS\system32\cmd.exe - mysql -u root -p
For info on MySQL books, utilities, consultants, etc., visit:
   http://www.mysql.com/portal

List of all MySQL commands:
Note that all text commands must be first on line and end with ';'
?         (\?) Synonym for `help'.
clear     (\c) Clear command.
connect   (\r) Reconnect to the server. Optional arguments are db and host.
delimiter (\d) Set query delimiter.
ego       (\G) Send command to mysql server, display result vertically.
exit      (\q) Exit mysql. Same as quit.
go        (\g) Send command to mysql server.
help      (\h) Display this help.
notee     (\t) Don't write into outfile.
print     (\p) Print current command.
prompt    (\R) Change your mysql prompt.
quit      (\q) Quit mysql.
rehash    (\#) Rebuild completion hash.
source    (\.) Execute a SQL script file. Takes a file name as an argument.
status    (\s) Get status information from the server.
tee       (\T) Set outfile [to_outfile]. Append everything into given outfile.
use       (\u) Use another database. Takes database name as argument.

For server side help, type 'help contents'

mysql> _
```

Figure 8-9 MySQL command help

Working with MySQL Databases

This section explains the basics of working with databases in MySQL.

Selecting a Database

When you first install MySQL, two databases are installed: `mysql` and `test`. The `mysql` database contains user accounts and other information that is required for your installation of the MySQL database server. The MySQL installation program installs the `test` database to ensure that the database server is working properly. To view the databases that are available, use the `SHOW DATABASES` statement, as follows:

```
mysql> SHOW DATABASES;
+-------------+
| Database    |
+-------------+
| mysql       |
| test        |
+-------------+
2 rows in set (0.00 sec)
```

If you are logged in with the `root` account and your installation of MySQL does not contain any additional databases, you should see the preceding output.

No database is selected when you first log in to MySQL. To work with a database, you must first select it by executing the `use` ***`database`*** statement. For example, the following statement selects the `guitars` database:

```
mysql> use guitars;
Database changed
```

You see the "Database changed" message if MySQL successfully changes to the specified database. User accounts that do not have permission to work with a specified database receive an error message similar to the following:

```
mysql> use guitars;
ERROR 1044 (42000): Access denied for user 'dongosselin'@'%' to
database 'guitars'
```

You study how to manage user accounts and permissions later in this chapter.

If you forget which database is selected, you can use the `SELECT DATABASE()` statement to display the name of the currently selected database, as follows:

```
mysql> SELECT DATABASE();
+------------+
| DATABASE() |
+------------+
| guitars    |
+------------+
1 row in set (0.00 sec)
```

Next, you log back in to the MySQL Monitor and select a database.

To log back in to the MySQL Monitor and select a database:

1. Return to your console window and log back in to MySQL with the `root` account or with the username and password supplied by your ISP or instructor.
2. Type the following command to display the databases that are available in your MySQL installation. By default, you should only see the `mysql` and `test` databases, although your installation might include additional databases.

   ```
   mysql> SHOW DATABASES;
   ```

3. Type the following at the MySQL command prompt to select the `mysql` database:

   ```
   mysql> use mysql;
   ```

4. After you see the "Database changed" message, type the following command to ensure that you selected the `mysql` database:

   ```
   mysql> SELECT DATABASE();
   ```

Your screen should appear similar to Figure 8-10.

```
C:\WINDOWS\system32\cmd.exe - mysql -u root -p
Welcome to the MySQL monitor.  Commands end with ; or \g.
Your MySQL connection id is 26 to server version: 4.1.9-nt

Type 'help;' or '\h' for help. Type '\c' to clear the buffer.

mysql> SHOW DATABASES;
+--------------+
| Database     |
+--------------+
| test         |
| mysql        |
+--------------+
2 rows in set (0.01 sec)

mysql> use mysql;
Database changed
mysql> SELECT DATABASE();
+------------+
| DATABASE() |
+------------+
| mysql      |
+------------+
1 row in set (0.00 sec)

mysql> _
```

Figure 8-10 MySQL Monitor after selecting a database

Creating Databases

You use the **CREATE DATABASE** statement to create a new database. The following statement creates the guitars database:

```
mysql> CREATE DATABASE guitars;
Query OK, 1 row affected (0.02 sec)
```

If the database is created successfully, you see the "Query OK" message shown in the preceding example. If the database already exists, you see the following message:

```
mysql> CREATE DATABASE guitars;
ERROR 1007 (HY000): Can't create database 'guitars'; database
exists
```

Creating a new database does not select it. To use a new database, you must select it by executing the use *database* statement.

Keep in mind that the **CREATE DATABASE** statement only creates a new directory for the specified database. Before you can add records to a new database, you must first define the tables and fields that will store your data. Later in this chapter, you learn how to define tables and fields in a database.

Next, you create a database named flightlog, which will store an airplane pilot's flight log entries.

To create a new database:

1. Return to the MySQL Monitor. You should still be logged in from the preceding exercise.
2. Enter the following command to create the `flightlog` database:

   ```
   mysql> CREATE DATABASE flightlog;
   ```

3. After you see the "Query OK" message, enter the following command to select the `flightlog` database:

   ```
   mysql> use flightlog;
   ```

4. After you see the "Database changed" message, type the following command to ensure that you selected the `flightlog` database:

   ```
   mysql> SELECT DATABASE();
   ```

Deleting Databases

To delete a database, you execute the `DROP DATABASE` statement, which removes all tables from the database and deletes the database itself. The syntax for the `DROP DATABASE` statement is as follows:

```
DROP DATABASE database;
```

The following statement deletes the `guitars` database:

```
mysql> DROP DATABASE guitars;
Query OK, 0 rows affected (0.00 sec)
```

You must be logged in as the `root` user or have `DROP` privileges to delete a database. You study privileges later in this chapter.

Next, you delete the `test` database that was created when you first installed MySQL.

If you are working with an instance of MySQL that is hosted by an ISP, the `test` database might have already been deleted or you might not have sufficient privileges to delete databases.

To delete the `test` database:

1. Return to the MySQL Monitor.
2. Type the following command to ensure that the `test` database exists in your MySQL installation:

   ```
   mysql> SHOW DATABASES;
   ```

3. If you see the `test` database in the list of available databases, enter the following command to delete it:

   ```
   mysql> DROP DATABASE test;
   ```

4. After you see the "Query OK" message, enter the following command again to ensure that the `test` database no longer exists:

   ```
   mysql> SHOW DATABASES;
   ```

MANAGING USER ACCOUNTS

Today, it is common to read about security breaches on the Internet. Corporate and government Web sites seem to be routinely invaded by unauthorized visitors, and credit card numbers and other personal information are often stolen during Internet transactions. One of the first steps in protecting your Web site is to require a username and password from anyone (including yourself) who needs to access your database. In this section, you learn how to secure the initial MySQL accounts and also how to manage user accounts and permissions.

Securing the Initial MySQL Accounts

As you learned earlier, when you first install MySQL, two accounts are created: an anonymous user account and a `root` account. The anonymous user account allows anyone to log in to MySQL without specifying a username or password, whereas the `root` account is created without a password. Instead of allowing anyone to access your databases anonymously, you need to delete the anonymous account and assign a password to the `root` account.

Deleting the Anonymous User Account

You can delete the anonymous account in several ways. The easiest way is to log in with the `root` account and execute the following SQL statements:

```
mysql> DELETE FROM mysql.user WHERE User = '';
mysql> FLUSH PRIVILEGES;
```

The first SQL statement in the preceding code uses the `DELETE` keyword to delete the anonymous user from the `user` table in the default `mysql` database. It deletes the anonymous user by deleting all records with an empty value in the `User` field. The `FLUSH PRIVILEGES` statement reloads the MySQL database server's **grant tables**, which contain the permissions assigned to each user account. In this case, the `FLUSH PRIVILEGES` statement removes the permissions assigned to the anonymous user account.

Next, you delete the anonymous user account.

If you are working with a hosted instance of MySQL, the anonymous user accounts might have already been deleted or you might not have sufficient privileges to delete users.

To delete the anonymous user account:

1. Return to the MySQL Monitor.
2. Enter the following command at the MySQL command prompt to delete the anonymous user accounts:

   ```
   mysql> DELETE FROM mysql.user WHERE User = '';
   ```

3. After you see the "Query OK" message, enter the following command to reload the grant tables:

   ```
   mysql> FLUSH PRIVILEGES;
   ```

Assigning a Password to the Root Account

As with deleting the anonymous user account, you have multiple ways to assign a password to the `root` account. The easiest way is to log in with the `root` account and execute the following SQL statements:

```
mysql> UPDATE mysql.user SET Password = PASSWORD('newpwd')
    -> WHERE User = 'root';
mysql> FLUSH PRIVILEGES;
```

The first SQL statement in the preceding code uses the `UPDATE` keyword to update the password for the `root` account, and the `FLUSH PRIVILEGES` statement reloads the grant tables.

The password you assign to the `root` account and other user accounts is case sensitive.

After you remove the anonymous user account and assign a password to the `root` account, you must specify the `root` account and password each time you access the MySQL database server with a program such as `mysqladmin` or the MySQL Monitor (`mysql`). For example, in Chapter 2 you used the `version` argument with the `mysqladmin` command to display the server version and other information about your installation of MySQL. Now that you have assigned a password to the `root` account, you must log in to use the `mysqladmin` command by specifying the `-u` and `-p` arguments, as follows:

```
mysqladmin status -u root -p
```

Next, you assign a password to the `root` account.

If you are working with a hosted instance of MySQL, you might not have sufficient privileges to modify the password for the `root` account.

To assign a password to the `root` account:

1. Return to the MySQL Monitor.
2. Enter the following command at the MySQL command prompt to assign a password to the `root` account. Replace *newpwd* with your own password and be sure to write it down in case you forget it.
```
mysql> UPDATE mysql.user SET Password = PASSWORD('newpwd')
     -> WHERE User = 'root';
```
3. After you see the "Query OK" message, enter the following command to reload the grant tables:
```
mysql> FLUSH PRIVILEGES;
```
4. Type **exit** or **quit** and press **Enter** to log out of MySQL.
5. Enter the following command to log back in to MySQL with the `root` account and password you just set.
```
mysql -u root -p
```
6. When prompted, enter the new password you assigned to the `root` account.

8

Creating Users

For security purposes, you should create an account that requires a password for each user who needs to access your database. However, one of the primary purposes of this book is to build Web applications that read from and write to databases on a server. For most Web sites, it's impossible to predict how many visitors might need to use a Web application to access a database. Therefore, instead of creating a separate database account for each visitor, you only need to create a single account that a PHP script uses to access the database for a user by proxy. The term **proxy** refers to someone or something that acts or performs a request for another person. In general, you should create a separate account for each Web application that needs to access a database. In Chapter 9, you learn how to create a PHP script that accesses a database by proxy.

Granting Privileges

You use a `GRANT` statement to create user accounts and assign **privileges**, which are the operations that a user can perform with a database. Table 8-2 lists common MySQL database privileges.

Table 8-2 Common MySQL database privileges

Privilege	Description
ALL	Assigns all privileges to the user
CREATE	Allows the user to create databases, tables, and indexes
DROP	Allows the user to delete databases and tables
ALTER	Allows the user to modify table structure
DELETE	Allows the user to delete records
INDEX	Allows the user to create and delete indexes
INSERT	Allows the user to add records
SELECT	Allows the user to select records
UPDATE	Allows the user to modify records
USAGE	Creates a user with no privileges

For information on additional privileges, including administrator privileges, refer to the MySQL Reference Manual at *http://dev.mysql.com/doc/mysql/en/index.html*.

Administrator accounts, such as the `root` account, are usually assigned all available privileges. For security purposes, user accounts should only be assigned the minimum necessary privileges to perform a given task. For example, if a user should only be able to view records from a table, you should only assign the `SELECT` privilege to his account. This helps secure your database by preventing the user from unintentionally (or maliciously) changing or tampering with database records.

The basic syntax for the `GRANT` statement is as follows:

```
GRANT privilege [(column)] [, privilege [(columns)]] ...
    ON {table | * | *.* | database.*}
    TO user [IDENTIFIED BY 'password'];
```

Privileges can be granted at the following levels: column, table, database, and global. The first line in the `GRANT` statement syntax allows you to specify individual columns to apply privileges. The `ON` portion of the `GRANT` statement determines the level to which privileges apply at the table, database, and global levels. You can specify the name of an individual table in the current database or an asterisk, which applies privileges to all the tables in the current database. If you specify `"*.*"`, privileges are applied at a global level to all databases in your MySQL installation. You can also indicate a specific table within another database by appending the table name to the database name with a period.

The `GRANT` statement creates the user account if it does not exist and assigns the specified privileges. If the user account already exists, the `GRANT` statement just updates the privileges. As an example, the following statement creates a new user named `dongosselin` and assigns `SELECT`, `INSERT`, and `UPDATE` privileges to the user for all tables in the currently selected database. The statement also assigns a password of `'rosebud'` to the `dongosselin` account.

```
mysql> GRANT SELECT, INSERT, UPDATE
    -> ON *
    -> TO dongosselin IDENTIFIED BY 'rosebud';
```

After you create a user account, you do not need to specify a password when updating privileges. However, if you specify a password other than the current password for an existing user account, the password is reset.

The following statement assigns privileges to a table named `students` in the currently selected database:

```
mysql> GRANT SELECT, INSERT, UPDATE
    -> ON students
    -> TO dongosselin;
```


The following statement assigns privileges at the global level to all databases in a MySQL installation:

```
mysql> GRANT SELECT, INSERT, UPDATE
    -> ON *.*
    -> TO dongosselin;
```

The following statement assigns privileges to the `inventory` table in the `guitars` database:

```
mysql> GRANT SELECT, INSERT, UPDATE
    -> ON guitars.inventory
    -> TO dongosselin;
```

Finally, the following statement uses a wildcard (`*`) to assign privileges to all tables in the `guitars` database:

```
mysql> GRANT SELECT, INSERT, UPDATE
    -> ON guitars.*
    -> TO dongosselin;
```

Next, you create a new user account with privileges to the `flightlog` database.

If you are working with a hosted instance of MySQL, you might not have sufficient privileges to create user accounts.

To create a new user account with privileges to the `flightlog` database:

1. Return to the MySQL Monitor.

2. Enter the following statement to create a new user account with `CREATE`, `DROP`, `ALTER`, `DELETE`, `INDEX`, `INSERT`, `SELECT`, and `UPDATE` privileges to all the tables in the `flightlog` database. The statement also assigns a password to the account. Enter your own name (as one word) and a password you won't forget.

```
mysql> GRANT CREATE, DROP, ALTER, DELETE, INDEX, INSERT, SELECT, UPDATE
    -> ON flightlog.*
    -> TO yourname IDENTIFIED BY 'password';
```

3. Type **exit** or **quit** and press **Enter** to log out of MySQL.
4. Enter the following command to log back in to MySQL with the user account and password you just created:

```
mysql -u yourname -p
```

5. When prompted, enter the new password you assigned to the user account.

Revoking Privileges

You use the `REVOKE` statement to take away privileges from an existing user account for a specified table or database. The syntax for the `REVOKE` statement is as follows:

```
REVOKE privilege [(column)] [, privilege [(columns)]] ...
    ON {table | * | *.* | database.*}
    FROM user;
```

The following example revokes `INSERT` and `UPDATE` privileges for the `inventory` table in the `guitars` database from the `dongosselin` user account:

```
mysql> REVOKE INSERT, UPDATE
    -> ON guitars.inventory
    -> FROM dongosselin;
```

The `REVOKE ALL PRIVILEGES` statement removes all privileges from a user account for a specified table or database. The following example takes away all privileges from the `inventory` table in the `guitars` database from the `dongosselin` user account:

```
mysql> REVOKE ALL PRIVILEGES
    -> ON guitars.inventory
    -> FROM dongosselin;
```

You must be logged in with the `root` account or have sufficient privileges to revoke privileges from another user account.

In this chapter, the user account you created does not need `ALTER` and `INDEX` privileges, so you revoke them in the next exercise.

To revoke privileges:

1. Return to the MySQL Monitor.
2. Type **exit** or **quit** and press **Enter** to log out of MySQL.
3. Log back in to MySQL with the `root` account.
4. When prompted, enter the password you assigned to the `root` account.
5. Enter the following command to revoke `ALTER` and `INDEX` privileges to the tables in the `flightlog` database from your user account:

```
mysql> REVOKE ALTER, INDEX
     -> ON flightlog.*
     -> FROM yourname;
```

6. Type **exit** or **quit** and press **Enter** to log out of MySQL.
7. Log back in to MySQL with your user account.
8. Enter the following command to select the `flightlog` database:

```
mysql> use flightlog;
```


Deleting Users

To delete an existing user, you execute the `DROP USER` statement. However, before you attempt to delete a user, you must first revoke all privileges assigned to the user account for all databases. The easiest way to do this is to use the `REVOKE ALL PRIVILEGES` statement that is described in the preceding section. However, keep in mind that you can assign privileges at different levels for the same user. For example, you may execute one `GRANT` statement that assigns privileges to all databases and another `GRANT` statement that assigns privileges to a specific database. To view the privileges assigned to a user account, execute the `SHOW GRANTS FOR` *`user`* statement. The following statement shows the grants for the `dongosselin` user account. Notice that the account is assigned all privileges at the global level and `SELECT` privileges for the `inventory` table in the `guitars` database.

```
mysql> SHOW GRANTS FOR dongosselin;
+--------------------------------------------------------------+
| Grants for dongosselin@%                                     |
+--------------------------------------------------------------+
| GRANT ALL PRIVILEGES ON *.* TO 'dongosselin'@'%'             |
| GRANT SELECT ON `guitars`.`inventory` TO 'dongosselin'@'%'   |
+--------------------------------------------------------------+
```

The following statements revoke both sets of privileges from the `dongosselin` account:

```
mysql> REVOKE ALL PRIVILEGES
    -> ON *.*
```

```
    -> FROM dongosselin;
mysql> REVOKE ALL PRIVILEGES
    -> ON guitars.inventory
    -> FROM dongosselin;
```

After you remove all privileges, you execute the `DROP USER` *`user`* statement, which deletes the account from the `user` table in the `mysql` database. The following statement deletes the `dongosselin` account:

```
mysql> DROP USER dongosselin;
```

DEFINING TABLES

This section explains how to select field data types, create tables, and delete existing tables. Remember that before you can add tables to a database, you must first create the database, as described earlier in this chapter.

Specifying Field Data Types

By now, you should thoroughly understand that PHP variables consist of different data types, which are the specific categories of information that a variable can contain. Just like PHP variables, the fields in a table also store data according to type. Recall that one of the most important purposes of a variable's specific data type is that it determines how much memory the computer allocates for the data stored in the variable. Similarly, the data types in database fields determine how much storage space the computer allocates for the data in the database. MySQL includes numerous data types that are categorized in numeric types, string types, and date/time types. Table 8-3 lists some of the common MySQL data types.

Table 8-3 Common MySQL data types

Type	Range	Storage
`BOOL`	-128 to 127; 0 is considered false	1 byte
`INT` or `INTEGER`	-2147483648 to 2147483647	4 bytes
`FLOAT`	-3.402823466E+38 to -1.175494351E-38, 0, and 1.175494351E-38 to 3.402823466E+38	4 bytes
`DOUBLE`	-1.7976931348623157E+308 to -2.2250738585072014E-308, 0, and 2.2250738585072014E-308 to 1.7976931348623157E+308	8 bytes
`DATE`	'1000-01-01' to '9999-12-31'	Varies
`TIME`	'-838:59:59' to '838:59:59'	Varies

Table 8-3 Common MySQL data types (continued)

Type	Range	Storage
`CHAR(m)`	Fixed length string between 0 to 255 characters	Number of bytes specified by *m*
`VARCHAR(m)`	Variable length string between 1 to 65,535 characters	Varies according to the number of bytes specified by *m*

You can find a complete listing of MySQL data types in the MySQL Reference Manual at *http://dev.mysql.com/doc/mysql/en/index.html*.

To keep your database from growing too large, you should choose the smallest data type possible for each field. For example, the `SMALLINT` data type stores integer values between -32768 and 32767 and occupies 2 bytes of storage space. In comparison, the `BIGINT` data type stores integer values between -9223372036854775808 and 9223372036854775807 and occupies 8 bytes of storage space. Regardless of how small the value is that you store in a `SMALLINT` field, it occupies 2 bytes of storage space. Similarly, the `BIGINT` data type occupies 8 bytes of storage space, no matter how small the value. If you know that a value you assign to a field will always be between -32768 and 32767, you should use the `SMALLINT` data type instead of the `BIGINT` data type, which saves 6 bytes per record. This might not seem like a huge savings, but imagine how much storage space is saved for a database with millions of records.

To store text in a field, you specify a data type of `CHAR(m)` or `VARCHAR(m)`. For both data types, you replace *m* with the maximum number of characters you anticipate the field will store. In general, you should use the `VARCHAR(m)` data type because the amount of storage space it occupies varies according to the number of characters in the field.

Creating Tables

To create a table, you use the `CREATE TABLE` statement, which specifies the table and column names and the data type for each column. The syntax for the `CREATE TABLE` statement is as follows:

```
CREATE TABLE table_name (column_name TYPE, ...);
```

Be sure you have executed the USE statement to select a database before executing the CREATE TABLE statement, or you might create your new table in the wrong database.

The following statement creates the inventory table in the guitars database. The first two columns in the table are VARCHAR data types; the make field can be a maximum of 25 characters and the model field can be a maximum of 50 characters. The price field is a FLOAT data type, and the quantity field is an INT data type.

```
mysql> CREATE TABLE inventory (make VARCHAR(25),
    -> model VARCHAR(50), price FLOAT, quantity INT);
```

After you create a table, you can use the DESCRIBE statement to display how the table is structured. The following DESCRIBE statement displays the structure of the inventory table shown below the command:

```
mysql> DESCRIBE inventory;
+----------+-------------+------+-----+---------+-------+
| Field    | Type        | Null | Key | Default | Extra |
+----------+-------------+------+-----+---------+-------+
| make     | varchar(25) | YES  |     | NULL    |       |
| model    | varchar(50) | YES  |     | NULL    |       |
| price    | float       | YES  |     | NULL    |       |
| quantity | int(11)     | YES  |     | NULL    |       |
+----------+-------------+------+-----+---------+-------+
4 rows in set (0.00 sec)
```

You can execute the SHOW TABLES statement to display a list of the tables in the current database.

Next, you create in the flightlog database a table named flightsessions, which will contain detailed information about every flight. The table will contain seven fields: flight_date, flight_time, origin, destination, weather, windows, and temp. The flight_date field will be a DATE data type, the flight_time field will be a TIME data type, the temp field will be an INTEGER data type, and the rest of the fields will be VARCHAR data types. Note that the TIME data type can be used to store a specific time or a measure of time. In the flightsessions table, the flight_time field will contain the duration of each flight. For the DATE data type, dates must be entered in the format YYYY-MM-DD, and for the TIME data type, times must be entered in the format HH:MM:SS.

To create the flightsessions table:

1. Return to the MySQL Monitor.

2. You should have selected the `flightlog` database in the preceding exercise. However, it's good practice to ensure that you have the correct database selected before creating new tables. Therefore, enter the following command to ensure that the `flightlog` database is selected:

   ```
   mysql> SELECT DATABASE();
   ```

3. If the `flightlog` database is not selected, select it with the `use` command. Then enter the following command to create the `flightsessions` table:

   ```
   mysql> CREATE TABLE flightsessions (flight_date DATE, flight_time TIME,
       -> origin VARCHAR(45), destination VARCHAR(45),
       -> weather VARCHAR(45), winds VARCHAR(45), temp INTEGER);
   ```

4. After you see the "Query OK" message, enter the following command to view the structure of the new table. Your screen should appear similar to Figure 8-11.

   ```
   mysql> DESCRIBE flightsessions;
   ```

```
C:\WINDOWS\system32\cmd.exe - mysql -u root -p
mysql> DESCRIBE flightsessions;
+-------------+-------------+------+-----+---------+-------+
| Field       | Type        | Null | Key | Default | Extra |
+-------------+-------------+------+-----+---------+-------+
| flight_date | date        | YES  |     | NULL    |       |
| flight_time | time        | YES  |     | NULL    |       |
| origin      | varchar(45) | YES  |     | NULL    |       |
| destination | varchar(45) | YES  |     | NULL    |       |
| weather     | varchar(45) | YES  |     | NULL    |       |
| winds       | varchar(45) | YES  |     | NULL    |       |
| temp        | int(11)     | YES  |     | NULL    |       |
+-------------+-------------+------+-----+---------+-------+
7 rows in set (0.00 sec)

mysql> _
```

Figure 8-11 `DESCRIBE` statement displaying the structure of the `flightsessions` table

Deleting Tables

To delete a table, you execute the `DROP TABLE` statement, which removes all data and the table definition. The syntax for the `DROP TABLE` statement is as follows:

```
DROP TABLE table;
```

The following statement deletes the `inventory` table in the `guitars` database:

```
mysql> DROP TABLE inventory;
Query OK, 0 rows affected (0.30 sec)
```

NOTE

You must be logged in as the `root` user or have `DROP` privileges to delete a table.

Working with Records

In this section, you learn how to add records to a table and how to update and delete existing records.

Adding Records

You add individual records to a table with the INSERT statement. The basic syntax for the INSERT statement is as follows:

```
INSERT INTO table_name VALUES(value1, value2, ...);
```

The values you enter in the VALUES list must be in the same order in which you defined the table fields. For example, the following statement adds a new row to the inventory table in the guitars database:

```
mysql> INSERT INTO inventory VALUES('Yamaha', 'FG720S',
    -> 279.99, 3);
```

Specify NULL in any fields for which you do not have a value. For example, if you do not know the quantity of guitars in stock for the Yamaha guitar, you can enter NULL as the last item in the VALUES list, as follows:

```
mysql> INSERT INTO inventory VALUES('Yamaha', 'FG720S',
    -> 279.99, NULL);
```

Next, you add two records to the flightsessions table in the flightlog database.

To add two records to the flightsessions table in the flightlog database:

1. Return to the MySQL Monitor.
2. Enter the following command to add a record to the flightsessions table:

   ```
   mysql> INSERT INTO flightsessions VALUES('2007-02-04', '01:30:00',
       -> 'Sonoma', 'Sonoma', 'Sunny', 'W 10 MPH', 58);
   ```

3. After you see the "Query OK" message, add another record, as follows:

   ```
   mysql> INSERT INTO flightsessions VALUES('2007-02-15', '02:15:00',
       -> 'Sonoma', 'Lake Tahoe', 'Partly cloudy', 'E 8 mph', 62);
   ```

   Your screen should appear similar to Figure 8-12.

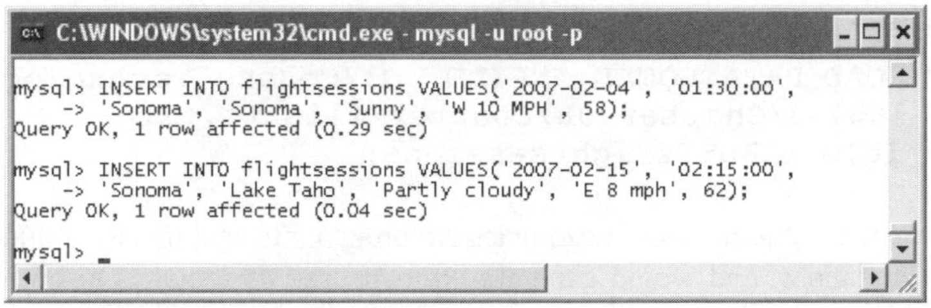

```
C:\WINDOWS\system32\cmd.exe - mysql -u root -p
mysql> INSERT INTO flightsessions VALUES('2007-02-04', '01:30:00',
    -> 'Sonoma', 'Sonoma', 'Sunny', 'W 10 MPH', 58);
Query OK, 1 row affected (0.29 sec)

mysql> INSERT INTO flightsessions VALUES('2007-02-15', '02:15:00',
    -> 'Sonoma', 'Lake Taho', 'Partly cloudy', 'E 8 mph', 62);
Query OK, 1 row affected (0.04 sec)

mysql> _
```

Figure 8-12 MySQL Monitor after adding two records to the `flightsessions` table

In most cases, you will probably add individual records to a database with the `INSERT INTO` statement. However, there will be times when you need to add more than one record at the same time. For example, you might need to load multiple records to a new database or append multiple records to an existing database. To add multiple records to a database, you use the `LOAD DATA` statement with a local text file containing the records you want to add. The syntax for the `LOAD DATA` statement is as follows:

```
LOAD DATA LOCAL INFILE 'file_path' INTO TABLE table_name;
```

Place each record in the text file on a separate line and place tabs between each field. The values on each line must be in the same order in which you defined the table fields. For missing field values, use `\N` instead of `NULL`; MySQL converts `\N` character sequences into `NULL` values when it loads the records. The following statement loads a file named inventory.txt into the `inventory` table in the `guitars` database:

```
LOAD DATA LOCAL INFILE 'inventory.txt' INTO TABLE inventory;
```

Next, you add new records to the `flightsessions` table in the `flightlog` database from a text file named flights.txt, located in your Chapter directory for Chapter 8.

To add new records to the `flightsessions` table in the `flightlog` database:

1. Return to the MySQL Monitor.
2. Enter a `LOAD DATA` statement that inserts records from the flights.txt file in your Chapter directory for Chapter 8. Be certain to enter the full path for where your data files are stored. By default, the directories and data files are installed for Windows platforms in C:\Course Technology\1687-5 and for UNIX/Linux platforms in usr/local/course/1687-5. On UNIX/Linux systems, enter the following command:

```
mysql> LOAD DATA LOCAL INFILE '/usr/local/course/
       1687-5/Chapter.08/Chapter/flights.txt'
    -> INTO TABLE flightsessions;
```

On Windows platforms, enter the following command:

```
mysql> LOAD DATA LOCAL INFILE 'C:/Course Technology/
       1687-5/Chapter.08/Chapter/flights.txt'
    -> INTO TABLE flightsessions;
```

The pathnames in the preceding examples are broken into multiple lines due to space limitations, and would generate errors if used as shown. On both UNIX/Linux and Windows platforms, you need to enter the pathname on a single line or you will receive an error. Also, on Windows platforms, be sure to escape the backward slashes in your path, or use forward slashes, as shown in the preceding example.

Retrieving Records

Earlier in this chapter, you saw an example of how to use a **SELECT** statement to retrieve records from a table. The basic syntax for a **SELECT** statement is as follows:

```
SELECT criteria FROM table_name;
```

As you also learned earlier, you use the asterisk (*) wildcard with the SELECT statement to retrieve all fields from a table. Instead of returning all records by specifying a wildcard, you can specify individual fields to return. To return multiple fields, separate field names with a comma. The following statement returns the `model` and `quantity` fields from the `inventory` table in the `guitars` database:

```
mysql> SELECT model, quantity FROM inventory;
+-------------------------+----------+
| model                   | quantity |
+-------------------------+----------+
| D15 Spruce and Rosewood |        2 |
| D30s                    |        5 |
| D100                    |       10 |
| D15 Limited Edition     |        1 |
| DG11                    |        8 |
| DX1 Dreadnought         |        9 |
| DG7                     |       14 |
| Baby Taylor Mahogany    |        7 |
| 210 Dreadnought         |        6 |
| D10s                    |       18 |
| FG720S                  |        3 |
+-------------------------+----------+
11 rows in set (0.00 sec)
```

Next, you enter several **SELECT** statements that return records from the `flightsessions` table in the `flightlog` database.

To enter `SELECT` statements that return records from the `flightsessions` table in the `flightlog` database:

1. Return to the MySQL Monitor.
2. Enter the following `SELECT` statement, which returns all records from the `flightsessions` table. Your output should appear similar to Figure 8-13, although the lines might wrap, depending on your screen resolution.

   ```
   mysql> SELECT * FROM flightsessions;
   ```

```
C:\WINDOWS\system32\cmd.exe - mysql -u root -p

mysql> SELECT * FROM flightsessions;
+-------------+-------------+----------------+----------------+---------------+----------+------+
| flight_date | flight_time | origin         | destination    | weather       | winds    | temp |
+-------------+-------------+----------------+----------------+---------------+----------+------+
| 2007-02-04  | 01:30:00    | Sonoma         | Sonoma         | Sunny         | W 10 mph |   58 |
| 2007-02-15  | 02:15:00    | Sonoma         | Lake Tahoe     | Partly cloudy | E 8 mph  |   62 |
| 2007-02-15  | 01:50:00    | Lake Tahoe     | Sonoma         | Partly cloudy | E 10 mph |   59 |
| 2007-02-18  | 00:45:00    | Sonoma         | Sonoma         | Sunny         | calm     |   60 |
| 2007-02-22  | 01:20:00    | Sonoma         | Redwood Shores | Mostly cloudy | S 5 mph  |   55 |
| 2007-02-22  | 01:10:00    | Redwood Shores | Sonoma         | Mostly cloudy | S 8 mph  |   57 |
| 2007-02-28  | 02:50:00    | Sonoma         | Santa Barbara  | Sunny         | Calm     |   72 |
| 2007-02-28  | 02:45:00    | Santa Barbara  | Sonoma         | Sunny         | Calm     |   72 |
+-------------+-------------+----------------+----------------+---------------+----------+------+
8 rows in set (0.00 sec)

mysql> _
```

Figure 8-13 `SELECT` statement that returns all records from the `flightsessions` table

3. Enter the following `SELECT` statement, which returns the `flight_date`, `origin`, and `destination` fields from the `flightsessions` table. Your output should appear similar to Figure 8-14.

   ```
   mysql> SELECT flight_date, origin, destination FROM
   flightsessions;
   ```

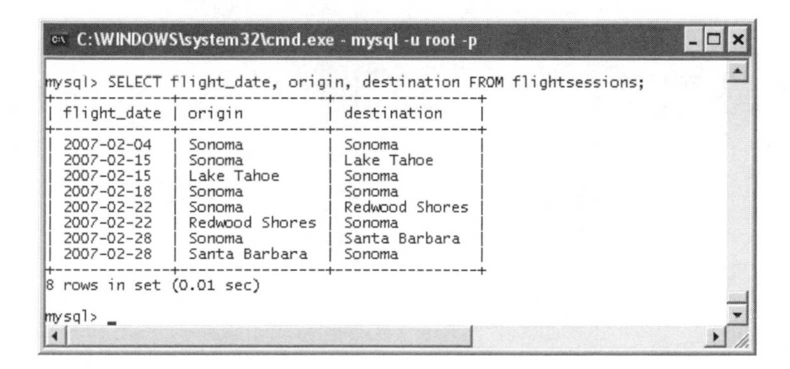

```
C:\WINDOWS\system32\cmd.exe - mysql -u root -p

mysql> SELECT flight_date, origin, destination FROM flightsessions;
+-------------+----------------+----------------+
| flight_date | origin         | destination    |
+-------------+----------------+----------------+
| 2007-02-04  | Sonoma         | Sonoma         |
| 2007-02-15  | Sonoma         | Lake Tahoe     |
| 2007-02-15  | Lake Tahoe     | Sonoma         |
| 2007-02-18  | Sonoma         | Sonoma         |
| 2007-02-22  | Sonoma         | Redwood Shores |
| 2007-02-22  | Redwood Shores | Sonoma         |
| 2007-02-28  | Sonoma         | Santa Barbara  |
| 2007-02-28  | Santa Barbara  | Sonoma         |
+-------------+----------------+----------------+
8 rows in set (0.01 sec)

mysql> _
```

Figure 8-14 `SELECT` statement that returns `flight_date`, `origin`, and `destination` fields from the `flightsessions` table

Sorting Query Results

You use the `ORDER BY` keyword with the `SELECT` statement to perform an alphanumeric sort of the results returned from a query. The following statement returns the `make` and model fields from the inventory table in the guitars database and sorts the results by the make field. The statement also performs a secondary sort on the model field:

```
mysql> SELECT make, model FROM inventory ORDER BY make, model;
+----------+-------------------------+
| make     | model                   |
+----------+-------------------------+
| Fender   | DG11                    |
| Fender   | DG7                     |
| Martin   | D15 Limited Edition     |
| Martin   | D15 Spruce and Rosewood |
| Martin   | DX1 Dreadnought         |
| Taylor   | 210 Dreadnought         |
| Taylor   | Baby Taylor Mahogany    |
| Washburn | D100                    |
| Washburn | D10s                    |
| Washburn | D30s                    |
| Yamaha   | FG720S                  |
+----------+-------------------------+
11 rows in set (0.00 sec)
```

To perform a reverse sort, add the DESC keyword after the name of the field by which you want to perform the sort. The following statement returns the make and model fields from the inventory table in the guitars database and reverse sorts the results by the make field:

```
mysql> SELECT make, model FROM inventory ORDER BY make DESC,
model;
+----------+-------------------------+
| make     | model                   |
+----------+-------------------------+
| Yamaha   | FG720S                  |
| Washburn | D100                    |
| Washburn | D10s                    |
| Washburn | D30s                    |
| Taylor   | 210 Dreadnought         |
| Taylor   | Baby Taylor Mahogany    |
| Martin   | D15 Limited Edition     |
| Martin   | D15 Spruce and Rosewood |
| Martin   | DX1 Dreadnought         |
| Fender   | DG11                    |
| Fender   | DG7                     |
+----------+-------------------------+
11 rows in set (0.01 sec)
```

Next, you enter several SELECT statements that sort records from the flightsessions table in the flightlog database.

To enter several **`SELECT`** statements that sort records from the **`flightsessions`** table in the **`flightlog`** database:

1. Return to the MySQL Monitor.
2. Enter the following **`SELECT`** statement, which returns the **`flight_date`**, **`origin`**, and **`destination`** fields from the **`flightsessions`** table, and sorts the returned records by **`origin`** and **`destination`**. Your output should appear similar to Figure 8-15.

```
mysql> SELECT flight_date, origin, destination
    -> FROM flightsessions ORDER BY origin, destination;
```

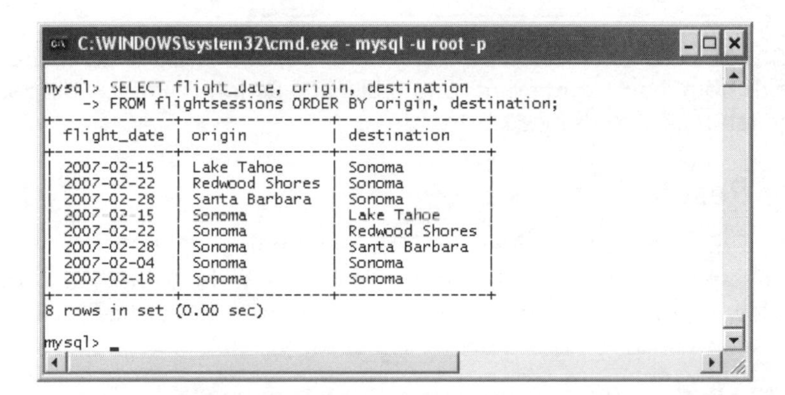

Figure 8-15 `SELECT` statement that returns `flight_date`, `origin`, and `destination` fields from the `flightsessions` table, and sorts the returned records by origin and destination

3. Enter the following **`SELECT`** statement, which returns the **`flight_date`**, **`origin`**, and **`destination`** fields from the **`flightsessions`** table, and performs a descending sort of the returned records by **`flight_date`**. Your output should appear similar to Figure 8-16.

```
mysql> SELECT flight_date, origin, destination
    -> FROM flightsessions ORDER BY flight_date DESC;
```

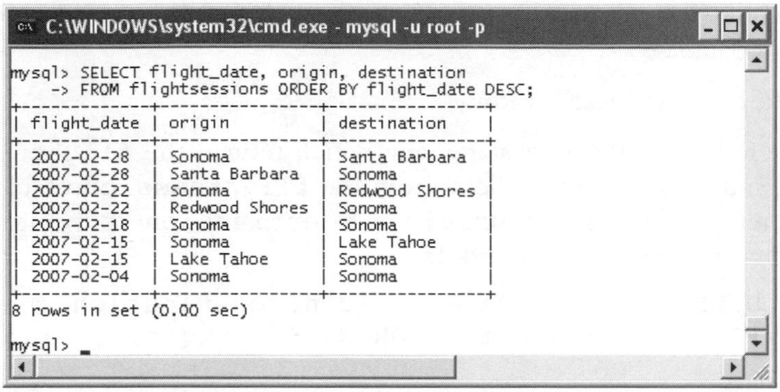

```
C:\WINDOWS\system32\cmd.exe - mysql -u root -p
mysql> SELECT flight_date, origin, destination
    -> FROM flightsessions ORDER BY flight_date DESC;
+-------------+----------------+----------------+
| flight_date | origin         | destination    |
+-------------+----------------+----------------+
| 2007-02-28  | Sonoma         | Santa Barbara  |
| 2007-02-28  | Santa Barbara  | Sonoma         |
| 2007-02-22  | Sonoma         | Redwood Shores |
| 2007-02-22  | Redwood Shores | Sonoma         |
| 2007-02-18  | Sonoma         | Sonoma         |
| 2007-02-15  | Sonoma         | Lake Tahoe     |
| 2007-02-15  | Lake Tahoe     | Sonoma         |
| 2007-02-04  | Sonoma         | Sonoma         |
+-------------+----------------+----------------+
8 rows in set (0.00 sec)

mysql> _
```

Figure 8-16 `SELECT` statement that returns `flight_date`, `origin`, and `destination` fields from the `flightsessions` table, and performs a descending sort of the returned records by `flight_date`

Filtering Query Results

The *criteria* portion of the `SELECT` statement determines which fields to retrieve from a table. You can also specify which records to return by using the `WHERE` keyword. For example, the following statement returns all records from the `inventory` table in the `guitars` database in which the `make` field is equal to 'Martin':

```
mysql> SELECT * FROM inventory WHERE make='Martin';
+--------+-------------------------+---------+----------+
| make   | model                   | price   | quantity |
+--------+-------------------------+---------+----------+
| Martin | D15 Spruce and Rosewood | 1370.00 |        2 |
| Martin | D15 Limited Edition     | 1138.00 |        1 |
| Martin | DX1 Dreadnought         |  699.00 |        9 |
+--------+-------------------------+---------+----------+
3 rows in set (0.00 sec)
```

SQL includes the keywords `AND` and `OR` that you can use to specify more detailed conditions about the records you want to return. For example, the following statement returns all records from the `inventory` table in the `guitars` database in which the `make` field is equal to 'Washburn' AND the price is less than $400.00:

```
mysql> SELECT * FROM inventory WHERE make='Washburn'
    -> AND price<400;
+----------+-------+--------+----------+
| make     | model | price  | quantity |
+----------+-------+--------+----------+
| Washburn | D100  | 329.90 |       10 |
| Washburn | D10s  | 349.99 |       18 |
+----------+-------+--------+----------+
2 rows in set (0.00 sec)
```

The following statement shows an example of how to use the `OR` keyword by returning all records from the `inventory` table in the `guitars` database in which the `make` field is equal to 'Martin' OR 'Fender'. The statement also sorts the returned records by price.

```
mysql> SELECT * FROM inventory WHERE make='Martin'
    -> OR make='Fender' ORDER BY price;
+--------+------------------------+---------+----------+
| make   | model                  | price   | quantity |
+--------+------------------------+---------+----------+
| Fender | DG7                    |  228.55 |       14 |
| Fender | DG11                   |  285.70 |        8 |
| Martin | DX1 Dreadnought        |  699.00 |        9 |
| Martin | D15 Limited Edition    | 1138.00 |        1 |
| Martin | D15 Spruce and Rosewood | 1370.00 |       2 |
+--------+------------------------+---------+----------+
5 rows in set (0.01 sec)
```

Next, you enter several `SELECT` statements that use the `WHERE` keyword to filter records from the `flightsessions` table in the `flightlog` database.

To enter several `SELECT` statements that use the `WHERE` keyword to filter records from the `flightsessions` table in the `flightlog` database:

1. Return to the MySQL Monitor.
2. Enter the following `SELECT` statement, which returns all records from the `flightsessions` table in which the `origin` field is equal to "Sonoma." Your output should appear similar to Figure 8-17.

   ```
   mysql> SELECT * FROM flightsessions WHERE origin='Sonoma';
   ```

```
C:\WINDOWS\system32\cmd.exe - mysql -u root -p

mysql> SELECT * FROM flightsessions WHERE origin='Sonoma';
+-------------+-------------+--------+----------------+---------------+----------+------+
| flight_date | flight_time | origin | destination    | weather       | winds    | temp |
+-------------+-------------+--------+----------------+---------------+----------+------+
| 2007-02-04  | 01:30:00    | Sonoma | Sonoma         | Sunny         | W 10 mph |   58 |
| 2007-02-15  | 02:15:00    | Sonoma | Lake Tahoe     | Partly cloudy | E 8 mph  |   62 |
| 2007-02-18  | 00:45:00    | Sonoma | Sonoma         | Sunny         | calm     |   60 |
| 2007-02-22  | 01:20:00    | Sonoma | Redwood Shores | Mostly cloudy | S 5 mph  |   55 |
| 2007-02-28  | 02:50:00    | Sonoma | Santa Barbara  | Sunny         | Calm     |   72 |
+-------------+-------------+--------+----------------+---------------+----------+------+
5 rows in set (0.00 sec)

mysql> _
```

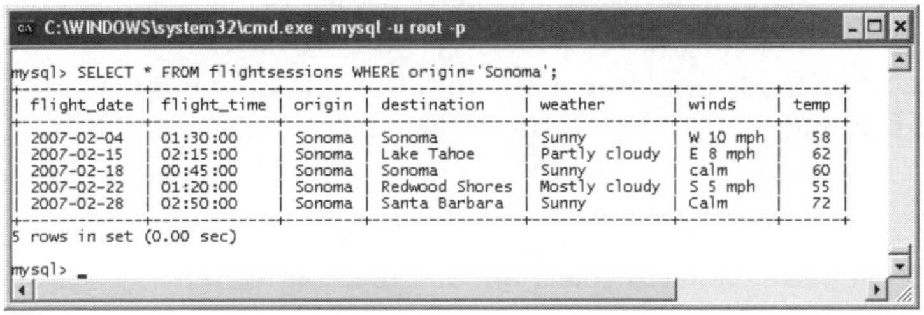

Figure 8-17 `SELECT` statement that returns all records from the `flightsessions` table in which the `origins` field is equal to "Sonoma"

3. Enter the following `SELECT` statement, which returns all records from the `flightsessions` table in which the `temp` field is greater than 60. Your output should appear similar to Figure 8-18.

   ```
   mysql> SELECT * FROM flightsessions WHERE temp>60;
   ```

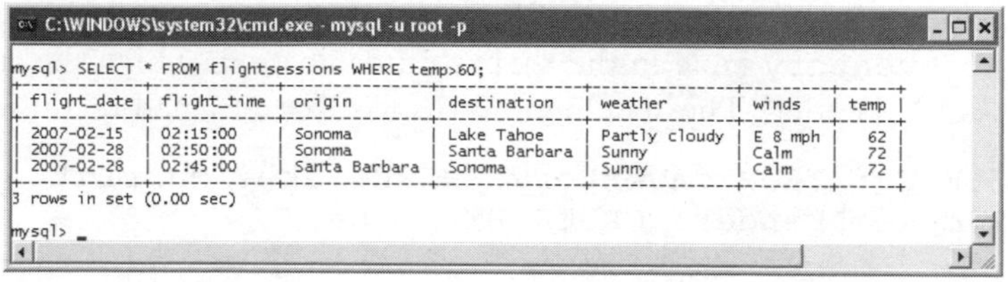

```
C:\WINDOWS\system32\cmd.exe - mysql -u root -p

mysql> SELECT * FROM flightsessions WHERE temp>60;
+-------------+-------------+---------------+---------------+---------------+---------+------+
| flight_date | flight_time | origin        | destination   | weather       | winds   | temp |
+-------------+-------------+---------------+---------------+---------------+---------+------+
| 2007-02-15  | 02:15:00    | Sonoma        | Lake Tahoe    | Partly cloudy | E 8 mph |   62 |
| 2007-02-28  | 02:50:00    | Sonoma        | Santa Barbara | Sunny         | Calm    |   72 |
| 2007-02-28  | 02:45:00    | Santa Barbara | Sonoma        | Sunny         | Calm    |   72 |
+-------------+-------------+---------------+---------------+---------------+---------+------+
3 rows in set (0.00 sec)

mysql> _
```

Figure 8-18 `SELECT` statement that returns all records from the `flightsessions` table in which the `temp` field is greater than 60

Updating Records

If you need to update records in a table, you use the **`UPDATE`** statement. The basic syntax for the **`UPDATE`** statement is as follows:

```
UPDATE table_name
SET column_name=value
WHERE condition;
```

The **`UPDATE`** keyword specifies the name of the table to update, and the **`SET`** keyword specifies the value to assign to the fields in the records that match the condition in the **`WHERE`** keyword. For example, the following statement modifies the price of the Fender DG7 guitar to $368.20:

```
mysql> UPDATE inventory SET price=368.20 WHERE make='Fender'
    -> AND model='DG7';
Query OK, 1 row affected (0.27 sec)
Rows matched: 1  Changed: 1  Warnings: 0
```

Notice in the preceding statement that to ensure that the correct record is updated, the statement uses the **`WHERE`** keyword to specify that the **`make`** field should be equal to 'Fender' and the **`model`** field should be equal to 'DG7.' If the statement only specified that the **`make`** field should be equal to 'Fender,' the **`price`** field for all other records in the table that included a **`make`** field with a value of 'Fender' would also have been updated to 368.20.

Next, you enter several **`UPDATE`** statements to modify records from the **`flightsessions`** table in the **`flightlog`** database. The table contains one record that includes a value of "Santa Barbara" in the **`origin`** field and another record that includes "Santa Barbara" in the **`destination`** field. Assume that the pilot made a mistake and meant to enter "San Luis Obispo."

To enter several **`UPDATE`** statements to modify records from the **`flightsessions`** table in the **`flightlog`** database:

1. Return to the MySQL Monitor.

2. Enter the following `UPDATE` statement to modify the `origin` field in records in the `flightsessions` database from "Santa Barbara" to "San Luis Obispo":

```
mysql> UPDATE flightsessions
    -> SET origin='San Luis Obispo'
    -> WHERE origin='Santa Barbara';
```

3. Now enter the following `UPDATE` statement to modify the `destination` field in records in the `flightsessions` database from "Santa Barbara" to "San Luis Obispo":

```
mysql> UPDATE flightsessions
    -> SET destination='San Luis Obispo'
    -> WHERE destination='Santa Barbara';
```

4. Enter the following `SELECT` statement to view all the records in the table. The "Santa Barbara" values should now be "San Luis Obispo."

```
mysql> SELECT * FROM flightsessions;
```


Deleting Records

To delete records in a table, you use the `DELETE` statement. The basic syntax for the `DELETE` statement is as follows:

```
DELETE FROM table_name
WHERE condition;
```

Be careful when you use the `DELETE` statement because it deletes all records that match the condition. Therefore, be certain to carefully construct the conditions assigned to the `WHERE` keyword. For example, the following statement deletes the "Taylor 210 Dreadnought" record from the `inventory` table in the `guitars` database:

```
mysql> DELETE FROM inventory WHERE make='Taylor'
    -> AND model='210 Dreadnought';
Query OK, 1 row affected (0.28 sec)
```

To delete all the records in a table, leave off the `WHERE` keyword. The following statement deletes all the records in the inventory table:

```
mysql> DELETE FROM inventory;
Query OK, 9 rows affected (0.28 sec)
```

Next, you delete several records from the `flightsessions` table in the `flightlog` database.

To delete several records from the `flightsessions` table in the `flightlog` database:

1. Return to the MySQL Monitor.

2. Enter the following statement to delete the first record in the table:

```
mysql> DELETE FROM flightsessions WHERE flight_date='2007-02-04'
    -> AND flight_time='01:30:00';
```

3. Enter the following statement to delete the next record in the table:

```
mysql> DELETE FROM flightsessions WHERE flight_date='2007-02-15'
    -> AND flight_time='02:15:00';
```

4. Enter the following `SELECT` statement to view all the records in the table. The table should now only consist of six records.

```
mysql> SELECT * FROM flightsessions;
```

CHAPTER SUMMARY

- A database is an ordered collection of information from which a computer program can quickly access information.
- A record in a database is a single complete set of related information.
- Fields are the individual categories of information stored in a record.
- A flat-file database stores information in a single table.
- A relational database stores information across multiple related tables.
- A query is a structured set of instructions and criteria for retrieving, adding, modifying, and deleting database information.
- Structured query language, or SQL (pronounced sequel), has become somewhat of a standard data manipulation language among many database management systems.
- The MySQL Monitor is a command-line program that you use to manipulate MySQL databases.
- To work with a database, you must first select it by executing the `USE DATABASE` statement.
- You use the `CREATE DATABASE` statement to create a new database.
- To delete a database, you execute the `DROP DATABASE` statement, which removes all tables from the database and deletes the database itself.
- With new installations of MySQL, you need to delete the anonymous account and assign a password to the `root` account.
- You use a `GRANT` statement to create user accounts and assign privileges, which refer to the operations that a user can perform with a database.
- You use the `REVOKE` statement to take away privileges from an existing user account for a specified table or database.

- You execute the DROP USER statement to delete an existing user.
- The fields in a table also store data according to type. To keep your database from growing too large, you should choose the smallest data type possible for each field.
- To create a table, you use the CREATE TABLE statement, which specifies the table and column names and the data type for each column.
- To delete a table, you execute the DROP TABLE statement, which removes all data and the table definition.
- You add individual records to a table with the INSERT statement.
- To add multiple records to a database, you use the LOAD DATA statement with a local text file containing the records you want to add.
- You use the SELECT statement to retrieve records from a table.
- You use the ORDER BY keyword with the SELECT statement to perform an alphanumeric sort of the results returned from a query. To perform a reverse sort, add the DESC keyword after the name of the field by which you want to perform the sort.
- You can specify which records to return from a database by using the WHERE keyword.
- You use the UPDATE statement to update records in a table.
- You use the DELETE statement to delete records in a table.

Review Questions

1. A flat-file database consists of a single table. True or False?
2. Explain how relational databases are organized.
3. What is the correct term for the individual pieces of information that are stored in a database record?
   a. element
   b. field
   c. section
   d. container
4. What is the name of one table's primary key when it is stored in another table? (Choose all that apply.)
   a. key symbol
   b. record link
   c. foreign key
   d. unique identifier

5. Breaking tables into multiple related tables to reduce redundant and duplicate information is called ________________.
   a. normalization
   b. redundancy design
   c. splitting
   d. simplification
6. Suppose you have a relational database for a dry cleaning company. Each customer of the dry cleaning company can have multiple items in a cleaning order. What type of relationship is this?
   a. one-to-one
   b. one-to-many
   c. many-to-one
   d. many-to-many
7. ________________ has become somewhat of a standard data manipulation language among many database management systems.
   a. Java
   b. SQL
   c. ASP.NET
   d. PERL
8. Files created by different database management systems are completely interchangeable. True or False?
9. What is the default value of the `mysql` command's `-h` argument?
   a. *`database`*
   b. *`mysqlmonitor`*
   c. *`mysqladmin`*
   d. *`localhost`*
10. What character must terminate SQL commands in the MySQL Monitor?
    a. colon (`:`)
    b. semicolon (`;`)
    c. ampersand (`&`)
    d. period (`.`)
11. With what characters do you quote identifiers that include special characters?
    a. quotation marks (')
    b. double quotation marks (")
    c. backticks (`)
    d. tildes (~)

12. SQL keywords are case sensitive in the MySQL Monitor. True or False?
13. Explain case sensitivity issues when it comes to file and directory names.
14. Which of the following statements displays the available databases in your MySQL installation?
    a. `SHOW DATABASES;`
    b. `SHOW DATABASES();`
    c. `LIST FILES;`
    d. `GET LIST();`
15. What's the first thing you should do after creating a new database?
    a. Save the database.
    b. Restart the MySQL Monitor.
    c. Select the database.
    d. Create a table.

16. Explain the required steps for securing the `root` account and anonymous account that are initially installed with MySQL.
17. Explain what the term "proxy" means in relation to user accounts.
18. A `GRANT` statement does not create new user accounts. True or False?
19. Explain how to add multiple records to a table by using a single SQL statement.
20. Which of the following keywords performs a reverse sort of database records?
    a. `DESC`
    b. `REVERSE`
    c. `DESCEND`
    d. `SORTR`
21. Which of the following is the correct string for a filter that narrows a recordset to include only records in which the `State` field is equal to Massachusetts?
    a. `"WHERE State = 'Massachusetts'"`
    b. `"State = 'Massachusetts'"`
    c. ``"WHERE `State` = Massachusetts"``
    d. ``"`State` = 'Massachusetts'"``

HANDS-ON PROJECTS

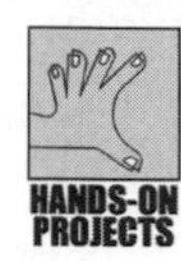

Hands-On Project 8-1

In this project, you create a database with a table containing hitting statistics for major league baseball teams.

1. Log in to the MySQL Monitor with your `root` account.
2. Enter the following command to create a database named `baseball_stats`:

```
mysql> CREATE DATABASE baseball_stats;
```

3. After you see the "Query OK" message, enter the following command to select the `baseball_stats` database:

```
mysql> use baseball_stats;
```

4. After you see the "Database changed" message, type the following command to ensure that you selected the `baseball_stats` database:

```
mysql> SELECT DATABASE();
```

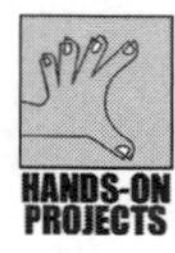

Hands-On Project 8-2

In this project, you create a table named `teamstats` in the `baseball_stats` database and add records to the new table from a file named baseball_team_stats.txt in your Projects directory for Chapter 8.

1. Return to the MySQL Monitor.
2. Enter the following command to create the `teamstats` table. The `Team` field uses the `VARCHAR` data type. Thirteen of the columns use `INT` data types, and the last three fields use `FLOAT` data types. Each of the statistical field names use common baseball acronyms, such as G for games, AB for at bats, R for runs, H for home runs, and so on.

```
mysql> CREATE TABLE teamstats (Team VARCHAR(50),  G INT,  AB INT,
     -> R INT,  H INT,  2B INT,  3B INT,  HR INT,  RBI INT,  TB INT,
     -> BB INT,  SO INT,  SB INT,  CS INT,  OBP FLOAT,  SLG FLOAT,
     -> AVG FLOAT);
```

3. After you see the "Query OK" message, enter the following command to display the structure of the new table:

```
mysql> DESCRIBE teamstats;
```

4. Enter a `LOAD DATA` statement that inserts records from the baseball_team_stats.txt file in your Projects directory for Chapter 8 into the `teamstats` table. Replace *path* with the path to your Projects directory for Chapter 8.

```
mysql> LOAD DATA LOCAL INFILE 'path/baseball_team_stats.txt'
     -> INTO TABLE teamstats;
```

5. After you see the "Query OK" message, enter the following command to view all the records in the teamstats table:

```
mysql> SELECT * FROM teamstats;
```

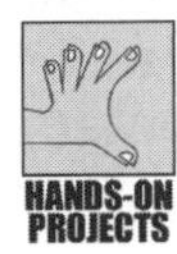

Hands-On Project 8-3

In this project, you write SQL statements that return team names, games played, and number of at bats from the teamstats in the baseball_stats database.

1. Return to the MySQL Monitor.
2. Enter the following SELECT statement, which returns the team, G (games played), and AB (at bats) fields from the teamstats table:

```
mysql> SELECT team, G, AB FROM teamstats;
```

3. Enter the following SELECT statement, which returns the team, G (games played), and AB (at bats) fields from the teamstats table, sorted by team name:

```
mysql> SELECT team, G, AB FROM teamstats ORDER BY team;
```

4. Enter the following SELECT statement, which returns the team, G (games played), and AB (at bats) fields from the teamstats table, reverse sorted by team name:

```
mysql> SELECT team, G, AB FROM teamstats ORDER BY team DESC;
```

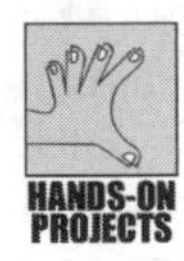

Hands-On Project 8-4

The LIMIT keyword restricts the number of records returned from the database. For example, if you specify a value of 10 with the LIMIT keyword, the database returns the first 10 records that match the conditions of your query. In this project, you write SQL statements that return teams that had the least and the most all time home runs scored.

1. Return to the MySQL Monitor.
2. Enter the following SELECT statement, which returns the team and HR (home runs) fields. The statement sorts the records by the HR field and includes the LIMIT keyword, assigned a value of 1. Because the records are sorted in ascending order, the statement returns the first record, which lists the team with the least all time home runs scored: the Tampa Bay Devil Rays with 981.

```
mysql> SELECT team, HR FROM teamstats ORDER BY HR LIMIT 1;
```

3. Enter the following SELECT statement, which also returns the team and HR (home runs) fields. The statement reverse sorts the records by the HR field and includes the LIMIT keyword, assigned a value of 1. Because the records are sorted in descending order, the statement returns the first record, which lists the team with the most all time home runs scored: the New York Yankees with 13,092.

```
mysql> SELECT team, HR FROM teamstats ORDER BY HR DESC LIMIT 1;
```

8

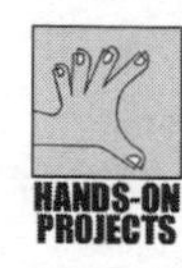

Hands-On Project 8-5

SQL offers various functions that you can include in statements, including the `SUM()` function, which returns the sum of an expression, and the `AVG()` function, which returns the average of an expression. Both functions can include field names in the expressions assigned to them. In this project, you write SQL statements that use the `SUM()` function to return the total number of games played by all teams and the `AVG()` function to return the common batting average for all teams.

1. Return to the MySQL Monitor.
2. Enter the following `SELECT` statement, which uses the `SUM()` function to return the total number of games played by summing the contents of the `G` fields. You should see a value of 346,316.

```
mysql> SELECT SUM(G) FROM teamstats;
```

3. Enter the following `SELECT` statement, which uses the `AVG()` function to return the batting average for all teams by averaging the contents of the `AVG` fields. You should see a value of 0.26186666538318.

```
mysql> SELECT AVG(AVG) FROM teamstats;
```

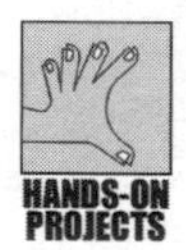

Hands-On Project 8-6

In this project, you add a new table for RBI leaders to the `baseball_stats` database. Before you create the new table, you create a text file using data from the `teamstats` table. You then import the data from the text file into MySQL to create a new table named `rbileaders`. To create the RBI leaders table, you use the `INTO OUTFILE` keywords with a `SELECT` statement. The `INTO OUTFILE` keywords copy the returned records into a specified file. You use the `FIELDS TERMINATED BY` and the `LINES TERMINATED BY` keywords to specify how the text file should be structured. Because you will import the RBI records into the new table, you separate each field by a tab and each line with a line break.

1. Return to the MySQL Monitor.
2. Enter the following SQL statement, which returns the `team` and `RBI` fields for the teams with the highest number of RBIs. Replace *path* with the path to your Projects directory for Chapter 8. Notice that the statement uses the `ORDER BY` and `DESC` keywords to perform a reverse sort of the fields. The results are sent to a text file named rbileaders.txt, with each field separated by a tab and each line separated by a line break escape sequence (\n).

```
mysql> SELECT team, RBI FROM teamstats
    -> ORDER BY RBI DESC LIMIT 10
    -> INTO OUTFILE 'path/rbileaders.txt'
    -> FIELDS TERMINATED BY '\t'
    -> LINES TERMINATED BY '\n';
```

3. Enter the following command to create a table named `rbileaders`:

```
mysql> CREATE TABLE rbileaders (Team VARCHAR(50),  RBI INT);
```

4. Enter the following `LOAD DATA` statement to import records from the rbileaders.txt file into the `rbileaders` table. Replace ***path*** with the path to your Projects directory for Chapter 8.

```
mysql> LOAD DATA LOCAL INFILE 'path/rbileaders.txt'
    -> INTO TABLE rbileaders;
```

5. After you see the "Query OK" message, enter the following command to view all the records in the `rbileaders` table:

```
mysql> SELECT * FROM rbileaders;
```

6. Finally, enter the following command to list the tables in the `baseball_stats` database. You should see the `rbileaders` and the `teamstats` tables listed.

```
mysql> SHOW TABLES;
```


Case Projects

Save the queries you write for the following projects in text files within the Cases directory for Chapter 8. Create a separate text file for each project.

Case Project 8-1

Create a demographics database with a table that contains the following fields: `country`, `primary language`, and `population`. Enter records for at least 10 countries. You can find demographic information for various countries in many places on the Internet, including Wikipedia, a free encyclopedia at *http://www.wikipedia.org/*. Write queries that return the following:

- A list of all records sorted by country name
- The country with the highest population
- The country with the lowest population
- Countries that share a common language, such as French

Case Project 8-2

Create a database for a used car dealership that includes a table for inventory. Include the following fields in the inventory table: `make`, `model`, `price`, and `mpg` (miles per gallon). Enter at least 10 records into the table. Write queries that return the following:

- All records
- Make, model, and price, sorted by make and model

- The make and model of the car that gets the best miles per gallon
- The make and model of the car that gets the worst miles per gallon
- The make and model of the highest and lowest priced cars

Case Project 8-3

Database design techniques include the process of being able to identify and design five normalization levels: first normal form, second normal form, third normal form, fourth normal form, and fifth normal form. Search the Internet or visit your local library for information on these techniques and describe how to identify and design each normalization level.

CHAPTER

9

MANIPULATING MYSQL DATABASES WITH PHP

In this chapter, you will:

- Connect to MySQL from PHP
- Learn how to handle MySQL errors
- Execute SQL statements with PHP
- Use PHP to work with MySQL databases and tables
- Use PHP to manipulate database records

One of PHP's greatest strengths is its ability to access and manipulate databases. With its strong ODBC support, you can use PHP to access any database that is ODBC compliant. PHP also includes functionality that allows you to work directly with different types of databases, without going through ODBC. Some of the databases that you can access directly from PHP include Oracle, Informix, PostgresSQL, and MySQL.

PHP also supports other methods of accessing data sources, including SQLite, database abstraction layer functions, and PEAR DB. SQLite and database abstraction layer functions work with file-based databases instead of server-based databases such as MySQL. The PHP Extension and Application Repository (PEAR) is a library of open source PHP code. One of the most popular PEAR code modules is PEAR DB, which simplifies access between PHP and a database server by providing a generic interface that works with various types of database systems, similar to the way ODBC works. Although PEAR DB and ODBC perform similar functions, the difference between the two languages is that PEAR is designed specifically to work with PHP, whereas ODBC is a more generic protocol that is used by many programming languages and database management systems.

With so many database connectivity options, how do you decide which method to use for accessing databases with PHP? First, you need to select a database management system. If you are new to database development, you should probably start with an open source database such as PostgresSQL or

MySQL, mainly because they are free and fairly easy to learn. After you select a database, you need to determine whether PHP can access it directly or whether it must go through a layer such as ODBC or PEAR DB. Going through ODBC or PEAR DB makes it easier for you to write PHP code that can be used with a variety of databases. However, your PHP script will be faster if it can access a database directly, without going through a PEAR DB or ODBC layer. Therefore, if you anticipate that your PHP script will need to access more than one type of database, you should use PEAR DB or ODBC. To be more precise, you should use PEAR DB over ODBC because PEAR is designed specifically for the PHP language. Yet, there are cases when ODBC is preferable, especially when you need to access Microsoft data source products such as Microsoft Access or Microsoft Excel. However, if you plan to work with a single database, such as MySQL, and you are more concerned with your Web application's performance than whether it is compatible with multiple database systems, use PHP's direct database access functionality if it's available for your database management system.

In this chapter, you study how to use PHP to directly access MySQL.

Connecting to MySQL with PHP

As you work through this chapter, keep in mind that almost everything you learned in the preceding chapter about MySQL is applicable to this chapter. Although you need to learn a few new functions to access MySQL with PHP, you will execute the same SQL statements that you used with the MySQL Monitor. The great benefit to using PHP or some other server-side scripting language to read from and write to a database server is that it allows you to create a Web-based interface that makes it much easier for visitors to interact with your database.

Before you can use PHP to read from and write to MySQL databases, you need to enable MySQL support in PHP and learn how to connect to the MySQL database server.

Enabling MySQL Support in PHP

In PHP versions earlier than PHP 5, support for MySQL was installed by default. However, starting with PHP 5, MySQL support no longer comes preinstalled with PHP. To enable MySQL support in PHP, you must configure your PHP installation to use the `mysqli` extension.

The `mysqli` extension is designed to work with MySQL version 4.1.3 and higher. If you are using a version of MySQL that is older that 4.1.3, you must use the `mysql` extension.

How you enable MySQL support in PHP depends on your operating system and how you installed PHP. On UNIX/Linux systems, you configure PHP to use the `mysqli` extension by specifying the `--with-mysqli` parameter when you run the `configure` command during the PHP installation process. If you followed the UNIX/Linux PHP installation instructions in Chapter 2, you should have specified the `--with-mysqli` parameter when you ran the `configure` command. If you did not specify the `--with-mysqli` parameter when you ran the `configure` command, you need to reinstall PHP to complete the exercises in this chapter.

To enable the `mysqli` extension on Windows installations of PHP, you must copy two files, libmysql.dll and php_mysqli.dll, to the directory where you installed PHP. You must also edit your php.ini configuration file and enable the `extension=php_mysqli.dll` directive. The libmysql.dll and php_mysqli.dll files are available in the full PHP Windows zip package (not the Windows binary installer) that is available on the PHP download page. The following instructions describe how to enable MySQL support on Windows installations of PHP.

If you are working with an installation of PHP that is hosted by an ISP, MySQL support should already be enabled.

The following steps assume that you followed the instructions in Chapter 2 to install PHP with the Windows binary installer. If you installed PHP by using the full PHP Windows zip package, the libmysql.dll file is installed by default in the PHP installation directory and the php_mysqli.dll file is installed in the ext directory beneath the PHP installation directory. You only need to copy the php_mysqli.dll file from the ext directory to the main PHP installation directory and enable the `extension=php_mysqli.dll` directive, as described in the following steps.

To enable MySQL support on Windows installations of PHP:

1. Start your Web browser, and enter the Web address for the PHP download page: **http://www.php.net/downloads.php**. Download the Windows zip package (not the Windows binary installer) containing the most recent Windows binary files. Save the file to a temporary folder on your computer.
2. Open **Windows Explorer** or **My Computer** and navigate to the folder where you downloaded the Windows zip package. Double-click the file to open it in WinZip, which is the archive utility for Windows.
3. Extract the **libmysql.dll** and **php_mysqli.dll** files to the directory where you installed PHP. By default, the PHP installation directory is C:\PHP. To extract individual files in WinZip, locate and click on a filename, and then click the **Extract** button. The Extract dialog box opens, which allows you to specify the location where you want to store the file.
4. Close **WinZip**.

5. Open your **php.ini** configuration file in your text editor. On Windows systems, this file is installed automatically in your main Windows directory, which is usually C:\WINDOWS or C:\WINNT.
6. In the php.ini file, locate the **`extension=php_mysqli.dll`** directive (not the `extension=php_mysql.dll` directive) and remove the semicolon at the beginning of the line to enable MySQL support. If the `extension=php_mysqli.dll` directive does not exist in your **php.ini** file, add it to the end of the Windows Extensions section.
7. Save and close the **php.ini** file.
8. Restart your Web server.

See Chapter 2 for information on how to restart your Web server.

Opening and Closing a MySQL Connection

Before you can use PHP to access the records in a database, you must first use the `mysqli_connect()` function to open a connection to a MySQL database server. Opening a connection to a database is similar to opening a handle to a text file, as you did in Chapter 6. However, instead of returning a file handle, the `mysqli_connect()` function returns a positive integer if it connects to the database successfully or false if it doesn't. You assign the return value from the `mysqli_connect()` function to a variable that you can use to access the database in your script. The basic syntax for the `mysqli_connect()` function is as follows:

```
$connection = mysqli_connect("host"[, "user ", "password", "database"])
```

In the preceding, the *host* argument allows you to specify the host name where your MySQL database server is installed. If you are working with an instance of MySQL database server that is installed on your local computer, use a value of "localhost" or "127.0.0.1" for the *host* argument. However, if you are working with a MySQL database server on an ISP's Web site, you need to enter your ISP's host name. The *user* and *password* arguments allow you to specify a MySQL account name and password, and the *database* argument allows you to select a database with which to work. For example, the following command connects the username *dongosselin* with a password of "rosebud" to a local instance of MySQL database server and opens a database named `real_estate`. The database connection is assigned to the `$DBConnect` variable.

```
$DBConnect = mysqli_connect("localhost", "dongosselin",
     "rosebud", "real_estate");
```

TIP

To change users after connecting to a database, use the `mysqli_change_user()` function.

When your PHP script ends, any open database connections close automatically. However, you should get into the habit of explicitly closing database connections with the `mysqli_close()` function when you are finished with them to ensure that the connection doesn't keep taking up space in your computer's memory while the script finishes processing. You close a database connection by passing the database connection variable to the `mysqli_close()` function. The following statement closes the `$DBConnect` database connection variable that was opened in the preceding statement:

```
mysqli_close($DBConnect);
```

TIP

If you receive a warning that PHP is unable to load a dynamic library or an error such as "Call to undefined function `mysqli_connect()`," MySQL support is not correctly enabled for your PHP installation. For more information, refer to the "Enabling MySQL Support in PHP" section earlier in this chapter.

9

After you connect to a database with the `mysqli_connect()` function, you can use the functions listed in Table 9-1 to return information about your installation of MySQL server.

Table 9-1 MySQL server information functions

Function	Description
`mysqli_get_client_info()`	Returns the MySQL client version
`mysqli_get_client_version()`	Returns the MySQL client version as an integer
`mysqli_get_host_info(`*connection*`)`	Returns the MySQL database server connection information
`mysqli_get_proto_info(`*connection*`)`	Returns the MySQL protocol version
`mysqli_get_server_info(`*connection*`)`	Returns the MySQL database server version
`mysqli_get_server_version(`*connection*`)`	Returns the MySQL database server version as an integer

NOTE

The `mysqli_get_client_info()` and `mysqli_get_client_version()` functions do not accept any arguments. However, you must pass the variable representing the database connection to the rest of the functions listed in Table 9-1.

Next, you create a PHP script that connects to MySQL and uses the functions listed in Table 9-1 to print information about your installation of MySQL.

To create a PHP script that connects to MySQL and uses the functions listed in Table 9-1 to print information about your installation of MySQL:

1. Create a new document in your text editor.
2. Type the `<!DOCTYPE>` declaration, `<html>` element, header information, and `<body>` element. Use the strict DTD and "MySQL Server Information" as the content of the `<title>` element.
3. Add the following `<link>` element above the closing `</head>` tag to link to the php_styles.css style sheet in your Chapter directory:

   ```
   <link rel="stylesheet" href="php_styles.css" type="text/css" />
   ```

4. Add the following heading element to the document body:

   ```
   <h1>MySQL Database Server Information</h1>
   ```

5. Add the following script section to the end of the document body:

   ```
   <?php
   ?>
   ```

6. Add the following `mysqli_connect()` statement to the script section. Replace *`user`* and *`password`* with the MySQL username and password you created in Chapter 8.

   ```
   $DBConnect = mysqli_connect("localhost", "user", "password");
   ```

7. Add to the end of the script section the following statements, which print information about your installation of MySQL server:

   ```
   echo "<p>MySQL client version: "
        . mysqli_get_client_info() . "</p>";
   echo "<p>MySQL connection: "
        . mysqli_get_host_info($DBConnect) . "</p>";
   echo "<p>MySQL protocol version: "
        . mysqli_get_proto_info($DBConnect) . "</p>";
   echo "<p>MySQL server version: "
        . mysqli_get_server_info($DBConnect) . "</p>";
   ```

8. Finally, add the following statement to the end of the script section to close the database connection:

   ```
   mysqli_close($DBConnect);
   ```

9. Save the document as **MySQLInfo.php** in the Chapter directory for Chapter 9, and then close it in your text editor.
10. Open the **MySQLInfo.php** file in your Web browser by entering the following URL: **http://localhost/PHP_Projects/Chapter.09/Chapter/MySQLInfo.php**. Your Web browser should appear similar to Figure 9-1, although the information printed from each function might be different for your MySQL installation.

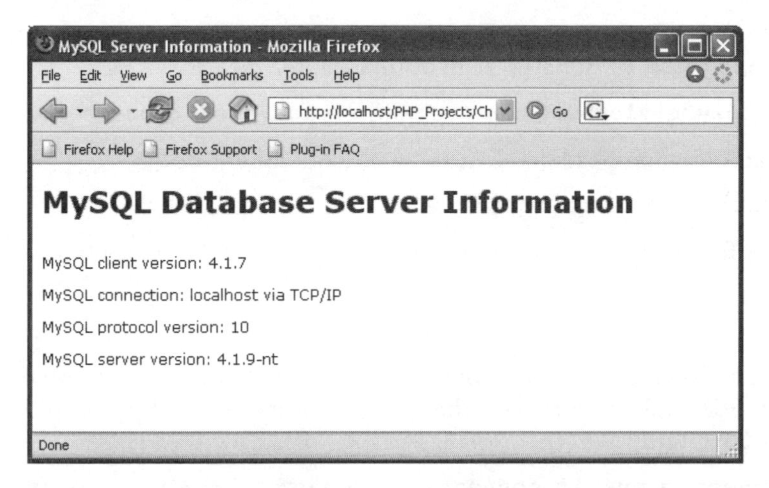

Figure 9-1 MySQLInfo.php in a Web browser

11. Close your Web browser window.

Selecting a Database

As you saw in Chapter 8, you must first select a database with the `use` ***`database`*** statement when you log on to the MySQL Monitor. Although you can select a database by passing a database name as the fourth argument to the `mysqli_connect()` function, you can also select or change a database with the `mysqli_select_db()` function. The syntax for the `mysqli_select_db()` function is `mysqli_select_db(`*`connection`*`, `*`database`*`)`. The function returns a value of true if it successfully selects a database or false if it doesn't. For example, instead of selecting a database by passing the database name as the fourth argument to the `mysqli_connect()` function, the following code uses a `mysqli_select_db()` statement to open the `real_estate` database from the `$DBConnect` database connection:

```
$DBConnect = mysqli_connect("localhost", "dongosselin", "rosebud");
mysqli_select_db($DBConnect, "real_estate");
// additional statements that access or manipulate the database
mysqli_close($DBConnect);
```

Next, you create a PHP script that selects the `flightlog` database you created in Chapter 8.

To create a PHP script that selects the `flightlog` database you created in Chapter 8:

1. Create a new document in your text editor.
2. Type the `<!DOCTYPE>` declaration, `<html>` element, header information, and `<body>` element. Use the strict DTD and "Flightlog Entries" as the content of the `<title>` element.

3. Add the following `<link>` element above the closing `</head>` tag to link to the php_styles.css style sheet in your Chapter directory:

```
<link rel="stylesheet" href="php_styles.css" type="text/css" />
```

4. Add the following heading element to the document body:

```
<h1>Flightlog Entries</h1>
```

5. Add the following script section to the end of the document body:

```
<?php
?>
```

6. Add the following `mysqli_connect()` statement to the script section. Replace *user* and *password* with the MySQL username and password you created in Chapter 8.

```
$DBConnect = mysqli_connect("localhost", "user", "password");
```

7. After the `mysqli_connect()` function, add the following statements to select the `flightlog` database:

```
$DBName = "flightlog";
mysqli_select_db($DBConnect, $DBName);
```

8. Add the following statement to the end of the script section to close the database connection:

```
mysqli_close($DBConnect);
```

9. Save the document as **FlightlogEntries.php** in the Chapter directory for Chapter 9, and then close it in your text editor.

Handling MySQL Errors

When accessing MySQL databases and other types of data sources, you need to understand the errors that can affect the execution of your script. One of the most important errors that you need to consider occurs when you cannot connect to a database server. Reasons that you may not be able to connect to a database server include the following:

- The database server is not running.
- You do not have sufficient privileges to access the data source.
- You entered an invalid username and/or password.

When it comes to connecting to a database server or selecting a database, your first instinct might be to check the value that is returned from the `mysqli_connect()` function and `mysqli_select_db()` function. The `mysqli_connect()` function returns a positive integer if it connects to the database successfully or false if it doesn't. Thus, you might make the mistake of trying to use the return value to determine if the connection is successful. As an example, consider the following code. The conditional expression in the `if` statement uses the Not operator (`!`) to determine if the `$DBConnect` variable is equal to false. If the variable is equal to false, a message prints to the Web browser informing the user that the database server is not available. If the variable is not equal to false, a message prints to the Web browser informing the user that she connected successfully to the database server.

```
$DBConnect = mysqli_connect("localhost", "dongosselin",
     "rosebud", "flightlog");
if (!$DBConnect)
      echo "<p>The database server is not available.</p>";
else   {
     echo "<p>Successfully connected to the database server.</p>";
     // additional statements that access the database server
     mysqli_close($DBConnect);
}
```

The problem with the preceding code is that, although it prints "The database server is not available" if you cannot connect to the database server, it also prints any error messages that may be caused by the `mysqli_connect()` function. For example, Figure 9-2 displays an error message that occurs if you attempt to access the database with an invalid username or password.

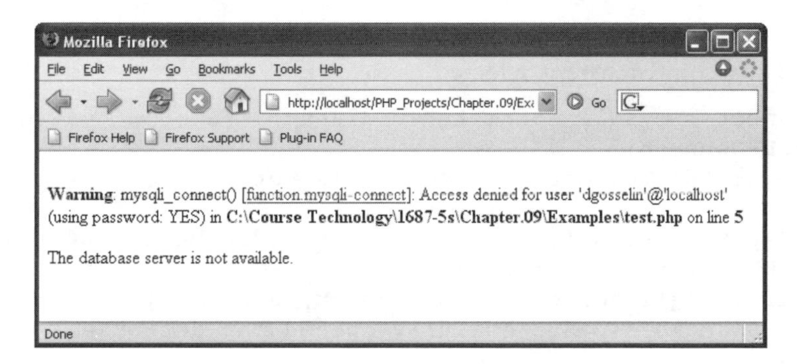

Figure 9-2 Database connection error message

As with the connection to the database server, you should also check to ensure that the `mysqli_select_db()` function successfully selects the database. Because the `mysqli_select_db()` function returns a value of true if it is successful, you can call the function from within an `if` statement's conditional expression. The following code demonstrates how to call the `mysqli_select_db()` function from within an `if` statement's conditional expression to determine whether the database was selected successfully:

```
$DBConnect = mysqli_connect("localhost", "dongosselin", "rosebud");
if (!$DBConnect)
      echo "<p>The database server is not available.</p>";
else   {
```

```
        echo "<p>Successfully connected to the database server.</p>";
        if (mysqli_select_db($DBConnect, "flightlog")) {
              echo "<p>Successfully opened the database.</p>";
              // additional statements that access the database
        }
        else
              echo "<p>The database is not available.</p>";
        mysqli_close($DBConnect);
}
```

In most cases, the `mysqli_select_db()` function does not print any error messages the way the `mysqli_connect()` function does. However, to be on the safe side, you should suppress any error codes that may appear for both the `mysqli_connect()` function and the `mysqli_select_db()` function. In the next section, you learn how to suppress errors with the error control operator.

Next, you modify the FlightlogEntries.php script so it verifies that the database is connected and that the `flightlog` database is selected.

To modify the FlightlogEntries.php script so it verifies that the database is connected and that the `flightlog` database is selected:

1. Return to the **FlightlogEntries.php** document in your text editor.
2. Modify the script section so it verifies that the database is connected and that the `flightlog` database is selected, as follows:

```
$DBConnect = mysqli_connect("localhost", "user", "password");
if (!$DBConnect)
     echo "<p>The database server is not available.</p>";
else  {
echo "<p>Successfully connected to the database server.</p>";
     $DBName = "flightlog";
     if (mysqli_select_db($DBConnect, $DBName))
          echo "<p>Successfully opened the database.</p>";
     else
          echo "<p>The database is not available.</p>";
     mysqli_close($DBConnect);
}
```

3. Save the **FlightlogEntries.php** file and open it in your Web browser by entering the following URL: **http://localhost/PHP_Projects/Chapter.09/Chapter/FlightlogEntries.php**. Your Web browser should appear similar to Figure 9-3.

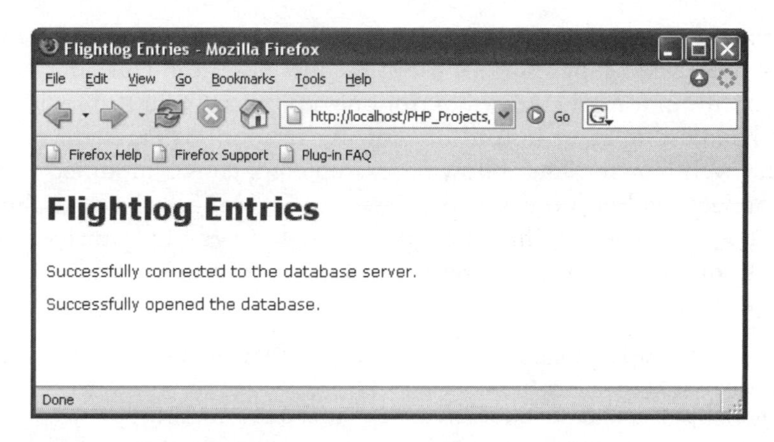

Figure 9-3 FlightlogEntries.php in a Web browser

4. Close your Web browser window.

Suppressing Errors with the Error Control Operator

Although standard error messages that are generated by programming languages such as PHP are very helpful to programmers, they tend to scare users, who might think that they somehow caused the error. Errors can and will occur, but you should never let your users think that they did something wrong. Your goal should be to write code that anticipates any problems that may occur and includes graceful methods of dealing with those problems. Writing code that anticipates and handles potential problems is often called **bulletproofing**. One bulletproofing technique you have already used has to do with validating submitted form data. For example, in Chapter 5, you saw the following code, which ensures that values submitted to a script that measures body mass contain numeric values. This example contains a nested `if` statement that tests whether the `$_GET['height']` and `$_GET['weight']` variables are numeric after the first `if` statement checks to see whether they are set.

```
if (isset($_GET['height']) && isset($_GET['weight'])) {
     if (!is_numeric($_GET['weight']) || !is_numeric($_GET['height'])) {
          $BodyMass = $_GET['weight'] / ($_GET['height']
                * $_GET['height']) * 703;
          printf("<p>Your body mass index is %d.</p>",
                $BodyMass);
     }
     else
          echo "<p>You must enter numeric values!</p>";
}
```

Another method of bulletproofing your code is to use the **error control operator (@)** to suppress error messages. You can place the error control operator before any expression, although it is most commonly used with built-in PHP functions, especially functions that access data sources such as the `mysqli_connect()` and `mysqli_select_db()` functions. Using the error control operator to suppress error messages does not mean you can then ignore errors that may occur. Instead, the error control operator allows you to provide a more graceful way of handling an error instead of allowing an intimidating error message to be printed to the Web browser. The following example contains a modified version of the code that connects with a username and password of "dongosselin" and "rosebud" to the `flightlog` database. In this example, both the `mysqli_connect()` and `mysqli_select_db()` functions are preceded by error control operators to suppress any error messages that may occur.

```
$DBConnect = @mysqli_connect("localhost", "dongosselin", "rosebud");
if (!$DBConnect)
     echo "<p>The database server is not available.</p>";
else   {
     echo "<p>Successfully connected to the database server.</p>";
     if (@mysqli_select_db($DBConnect, "flightlog")) {
          echo "<p>Successfully opened the database.</p>";
     // additional statements that access the database
    }
    else
         echo "<p>The database is not available.</p>";
    mysqli_close($DBConnect);
}
```

Next, you add error control operators to the `mysqli_connect()` and `mysqli_select_db()` functions in the FlightlogEntries.php script.

To add error control operators to the `mysqli_connect()` and `mysqli_select_db()` functions in the FlightlogEntries.php script:

1. Return to the **FlightlogEntries.php** document in your text editor.
2. Add error control operators before the `mysqli_connect()` and `mysqli_select_db()` functions.
3. Save the **FlightlogEntries.php** file and open it in your Web browser by entering the following URL: **http://localhost/PHP_Projects/Chapter.09/Chapter/FlightlogEntries.php**. The Web page should appear the same as it did before you added the error control operators.
4. Close your Web browser window.

Terminating Script Execution

Up to this point in this book, you have relied on `if...else` statements to execute code only when certain conditions have been met. For example, the `else` clause in the preceding example executes only if the `mysqli_connect()` successfully connects to a database server. The `else` clause also contains a nested `if` statement, which executes only if the mysqli_select_db() function successfully opens a database. Instead of relying on if...else statements to execute code, you can more easily terminate script execution with the die() or exit() functions. The die() and exit() functions perform the same task of terminating script execution, although the die() version is usually used when attempting to access a data source. Both functions accept a single string argument, which is printed to the Web browser when the script ends. You can call the die() and exit() functions as separate statements or by appending either function to an expression with the Or operator. The following code demonstrates how to call the die() function by using if statements. Notice that the code does not require else clauses because the script terminates when the conditional expressions in the if statements are true.

```
$DBConnect = @mysqli_connect("localhost", "root", "paris");
if (!$DBConnect)
     die("<p>The database server is not available.</p>");
echo "<p>Successfully connected to the database server.</p>";
$DBSelect = @mysqli_select_db($DBConnect, "flightlog");
if (!$DBSelect)
     die("<p>The database is not available.</p>");
echo "<p>Successfully opened the database.</p>";
// additional statements that access the database
mysqli_close($DBConnect);
```

The following code demonstrates how to use an Or operator to append the die() function to the statements that call the mysqli_connect() and mysqli_select_db() functions:

```
$DBConnect = @mysqli_connect("localhost", "dongosselin",
"rosebud")
     Or die("<p>The database server is not available.</p>");
echo "<p>Successfully connected to the database server.</p>";
@mysqli_select_db($DBConnect, "flightlog")
     Or die("<p>The database is not available.</p>");
echo "<p>Successfully opened the database.</p>";
// additional statements that access the database server
mysqli_close($DBConnect);
```

Next, you modify the mysqli_connect() and mysqli_select_db() functions in the FlightlogEntries.php script so they use die() functions to terminate the script in the event of an error.

To modify the `mysqli_connect()` and `mysqli_select_db()` functions in the FlightlogEntries.php script so they use `die()` functions to terminate the script in the event of an error:

1. Return to the **FlightlogEntries.php** document in your text editor.
2. Modify the contents of the script section so it uses `die()` functions to terminate the script in the event of an error. Your modified script section should appear as follows:

```
$DBConnect = @mysqli_connect("localhost", "user", "password")
     Or die("<p>The database server is not available.</p>");
echo "<p>Successfully connected to the database server.</p>";
$DBName = "flightlog";
@mysqli_select_db($DBConnect, $DBName)
     Or die("<p>The database is not available.</p>");
echo "<p>Successfully opened the database.</p>";
mysqli_close($DBConnect);
```

3. Save the **FlightlogEntries.php** file and open it in your Web browser by entering the following URL: **http://localhost/PHP_Projects/Chapter.09/Chapter/FlightlogEntries.php**. The Web page should appear the same as it did before you added the error control operators.
4. Close your Web browser window.

Reporting MySQL Errors

The preceding section emphasized the importance of using the error control operator to prevent PHP from spitting out errors wherever they occur. However, that does not mean error messages are useless. In fact, when displayed correctly, error numbers and codes can be invaluable in providing useful feedback and in helping you track down problems with your script or database. PHP includes the functions listed in Table 9-2 for reporting MySQL error numbers and codes.

Table 9-2 MySQL error reporting functions

Function	Description
`mysqli_connect_errno()`	Returns the error code from the last database connection attempt or zero if no error occurred
`mysqli_connect_error()`	Returns the error message from the last database connection attempt or an empty string if no error occurred
`mysqli_errno(connection)`	Returns the error code from the last attempted MySQL function call or zero if no error occurred
`mysqli_error(connection)`	Returns the error message from the last attempted MySQL function call or an empty string if no error occurred
`mysqli_sqlstate(connection)`	Returns a string of five characters representing an error code from the last MySQL operation or 00000 if no error occurred

You can find a list of error codes that may be returned from the `mysqli_sqlstate()` function at *http://dev.mysql.com/doc/mysql/en/error-handling.html*.

As an example of how you might use a MySQL error reporting function, consider a PHP script that allows users to submit a username and password that will be used to log on to MySQL. For example, a Web page may contain the following simple form that will be submitted to a PHP script named dblogin.php:

```
<form action="dblogin.php" method="GET"
enctype="application/x-www-form-urlencoded">
<p>Username <input type="text" name="username" /><br />
Password <input type="password" name="password" /></p>
<p><input type="submit" value="Log In" /></p>
</form>
```

If a user enters an invalid username or password with the preceding form, printing a generic message such as "The database server is not available" doesn't help him determine what's wrong. When connecting to the MySQL database server, you should at least use the `mysqli_connect_error()` function to give the user more information about the error that occurred. For example, the `die()` function in the following code uses the `mysqli_connect_errno()` and the `mysqli_connect_error()` functions to print an error code and message if the connection attempt fails. Both of these functions report on the most recent database connection attempt. If the user enters an invalid username or password in the form, he will see the error number and description shown in Figure 9-4. As you can see in the figure, the error description informs users that access was denied for the submitted username and password, which should point out that either a typo occurred in the submitted username or password, or that the user doesn't have authorization to access the database.

```
$User = $_GET['username'];
$Password = $_GET['password'];
$DBConnect = @mysqli_connect("localhost", $User, $Password)
     Or die("<p>Unable to connect to the database server.</p>"
     . "<p>Error code " . mysqli_connect_errno()
     . ": " . mysqli_connect_error()) . "</p>";
echo "<p>Successfully connected to the database server.</p>";
@mysqli_select_db($DBConnect, "flightlog")
     Or die("<p>The database is not available.</p>");
echo "<p>Successfully opened the database.</p>";
// additional statements that access the database
mysqli_close($DBConnect);
```

9

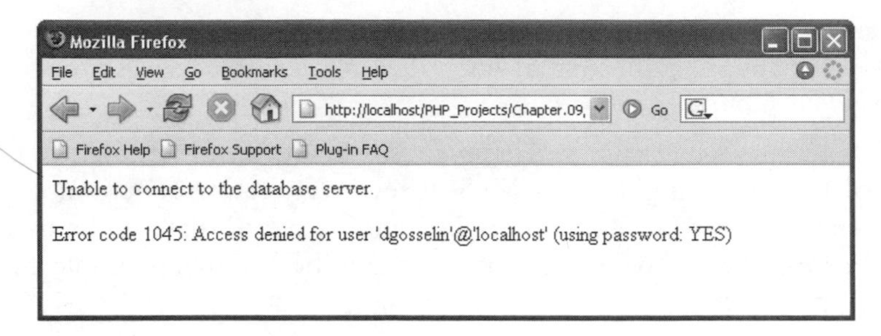

Figure 9-4 Error number and message generated by an invalid username and password

The `mysqli_connect_errno()` and `mysqli_connect_error()` functions only report errors that occur when you attempt to connect to a MySQL database server with the `mysqli_connect()`function. To obtain error information for any other functions that access a MySQL database, such as the `mysqli_select_db()` function, you use the `mysqli_errno()` and the `mysqli_error()` functions. Unlike the `mysqli_connect_errno()` and the `mysqli_connect_error()` functions, you pass to the the `mysqli_errno()` and the `mysqli_error()` functions the variable representing the database connection. The following example demonstrates how to display error codes and messages that may occur when you call the `mysqli_select_db()` function:

```
$User = $_GET['username'];
$Password = $_GET['password'];
$DBConnect = @mysqli_connect("localhost", $User, $Password)
     Or die("<p>Unable to connect to the database server.</p>"
     . "<p>Error code " . mysqli_connect_errno()
     . ": " . mysqli_connect_error()) . "</p>";
echo "<p>Successfully connected to the database server.</p>";
@mysqli_select_db($DBConnect, "flightplan")
     Or die("<p>Unable to select the database.</p>"
     . "<p>Error code " . mysqli_errno($DBConnect)
     . ": " . mysqli_error($DBConnect)) . "</p>";
echo "<p>Successfully opened the database.</p>";
// additional statements that access the database
mysqli_close($DBConnect);
```

The preceding script attempts to select a database named `flightplan`. Figure 9-5 shows the output in a Web browser if the `flightplan` database does not exist on the MySQL database server.

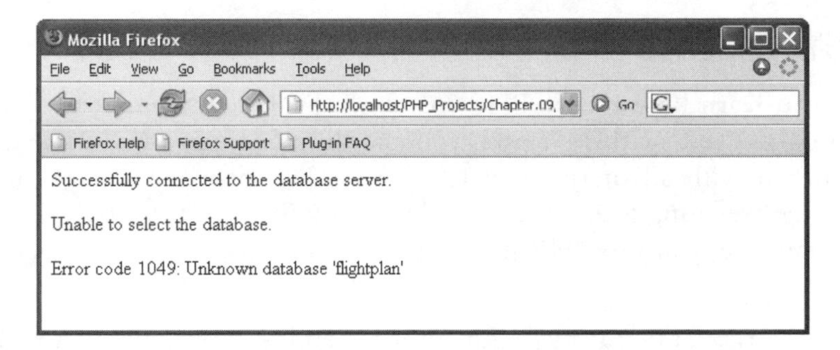

Figure 9-5 Error code and message generated when attempting to select a database that does not exist

Next, you modify the `die()` functions in the FlightlogEntries.php script so they print error codes and messages in the event of an error.

To modify the `die()` functions in the FlightlogEntries.php script so they print error codes and messages in the event of an error:

1. Return to the **FlightlogEntries.php** document in your text editor.
2. Modify the `die()` function in the `mysqli_connect()` statement so it includes the `mysqli_connect_errno()` and `mysqli_connect_error()` functions, as follows:

```
$DBConnect = @mysqli_connect("localhost",
"dongosselin","rosebud")
     Or die("<p>Unable to connect to the database server.</p>"
     . "<p>Error code " . mysqli_connect_errno()
     . ": " . mysqli_connect_error()) . "</p>";
```

3. Modify the `die()` function in the `mysqli_select_db()` statement so it includes the `mysqli_errno()` and `mysqli_error()` functions, as follows:

```
@mysqli_select_db($DBConnect, $DBName)
     Or die("<p>Unable to select the database.</p>"
     . "<p>Error code " . mysqli_errno($DBConnect)
     . ": " . mysqli_error($DBConnect)) . "</p>";
```

4. Save the **FlightlogEntries.php** file and open it in your Web browser by entering the following URL: **http://localhost/PHP_Projects/Chapter.09/Chapter/FlightlogEntries.php**. The Web page should appear the same as it did before you added the error functions.
5. Close your Web browser window.

EXECUTING SQL STATEMENTS

In this section, you learn how to use PHP to submit SQL statements to MySQL. As you work through the rest of this chapter, you should recognize the SQL statements because you worked with all of them in Chapter 8. The primary difference is that instead of manually executing SQL statements by typing them in the MySQL Monitor as you did in Chapter 8, you use PHP statements to access MySQL and execute SQL statements for you.

In PHP, you use the `mysqli_query()` function to send SQL statements to MySQL. The `mysqli_query()` function is the workhorse of PHP connectivity with MySQL; almost every SQL command you send to MySQL from PHP is executed with the `mysqli_query()` function. The basic syntax for the `mysqli_query()` function is `mysqli_query(connection, query)`. The `mysqli_query()` function returns one of three values, depending on the type of query executed. For SQL statements that do not return results, such as the `CREATE DATABASE` and `CREATE TABLE` statements, the `mysqli_query()` function returns a value of true if the statement executes successfully. For SQL statements that return results, such as `SELECT` and `SHOW` statements, the `mysqli_query()` function returns a result pointer that represents the query results. A **result pointer** is a special type of variable that refers to the currently selected row in a resultset. The query pointer is a way of keeping track of where you are in a resultset. You assign the result pointer to a variable, which you can use to access the resultset in PHP. The `mysqli_query()` function returns a value of false for any SQL statements that fail, regardless of whether they return results. As an example, the following code queries the `guitars` database you saw in Chapter 8. The code then executes the `mysqli_query()` function and assigns the result pointer to a variable named `$QueryResult`.

```
@mysqli_select_db($DBConnect, "guitars")
     Or die("<p>Unable to select the database.</p>"
     . "<p>Error code " . mysqli_errno($DBConnect)
     . ": " . mysqli_error($DBConnect)) . "</p>";
echo "<p>Successfully opened the database.</p>";
$SQLstring = "SELECT model, quantity FROM inventory";
$QueryResult = mysqli_query($DBConnect, $SQLstring)
mysqli_close($DBConnect);
```

You use the same techniques to handle errors with the `mysqli_query()` function that you use with the `mysqli_connect()` and `mysqli_select_db()` functions. For example, the following code uses the error control operator to suppress errors and terminates the script with the `die()` function if the query is unsuccessful. The example also uses the `mysqli_errno()` and `mysqli_error()` functions to report the error code and message.

```
$SQLstring = "SELECT model, quantity FROM inventory";
$QueryResult = @mysqli_query($DBConnect, $SQLstring)
```

```
        Or die("<p>Unable to execute the query.</p>"
        . "<p>Error code " . mysqli_errno($DBConnect)
        . ": " . mysqli_error($DBConnect)) . "</p>";
    echo "<p>Successfully executed the query.</p>";
    mysqli_close($DBConnect);
```

When you use a PHP variable to represent a field name in a SQL query, you must enclose the variable name within single quotes or you receive an error. For example, the following statement raises an error because the `$Make` variable is not enclosed within single quotes:

```
$Make = "Ovation";
$SQLstring = "SELECT model, quantity FROM $DBTable
     WHERE model=$Make";
```

To fix the preceding code, enclose the `$Make` variable in single quotes, as follows:

```
$Make = "Ovation";
$SQLstring = "SELECT model, quantity FROM $DBTable
     WHERE model='$Make'";
```


Next, you add query statements to the FlightlogEntries.php script that select all the records in the `flightsessions` table.

To query statements to the FlightlogEntries.php script that select all the records in the `flightsessions` table:

1. Return to the **FlightlogEntries.php** document in your text editor.
2. Add the following statements above the `mysqli_close()` statement. The first statement creates a SQL query that selects all records from the `flightsessions` table. The second statement executes the query with the `mysqli_query()` function, and the third statement prints a message if the query is successful.

```
$SQLstring = "SELECT * FROM flightsessions";
$QueryResult = @mysqli_query($DBConnect, $SQLstring)
     Or die("<p>Unable to execute the query.</p>"
     . "<p>Error code " . mysqli_errno($DBConnect)
     . ": " . mysqli_error($DBConnect)) . "</p>";
echo "<p>Successfully executed the query.</p>";
```

3. Save the **FlightlogEntries.php** file and open it in your Web browser by entering the following URL: **http://localhost/PHP_Projects/Chapter.09/Chapter/FlightlogEntries.php**. You should see the three success messages printed to the Web browser window.
4. Close your Web browser window.

Working with Query Results

Recall that for SQL statements that return results, such as `SELECT` and `SHOW` statements, the `mysqli_query()` function returns a result pointer that represents the query results. You assign the result pointer to a variable, which you can use to access the resultset in PHP. To access the database records through the result pointer, you must use one of the functions listed in Table 9-3.

Table 9-3 Common PHP functions for accessing database results

Function	Description
`mysqli_data_seek($Result, position)`	Moves the result pointer to a specified row in the resultset
`mysqli_fetch_array($Result, MYSQLI_ASSOC | MYSQLI_NUM | MYSQLI_BOTH)`	Returns the fields in the current row of a resultset into an indexed array, associative array, or both and moves the result pointer to the next row
`mysqli_fetch_assoc($Result)`	Returns the fields in the current row of a resultset into an associative array and moves the result pointer to the next row
`mysqli_fetch_lengths($Result)`	Returns the field lengths for the current row in a resultset into an indexed array
`mysqli_fetch_row($Result)`	Returns the fields in the current row of a resultset into an indexed array and moves the result pointer to the next row

First, you learn how to use the `mysqli_fetch_row()` function to retrieve fields into an indexed array.

Retrieving Records into an Indexed Array

In Chapter 6, you learned how to use the `fgets()` function, which returns a line from a text file and moves the file pointer to the next line. The `mysqli_fetch_row()` function is very similar in that it returns the fields in the current row of a resultset into an indexed array and moves the result pointer to the next row. You can then use the array to access the individual fields in the row. As an example, the following code prints the contents of the fields in the first row in the `inventory` table of the `guitars` database:

```
$SQLstring = "SELECT * FROM inventory";
$QueryResult = @mysqli_query($DBConnect, $SQLstring)
     Or die("<p>Unable to execute the query.</p>"
     . "<p>Error code " . mysqli_errno($DBConnect)
     . ": " . mysqli_error($DBConnect)) . "</p>";
$Row = mysqli_fetch_row($QueryResult);
```

```
echo "<p><strong>Make</strong>: {$Row[0]}<br />";
echo "<strong>Model</strong>: {$Row[1]}<br />";
echo "<strong>Price</strong>: {$Row[2]}<br />";
echo "<strong>Quantity</strong>: {$Row[3]}</p>";
```

The `mysqli_fetch_row()` function returns the fields in the current row or a value of false when it reaches the last row in the resultset. This allows you to iterate through all the rows in a resultset. The following code shows a more complex example that uses a `do...while` statement to print all of the rows in the `inventory` table to an HTML table. Figure 9-6 shows how the table appears in a Web browser.

```
echo "<table width='100%' border='1'>";
echo "<tr><th>Make</th><th>Model</th>
     <th>Price</th><th>Quantity</th></tr>";
$Row = mysqli_fetch_row($QueryResult);
do {
     echo "<tr><td>{$Row[0]}</td>";
     echo "<td>{$Row[1]}</td>";
     echo "<td align='right'>{$Row[2]}</td>";
     echo "<td align='right'>{$Row[3]}</td></tr>";
     $Row = mysqli_fetch_row($QueryResult);
} while ($Row);
```


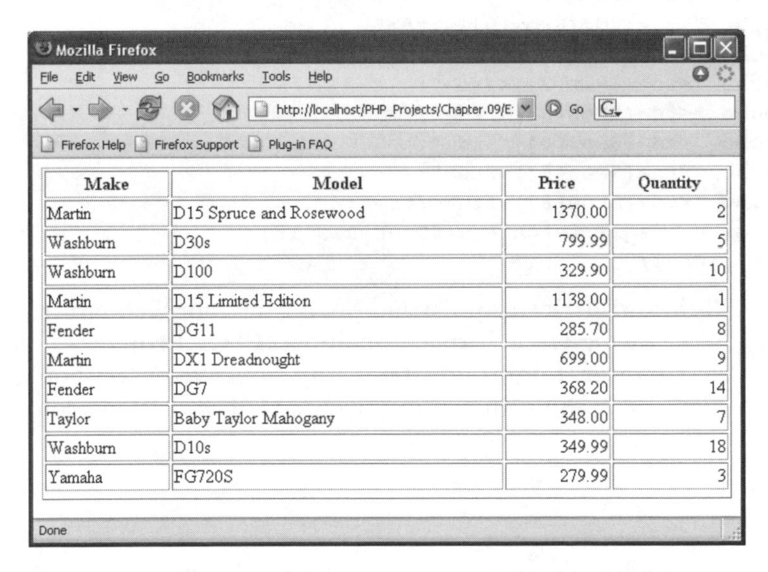

Make	Model	Price	Quantity
Martin	D15 Spruce and Rosewood	1370.00	2
Washburn	D30s	799.99	5
Washburn	D100	329.90	10
Martin	D15 Limited Edition	1138.00	1
Fender	DG11	285.70	8
Martin	DX1 Dreadnought	699.00	9
Fender	DG7	368.20	14
Taylor	Baby Taylor Mahogany	348.00	7
Washburn	D10s	349.99	18
Yamaha	FG720S	279.99	3

Figure 9-6 Output of the `inventory` table in a Web browser

Next, you add query statements to the FlightlogEntries.php script that select all the records in the `flightsessions` table.

To add query statements to the FlightlogEntries.php script that select all the records in the `flightsessions` table:

1. Return to the **FlightlogEntries.php** document in your text editor.
2. Delete the following `echo()` statement that prints when the script successfully connects to the database server:

```
echo "<p>Successfully connected to the database server.</p>";
```

3. Delete the following `echo()` statement that prints when the database opens successfully:

```
echo "<p>Successfully opened the database.</p>";
```

4. Replace the statement that prints when the query executes successfully with the following statements, which use the `mysqli_fetch_row()` function to print the results in a table:

```
echo "<table width='100%' border='1'>";
echo "<tr><th>Flight Date</th><th>Flight Time</th>
<th>Origin</th><th>Destination</th><th>Weather</th><th>Winds</th>
<th>Temp</th></tr>";
$Row = mysqli_fetch_row($QueryResult);
do {
      echo "<tr><td>{$Row[0]}</td>";
      echo "<td>{$Row[1]}</td>";
      echo "<td>{$Row[2]}</td>";
      echo "<td>{$Row[3]}</td>";
      echo "<td>{$Row[4]}</td>";
      echo "<td>{$Row[5]}</td>";
      echo "<td>{$Row[6]}</td></tr>";
      $Row = mysqli_fetch_row($QueryResult);
} while ($Row);
```

5. Save the **FlightlogEntries.php** file and open it in your Web browser by entering the following URL: **http://localhost/PHP_Projects/Chapter.09/Chapter/FlightlogEntries.php**. Your Web page should be similar to Figure 9-7, although you may have added or deleted additional entries.

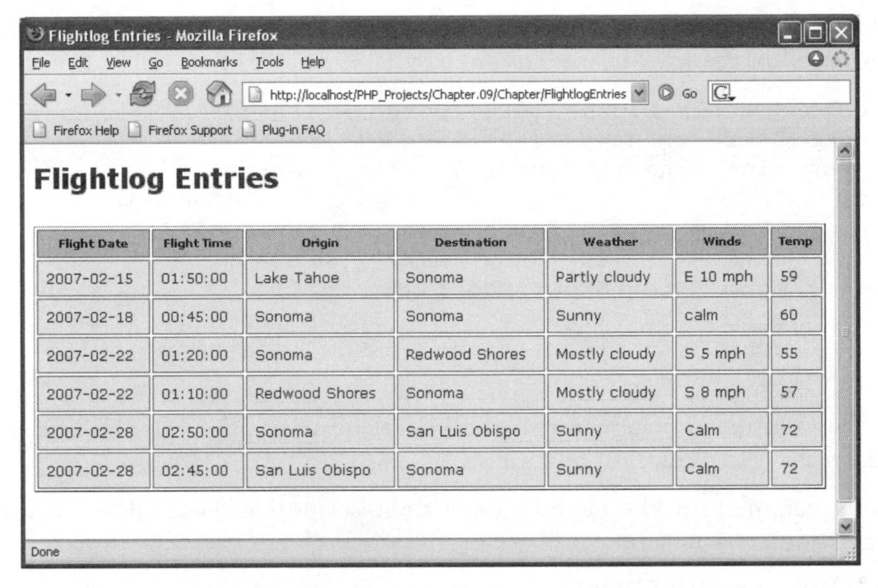

Flight Date	Flight Time	Origin	Destination	Weather	Winds	Temp
2007-02-15	01:50:00	Lake Tahoe	Sonoma	Partly cloudy	E 10 mph	59
2007-02-18	00:45:00	Sonoma	Sonoma	Sunny	calm	60
2007-02-22	01:20:00	Sonoma	Redwood Shores	Mostly cloudy	S 5 mph	55
2007-02-22	01:10:00	Redwood Shores	Sonoma	Mostly cloudy	S 8 mph	57
2007-02-28	02:50:00	Sonoma	San Luis Obispo	Sunny	Calm	72
2007-02-28	02:45:00	San Luis Obispo	Sonoma	Sunny	Calm	72

Figure 9-7 Output of FlightlogEntries.php with the `mysqli_fetch_row()` function

6. Close your Web browser window.

Retrieving Records into an Associative Array

The `mysqli_fetch_assoc()` function returns the fields in the current row of a resultset into an associative array and moves the result pointer to the next row. The primary difference between the `mysqli_fetch_assoc()` function and the `mysqli_fetch_row()` function is that instead of returning the fields into an indexed array, the `mysqli_fetch_assoc()` function returns the fields into an associate array and uses each field name as the array key. For example, the following code uses the `mysqli_fetch_assoc()` function to print the contents of the fields in the first row in the `inventory` table of the `guitars` database. Notice that the `echo()` statements refer to keys instead of indexes in the `$Row[]` array.

```
$Row = mysqli_fetch_assoc($QueryResult);
echo "<p><strong>Make</strong>: {$Row['make']}<br />";
echo "<strong>Model</strong>: {$Row['model']}<br />";
echo "<strong>Price</strong>: {$Row['price']}<br />";
echo "<strong>Quantity</strong>: {$Row['quantity']}</p>";
```

The following code shows an associative array version of the `do...while` statement that prints all of the rows in the `inventory` table to an HTML table:

```
echo "<table width='100%' border='1'>";
echo "<tr><th>Make</th><th>Model</th>
<th>Price</th><th>Quantity</th></tr>";
do {
     $Row = mysqli_fetch_assoc($QueryResult);
     echo "<tr><td>{$Row['make']}</td>";
     echo "<td>{$Row['model']}</td>";
     echo "<td align='right'>{$Row['price']}</td>";
     echo "<td align='right'>{$Row['quantity']}</td></tr>";
} while ($Row);
```

Next, you add query statements to the FlightlogEntries.php script that select all the records in the `flightsessions` table.

To query statements to the FlightlogEntries.php script that select all the records in the `flightsessions` table:

1. Return to the **FlightlogEntries.php** document in your text editor.
2. Replace the two `mysqli_fetch_row()` functions with `mysqli_fetch_assoc()` functions.
3. Modify the `echo()` statements in the `do...while` statement so they reference the keys in the associative array instead of the index values. Your modified code should appear as follows:

```
echo "<table width='100%' border='1'>";
echo "<tr><th>Flight Date</th><th>Flight Time</th>
<th>Origin</th><th>Destination</th><th>Weather</th><th>Winds</th>
<th>Temp</th></tr>";
$Row = mysqli_fetch_assoc($QueryResult);
do {
     echo "<tr><td>{$Row['flight_date']}</td>";
     echo "<td>{$Row['flight_time']}</td>";
     echo "<td>{$Row['origin']}</td>";
     echo "<td>{$Row['destination']}</td>";
     echo "<td>{$Row['weather']}</td>";
     echo "<td>{$Row['winds']}</td>";
     echo "<td>{$Row['temp']}</td></tr>";
     $Row = mysqli_fetch_assoc($QueryResult);
} while ($Row);
```

4. Save the **FlightlogEntries.php** file and open it in your Web browser by entering the following URL: **http://localhost/PHP_Projects/Chapter.09/Chapter/FlightlogEntries.php**. Your Web page should appear the same as it did before you modified the code to use `mysqli_fetch_assoc()` functions.
5. Close your Web browser window.

Accessing Query Result Information

PHP includes numerous functions for working with query results, including the `mysqli_num_rows()` function, which returns the number of rows in a query result, and the `mysqli_num_fields()` function, which returns the number of fields in a query result. Both functions accept a database connection variable as an argument. The following code demonstrates how to use both functions with the query results returned from the `guitars` database. If the number of rows and fields in the query result are not equal to zero, an `echo()` statement prints the number of rows and fields. However, if the number of rows and fields in the query result are equal to zero, an `echo()` statement prints "Your query returned no results." Figure 9-8 shows the output if the `guitars` database contains 10 rows and 4 fields.

```
$SQLstring = "SELECT * FROM inventory";
$QueryResult = @mysqli_query($DBConnect, $SQLstring)
     Or die("<p>Unable to execute the query.</p>"
     . "<p>Error code " . mysqli_errno($DBConnect)
     . ": " . mysqli_error($DBConnect)) . "</p>";
echo "<p>Successfully executed the query.</p>";
$NumRows = mysqli_num_rows($QueryResult);
$NumFields = mysqli_num_fields($QueryResult);
if ($NumRows != 0 && $NumFields != 0)
     echo "<p>Your query returned " .
mysqli_num_rows($QueryResult) . " rows and "
     . mysqli_num_fields($QueryResult) . " fields.</p>";
else
     echo "<p>Your query returned no results.</p>";
mysqli_close($DBConnect);
```


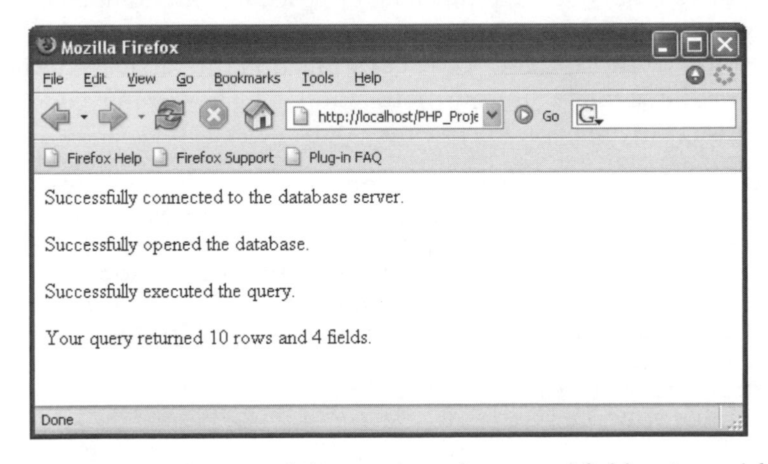

Figure 9-8 Output of the number of rows and fields returned from a query

Next, you add statements to the FlightlogEntries.php script that print the number of returned rows and fields.

To add statements to the FlightlogEntries.php script that print the number of returned rows and fields:

1. Return to the **FlightlogEntries.php** document in your text editor.
2. Add the following statements above the above the `mysqli_close($DBConnect);` statement:

```
$NumRows = mysqli_num_rows($QueryResult);
$NumFields = mysqli_num_fields($QueryResult);
echo "<p>Your query returned the following "
     . mysqli_num_rows($QueryResult)
     . " rows and ". mysqli_num_fields($QueryResult)
     . " fields:</p>";
```

3. Save the **FlightlogEntries.php** file and open it in your Web browser by entering the following URL: **http://localhost/PHP_Projects/Chapter.09/Chapter/FlightlogEntries.php**. Your Web page should appear the same as it did before you added modified the code to use `mysqli_fetch_assoc()` functions.
4. Close your Web browser window.

Closing Query Results

When you are finished working with query results retrieved with the `mysqli_query()` function, you should use the `mysqli_free_result()` function to close the resultset. This ensures that the resultset doesn't keep taking up space in your computer's memory. (As you'll recall, you need to close a database connection for the same reason.) To close the resultset, pass to the `mysqli_free_result()` function the variable containing the result pointer from the `mysqli_query()` function. The following code uses the `mysqli_free_result()` function to close the `$QueryResult` variable:

```
$SQLstring = "SELECT * FROM inventory";
$QueryResult = @mysqli_query($DBConnect, $SQLstring)
     Or die("<p>Unable to execute the query.</p>"
     . "<p>Error code " . mysqli_errno($DBConnect)
     . ": " . mysqli_error($DBConnect)) . "</p>";
echo "<p>Successfully executed the query.</p>";
...
mysqli_free_result($QueryResult);
mysqli_close($DBConnect);
```

You can only use the `mysqli_free_result()` function with SQL statements that return results, such as `SELECT` queries. If you attempt to use the `mysqli_free_result()` function with SQL statements that do not return results, such as the `CREATE DATABASE` and `CREATE TABLE` statements, you receive an error.

Next, you add a `mysqli_free_result()` function to the FlightlogEntries.php script.

To add a `mysqli_free_result()` function to the FlightlogEntries.php script:

1. Return to the **FlightlogEntries.php** document in your text editor.
2. Add the following statement above the `mysqli_close()` statement:

   ```
   mysqli_free_result($QueryResult);
   ```

3. Save the **FlightlogEntries.php** file and close it in your text editor. Then open the script in your Web browser by entering the following URL: **http://localhost/PHP_Projects/Chapter.09/Chapter/FlightlogEntries.php**. Your Web page should appear the same as it did before you added the `mysqli_free_result()` function.
4. Close your Web browser window.

WORKING WITH DATABASES AND TABLES

In this section, you learn how to use PHP to work with MySQL databases and tables. More specifically, you learn how to create and delete databases and tables. Again, keep in mind that the SQL statements in this section are identical to the SQL statements you saw in Chapter 8. The only difference is that they are executed with PHP instead of with the MySQL Monitor.

For information that you want to store permanently, you should use the MySQL Monitor instead of PHP to create and delete databases and tables. Creating and deleting databases and tables with PHP is most useful when you only need to temporarily store information for the current Web browser session.

Creating and Deleting Databases

You use the `CREATE DATABASE` statement with the `mysqli_query()` function to create a new database. The following statements create a database named `real_estate`:

```
$SQLstring = "CREATE DATABASE real_estate";
$QueryResult = @mysqli_query($DBConnect, $SQLstring)
     Or die("<p>Unable to execute the query.</p>"
     . "<p>Error code " . mysqli_errno($DBConnect)
     . ": " . mysqli_error($DBConnect)) . "</p>";
echo "<p>Successfully executed the query.</p>";
mysqli_close($DBConnect);
```

If the `mysqli_query()` function successfully creates the database, you see the "Successfully executed the query" message shown in the preceding example. If the database already exists, you see the error code and message shown in Figure 9-9.

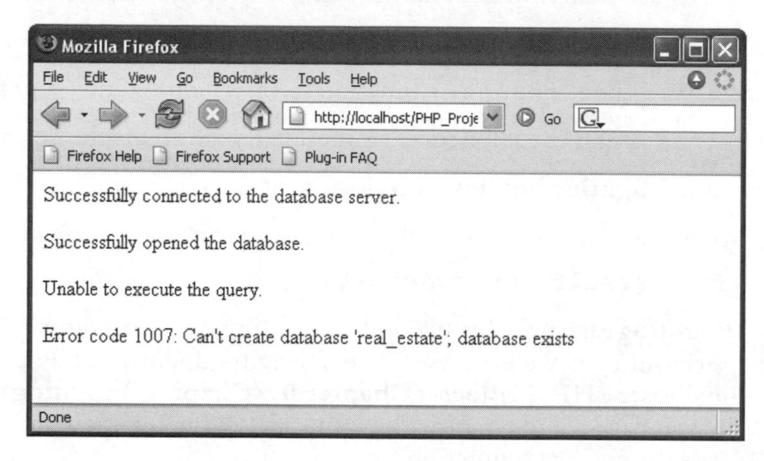

Figure 9-9 Error code and message that prints when you attempt to create a database that already exists

To avoid the error message shown in Figure 9-9, you should use the `mysqli_db_select()` function to check whether a database exists before you create or delete it. The following code attempts to select the real_estate database with the `mysqli_db_select()` function. Notice that the `mysqli_db_select()` function is preceded by the error control operator to suppress errors. If the `mysqli_db_select()` function successfully selects the `real_estate` database, the message "The real_estate database already exists!" prints to the Web browser. Otherwise, the statements in the `else` clause create the database.

```
$DBName = "real_estate";
if (@mysqli_select_db($DBConnect, $DBName))
     echo "<p>The $DBName database already exists!</p>";
else {
     $SQLstring = "CREATE DATABASE $DBName";
     $QueryResult = @mysqli_query($DBConnect, $SQLstring)
           Or die("<p>Unable to execute the query.</p>"
           . "<p>Error code " . mysqli_errno($DBConnect)
           . ": " . mysqli_error($DBConnect)) . "</p>";
     echo "<p>Successfully created the database.</p>";
mysqli_select_db($DBConnect, $DBName)
}
mysqli_close($DBConnect);
```

As with the MySQL Monitor, creating a new database does not select it. To use a new database, you must select it by executing the **mysqli_select_db()** function. The **real_estate** database is selected at the end of the **else** clause in the preceding code.

Deleting a database is almost identical to creating one, except that you use the **DROP DATABASE** statement instead of the **CREATE DATABASE** statement with the **mysqli_query()** function. The following code demonstrates how to delete the **real_estate** database. Notice that the code uses the same error-handling functionality as the code that created the database.

```
$DBName = "real_estate";
...
if (@!mysqli_select_db($DBConnect, $DBName))
     echo "<p>The $DBName database does not exist!</p>";
else {
     $SQLstring = "DROP DATABASE $DBName";
     $QueryResult = @mysqli_query($DBConnect, $SQLstring)
           Or die("<p>Unable to execute the query.</p>"
           . "<p>Error code " . mysqli_errno($DBConnect)
           . ": " . mysqli_error($DBConnect)) . "</p>";
     echo "<p>Successfully deleted the database.</p>";
}
mysqli_close($DBConnect);
```

In the rest of this chapter, you work on a Web site for registering students in scuba diving classes for a company named Aqua Don's Scuba School. Student information and class registrations will be stored in a MySQL database named **scuba_school** consisting of two tables: **divers** and **registration**. The **divers** table contains each diver's ID, along with other personal information. The **registration** table contains a record for each class in which a diver enrolls. The **divers** table is the primary table, and the **diverID** field acts as the primary key. The **diverID** field also acts as the foreign key in the **registration** table. Because each student can enroll in more than one class, the relationship between the **students** table and the **registration** table is one-to-many; the **students** table is the one side of the relationship, and the **registration** table is the many side of the relationship. Your Chapter directory for Chapter 9 contains a document named Registration.html that you will use to call some PHP scripts that access the MySQL database. Figure 9-10 shows the Registration.html page in a Web browser.

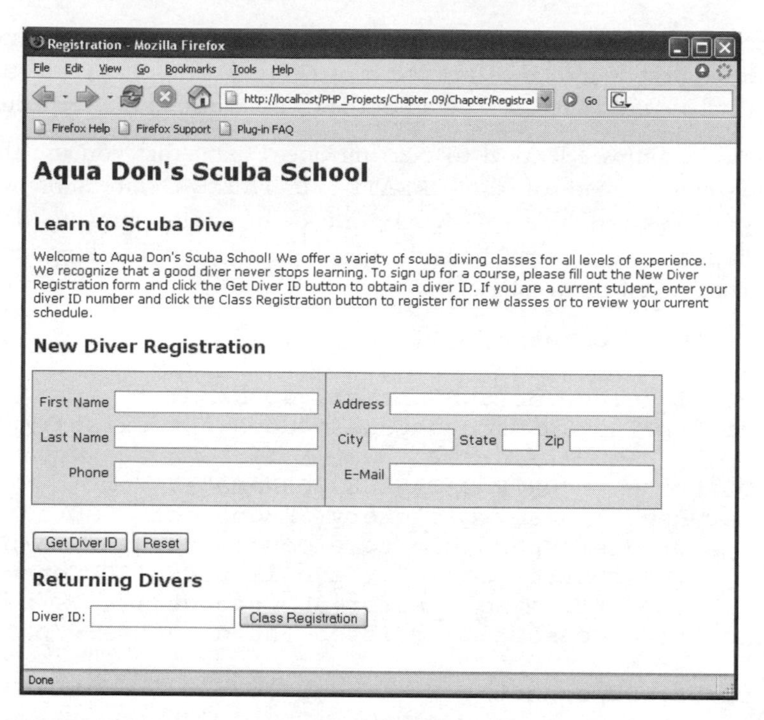

Figure 9-10 Registration.html page in a Web browser

First, you create a script named GetDiverID.php that registers divers with Aqua Don's Scuba School. You add code to the GetDiverID.php script that creates the `scuba_school` database the first time the script is called.

To create the GetDiverID.php script:

1. Create a new document in your text editor.
2. Type the `<!DOCTYPE>` declaration, `<html>` element, header information, and `<body>` element. Use the strict DTD and "Register Diver" as the content of the `<title>` element.
3. Add the following `<link>` element above the closing `</head>` tag to link to the php_styles.css style sheet in your Chapter directory:

```
<link rel="stylesheet" href="php_styles.css" type="text/css" />
```

4. Add the following heading element to the document body:

```
<h1>Aqua Don's Scuba School Registration</h1>
```

5. Add the following script section to the end of the document body:

```
<?php
?>
```

6. Add the following statements to the script section to ensure that users enter all the fields in New Diver Registration form:

```
if (empty($_GET['first_name']) || empty($_GET['last_name']) ||
empty($_GET['phone']) || empty($_GET['address']) ||
empty($_GET['city']) || empty($_GET['state']) ||
empty($_GET['zip']) || empty($_GET['email']))
     exit("<p>You must enter values in all fields of the New
Diver Registration form! Click your browser's Back button to
return to the previous page.</p>");
```

7. Add the following statements to the end of the script section to connect to the database server. Replace `user` and `password` with the MySQL user-name and password you created in Chapter 8.

```
$DBConnect = @mysqli_connect("localhost", "user", "password")
     Or die("<p>Unable to connect to the database server.</p>"
     . "<p>Error code " . mysqli_connect_errno()
     . ": " . mysqli_connect_error()) . "</p>";
```


8. Add the following statements, which create and select the `scuba_school` database. The contents of the conditional expression in the `if` statement only execute if the `mysqli_select_db()` function returns a value of false, which means the database does not exist. Because the contents of the `if` statement only execute the first time you open the script, the "Successfully created the database" message only appears once.

```
$DBName = "scuba_school";
if (!@mysqli_select_db($DBConnect, $DBName)) {
     $SQLstring = "CREATE DATABASE $DBName";
     $QueryResult = @mysqli_query($DBConnect, $SQLstring)
          Or die("<p>Unable to execute the query.</p>"
          . "<p>Error code " . mysqli_errno($DBConnect)
          . ": " . mysqli_error($DBConnect)) . "</p>";
     echo "<p>Successfully created the database.</p>";
     mysqli_select_db($DBConnect, $DBName);
}
```

9. Add the following statement to the end of the script section to close the database connection:

```
mysqli_close($DBConnect);
```

10. Save the document as **GetDiverID.php** in the Chapter directory for Chapter 9.

Creating and Deleting Tables

To create a table, you use the `CREATE TABLE` statement with the `mysqli_query()` function. Be sure you have executed the `mysqli_select_db()` function before executing the `CREATE TABLE` statement or you might create your new table in the wrong database. The following code creates a table named `commercial` in the `real_estate` database.

```
$DBName = "real_estate";
...
$SQLstring = "CREATE TABLE commercial (city VARCHAR(25), state
VARCHAR(25), sale_or_lease VARCHAR(25), type_of_use VARCHAR(40),
price INT, size INT)";
$QueryResult = @mysqli_query($DBConnect, $SQLstring)
     Or die("<p>Unable to execute the query.</p>"
     . "<p>Error code " . mysqli_errno($DBConnect)
     . ": " . mysqli_error($DBConnect)) . "</p>";
echo "<p>Successfully created the table.</p>";
mysqli_close($DBConnect);
```

With the preceding code, if the table already exists in the selected database, you will see the error code and message shown in Figure 9-11.

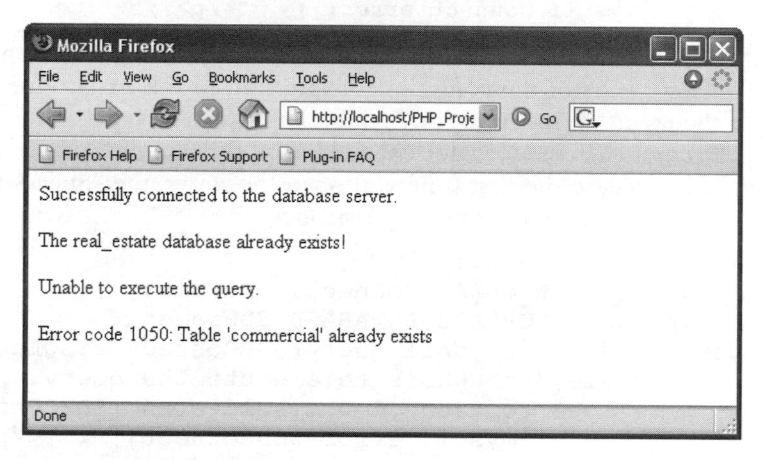

Figure 9-11 Error code and message that prints when you attempt to create a table that already exists

To prevent your code from attempting to create a table that already exists, use a `mysqli_query()` function that attempts to select records from the table. If the function executes successfully and returns a value of true, the table already exists. The following code demonstrates how to check whether a table exists before attempting to create it:

```
$DBName = "real_estate";
...
$TableName = "commercial";
$SQLstring = "SELECT * FROM $TableName";
$QueryResult = @mysqli_query($DBConnect, $SQLstring);
```

```
if ($QueryResult)
     echo "<p>The $TableName table already exists!</p>";
else {
     $SQLstring = "CREATE TABLE commercial (city VARCHAR(25),
     state VARCHAR(25), sale_or_lease VARCHAR(25),
     type_of_use VARCHAR(40), price INT, size INT)";
     $QueryResult = @mysqli_query($DBConnect, $SQLstring)
          Or die("<p>Unable to execute the query.</p>"
          . "<p>Error code " . mysqli_errno($DBConnect)
          . ": " . mysqli_error($DBConnect)) . "</p>";
     echo "<p>Successfully created the table.</p>";
}
 mysqli_close($DBConnect);
```

Next, you add code to the GetDiverID.php script that creates the `divers` table the first time the script is called. The `divers` table will use the `diverID` field as the primary key. To identify a field as a primary key in MySQL, you include the `PRIMARY KEY` keywords when you first define a field with the `CREATE TABLE` statement. The `AUTO_INCREMENT` keyword is often used with a primary key to generate a unique ID for each new row in a table. The first row in a field that is created with the `AUTO_INCREMENT` keyword is assigned a value of 1. The value for each subsequently added row is incremented by 1 from the preceding row. Another keyword that is often used with primary keys is the `NOT NULL` keyword, which requires a field to include a value. As an example, the following SQL statement defines a primary key named `id` for the `inventory` table using the `SMALLINT` data type. The `id` field definition also includes the `NOT NULL` and `AUTO_INCREMENT` keywords.

```
CREATE TABLE inventory (id SMALLINT NOT NULL AUTO_INCREMENT
PRIMARY KEY, make VARCHAR(25), model VARCHAR(50), price FLOAT,
quantity INT);
```

When you add records to a table that includes an `AUTO_INCREMENT` field, you specify `NULL` as the field value. The following SQL statement inserts a new record into the `inventory` table of the `guitars` database. If this is the first record added to the table, its primary key will be a value of 1.

```
INSERT INTO inventory VALUES(NULL, 'Ovation',
'1777 LX Legend', 1049.00, NULL);
```

Next, you add code to the GetDiverID.php script that creates the `divers` table the first time the script is called. The `divers` table includes an autoincrementing primary key.

To add code to the GetDiverID.php script that creates the `divers` table the first time the script is called:

1. Return to the **GetDiverID.php** document in your text editor.

2. Add the following variable declarations and `mysqli_query()` statement to the end of the script section. The `mysqli_query()` statement selects all existing records from the `divers` table.

```
$TableName = "divers";
$SQLstring = "SELECT * FROM $TableName";
$QueryResult = @mysqli_query($DBConnect, $SQLstring);
```

3. Add the following `if` statement to the end of the script section. The statements in the `if` statement only execute if the `$QueryResult` variable contains a value of false, which means that it does not yet exist. Notice that the `CREATE TABLE` statement creates the `diverID` field as an autoincrementing primary key.

```
if (!$QueryResult) {
     $SQLstring = "CREATE TABLE divers (diverID SMALLINT NOT
          NULL AUTO_INCREMENT PRIMARY KEY, first VARCHAR(40),
          last VARCHAR(40), phone VARCHAR(40),
          address VARCHAR(40), city VARCHAR(40),
          state VARCHAR(2), zip VARCHAR(10))";
     $QueryResult = @mysqli_query($DBConnect, $SQLstring)
          Or die("<p>Unable to create the divers table.</p>"
          . "<p>Error code " . mysqli_errno($DBConnect)
          . ": " . mysqli_error($DBConnect)) . "</p>";
     echo "<p>Successfully created the divers table.</p>";
}
```

4. Save the **GetDiverID.php** document.

To delete a table, you use the `DROP TABLE` statement with the `mysqli_query()` function. The following code demonstrates how to delete the `commercial` table using similar error-handling functionality as the code that created the table:

```
$DBName = "real_estate";
...
$TableName = "commercial";
$SQLstring = "SELECT * FROM $TableName";
$QueryResult = @mysqli_query($DBConnect, $SQLstring);
if (!$QueryResult)
     echo "<p>The $TableName table does not exist!</p>";
else {
     $SQLstring = "DROP TABLE commercial";
     $QueryResult = @mysqli_query($DBConnect, $SQLstring)
           Or die("<p>Unable to execute the query.</p>"
           . "<p>Error code " . mysqli_errno($DBConnect)
           . ": " . mysqli_error($DBConnect)) . "</p>";
     echo "<p>Successfully deleted the table.</p>";
}
mysqli_close($DBConnect);
```

MANIPULATING RECORDS

In this section, you learn how to use PHP to add, update, and delete database records.

Adding, Deleting, and Updating Records

To add records to a table, you use the **INSERT** and **VALUES** keywords with the mysqli_query() function. Remember that the values you enter in the VALUES list must be in the same order in which you defined the table fields. For example, the following statements add a new row to the inventory table in the guitars database:

```
$SQLstring = "INSERT INTO inventory VALUES('Ovation',
      '1777 LX Legend', 1049.00, 2)";
$QueryResult = @mysqli_query($DBConnect, $SQLstring)
      Or die("<p>Unable to execute the query.</p>"
      . "<p>Error code " . mysqli_errno($DBConnect)
      . ": " . mysqli_error($DBConnect)) . "</p>";
echo "<p>Successfully added the record.</p>";
```

Also remember that you must specify NULL in any fields for which you do not have a value. For example, if you do not know the quantity of guitars in stock for the Ovation guitar, you can enter NULL as the last item in the VALUES list, as follows:

```
$SQLstring = "INSERT INTO inventory VALUES('Ovation',
      '1777 LX Legend', 1049.00, NULL)";
```

To add multiple records to a database, you use the LOAD DATA statement and the mysqli_query() function with a local text file containing the records you want to add. The following statement loads a file named inventory.txt into the inventory table in the guitars database:

```
$SQLstring = "LOAD DATA LOCAL INFILE 'inventory.txt'
     INTO TABLE inventory";
```

To update records in a table, you use the UPDATE, SET, and WHERE keywords with the mysqli_query() function. The UPDATE keyword specifies the name of the table to update and the SET keyword specifies the value to assign to the fields in the records that match the condition in the WHERE keyword. For example, the following statements modify the price of the Fender DG7 guitar to $368.20:

```
$SQLstring = "UPDATE inventory SET price=368.20
     WHERE make='Fender' AND model='DG7'";
$QueryResult = @mysqli_query($DBConnect, $SQLstring)
     Or die("<p>Unable to execute the query.</p>"
     . "<p>Error code " . mysqli_errno($DBConnect)
     . ": " . mysqli_error($DBConnect)) . "</p>";
echo "<p>Successfully modified the records.</p>";
```

To delete records in a table, you use the DELETE and WHERE keywords with the mysqli_query() function. Remember that the WHERE keyword determines which records to delete in the table. For example, the following statement deletes the "Taylor 210 Dreadnought" record from the inventory table in the guitars database:

```
$SQLstring = "DELETE FROM inventory WHERE make='Taylor'
     AND model='210 Dreadnought'";
$QueryResult = @mysqli_query($DBConnect, $SQLstring)
     Or die("<p>Unable to execute the query.</p>"
     . "<p>Error code " . mysqli_errno($DBConnect)
     . ": " . mysqli_error($DBConnect)) . "</p>";
echo "<p>Successfully deleted the records.</p>";
```

To delete all the records in a table, omit the WHERE keyword. For example, the following statement deletes all the records in the inventory table:

```
$SQLstring = "DELETE FROM inventory";
```

Next, you add code to the GetDiverID.php script that adds a new diver record to the divers table in the scuba_school database. You also use the mysqli_insert_id() function, which returns the ID created with AUTO_INCREMENT in the last INSERT operation. You pass to the mysqli_insert_id() function the variable to which you assigned the database connection with the mysqli_connect() function. The mysqli_insert_id() function is useful when you need to find the primary key created for new records you add to a database table.

To add code to the GetDiverID.php script that adds a new diver record to the divers table in the scuba_school database:

1. Return to the **GetDiverID.php** document in your text editor.
2. Add the following statements above the mysqli_close() statement to copy the values that were passed from the form in the Registration.html to PHP variables:

```
$First = addslashes($_GET['first_name']);
$Last = addslashes($_GET['last_name']);
$Phone = addslashes($_GET['phone']);
$Address = addslashes($_GET['address']);
$City = addslashes($_GET['city']);
$State = addslashes($_GET['state']);
$Zip = addslashes($_GET['zip']);
$Email = addslashes($_GET['email']);
```

3. Add the following statements above the `mysqli_close()` statement to build a query string that will insert the values into the `diver` table:

```
$SQLstring = "INSERT INTO divers VALUES(NULL, '$First', '$Last',
'$Phone', '$Address', '$City', '$State', '$Zip')";
```

4. Add the following statements above the `mysqli_close()` statement to execute the query:

```
$QueryResult = @mysqli_query($DBConnect, $SQLstring)
     Or die("<p>Unable to execute the query.</p>"
          . "<p>Error code " . mysqli_errno($DBConnect)
          . ": " . mysqli_error($DBConnect)) . "</p>";
```

5. Add the following `mysqli_insert_id()` statement above the `mysqli_close()` statement to assign the new primary key to the `$DiverID` variable:

```
$DiverID = mysqli_insert_id($DBConnect);
```

6. Finally, add the following text and elements to the end of the document body. The form allows users to register for classes by clicking the Register for Classes button, which opens a script named CourseListings.php. Notice that the form includes a hidden variable that is assigned the value of the `$DiverID` variable. This ensures that the diver ID is passed to the CourseListings.php script when the user clicks the Register for Classes button.

```
<p>Thanks <?= $First ?>! Your new diver ID is <strong><?=
$DiverID ?></strong>.</p>
<form action="CourseListings.php" method="get">
<p><input type="submit" value="Register for Classes" />
<input type="hidden" name="diverID" value="<?= $DiverID ?>"
/></p>
</form>
```

7. Save the **GetDiverID.php** document and close it in your text editor.

8. Open the **Registration.html** file in your Web browser by entering the following URL: **http://localhost/PHP_Projects/Chapter.09/Chapter/Registration.html**. Enter values into the New Diver Registration form and click the **Get Diver ID** button. You should be assigned a new diver ID of 1. You should see the Web page shown in Figure 9-12.

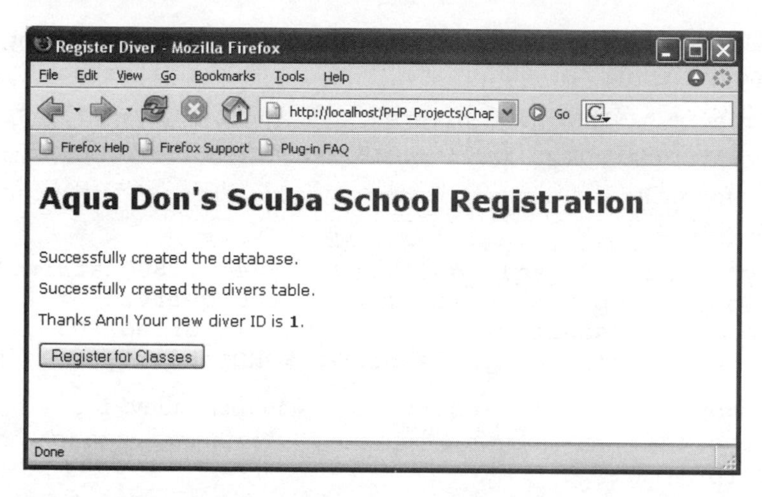

Figure 9-12 Register Diver Web page

9. Click your browser's Back button, enter some new values in the New Diver Registration form, and then click the **Get Diver ID** button. The new diver ID should be 2. Notice that the messages about successfully creating the database and `divers` table do not appear this time.
10. Close your Web browser window.

Next, you create the CourseListings.php script, which divers can use to register for classes.

To create the CourseListings.php script:

1. Create a new document in your text editor.
2. Type the `<!DOCTYPE>` declaration, `<html>` element, header information, and `<body>` element. Use the strict DTD and "Course Listings" as the content of the `<title>` element.
3. Add the following `<link>` element above the closing `</head>` tag to link to the php_styles.css style sheet in your Chapter directory:

```
<link rel="stylesheet" href="php_styles.css" type="text/css" />
```

4. Add the following heading element to the document body:

```
<h1>Aqua Don's Scuba School</h1>
<h2>Class Registration Form</h2>
```

5. Add the following script section to the end of the document body:

```
<?php
?>
```

6. Add the following statements to the script section to connect to the database server and open the `scuba_school` database. Replace *`user`* and *`password`* with the MySQL username and password you created in Chapter 8.

```
$DBConnect = @mysqli_connect("localhost", "user", "password")
     Or die("<p>Unable to connect to the database server.</p>"
     . "<p>Error code " . mysqli_connect_errno()
     . ": " . mysqli_connect_error()) . "</p>";
$DBName = "scuba_school";
@mysqli_select_db($DBConnect, $DBName)
     Or die("<p>Unable to select the database.</p>"
     . "<p>Error code " . mysqli_errno($DBConnect)
     . ": " . mysqli_error($DBConnect)) . "</p>";
```

7. Add the following statements to the end of the script section to ensure that users open the page with a valid diver ID:

```
$DiverID = $_GET['diverID'];
if (empty($DiverID))
     exit("<p>You must enter a diver ID! Click your browser's
Back button to return to the previous page.</p>");
$TableName = "divers";
$SQLstring = "SELECT * FROM $TableName WHERE diverID='$DiverID'";
$QueryResult = @mysqli_query($DBConnect, $SQLstring)
     Or die("<p>Unable to execute the query.</p>"
     . "<p>Error code " . mysqli_errno($DBConnect)
     . ": " . mysqli_error($DBConnect)) . "</p>";
if (mysqli_num_rows($QueryResult) == 0)
     die("<p>You must enter a valid diver ID! Click your
browser's Back button to return to the Registration form.</p.");
```

8. Add the following statement to the end of the script section to close the database connection:

```
mysqli_close($DBConnect);
```

9. Add the following form to the end of document body. This form allows divers to review their current schedule with the ReviewSchedule.php script.

```
<form method="get" action="ReviewSchedule.php">
<p><strong>Student ID: <?= $DiverID ?></strong>
<input type="submit" value=" Review Current Schedule " /><input
type="hidden" name="diverID" value="<?= $DiverID ?>" /></p>
</form>
```

9

10. Add the following form to the end of document body. This is the form divers use to register for classes with the RegisterDiver.php script.

```
<form method="get" action="RegisterDiver.php">
<p><strong>Select the class you would like to take:</strong><br />
<input type="radio" name="class" value="Beginning Open Water"
checked="checked" />Beginning Open Water<br />
<input type="radio" name="class" value="Advanced Open Water" />
Advanced Open Water<br />
<input type="radio" name="class" value="Rescue Diving" />
Rescue Diving<br />
<input type="radio" name="class"
value="Divemaster Certification" />Divemaster Certification<br />
<input type="radio" name="class"
value="Instructor Certification" />Instructor Certification</p>
<p><strong>Available Days and Times:</strong><br />
<select name="days">
<option selected="selected" value="Mondays and Wednesdays">
Mondays and Wednesdays</option>
<option value="Tuesdays and Thursdays">
Tuesdays and Thursdays</option>
<option value="Wednesdays and Fridays">
Wednesdays and Fridays</option>
</select>
<select name="time">
<option selected="selected" value="9 a.m. - 11 a.m.">9 a.m. - 11
a.m.</option>
<option value="1 p.m. - 3 p.m.">1 p.m. - 3 p.m.</option>
<option value="6 p.m. - 8 p.m.">6 p.m. - 8 p.m.</option>
</select><input type="hidden" name="diverID"
value="<?= $DiverID ?>" /></p>
<p><input type="submit" value=" Register " />
<input type="reset" /></p>
</form>
```

11. Save the document as **CourseListings.php** in the Chapter directory for Chapter 9, and then close it in your text editor.

12. Open the **Registration.html** file in your Web browser by entering the following URL: **http://localhost/PHP_Projects/Chapter.09/Chapter/Registration.html**. Enter an existing diver ID into the Returning Divers form and click the **Class Registration** button. You should see the Web page shown in Figure 9-13.

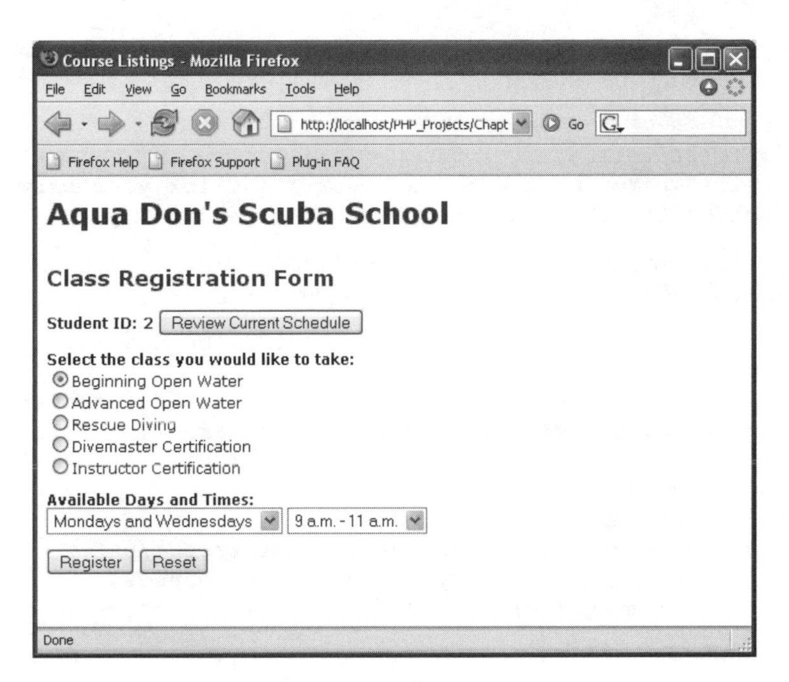

Figure 9-13 Course Listings Web page

13. Leave the Course Listings page open in your Web browser.

Next, you create the RegisterDiver.php script, which adds diver registration information to the `registration` table.

To create the RegisterDiver.php script:

1. Create a new document in your text editor.
2. Type the `<!DOCTYPE>` declaration, `<html>` element, header information, and `<body>` element. Use the strict DTD and "Register Diver" as the content of the `<title>` element.
3. Add the following `<link>` element above the closing `</head>` tag to link to the php_styles.css style sheet in your Chapter directory:

```
<link rel="stylesheet" href="php_styles.css" type="text/css" />
```

4. Add the following heading element to the document body:

```
<h1>Aqua Don's Scuba School</h1>
<h2>Registration Confirmation</h2>
```

5. Add the following script section to the end of the document body:

```
<?php
?>
```

6. Add the following statements to the script section to ensure that users open the page with a valid diver ID:

```
$DiverID = $_GET['diverID'];
if (empty($DiverID))
     exit("<p>You must enter a diver ID! Click your browser's
Back button to return to the previous page.</p>");
```

7. Add the following statements to the end of the script section to connect to the database server and open the `scuba_school` database:

```
$DBConnect = @mysqli_connect("localhost", "dongosselin",
"rosebud")
     Or die("<p>Unable to connect to the database server.</p>"
     . "<p>Error code " . mysqli_connect_errno()
     . ": " . mysqli_connect_error()) . "</p>";
$DBName = "scuba_school";
@mysqli_select_db($DBConnect, $DBName)
     Or die("<p>Unable to select the database.</p>"
     . "<p>Error code " . mysqli_errno($DBConnect)
     . ": " . mysqli_error($DBConnect)) . "</p>";
```

8. Add the following statements to the end of the script section to create the registration table if it does not exist:

```
$TableName = "registration";
$SQLstring = "SELECT * FROM $TableName";
$QueryResult = @mysqli_query($DBConnect, $SQLstring);
if (!$QueryResult) {
     $SQLstring = "CREATE TABLE registration (diverID SMALLINT,
class VARCHAR(40), days VARCHAR(40), time VARCHAR(40))";
     $QueryResult = @mysqli_query($DBConnect, $SQLstring)
           Or die("<p>Unable to create the registration
           table.</p>"
          . "<p>Error code " . mysqli_errno($DBConnect)
          . ": " . mysqli_error($DBConnect)) . "</p>";
     echo "<p>Successfully created the registration table.</p>";
}
```

9. Add the following statements to the end of the script section to register the diver in the selected class:

```
$Class = $_GET['class'];
$Days = $_GET['days'];
$Time = $_GET['time'];
$SQLstring = "INSERT INTO $TableName VALUES('$DiverID', '$Class',
     '$Days', '$Time')";
$QueryResult = @mysqli_query($DBConnect, $SQLstring)
     Or die("<p>Unable to execute the query.</p>"
     . "<p>Error code " . mysqli_errno($DBConnect)
     . ": " . mysqli_error($DBConnect)) . "</p>";
```

10. Add the following statement to the end of the script section to close the database connection:

```
mysqli_close($DBConnect);
```

11. Finally, add the following text and elements to the end of the document body:

```
<p>You are registered for <?= "$Class on $Days, $Time" ?>. Click
your browser's Back button to register for another course or
review your schedule.</p>
```

12. Save the document as **RegisterDiver.php** in the Chapter directory for Chapter 9, and then close it in your text editor.

13. Return to the **Course Listings** page in your Web browser. Select a class, as well as the days and times you want to take it, and then click the **Register** button. You should see a message indicating that the `registration` table was created successfully, along with a message confirming your registration in the class, as shown in Figure 9-14.

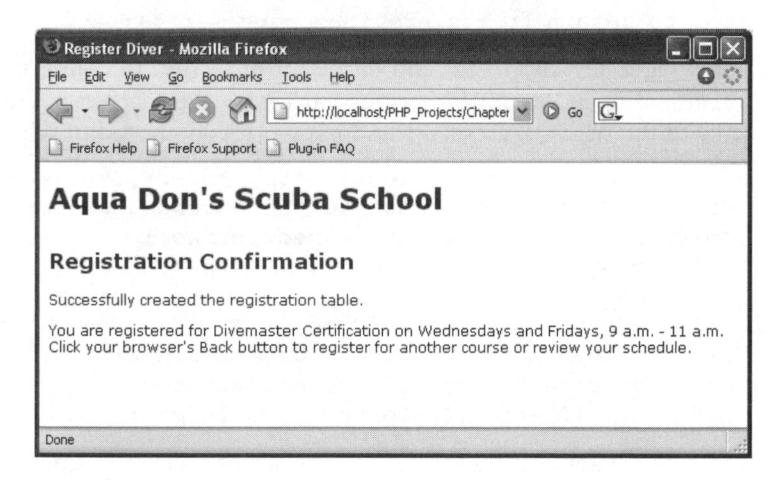

Figure 9-14 Registration Confirmation Web page

14. Click your browser's **Back** button to return to the Course Listings page.

The last script you create is the ReviewSchedule.php script, which allows divers to review the classes in which they are registered.

To create the ReviewSchedule.php script:

1. Create a new document in your text editor.
2. Type the `<!DOCTYPE>` declaration, `<html>` element, header information, and `<body>` element. Use the strict DTD and "Review Schedule" as the content of the `<title>` element.

3. Add the following `<link>` element above the closing `</head>` tag to link to the php_styles.css style sheet in your Chapter directory:

```
<link rel="stylesheet" href="php_styles.css" type="text/css" />
```

4. Add the following heading element to the document body:

```
<h1>Aqua Don's Scuba School</h1>
<h2>This is your current schedule:</h2>
```

5. Add the following script section to the end of the document body:

```
<?php
?>
```

6. Add the following statements to the script section to ensure that users open the page with a valid diver ID:

```
$DiverID = $_GET['diverID'];
if (empty($DiverID))
     exit("<p>You must enter a diver ID! Click your browser's
Back button to return to the previous page.</p>");
```

7. Add the following statements to the end of the script section to connect to the database server and open the `scuba_school` database. Replace *`user`* and *`password`* with the MySQL username and password you created in Chapter 8.

```
$DBConnect = @mysqli_connect("localhost", "user", "password")
     Or die("<p>Unable to connect to the database server.</p>"
     . "<p>Error code " . mysqli_connect_errno()
     . ": " . mysqli_connect_error()) . "</p>";
$DBName = "scuba_school";
@mysqli_select_db($DBConnect, $DBName)
     Or die("<p>Unable to select the database.</p>"
     . "<p>Error code " . mysqli_errno($DBConnect)
     . ": " . mysqli_error($DBConnect)) . "</p>";
```

8. Add the following statements to the end of the script section to query the database for all records that match the diver ID:

```
$TableName = "registration";
$SQLstring = "SELECT * FROM $TableName WHERE diverID='$DiverID'";
$QueryResult = @mysqli_query($DBConnect, $SQLstring)
     Or die("<p>Unable to execute the query.</p>"
     . "<p>Error code " . mysqli_errno($DBConnect)
     . ": " . mysqli_error($DBConnect)) . "</p>";
```

9. Next, add the following statements to the end of the script section, which print a message if the diver has not yet registered for any classes:

```
if (mysqli_num_rows($QueryResult) == 0)
     die("<p>You have not registered for any classes! Click your
     browser's Back button to return to the previous page.</p>");
```

10. Add the following statements to the end of the script section to print the results in an HTML table:

```
echo "<table width='100%' border='1'>";
echo "<tr><th>Class</th><th>Days</th>
<th>Time</th></tr>";
$Row = mysqli_fetch_assoc($QueryResult);
do {
     echo "<tr><td>{$Row['class']}</td>";
     echo "<td>{$Row['days']}</td>";
     echo "<td>{$Row['time']}</td></tr>";
     $Row = mysqli_fetch_assoc($QueryResult);
} while ($Row);
```

11. Finally, add the following statements to the end of the script section to close the database connection and the query results:

```
mysqli_free_result($QueryResult);
mysqli_close($DBConnect);
```


12. Save the document as **ReviewSchedule.php** in the Chapter directory for Chapter 9, and then close it in your text editor.

13. Return to the **Course Listings** page in your Web browser and register for several other classes. After you have registered for a few classes, click the Review Current Schedule button to display your schedule. Figure 9-15 shows the Review Schedule Web page for a diver who is signed up for three classes.

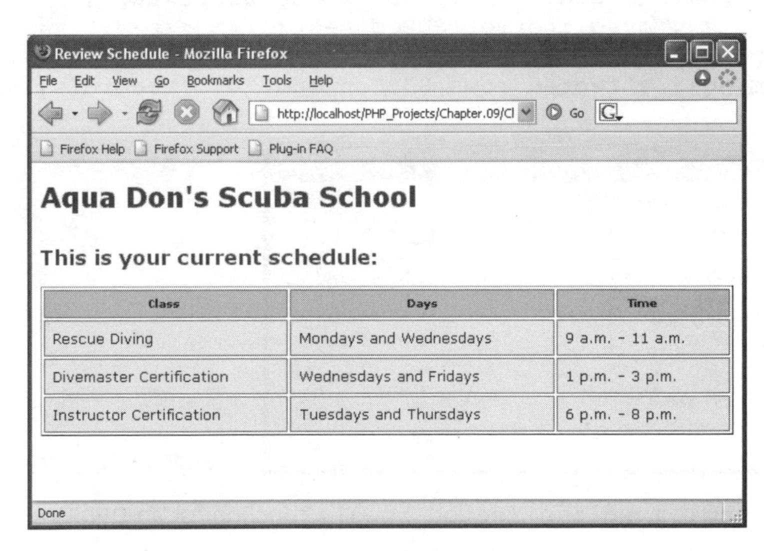

Figure 9-15 Review Schedule Web page

Returning Information on Affected Records

As you have learned, the `mysqli_num_rows()` function returns the number of rows in a query result and the `mysqli_num_fields()` function returns the number of fields in a query result. In addition, PHP includes two functions, `mysqli_affected_rows()` and `mysqli_info()`, which you can use to return information on the records that were affected by a query. First, you learn how to use the `mysqli_affected_rows()` function.

Using the mysqli_affected_rows() Function

With queries that return results, such as `SELECT` queries, you can use the `mysqli_num_rows()` function to find the number of records returned from the query. However, with queries that modify tables but do not return results, such as `INSERT`, `UPDATE`, and `DELETE` queries, you can use the `mysqli_affected_rows()` function to determine the number of affected rows.You pass to the `mysqli_affected_rows()` function the variable containing the database connection returned from the `mysqli_connect()` function—not the variable containing the result pointer from the `mysqli_query()` function. For example, the following statements print the number of rows affected by an `UPDATE` query. Figure 9-16 shows the output in a Web browser.

```
$SQLstring = "UPDATE inventory SET price=368.20
     WHERE make='Fender' AND model='DG7'";
$QueryResult = @mysqli_query($DBConnect, $SQLstring)
     Or die("<p>Unable to execute the query.</p>"
     . "<p>Error code " . mysqli_errno($DBConnect)
     . ": " . mysqli_error($DBConnect)) . "</p>";
echo "<p>Successfully updated "
     . mysqli_affected_rows($DBConnect) . " record(s).</p>";
```

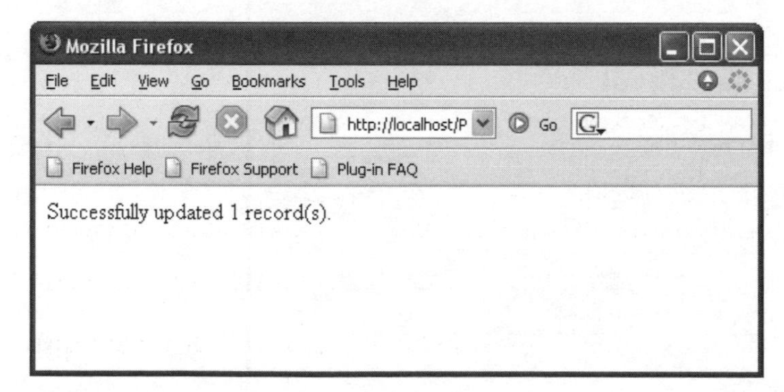

Figure 9-16 Output of `mysqli_affected_rows()` function for an `UPDATE` query

The following code contains another example of the `mysqli_affected_rows()` function, this time with a `DELETE` query:

```
$SQLstring = "DELETE FROM inventory WHERE make='Washburn'";
$QueryResult = @mysqli_query($DBConnect, $SQLstring)
     Or die("<p>Unable to execute the query.</p>"
     . "<p>Error code " . mysqli_errno($DBConnect)
     . ": " . mysqli_error($DBConnect)) . "</p>";
echo "<p>Successfully deleted "
     . mysqli_affected_rows($DBConnect) . " record(s).</p>";
```

Using the `mysqli_info()` Function

For queries that add or update records, or that alter a table's structure, you can use the `mysqli_info()` function to return information about the query. The `mysqli_info()` function returns the number of operations for various types of actions, depending on the type of query. For example, with `INSERT` queries, the `mysqli_info()` function returns the number of records added and duplicated, along with the number of warnings. However, for `LOAD DATA` queries, the `mysqli_info()` function returns the number of records added, deleted, and skipped, along with the number of warnings. As with the `mysqli_affected_rows()` function, you pass to the `mysqli_info()` function the variable containing the database connection from the `mysqli_connect()` function. The `mysqli_info()` function returns information about the last query that was executed on the database connection. However, the `mysqli_info()` function returns information about queries that match one of the following formats:

9

- `INSERT INTO...SELECT...`
- `INSERT INTO...VALUES (...),(...),(...)`
- `LOAD DATA INFILE ...`
- `ALTER TABLE ...`
- `UPDATE ...`

For any queries that do not match one of the preceding formats, the `mysqli_info()` function returns an empty string. Notice that the format for adding records with the `INSERT` and `VALUES` keywords includes multiple value sets. The `mysqli_info()` function only returns query information when you add multiple records with the `INSERT` keyword. For example, the `mysqli_info()` function in the following example returns an empty string because the `INSERT` query only adds a single record:

```
$SQLstring = "INSERT INTO inventory VALUES('Ovation',
      '1777 LX Legend', 1049.00, 2)";
$QueryResult = @mysqli_query($DBConnect, $SQLstring)
      Or die("<p>Unable to execute the query.</p>"
      . "<p>Error code " . mysqli_errno($DBConnect)
      . ": " . mysqli_error($DBConnect)) . "</p>";
echo "<p>Successfully added the record.</p>";
echo "<p>" . mysqli_info($DBConnect) . "</p>";
```

In comparison, the following statements print the query information shown in Figure 9-17 because the INSERT query adds multiple records:

```
$SQLstring = "INSERT INTO inventory
     VALUES('Ovation', '1777 LX Legend', 1049.00, 2),
     ('Ovation', '1861 Standard Balladeer', 699.00, 1),
     ('Ovation', 'Tangent Series T357', 569.00, 3)";
$QueryResult = @mysqli_query($DBConnect, $SQLstring)
     Or die("<p>Unable to execute the query.</p>"
     . "<p>Error code " . mysqli_errno($DBConnect)
     . ": " . mysqli_error($DBConnect)) . "</p>";
echo "<p>Successfully added the records.</p>";
echo "<p>" . mysqli_info($DBConnect) . "</p>";
```

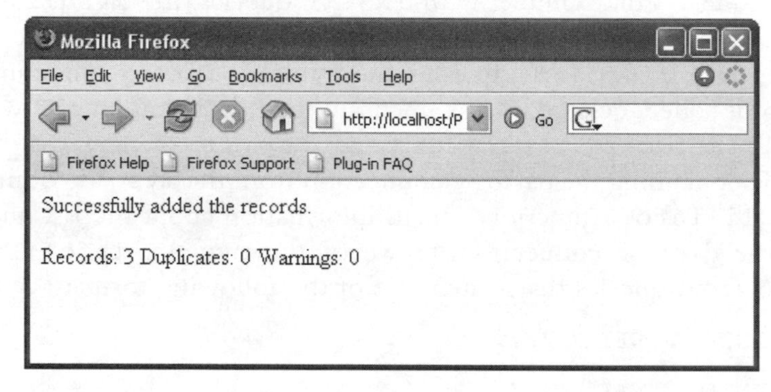

Figure 9-17 Output of `mysqli_info()` function for an INSERT query that adds multiple records

The `mysqli_info()` function also returns information for LOAD DATA queries. The following statements print the output shown in Figure 9-18:

```
$SQLstring = "LOAD DATA LOCAL INFILE 'c:/temp/inventory.txt'
     INTO TABLE inventory;";
$QueryResult = @mysqli_query($DBConnect, $SQLstring)
     Or die("<p>Unable to execute the query.</p>"
     . "<p>Error code " . mysqli_errno($DBConnect)
     . ": " . mysqli_error($DBConnect)) . "</p>";
echo "<p>Successfully added the records.</p>";
echo "<p>" . mysqli_info($DBConnect) . "</p>";
```

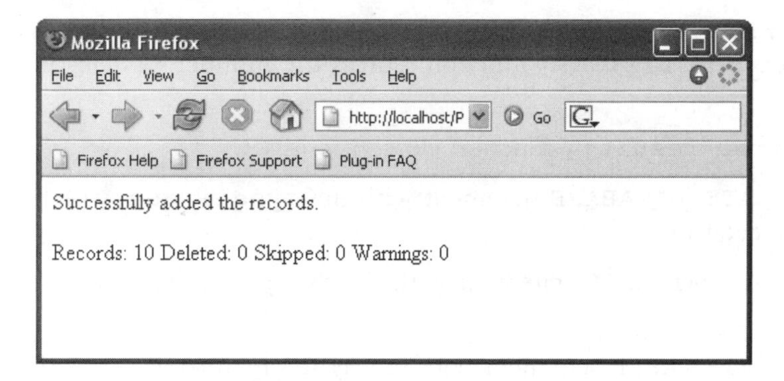

Figure 9-18 Output of `mysqli_info()` function for a `LOAD DATA` query

Chapter Summary

- The `mysqli_connect()` function opens a connection to a MySQL database server.
- The `mysqli_close()` function closes a database connection.
- The `mysqli_select_db()` function selects a database.
- Writing code that anticipates and handles potential problems is often called bulletproofing.
- The error control operator (@) suppresses error messages.
- The `die()` and `exit()` functions terminate script execution.
- The `mysqli_connect_errno()` function returns the error code from the last database connection attempt or zero if no error occurred.
- The `mysqli_connect_error()` function returns the error message from the last database connection attempt or an empty string if no error occurred.
- The `mysqli_errno()` function returns the error code from the last attempted MySQL function call or zero if no error occurred.
- The `mysqli_error()` function returns the error message from the last attempted MySQL function call or an empty string if no error occurred.
- The `mysqli_query()` function sends SQL statements to MySQL.
- A result pointer is a special type of variable that refers to the currently selected row in a resultset.
- The `mysqli_fetch_row()` function returns the fields in the current row of a resultset into an indexed array and moves the result pointer to the next row.
- The `mysqli_fetch_assoc()` function returns the fields in the current row of a resultset into an associative array and moves the result pointer to the next row.

- The `mysqli_num_rows()` function returns the number of rows in a query result, and the `mysqli_num_fields()` function returns the number of fields in a query result.
- The `mysqli_free_result()` function closes a resultset.
- You use the `CREATE DATABASE` statement with the `mysqli_query()` function to create a new database.
- You use the `DROP DATABASE` statement with the `mysqli_query()` function to delete a database.
- You use the `CREATE TABLE` statement with the `mysqli_query()` function to create a table.
- You use the `DROP TABLE` statement with the `mysqli_query()` function to delete a table.
- To identify a field as a primary key in MySQL, you include the `PRIMARY KEY` keywords when you first define a field with the `CREATE TABLE` statement. The `AUTO_INCREMENT` keyword is often used with a primary key to generate a unique ID for each new row in a table.
- You use the `INSERT` and `VALUES` keywords with the `mysqli_query()` function to add records to a table.
- You use the `LOAD DATA` statement and the `mysqli_query()` function with a local text file to add multiple records to a database.
- You use the `UPDATE`, `SET`, and `WHERE` keywords with the `mysqli_query()` function to update records in a table.
- You use the `DELETE` and `WHERE` keywords with the `mysqli_query()` function to delete records in a table.
- With queries that return results, such as `SELECT` queries, you can use the `mysqli_num_rows()` function to find the number of records returned from the query.
- The `mysqli_info()` function returns the number of operations for various types of actions, depending on the type of query.

Review Questions

1. MySQL support is enabled in PHP by default. True or False?
2. Which of the following functions closes a database connection?
   a. `close()`
   b. `mysqli_close()`
   c. `mysqli_free()`
   d. `mysqli_free_connect()`

3. To which of the following functions do you need to pass a variable representing the database connection? (Choose all that apply.)
   a. `mysqli_get_client_info()`
   b. `mysqli_get_host_info()`
   c. `mysqli_get_proto_info()`
   d. `mysqli_get_server_info()`
4. What is the correct syntax for selecting a database with the `mysqli_select_db()` function?
   a. `mysqli_select_db(connection)`
   b. `mysqli_select_db(database)`
   c. `mysqli_select_db(connection, database)`
   d. `database = mysqli_select_db(connection)`
5. Explain the types of errors that can occur when accessing MySQL databases and other types of data sources with PHP.
6. The following code structure prevents error messages from printing in the event that the database connection is not available. True or False?

```
$DBConnect = mysqli_connect("localhost", "dongosselin",
     "rosebud", "flightlog");
if (!$DBConnect)
      echo "<p>The database server is not available.</p>";
else  {
     echo "<p>Successfully connected to the database server.</p>";
     mysqli_close($DBConnect);
}
```

7. Explain the concept of bulletproofing your code.
8. Which of the following characters suppresses error messages in PHP?
   a. *
   b. &
   c. #
   d. @
9. Which of the following functions terminate script execution? (Choose all that apply.)
   a. `exit()`
   b. `bye()`
   c. `die()`
   d. `quit()`

10. Which of the following functions reports the error message from the last failed database connection attempt?
    a. `mysqli_connect_errno()`
    b. `mysqli_connect_error()`
    c. `mysqli_errno()`
    d. `mysqli_error()`
11. Explain what a result pointer is and how to create and use one.
12. Which of the following functions returns the fields in the current row of a resultset into an indexed array?
    a. `mysqli_data_fetch()`
    b. `mysqli_data_seek()`
    c. `mysqli_index_row()`
    d. `mysqli_fetch_row()`
13. Which of the following functions returns the fields in the current row of a resultset into an associative array?
    a. `mysqli_assoc_fetch()`
    b. `mysqli_fetch_keys()`
    c. `mysqli_fetch_assoc()`
    d. `mysqli_fetch_index()`
14. Write a simple code segment that demonstrates how to use the `mysqli_num_rows()` and `mysqli_num_fields()` functions to determine whether a SQL query returned results.
15. Which of the following functions closes a resultset to ensure that it doesn't keep taking up space in your computer's memory?
    a. `mysqli_free_result()`
    b. `mysqli_result_close()`
    c. `mysqli_free()`
    d. `mysqli_close_result()`
16. Write a simple code segment that demonstrates how to use the `mysqli_db_select()` function to check whether a database exists before you create or delete it.
17. Write a simple code segment that demonstrates how to use a `mysqli_query()` function to prevent your code from attempting to create a table that already exists.

18. Which of the following SQL keywords creates an autoincrementing field?
    a. `AUTO`
    b. `INCREMENT`
    c. `AUTO_INCREMENT`
    d. `AUTOINCREMENT`
19. Which of the following functions returns the number of rows affected by queries that do not return results, such as `INSERT`, `UPDATE`, and `DELETE` queries?
    a. `mysqli_affected_rows()`
    b. `mysqli_rows()`
    c. `mysqli_get_changed()`
    d. `mysqli_fetch_rows()`
20. The ________________ function returns the number of operations for various types of actions, depending on the type of query.
    a. `mysqli_get_info()`
    b. `mysqli_operations()`
    c. `mysqli_info()`
    d. `mysqli_fetch_actions()`

HANDS-ON PROJECTS

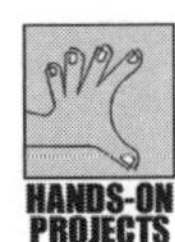

Hands-On Project 9-1

In this project, you create a hit counter script that keeps track of the number of hits a Web page receives. The number of hits will be stored as autoincrementing primary keys in MySQL.

1. Create a new document in your text editor and type the `<!DOCTYPE>` declaration, `<html>` element, document head, and `<body>` element. Use the strict DTD and "Hit Counter" as the content of the `<title>` element.
2. Add the following script section to the document body:

```
<?php
?>
```

3. Add the following statement to the script section to connect to the database. Replace *user* and *password* with the MySQL username and password you created in Chapter 8.

```
$DBConnect = @mysqli_connect("localhost", "user", "password")
     Or die("<p>Unable to connect to the database server.</p>"
     . "<p>Error code " . mysqli_connect_errno()
     . ": " . mysqli_connect_error()) . "</p>";
```

4. Add the following statements to the end of the script section to create a database named `hit_counter` if it does not already exist:

```
$DBName = "hit_counter";
if (!@mysqli_select_db($DBConnect, $DBName)) {
     $SQLstring = "CREATE DATABASE $DBName";
     $QueryResult = @mysqli_query($DBConnect, $SQLstring)
          Or die("<p>Unable to execute the query.</p>"
          . "<p>Error code " . mysqli_errno($DBConnect)
          . ": " . mysqli_error($DBConnect)) . "</p>";
     echo "<p>You are the first visitor!</p>";
     mysqli_select_db($DBConnect, $DBName);
}
```

5. Add the following statements to the end of the script section to create a table named `count` if it does not already exist. The table consists of a single autoincrementing primary key field named `countID`.

```
$TableName = "count";
$SQLstring = "SELECT * FROM $TableName";
$QueryResult = @mysqli_query($DBConnect, $SQLstring);
if (!$QueryResult) {
     $SQLstring = "CREATE TABLE $TableName (countID SMALLINT NOT
NULL AUTO_INCREMENT PRIMARY KEY)";
     $QueryResult = @mysqli_query($DBConnect, $SQLstring)
          Or die("<p>Unable to create the table.</p>"
          . "<p>Error code " . mysqli_errno($DBConnect)
          . ": " . mysqli_error($DBConnect)) . "</p>";
}
```

6. Add the following statements to the end of the script section to add a new row to the count table, which increments the `countID` field by one:

```
$SQLstring = "INSERT INTO $TableName VALUES(NULL)";
$QueryResult = @mysqli_query($DBConnect, $SQLstring)
     Or die("<p>Unable to execute the query.</p>"
          . "<p>Error code " . mysqli_errno($DBConnect)
          . ": " . mysqli_error($DBConnect)) . "</p>";
```

7. Finally, add the following statements to the end of the script section. The first statement uses the `mysqli_insert_id()` function to return the last value assigned to the `countID` field and the `echo()` statement prints the number of hits. The last statement closes the database connection.

```
$Hits = mysqli_insert_id($DBConnect);
echo "<h1>There have been $Hits hits to this page!</h1>";
mysqli_close($DBConnect);
```

8. Save the document as **HitCounter.php** in the Projects directory for Chapter 9.

9. Open **HitCounter.php** file in your Web browser by entering the following URL: **http://localhost/PHP_Projects/Chapter.09/Projects/HitCounter.php**. The first time you open the Web page, you should see the message about being the first visitor to the Web site, along with a hit count of 1. Reload the Web page a few times to see if the count increases.
10. Close your Web browser window.

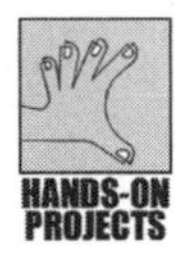

Hands-On Project 9-2

In this project, you create a Web page that allows visitors to your site to sign a guest book that is saved to a database.

1. Create a new document in your text editor and type the `<!DOCTYPE>` declaration, `<html>` element, document head, and `<body>` element. Use the strict DTD and "Guest Book" as the content of the `<title>` element.
2. Add the following text and elements to the document body:

```
<h2>Enter your name to sign our guest book</h2>
<form method="get" action="SignGuestBook.php">
<p>First Name <input type="text" name="first_name" /></p>
<p>Last Name <input type="text" name="last_name" /></p>
<p><input type="submit" value="Submit" /></p>
</form>
```

3. Save the document as **GuestBook.html** in the Projects directory for Chapter 9.
4. Create a new document in your text editor and type the `<!DOCTYPE>` declaration, `<html>` element, document head, and `<body>` element. Use the strict DTD and "Guest Book" as the content of the `<title>` element.
5. Add the following script section to the document body:

```
<?php
?>
```

6. Add the following statements to the script section to ensure that visitors enter their first and last names:

```
if (empty($_GET['first_name']) || empty($_GET['last_name']))
     die("<p>You must enter your first and last name! Click your
browser's Back button to return to the Guest Book form.</p>");
```

7. Add the following statement to the script section to connect to the database. Replace *user* and *password* with the MySQL username and password you created in Chapter 8.

```
$DBConnect = @mysqli_connect("localhost", "user", "password")
     Or die("<p>Unable to connect to the database server.</p>"
     . "<p>Error code " . mysqli_connect_errno()
     . ": " . mysqli_connect_error()) . "</p>";
```

8. Add the following statements to the end of the script section to create a database named `hit_counter` if it does not already exist:

```
$DBName = "guestbook";
if (!@mysqli_select_db($DBConnect, $DBName)) {
     $SQLstring = "CREATE DATABASE $DBName";
     $QueryResult = @mysqli_query($DBConnect, $SQLstring)
           Or die("<p>Unable to execute the query.</p>"
           . "<p>Error code " . mysqli_errno($DBConnect)
           . ": " . mysqli_error($DBConnect)) . "</p>";
     echo "<p>You are the first visitor!</p>";
     mysqli_select_db($DBConnect, $DBName);
}
```

9. Add the following statements to the end of the script section to create a table named `count` if it does not already exist. The table consists of a single autoincrementing primary key field named `countID`.

```
$TableName = "visitors";
$SQLstring = "SELECT * FROM $TableName";
$QueryResult = @mysqli_query($DBConnect, $SQLstring);
if (!$QueryResult) {
     $SQLstring = "CREATE TABLE $TableName (countID SMALLINT
     NOT NULL AUTO_INCREMENT PRIMARY KEY,
     last_name VARCHAR(40), first_name VARCHAR(40))";
     $QueryResult = @mysqli_query($DBConnect, $SQLstring)
     Or die("<p>Unable to create the table.</p>"
     . "<p>Error code " . mysqli_errno($DBConnect)
     . ": " . mysqli_error($DBConnect)) . "</p>";
}
```

10. Finally, add the following statements to the end of the script section. These `mysqli_query()` statements add the visitor to the database and the last statement closes the database connection.

```
$LastName = addslashes($_GET['last_name']);
$FirstName = addslashes($_GET['first_name']);
$SQLstring = "INSERT INTO $TableName VALUES(NULL, '$LastName',
     '$FirstName')";
$QueryResult = @mysqli_query($DBConnect, $SQLstring)
     Or die("<p>Unable to execute the query.</p>"
          . "<p>Error code " . mysqli_errno($DBConnect)
          . ": " . mysqli_error($DBConnect)) . "</p>";
echo "<h1>Thank you for signing our guest book!</h1>";
mysqli_close($DBConnect);
```

11. Save the document as **SignGuestBook.php** in the Projects directory for Chapter 9.
12. Open **GuestBook.html** file in your Web browser by entering the following URL:
    http://localhost/PHP_Projects/Chapter.09/Projects/GuestBook.html. Test the form to see if you can add your name to the database.
13. Close your Web browser window.

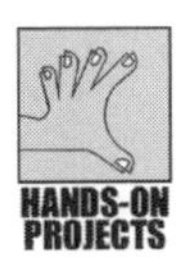

Hands-On Project 9-3

In this project, add a document to the Guest Book program you created in Hands-On Project 9-2. This document displays the entries in the guest book.

1. Create a new document in your text editor and type the `<!DOCTYPE>` declaration, `<html>` element, document head, and `<body>` element. Use the strict DTD and "Guest Book" as the content of the `<title>` element.
2. Add the following script section to the document body:

```
<?php
?>
```

3. Add the following statement to the script section to connect to the database. Replace *user* and *password* with the MySQL username and password you created in Chapter 8.

```
$DBConnect = @mysqli_connect("localhost", "user", "password")
     Or die("<p>Unable to connect to the database server.</p>"
     . "<p>Error code " . mysqli_connect_errno()
     . ": " . mysqli_connect_error()) . "</p>";
```

4. Add the following statements to the end of the script section to connect to the `guestbook` database. If the database does not exist, a message prints that the guest book does not contain any entries.

```
$DBName = "guestbook";
if (!@mysqli_select_db($DBConnect, $DBName))
     die("<p>There are no entries in the guest book!</p>");
```

5. Add the following statements to the end of the script section to select all the records in the `visitors` table. If no records are returned, a message prints that the guest book does not contain any entries.

```
$TableName = "visitors";
$SQLstring = "SELECT * FROM $TableName";
$QueryResult = @mysqli_query($DBConnect, $SQLstring);
if (mysqli_num_rows($QueryResult) == 0)
     die("<p>There are no entries in the guest book!</p>");
```

9

6. Add the following statements to the end of the script section to print the records returned from the `visitors` table:

```
echo "<p>The following visitors have signed our guest book:</p>";
echo "<table width='100%' border='1'>";
echo "<tr><th>First Name</th><th>Last Name</th></tr>";
$Row = mysqli_fetch_assoc($QueryResult);
do {
     echo "<tr><td>{$Row['first_name']}</td>";
     echo "<td>{$Row['last_name']}</td></tr>";
     $Row = mysqli_fetch_assoc($QueryResult);
} while ($Row);
```

7. Add the following statements to the end of the script section to close the database connection and the result pointer:

```
mysqli_free_result($QueryResult);
mysqli_close($DBConnect);
```

8. Save the document as **ShowGuestBook.php** in the Projects directory for Chapter 9.
9. Return to the **GuestBook.html** document in your text editor and add the following text and elements to the end of the document body:

```
<p><a href="ShowGuestBook.php">Show Guest Book</a></p>
```

10. Save the **GuestBook.html** file, and then open it in your Web browser by entering the following URL: **http://localhost/PHP_Projects/Chapter.09/Projects/GuestBook.html**. Click the Show Guest Book link to see if the script functions correctly.
11. Close your Web browser window.

Case Projects

In Chapter 6, you created versions of the following projects that saved data to text files. Create new versions of each project that store data in MySQL databases instead of text files. Save the documents you create for the following projects in the Cases directory for Chapter 9.

Case Project 9-1

Create a document with a form that registers users for a professional conference.

Case Project 9-2

Create a telephone directory application that saves entries to a single text file. You should include standard telephone directory fields in the database, such as first name, last name, address, city, state, zip, telephone number, and so on. Create a document as a main "directory," where you can select and retrieve records. Also, create one document that you can use to add new entries to the database and another document that you can use to edit entries.

Case Project 9-3

Create a Web page to be used for storing software development bug reports in a MySQL database. Include fields such as product name and version, type of hardware, operating system, frequency of occurrence, and proposed solutions. Include links on the main page that allow you to create a new bug report and update an existing bug report.

Case Project 9-4

Create a Web site for tracking, documenting, and managing the process of interviewing candidates for professional positions. On the main page, include a form with fields for the interviewer's name, position, and date of interview. Also include fields for entering the candidate's name, communication abilities, professional appearance, computer skills, business knowledge, and interviewer's comments. Clicking the Submit button should save the data in a MySQL database. Include a link for opening a document that displays each candidate's interview information.

Case Project 9-5

Create a Web page that stores airline surveys in a MySQL database. Include fields for the date and time of the flight, flight number, and so on. Also, include groups of radio buttons that allow the user to rate the airline on the following criteria:

- Friendliness of customer staff
- Space for luggage storage
- Comfort of seating
- Cleanliness of aircraft
- Noise level of aircraft

The radio buttons for each question should consist of the following options: No Opinion, Poor, Fair, Good, or Excellent. Separate text files should store the results of a single survey. Include a View Past Survey Results button on the main survey page that displays a list of past survey results.

Case Project [illegible]

[illegible]

Case Project [illegible]

[illegible]

Case Project [illegible]

[illegible]

Case Project [illegible]

[illegible]

Case Project [illegible]

[illegible]

CHAPTER

10

MANAGING STATE INFORMATION

In this chapter, you will:

- Learn about state information
- Use hidden form fields to save state information
- Use query strings to save state information
- Use cookies to save state information
- Use sessions to save state information

Information about individual visits to a Web site is called **state information**. HTTP was originally designed to be **stateless**, which means that Web browsers stored no persistent data about a visit to a Web site. In this chapter, you learn how to **maintain state**, or store persistent data about a Web site visit, with hidden form fields, query strings, cookies, and sessions.

UNDERSTANDING STATE INFORMATION

The original stateless design of the Web allowed early Web servers to quickly process requests for Web pages because they did not need to remember any unique requirements for different clients. Similarly, Web browsers did not need to know any special information to load a particular Web page from a server. Although this stateless design was efficient, it was also limiting; because a Web server could not remember individual user information, the Web browser was forced to treat every visit to a Web page as an entirely new session. This was true regardless of whether the browser had just opened a different Web page on the same server. This design hampered interactivity and limited the amount of personal attention a Web site could provide.

Today, there are many reasons for maintaining state information. Among other things, a server that maintains state information can:

- Customize individual Web pages based on user preferences.
- Temporarily store information for a user as a browser navigates within a multipart form.
- Allow a user to create bookmarks for returning to specific locations within a Web site.
- Provide shopping carts that store order information.
- Store user IDs and passwords.
- Use counters to keep track of how many times a user has visited a site.

The four tools for maintaining state information with PHP are hidden form fields, query strings, cookies, and sessions. To learn how to use these tools to maintain state information, in this chapter you work on the Skyward Aviation Frequent Flyer Web site, which consists of eight Web pages. Figure 10-1 illustrates how visitors navigate through the pages on the Skyward Aviation Frequent Flyer Web site.

The first page that visitors to the Web site open is the Registration/Log In page, which is located in the upper-left corner of Figure 10-1. New visitors to the Web site must first get a frequent flyer ID number and enter their contact information before accessing the Frequent Flyer Club home page, which is the site's main page. Visitors are required to use a valid e-mail address as their user name. Returning visitors can enter their login information and access the Frequent Flyer Club home page directly. Figure 10-2 shows the Registration/Log In Web page, and Figure 10-3 shows the Frequent Flyer Club home page.

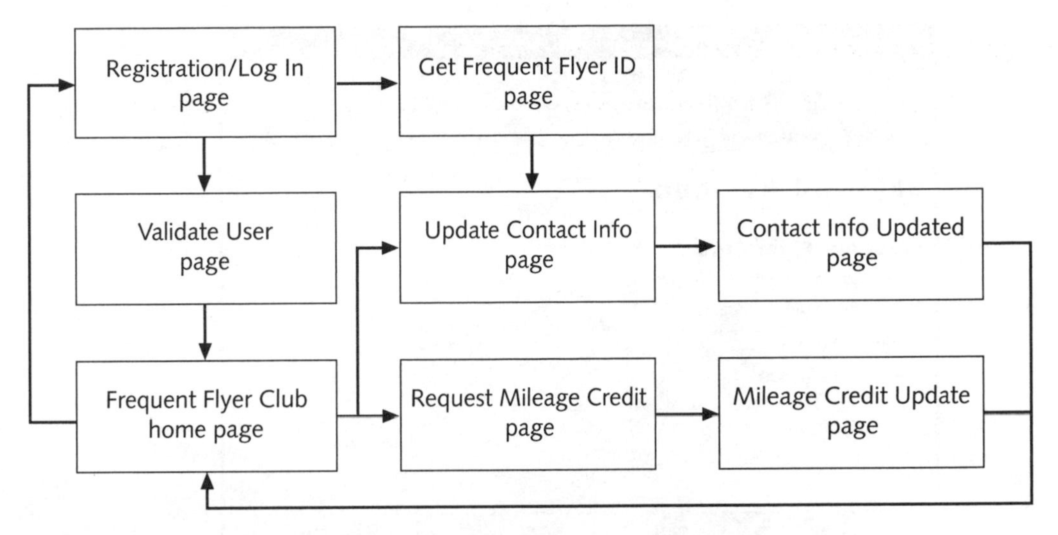

Figure 10-1 Skyward Aviation Frequent Flyer Web site page flow

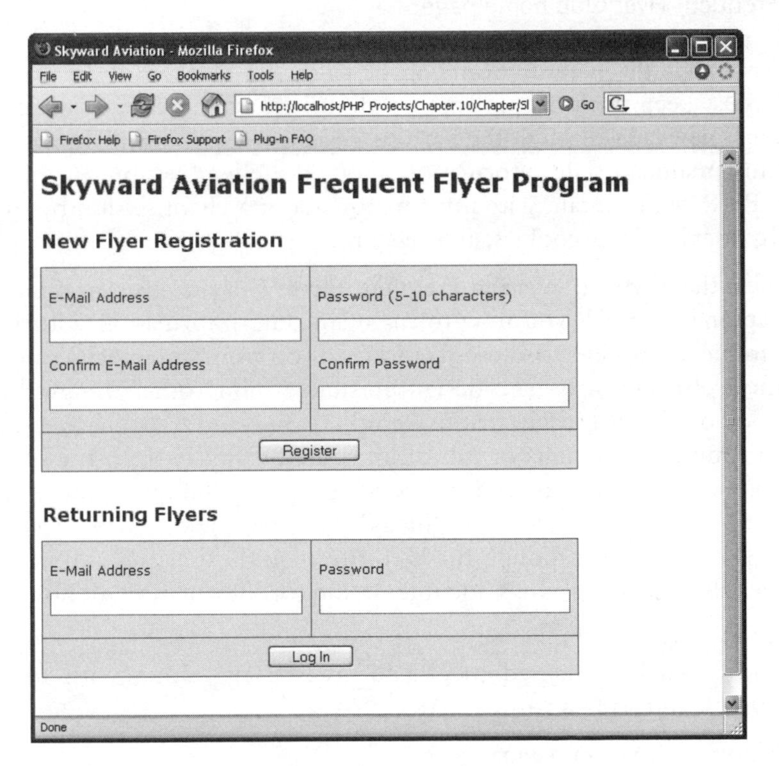

Figure 10-2 Registration/Log In Web page

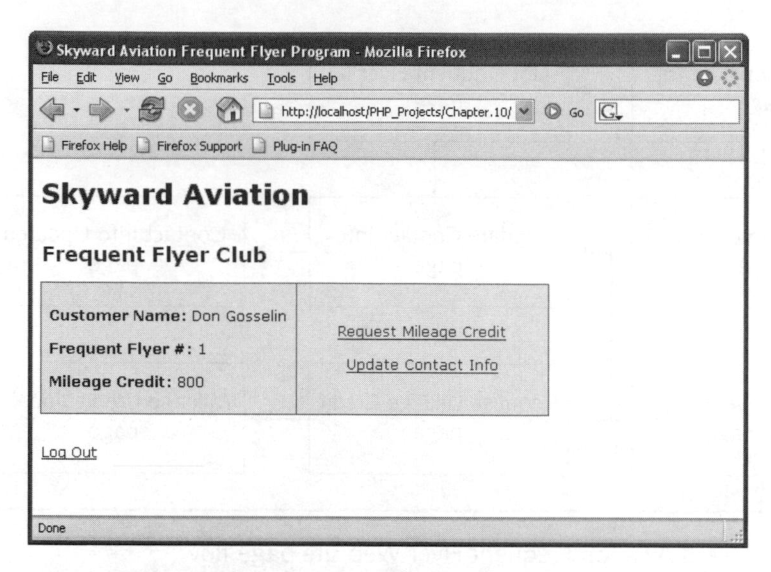

Figure 10-3 Frequent Flyer Club home page

After a user logs in via the Registration/Log In page, the Skyward Aviation Frequent Flyer Web site must keep track of information about the user the entire time the user (that is, the client) navigates through the various pages on the Web site. In other words, the Web site must maintain state information about the client session. In this chapter, you learn how PHP can maintain state information about a client session by using hidden form fields, query strings, cookies, and sessions.

As you work with the Skyward Aviation Frequent Flyer Web site, keep in mind that the goal of this chapter is to teach you how to maintain state information with PHP. The Web site is as simple as possible, to allow you to focus on using state techniques. It does not have the most efficient or elegant design possible. Among other things, this means that the PHP code on the Web pages that make up the Skyward Aviation Frequent Flyer Web site contain minimal amounts of validation functionality to keep the code structure as simple as possible; this way, you can focus on the techniques presented in this chapter. If you try to cause an error (or "break" the scripts), you will succeed. Most important, remember that even though the Web site requires user IDs and passwords, *it is not secure*. Refer to your Web server's documentation for information on how to secure your Web site.

First, you create a database named `skyward_aviation` along with two tables, `frequent_flyers` and `mileage`.

To create the Skyward Aviation database:

1. Log in to the MySQL Monitor with the MySQL user name and password you created in Chapter 8.

2. Enter the following command to create a database named `skyward_aviation`:

```
mysql> CREATE DATABASE skyward_aviation;
```

3. After you see the "Query OK" message, enter the following command to select the `skyward_aviation` database:

```
mysql> use skyward_aviation;
```

4. Enter the following command to create the `frequent_flyers` table:

```
mysql> CREATE TABLE frequent_flyers (flyerID SMALLINT NOT NULL
          AUTO_INCREMENT PRIMARY KEY, email VARCHAR(40),
          password VARCHAR(10), first VARCHAR(40), last VARCHAR(40),
          phone VARCHAR(40), address VARCHAR(40), city VARCHAR(40),
          state VARCHAR(2), zip VARCHAR(10));
```

5. Enter the following command to create the `mileage` table:

```
mysql> CREATE TABLE mileage (mileageID SMALLINT
          NOT NULL AUTO_INCREMENT PRIMARY KEY,
          flyerID SMALLINT, travelDate DATE,
          mileage SMALLINT);
```

6. After you see the "Query OK" message, type **`exit`** or **`quit`** and press **Enter** to log out of the MySQL Monitor.

The Registration/Log In page, named SkywardFlyers.php, is already created for you in your Chapter directory for Chapter 10. Next, you create the Get Frequent Flyer ID page, which registers users and assigns frequent flyer numbers.

To create the Get Frequent Flyer ID page:

1. Create a new document in your text editor and type the `<!DOCTYPE>` declaration, `<html>` element, header information, and `<body>` element. Use the strict DTD and "Skyward Aviation" as the content of the `<title>` element.
2. Add the following `<link>` element above the closing `</head>` tag to link to the php_styles.css style sheet in your Chapter directory:

```
<link rel="stylesheet" href="php_styles.css" type="text/css" />
```

3. Add the following text, elements, and script section to the document body:

```
<h1>Skyward Aviation</h1>
<h2>Frequent Flyer Registration</h2>
<?php
?>
```

4. Add the following statements to the script section to validate the submitted data. The first `if` statement confirms that all the fields in the New Flyer Registration form contain values. The first `else...if` statement uses a regular expression to validate the e-mail address and the second `else...if` statement confirms that the user entered the same e-mail address in the

E-Mail Address and Confirm E-Mail Address fields. The third and fourth `else...if` statements validate the password.

```
if (empty($_GET['email']) || empty($_GET['email_confirm'])
     || empty($_GET['password'])
     ||  empty($_GET['password_confirm']))
     exit("<p>You must enter values in all fields of the
          Frequent Flyer Registration form! Click your
          browser's Back button to return to the
          previous page.</p>");
else if (!eregi("^[_a-z0-9-]+(\.[_a-z0-9-]+)*@[a-z0-9-]+(\.[a-z0-9-]
     +)*(\.[a-z]{2,3})$", $_GET['email']))
     exit("<p>You must enter a valid e-mail address! Click
  your browser's Back button to return to the
  previous page.</p>");
else if ($_GET['email'] != $_GET['email_confirm'])
     exit("<p>You did not enter the same e-mail address!
          Click your browser's Back button to return to
          the previous page.</p>");
else if ($_GET['password'] != $_GET['password_confirm'])
     exit("<p>You did not enter the same password! Click
          your browser's Back button to return to the
          previous page.</p>");
else if (strlen($_GET['password']) < 5
     || strlen($_GET['password']) > 10)
     exit("<p>Your password must be between 5 and 10
          characters! Click your browser's Back button
          to return to the previous jpage.</p>");
```

5. Add the following statements to the end of the script section to connect to the database server and open the `skyward_aviation` database. Be sure to replace *`user`* and *`password`* with your username and password.

```
$DBConnect = @mysqli_connect("localhost", "user", "password")
     Or die("<p>Unable to connect to the database server.</p>"
     . "<p>Error code " . mysqli_connect_errno()
     . ": " . mysqli_connect_error()) . "</p>";
$DBName = "skyward_aviation";
@mysqli_select_db($DBConnect, $DBName)
     Or die("<p>Unable to select the database.</p>"
     . "<p>Error code " . mysqli_errno($DBConnect)
     . ": " . mysqli_error($DBConnect)) . "</p>";
```

6. Add the following statements to the end of the script section to open a table named `frequent_flyers`, which contains each user's contact information:

```
$TableName = "frequent_flyers";
$Email = addslashes($_GET['email']);
$Password = addslashes($_GET['password']);
$SQLstring = "SELECT * FROM $TableName";
$QueryResult = @mysqli_query($DBConnect, $SQLstring);
```

7. Add to the end of the script section the following `if` statement, which prevents the same e-mail address from being entered twice:

```
if (mysqli_num_rows($QueryResult) > 0) {
      $Row = mysqli_fetch_row($QueryResult);
      do {
            if (in_array($Email, $Row))
                  exit("<p>The e-mail address you entered is already
                        registered! Click your browser's Back button to
                        return to the previous page.</p>");
            $Row = mysqli_fetch_row($QueryResult);
      } while ($Row);
      mysqli_free_result($QueryResult);
}
```

8. Finally, add to the end of the script section the following statements, which add the new user to the `frequent_flyers` table. Because you only know the user's e-mail address and password, the SQL statement uses `NULL` values for the other fields. Each user's frequent flyer number is the primary key of the row in which their personal information is stored. Therefore, the `mysqli_insert_id()` function returns the primary key to the `$FlyerID` variable. The last statement closes the database connection.

```
$SQLstring = "INSERT INTO $TableName VALUES(NULL, '$Email',
    '$Password', NULL, NULL, NULL, NULL, NULL, NULL, NULL)";
$QueryResult = @mysqli_query($DBConnect, $SQLstring)
      Or die("<p>Unable to execute the query.</p>"
            . "<p>Error code " . mysqli_errno($DBConnect)
            . ": " . mysqli_error($DBConnect)) . "</p>";
$FlyerID = mysqli_insert_id($DBConnect);
mysqli_close($DBConnect);
```

9. Add the following text and elements to the end of the document body, below the script section:

```
<p>Your new frequent flyer ID is <strong>
<?= $FlyerID ?></strong>.</p>
```

10. Save the document as **RegisterFlyer.php** in the Chapter directory for Chapter 10.

11. Open the **SkywardFlyers.php** file in your Web browser by entering the following URL: **http://localhost/PHP_Projects/Chapter.10/Chapter/SkywardFlyers.php**. Enter an e-mail address and password in the New Flyer Registration form. Be sure to enter a valid e-mail address and a password between 5 and 10 characters, and be sure to enter the same e-mail address and password in the confirmation fields or you will receive an error. Click the **Register** button to obtain a frequent flyer number. You should see the Web page shown in Figure 10-4. (The first frequent flyer number should be a value of 1.)

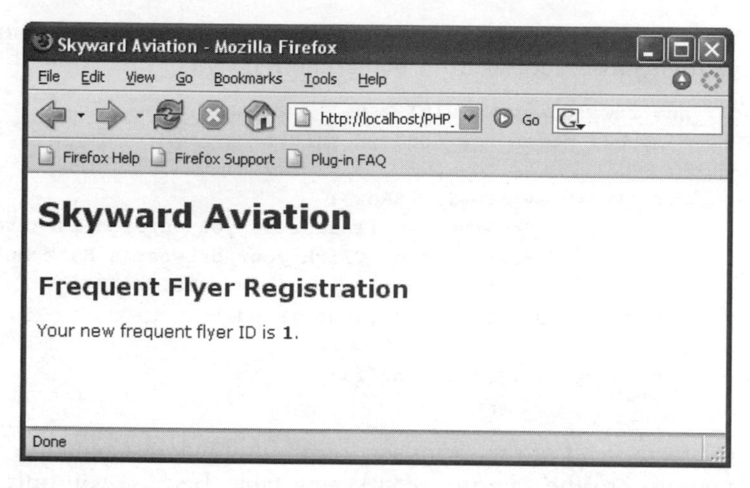

Figure 10-4 Frequent Flyer Registration Web page

12. Close your Web browser window.

Using Hidden Form Fields to Save State Information

As you should know from your study of HTML, a hidden form field is not displayed by the Web browser and, therefore, allows you to hide information from users. You create hidden form fields with the `<input>` element. Hidden form fields temporarily store data that needs to be sent to a server along with the rest of a form, but that a user does not need to see. Examples of data stored in hidden fields include the result of a calculation or some other type of information that a program on the Web server might need. You create hidden form fields using the same syntax used for other fields created with the `<input>` element: `<input type="hidden">`. The only attributes that you can include with a hidden form field are the *name* and *value* attributes.

When you submit a form to a PHP script, you can access the values submitted from the form by using the `$_GET[]` and `$_POST[]` autoglobals. If you then want to pass form values from one PHP script to another PHP script, you can store the values in hidden form fields, which are submitted along with other types of form fields. If fact, you already used this technique in Chapter 9 with the Aqua Don's Scuba School project. In that project, the primary key from the `divers` table was assigned to a variable named `$DiverID` with the `mysqli_insert_id()` function, as shown in the following statement:

```
$DiverID = mysqli_insert_id($DBConnect);
```

The script also included the following statements, which stored the value of the `$DiverID` variable in a hidden form field:

```
<form action="CourseListings.php" method="get">
<p><input type="submit" value="Register for Classes" />
<input type="hidden" name="diverID"
    value="<?= $DiverID ?>" /></p>
</form>
```

The preceding hidden form field allowed you to pass the `$DiverID` variable to the CourseListings.php script when the user clicked the Register for Classes button, which submitted the form.

Next, you create the Validate User page and the Frequent Flyer Club home page. A user logs in by entering his e-mail address and password in the Returning Flyers form on the Registration/Log In page. The Validate User page uses the e-mail address and password to retrieve the user's frequent flyer number, which it then stores in a hidden form field. When the user clicks a Submit button on the Validate User page, the frequent flyer number is submitted to the Frequent Flyer Club home page.

To create the Validate User page:

1. Create a new document in your text editor and type the `<!DOCTYPE>` declaration, `<html>` element, header information, and `<body>` element. Use the strict DTD and "Skyward Aviation" as the content of the `<title>` element.

2. Add the following `<link>` element above the closing `</head>` tag to link to the php_styles.css style sheet in your Chapter directory:

   ```
   <link rel="stylesheet" href="php_styles.css" type="text/css" />
   ```

3. Add the following heading element and script section to the document body:

   ```
   <h1>Skyward Aviation</h1>
   <?php
   ?>
   ```

4. Add the following statements to the script section, which retrieve and validate the e-mail address and password submitted by the user:

   ```
   $FlyerEmail = $_GET['email'];
   $FlyerPassword = $_GET['password'];
   if (empty($FlyerEmail) || empty($FlyerPassword))
        exit("<p>You must enter your e-mail address and password!
             Click your browser's Back button to return to the
             previous page.</p>");
   ```

10

5. Add the following statements to the end of the script section to connect to the database server and open the `skyward_aviation` database. Be sure to replace *user* and *password* with your username and password.

```
$DBConnect = @mysqli_connect("localhost", "user", "password")
     Or die("<p>Unable to connect to the database server.</p>"
     . "<p>Error code " . mysqli_connect_errno()
     . ": " . mysqli_connect_error()) . "</p>";
$DBName = "skyward_aviation";
@mysqli_select_db($DBConnect, $DBName)
     Or die("<p>Unable to select the database.</p>"
     . "<p>Error code " . mysqli_errno($DBConnect)
     . ": " . mysqli_error($DBConnect)) . "</p>";
```

6. Add the following statements to the end of the script section to retrieve the user's information from the `frequent_flyers` table:

```
$TableName = "frequent_flyers";
$SQLstring = "SELECT * FROM $TableName WHERE
email='$FlyerEmail'";
$QueryResult = @mysqli_query($DBConnect, $SQLstring)
     Or die("<p>Unable to execute the query.</p>"
     . "<p>Error code " . mysqli_errno($DBConnect)
     . ": " . mysqli_error($DBConnect)) . "</p>";
if (mysqli_num_rows($QueryResult) == 0)
     die("<p>You must enter a registered e-mail address! Click
          your browser's Back button to return to the
          Registration form.</p.");
```

7. Add the following statements to the end of the script section to assign the user's frequent flyer number to the `$FlyerID` variable:

```
$Row = mysqli_fetch_row($QueryResult);
if ($FlyerPassword != $Row[2])
     die("<p>You did not enter a valid password! Click your
browser's Back button to return to the Registration form.</p.");
else
     $FlyerID = $Row[0];
```

8. Add the following heading element and form to the end of the document body, after the script section. The form assigns the `$FlyerID` variable as the value of a hidden form field named `flyerID`. The form is submitted to the FrequentFlyerClub.php script.

```
<h2>Login Successful</h2>
<form action="FrequentFlyerClub.php" method="get">
<p><input type="hidden" name="flyerID" value="<?= $FlyerID ?>" />
<input type="submit" value="Frequent Flyer Club Home Page" /></p>
</form>
```

9. Save the document as **ValidateUser.php** in the Chapter directory for Chapter 10.

Next, you create the Frequent Flyer Club home page.

To create the Frequent Flyer Club home page:

1. Create a new document in your text editor and type the `<!DOCTYPE>` declaration, `<html>` element, header information, and `<body>` element. Use the strict DTD and "Skyward Aviation" as the content of the `<title>` element.
2. Add the following `<link>` element above the closing `</head>` tag to link to the php_styles.css style sheet in your Chapter directory:

```
<link rel="stylesheet" href="php_styles.css" type="text/css" />
```

3. Add the following text, elements, and script section to the document body:

```
<h1>Skyward Aviation</h1>
<h2>Frequent Flyer Club</h2>
<?php
?>
```

4. Add the following statement to the script section, which retrieves the frequent flyer ID submitted in the hidden form field:

```
if (isset($_GET['flyerID']))
     $FlyerID = $_GET['flyerID'];
```

5. Add the following statements to the end of the script section to connect to the database server and open the `skyward_aviation` database. Be sure to replace *`user`* and *`password`* with your username and password.

```
$DBConnect = @mysqli_connect("localhost", "user", "password")
     Or die("<p>Unable to connect to the database server.</p>"
     . "<p>Error code " . mysqli_connect_errno()
     . ": " . mysqli_connect_error()) . "</p>";
$DBName = "skyward_aviation";
@mysqli_select_db($DBConnect, $DBName)
     Or die("<p>Unable to select the database.</p>"
     . "<p>Error code " . mysqli_errno($DBConnect)
     . ": " . mysqli_error($DBConnect)) . "</p>";
```

6. Add the following statements to the end of the script section to retrieve the user's information from the `frequent_flyers` table. Notice in this version that the SQL statement uses the frequent flyer ID, which is stored in the `$FlyerID` variable, to retrieve user information from the table.

```
$TableName = "frequent_flyers";
$SQLstring = "SELECT * FROM $TableName WHERE flyerID='$FlyerID'";
$QueryResult = @mysqli_query($DBConnect, $SQLstring)
     Or die("<p>Unable to execute the query.</p>"
     . "<p>Error code " . mysqli_errno($DBConnect)
     . ": " . mysqli_error($DBConnect)) . "</p>";
if (mysqli_num_rows($QueryResult) == 0)
     exit("<p>Invalid frequent flyer number!</p>");
```

7. Add the following statements to the end of the script section to retrieve the user's first and last name from the resultset:

```
$Row = mysqli_fetch_row($QueryResult);
$CustomerName = $Row[3] . " " . $Row[4];
```

8. Add the following statements to the end of the script section. The query uses the SQL `SUM()` function to query the `mileage` table to return the amount of airline miles the user has accumulated. The `mileage` table is the "many" side in a one-to-many relationship and stores individual records for each trip a user takes. The last statement closes the database connection.

```
$TableName = "mileage";
$Mileage = 0;
$SQLstring = "SELECT SUM(mileage) FROM $TableName WHERE
flyerID='$FlyerID'";
$QueryResult = @mysqli_query($DBConnect, $SQLstring);
if (mysqli_num_rows($QueryResult) > 0) {
     $Row = mysqli_fetch_row($QueryResult);
     $Mileage = number_format($Row[0], 0) ;
     mysqli_free_result($QueryResult);
}
mysqli_close($DBConnect);
```

9. Add the following text and elements to the end of the document body, after the script section. The table prints the values assigned to the `$CustomerName`, `$FlyerID`, and `$Mileage` variables. The table also contains links to two scripts: RequestMileage.php and UpdateContactInfo.php. You create both scripts later in this chapter. The last paragraph element contains a link back to the Registration/Log In page.

```
<table frame="border" rules="cols">
<colgroup width="50%" />
<colgroup width="50%" />
<tr><td align="left">
<p><strong>Customer Name:</strong> <?= $CustomerName ?> </p>
<p><strong>Frequent Flyer #:</strong> <?= $FlyerID ?></p>
<p><strong>Mileage Credit:</strong> <?= $Mileage ?></p>
</td>
<td align="center">
<p><a href="RequestMileage.php">Request Mileage Credit</a></p>
<p><a href="UpdateContactInfo.php">Update Contact Info</a></p>
</td></tr></table>
<p><a href="SkywardFlyers.php">Log Out</a></p>
```

10. Save the document as **FrequentFlyerClub.php** in the Chapter directory for Chapter 10.

11. Open the **SkywardFlyers.php** file in your Web browser by entering the following URL: **http://localhost/PHP_Projects/Chapter.10/Chapter/SkywardFlyers.php**. Enter the e-mail address and password in the Returning Flyers form that you registered with the New Flyer Registration form and

click the **Log In** button. You should see the Login Successful page shown in Figure 10-5.

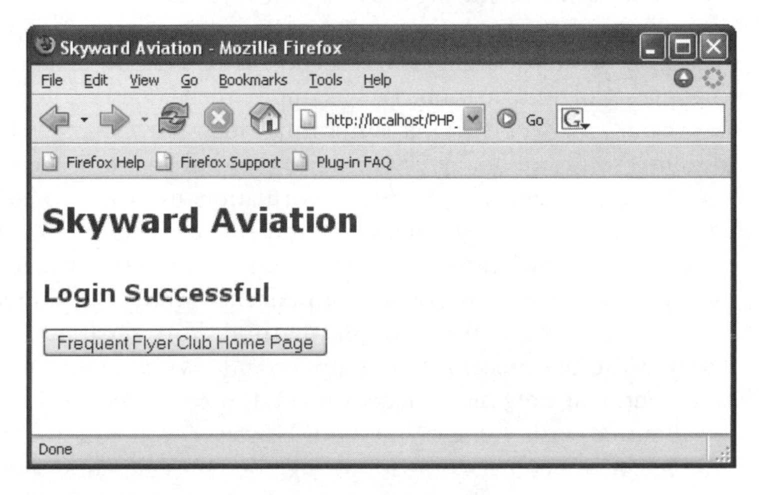

Figure 10-5 Login Successful Web page

12. Click the **Frequent Flyer Club Home Page** button to open the Frequent Flyer Club home page, which is shown in Figure 10-6. Because you have not yet added functionality to store contact information or update airline miles, the Customer Name field is empty and the Mileage Credit field displays a value of 0.

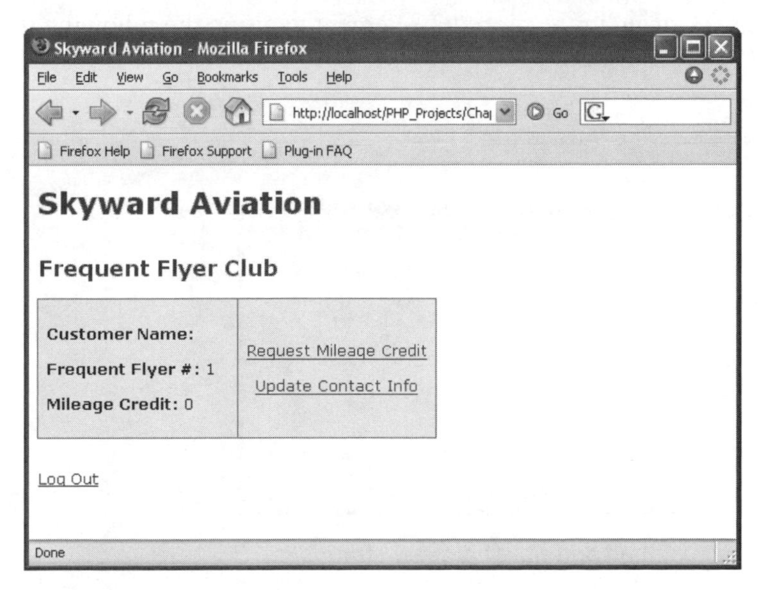

Figure 10-6 Frequent Flyer Club home page displaying a frequent flyer number

13. Close your Web browser window.

USING QUERY STRINGS TO SAVE STATE INFORMATION

One way to preserve information following a user's visit to a Web page is to append a query string to the end of a URL. As you learned in Chapter 5, a query string is a set of name=value pairs appended to a target URL. It consists of a single text string containing one or more pieces of information. For example, the name=value pairs for a user's first and last name may consist of something like "firstName=Don" and "secondName=Gosselin". You can use a query string to pass information, such as search criteria, from one Web page to another. To pass information from one Web page to another using a query string, add a question mark (`?`) immediately after a URL, followed by the query string containing the information you want to preserve in name=value pairs. In this manner, you are passing information to another Web page, similar to the way you can pass arguments to a function or method. You separate individual name=value pairs within the query string using ampersands (`&`). A question mark (`?`) and a query string are automatically appended to the URL of a server-side script for any forms that are submitted with the `GET` method. However, you can also append a query string to any URL on a Web page. The following code provides an example of an `<a>` element that contains a query string consisting of three name=value pairs:

```
<a href="http://www.URL.com/TargetPage.php?firstName=Don
&lastName=Gosselin&occupation=writer ">Link Text</a>
```

You can access any query string data that is appended to a URL from PHP by using the `$_GET[]` autoglobal, the same as for any forms that are submitted with the `GET` method. For example, the TargetPage.php script (which is the target of the link) can print the values from the query string in the preceding element by using the following statements. Figure 10-7 shows the output in a Web browser.

```
echo "{$_GET['firstName']} {$_GET['lastName']}
 is a {$_GET['occupation']}.";
```

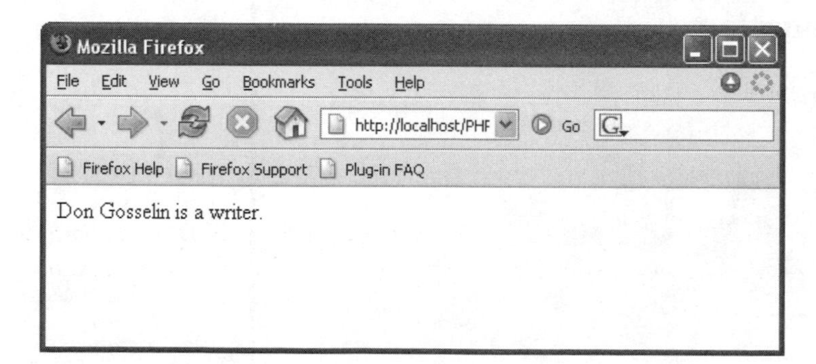

Figure 10-7 Output of the contents of a query string

Next, you modify the Validate User page so the frequent flyer ID is passed as a query string instead of being stored in a hidden form field.

To modify the Validate User page so the frequent flyer ID is passed as a query string instead of being stored in a hidden form field:

1. Return to the **ValidateUser.php** document in your text editor.
2. Replace the form containing the hidden form fields with the following text and elements. The PHP output directive appends a query string to the FrequentFlyerClub.php URL consisting of a name=value pair of `flyerID=$FlyerID`.

```
<p><a href='<?= "FrequentFlyerClub.php?flyerID=$FlyerID"
?>'>Frequent Flyer Club Home Page</a></p>
```

3. Save the **ValidateUser.php** document.
4. Open the **SkywardFlyers.php** file in your Web browser by entering the following URL: **http://localhost/PHP_Projects/Chapter.10/Chapter/SkywardFlyers.php**. Enter the e-mail address and password in the Returning Flyers form that you registered with the New Flyer Registration form and click the **Log In** button. You should see the Login Successful Web page with a link instead of the Submit button, as shown in Figure 10-8.

10

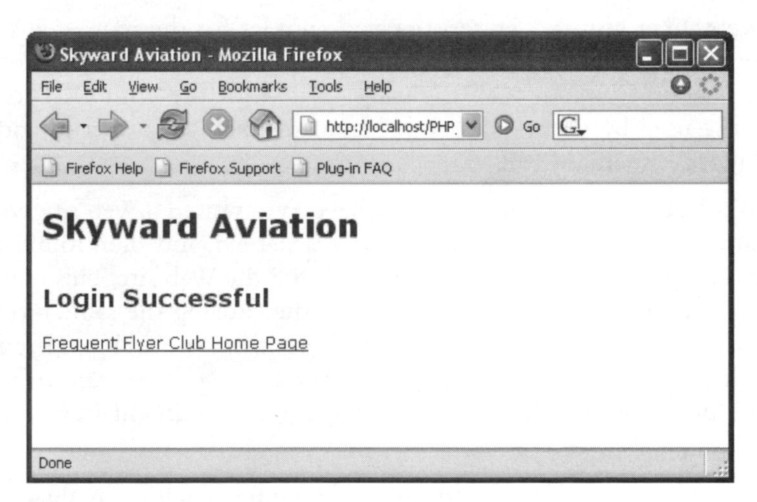

Figure 10-8 Login Successful Web page after replacing the form with a link

5. Click the **Frequent Flyer Club Home Page** link to open the Frequent Flyer Club home page. The Frequent Flyer Club home page should open just as it did with the hidden form field.

Using Cookies to Save State Information

When choosing a method of saving state information, you need to consider whether you want the state information to be available after the current session of a Web page has ended—in other words, whether you want the state information to be permanent. Query strings do not permanently maintain state information. That's because the information contained in a query string is available only during the current session of a Web page. After a Web page that reads a query string closes, the query string is lost. Hidden form fields maintain state information between Web pages, but the data they contain is also lost when the Web page that reads the hidden fields closes. You can save the contents of a query string or hidden form fields by submitting the form data using a server-side scripting language, but that method requires a separate server-based application. To make it possible to store state information beyond the current Web page session, Netscape created cookies. **Cookies**, or magic cookies, are small pieces of information about a user that are stored by a Web server in text files on the user's computer. Cookies can be temporary or persistent. **Temporary cookies** remain available only for the current browser session. **Persistent cookies** remain available beyond the current browser session and are stored in a text file on a client computer.

Each time the Web client visits a Web server, saved cookies for the requested Web page are sent from the client to the server. The server then uses the cookies to customize the Web page for the client. Cookies were originally created for use with CGI scripts, but are now commonly used by client-side script languages such as JavaScript and server-side scripting languages such as PHP.

You have probably seen cookies in action if you have ever visited a Web site where you entered a username in a prompt dialog box or in a text field, and then found that you were greeted by that username the next time you visited the Web site. This could occur with each subsequent visit to the same Web site, whether during the same browser session or during a different browser session days or weeks later. The Web page remembers this information by storing it locally on your computer in a cookie. Another example of a cookie is a counter that counts the number of times an individual user has visited a Web site.

There are a number of limitations on the use of cookies. Each individual server or domain can store only a maximum of 20 cookies on a user's computer. In addition, the total cookies per browser cannot exceed 300, and the largest cookie size is 4 kilobytes. If these limits are exceeded, a Web browser may start discarding older cookies.

Creating Cookies

You use the `setcookie()` function to create cookies in PHP. The syntax for the `setcookie()` function is as follows:

```
setcookie(name [,value ,expires, path, domain, secure])
```

You create a cookie by passing to the **setcookie()** function a required **name** argument and five optional arguments: **value**, **expires**, **path**, **domain**, and **secure**. You must pass each of the arguments in the order specified in the preceding syntax. To skip the **value**, **path**, and **domain** arguments, specify an empty string as the argument value. To skip the **expires** and **secure** arguments, specify 0 as the argument value.

You must call the **setcookie()** function before you send the Web browser any output, including white space, HTML elements, or output from the **echo()** or **print()** statements. If any output exists before you call the **setcookie()** function, you receive an error and the function returns a value of false. Also, keep in mind that users can choose whether to accept cookies that a script attempts to write to their system. If the **setcookie()** function runs successfully, it returns a value of true, even if a user rejects the cookie.

The name and value Arguments

Although the only required argument of the **setcookie()** function is the *name* attribute, a cookie is not of any use if you do not specify the **value** argument. Cookies created with only the **name** and **value** arguments are temporary cookies because they are available for only the current browser session. The following code creates a cookie named **firstName** and assigns it a value of "Don":

```
<?php
setcookie("firstName", "Don");
?>
<!DOCTYPE html PUBLIC "-//W3C//DTD XHTML 1.0 Strict//EN"
     "http://www.w3.org/TR/xhtml1/DTD/xhtml1-strict.dtd">
<html xmlns="http://www.w3.org/1999/xhtml">
<head>
<title>Skyward Aviation</title>
...
```

Notice that the script section is placed above the HTML elements in the preceding example. Remember that you must call the **setcookie()** function before you send the Web browser any output, including white space, HTML elements, or output from the **echo()** or **print()** statements, or you receive an error.

You can call the **setcookie()** function multiple times to create additional cookies—but again, remember that **setcookie()** statements must come before any other output on a Web page. The following example creates three cookies:

```
setcookie("firstName", "Don");
setcookie("lastName", "Gosselin");
setcookie("occupation", "writer");
```

PHP also allows you to store cookie values in indexed or associative arrays by appending array operators ([ ]) and an index or key to the cookie name within the setcookie() function. The following statements create an indexed cookie array named professional[] that contains three cookie values:

```
setcookie("professional[0]", "Don");
setcookie("professional[1]", "Gosselin");
setcookie("professional[2]", "writer");
```

The following statements create an associative version of the professional[] cookie array:

```
setcookie("professional['firstName']", "Don");
setcookie("professional['lastName']", "Gosselin");
setcookie("professional['occupation']", "writer");
```

By default, cookies themselves cannot include semicolons or other special characters, such as commas or spaces. Cookies cannot include special characters because they are transmitted between Web browsers and Web servers using HTTP, which does not allow certain nonalphanumeric characters to be transmitted in their native format. However, you can use special characters in cookies you create with PHP because the setcookie() function automatically encodes, or converts, special characters in a text string to their corresponding hexadecimal ASCII value, preceded by a percent sign. For example, 20 is the hexadecimal ASCII equivalent of a space character, and 25 is the hexadecimal ASCII equivalent of a percent sign (%). In URL encoded format, each space character is represented by %20, and each percent sign is represented by %25. After encoding, the contents of the string "tip=A standard tip is 15%" would read as follows:

```
tip=A%20standard%20tip%20is%2015%25
```

More specifically, encoding converts special characters in a text string to their corresponding hexadecimal ASCII value, preceded by a percent sign. Encoding does not encode standard alphanumeric characters such as A, B, C, or 1, 2, 3, or any of the following special characters: - _ . ! ~ * ' ( ). It also does not encode the following characters that have special meaning in a URI: ; / ? : @ & = + $,. For example, the / character is not encoded because it is used for designating a path on a file system. PHP automatically decodes special characters when you read cookie values. (You learn how to read cookies later in this chapter.)

Next, you modify the Get Frequent Flyer ID page so the frequent flyer ID is stored in a temporary cookie.

To modify the Get Frequent Flyer ID page so the frequent flyer ID is stored in a temporary cookie:

1. Return to the **RegisterFlyer.php** document in your text editor.
2. Cut and paste the existing PHP script section above the <!DOCTYPE> declaration. You need to do this because the setcookie() function, which you add in the next step, must be called before any output statements.

3. Add the following `setcookie()` statement above the `mysqli_close()` statement at the end of the script section. This statement creates a new cookie named `flyerID` that contains the newly assigned frequent flyer ID.

```
setcookie("flyerID", $FlyerID);
```

4. Add to the end of the document body the following text and elements, which link to the Update Contact Info page:

```
<p><a href="UpdateContactInfo.php">Enter Contact
Information</a></p>
```

5. Save the **RegisterFlyer.php** document.

Next, you create the Update Contact Info page.

To create the Update Contact Info page:

1. Create a new document in your text editor and type the `<!DOCTYPE>` declaration, `<html>` element, header information, and `<body>` element. Use the strict DTD and "Skyward Aviation" as the content of the `<title>` element.
2. Add the following `<link>` element above the closing `</head>` tag to link to the php_styles.css style sheet in your Chapter directory:

```
<link rel="stylesheet" href="php_styles.css" type="text/css" />
```


3. Add the following heading element and script section to the document body:

```
<h1>Skyward Aviation</h1>
<?php
?>
```

4. Add the following statements to the script section to connect to the database server and open the `skyward_aviation` database. Be sure to replace *`user`* and *`password`* with your username and password.

```
$DBConnect = @mysqli_connect("localhost", "user", "password")
     Or die("<p>Unable to connect to the database server.</p>"
     . "<p>Error code " . mysqli_connect_errno()
     . ": " . mysqli_connect_error()) . "</p>";
$DBName = "skyward_aviation";
@mysqli_select_db($DBConnect, $DBName)
     Or die("<p>Unable to select the database.</p>"
     . "<p>Error code " . mysqli_errno($DBConnect)
     . ": " . mysqli_error($DBConnect)) . "</p>";
```

5. Add the following statements to the end of the script section to retrieve the user's information from the `frequent_flyers` table:

```
$TableName = "frequent_flyers";
$SQLstring = "SELECT * FROM $TableName WHERE flyerID='$FlyerID'";
$QueryResult = @mysqli_query($DBConnect, $SQLstring)
     Or die("<p>Unable to execute the query.</p>"
          . "<p>Error code " . mysqli_errno($DBConnect)
          . ": " . mysqli_error($DBConnect)) . "</p>";
```

6. Add the following statements to the end of the script section to assign the user information to variables. The last statement closes the database connection.

```
if (mysqli_num_rows($QueryResult) > 0) {
     $Row = mysqli_fetch_row($QueryResult);
     $First = stripslashes($Row[3]);
     $Last = stripslashes($Row[4]);
     $Phone = stripslashes($Row[5]);
     $Address = stripslashes($Row[6]);
     $City = stripslashes($Row[7]);
     $State = stripslashes($Row[8]);
     $Zip = stripslashes($Row[9]);
     mysqli_free_result($QueryResult);
}
else {
     $First = "";
     $Last = "";
     $Phone = "";
     $Address = "";
     $City = "";
     $State = "";
     $Zip = "";
}
mysqli_close($DBConnect);
```

7. Add the following text and elements to the end of the document body. The statements contain PHP output directives, which assign the values of the PHP variables to the form fields.

```
<h2>Contact Information</h2>
<form action="ContactUpdate.php" method="get">
<table frame="border" rules="cols">
<colgroup width="50%" />
<colgroup width="50%" />
<tr><td align="right" valign="top">
<p>First Name <input type="text" name="first_name"
     value="<?= $First ?>" size="36" /></p>
<p>Last Name <input type="text" name="last_name"
     value="<?= $Last ?>" size="36" /></p>
<p>Phone <input type="text" name="phone"
     value="<?= $Phone ?>" size="36" /></p></td>
<td align="right" valign="top">
<p>Address <input type="text" name="address"
     value="<?= $Address ?>" size="40" /></p>
<p>City <input type="text" name="city" value="<?= $City ?>"
     size="10" />
State <input type="text" name="state" value="<?= $State ?>"
     size="2" maxlength="2" />
Zip <input type="text" name="zip" value="<?= $Zip ?>" size="10"
     maxlength="10" /></p>
```

```
</td></tr>
</table>
<p><input type="submit" value="Submit" /></p>
</form>
```

8. Save the document as **UpdateContactInfo.php** in the Chapter directory for Chapter 10.

The `expires` Argument

For a cookie to persist beyond the current browser session, you must use the `expires` argument with the `setcookie()` function. You might use a cookie that expires after one week (or less) to store data that needs to be maintained for a limited amount of time. For example, a travel agency may store data in a cookie that temporarily holds a travel reservation that expires after one week. Or, an online retail site may store shopping cart information in cookies that expire after a much shorter period of time, for example 15 minutes. The `expires` argument determines how long a cookie can remain on a client system before it is deleted. Cookies created without an `expires` argument are available for only the current browser session. You assign to the `expires` argument a value representing the date or time when the client system is to delete the cookie. To specify a cookie's expiration time, you use PHP's `time()` function to return the current time and add to it an integer in seconds to specify the time to delete the cookie. The following `setcookie()` function specifies that the `firstName` cookie expires in 3600 seconds, or one hour from now:


```
setcookie("firstName", "Don", time()+3600);
```

Multiplying the number of seconds in a minute and an hour, then multiplying that value by the number of hours or days can make it easier to specify an expiration time. The following example specifies that the `firstName` cookie expires in one week by multiplying the number of seconds in a minute (60), the number of minutes in an hour (60), the number of hours in a day (24), and then the number of days in a week (7).

```
setcookie("firstName", "Don", time()+60*60*24*7);
```

When developing a PHP script, you may accidentally create, but not delete, persistent cookies that your program does not need. Unused persistent cookies can sometimes interfere with the execution of a PHP script. For this reason, you may periodically want to delete your browser cookies, especially while developing a PHP script that use cookies. To delete cookies in Firefox, click Tools on the menu bar, click Options, click the Privacy category, and then click Remove next to the Cookies option. To delete cookies in Microsoft Internet Explorer, click Tools on the menu bar, click Internet Options, click the General tab of the Internet Options dialog box, and then click the Delete Cookies button.

Next, you create the Contact Info Updated page, which creates a persistent cookie containing the visitor's name.

To create the Contact Info Updated page:

1. Create a new document in your text editor and type the <!DOCTYPE> declaration, <html> element, header information, and <body> element. Use the strict DTD and "Skyward Aviation" as the content of the <title> element.
2. Add the following <link> element above the closing </head> tag to link to the php_styles.css style sheet in your Chapter directory:

```
<link rel="stylesheet" href="php_styles.css" type="text/css" />
```

3. Add the following text and elements to the document body:

```
<h1>Skyward Aviation</h1>
<h2>Contact Info Updated</h2>
<p>Your contact information was successfully updated.</p>
<p><a href="FrequentFlyerClub.php">Frequent Flyer Club Home
Page</a></p>
```

4. Add a script section above the opening <!DOCTYPE> declaration:

```
<?php
?>
```

The script section will contain a setcookie() function, so be sure to create the script section above the opening <!DOCTYPE> declaration or you will receive an error.

5. Add the following statements to the script section to validate and add slashes to the submitted data:

```
if (empty($_GET['first_name']) || empty($_GET['last_name']) ||
      empty($_GET['phone']) || empty($_GET['address']) ||
      empty($_GET['city']) || empty($_GET['state']) ||
      empty($_GET['zip']))
exit("<p>You must enter values in all fields of the Contact
      Information form! Click your browser's Back button
      to return to the previous page.</p>");
$First = addslashes($_GET['first_name']);
$Last = addslashes($_GET['last_name']);
$Phone = addslashes($_GET['phone']);
$Address = addslashes($_GET['address']);
$City = addslashes($_GET['city']);
$State = addslashes($_GET['state']);
$Zip = addslashes($_GET['zip']);
```

6. Add the following statement to the end of the script section to create a persistent cookie named customerName. The cookie is set to expire one week from now.

```
setcookie("customerName", $First . " " . $Last,
     time()+60*60*24*7);
```

7. Add the following statements to the end of the script section to connect to the database server and open or create the `skyward_aviation` database. Be sure to replace *`user`* and *`password`* with your username and password.

```
$DBConnect = @mysqli_connect("localhost", "user", "password")
     Or die("<p>Unable to connect to the database server.</p>"
     . "<p>Error code " . mysqli_connect_errno()
     . ": " . mysqli_connect_error()) . "</p>";
$DBName = "skyward_aviation";
@mysqli_select_db($DBConnect, $DBName)
     Or die("<p>Unable to select the database.</p>"
     . "<p>Error code " . mysqli_errno($DBConnect)
     . ": " . mysqli_error($DBConnect)) . "</p>";
```

8. Add the following statements to the end of the script section to update the user information in the `frequent_flyers` table and to close the database connection:

```
$TableName = "frequent_flyers";
$SQLstring = "UPDATE $TableName SET first='$First', last='$Last',
phone='$Phone', address='$Address', city='$City', state='$State',
zip='$Zip' WHERE flyerID='$FlyerID'";
$QueryResult = @mysqli_query($DBConnect, $SQLstring)
     Or die("<p>Unable to execute the query.</p>"
          . "<p>Error code " . mysqli_errno($DBConnect)
          . ": " . mysqli_error($DBConnect)) . "</p>";
mysqli_close($DBConnect);
```

9. Save the document as **ContactUpdate.php** in the Chapter directory for Chapter 10.

10

The `path` Argument

The `path` argument determines the availability of a cookie to other Web pages on a server. By default, a cookie is available to all Web pages in the same directory. However, if you specify a path, a cookie is available to all Web pages in the specified path as well as to all Web pages in all subdirectories in the specified path. For example, the following statement makes the cookie named `firstName` available to all Web pages located in the marketing directory or any of its subdirectories:

```
setcookie("firstName", "Don", time()+3600, "/marketing/");
```

To make a cookie available to all directories on a server, use a slash to indicate the root directory, as in the following example:

```
setcookie("firstName", "Don", time()+3600, "/");
```

When you are developing PHP scripts that create cookies, your programs may not function correctly if the directory containing your Web page contains other programs that create cookies. Cookies from other programs that are stored in the same directory along with unused cookies you created during development can cause your PHP cookie script to run erratically. Therefore, it is a good idea to always place PHP cookie scripts in their own directory and use the *path* argument to specify any subdirectories your program requires.

The domain Argument

Using the `path` argument allows cookies to be shared across a server. Some Web sites, however, are very large and use a number of servers. The `domain` argument is used for sharing cookies across multiple servers in the same domain. Note that you cannot share cookies outside of a domain. For example, if the Web server `programming.gosselin.com` needs to share cookies with the Web server `writing.gosselin.com`, the `domain` argument for cookies set by `programming.gosselin.com` should be set to `.gosselin.com`. That way, cookies created by `programming.gosselin.com` are available to `writing.gosselin.com` and to all other servers in the domain `gosselin.com`.

The following code shows how to make a cookie at `programming.gosselin.com` available to all servers in the `gosselin.com` domain:

```
setcookie("firstName", "Don", time()+3600, "/", ".gosselin.com");
```

The secure Argument

Internet connections are not always considered safe for transmitting sensitive information. It is possible for unscrupulous people to steal personal information, such as credit card numbers, passwords, Social Security numbers, and other types of private information online. To protect private data transferred across the Internet, Netscape developed Secure Sockets Layer, or SSL, to encrypt data and transfer it across a secure connection. Web sites that support SSL usually start with HTTPS instead of HTTP. The `secure` argument indicates that a cookie can only be transmitted across a secure Internet connection using HTTPS or another security protocol. To use this argument, you assign a value of 1 (for true) or 0 (for false) as the last argument of the `setcookie()` function. For example, to activate the *secure* attribute for a cookie, you use a statement similar to the following:

```
setcookie("firstName", "Don", time()+3600, "/", ".gosselin.com", 1);
```

Reading Cookies

Cookies that are available to the current Web page are automatically assigned to the `$_COOKIE` autoglobal. You can then access each cookie by using the cookie name as a key in the associative `$_COOKIE[]` array. (Recall that autoglobals are associative arrays.) The following statement prints the value assigned to the `firstName` cookie:

```
echo $_COOKIE['firstName'];
```

When you first create a cookie with the `setcookie()` function, the cookie is not available to the current Web page until you reload it. For example, the following statement causes an error when the Web page first loads because you cannot access the `firstName`, `lastName`, and `occupation` cookies until you reload the Web page:

```
setcookie("firstName", "Don");
setcookie("lastName", "Gosselin");
setcookie("occupation", "writer");
echo "{$_COOKIE['firstName']} {$_COOKIE['lastName']} is a
{$_COOKIE['occupation']}.";
```

To ensure that a cookie is set before you attempt to use it, you can use the `isset()` function, the same as when you check whether form variables contain values.

```
setcookie("firstName", "Don");
setcookie("lastName", "Gosselin");
setcookie("occupation", "writer");
if (isset($_COOKIE['firstName'])
     && isset($_COOKIE['lastName'])
     && isset($_COOKIE['occupation']))
     echo "{$_COOKIE['firstName']} {$_COOKIE['lastName']}
           is a {$_COOKIE['occupation']}.";
```

When you store cookies in indexed or associative arrays, PHP stores the cookies as two-dimensional arrays within the `$_COOKIE[]` autoglobal. Therefore, you must use multi-dimensional array syntax to read each cookie value. You refer to cookie arrays by using the cookie name as the first dimension and each index or key that represents a cookie value as the second dimension. For example, the following statements create and print an indexed version of the `professional[]` cookie array:


```
setcookie("professional[0]", "Don");
setcookie("professional[1]", "Gosselin");
setcookie("professional[2]", "writer");
if (isset($_COOKIE['professional']))
     echo "{$_COOKIE['professional'][0]}
          {$_COOKIE['professional'][1]} is a
          {$_COOKIE['professional'][2]}.";
```

The following statements create and print an associative version of the `professional[]` cookie array:

```
setcookie("professional[firstName]", "Don");
setcookie("professional[lastName]", "Gosselin");
setcookie("professional[occupation]", "writer");
if (isset($_COOKIE['professional']))
     echo "{$_COOKIE['professional']['firstName']}
     {$_COOKIE['professional']['lastName']} is a
     {$_COOKIE['professional']['occupation']}.";
```

Next, you add statements to the Update Contact Info page, Contact Info Updated page, and Frequent Flyer Club home page that read the stored cookies. First, you modify the Update Contact Info page so it reads the stored `flyerID` cookie.

To modify the Update Contact Info page so it reads the stored `flyerID` cookie:

1. Return to the **UpdateContactInfo.php** document in your text editor.
2. Add the following statements to the beginning of the script section, above the `mysqli_connect()` statement, to read the `flyerID` cookie:

   ```
   if (isset($_COOKIE['flyerID']))
        $FlyerID = $_COOKIE['flyerID'];
   ```

3. Save the **UpdateContactInfo.php** document.

Next, you modify the Contact Info Update page so it reads the stored `flyerID` cookie.

To modify the Contact Info Update page so it reads the stored `flyerID` cookie:

1. Return to the **ContactUpdate.php** document in your text editor.
2. Add the following statements to the beginning of the script section, above the first `if` statement, to read the `flyerID` cookie:

   ```
   if (isset($_COOKIE['flyerID']))
        $FlyerID = $_COOKIE['flyerID'];
   ```

3. Save the **ContactUpdate.php** document.

Next, you modify the Frequent Flyer Club home page so it reads the stored `flyerID` and the `customerName` cookies.

To modify the Frequent Flyer Club home page so it reads the stored `flyerID` and the `customerName` cookies:

1. Return to the **FrequentFlyerClub.php** document in your text editor.
2. Add the following statements, which read the `flyerID` cookie from the `$_COOKIE` autoglobal, immediately after the statement that retrieves the frequent flyer ID from the `$_GET` autoglobal. You need both sets of code because the Validate User page still uses a query string to log in existing users.

   ```
   if (isset($_COOKIE['flyerID']))
        $FlyerID = $_COOKIE['flyerID'];
   ```

3. Delete the following statements from the script section:

   ```
   $TableName = "frequent_flyers";
   $SQLstring = "SELECT * FROM $TableName WHERE flyerID='$FlyerID'";
   $QueryResult = @mysqli_query($DBConnect, $SQLstring)
        Or die("<p>Unable to execute the query.</p>"
        . "<p>Error code " . mysqli_errno($DBConnect)
        . ": " . mysqli_error($DBConnect)) . "</p>";
   if (mysqli_num_rows($QueryResult) == 0)
        exit("<p>Invalid frequent flyer number!</p>");
   $Row = mysqli_fetch_row($QueryResult);
   $CustomerName = $Row[3] . " " . $Row[4];
   ```

4. Add the following statements above the statement that declares the `$TableName` variable. These statements read the value stored in the `customerName` cookie.

```
$CustomerName = "";
if (isset($_COOKIE['customerName']))
     $CustomerName = $_COOKIE['customerName'];
```

5. Save the **FrequentFlyerClub.php** document.

Next, you modify the Registration/Log In page so it reads the persistent `customerName` cookie.

To modify the Registration/Log In page so it reads the persistent `customerName` cookie:

1. Open the **SkywardFlyers.php** document, located in the Chapter directory for Chapter 10, in your text editor.
2. Add the following script section immediately after the `<h2>` element for the Returning Flyers section.

```
<?php if(isset($_COOKIE['customerName'])) echo "<p>Welcome bac
{$_COOKIE['customerName']}!"; ?>
```

3. Save the **SkywardFlyers.php** document.
4. Open the **SkywardFlyers.php** document in your Web browser by entering the following URL: **http://localhost/PHP_Projects/Chapter.10/Chapter/SkywardFlyers.php**. Create a new frequent flyer account by entering an e-mail address and password in the New Flyer Registration form. You need to enter a different e-mail address than the one you used earlier. Click the **Register** button to obtain a frequent flyer number. The Frequent Flyer Registration page appears.
5. Click the **Enter Contact Information** link in the Frequent Flyer Registration page. The Contact Information Web page appears, as shown in Figure 10-9.

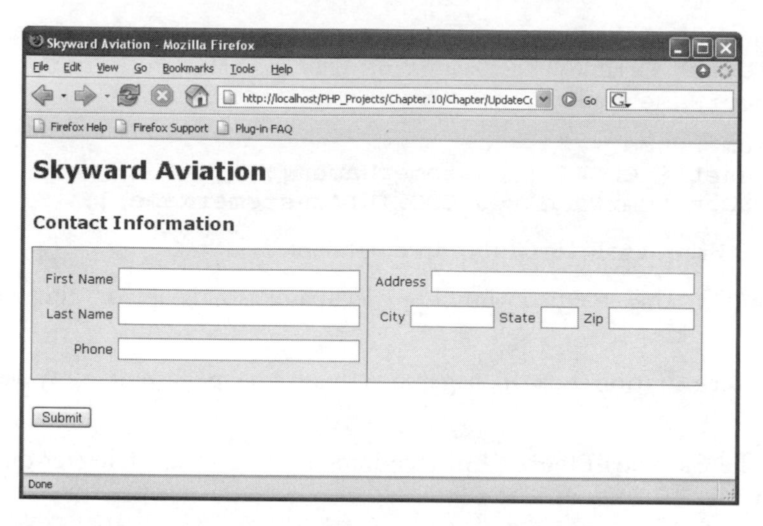

Figure 10-9 Contact Information Web page

6. Enter some contact information in the Contact Information page and click the **Submit** button. The Contact Info Updated Web page appears, as shown in Figure 10-10.

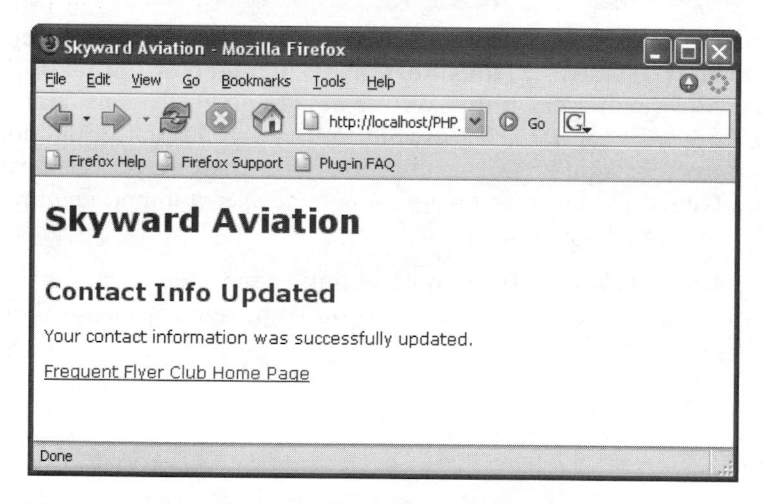

Figure 10-10 Contact Info Updated Web page

7. Click the **Frequent Flyer Club Home Page** link in the Contact Info Updated page. The Frequent Flyer Club home page appears. The customer name and frequent flyer number, which the script obtains from the cookies, should appear, as shown in Figure 10-11.

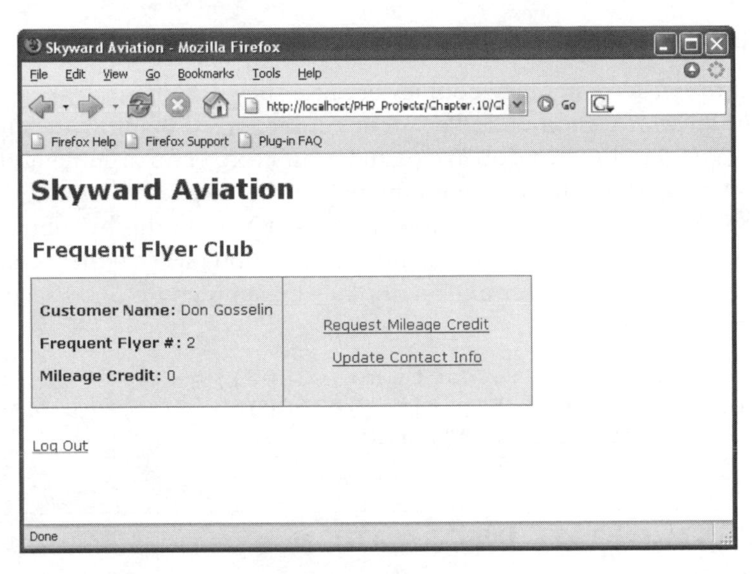

Figure 10-11 Frequent Flyer Club home page displaying the customer name and frequent flyer number

8. If you click the **Update Contact Info** link, you should be brought back to the Contact Information page. Click the **Submit** button to return to the Frequent Flyer Club home page.
9. Click the **Log Out** link on the Frequent Flyer Club home page. The Registration/Log In Web page appears. The name you entered on the Contact Information page should display beneath the Returning Flyers heading, as shown in Figure 10-12.

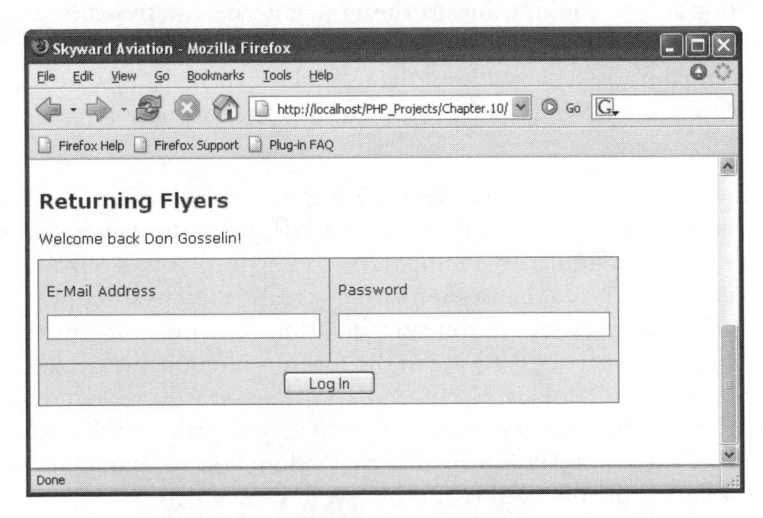

Figure 10-12 Registration/Log In Web page displaying text from a persistent cookie

10. Close your Web browser window.

Deleting Cookies

You do not need to delete temporary cookies because they automatically cease to exist when the current browser session ends. Persistent cookies are also automatically deleted when the time assigned to the `setcookie()` function's `expires` argument elapses. To delete a persistent cookie before the time assigned to the `expires` argument elapses, assign a new expiration value that is sometime in the past. You do this by subtracting any number of seconds from the `time()` function. The following statements delete the `firstName`, `lastName`, and `occupation` cookies by subtracting 3600 seconds (one hour) from the current time:

```
setcookie("firstName", "", time()-3600);
setcookie("lastName", "", time()-3600);
setcookie("occupation", "", time()-3600);
```

USING SESSIONS TO SAVE STATE INFORMATION

Saving state information with cookies is a common state preservation technique that is used by various Web development tools in addition to PHP. However, several security issues are involved with saving state in cookies on a client computer. The first issue is that you cannot ensure that every client computer on which your PHP scripts will run is properly secured. This means that any private information stored in cookies, including Social Security numbers and credit card information, may be accessible by hackers. Because of the security risks involved with cookies, many clients configure their Web browsers not to accept cookies. (You can disable cookies in every current Web browser.) Unfortunately, this also prevents any cookie preservation code in your PHP scripts from working.

Many clients do not accept cookies due to the rampant rise of **spyware**, which is an annoying type of software that gathers user information from a local computer for marketing and advertising purposes, but without the user's knowledge. Users are increasingly choosing to disable cookies to prevent spyware from gathering user information from stored cookies.

PHP offers more secure alternative to cookies: storing state information in sessions. The term **session** refers to a period of activity when a PHP script stores state information on a Web server. A session is similar to a temporary cookie in that it is only available for the current browser session. Note that sessions are not really used to store persistent data beyond the current browser session. If you want to store state information that will be available when a client revisits your Web site in the future, you must use cookies. Sessions are a little harder to use than cookies. However, because sessions store state information on a Web server, they are much safer to use—provided you properly secure your Web server. Another benefit to using sessions is that they allow you to maintain state information even when clients disable cookies in their Web browsers.

The php.ini configuration file contains numerous directives that you can use to control how sessions behave in your environment.

Starting a Session

Whenever you need to work with sessions in a PHP script, you must call the `session_start()` function, which starts a new session or continues an existing one. When you start a new session, the `session_start()` function generates a unique session ID to identify the session. A **session ID** is a random alphanumeric string that looks something like `7f39d7dd020773f115d753c71290e11f`. In addition to generating a session ID, the `session_start()` function creates a text file on the Web server that is the same name as the session ID, preceding by `sess_`. For example, the session ID text file for the preceding session ID would be `sess_7f39d7dd020773f115d753c71290e11f`. Any variables that are generated for a session are stored on the Web server in the text file whose name matches the session ID.

Session ID text files are stored in the Web server directory specified by the `session.save_path` directive in your php.ini configuration file.

The `session_start()` function does not accept any functions, nor does it return a value that you can use in your script. Instead, you simply call the `session_start()` function by itself in your PHP script, as follows:


```
<?php
session_start();
...
```

Like the `setcookie()` function, you must call the `session_start()` function before you send the Web browser any output, including white space, HTML elements, or output from the `echo()` or `print()` statements. If any output exists before you call the `session_start()` function, you receive an error and the function returns a value of false.

If a client's Web browser is configured to accept cookies, the session ID is assigned to a temporary cookie named `PHPSESSID`. However, because you cannot be certain that every client accepts cookies, you should also pass the session ID as a query string or hidden form field to any Web pages that are called as part of the current session. You pass a session ID in a name=value pair of PHPSESSID=*session ID*. You use the `session_id()` function to retrieve the session ID for the current session. For example, the following code starts a session and uses the `session_id()` function to pass the session ID as a query string to a Web page named Occupation.php:

```
<?php
session_start();
...
?>
<p><a href='<?php echo "Occupation.php?PHPSESSID="
     . session_id() ?>'>Occupation</a></p>
```

You can also use the constant SID, which contains a string consisting of "PHPSESSID=" and the session ID. The following example demonstrates how to use the constant `SID` to pass the session ID as a query string to another page:

```
<?php
session_start();
...
?>
<p><a href='<?php echo "Occupation.php?"
     . SID ?>'>Occupation</a></p>
```

For hidden form fields, assign a value of "PHPSESSID" to the *name* attribute and use the `session_id()` function to assign the session ID to the *value* attribute of the `<input>` element, as follows:

```
<input type="hidden" name="PHPSESSID"
     value='<?php echo session_id() ?>' />
```

Next, you modify the Validate Users page so it uses a session that tracks the frequent flyer ID number of the current user.

To modify the Validate Users page so it uses a session that tracks the frequent flyer ID number of the current user:

1. Return to the **ValidateUser.php** document in your text editor.
2. Cut and paste the entire PHP script section above the opening `<!DOCTYPE>` declaration.
3. Add the following `session_start()` statement to the beginning of the script section:

   ```
   session_start();
   ```

4. Modify the link to the FrequentFlyerClub.php script in the document body so it passes the session ID instead of the query string containing the frequent flyer ID. The modified link should appear as follows:

   ```
   <p><a href='<?php echo "FrequentFlyerClub.php?"
        . SID ?>'>Frequent Flyer Club Home Page</a></p>
   ```

5. Save the **ValidateUser.php** document.

Working with Session Variables

You store session state information in the `$_SESSION` autoglobal. When you call the `session_start()` function, PHP either initializes a new `$_SESSION` autoglobal or retrieves any variables for the current session (based on the session ID) into the

`$_SESSION` autoglobal. For example, the following code declares and initializes three variables, `firstName`, `lastName`, and `occupation`, in the `$_SESSION` autoglobal:

```
<?php
session_start();
session_set_cookie_params(3600);
$_SESSION['firstName'] = "Don";
$_SESSION['lastName'] = "Gosselin";
$_SESSION['occupation'] = "writer";
?>
<p><a href='<?php echo "Occupation.php?"
 . session_id() ?>'>Occupation</a></p>
```

When a user clicks the Occupation link, the `firstName`, `lastName`, and `occupation` variables are available in the `$_SESSION` autoglobal on the Occupation.html page. If the Occupation.html page contains the following script section, it prints *Don Gosselin is a writer.*

```
<?php
session_start();
echo "<p>" . $_SESSION['firstName'] . " " . $_SESSION['lastName']
 . " is a " . $_SESSION['occupation'] . "</p>";
?>
```

As with cookies, you can use the `isset()` function to ensure that a session variable is set before you attempt to use it, as follows:

```
<?php
session_start();
if (isset($_SESSION['firstName']) && isset($_SESSION['lastName'])
      && isset($_SESSION['occupation']))
     echo "<p>" . $_SESSION['firstName'] . " "
          . $_SESSION['lastName'] . " is a "
          . $_SESSION['occupation'] . "</p>";
?>
```

Next, you modify the Get Frequent Flyer ID page so it stores the frequent flyer ID number in the `$_SESSION` autoglobal.

To modify the Get Frequent Flyer ID page so it stores the frequent flyer ID number in the `$_SESSION` autoglobal:

1. Return to the **RegisterFlyer.php** document in your text editor.
2. Add a `session_start()` statement to the beginning of the script section:

   `session_start();`

3. Locate the statement at the end of the script section that declares the `$FlyerID` variable and modify it so the ID that is returned from the `mysqli_insert_id()` function is assigned to the `$_SESSION` autoglobal, as follows:

   `$_SESSION['flyerID'] = mysqli_insert_id($DBConnect);`

4. Delete the following statement:

```
setcookie("flyerID", $FlyerID);
```

5. Modify the paragraph element in the document body that prints the frequent flyer number so it refers to the `$_SESSION['flyerID']` autoglobal variable instead of to the `$FlyerID` variable, as follows:

```
<p>Your new frequent flyer ID is <strong>
     <?= $_SESSION['flyerID'] ?></strong>.</p>
```

6. Save the **RegisterFlyer.php** document, and then close it in your text editor.
7. Return to the **FrequentFlyerClub.php** document in your text editor.
8. Modify the links to the RequestMileage.php and the UpdateContactInfo.php so the session ID passes to each script as a query string. The modified links should appear as follows:

```
<p><a href='<?php echo "RequestMileage.php?"
     . SID ?>'>Request Mileage Credit</a></p>
<p><a href='<?php echo "UpdateContactInfo.php?"
     . SID ?>'>Update Contact Info</a></p>
```

9. Save the **FrequentFlyerClub.php** document.

Next, you modify the Validate User page so it stores the frequent flyer ID number in the `$_SESSION` autoglobal.

To modify the Validate User page so it stores the frequent flyer ID number in the `$_SESSION` autoglobal:

1. Return to the **ValidateUser.php** document in your text editor.
2. Modify the last statement in the script section so it assigns the frequent flyer ID to the `$_SESSION['flyerID']` autoglobal variable instead of to the `$FlyerID` variable, as follows:

```
...
else
     $_SESSION['flyerID'] = $Row[0];
?>
```

3. Save the **ValidateUser.php** document, and then close it in your text editor.

Next, you modify the Frequent Flyer Club Home page .php document so it uses the session ID to retrieve user information:

To modify the Frequent Flyer Club Home page .php document so it uses the session ID to retrieve user information:

1. Return to the **FrequentFlyerClub.php** document in your text editor.
2. Cut and paste the entire PHP script section above the opening `<!DOCTYPE>` declaration.

3. Replace the two `if` statements at the beginning of the script section with the following statement to start the session:

```
session_start();
```

4. Modify the statement that declares the SQL string so it refers to the `$_SESSION['flyerID']` autoglobal variable instead of to the `$FlyerID` variable, as follows:

```
$SQLstring = "SELECT SUM(mileage) FROM $TableName
      WHERE flyerID='{$_SESSION['flyerID']}'";
```

5. Modify the **Frequent Flyer #** paragraph element in the document body so it refers to the `$_SESSION['flyerID']` autoglobal variable instead of to the `$FlyerID` variable, as follows:

```
<p><strong>Frequent Flyer #:</strong>
     <?= $_SESSION['flyerID'] ?></p>
```

6. Save the **FrequentFlyerClub.php** document, and then close it in your text editor.

Next, you modify the Update Contact Info page so it uses the session ID to retrieve user information:

To modify the Update Contact Info page so it uses the session ID to retrieve user information:

1. Return to the **UpdateContactInfo.php** document in your text editor.
2. Cut and paste the entire PHP script section above the opening `<!DOCTYPE>` declaration.
3. Replace the `if` statement at the beginning of the script section that assigns the `flyerID` variable from the `$_COOKIE` autoglobal to the `$FlyerID` variable with the following statement to start the session:

```
session_start();
```

4. Modify the statement that declares the SQL string so it refers to the `$_SESSION['flyerID']` autoglobal variable instead of to the `$FlyerID` variable, as follows:

```
$SQLstring = "SELECT * FROM $TableName WHERE
      flyerID='{$_SESSION['flyerID']}'";
```

5. Add the following hidden form element, which passes the session ID to the Contact Info Updated page, to the end of the form:

```
<p><input type="hidden" name="PHPSESSID"
     value='<?php echo session_id() ?>' />
     <input type="submit" value="Submit" /></p>
```

6. Save the **UpdateContactInfo.php** document, and then close it in your text editor.

Next, you modify the Contact Info Updated page so it uses the session ID to retrieve user information:

To modify the Contact Info Updated page so it uses the session ID to retrieve user information:

1. Return to the **ContactUpdate.php** document in your text editor.
2. Replace the `if` statement at the beginning of the script section that assigns the `flyerID` variable from the `$_COOKIE` autoglobal to the `$FlyerID` variable with the following statement to start the session:

   ```
   session_start();
   ```
3. Modify the statement that declares the SQL string so it refers to the `$_SESSION['flyerID']` autoglobal variable instead of to the `$FlyerID` variable, as follows:

   ```
   $SQLstring = "UPDATE $TableName SET first='$First', last='$Last'
    phone='$Phone', address='$Address', city='$City',
    state='$State', zip='$Zip' WHERE flyerID='{$_SESSION['flyerID']}'";
   ```
4. Modify the link to the FrequentFlyerClub.php script so it passes the session ID as a query string. The modified link should appear as follows:

   ```
   <p><a href='<?php echo "FrequentFlyerClub.php?"
         . SID ?>'>Frequent Flyer Club Home Page</a></p>
   ```
5. Save the **ContactUpdate.php** document, and then close it in your text editor.
6. Open the **SkywardFlyers.php** file in your Web browser by entering the following URL: **http://localhost/PHP_Projects/Chapter.10/Chapter/SkywardFlyers.php**. Create a new frequent flyer registration and navigate through the various Web pages to test the session handling functionality. The state information should be saved just as it was with hidden form fields, query strings, and cookies.

The Request Mileage Credit link on the Frequent Flyer Club home page does not work yet. You add the Request Mileage Credit and Mileage Credit Updated pages in the Hands-On Projects later in this chapter.

7. Close your Web browser window.

Deleting a Session

Although a session automatically ends when the current browser session ends, there will be times when you need to delete a session manually. For example, you might want to give users the opportunity to end a session by clicking a Log Out button or link, or you might want a session to end if it is inactive for a specified period of time. To delete a session, you must perform the following steps:

1. Execute the `session_start()` function. (Remember that you must call the `session_start()` function whenever you need to work with sessions in a PHP script.)
2. Use the `array()` construct to reinitialize the `$_SESSION` autoglobal.
3. Use the `session_destroy()` function to delete the session.

For example, the following code deletes a session:

```
<?php
session_start();
$_SESSION = array();
session_destroy();
?>
```

Next, you modify the Registration/Log In page so it deletes any existing user sessions whenever a user opens it.

To modify the Registration/Log In page so it deletes any existing sessions whenever a user opens it:

1. Return to the **SkywardFlyers.php** document in your text editor.
2. Add the following script section and session deletion code to the beginning of the document, above the `<!DOCTYPE>` declaration:

```
<?php
session_start();
$_SESSION = array();
session_destroy();
?>
```

3. Save the **SkywardFlyers.php** document, and then close it in your text editor.
4. Open the **SkywardFlyers.php** file in your Web browser by entering the following URL: **http://localhost/PHP_Projects/Chapter.10/Chapter/SkywardFlyers.php**. Enter the e-mail address and password for a registered user and click the **Log In** button. You should see the Login Successful page. Click the **Frequent Flyer Club Home Page** link to open the Frequent Flyer Club home page. Notice the session ID appended to the URL in your browser's Address box.
5. Click the **Log Out** link on the Frequent Flyer Club home page to execute the session deletion code.
6. Close your Web browser window and text editor.

Chapter Summary

- Information about individual visits to a Web site is called state information. Maintaining state means to store persistent information about Web site visits.
- To pass form values from one PHP script to another PHP script, you can store the values in hidden form fields, which are submitted along with other types of form fields.
- One way to preserve information following a user's visit to a Web page is to append a query string to the end of a URL. To pass information from one Web page to another using a query string, add a question mark (`?`) immediately after a URL, followed by the query string containing the information you want to preserve in name=value pairs.
- Cookies, also called magic cookies, are small pieces of information about a user that are stored by a Web server in text files on the user's computer. Cookies can be temporary or persistent. Temporary cookies remain available only for the current browser session. Persistent cookies remain available beyond the current browser session and are stored in a text file on a client computer.
- You use the `setcookie()` function to create cookies in PHP. You must call the `setcookie()` function before you send the Web browser any output, including white space, HTML elements, or output from the `echo()` or `print()` statements.
- Cookies created with only the `name` and `value` arguments of the `setcookie()` function are temporary cookies, because they are available for only the current browser session.
- For a cookie to persist beyond the current browser session, you must use the `expires` argument with the `setcookie()` function.
- The `path` argument of the `setcookie()` function determines the availability of a cookie to other Web pages on a server.
- The `secure` argument of the `setcookie()` function indicates that a cookie can only be transmitted across a secure Internet connection using HTTPS or another security protocol.
- To delete a persistent cookie before the time assigned to the `expires` argument elapses, assign a new expiration value that is sometime in the past. You do this by subtracting any number of seconds from the `time()` function.
- Sessions refer to a period of activity when a PHP script stores state information on a Web server. When you start a new session, the `session_start()` function generates a unique session ID to identify the session. If a client's Web browser is configured to accept cookies, the session ID is assigned to a temporary cookie named `PHPSESSID`.
- You must call the `session_start()` function before you send the Web browser any output, including white space, HTML elements, or output from the `echo()` or `print()` statements.

- You store session state information in the `$_SESSION` autoglobal.
- To delete a session, you execute the `session_start()` function, use the `array()` construct to reinitialize the `$_SESSION` autoglobal, and then call the `session_destroy()` function to delete the session.

Review Questions

1. HTTP was originally designed to store data about individual visits to a Web site. True or False?
2. Stored information about a previous visit to a Web site is called ______________ information.
   a. HTTP
   b. client-side
   c. state
   d. prior
3. Describe the different types of information about a user that a Web server might need to store.
4. Explain how to use form fields to temporarily store user information.
5. In what format are items in a query string appended to a target URL?
   a. in comma-delimited format
   b. as name&value pairs
   c. as name=value pairs
   d. in name, value, length format
6. Explain how to use PHP to access query string data that is appended to a URL.
7. What is the correct syntax for creating a temporary cookie containing a value of "blue"?
   a. `$Color = setcookie("blue");`
   b. `setcookie("color", "blue");`
   c. `setcookie("blue", "color");`
   d. `setcookie("blue");`
8. You must manually encode and decode cookie values. True or False?
9. By default, cookies created without the `expires` argument of the `setcookie()` function are available for 24 hours. True or False?

10. Cookies created without the **expires** argument of the **setcookie()** function are called ______________.
    a. transient
    b. temporary
    c. permanent
    d. persistent
11. Which of the following examples specifies that a cookie should expire in three days?
    a. `time()+48h`
    b. `time()+24h*3`
    c. `time()+60*60*24*7`
    d. `time()+60*60*24*3`
12. The availability of a cookie to other Web pages on a server is determined by the ______________ argument of the **setcookie()** function.
    a. **path**
    b. **directory**
    c. **system**
    d. **server**
13. Which argument of the **setcookie()** function is used for sharing cookies outside of a domain?
    a. **domain**
    b. **share**
    c. **secure**
    d. You cannot share cookies outside of a domain.
14. You use the ______________ to read cookies in PHP.
    a. **$_COOKIE** autoglobal
    b. **$_COOKIES** autoglobal
    c. **cookie()** function
    d. **getcookie()** function
15. How do you delete cookies before the time assigned to the **setcookie()** function's **expires** argument elapses?
    a. Assign a **NULL** value with the **setcookie()** function.
    b. Subtract any number of seconds from the **time()** function.
    c. Execute the **deletecookie()** function.
    d. You cannot delete a cookie before the time assigned to the **setcookie()** function's **expires** argument elapses.

16. Explain the security risks involved with cookies and how sessions offer a more secure method of maintaining state.
17. Unlike the `setcookie()` function, you can call the `session_start()` function from any location on a Web page. True or False?
18. What is the name of the cookie that PHP creates for a session?
    a. `SESSION`
    b. `PHPSESSION`
    c. `SESSIONID`
    d. `PHPSESSID`
19. Explain how to pass a session ID to other PHP scripts when cookies are not available.
20. You use the ________________ to access session variables in PHP.
    a. `$_SESSION` autoglobal
    b. `$_SESSIONS` autoglobal
    c. `session()` function
    d. `getsession()` function

HANDS-ON PROJECTS

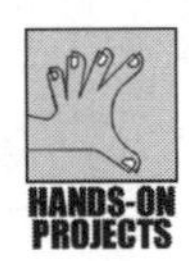

Hands-On Project 10-1

In this project, you complete the Request Mileage Credit page for the Skyward Aviation Frequent Flyer Web site. Your Chapter directory for Chapter 10 includes a document named RequestMileage.php that contains the HTML you will need for the page.

1. Open the **RequestMileage.php** document from your Chapter directory for Chapter 10.
2. Add the following script section, which contains a single `session_start()` statement, above the `<!DOCTYPE>` declaration:

```
<?php
session_start();
?>
```

3. Add the following hidden form field, which passes the session ID to the Mileage Credit Updated page, to the end of the form:

```
<p><input type="hidden" name="PHPSESSID"
     value='<?php echo session_id() ?>' /></p>
```

4. Save the document as **RequestMileage.php** in the Chapter directory for Chapter 10, and then close it in your text editor.

Hands-On Project 10-2

In this project, you create the Mileage Credit Updated page for the Skyward Aviation Frequent Flyer Web site.

1. Create a new document in your text editor and type the `<!DOCTYPE>` declaration, `<html>` element, header information, and `<body>` element. Use the strict DTD and "Skyward Aviation" as the content of the `<title>` element.
2. Add the following `<link>` element above the closing `</head>` tag to link to the php_styles.css style sheet in your Chapter directory:

```
<link rel="stylesheet" href="php_styles.css" type="text/css" />
```

3. Add the following text, elements, and script section to the document body:

```
<h1>Skyward Aviation</h1>
<h2>Mileage Credit Updated!</h2>
<p><a href='<?php echo "FrequentFlyerClub.php?" . SID
?>'>Frequent Flyer Club Home Page</a></p>
```

4. Add the following script section above the `<!DOCTYPE>` declaration:

```
<?php

?>
```

5. Add the following statements to the script section to start the session and to build variables containing the date and mileage submitted from the Request Mileage Credit page:

```
session_start();
$TravelDate = $_GET['year'] . "-" . $_GET['month']
     . "-" . $_GET['date'];
$Mileage = $_GET['mileage'];
```

6. Add the following statements to the end of the script section to connect to the database server and open the `skyward_aviation` database. Be sure to replace *`user`* and *`password`* with your username and password.

```
$DBConnect = @mysqli_connect("localhost", "user", "password")
     Or die("<p>Unable to connect to the database server.</p>"
     . "<p>Error code " . mysqli_connect_errno()
     . ": " . mysqli_connect_error()) . "</p>";
$DBName = "skyward_aviation";
@mysqli_select_db($DBConnect, $DBName)
     Or die("<p>Unable to select the database.</p>"
     . "<p>Error code " . mysqli_errno($DBConnect)
     . ": " . mysqli_error($DBConnect)) . "</p>";
```

7. Add the following statements to the end of the script section to open the `mileage` table, which records the mileage for each trip the user takes:

```
$TableName = "mileage";
$SQLstring = "SELECT * FROM $TableName";
$QueryResult = @mysqli_query($DBConnect, $SQLstring);
```

8. Add the following statements to the end of the script section to add records to the `mileage` table and close the database connection:

```
$SQLstring = "INSERT INTO $TableName VALUES(NULL,
 '{$_SESSION['flyerID']}', '$TravelDate', $Mileage)";
$QueryResult = @mysqli_query($DBConnect, $SQLstring)
     Or die("<p>Unable to execute the query.</p>"
          . "<p>Error code " . mysqli_errno($DBConnect)
          . ": " . mysqli_error($DBConnect)) . "</p>";
mysqli_close($DBConnect);
```

9. Save the document as **UpdateMileage.php** in the Chapter directory for Chapter 10, and then close it in your text editor.

10. Open the **SkywardFlyers.php** file in your Web browser by entering the following URL: **http://localhost/PHP_Projects/Chapter.10/Chapter/SkywardFlyers.php**. Enter the e-mail address and password for a registered user and click the **Log In** button. You should see the Login Successful page. Click the **Frequent Flyer Club Home Page** link to open the Frequent Flyer Club home page, and then click the **Request Mileage Credit** link to open the Request Mileage Credit Web page, which is shown in Figure 10-13.

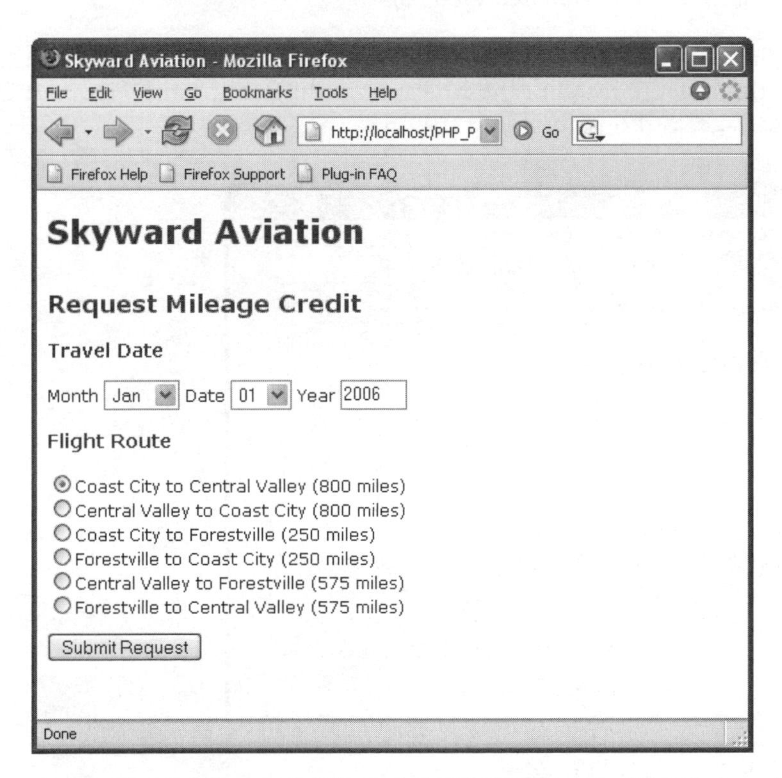

Figure 10-13 Request Mileage Credit Web page of the Skyward Aviation Frequent Flyer Web site

11. Select the travel date and a flight route and click the **Submit Request** button. You should see the Mileage Credit Update Web page, as shown in Figure 10-14.

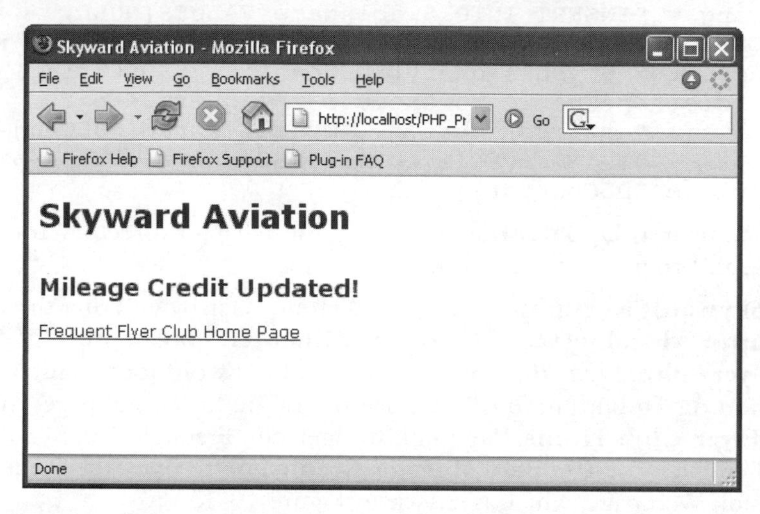

Figure 10-14 Mileage Credit Updated Web page

12. Click the **Frequent Flyer Club Home Page** link to return the home page. You should see the mileage listed in the Mileage Credit field on the Frequent Flyer Club home page, as shown in Figure 10-15.

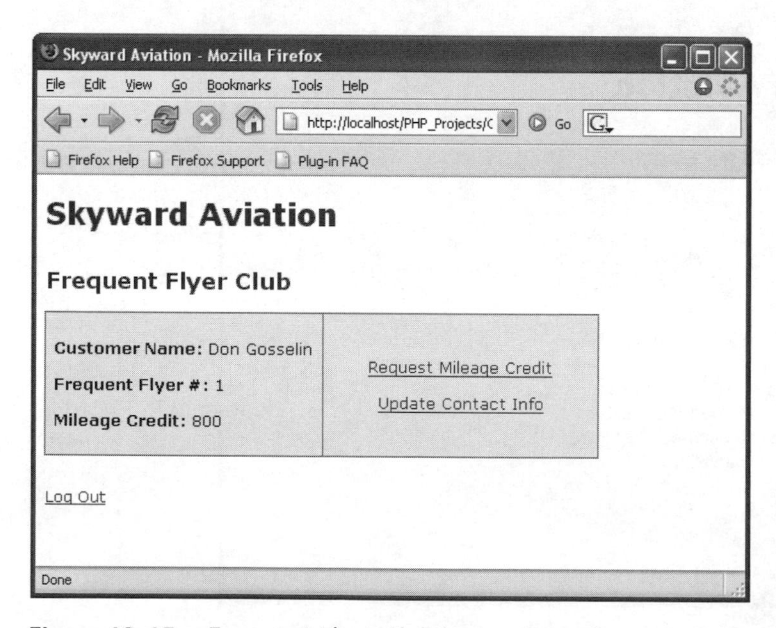

Figure 10-15 Frequent Flyer Club home page after requesting mileage credit

13. Close your Web browser window.

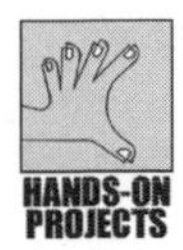

Hands-On Project 10-3

The Get Frequent Flyer ID page and the Validate User page of the Skyward Aviation Frequent Flyer Web site contain validation code to ensure that users enter valid e-mail addresses and passwords in the Registration/Log In page before assigning a frequent flyer ID to the `$_SESSION['flyerID']` variable. However, the other pages on the Web site assume that the `$_SESSION['flyerID']` variable is already set. If users attempt to open these pages directly instead of going through the Registration/Log In page, they receive errors. In this project, you modify the pages that make up the Skyward Aviation Frequent Flyer Web site so they use an `isset()` function to confirm that the `$_SESSION['flyerID']` variable is already set. If the variable is not set, a `header("location:`*`URL`*`")` function redirects users to the Registration/Log In page.

1. Open the **UpdateContactInfo.php** document from the Chapter directory for Chapter 10.
2. Immediately after the `session_start()` statement, add the following `isset()` function to confirm that the `$_SESSION['flyerID']` variable is already set and to redirect users to the Registration/Log In page if it is not:

   ```
   if (!isset($_SESSION['flyerID']))
        header("location:SkywardFlyers.php");
   ```

3. Save and close the **UpdateContactInfo.php** document.
4. Open the **ContactUpdate.php** document from the Chapter directory for Chapter 10 and add the same validation code immediately after the `session_start()` statement, and then save and close the document.
5. Open the **FrequentFlyerClub.php** document from the Chapter directory for Chapter 10 and add the same validation code immediately after the `session_start()` statement, and then save and close the document.
6. Open the **RequestMileage.php** document from the Chapter directory for Chapter 10 and add the same validation code immediately after the `session_start()` statement, and then save and close the document.
7. Open the **UpdateMileage.php** document from the Chapter directory for Chapter 10 and add the same validation code immediately after the `session_start()` statement, and then save and close the document.
8. Open the **SkywardFlyers.php** file in your Web browser by entering the following URL: **http://localhost/PHP_Projects/Chapter.10/Chapter/SkywardFlyers.php**. Enter the e-mail address and password for a registered user and click the **Log In** button. Test the Web site to ensure it works properly, and then close your Web browser.

9. Open your Web browser again and try directly opening one of the pages in the Skyward Aviation Frequent Flyer Web site, without going through the Registration/Log In page. For example, try opening the Request Mileage Credit page by entering the following URL: **http://localhost/PHP_Projects/Chapter.10/Chapter/RequestMileage.php**. You should be redirected to the Registration/Log In page.
10. Close your Web browser window.

Hands-On Project 10-4

In this project, you create a cookies program that stores the date and time of a user's last visit.

1. Create a new document in your text editor and type the `<!DOCTYPE>` declaration, `<html>` element, header information, and `<body>` element. Use the strict DTD and "Last Visit" as the content of the `<title>` element.
2. Add the following script section above the `<!DOCTYPE>` declaration:

```
<?php
?>
```

3. Add the following `if...else` statement to the script section to assign a value to the `$LastVisit` variable. If the `$_COOKIE['lastVisit']` variable is set, the date and time of the last visit is assigned to the `$LastVisit` variable. Otherwise, the variable is assigned a value of "This is your first visit!"

```
if (isset($_COOKIE['lastVisit']))
     $LastVisit = "<p>Your last visit was on "
          . $_COOKIE['lastVisit'];
else
     $LastVisit = "<p>This is your first visit!</p>";
```

4. Add the following statement to the end of the script section. The statement uses the `date()` function with the `setcookie()` function to assign the date to the `$LastVisit` variable.

```
setcookie("lastVisit", date("F j, Y, g:i a"),
     time()+60*60*24*365);
```

5. Add to the document body the following output directive, which prints the value of the `$LastVisit` variable:

```
<? = $LastVisit ?>
```

6. Save the document as **LastVisit.php** in the Projects directory for Chapter 10, and then close it in your text editor.

7. Open the **LastVisit.php** file in your Web browser by entering the following URL: **http://localhost/PHP_Projects/Chapter.10/Projects/LastVisit.php**. The first time you open the page, you should see "This is your first visit!" print to the browser window. Reload the Web page, and you should see the date and time print to the browser window.
8. Close your Web browser window.

CASE PROJECTS

Save the documents you create for the following projects in the Cases directory for Chapter 10.

Case Project 10-1

Create a document that stores and reads cookies containing a user's name and the number of times he or she has visited your Web site. Whenever a user visits the site, print the cookies, increment the counter cookie by one, and then reset the counter cookie expiration date to one year from the current date.

Case Project 10-2

Create a document with a "nag" counter that reminds users to register. Save the counter in a cookie and display a message reminding users to register every fifth time they visit your site. Create a form in the body of the document that includes text boxes for a user's name and e-mail address along with a Registration button, and store the information in a database. After a user fills in the text boxes and clicks the Registration button, delete the nag counter cookie and replace it with cookies containing the user's name and e-mail address. After registering, print the name and e-mail address cookies whenever the user revisits the site.

Case Project 10-3

You can use PHP's `rand()` function to generate a random integer. The `rand()` function accepts two arguments. The first argument specifies the minimum integer to generate, and the second argument specifies the maximum integer to generate. For example, the statement `$RandNum = rand(10, 20)` generates a random integer between 10 and 20 and assigns the number to the `$RandNum` variable. Create a guessing game that uses sessions to store a random number between 0 and 100, along with the number of guesses the user has attempted. Each time the user guesses wrong, display the number of times he or she has guessed. Include a Give Up link that displays the generated number for the current game. Also include a Start Over link that deletes the user session and uses the `header("location:URL")` function to navigate to the main page.

Case Project 10-4

Create a set of Web pages that registers users for a professional conference. Use a session to track users as they navigate through the Web pages. Include three separate Web pages containing forms: The first form gathers the user's name and contact information, the second form gathers the user's company information, and the third form prompts users to select the seminars they want to attend at the conference. Include a fourth page that displays the submitted information. The fourth page should include links that allow users to edit the submitted data, along with a Submit button that saves the information to a database. A fifth page should display a confirmation that the information was successfully saved. Include code that prevents the same user from registering twice, based on an e-mail address.

Case Project 10-5

Create a set of Web pages that reserves hotel rooms. Store room rates in a database, and calculate rates according to the number of guests, room size (standard, suite, junior suite), and discounts for corporations and for members of AAA and AARP. Require users to register and log in before making any reservations. Use a session to track users as they navigate through the Web pages and save the reservation information to a database. Include functionality that allows users to view, change, and cancel their reservations.

CHAPTER

11

DEVELOPING OBJECT-ORIENTED PHP

In this chapter, you will:

- Study object-oriented programming concepts
- Use objects in PHP scripts
- Declare data members in classes
- Work with class member functions

The PHP programs you have written so far have mostly been self-contained—that is, most of the code, such as variables, statements, and functions, exists within a script section. For example, you might create a Web page for an online retailer that uses PHP to calculate the total for a sales order that includes state sales tax and shipping. However, suppose the retailer sells different types of products on different Web pages, with one page selling baseball uniforms, another page selling jellybeans, and so on. If you want to reuse the PHP sales total code on multiple Web pages, you must copy all of the statements or re-create them from scratch for each Web page. Object-oriented programming takes a different approach. Essentially, object-oriented programming allows you to use and create self-contained sections of code—known as objects—that can be reused in your programs. In other words, object-oriented programming allows you to reuse code without having to copy or re-create it.

PHP 5 added many new object-oriented programming capabilities to the PHP language. In fact, PHP's object-oriented programming features now rival those found in more advanced languages, such as Java and C++. However, as you work through this chapter, keep in mind that entire books are written on object-oriented programming. This chapter only covers enough of the basics to get you started in creating object-oriented PHP scripts.

INTRODUCTION TO OBJECT-ORIENTED PROGRAMMING

The term **object-oriented programming (OOP)** refers to the creation of reusable software objects that can be easily incorporated into multiple programs. The term **object** specifically refers to programming code and data that can be treated as an individual unit or component. (Objects are often also called **components**.) For example, you might create a `Loan` object that calculates the number of payments required to pay off a loan. The `Loan` object might also store information such as the principal loan amount and the interest rate. The term **data** refers to information contained within variables or other types of storage structures. The functions associated with an object are called **methods**, and the variables that are associated with an object are called **properties** or **attributes**. In the `Loan` object example, a function that calculates the number of payments required to pay off the loan is a method. The principal loan amount and the interest rate are properties of the `Loan` object.

Objects can range from simple controls, such as a button, to entire programs, such as a database application. In fact, some programs consist entirely of other objects. You'll often encounter objects that have been designed to perform a specific task. For example, in a retail sales program, you could refer to all of the code that calculates the sales total as a single object. You could then reuse that object over and over again in the same program just by typing the object name.

Popular object-oriented programming languages include C++, Java, and Visual Basic. Using any of these or other object-oriented languages, programmers can create objects themselves or use objects created by other programmers. For example, if you are creating an accounting program in Visual Basic, you can use an object named `Payroll` that was created in C++. The `Payroll` object might contain one method that calculates the amount of federal and state tax to deduct, another function that calculates the FICA amount to deduct, and so on. Properties of the `Payroll` object might include an employee's number of tax withholding allowances, federal and state tax percentages, and the cost of insurance premiums. You do not need to know how the `Payroll` object was created in C++, nor do you need to re-create it in Visual Basic. You only need to know how to access the methods and properties of the `Payroll` object from the Visual Basic program.

An object-oriented accounting program is conceptually illustrated in Figure 11-1. In the figure, the accounting program is composed of three separate objects, or components: an `AccountsReceivable` object, the `Payroll` object, and an `AccountsPayable` object. The important thing to understand is that you do not need to rewrite the `Payroll`, `AccountsPayable`, and `AccountsReceivable` objects for the accounting program; the accounting program only needs to call their methods and provide the correct data to their properties.

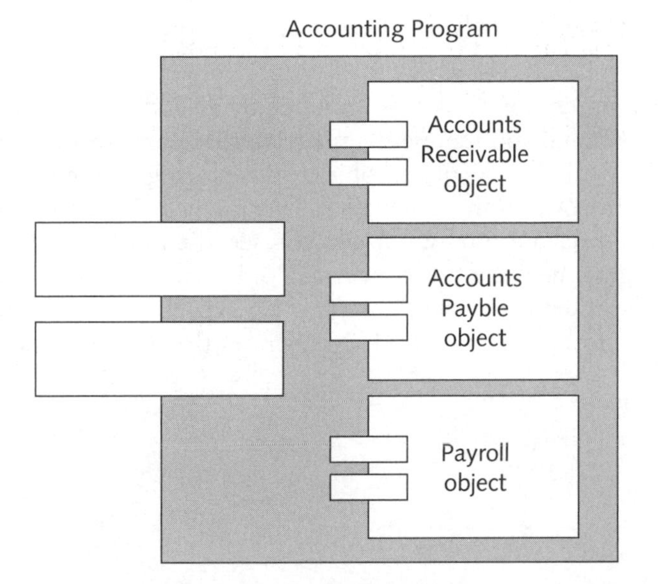

Figure 11-1 Accounting program

The diagram in Figure 11-1 is created in Unified Modeling Language, or UML, which is a modeling language that uses symbols to represent software elements, such as objects, methods, and properties. UML is very useful for visually designing and documenting software and other types of engineering systems.

11

Understanding Encapsulation

Objects are **encapsulated**, which means that all code and required data are contained within the object itself. In most cases, an encapsulated object consists of a single computer file that contains all code and required data. Encapsulation places code inside what programmers like to call a "black box." When an object is encapsulated, you cannot see "inside" it—all internal workings are hidden. The code (methods and statements) and data (variables and constants) contained in an encapsulated object are accessed through an interface. An **interface** refers to the methods and properties that are required for a source program to communicate with an object. For example, interface elements required to access a `Payroll` object might be a method named `calcNetPay()`, which calculates an employee's net pay, and properties containing the employee's name and pay rate.

When you include encapsulated objects in your programs, users can see only the methods and properties of the object that you allow them to see. By removing the ability to see inside the black box, encapsulation reduces the complexity of the code, allowing programmers who use the code to concentrate on the task of integrating the code into their programs. Encapsulation also prevents other programmers from accidentally introducing a bug into a program, or from possibly even stealing the code and claiming it as their own.

You can compare a programming object and its interface to a handheld calculator. The calculator represents an object, and you represent a program that wants to use the object. You establish an interface with the calculator object by entering numbers (the data required by the object) and then pressing calculation keys (which represent the methods of the object). You do not need to know, nor can you see, the inner workings of the calculator object. As a programmer, you are concerned only with an object's methods and properties. To continue the analogy, you are only concerned with the result you expect the calculator object to return. Figure 11-2 illustrates the idea of the calculator interface.

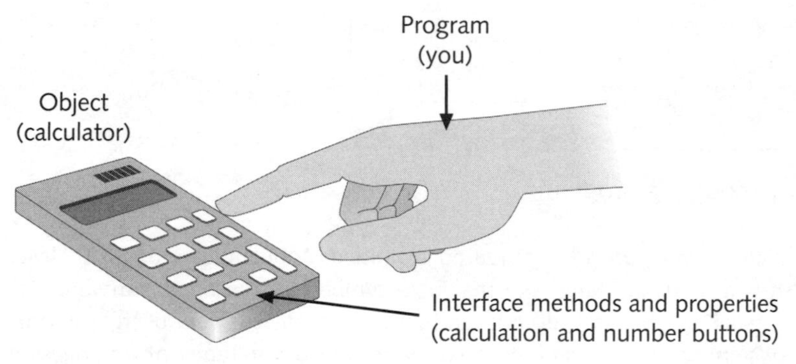

Figure 11-2 Calculator interface

Another example of an object and its interface is Microsoft Word. Word itself is actually an object made up of numerous other objects. The program window (or user interface) is one object. The items you see in the interface, such as the menu and toolbars, are used to execute methods. For example, the Bold button on the toolbar executes a bold method. The text of your document is the data you provide to the program. Word is a helpful tool that you can use without knowing how the various methods work. You only need to know what each method does. To get full satisfaction out of Word, you only need to provide the data (text) and execute the appropriate methods (such as the bold method), when necessary. In the same way, when using objects in your code, you only need to provide the necessary data (such as an employee's gross pay) and execute the appropriate method (such as the `calcNetPay()` method).

Object-Oriented Programming and Classes

In object-oriented programming, the code, methods, attributes, and other information that make up an object are organized into **classes**. Essentially, a class is a template, or blueprint, that serves as the basis for new objects. When you use an object in your program, you actually create an instance of the class of the object. An **instance** is an object that has been created from an existing class. When you create an object from an existing class, you are said to be **instantiating** the object.

Later in this chapter, you learn how to create, or instantiate, an object from built-in PHP classes and from custom classes that you write yourself. However, as a conceptual example, consider an object named `BankAccount` that contains methods and properties that you might use to record transactions associated with a checking or savings account. The `BankAccount` object is created from a `BankAccount` class. To use the `BankAccount` class, you create an instance of the class. A particular instance of an object **inherits** its methods and properties from a class—that is, it takes on the characteristics of the class on which it is based. The `BankAccount` object, for instance, would inherit all of the methods and properties of the `BankAccount` class. To give another example, when you create a new word-processing document, which is a type of object, it usually inherits the properties of a template on which it is based. The template is a type of class. The document inherits characteristics of the template, such as font size, line spacing, and boilerplate text. In the same manner, programs that include instances of objects inherit the object's functionality.

Class names in traditional object-oriented programming usually begin with an uppercase letter. This convention is also followed in PHP.

In this chapter, you create the Web site for an online grocery store named Gosselin Gourmet Grocers. The store includes three shopping categories: gourmet coffees, specialty olives, and gourmet spices. The purpose of the Web site is to demonstrate code reuse with classes. As you progress through this chapter, you develop a class named `ShoppingCart` that handles the functionality of building and updating a shopping cart as a user selects items to purchase. Shopping cart classes are very popular with PHP development because of the many Web sites that offer online shopping. Rather than re-creating shopping cart functionality for each online Web site you develop, you can much more easily develop the Web site by reusing an existing shopping cart class. As you create the `ShoppingCart` class, notice that its functionality has nothing to do with the products sold by Gosselin Gourmet Grocers. Instead, the code is generic enough that it can be used with any Web site that sells products, provided the pages in the site and the associated database conform to the requirements of the class.

First, you create the database and tables that store the products sold by Gosselin Gourmet Grocers. The `ShoppingCart` class requires that product information is stored in tables containing four fields: `productID`, `name`, `description`, and `price`. The `productID` field is the primary key and consists of a unique text field. For example, the primary key for the first coffee product is COFFEE001. To keep things simple, the `ShoppingCart` class does not store customer or payment information. Instead, the class simply uses session IDs to keep track of each user's shopping cart.

Next, you create a database named `gosselin_gourmet` along with three tables, `coffee`, `olives`, and `spices`, to contain product information. Your Chapter directory for Chapter 11 contains three text files, coffee.txt, olives.txt, and spices.txt, containing product information to load into each database table.

To create the Gosselin Gourmet Grocers database:

1. Log in to the MySQL Monitor with the MySQL username and password you created in Chapter 8.
2. Enter the following command to create a database named `gosselin_gourmet`:

   ```
   mysql> CREATE DATABASE gosselin_gourmet;
   ```

3. After you see the "Query OK" message, enter the following command to select the `gosselin_gourmet` database:

   ```
   mysql> use gosselin_gourmet;
   ```

4. Enter the following command to create the `coffee` table:

   ```
   mysql> CREATE TABLE coffee (productID VARCHAR(10) PRIMARY KEY,
        -> name VARCHAR(100), description VARCHAR(200), price FLOAT);
   ```

5. After you see the "Query OK" message, enter a `LOAD DATA` statement that inserts records from the coffee.txt file in your Chapter directory for Chapter 11 into the `gosselin_gourmet` table. Replace *`path`* with the path to your Chapter directory for Chapter 11.

   ```
   mysql> LOAD DATA LOCAL INFILE 'path/coffee.txt'
        -> INTO TABLE coffee;
   ```

6. Enter the following command to create the `olives` table:

   ```
   mysql> CREATE TABLE olives (productID VARCHAR(10) PRIMARY KEY,
        -> name VARCHAR(100), description VARCHAR(200), price FLOAT);
   ```

7. After you see the "Query OK" message, enter a `LOAD DATA` statement that inserts records from the olives.txt file in your Chapter directory for Chapter 11 into the `gosselin_gourmet` table. Replace *`path`* with the path to your Chapter directory for Chapter 11.

   ```
   mysql> LOAD DATA LOCAL INFILE 'path/olives.txt'
        -> INTO TABLE olives;
   ```

8. Enter the following command to create the `spices` table:

   ```
   mysql> CREATE TABLE spices (productID VARCHAR(10) PRIMARY KEY,
        -> name VARCHAR(100), description VARCHAR(200), price FLOAT);
   ```

9. After you see the "Query OK" message, enter a **LOAD DATA** statement that inserts records from the spices.txt file in your Chapter directory for Chapter 11 into the **gosselin_gourmet** table. Replace *path* with the path to your Chapter directory for Chapter 11.

```
mysql> LOAD DATA LOCAL INFILE 'path/spices.txt'
    -> INTO TABLE spices;
```

10. Type **exit** or **quit** and press **Enter** to log out of the MySQL Monitor.

Next, you create a PHP script named GosselinGourmetGoods.php that acts as the main entry point for the Web site.

To create the GosselinGourmetGoods.php script:

1. Create a new document in your text editor and type the <!DOCTYPE> declaration, <html> element, header information, and <body> element. Use the strict DTD and "Gosselin Gourmet Goods" as the content of the <title> element.
2. Add the following <link> element above the closing </head> tag to link to the php_styles.css style sheet in your Chapter directory:

```
<link rel="stylesheet" href="php_styles.css" type="text/css" />
```

3. Add the following text and elements to the document body:

```
<h1>Gosselin Gourmet Goods</h1>
<h2>Shop by Category</h2>
<p><a href="GosselinGourmetCoffees.php">Gourmet Coffees</a><br />
<a href="GosselinGourmetOlives.php">Specialty Olives</a><br />
<a href="GosselinGourmetSpices.php">Gourmet Spices</a></p>
```

4. Save the document as **GosselinGourmetGoods.php** in the Chapter directory for Chapter 11 and then close it in your text editor.

Using Objects in PHP Scripts

Up to this point, all of the PHP scripts you have written have contained procedural statements that did not rely on objects. This does not mean that the skills you have learned so far are useless in constructing object-oriented programs. However, object-oriented techniques will help you build more extensible code that is easier to reuse, modify, and enhance. In this section, you first learn how to work with database connections as objects to help you understand how to use objects in your scripts. Then, you learn how to define your own custom classes.

Before you begin working with database connections as objects, you first need to understand a few basics of how to work with objects in PHP. You declare an object in PHP by using the new operator with a class constructor. A **class constructor** is a special function with the same name as its class that is called automatically when an object from the class is instantiated. For example, the class constructor for the `BankAccount` class is `BankAccount()`. The syntax for instantiating an object is as follows:

```
$ObjectName = new ClassName();
```

The identifiers you use for an object name must follow the same rules as identifiers for variables: They must begin with a dollar sign, can include numbers or an underscore (but not as the first character after the dollar sign), cannot include spaces, and are case sensitive. The following statement instantiates an object named `$Checking` from the `BankAccount` class:

```
$Checking = new BankAccount();
```

Class constructors are primarily used to initialize properties when an object is first instantiated. For this reason, you can pass arguments to many constructor functions. For example, the `BankAccount` class might require you to pass three arguments: the checking account number, a check number, and a check amount, as follows:

```
$Checking = new BankAccount(01234587, 1021, 97.58);
```

After you instantiate an object, you use a hyphen and a greater-than symbol (`->`) to access the methods and properties contained in the object. Together, these two characters are referred to as **member selection notation**. Using member selection notation is similar to using an operator in that you append one or more characters (in this case, `->`) to an object, followed by the name of a method or property. With methods, you must also include a set of parentheses at the end of the method name, just as you would with functions. Like functions, methods can also accept arguments.

The following statements demonstrate how to call two methods, `getBalance()` and `getCheckAmount()`, from the `$Checking` object. The `getBalance()` method does not require any arguments, whereas the `getCheckAmount()` function requires an argument containing the check number.

```
$Checking->getBalance();
$CheckNumber = 1022;
$Checking->getCheckAmount($CheckNumber);
```

To access property values in an object, you do not include parentheses at the end of the property name, as you do with functions and methods, nor do you include a dollar sign before the property name. For example, the following statements update and display the value in a property named `$Balance` in the `$Checking` object:

```
$CheckAmount = 124.75;
$Checking->Balance = $Checking->Balance + $CheckAmount;
printf("<p>Your updated checking account balance is $%.2f.</p>",
     $Checking->Balance);
```

Next, you start creating the GosselinGourmetCoffees.php script, which displays the coffee products available for purchase. The first version of the script simply queries the database and prints a table with the product information. Later in this chapter, you modify the script so it uses the `ShoppingCart` class.

To create the GosselinGourmetCoffees.php script:

1. Create a new document in your text editor and type the `<!DOCTYPE>` declaration, `<html>` element, header information, and `<body>` element. Use the strict DTD and "Gosselin Gourmet Goods" as the content of the `<title>` element.
2. Add the following `<link>` element above the closing `</head>` tag to link to the php_styles.css style sheet in your Chapter directory:

   ```
   <link rel="stylesheet" href="php_styles.css" type="text/css" />
   ```

3. Add the following text and elements to the document body:

   ```
   <h1>Gosselin Gourmet Goods</h1>
   <h2>Shop by Category</h2>
   <p><a href="GosselinGourmetCoffees.php">Gourmet Coffees</a><br />
   <a href="GosselinGourmetOlives.php">Specialty Olives</a><br />
   <a href="GosselinGourmetSpices.php">Gourmet Spices</a></p>
   ```

4. Save the document as **GosselinGourmetCoffees.php** in the Chapter directory for Chapter 11.

Working with Database Connections as Objects

PHP allows you to connect to and manipulate MySQL and other types of databases using either procedural statements or object-oriented techniques. Although you should not notice any performance issues when using procedural statements or object-oriented techniques to access MySQL databases, you can expect the object-oriented techniques to become the preferred method as PHP continues to evolve as an object-oriented programming language. For this reason, you should get used to the object-oriented method of accessing MySQL databases.

You access MySQL database connections as objects by instantiating an object from the `mysqli` class. The `mysqli` class contains methods and properties that perform the same functionality as the procedural MySQL database connection statements you have used so far. For example, the `mysqli_query()` function is a method named `query()` in the `mysqli` class and the `mysqli_affect_rows()` function is a property named `affected_rows` in the `mysqli` class. Next, you learn how to instantiate and close a MySQL database connection object.

Instantiating and Closing a MySQL Database Object

In Chapter 9, you learned how to use the `mysqli_connect()` function to open a connection to a MySQL database server. When connecting to the MySQL database server using object-oriented techniques, you instantiate an object from the `mysqli` class. You pass to the `mysqli` class the same *host*, *user*, *password*, and *database* arguments that you pass to the `mysqli_connect()` function. For example, the following statement uses the `mysqli_connect()` function to connect to a MySQL database server:

```
$DBConnect = mysqli_connect("localhost", "dongosselin",
     "rosebud", "real_estate");
```

In comparison, you use the following statement to connect to the MySQL database server using object-oriented style:

```
$DBConnect = new mysqli("localhost", "dongosselin",
      "rosebud", "real_estate");
```

The preceding statement uses the `mysqli()` constructor function to instantiate a `mysqli` class object named `$DBConnect`. Instead of using the `mysqli_close()` function to explicitly close the database connection when you are through working with it, you call the `close()` method of the `mysqli` class. For example, the following statement closes the database connection represented by the `$DBConnect` object (remember that `$DBConnect` is an object of the `mysqli` class):

```
$DBConnect->close();
```

Next, you add statements to the GosselinGourmetCoffees.php script that instantiate and close a database connection to the MySQL database server using object-oriented style.

To add statements to the GosselinGourmetCoffees.php script that instantiate and close a database connection to the MySQL database server using object-oriented style:

1. Return to the **GosselinGourmetCoffees.php** script in your text editor.
2. Add the following text, elements, and script section to the end of the document body:

```
<h2>Gourmet Coffees</h2>
<?php
?>
```

3. Add the following statements to the script section to connect to the database server using object-oriented style. The code uses an `if...else` statement to print `echo()` statements that verify whether the script connected to the database successfully. Be sure to replace *`user`* and *`password`* with your username and password.

```
$DBConnect = new mysqli("localhost", "user", "password",
     "gosselin_gourmet");
if (!$DBConnect)
   echo "<p>The database server is not available.</p>";
else
     echo "<p>Successfully connected to the database server.</p>";
```

4. Add the following statement to the end of the script section to close the database connection:

   ```
   $DBConnect->close();
   ```

5. Save the **GosselinGourmetCoffees.php** file and then open the **GosselinGourmetGoods.php** script in your Web browser by entering the following URL: **http://localhost/PHP_Projects/Chapter.11/Chapter/GosselinGourmetGoods.php**.

6. Click the **Gourmet Coffees** link. You should see the message about successfully connecting to the database server that is shown in Figure 11-3.

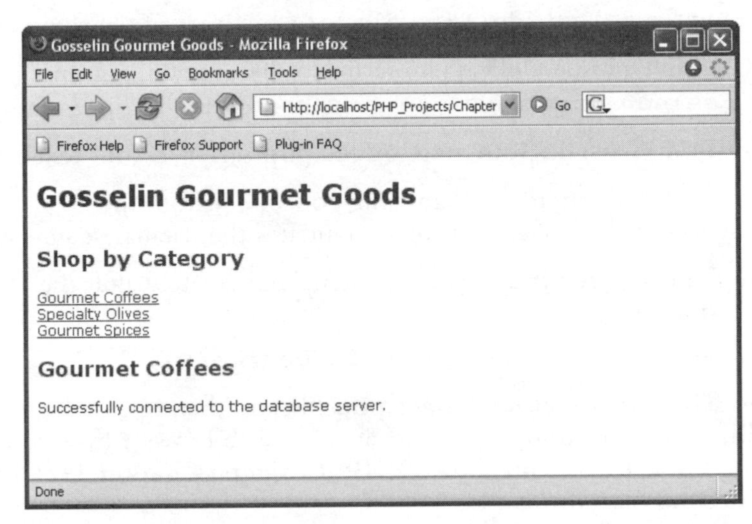

Figure 11-3 Gourmet Coffees Web page after connecting to the database server

7. Close your Web browser window.

Selecting a Database

With procedural syntax, instead of passing a database name as the fourth argument to the `mysqli_connect()` function, you can select or change a database with the `mysqli_select_db()` function. You pass two arguments to the `mysqli_select_db()` function: The first argument is the variable representing the database connection, and the second argument represents the name of the database you want to use. For example, the following statements use procedural syntax to open a connection to a MySQL database server, select a database named `real_estate`, and then close the database connection:

```
$DBConnect = mysqli_connect("localhost", "dongosselin", "rosebud");
mysqli_select_db($DBConnect, "real_estate");
// additional statements that access or manipulate the database
mysqli_close($DBConnect);
```

11

Similarly, you can also call the `select_db()` and `close()` methods of the `mysqli` class to select and close a database with object-oriented style. With object-oriented style, you only need to pass to the `select_db()` and `close()` methods a single argument representing the name of the database you want to use. The following statements show an object-oriented version of the preceding code:

```
$DBConnect = mysqli_connect("localhost", "dongosselin", "rosebud");
$DBConnect->select_db("real_estate");
// additional statements that access or manipulate the database
$DBConnect->close();
```

Next, you modify the GosselinGourmetCoffees.php script so the gosselin_gourmet database is opened using the `select_db()` and `close()` methods of the `mysqli` class.

To modify the GosselinGourmetCoffees.php script so the gosselin_gourmet database is opened using the `select_db()` and `close()` methods of the `mysqli` class:

1. Return to the **GosselinGourmetCoffees.php** script in your text editor.
2. Remove the fourth argument ("gosselin_gourmet") from the `mysqli_connect()` statement that instantiates the database connection.
3. Add the following `select_db()` statement immediately after the `mysqli_connect()` statement:

   ```
   $DBConnect->select_db("gosselin_gourmet");
   ```

4. Save the **GosselinGourmetCoffees.php** file and then open the **GosselinGourmetGoods.php** script in your Web browser by entering the following URL: **http://localhost/PHP_Projects/Chapter.11/Chapter/GosselinGourmetGoods.php**.
5. Click the **Gourmet Coffees** link. The Web page should appear the same as it did before you replaced the fourth argument in the `mysqli_connect()` statement with a `select_db()` statement.
6. Close your Web browser window.

Handling MySQL Errors

When you use procedural syntax to connect to the MySQL database server, the `mysqli_connect()` function returns a value of false if the database connection attempt fails. However, when you use the `mysqli()` constructor function to instantiate a new database object from the `mysqli` class, an object is instantiated even if the database connection fails. For this reason, with object-oriented style, you cannot simply terminate script execution with the `die()` or `exit()` functions in the event that the database connection fails, as you do with procedural syntax. For example, the following statements use procedural syntax to attempt to connect to the MySQL database server. If the connection attempt fails, the `die()` function terminates script execution and calls the `mysqli_connect_errno()` and `mysqli_connect_error()` functions to print an error code and message.

```
$DBConnect = @mysqli_connect("localhost", "dongosselin", "rosebud")
     Or die("<p>Unable to connect to the database server.</p>"
     . "<p>Error code " . mysqli_connect_errno()
     . ": " . mysqli_connect_error()) . "</p>";
```

With object-oriented style, you must check whether a value is assigned to the `mysqli_connect_errno()` or `mysqli_connect_error()` functions and then call the `die()` function to terminate script execution, as shown in the following example:

```
$DBConnect = @new mysqli("localhost", "dgosselin", "rosebud");
if (mysqli_connect_errno())
     die("<p>Unable to connect to the database server.</p>"
     . "<p>Error code " . mysqli_connect_errno()
     . ": " . mysqli_connect_error()) . "</p>";
```

Notice in the preceding example that the first statement, which instantiates the database connection object, uses the error control operator, `@`, to suppress error messages. Recall that you can place the error control operator before any expression to suppress error messages. The error control operator in the preceding example is placed before the `new` operator because the `new` operator begins the expression that instantiates the database connection object.

Most of the methods of the `mysqli` class return values of true or false, depending on whether the operation was successful. Therefore, for any methods of the `mysqli` class that fail (as indicated by a return value of false), you can terminate script execution by appending `die()` or `exit()` functions to method call statements. For example, the following statement uses an `Or` operator and the `die()` function to terminate script execution if the `select_db()` method returns a value of false. Notice that the statement which calls the `select_db()` method also uses the error control operator to suppress error messages.

```
$DBName = "guitars";
@$DBConnect->select_db($DBName)
     Or die("<p>Unable to select the database.</p>"
     . "<p>Error code " . mysqli_errno($DBConnect)
     . ": " . mysqli_error($DBConnect)) . "</p>";
```

Next, you add MySQL error-checking functionality to the GosselinGourmetCoffees.php script.

To add MySQL error-checking functionality to the GosselinGourmetCoffees.php script:

1. Return to the **GosselinGourmetCoffees.php** script in your text editor.
2. Delete the `if...else` statement that prints a message about whether the database connection is successful.

3. Add the error control operator (`@`) before the new keyword in the `mysqli_connect()` statement to suppress error messages, as follows:

```
$DBConnect = @new mysqli("localhost", "dongosselin", "rosebud");
```

4. Add the following error-checking statements immediately after the `mysqli_connect()` statement that instantiates the database object:

```
if (mysqli_connect_errno())
     die("<p>Unable to connect to the database server.</p>"
     . "<p>Error code " . mysqli_connect_errno()
     . ": " . mysqli_connect_error()) . "</p>";
```

5. Add the error control operator (@) to the beginning of the `select_db()` statement, as follows:

```
@$DBConnect->select_db("gosselin_gourmet");
```

6. Modify the `select_db()` statement so it includes error checking, as follows:

```
@$DBConnect->select_db("gosselin_gourmet")
     Or die("<p>Unable to select the database.</p>"
     . "<p>Error code " . mysqli_errno($DBConnect)
     . ": " . mysqli_error($DBConnect)) . "</p>";
```

7. Save the **GosselinGourmetCoffees.php** file and then open the **GosselinGourmetGoods.php** script in your Web browser by entering the following URL: **http://localhost/PHP_Projects/Chapter.11/Chapter/GosselinGourmetGoods.php**.

8. Click the **Gourmet Coffees** link. The Web page should appear the same as it did before you added the MySQL error-checking functionality with the exception of the "Successfully connected to the database server" message, which no longer appears.

9. Close your Web browser window.

Executing SQL Statements

Recall that you send SQL statements to MySQL with procedural syntax by using the `mysqli_query()` function. With object-oriented style, you use the `query()` method of the `mysqli` class. The `query()` method accepts a single argument representing the SQL statement you want to send to the MySQL database server. For queries that return results using procedural syntax, you use the `mysqli_fetch_row()` function to return the fields in the current row of a resultset into an indexed array and the `mysqli_fetch_assoc()` function returns the fields in the current row of a resultset into an associative array. In comparison, with object-oriented style, you call the `fetch_row()` and `fetch_assoc()` methods of the `mysqli` class.

The following code demonstrates how to use object-oriented style to execute a query that returns all the records from the `inventory` table of the `guitars` database. The code builds a table and uses the `fetch_row()` method to return the fields in the current row into an indexed array. The code is very similar to examples you have seen in the past few chapters. The only difference is that the SQL statement is executed and retrieved with the object-oriented `query()` and `fetch_row()` methods of the `mysqli` class instead of with the procedural `mysqli_query()` and `mysqli_fetch_row()` functions.

```
$TableName = "inventory";
$SQLstring = "SELECT * FROM inventory";
$QueryResult = $DBConnect->query($SQLstring)
     Or die("<p>Unable to execute the query.</p>"
          . "<p>Error code " . $DBConnect->errno
          . ": " . $DBConnect->error) . "</p>";

echo "<table width='100%' border='1'>";
echo "<tr><th>Make</th><th>Model</th>
<th>Price</th><th>Inventory</th></tr>";
$Row = $QueryResult->fetch_row();
do {
     echo "<tr><td>{$Row[0]}</td>";
     echo "<td>{$Row[1]}</td>";
     echo "<td align='right'>{$Row[2]}</td>";
     echo "<td align='right'>{$Row[3]}</td></tr>";
     $Row = $QueryResult->fetch_row();
} while ($Row);
```

Next, you add code to the GosselinGourmetCoffees.php script that uses an object-oriented style query to retrieve product information from the `coffee` table in the `gosselin_gourmet` database.

To add code that uses an object-oriented style query to the GosselinGourmetCoffees.php script:

1. Return to the **GosselinGourmetCoffees.php** script in your text editor.
2. Add the following statements above the statement that closes the database connection. The first statement creates a SQL string, and the second statement uses object-oriented style syntax to perform the query.

```
$SQLstring = "SELECT * FROM coffee";
$QueryResult = $DBConnect->query($SQLstring)
     Or die("<p>Unable to perform the query.</p>"
     . "<p>Error code " . mysqli_errno($DBConnect)
     . ": " . mysqli_error($DBConnect)) . "</p>";
```

3. Add the following statements above the statement that closes the database connection. These statements build a table that displays the results returned from the query.

```
echo "<table width='100%' border='1'>";
echo "<tr><th>Product</th><th>Description</th>
<th>Price Each</th></tr>";
$Row = $QueryResult->fetch_row();
do {
     echo "<tr><td>{$Row[1]}</td>";
     echo "<td>{$Row[2]}</td>";
     printf("<td align='center'>$%.2f</td></tr>", $Row[3]);
     $Row = $QueryResult->fetch_row();
} while ($Row);
echo "</table>";
```

4. Save the **GosselinGourmetCoffees.php** file and then open the **GosselinGourmetGoods.php** script in your Web browser by entering the following URL: **http://localhost/PHP_Projects/Chapter.11/Chapter/GosselinGourmetGoods.php**.

5. Click the **Gourmet Coffees** link. You should see the table shown in Figure 11-4.

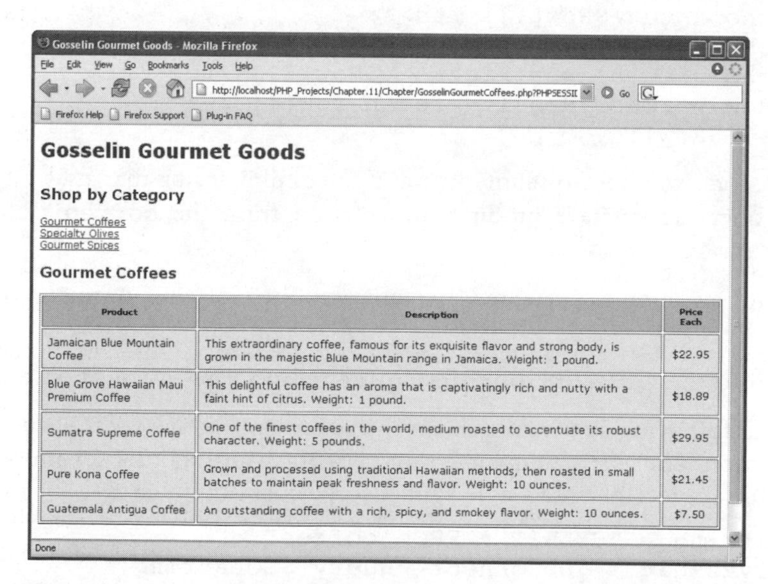

Figure 11-4 Gourmet Coffees Web page displaying query results

6. Close your Web browser window.

Defining Custom PHP Classes

Classes were defined earlier in this chapter as the code, methods, attributes, and other information that make up an object. In PHP, classes more specifically refer to data structures that contain variables along with functions for manipulating the variables. The term **data structure** refers to a system for organizing data. Some of the data structures you have already used include arrays, text files, and database records. The functions and variables defined in a class are called **class members**. Class variables are referred to as **data members** or **member variables**, whereas class functions are referred to as **member functions** or **function members**. To use the variables and functions in a class, you declare an object from that class. After you instantiate a class object, class data members are referred to as properties of the object and class member functions are referred to as methods of the object.

Classes themselves are also referred to as user-defined data types or programmer-defined data types. These terms can be somewhat misleading, however, because they do not accurately reflect the fact that classes can contain member functions. In addition, classes usually contain multiple data members of different data types, so calling a class a data type becomes even more confusing. One reason classes are referred to as user-defined data types or programmer-defined data types is that you can work with a class as a single unit, or object, in the same way you work with a variable. In fact, the terms variable and object are often used interchangeably in object-oriented programming. The term object-oriented programming comes from the fact that you can bundle variables and functions together and use the result as a single unit (a variable or object).

What this means will become clearer to you as you progress through this chapter. For now, think of the handheld calculator example. A calculator could be considered an object of a `Calculation` class. You access all of the `Calculation` class functions (such as addition and subtraction) and its data members (operands that represent the numbers you are calculating) through your calculator object. You never actually work with the `Calculation` class yourself, only with an object of the class (your calculator).

But why do you need to work with a collection of related variables and functions as a single object? Why not simply call each individual variable and function as necessary, without bothering with all this class business? The truth is, you are not required to work with classes; you can create much of the same functionality without classes as you can by using classes. In fact, many of the scripts that you create—and that you find in use today—do not require object-oriented techniques to be effective. Classes help make complex programs easier to manage, however, by logically grouping related functions and data and by allowing you to refer to that grouping as a single object. Another reason for using classes is to hide information that users of a class do not need to access or know about. Information hiding helps minimize the amount of information that needs to pass in and out of an object, which helps increase program speed and efficiency. Classes also make it much easier to reuse code or distribute your code to others for use in their programs. (You learn how to create your own classes and include them in your scripts shortly.) Without a way to package variables and functions in classes and include those classes in a new program, you would need to copy and paste each segment of code you wanted to reuse (functions, variables, and so on) into any new program.

An additional reason to use classes is that instances of objects inherit their characteristics, such as class members, from the class upon which they are based. This inheritance allows you to build new classes based on existing classes without having to rewrite the code contained in the existing classes. You learn more about inheritance later in this chapter. For now, you should understand that an object has the same characteristics as its class.

Creating a Class Definition

To create a class in PHP, you use the `class` keyword to write a **class definition**, which contains the data members and member functions that make up the class. The basic syntax for defining a class is as follows:

```
class ClassName {
data member and member function definitions
}
```

The *`ClassName`* portion of the class definition is the name of the new class. You can use any name you want for a structure, as long as you follow the same naming conventions that you use when declaring other identifiers, such as variables and functions. Also, keep in mind that class names usually begin with an uppercase letter to distinguish them from other identifiers. Within the class's curly braces, you declare the data type and field names for each piece of information stored in the structure, the same way you declare data members and member functions that make up the class.

The following code demonstrates how to declare a class named `BankAccount`. The statement following the class definition instantiates an object of the class named `$Checking`.

```
class BankAccount {
data member and member function definitions
}
$Checking = new BankAccount();
```

Class names in a class definition are not followed by parentheses, as are function names in a function definition.

Because the `BankAcccount` class does not yet contain any data members of member functions, there isn't much you can do with the `$Checking` object. However, PHP includes a number of built-in functions that you can use to return information about the class that instantiated the object. For example, the `get_class()` function returns the name of the class that instantiated the object. You pass the name of the object to the `get_class()` function, as follows:

```
$Checking = new BankAccount();
echo 'The $Checking object is instantiated from the '
     . get_class($Checking) . " class.</p>";
```

TIP

See the Class/Object Functions reference in the online PHP documentation at *http://www.php.net/docs.php* for more information on the functions you can use with classes and objects.

You can also use the `instanceof` operator to determine whether an object is instantiated from a given class. The syntax for using the `instanceof` operator is *object_name* `instanceof` *class_name*. For example, the following code uses an `if` statement and the `instanceof` operator to determine whether the `$Checking` object is an instance of the `BankAccount` class:

```
$Checking = new BankAccount();
if ($Checking instanceof BankAccount)
     echo 'The $Checking object is instantiated from the '
          . get_class($Checking) . " class.</p>";
```

One built-in class function that you should use whenever you declare an object is the `class_exists()` function, which determines whether a class exists and is available to the current script. You pass to the `class_exists()` function a string value containing the name of the class you want to use. The function returns a value of true if the class exists and false if it doesn't. For example, the following code uses the `class_exists()` function within an `if` statement's conditional expression to check for the existence of the `BankAccount` class. If the class exists, the `$Checking` object is instantiated. If the class does not exist, the `exit()` function halts script execution.

```
if (class_exists("BankAccount"))
     $Checking = new BankAccount();
else
     exit("<p>The BankAccount class is not available!</p>");
```

Storing Classes in External Files

Although you can define a class within the same document that instantiates an object of the class, this somewhat defeats the purpose of writing code that can be easily modified and reused. If you want to reuse the class, you need to copy and paste it between scripts. Further, if you want to modify the class, you need to modify it within every script that uses it. A better solution is to define a class within a single external file that is called from each script that needs the class. This technique allows you to easily use the class with multiple scripts, and makes it easier to modify the class because you only need to update the single external file where it is defined.

PHP provides the following functions that allow you to use external files in your PHP scripts: `include()`, `require()`, `include_once()`, and `require_once()`. You pass to each function the name and path of the external file you want to use. The `include()` and `require()` functions both insert the contents of an external file, called an include file, into a PHP script. The difference between the two functions is that the `include()` function only generates a warning if the file isn't available, whereas the `require()` function halts the processing of the Web page if the file isn't available. The `include_once()` and `require_once()` functions are similar to the `include()` and `require()` functions, except they only include an external file once during the processing of a script. The external files you call with these statements usually contain PHP code or HTML code. Any PHP code must be contained within a PHP script section (`<?php ... ?>`) in an external file. In general, you should use the `include()` and `include_once()` functions for HTML code that will not prevent a script from running if the external file is not available. For PHP code that is required for your script to execute, you should use the `require()` or `require_once()` functions, which halt the processing of the Web page if the external file is not available.

External files can be used not only for classes, but also for any type of PHP code or HTML code that you want to reuse on multiple Web pages.

You can use any file extension you want for include files. Many programmers use an extension of .inc for HTML and other types of information that do not need to be processed by the Web server. Although you can use the .inc extension for external files containing PHP scripts, you should avoid doing so unless your Web server is configured to process .inc files as PHP scripts. If your Web server is not configured to process .inc files as PHP scripts, anyone can view the contents of the file simply by entering the full URL in a Web browser. This creates a potential security risk, especially if the external file contains proprietary code or sensitive information such as passwords. Because most Web servers process the contents of a PHP script and only return HTML to the client, your safest bet is to always use an extension of .php for external files that contain PHP code.

Next, you start creating the `ShoppingCart` class.

To start creating the `ShoppingCart` class:

1. Create a new document in your text editor and add a PHP script section, as follows:

```
<?php
?>
```

2. Add the following class definition for the `ShoppingCart` class to the script section:

```
class ShoppingCart {
}
```

3. Save the document as **ShoppingCart.php** in the Chapter directory for Chapter 11.

Next, you modify the GosselinGourmetCoffees.php script so it instantiates an object of the `ShoppingCart` class.

To modify the GosselinGourmetCoffees.php script so it instantiates an object of the `ShoppingCart` class:

1. Return to the **GosselinGourmetCoffees.php** script in your text editor.
2. Add the following PHP script section to the beginning of the file, above the `<!DOCTYPE>` declaration. The script section contains a `require_once()` statement that makes the `ShoppingCart` class available to the GosselinGourmetCoffees.php script.

```
<?php
require_once("ShoppingCart.php");
?>
```

3. Delete the following statements from the script section in the document body:

```
$SQLstring = "SELECT * FROM coffee";
$QueryResult = $DBConnect->query($SQLstring)
     Or die("<p>Unable to perform the query.</p>"
     . "<p>Error code " . mysqli_errno($DBConnect)
     . ": " . mysqli_error($DBConnect)) . "</p>";
echo "<table width='100%' border='1'>";
echo "<tr><th>Product</th><th>Description</th>
<th>Price Each</th></tr>";
$Row = $QueryResult->fetch_row();
do {
     echo "<tr><td>{$Row[1]}</td>";
     echo "<td>{$Row[2]}</td>";
     printf("<td align='center'>$%.2f</td></tr>", $Row[3]);
     $Row = $QueryResult->fetch_row();
} while ($Row);
echo "</table>";
```

4. Add the following statements above the statement that closes the database connection. These statements instantiate an object of the `ShoppingCart` class.

```
if (class_exists("ShoppingCart")) {
     $Cart = new ShoppingCart();
     echo "<p>Successfully instantiated an object of
          the ShoppingCart class.</p>";
}
else
     exit("<p>The ShoppingCart class is not available!</p>");
```

5. Save the **GosselinGourmetCoffees.php** script and then open the **GosselinGourmetGoods.php** script in your Web browser by entering the following URL: **http://localhost/PHP_Projects/Chapter.11/Chapter/GosselinGourmetGoods.php**.
6. Click the **Gourmet Coffees** link. You should see the message shown in Figure 11-5:

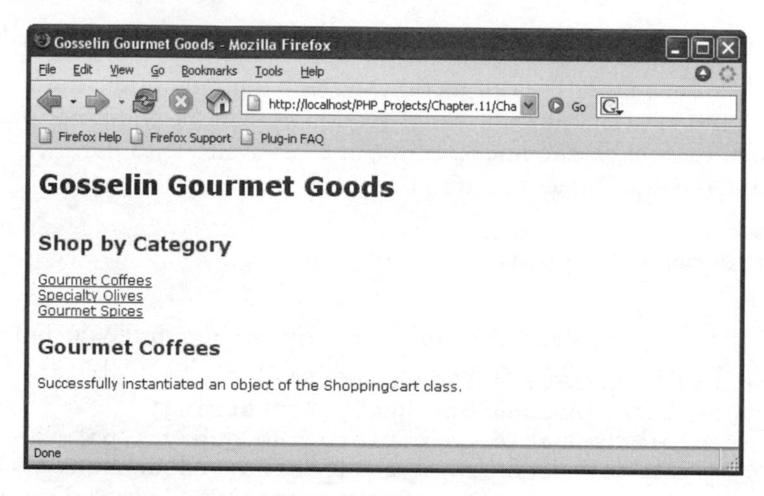

Figure 11-5 Gourmet Coffees Web page after instantiating a `ShoppingCart` object

7. Close your Web browser window.

Collecting Garbage

If you have worked with other object-oriented programming languages, you might be familiar with the term **garbage collection**, which refers to cleaning up, or reclaiming, memory that is reserved by a program. When you declare a variable or instantiate a new object, you are actually reserving computer memory for the variable or object. With some programming languages, you must write code that deletes a variable or object after you are through with it to free the memory for use by other parts of your program, or by other programs running on your computer. With PHP, you do not need to worry about reclaiming memory that is reserved for your variables or objects. Although you can manually remove a variable or object with the `unset()` function, there is usually no reason to do so because PHP knows when your program no longer needs a variable or object and automatically cleans up the memory for you. The one exception has to do with open database connections. As you learned in Chapter 9, because database connections can take up a lot of memory, you should explicitly close a database connection when you are through with it by calling the procedural `mysqli_close()` function or the `close()` method of the `mysqli` class. This ensures that the connection doesn't keep taking up space in your computer's memory while the script finishes processing.

Declaring Data Members

In this section, you learn how to declare data members within a class. Declaring and initializing data members is a little more involved than declaring and instantiating standard PHP variables. To be able to declare data members, you must first understand the principle of information hiding, which you study first.

What Is Information Hiding?

One of the fundamental principles in object-oriented programming is the concept of information hiding. Information hiding gives an encapsulated object its black box capabilities so that users of a class can see only the members of the class that you allow them to see. Essentially, the principle of **information hiding** states that any class members that other programmers, sometimes called clients, do not need to access or know about should be hidden. Information hiding helps minimize the amount of information that needs to pass in and out of an object, which helps increase program speed and efficiency. Information hiding also reduces the complexity of the code that clients see, allowing them to concentrate on the task of integrating an object into their programs. For example, if a client wants to add to her Accounting program a Payroll object, she does not need to know the underlying details of the Payroll object's member functions, nor does she need to modify any local data members that are used by those functions. The client only needs to know which of the object's member functions to call and what data (if any) needs to be passed to those member functions.

Now consider information hiding on a larger scale. Professionally developed software packages are distributed in an encapsulated format, which means that the casual user—or even an advanced programmer—cannot see the underlying details of how the software is developed. Imagine what would happen if Microsoft distributed Excel without hiding the underlying programming details. Most users of the program would be bewildered if they accidentally opened the source files. There is no need for Microsoft to allow users to see the underlying details of Excel, because users do not need to understand how the underlying code performs the various types of spreadsheet calculations. Microsoft also has a critical interest in protecting proprietary information, as do you. The design and sale of software components is big business. You certainly do not want to spend a significant amount of time designing an outstanding software component, only to have an unscrupulous programmer steal the code and claim it as his own.

This same principle of information hiding needs to be applied in object-oriented programming. There are few reasons why clients of your classes need to know the underlying details of your code. Of course, you cannot hide all of the underlying code, or other programmers will never be able to integrate your class with their applications. But you need to hide most of it.

Information hiding on any scale also prevents other programmers from accidentally introducing a bug into a program by modifying a class's internal workings. Programmers are curious creatures and will often attempt to "improve" your code, no matter how well it is written. Before you distribute your classes to other programmers, your classes should be thoroughly tested and bug-free. With tested and bug-free classes, other programmers can focus on the more important task of integrating your code into their programs using the data members and member functions you designate.

To enable information hiding in your classes, you must designate access specifiers for each of your class members. You learn about access specifiers next.

Using Access Specifiers

The first step in hiding class information is to set access specifiers for class members. **Access specifiers** control a client's access to individual data members and member functions. There are three levels of access specifiers in PHP: `public`, `private`, and `protected`. In this chapter, you study the `public` and `private` access specifiers.

The `protected` access specifier is used with a more advanced object-oriented programming technique called inheritance.

The **`public` access specifier** allows anyone to call a class's member function or to modify a data member. The **`private` access specifier** prevents clients from calling member functions or accessing data members and is one of the key elements in information hiding. Private access does not restrict a class's internal access to its own members; a class's member function can modify any private data member or call any private member function. Private access restricts clients from accessing class members.

Prior to PHP 5, the `var` keyword was used to declare class data members. If you use the `var` keyword to declare a data member in PHP 5, it is created with public access.

You include an access specifier at the beginning of a data member declaration statement. For example, the following statement declares a public data member named `$Balance` in the `BankAccount` class and initializes it with a value of 0:

```
class BankAccount {
     public $Balance = 0;
}
```

It is common practice to list public class members first to clearly identify the parts of the class that can be accessed by clients.

It is considered good programming practice to always assign an initial value to a data member when you first declare it. The best way to initialize a data member is with a constructor function (discussed later in this chapter). You can also assign simple values to data members when you first declare them, although an error occurs if you attempt to use any type of expression to initialize the data member. The preceding statement is valid because it only assigns a value of 0 to the `$Balance` data member. However, the following statement is invalid because it attempts to use an expression (the addition operation) to assign a value to the `$Balance` data member:

```
class BankAccount {
     public $Balance = 1 + 2;
}
```

Similarly, if you have a data member named `$CustomerName` in the `BankAccount` class, you can assign a simple text string to the data member as follows:

```
class BankAccount {
     public $CustomerName = "Don Gosselin";
}
```

In comparison, the following statement is invalid because it attempts to use an expression to assign a value to the `$CustomerName` data member:

```
class BankAccount {
     public $CustomerName = "Don" . " " . "Gosselin";
}
```


Recall that to access a data member, you use member selection notation. Keep in mind that when you use member selection notation, you do not include a dollar sign before the data member name. For example, the following statements assign a new value to the `$Balance` data member and then print its value:

```
$Checking->Balance = 958.20;
printf("<p>Your checking account balance is $%.2f.</p>",
     $Checking->Balance);
```

PHP does not define a default access specifer for data members. If you attempt to declare a data member without an access specifier, an error occurs. For example, the data member declaration in the following class is invalid because it does not include an access specifier:

```
class BankAccount {
     $Balance = 0; // invalid
}
```

Next, you declare three data members, `$DBConnect`, `$DBName`, `$TableName`, `$Orders[]`, and `$OrdersTable[]` in the `ShoppingCart` class. The `$DBConnect`, `$DBName`, and `$TableName` data members store the database connection details. The `$Orders[]` and `$OrdersTable[]` arrays keep track of the products in a customer's shopping cart. Both arrays use `productID` fields from the `gosselin_gourmet` database as element keys. The `$Orders[]` array stores the quantity of each product purchased and the `$OrdersTable[]` stores the table in the `gosselin_gourmet` database that contains the product information. To adhere to the principles of information hiding, you must declare all of the data members as private. Later in this chapter, you write member functions that access and manipulate the values in each array.

To add data members to the `ShoppingCart` class:

1. Return to the **ShoppingCart.php** script in your text editor.
2. Add the following private data member declarations to the class definition:

```
private $DBConnect = "";
private $DBName = "";
private $TableName = "";
private $Orders = array();
private $OrderTable = array();
```

3. Save the **ShoppingCart.php** script.

Serializing Objects

In Chapter 10, you learned about PHP's various state preservation techniques, including how to use sessions. In addition to keeping track of current Web site visitors, session variables can store information that can be shared among multiple scripts that are called as part of the same session. But how do you share objects within the same session? You could assign the value of an object's data members to session variables, but you would need to instantiate a new object and reassign the session variable values to the data members each time you call a new script. However, this approach would be difficult if you have an object with dozens of data members. A better choice is to serialize the object between script calls within the same session. **Serialization** refers to the process of converting an object into a string that you can store for reuse. Serialization stores both data members and member functions into strings, which can be stored in text files and databases or passed to another script. To serialize an object, you pass an object name to the `serialize()` function. The following statement serializes the `$Checking` objects and assigns the returned string to a variable named `$SavedAccount`:

```
$SavedAccount = serialize($Checking);
```

To convert serialized data back into an object, you use the `unserialize()` function. The following statement converts the serialized data in the `$SavedAccount` variable back into the `$Checking` object:

```
$Checking = unserialize($SavedAccount);
```

Serialization is also used to store the data in large arrays.

To use serialized objects between scripts, you assign a serialized object to a session variable. For example, the following statements serialize the `$Checking` object and assign the returned string to a variable named `savedAccount` in the `$_SESSION` autoglobal:

```
session_start();
$_SESSION('SavedAccount') = serialize($Checking);
```

Converting a serialized value in a session variable is very similar to converting a serialized value in a standard variable. The following statement converts the serialized data in the `savedAccount` session variable back into the `$Checking` object:

```
$Checking = unserialize($_SESSION('SavedAccount'));
```

NOTE

Later in this chapter, you learn how to use two special serialization methods, `__sleep()` and `__wakeup()`, in your classes.

Next, you modify the GosselinGourmetCoffees.php script so it uses sessions to store serialized `ShoppingCart` objects.

To modify the GosselinGourmetCoffees.php script so it uses sessions to store serialized `ShoppingCart` objects:

1. Return to the **GosselinGourmetCoffees.php** script in your text editor.
2. Add a `session_start()` statement to the first script section at the start of the file:

   ```
   <?php
   require_once("ShoppingCart.php");
   session_start();
   ?>
   ```

3. Add the following statement to the end of the second script section to serialize the `$Cart` object into a variable named `curCart` in the `$_SESSION` autoglobal:

   ```
   $_SESSION['curCart'] = serialize($Cart);
   ```

4. In the second script section, replace the `if...else` statement that instantiates the `$Cart` object with the following version, which calls the `unserialize()` function if the `curCart` variable exists in the `$_SESSION` autoglobal:

   ```
   if (isset($_SESSION['curCart']))
        $Cart = unserialize($_SESSION['curCart']);
   else {
        if (class_exists("ShoppingCart"))
             $Cart = new ShoppingCart();
   ```

```
          else
               exit("<p>The ShoppingCart class is
                    not available!</p>");
     }
```

5. Save the **GosselinGourmetCoffees.php** script.

WORKING WITH MEMBER FUNCTIONS

Because member functions perform most of the work in a class, you now learn about the various techniques associated with them. Member functions are usually declared as public, but they can also be declared as private. Public member functions can be called by anyone, whereas private member functions can be called only by other member functions in the same class.

You might wonder about the usefulness of a private member function, which cannot be accessed by a client of the program. Suppose your program needs some sort of utility function that clients have no need to access. For example, the `BankAccount` class might need to calculate interest by calling a function named `calcInterest()`. To use your program, the client does not need to access the `calcInterest()` function. By making the `calcInterest()` function private, you protect your program and add another level of information hiding. A general rule of thumb is to create public member functions for any functions that clients need to access and to create private member functions for any functions that clients do not need to access.

You declare a member function within the body of a class definition and include an access specifier before the `function` keyword. Other than including an access specifier, there is little difference between standard functions and member functions. Unlike data members, you are not required to define a member function with an access specifier. If you do exclude the access specifier, the member function's default access is public. However, it's good programming practice to include an access specifier with any member function definition to clearly identify the scope of the function. The following statement demonstrates how to declare a member function named `withdrawal()` in the `BankAccount` class:

```
class BankAccount {
     public $Balance = 958.20;
     public function withdrawal($Amount) {
          $this->Balance -= $Amount;
     }
}
if (class_exists("BankAccount"))
     $Checking = new BankAccount();
else
     exit("<p>The BankAccount class is not available!</p>");
```

```
printf("<p>Your checking account balance is $%.2f.</p>",
     $Checking->Balance);
     $Cash = 200;
     $Checking->withdrawal(200);
     printf("<p>After withdrawing $%.2f, your checking account balance
          is $%.2f.</p>", $Cash, $Checking->Balance);
```

Notice that the preceding example uses `$this` to refer to the `$Balance` data member. The `$this` reference is a special type of variable that refers to the current object. Notice that the `$this` reference uses member selection notation to access the data member in the same way you use an instantiated object to refer to a data member. If you do not use the `$this` reference to refer to a data member from within a member function, PHP treats the data member as a variable that is local to the scope of the function. The following version of the `withdrawal()` function raises an error because the statement within the function attempts to subtract a value from the undefined local variable named `$Balance`:

```
public function withdrawal($Amount) {
     $Balance -= $Amount;
}
```

Initializing with Constructor Functions

When you first instantiate an object from a class, you will often want to assign initial values to data members or perform other types of initialization tasks, such as calling a function member that might calculate and assign values to data members. Although you can assign simple values to data members when you declare them, a better choice is to use a constructor function. A **constructor function** is a special function that is called automatically when an object from a class is instantiated. You define and declare constructor functions the same way you define other functions, although you do not include a return type because constructor functions do not return values. Each class definition can contain its own constructor function, named either `__construct()` or the same name as the class. PHP first searches for the `__construct()` function within a class definition. You do not need to specify an access specifier with a constructor function, although if you do, you can only specify public access. The following code demonstrates how to use the `__construct()` function to initialize the data members in the `BankAccount` class:

```
class BankAccount {
     private $AccountNumber;
     private $CustomerName;
     private $Balance;
     function __construct() {
          $this->AccountNumber = 0;
          $this->Balance = 0;
          $this->CustomerName = "";
     }
```

The following code demonstrates how to create a constructor function using the same name as its class:

```
class BankAccount {
     private $AccountNumber;
     private $CustomerName;
     private $Balance;
     function BankAccount() {
           $this->AccountNumber = 0;
           $this->Balance = 0;
           $this->CustomerName = "";
     }
```

NOTE

The `__construct()` function takes precedence over a function with the same name as the class.

Constructor functions are commonly used in PHP to handle database connection tasks. Next, you add to the `ShoppingCart` class a `__construct()` function that contains statements that instantiate a new database object.

To add a `__construct()` function to the `ShoppingCart` class:

1. Return to the **ShoppingCart.php** script in your text editor.
2. Add the following `__construct()` function definition to the end of the class declaration:

```
function __construct() {
}
```

3. Add the following statements to the `__construct()` function to instantiate a database object. Notice that the first statement uses the `$this` reference to refer to the `$DBConnect` data member that you declared earlier. Be sure to replace *`user`* and *`password`* with your username and password.

```
$this->DBConnect = @new mysqli("localhost", "user", "password");
if (mysqli_connect_errno())
     die("<p>Unable to connect to the database server.</p>"
     . "<p>Error code " . mysqli_connect_errno()
     . ": " . mysqli_connect_error()) . "</p>";
```

4. Save the **ShoppingCart.php** script.
5. Return to the **GosselinGourmetCoffees.php** script and delete the following database connection statements. You no longer need them because the `ShoppingCart` class handles the database connection details.

```
$DBConnect = @new mysqli("localhost", "dongosselin", "rosebud");
if (mysqli_connect_errno())
     die("<p>Unable to connect to the database server.</p>"
```

```
        . "<p>Error code " . mysqli_connect_errno()
        . ": " . mysqli_connect_error()) . "</p>";
@$DBConnect->select_db("gosselin_gourmet")
        Or die("<p>Unable to select the database.</p>"
        . "<p>Error code " . mysqli_errno($DBConnect)
```

6. Also delete the `$DBConnect->close();` statement from the end of the script section.
7. Save the **GosselinGourmetCoffees.php** script.

Cleaning Up with Destructor Functions

Just as a default constructor function is called when a class object is first instantiated, a destructor function is called when the object is destroyed. A **destructor function** cleans up any resources allocated to an object after the object is destroyed. A destructor function is commonly called in two ways: when a script ends or when you manually delete an object with the `unset()` function. You generally do not need to use a destructor function, although many programmers use one to close file handles and open database connections. To add a destructor function to a PHP class, create a function named `__destruct()`. The following code contains a destructor function that closes a database connection that was opened with a constructor function:

```
function __construct() {
     $DBConnect = new mysqli("localhost", "dongosselin",
          "rosebud", "real_estate")
}
function __destruct() {
     $DBConnect->close();
}
```

Next, you add to the `ShoppingCart` class a `__destruct()` function that closes the database object that you instantiated with the `__construct()` function.

To add a `__destruct()` function to the `ShoppingCart` class:

1. Return to the **ShoppingCart.php** script in your text editor.
2. Add the following `__destruct()` function definition to the end of the class declaration:

```
function __destruct() {
}
```

3. Add the following statement to the __destruct() function to close the database object. Again notice that the statement uses the `$this` reference to refer to the `$DBConnect` data member.

```
$this->DBConnect->close();
```

4. Save the **ShoppingCart.php** script.

11

Writing Accessor Functions

Even if you make all data members in a class private, you can still allow your program's clients to retrieve or modify the value of data members via accessor functions. **Accessor functions** are public member functions that a client can call to retrieve or modify the value of a data member. (You learn more about how to use access specifiers with member functions later in this chapter.) Because accessor functions often begin with the words "set" or "get," they are also referred to as set or get functions. Set functions modify data member values; get functions retrieve data member values. To allow a client to pass a value to your program that will be assigned to a private data member, you include parameters in a set function's definition. You can then write code in the body of the set function that validates the data passed from the client, prior to assigning values to private data members. For example, if you write a class named `Payroll` that includes a private data member containing the current state income-tax rate, you could write a public accessor function named `getStateTaxRate()` that allows clients to retrieve the variable's value. Similarly, you could write a `setStateTaxRate()` function that performs various types of validation on the data passed from the client (such as making sure the value is not null, is not greater than 100%, and so on) prior to assigning a value to the private state tax rate data member.

The following code demonstrates how to use set and get member functions with the `$Balance` data member in the `BankAccount` class. The `setBalance()` function is declared with an access specifier of `public` and accepts a single parameter containing the value to assign to the `$Balance` data member. The `getBalance()` function is also declared as `public` and contains a single statement that returns the value assigned to the `$Balance` data member. Statements at the end of the example call the functions to set and get the `$Balance` data member.

```
class BankAccount {
     private $Balance = 0;
     public function setBalance($NewValue) {
          $this->Balance = $NewValue;
     }
     public function getBalance() {
          return $this->Balance;
     }
}
if (class_exists("BankAccount"))
     $Checking = new BankAccount();
else
     exit("<p>The BankAccount class is not available!</p>");
$Checking->setBalance(100);
echo "<p>Your checking account balance is "
     . $Checking->getBalance() . "</p>";
```

Next, you add four accessor functions to the `ShoppingCart` class: `setDatabase()`, `setTable()`, `getProductList()`, and `addItem()`. The `setDatabase()` assigns a value to the `$DBName` data member, and then executes the `select_db()` function. The `setTable()` function assigns a value to the `$TableName` data members. The `getProductList()` function queries the database and prints a table with the product information. The `addItem()` function allows users to add an item in the table to their shopping cart.

To add the `setDatabase()`, `setTable()`, `getProductList()`, and `addItem()` functions to the `ShoppingCart` class:

1. Return to the **ShoppingCart.php** script in your text editor.
2. Add the following `setDatabase()` function to the end of the class definition:

```
public function setDatabase($Database) {
     $this->DBName = $Database;
     @$this->DBConnect->select_db($this->DBName)
          Or die("<p>Unable to select the database.</p>"
          . "<p>Error code " . mysqli_errno($this->DBConnect)
          . ": " . mysqli_error($this->DBConnect)) . "</p>";
}
```

3. Add the following `setTable()` function to the end of the class definition:

```
public function setTable($Table) {
     $this->TableName = $Table;
}
```

4. Add the following `getProductList()` function to the end of the class definition. This code is similar to the statements you added earlier to the GosselinGourmetCoffees.php script, except this version adds an Add link to each row in the table that executes the `addItem()` function to add a product to the shopping cart. Notice that the statements that build the Add link append the session ID variable to the link to keep track of the current session in the event that cookies are disabled on the user's Web browser. The link is also appended with the product ID of the current product and the type of operation, which other Web pages that utilize the class will use to determine which member function to call.

```
public function getProductList() {
     $SQLstring = "SELECT * FROM $this->TableName";
     $QueryResult = $this->DBConnect->query($SQLstring)
          Or die("<p>Unable to perform the query.</p>"
          . "<p>Error code " . mysqli_errno($this->DBConnect)
          . ": " . mysqli_error($DBConnect)) . "</p>";
     echo "<table width='100%' border='1'>";
     echo "<tr><th>Product</th><th>Description</th>
```

11

```
            <th>Price Each</th><th>Select Item</th></tr>";
            $Row = $QueryResult->fetch_row();
            do {
                  echo "<tr><td>{$Row[1]}</td>";
                  echo "<td>{$Row[2]}</td>";
                  printf("<td align='center'>$%.2f</td>", $Row[3]);
                  echo "<td align='center'>
                        <a href='ShowCart.php?PHPSESSID=" . session_id()
                        . "&operation=addItem&productID=" . $Row[0]
                        . "'>Add</a></td></tr>";
                  $Row = $QueryResult->fetch_row();
            } while ($Row);
            echo "</table>";
      }
```

5. Add the following `addItem()` function to the end of the class definition. The first statement retrieves the product ID that was appended to the Add link in the `getProductList()` function you added in the last step. The `if` statement then uses the `array_key_exists()` function to determine whether the user already selected the current product. The third statement assigns an initial quantity of 1 to the `Orders[]` array and the fourth statement assigns the value assigned to the `$TableName` data member to the `$OrderTable[]` array.

```
public function addItem() {
     $ProdID = $_GET['productID'];
     if (array_key_exists($ProdID, $this->Orders))
           exit("<p>You already selected that item! Click your
                 browser's back button to return to the
                 previous page.</p>");
     $this->Orders[$ProdID] = 1;
     $this->OrderTable[$ProdID] = $this->TableName;
}
```

6. Save the **ShoppingCart.php** script.

Next, you modify the GosselinGourmetCoffees.php script so it calls the member functions you just added to the `ShoppingCart` class.

To add member function calls to the GosselinGourmetCoffees.php script:

1. Return to the **GosselinGourmetCoffees.php** script in your text editor.
2. Add the following variable declarations to the beginning of the second script section:

```
$Database = "gosselin_gourmet";
$Table = "coffee";
```

3. Add a statement to the end of the nested `if` statement that calls the `setDatabase()` method and passes to it the `$Database` variable. The entire `if...else` statement should appear as follows:

```
if (isset($_SESSION['curCart']))
      $Cart = unserialize($_SESSION['curCart']);
else {
      if (class_exists("ShoppingCart")) {
            $Cart = new ShoppingCart();
            $Cart->setDatabase($Database);
      }
      else
            exit("<p>The ShoppingCart class is not available!</p>");
}
```

Be sure to add curly braces around the statements in the nested `if` statement.

4. Add the following two statements above the statement that serializes the `$Cart` object. The first statement calls the `setTable()` function and the second statement calls the `getProductList()` function.

```
$Cart->setTable($Table);
$Cart->getProductList();
```


5. Finally, add the following text and elements to the end of the document body. The link calls a script named ShowCart.php, which you create in the next section.

```
<p><a href='<?php echo "ShowCart.php?PHPSESSID=" . session_id()
?>'>Show Shopping Cart</a></p>
```

6. Save the **GosselinGourmetCoffees.php** script and then open the **GosselinGourmetGoods.php** script in your Web browser by entering the following URL: **http://localhost/PHP_Projects/Chapter.11/Chapter/GosselinGourmetGoods.php**.

7. Click the **Gourmet Coffees** link. Your Web browser should be similar to Figure 11-6. Do not click any of the links or reload the Web page. If you do, you will receive error messages because you still need to add several other functions to the `ShoppingCart` class.

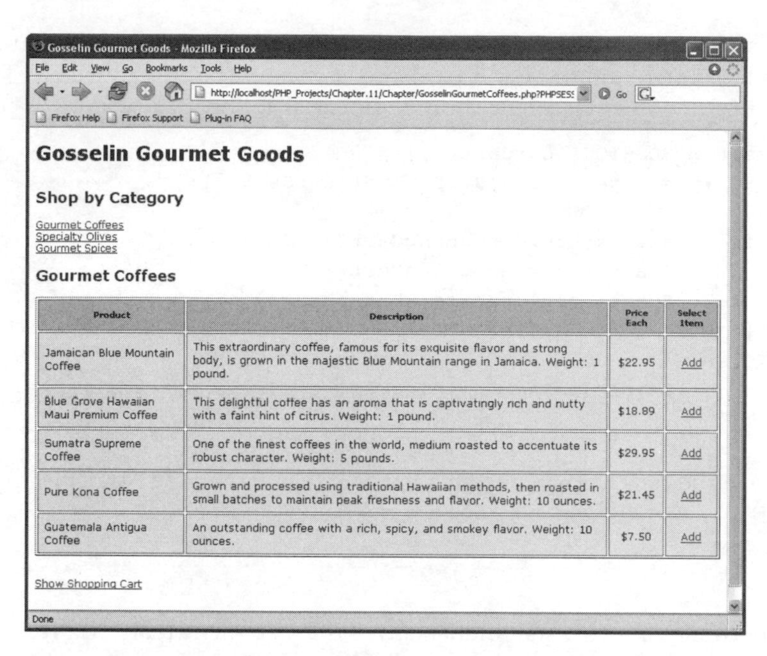

Figure 11-6 Gourmet Coffees Web page after adding member function calls

8. Close your Web browser window.

Serialization Functions

When you serialize an object with the `serialize()` function, PHP looks in the object's class for a special function named `__sleep()`, which you can use to perform many of the same tasks as a destructor function. However, because a destructor function is always called when a script that instantiates an object of a class ends, you do not need to duplicate any functionality between a destructor function and the `__sleep()` function. The primary reason for including a `__sleep()` function in a class is to specify which data members of the class to serialize. If you do not include a `__sleep()` function in your class, the `serialize()` function serializes all of its data members.

You don't necessarily have to serialize each and every data member in a class, particularly for large objects that contain numerous data members. Instead, you could use a `__sleep()` function to specify which data members to serialize. If you do include a `__sleep()` function in your class, the function must return an array of the data members to serialize or you will receive an error. For example, the following code demonstrates how to use a `__sleep()` function to serialize only the `$Balance` data member in the `BankAccount` class. Notice how the name `$Balance` data member is passed to the array constructor: It does not include the `$this` reference or a dollar sign. Instead, you simply pass the name of the data member surrounded by single (not double) quotation marks. Recall that double quotation marks surrounding a variable name return the variable's value, whereas single quotation marks return the variable name itself.

```
function __sleep() {
     $SerialVars = array('Balance');
     return $SerialVars;
}
```

Although the destructor function is always called, a constructor function is only called when you instantiate a new class object. This means that when you use the `unserialize()` function to restore a serialized class object, the constructor function does not execute. However, when the `unserialize()` function executes, PHP looks in the object's class for a special function named `__wakeup()`, which you can use to perform many of the same tasks as a constructor function. You use the `__wakeup()` function to perform any initialization the class requires when the object is restored. You do not typically need to use the `__wakeup()` function to initialize data members because they are normally saved with the serialization process. One of the primary uses of the `__wakeup()` function is to restore any database or file connections that were lost during object serialization.

Next, you add a `__wakeup()` function to the `ShoppingCart` class that restores the connection to the `gosselin_gourmet` database when an object is restored with the `unserialize()` function.

To add a `__wakeup()` function to the `ShoppingCart` class:

1. Return to the **ShoppingCart.php** script in your text editor.
2. Add the following `__wakeup()` function definition to the end of the class declaration:

   ```
   function __wakeup() {
   }
   ```

3. Add the following statements to the `__wakeup()` function to restore the database connection. Be sure to replace *`user`* and *`password`* with your user-name and password.

   ```
   $this->DBConnect = @new mysqli("localhost", "user", "password");
   if (mysqli_connect_errno())
        die("<p>Unable to connect to the database server.</p>"
        . "<p>Error code " . mysqli_connect_errno()
        . ": " . mysqli_connect_error()) . "</p>";
   @$this->DBConnect->select_db($this->DBName)
        Or die("<p>Unable to select the database.</p>"
        . "<p>Error code " . mysqli_errno($this->DBConnect)
        . ": " . mysqli_error($this->DBConnect)) . "</p>";
   ```

4. Save the **ShoppingCart.php** script.

Next, you add an additional member function named `showCart()` to the `ShoppingCart` class. The `showCart()` function displays the items in the user's shopping cart. You call the function from a script named ShowCart.php, which you create shortly.

To add the `showCart()` function to the `ShoppingCart` class:

1. Return to the **ShoppingCart.php** script in your text editor.
2. Add the following `showCart()` function definition to the end of the class declaration:

```
public function showCart() {
}
```

3. Add the following statements to the `showCart()` function to check whether the `$Orders[]` data member is empty. If it is empty, a message prints indicating that the shopping cart is empty.

```
if (empty($this->Orders))
echo "<p>Your shopping cart is empty!</p>";
```

4. Add the following statements to the end of the `showCart()` function. The first two statements start building a table that displays the orders in the shopping cart. The third statement declares a variable named `$Total` that contains the order total. Additional statements in the function update the value assigned to the `$Total` variable.

```
else {
     echo "<table width='100%' border='1'>";
     echo "<tr><th>Product</th><th>Quantity</th><th>
          Price Each</th></tr>";
     $Total = 0;
```

5. Add the following `foreach` loop to the end of the `showCart()` function. The code loops through each element in the `$Orders[]` data member and performs a query to return the name and price of each product according to its product ID. The code also builds a table to display the product information. Although the code might appear complex at first, you have already worked with every function and language construct it contains. As you examine the code, keep in mind that its purpose is simply to retrieve and output records.

```
foreach($this->Orders as $Order) {
     $SQLstring = "SELECT * FROM "
          . $this->OrderTable[key($this->Orders)] . "
          WHERE productID='" . key($this->Orders) . "'";
     $QueryResult = @mysqli_query($this->DBConnect, $SQLstring)
          Or die("<p>Unable to perform the query.</p>"
          . "<p>Error code " . mysqli_errno($this->DBConnect)
          . ": " . mysqli_error($this->DBConnect)) . "</p>";
```

```
        $Row = mysqli_fetch_row($QueryResult);
        echo "<td>{$Row[1]}</td>";
        echo "<td align='center'>$Order ";
        echo "</td>";
        printf("<td align='center'>$%.2f</td></tr>", $Row[3]);
        $Total += $Row[3] * $Order;
        next($this->Orders);
}
```

6. Add the following statements to the end of the `showCart()` function to complete the table:

```
        echo "<td align='center' colspan='2'><strong>Your shopping
              cart contains " . count($this->Orders)
              . " product(s).</strong></td>";
        printf("<td align='center'><strong>Total: $%.2f</strong>
              </td>", $Total);
        echo "</table>";
}
```

7. Save the **ShoppingCart.php** script and then close it in your text editor.

Next, you create the ShowCart.php script, which displays when the user clicks an Add link or the Show Shopping Cart link on the Gourmet Coffees page.

To create the ShowCart.php script:

1. Create a new document in your text editor and type the `<!DOCTYPE>` declaration, `<html>` element, header information, and `<body>` element. Use the strict DTD and "Gosselin Gourmet Goods" as the content of the `<title>` element.

2. Add the following `<link>` element above the closing `</head>` tag to link to the php_styles.css style sheet in your Chapter directory:

```
<link rel="stylesheet" href="php_styles.css" type="text/css" />
```

3. Add the following text and elements to the document body:

```
<h1>Gosselin Gourmet Goods</h1>
<h2>Shop by Category</h2>
<p><a href="GosselinGourmetCoffees.php">Gourmet Coffees</a><br />
<a href="GosselinGourmetOlives.php">Specialty Olives</a><br />
<a href="GosselinGourmetSpices.php">Gourmet Spices</a></p>
```

4. Add the following PHP script section to the beginning of the file, above the `<!DOCTYPE>` declaration. The script section contains a `require_once()` statement that makes the `ShoppingCart` class available to the GosselinGourmetCoffees.php script along with a `session_start()` function to begin or restore a session. The `if` statement determines whether the `$_SESSION['curCart']` variable is set. If it's not set, the user did not access this page through one of the shopping category pages, so she is redirected to the main Gosselin Gourmet Goods page.

```
<?php
require_once("ShoppingCart.php");
session_start();
if (!isset($_SESSION['curCart']))
     header("location:GosselinGourmetGoods.php");
?>
```

5. Add the following PHP script section to the end of the document body. The first statement restores the serialized `$Cart` object. The `if` statement checks the `$_GET['operation']` variable. If it contains a value of "addItem", the `addItem()` method of the `$Cart` object executes. (You add additional operations in the Hands-On Projects section later in this chapter.) The `showCart()` method then displays the shopping cart and the last statement serializes the `$Cart` object.

```
<?php
$Cart = unserialize($_SESSION['curCart']);
if (isset($_GET['operation'])) {
     if ($_GET['operation'] == "addItem")
          $Cart->addItem();
}
$Cart->showCart();
$_SESSION['curCart'] = serialize($Cart);
?>
```

6. Save the document as **ShowCart.php** in the Chapter directory for Chapter 11 and then close it in your text editor.

In studying the various class techniques presented in this chapter, you might have forgotten that the goal of object-oriented program is code reuse. Now that you have developed the `ShoppingCart` class, you will see how easy it is to reuse the code on other Web pages by creating the GosselinGourmetOlives.php and GosselinGourmetSpices.php scripts.

To create the GosselinGourmetOlives.php and GosselinGourmetSpices.php scripts:

1. Return to the **GosselinGourmetCoffees.php** script in your text editor and immediately save it as **GosselinGourmetOlives.php**.

2. Change the text in the `<h2>` heading in the document body to **Specialty Olives**.

3. Change the value assigned to the `$Table` variable in the second PHP script section from coffee to **olives**.
4. Save the **GosselinGourmetOlives.php** script and then immediately save it as **GosselinGourmetSpices.php**.
5. Change the text in the `<h2>` heading in the document body to **Gourmet Spices**.
6. Change the value assigned to the `$Table` variable in the second PHP script section to **spices**.
7. Save the **GosselinGourmetSpices.php** script and close it in your text editor.
8. Open the **GosselinGourmetGoods.php** script in your Web browser by entering the following URL: **http://localhost/PHP_Projects/Chapter.11/Chapter/GosselinGourmetGoods.php**.
9. Click each of the shopping category links and click the **Add** button for various products on each page. The Your Shopping Cart Web page appears each time you click an Add button or when you click the Show Shopping Cart link on any of the product pages. Figure 11-7 shows the Your Shopping Cart Web page after selecting several products.

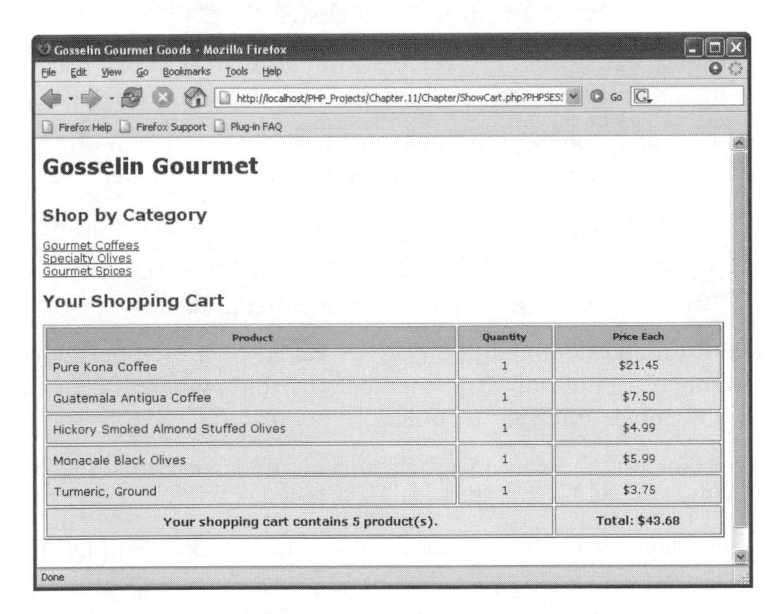

Figure 11-7 Your Shopping Cart Web page after selecting several products

10. Close your Web browser window and text editor.

Chapter Summary

- The term "object-oriented programming" (OOP) refers to the creation of reusable software objects that can be easily incorporated into multiple programs. The term "object" specifically refers to programming code and data that can be treated as an individual unit or component. (Objects are often also called components.)
- The term "data" refers to information contained within variables or other types of storage structures.
- The functions associated with an object are called methods, and the variables that are associated with an object are called properties or attributes.
- Objects are encapsulated, which means that all code and required data are contained within the object itself.
- An interface represents elements required for a source program to communicate with an object.
- The principle of information hiding states that any class members that other programmers do not need to access or know about should be hidden.
- In object-oriented programming, the code, methods, attributes, and other information that make up an object are organized into classes.
- An instance is an object that has been created from an existing class. When you create an object from an existing class, you are said to be instantiating the object.
- A particular instance of an object inherits its methods and properties from a class—that is, it takes on the characteristics of the class on which it is based.
- A constructor is a special function with the same name as its class that is called automatically when an object from the class is instantiated.
- The term "data" structure refers to a system for organizing data.
- The functions and variables defined in a class are called class members. Class variables are referred to as data members or member variables, whereas class functions are referred to as member functions or function members.
- A class definition contains the data members and member functions that make up the class.
- PHP provides the following functions that allow you to use external files in your PHP scripts: `include()`, `require()`, `include_once()`, and `require_once()`.
- Access specifiers control a client's access to individual data members and member functions.
- Serialization refers to the process of converting an object into a string that you can store for reuse.

- A constructor function is a special function that is called automatically when an object from a class is instantiated.
- A destructor cleans up any resources allocated to an object after the object is destroyed.
- Accessor functions are public member functions that a client can call to retrieve or modify the value of a data member.
- When you serialize an object with the `serialize()` function, PHP looks in the object's class for a special function named `__sleep()`, which you can use to perform many of the same tasks as a destructor function.
- When the `unserialize()` function executes, PHP looks in the object's class for a special function named `__wakeup()`, which you can use to perform many of the same tasks as a constructor function.

Review Questions

1. Reusable software objects are often referred to as ________________.
   a. methods
   b. components
   c. widgets
   d. functions
2. Explain the benefits of object-oriented programming.
3. The functions associated with an object are called ________________.
   a. properties
   b. fields
   c. methods
   d. attributes
4. The term "black box" refers to ________________.
   a. a property
   b. debugging
   c. encapsulation
   d. an interface
5. A(n) ________________ is an object that has been created from an existing class.
   a. pattern
   b. structure
   c. replica
   d. instance

6. An object inherits its characteristics from a class. True or False?
7. A function that is used as the basis for an object is called a(n) ________.
   a. method
   b. class
   c. class constructor
   d. object variable
8. Which of the following characters are used in member selection notation?
   a. `>`
   b. `->`
   c. `=>`
   d. `.`
9. What is the correct syntax to connect to the MySQL database server using object-oriented style?
   a. `$Variable = mysqli_connect("localhost", "user", "password", "database_name");`
   b. `$Variable = new mysqli_connect("localhost", "user", "password", "database_name");`
   c. `$Variable = mysqli("localhost", "user", "password", "database_name");`
   d. `$Variable = new mysqli("localhost", "user", "password", "database_name");`
10. Explain how to handle MySQL errors using object-oriented database style.
11. The terms variable and object are often used interchangeably in object-oriented programming. True or False?
12. Class names usually begin with a(n) ________ to distinguish them from other identifiers.
    a. number
    b. exclamation mark (!)
    c. ampersand (&)
    d. uppercase letter
13. Which of the following functions returns the name of the class upon which an object is based?
    a. `class_of()`
    b. `instanceof()`
    c. `class_name()`
    d. `get_class()`

14. What extensions should you use for external HTML files and PHP scripts and why?
15. Explain the principle of information hiding.
16. Which of the following access specifiers prevents clients from calling member functions or accessing data members?
    a. `public`
    b. `private`
    c. `protected`
    d. `privileged`
17. You name a constructor function as the same name as its class or as ________________.
    a. `construct()`
    b. `__construct()`
    c. `constructor()`
    d. `__constructor()`
18. When is a destructor called? (Choose all that apply.)
    a. when a script ends
    b. when the constructor function ends
    c. when you delete a class object with the `unset()` function
    d. when you call the `serialize()` function
19. Explain the use of accessor functions. How are accessor functions often named?
20. When serializing objects, how do you specify which data members to serialize?

HANDS-ON PROJECTS

Hands-On Project 11-1

In this project, you add two member functions, `removeItem()` and `emptyCart()`, to the `ShoppingCart` class. These functions allow you to remove individual items or empty all items from the shopping cart.

To add the `removeItem()` and `emptyCart()` member functions to the `ShoppingCart` class:

1. Open the **ShoppingCart.php** script from your Chapter directory for Chapter 11 in your text editor.

2. Add the following `removeItem()` function definition to the end of the class definition. The statements use the `$_GET['productID']` variable and `unset()` function to remove the element that represents the product from the `$Orders[]` and `$OrderTable[]` arrays.

```
public function removeItem() {
        $ProdID = $_GET['productID'];
        unset($this->Orders[$ProdID]);
        unset($this->OrderTable[$ProdID]);
}
```

3. Add the following `emptyCart()` function definition to the end of the class declaration. The statements empty the cart by assigning the `array()` construct to the `$Orders[]` and `$OrderTable[]` data members, which reinitializes the array.

```
function emptyCart() {
        $this->Orders = array();
        $this->OrderTable = array();
}
```

4. Next, you need to modify the `showCart()` function so it displays links that call the `removeItem()` and `emptyCart()` functions. First, modify the `echo()` statement that creates the table header (<th>) elements so it includes another column for the Remove Item links, as follows:

```
echo "<tr><th>Remove Item</th><th>Product</th>
<th>Quantity</th><th>Price Each</th></tr>";
```

5. Add the following `echo()` statements immediately after the statement that calls the `mysqli_fetch_row()` function. These statements create new table cells containing Remove Item links.

```
echo "<td align='center'>";
echo "<a href='ShowCart.php?PHPSESSID=" . session_id()
        . "&operation=removeItem&productID=" . $Row[0]
        . "'>Remove</a></td>";
```

6. Add the following statement after the `foreach` loop's closing brace. This statement adds an Empty Cart link to the end of the shopping cart table.

```
echo "<tr><td align='center'><a href='ShowCart.php?PHPSESSID="
        . session_id() . "&operation=emptyCart'><strong>
        Empty Cart</strong></a></td>";
```

7. Save the **ShoppingCart.php** script and then open the **ShowCart.php** script from your Chapter directory for Chapter 11 in your text editor. The final step is to modify the ShowCart.php script so it calls the `removeItem()` or `emptyCart()` methods if the value assigned to the `$_GET['operation']` variable is either "removeItem" or "emptyCart".

8. Modify the `if` statement that checks the value of the `$_GET['operation']` variable so it includes nested `if` statements that call the `removeItem()` and `emptyCart()` methods, as follows:

```
if (isset($_GET['operation'])) {
        if ($_GET['operation'] == "addItem")
              $Cart->addItem();
        if ($_GET['operation'] == "removeItem")
              $Cart->removeItem();
        if ($_GET['operation'] == "emptyCart")
              $Cart->emptyCart();
}
```

9. Save the **ShowCart.php** script and then open the **GosselinGourmetGoods.php** script in your Web browser by entering the following URL: **http://localhost/PHP_Projects/Chapter.11/Chapter/GosselinGourmetGoods.php**.
10. Click each of the shopping category links and click the **Add** button for various products on each page. Figure 11-8 shows the Your Shopping Cart Web page after adding remove item and empty cart functionality. Notice the Remove and Empty Cart links.

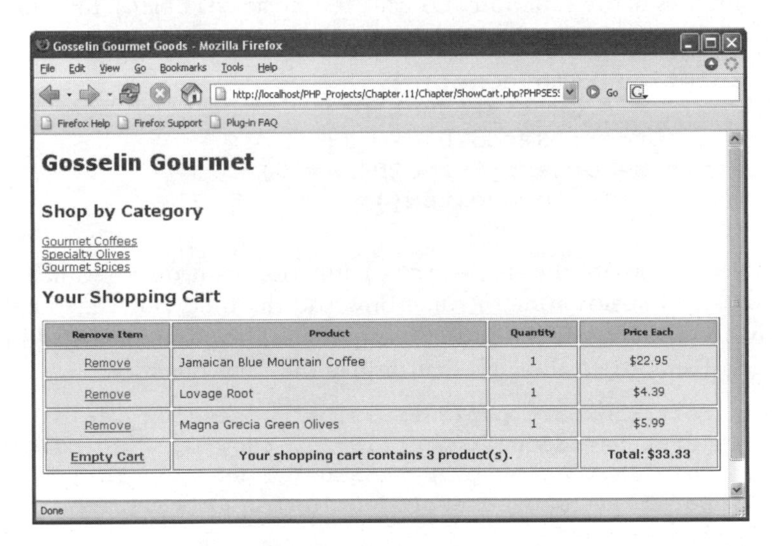

Figure 11-8 Your Shopping Cart Web page after adding remove item and empty cart functionality

11. Verify that the individual **Remove** links work, and then click the **Empty Cart** link to empty the entire cart.
12. Close your Web browser window.

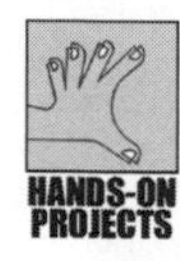

Hands-On Project 11-2

In this project, you add two member functions, `addOne()` and `removeOne()`, to the `ShoppingCart` class that allow you to change the quantities of products in the shopping cart.

To add the `addOne()` and `removeOne()` member functions to the `ShoppingCart` class:

1. Return to the **ShoppingCart.php** script in your text editor.
2. Add the following `addOne()` function definition to the end of the class definition. The statements use the `$_GET['productID']` variable to increment the value assigned to the element that represents the product.

```
public function addOne() {
     $ProdID = $_GET['productID'];
     $this->Orders[$ProdID] += 1;
}
```

3. Add the following `removeOne()` function definition to the end of the class definition. The statements use the `$_GET['productID']` variable to decrement the value assigned to the element that represents the product. If the quantity of a particular item reaches 0, the function also calls the `removeItem()` function to remove the product from the shopping cart.

```
public function removeOne() {
     $ProdID = $_GET['productID'];
     $this->Orders[$ProdID] -= 1;
     if ($this->Orders[$ProdID] == 0)
          $this->removeItem();
}
```

4. Next, you need to modify the `showCart()` function so it displays links that call the `addOne()` and `removeOne()` functions. Add the following statements immediately above the `echo "</td>";` statement. These statements add two links, Add and Remove, to the cells that display the item quantity.

```
echo "<a href='ShowCart.php?PHPSESSID=" . session_id()
     . "&operation=addOne&productID=" . $Row[0] . "'>Add</a> ";
echo "<a href='ShowCart.php?PHPSESSID=" . session_id()
     . "&operation=removeOne&productID=" . $Row[0]
     . "'>Remove</a>";
```

5. Save the **ShoppingCart.php** script and return to the **ShowCart.php** script in your text editor.
6. Modify the `if` statement that checks the value of the `$_GET['operation']` variable so it includes nested `if` statements that call the `addOne()` and `removeOne()` methods, as follows:

```
if (isset($_GET['operation'])) {
     if ($_GET['operation'] == "addItem")
          $Cart->addItem();
```

```
            if ($_GET['operation'] == "removeItem")
                  $Cart->removeItem();
            if ($_GET['operation'] == "emptyCart")
                  $Cart->emptyCart();
            if ($_GET['operation'] == "addOne")
                  $Cart->addOne();
            if ($_GET['operation'] == "removeOne")
                  $Cart->removeOne();
}
```

7. Save the **ShowCart.php** script and then open the **GosselinGourmetGoods.php** script in your Web browser by entering the following URL: **http://localhost/PHP_Projects/Chapter.11/Chapter/GosselinGourmetGoods.php**.
8. Click each of the shopping category links and click the **Add** button for various products on each page. Then, use the Add and Remove links for each product on the Your Shopping Cart page to test the modify quantity functionality. Figure 11-9 shows the Your Shopping Cart Web page after changing the quantities for several products.

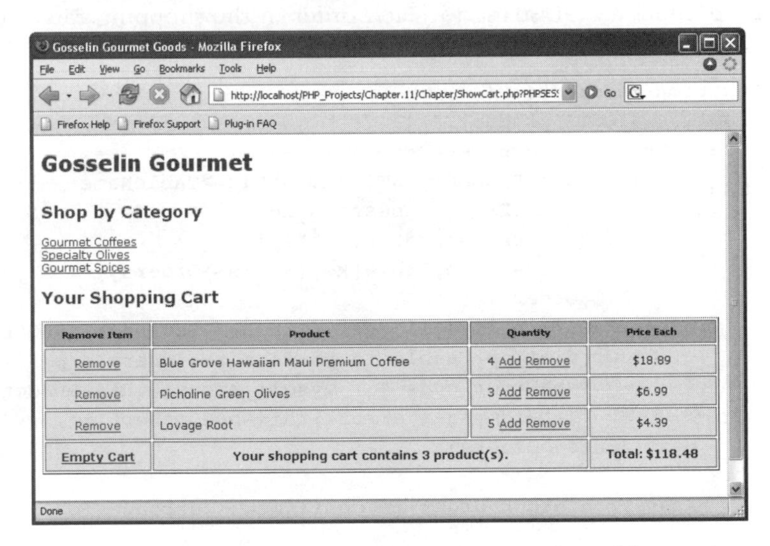

Figure 11-9 Your Shopping Cart Web page after adding quantity modification functionality

9. Close your Web browser window.

Hands-On Project 11-3

In this project, you add a `checkout()` function to the `ShoppingCart` class that allows customers to check out by saving order information to a database table. For the sake of simplicity, the `checkout()` function does not record customer information, although it does use the session ID to uniquely identify each order. The session ID also acts as the primary key for each order.

To add a `checkout()` function to the `ShoppingCart` class:

1. Return to the **ShoppingCart.php** script in your text editor.
2. Log in to the MySQL Monitor with the MySQL username and password you created in Chapter 8.
3. Enter the following command to select the `gosselin_gourmet` database:

```
mysql> use gosselin_gourmet;
```

4. Enter the following command to create a table named `orders`, which will contain each shopping cart order. The table consists of four columns: `orderID`, `productID`, `productTable`, and `quantity`. The `orderID` field is the primary key and will contain the session ID that represents each order.

```
mysql> CREATE TABLE orders (productID VARCHAR(100) PRIMARY KEY,
     -> orderID VARCHAR(25), productTable VARCHAR(50),
     -> quantity INT);
```

5. Return to the **ShoppingCart.php** script in your text editor and add the following `checkout()` function definition to the end of the class definition. The `foreach` loop builds a SQL string for each order in the shopping cart and inserts it into the database.

```
public function checkout() {
      $ProdID = $_GET['productID'];
      foreach($this->Orders as $Order) {
            $SQLstring = "INSERT INTO " . $this->TableName
                  . " VALUES('" . session_id() . "','"
                  . key($this->Orders) . "','"
                  . $this->OrderTable[key($this->Orders)] . "',"
                  . $Order . ")";
            $QueryResult = @mysqli_query($this->DBConnect, $SQLstring)
                  Or die("<p>Unable to perform the query.</p>"
                  . "<p>Error code " . mysqli_errno($this->DBConnect)
                  . ": " . mysqli_error($this->DBConnect)) . "</p>";
            next($this->Orders);
      }
      echo "<p><strong>Your order is confirmed.</strong></p>";
}
```

6. Save the **ShoppingCart.php** script and close it in your text editor.
7. Return to the **ShowCart.php** script in your text editor and add the following text and elements to the end of the document body. The code calls a script named Checkout.php, which you create next.

```
<p><a href='<?php echo "Checkout.php?PHPSESSID=" . session_id() .
"&operation=checkout&productID=" . $_GET["productID"]
?>'>Checkout</a>
```

8. Save the **ShowCart.php** script.

Hands-On Project 11-4

In this project, you create a script named Checkout.php that calls the `checkout()` function you created in Hands-On Project 11-3.

To create the Checkout.php script:

1. Create a new document in your text editor and type the `<!DOCTYPE>` declaration, `<html>` element, header information, and `<body>` element. Use the strict DTD and "Gosselin Gourmet Goods" as the content of the `<title>` element.
2. Add the following `<link>` element above the closing `</head>` tag to link to the php_styles.css style sheet in your Chapter directory:

```
<link rel="stylesheet" href="php_styles.css" type="text/css" />
```

3. Add the following text and elements to the document body:

```
<h1>Gosselin Gourmet Goods</h1>
```

4. Add the following PHP script section to the beginning of the file, above the `<!DOCTYPE>` declaration. The script section contains a `require_once()` statement that makes the `ShoppingCart` class available to the GosselinGourmetCoffees.php script along with a `session_start()` function to begin or restore a session. The `if` statement determines whether the `$_SESSION['curCart']` variable is set and whether the operation variable contains a value of "checkout". If not, the user did not access this page through one of the shopping category pages, so he is redirected to the main Gosselin Gourmet Goods page.

```
<?php
require_once("ShoppingCart.php");
session_start();
if (!isset($_SESSION['curCart']) && $_GET['operation'] !=
"checkout")
     header("location:GosselinGourmetGoods.php");
?>
```

5. Add the following PHP script section to the end of the document body. The statements in the script section restore the serialized `$Cart` object, set the table name to "orders," and then call the `checkout()` method.

```
<?php
$Cart = unserialize($_SESSION['curCart']);
$Cart->setTable("orders");
$Cart->checkout();
?>
```

6. Add the following text and elements to the end of the document body:

```
<p><a href="GosselinGourmetGoods.php">Gosselin Gourmet
Goods</a></p>
```

7. Save the document as **Checkout.php** in the Chapter directory for Chapter 11 and then close it in your text editor.
8. Open the **GosselinGourmetGoods.php** script in your Web browser by entering the following URL: **http://localhost/PHP_Projects/Chapter.11/Chapter/GosselinGourmetGoods.php**. Use the shopping category links to add several products to your shopping cart, and then click the Checkout link on the Your Shopping Cart page. You should see the message confirming your order.
9. Close your Web browser window.
10. Return to the MySQL monitor in your console window and enter the following command. The products you entered should appear in the database table.

```
mysql> SELECT * FROM orders;
```

11. Type **exit** or **quit** and press **Enter** to log out of the MySQL Monitor.

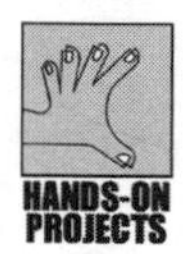

Hands-On Project 11-5

In this project, you add code to the Gosselin Gourmet Goods Web site that cancels the current order.

To add cancellation code to the Gosselin Gourmet Goods Web site:

1. Return to the **ShowCart.php** script in your text editor and add the following text and elements to the document body. The link simply calls the main Gosselin Gourmet Goods Web page, GosselinGourmetGoods.php.

```
<p><a href="GosselinGourmetGoods.php">Cancel Order</a></p>
```

2. Save the **ShowCart.php** script and close it in your text editor.
3. Open the **GosselinGourmetGoods.php** document in your text editor.
4. Add the following script section and session deletion code to the beginning of the document, above the `<!DOCTYPE>` declaration:

```
<?php
session_start();
$_SESSION = array();
session_destroy();
?>
```

5. Save the **GosselinGourmetGoods.php** script and close it in your text editor.
6. Open the **GosselinGourmetGoods.php** script in your Web browser by entering the following URL: **http://localhost/PHP_Projects/Chapter.11/Chapter/GosselinGourmetGoods.php**. Use the shopping category links to add several products to your shopping cart, and then click the **Cancel Order** link on the Your Shopping Cart page to test the cancellation code.
7. Close your Web browser window.

CASE PROJECTS

Save the documents you create for the following projects in the Cases directory for Chapter 11.

Case Project 11-1

Create a `HitCounter` class that counts the number of hits to a Web page and stores the results in a MySQL database. Use a private data member to store the number of hits and include public set and get member functions to access the private counter member variable.

Case Project 11-2

Create a `GuestBook` class that stores Web site visitor names in a MySQL database. Use a private data member to store visitor names and include public set and get member functions to access the private visitor name member variable.

Case Project 11-3

Create a `Movies` class that determines the cost of a ticket to a cinema, based on the moviegoer's age. Assume that the cost of a full-price ticket is $10. Assign the age to a private data member. Use a public member function to determine the ticket price, based on the following schedule:

Age	Price
Under 5	Free
5 to 17	Half price
18 to 55	Full price
Over 55	$2 off

Case Project 11-4

In Chapter 5, you wrote a script that calculates how long it takes to travel a specified number of miles, based on speed, number of stops, and weather conditions for a passenger train that averages a speed of 50 mph. Each stop of the train adds an additional five minutes to the train's schedule. In addition, during bad weather the train can only average a speed of 40 mph. Write a class-based version of this script with a class named `Train`. Save each piece of information you gather from the user in a private data member, and write the appropriate get and set functions for setting and retrieving each data member.

Case Project 11-5

In Chapter 5, you wrote a script that calculates the correct amount of change to return when performing a cash transaction. Write a class-based version of this script with a class named `Change`. Allow the user (a cashier) to enter the cost of a transaction and the exact amount of money that the customer hands over to pay for the transaction. Use set and get functions to store and retrieve both amounts to and from private data members. Then use member functions to determine the largest amount of each denomination to return to the customer. Assume that the largest denomination a customer will use is a $100 bill. Therefore, you need to calculate the correct amount of change to return for $50, $20, $10, $5, and $1 bills, along with quarters, dimes, nickels, and pennies. For example, if the price of a transaction is $5.65 and the customer hands the cashier $10, the cashier should return $4.35 to the customer. Include code that requires the user to enter a numeric value for the cash transaction.

Case Project 11-6

Create a `BankAccount` class that allows users to calculate the balance in a bank account. The user should be able to enter a starting balance, and then calculate how that balance changes when they make a deposit, withdraw money, or enter any accumulated interest. Add the appropriate data members and member functions to the `BankAccount` class that will enable this functionality. Also, add code to the class that ensures that the user does not overdraw her account. Be sure that the program adheres to the information hiding techniques that were discussed in this chapter.

CHAPTER

12

ERROR HANDLING AND DEBUGGING

In this chapter, you will:

- Study debugging concepts
- Handle and report errors
- Learn how to use basic debugging techniques

The more PHP programs you write, the more likely you are to write programs that generate error messages. At times, it might seem like your programs never function quite the way you want. Regardless of experience, knowledge, and ability, all programmers incorporate errors into their programs at one time or another. Thus, all programmers must devote part of their programming education to mastering the art of debugging. As you learned at the beginning of this book, debugging is the act of tracing and resolving errors in a program. Debugging is an essential skill for any programmer, regardless of the programming language.

In this chapter, you learn how to handle and report error messages. You also learn techniques and tools that you can use to trace and resolve errors in PHP programs. However, you do not create any new programs. Instead, you learn how to use PHP error-handling and debugging techniques to locate errors in an existing program named MovingEstimator. The Moving Estimator program is designed to be used by a shipping company to calculate the costs of moving a household from one location to another, based on distance, weight, and several other factors. The program consists of two scripts: one script containing a class named `MovingEstimate` and another script that uses the `MovingEstimate` class to calculate the various types of moving costs.

Before you proceed with this chapter, try out the completed version of the program named MovingEstimatorNoBugs.php in the Chapter directory for Chapter 12. MovingEstimatorNoBugs.php calls the EstimatorClassNoBugs.php script, which contains the MovingEstimator class. After a user enters values into each of the text boxes and clicks the Calculate button, the `MovingEstimator` class calculates the total estimated moving cost. Figure 12-1 shows an example of the program running in a Web browser after some moving costs have been entered.

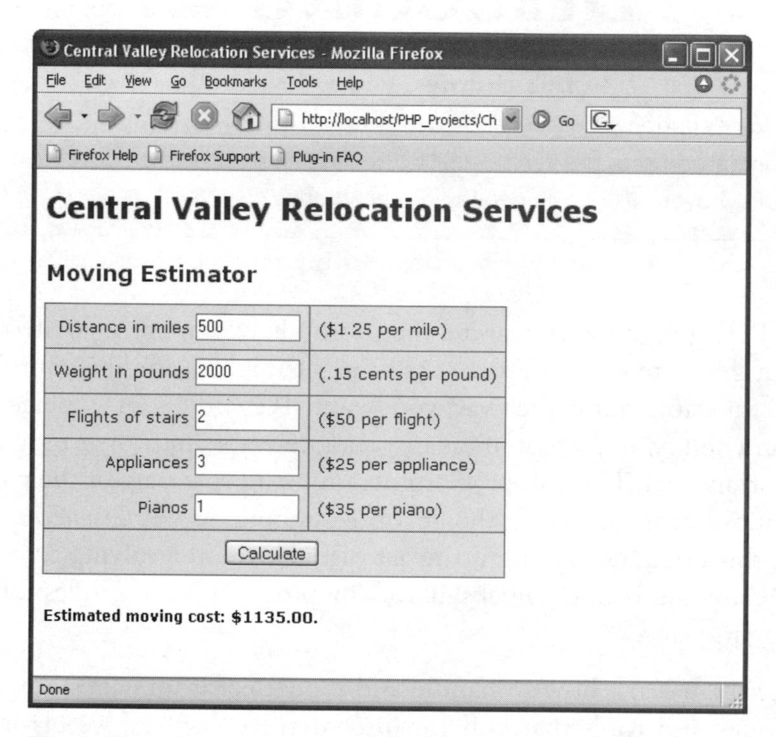

Figure 12-1 Moving Estimator program

Note that you will not be working with the MovingEstimatorNoBugs.php or the EstimatorClassNoBugs.php scripts in this chapter. Rather, you work with versions of each script, MovingEstimatorWithBugs.php and EstimatorClassWithBugs.php, that contain bugs. You need to use the "buggy" version to learn the debugging techniques presented in this chapter. If you get stuck, however, you can use the no-bugs version as a reference.

Understanding Logic and Debugging

To write a program, you must understand the syntax of the programming language you are using. You must also understand computer-programming logic. The term **logic** refers to the order in which various parts of a program run, or execute. The statements in a program must execute in the correct order to produce the desired results. In an analogous situation, although you know how to drive a car well, you might not reach your destination if you do not follow the correct route. Similarly, you might be able to write statements using the correct syntax, but be unable to construct an entire, logically executed program that works the way you want. Or, you might be able to use a programming language's syntax correctly, but be unable to execute a logically constructed, workable program. A typical logical error might be multiplying two values when you meant to divide them. Another might be producing output before obtaining the appropriate input (for example, printing an order confirmation on the screen before asking the user to enter the necessary order information).

Any error in a program that causes it to function incorrectly, whether because of incorrect syntax or flaws in logic, is called a **bug**. The term **debugging** refers to the act of tracing and resolving errors in a program. Grace Murray Hopper, a mathematician who was instrumental in developing the Common Business-Oriented Language (COBOL) programming language, is said to have first coined the term "debugging." As the story from the 1940s goes, a moth short-circuited a primitive computer that Hopper was using. Removing the moth from the computer "debugged" the system and resolved the problem. Today, the term "bug" refers to any sort of problem in the design and operation of a program.

Do not confuse bugs with computer viruses. Viruses are self-contained programs designed to "infect" a computer system and cause mischievous or malicious damage. Virus programs themselves can contain bugs (and do damage) if they contain syntax errors or do not perform as their creators envisioned.

What can you do to mitigate bugs in your PHP programs? First, always use good syntax, such as ending statements with semicolons, and always initialize variables when you first declare them to ensure they contain data if your script attempts to use them. When you create structures such as functions and `for` statements, be sure to type the opening and closing braces before adding any code to the body of the structure. Also, take care to include the opening and closing parentheses and correct number of arguments when you call a function. Remember that the more disciplined you are in your programming technique, the fewer bugs you will find in your programs. Finally, develop good debugging skills. As you work through this chapter, keep in mind that debugging is not an exact science—every program you write is different and requires different methods of debugging. Although there are some tools available to help you debug your PHP code, your own logical and analytical skills are the best debugging resources you have.

Next, you study the three types of errors that can occur in a program: syntax errors, runtime errors, and logic errors.

Syntax Errors

Syntax errors, or **parse errors**, occur when the scripting engine fails to recognize code. In PHP, statements that are not recognized by the PHP scripting engine generate syntax errors. Syntax errors can be caused by incorrect use of PHP code or references to objects, methods, and variables that do not exist. For example, if a programmer attempts to use a method that does not exist or omits a method's closing parenthesis, the scripting engine generates a syntax error. Many syntax errors are generated by incorrectly spelled or mistyped words. For example, the statement eco "<p>Hello World!</p>"; causes a syntax error because the echo() statement is misspelled as *eco*. Similarly, the following statements cause a syntax error because the $Hello variable is incorrectly typed with a lowercase 'h'. (Remember that identifiers in PHP are case sensitive.)

```
$Hello = "<p>Hello World!</p>";
echo $hello;
```

NOTE

Syntax errors in compiled languages, such as C++, are also called compile-time errors because they are usually discovered when a program is compiled. Because PHP is an interpreted language, syntax errors are not discovered until a program executes.

Run-Time Errors

The second type of error, a **run-time error**, occurs when the PHP scripting engine encounters a problem while a program is executing. Run-time errors differ from syntax errors in that they do not necessarily represent PHP language errors. Instead, run-time errors occur when the scripting engine encounters code that it cannot execute. For example, consider the statement customFunction();, which calls a custom PHP function named customFunction(). This statement does not generate a syntax error, because it is legal (and usually necessary) to create and then call custom functions in a PHP program. However, if your program includes the call statement but does not include code that creates the function in the first place, your program generates a run-time error. The error occurs when the scripting engine attempts to call the function and is unable to find the function.

The following code shows another example of a run-time error. In this example, an echo() statement attempts to print the contents of a variable named $MessageVar. Because the $MessageVar variable is not declared (you can assume it has not been declared in another script section elsewhere in the document), a run-time error occurs.

```
<?php
echo $MessageVar;
?>
```

When investigating a run-time error, keep in mind that the culprit might in fact be a syntax error. Because syntax errors do not occur until the scripting engine attempts to execute the code, they often manifest as run-time errors. For example, suppose your code includes a function that contains a statement with a syntax error. This syntax error will not be caught until the function executes at run time. When the function does execute, it generates a run-time error because of the syntax error within the function.

Logic Errors

The third type of error, **logic errors**, are flaws in a program's design that prevent the program from running as you anticipate. In this context, the term "logic" refers to the execution of program statements and procedures in the correct order to produce the desired results. You're already accustomed to performing ordinary, nonprogramming tasks according to a certain logic. For example, when you do the laundry, you normally wash, dry, iron, and then fold your clothes. If you decided to iron, fold, dry, and then wash the clothes, you would end up with a pile of wet laundry rather than the clean and pressed garments you desired. The problem, in that case, would be a type of logic error—you performed the steps in the wrong order.

One example of a logic error in a computer program is multiplying two values when you mean to divide them, as in the following code:

```
$DivisionResult = 10 * 2;
echo "<p>Ten divided by two is equal to $DivisionResult.</p>"
```

Another example of a logic error is the creation of an infinite loop, in which a loop statement never ends because its conditional expression is never updated or is never false. The following code creates a `for` statement that results in the logic error of an infinite loop. The cause of the infinite loop is that the third argument in the `for` statement's parentheses never changes the value of the `$Count` variable.

```
for($Count = 10; $Count >= 0; $Count) {
     if ($Count == 0)
          echo "<p>We have liftoff!</p>";
     else
          echo "<p>Liftoff in $Count seconds.</p>";
}
```

Because the `$Count` variable is never updated in the preceding example, it continues to have a value of 10 through each iteration of the loop, resulting in the repeated printing of the text "Liftoff in 10 seconds" in a browser window. To correct this logic error, you add a decrement operator to the third argument in the `for` statement's constructor, as follows:

```
for($Count = 10; $Count >= 0; —$Count) {
     if ($Count == 0)
          echo "<p>We have liftoff!</p>";
     else
          echo "<p>Liftoff in $Count seconds.</p>";
}
```

Handling and Reporting Errors

The first line of defense in locating bugs in PHP programs are the error messages you receive when the PHP scripting engine encounters an error. PHP generates four basic types of errors: parse errors, fatal errors, notices, and warnings. Parse errors are syntax errors, whereas the other three types of errors are run-time errors.

Parse error messages occur when a PHP script contains a syntax error that prevents your script from running. For example, the following code raises a parse error because the `for()` statement is missing its opening brace ({). Figure 12-2 shows the resulting parse error message in a Web browser.

```
<?php
for ($Count = 10; $Count >= 0; –$Count)
     if ($Count == 0)
          echo "<p>We have liftoff!</p>";
     else
          echo "<p>Liftoff in $Count seconds.</p>";
}
?>
```

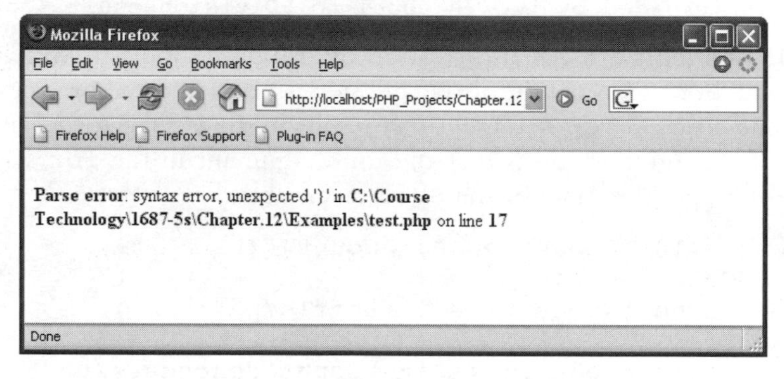

Figure 12-2 PHP parse error message in a Web browser

Two important pieces of information displayed with a parse error are the line number in the document where the error occurred and a description of the error. Note that the line number in an error message is counted from the start of the document, not just from the start of a script section. For example, the PHP script that generated the error message displayed in Figure 12-2 is located within the body of the document shown in Figure 12-3. As the line numbers in the figure illustrate, the line number that caused the error (line 17) is counted from the start of the document.

```
 1  <!DOCTYPE html PUBLIC '-//W3C//DTD XHTML 1.0 Strict//EN'
 2       'http://www.w3.org/TR/xhtml1/DTD/xhtml1-strict.dtd'>
 3  <html xmlns='http://www.w3.org/1999/xhtml'>
 4  <head>
 5  <title>Countdown Script</title>
 6  <link rel='stylesheet' href='php_styles.css' type='text/css' />
 7  <meta http-equiv='content-type'
 8  content='text/html; charset=iso-8859-1' />
 9  </head>
10  <body>
11  <?php
12  for($Count = 10; $Count >= 0; --$Count)
13       if ($Count == 0)
14            echo '<p>We have liftoff!</p>';
15       else
16            echo '<p>Liftoff in $Count seconds.</p>';
17  }
18  ?>
19  </body>
20  </html>
```

Figure 12-3 Web page document illustrating line numbers

Keep in mind that you can rely on error messages only to find the general location of an error in a program; an error message does not tell you the exact nature of an error. You cannot always assume that the line specified by an error message is the actual problem. The parse error message shown in Figure 12-2 lists the error as occurring on line 17. This is because the PHP scripting engine searches to the end of the script for the `for()` statement's opening brace. However, the real problem is that the opening brace should be the first character following the closing parenthesis in the `for()` statement's conditional expression.

Fatal error messages are raised when a script contains a run-time error that prevents it from executing. A typical fatal error message occurs when a script attempts to call a function that does not exist. The following code generates the fatal error message shown in Figure 12-4 because the last statement misspells the name of the `beginCountdown()` function as `beginCntdown()`:


```
function beginCountdown() {
     for($Count = 10; $Count >= 0; –$Count) {
          if ($Count == 0)
               echo "<p>We have liftoff!</p>";
          else
               echo "<p>Liftoff in $Count seconds.</p>";
     }
}
beginCntdown();
```

Warning messages are raised for run-time errors that do not prevent a script from executing. For example, a warning message occurs when you attempt to divide a number by 0. Warning messages are also raised if you pass the wrong number of arguments to a function. The following code raises a warning message because the function call does not pass an argument for the `$Time` parameter. However, the code executes correctly because the `beginCountdown()` function assigns a default value of 10 to the `$Time` parameter if a value is not passed with the function call. Figure 12-5 shows the output.

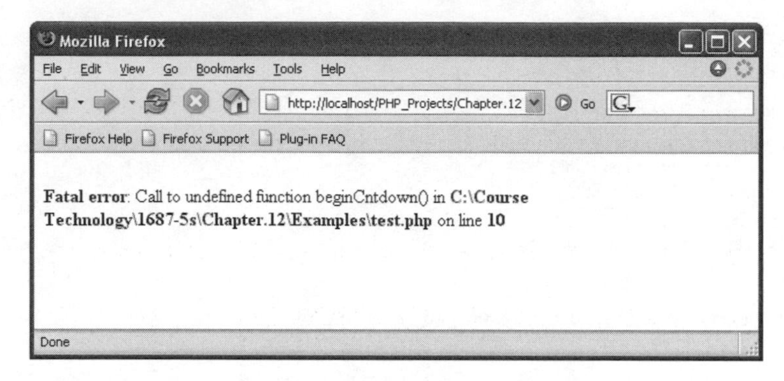

Figure 12-4 PHP fatal error message in a Web browser

```
function beginCountdown($Time) {
     if (!isset($Time))
          $Time = 10;
     for($Count = $Time; $Count >= 0; –$Count) {
          if ($Count == 0)
               echo "<p>We have liftoff!</p>";
          else
               echo "<p>Liftoff in $Count seconds.</p>";
     }
}
beginCountdown();
```

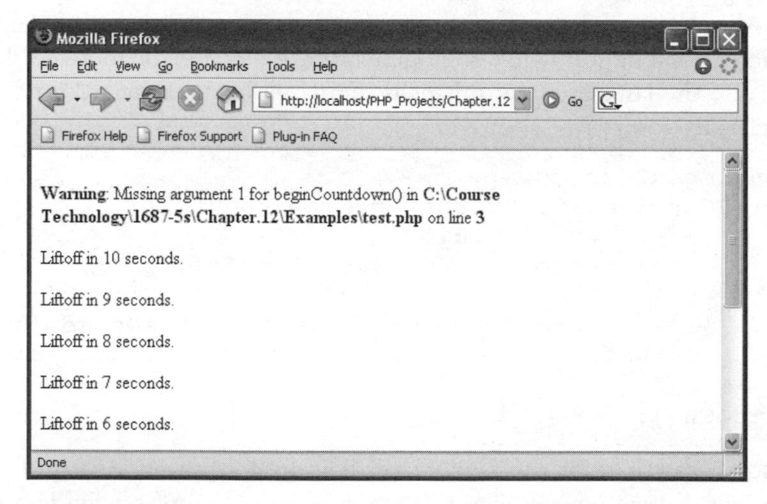

Figure 12-5 PHP warning message in a Web browser

Notice messages are raised for potential run-time errors that do not prevent a script from executing. Notices are less severe than warnings and are typically raised when a script attempts to use an undeclared variable. The following code raises the notice shown in Figure 12-6 because the `echo()` statement misspells the `$LastName` variable as `$Last`:

```
$FirstName = "Don";
$LastName = "Gosselin";
echo "<p>Hello, my name is $FirstName $Last.</p>";
```

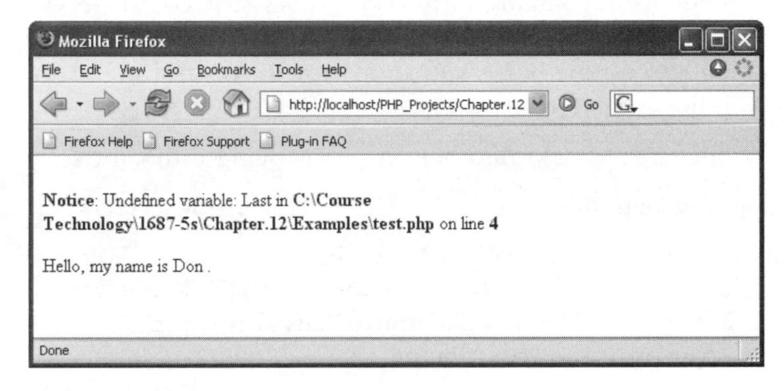

Figure 12-6 PHP notice message in a Web browser

Like parse errors, warnings and notices help you find the general location of an error in a program; they do not pinpoint the error precisely. You cannot always assume that the line specified by an error message is the actual problem in your program. For example, the `$Result = $Amount * $Percentage;` statement in the following code causes a run-time error because the scripting engine cannot locate the `$Amount` and `$Percentage` variables included in the statement. The `$Amount` and `$Percentage` variables are declared within the `variableDeclarations()` function, making them local variables that are only available inside the function. Because the `$Amount` and `$Percentage` variables are not global variables, they are not visible to the `calculatePercentage()` function, which causes a run-time error. The `$Result = $Amount * $Percentage;` statement generates the run-time error because it attempts to access variables that are local to another function. However, the real problem is that the `$Amount` and `$Percentage` variables are not declared at a global level.

```
function variableDeclarations() {
     $Percentage = .25;
     $Amount = 1600;
}
function calculatePercentage() {
     $Result = $Amount * $Percentage;
     echo "<p>Twenty-five percent of 1,600 is $Result.</p>";
}
variableDeclarations();
calculatePercentage();
```

Logic errors do not generate error messages because they do not prevent the script from running (as syntax errors do) or from executing properly (as run-time errors do). Instead, they prevent the program from running the way you anticipated. Computers are not smart enough (yet) to identify a flaw in a program's logic. For example, if you create an infinite loop with a `for` statement, the scripting engine has no way of telling whether you really wanted to continually execute the `for` statement's code. Later in this chapter, you learn how to trace the flow of your program's execution to locate logic errors.

The php.ini configuration file contains various directives that control how the PHP scripting engine handles errors. PHP also includes various functions that you can use to control error handling at run time. First, you study how to control the error messages that print to the Web browser.

Next, you use error messages to help find bugs in the Moving Estimator script.

To use error messages to help find bugs in the Moving Estimator script:

1. Open the **MovingEstimatorWithBugs.php** script in your Web browser by entering the following URL: **http://localhost/PHP_Projects/Chapter.12/Chapter/MovingEstimatorWithBugs.php**. You should receive the parse error shown in Figure 12-7.

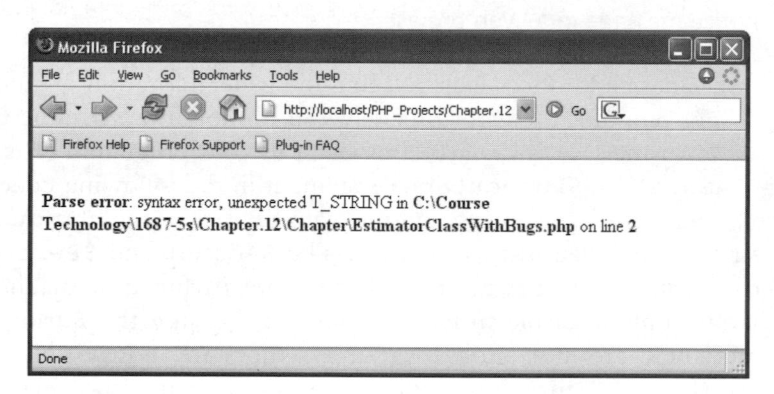

Figure 12-7 Parse error on line 2 in EstimatorClassWithBugs.php script

2. The parse error occurs in the EstimatorClassWithBugs.php script. Leave the MovingEstimatorWithBugs.php script open in your Web browser, but open the **EstimatorClassWithBugs.php** script in your text editor. As shown in Figure 12-7, the error is located on line 2, although it doesn't tell you much else other than there is an unexpected `T_STRING`. Locate line 2 and notice that the opening class definition statement is missing a letter *s* in the `class` keyword. Add the missing s so the line reads as follows:

```
class MovingEstimator {
```

3. Save the **EstimatorClassWithBugs.php** script, and then return to your Web browser and reload the **MovingEstimatorWithBugs.php** script. You should receive another parse error, this time on line 7, as shown in Figure 12-8.

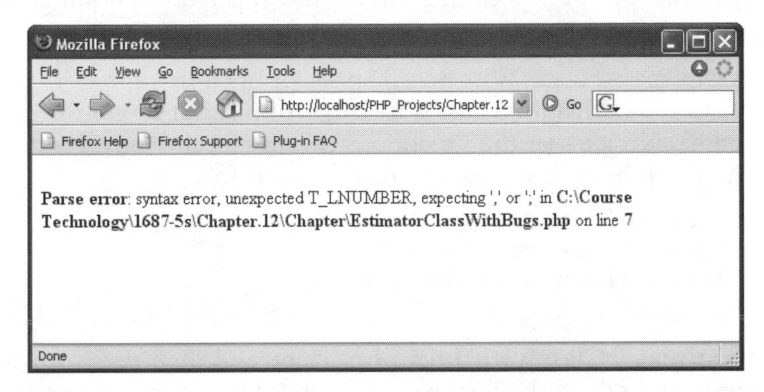

Figure 12-8 Parse error on line 7 in EstimatorClassWithBugs.php script

4. Leave the MovingEstimatorWithBugs.php script open in your Web browser and return to the **EstimatorClassWithBugs.php** script in your text editor. As with the first error, it's difficult to tell from the message shown in Figure 12-8 what is causing the error. However, if you examine line 7, you can see that the variable declaration statement is missing the assignment operator. Add an assignment operator to the statement, as follows:

```
private $PianosCost = 0;
```

5. Save the **EstimatorClassWithBugs.php** script, and then return to your Web browser and reload the **MovingEstimatorWithBugs.php** script. You should receive another parse error, this time on line 33. This error message is a little more helpful in that it tells you the PHP scripting engine was expecting to find an opening brace.

6. Leave the MovingEstimatorWithBugs.php script open in your Web browser and return to the **EstimatorClassWithBugs.php** script in your text editor. If you examine the function that contains line 33, you can see that the function is missing its opening brace. Add the missing opening brace to the function definition, as follows:

```
function calcLaborCost() {
     $this->LaborCost *= .15;
     $this->calcTotalEstimate();
}
```

12

7. Save the **EstimatorClassWithBugs.php** script, and then return to your Web browser and reload the **MovingEstimatorWithBugs.php** script. You should receive another parse error, this time on line 45. This error message informs you that the PHP scripting engine unexpectedly encountered an opening brace.
8. Leave the MovingEstimatorWithBugs.php script open in your Web browser and return to the **EstimatorClassWithBugs.php** script in your text editor. Locate line 47. Notice that the function is missing its closing parenthesis. Add the missing parenthesis so the statement appears as follows:

```
function calcPianosCost() {
     $this->PianosCost *= 3.5;
     $this->calcTotalEstimate();
}
```

9. Save the **EstimatorClassWithBugs.php** script, and then return to your Web browser and reload the Web page. You should receive no more error messages, although you will receive a few notice messages. Do not try to use the program yet because it still contains plenty of bugs. Leave the **MovingEstimatorWithBugs.php** page open in your Web browser.

Printing Errors to the Web Browser

The php.ini configuration file contains two directives, `display_errors` and `display_startup_errors`, that determine whether error messages print to a Web browser. The `display_errors` directive prints script error messages, whereas the `display_startup_errors` directive displays errors that occur when PHP first starts. By default, the `display_errors` directive is assigned a value of "On," and the `display_startup_errors` directive is assigned a value of "Off." Although displaying error messages is useful when you develop PHP scripts, the PHP Group strongly recommends that you turn this feature off for scripts that run in production environments and instead save any errors in a log file. The reason for this is because hackers can use any displayed error messages to identify potential weaknesses in your Web site. The PHP Group also recommends that you only turn the `display_startup_errors` directive on when debugging a script.

You learn how to write errors to a log file shortly.

For the rest of this chapter, you should leave display errors turned on in your php.ini configuration file to help you with your debugging efforts. However, remember to turn display errors off for any PHP production environments.

Setting the Error Reporting Level

The `error_reporting` directive in the php.ini configuration file determines which types of error messages PHP should generate. Setting the error reporting level can be useful in helping you debug your scripts. However, keep in mind that changing the error messages PHP generates does not prevent errors from occurring; it only prevents the error messages from being printed to the Web browser or written to a log file.

By default, the `error_reporting` directive is assigned a value of "E_ALL," which generates all errors, warnings, and notices to the Web browser. You can also assign to the `error_reporting` directive the error levels listed in Table 12-1. Note that each error level can be set using either the constant or integer listed in the table.

Table 12-1 Error reporting levels

Constant	Integer	Description
--	0	Turns off all error reporting
E_ERROR	1	Reports fatal run-time errors
E_WARNING	2	Reports run-time warnings
E_PARSE	4	Reports syntax errors
E_NOTICE	8	Reports run-time notices
E_CORE_ERROR	16	Reports fatal errors that occur when PHP first starts
E_CORE_WARNING	32	Reports warnings that occur when PHP first starts
E_COMPILE_WARNING	32	Reports warnings generated by the Zend Scripting Engine
E_COMPILE_ERROR	64	Reports errors generated by the Zend Scripting Engine
E_USER_ERROR	256	Reports user-generated error messages
E_USER_WARNING	512	Reports user-generated warnings
E_USER_NOTICE	1024	Reports user-generated notices
E_ALL	2047	Reports errors, warnings, and notices with the exception of `E_STRICT` notices
E_STRICT	2048	Reports strict notices, which are code recommendations that ensure compatibility with PHP 5

To generate a combination of error levels, separate the levels assigned to the `error_reporting` directive with the bitwise `Or` operator (|). For example, the following statement specifies that PHP only report fatal and parse errors:

```
error_reporting = E_ERROR | E_PARSE
```

To specify that the `E_ALL` error should exclude certain types of messages, separate the levels with bitwise `And` (`&`) and `Not` operators (~). The following statement specifies that PHP report all errors except run-time notices:

```
error_reporting = E_ALL &~ E_NOTICE
```

Instead of modifying the values assigned to the `error_reporting` directive in the php.ini configuration file, you can use the `error_reporting()` function to specify the messages to report in a particular script. Use the same bitwise operators to separate reporting levels that you pass to the `error_reporting()` function. The following statement uses the `error_reporting()` function so that PHP only report fatal and parse errors:

```
error_reporting(E_ERROR | E_PARSE);
```

The following statement uses the `error_reporting()` function to specify that PHP report all errors except run-time notices:

```
error_reporting(E_ALL &~ E_NOTICE);
```

To disable error messages for a particular script, place the `error_reporting()` function at the beginning of a script section and pass to it a value of 0, as follows:

```
error_reporting(0);
```

The notice messages displayed in the Moving Estimator script are caused by the references to the `$_GET` autoglobal variables in the `MovingEstimator` class constructor function. Each `$_GET` variable is missing quotations around the variable names within the array brackets. For example, the `$_GET['distance']` is referred to as `$_GET[distance]`, without the quotations around *distance*. This syntax is not illegal in PHP, although it is considered bad programming style, which is why the PHP scripting engine issues the notice messages. Although your best bet is to add the missing quotation marks around the variable names, for this exercise you instead modify the error reporting level for the Moving Estimator script so it does not display notice messages.

To modify the Moving Estimator script so it does not display notice messages:

1. Open the **MovingEstimatorWithBugs.php** script in your text editor.
2. Add the following `error_reporting()` statement to the beginning of the first script section. This statement specifies that PHP report all errors except run-time notices.

   ```
   error_reporting(E_ALL &~ E_NOTICE);
   ```

3. Save the **MovingEstimatorWithBugs.php** script, and then return to your Web browser and reload the Web page. The page should open without any notice messages. Leave the **MovingEstimatorWithBugs.php** script open in your Web browser.

Logging Errors to a File

Remember that for security reasons, you should disable the printing of error messages for any scripts that run in a production environment. Unless you work for a large company with separate development and production systems, chances are you will use the same server to execute scripts in development that you will use to execute scripts in production. In this situation, it's not feasible to use your php.ini configuration file to turn the display_errors and display_startup_errors directives on and off each time you want to work on a script you are writing. A better choice is to log all errors to a text file.

PHP logs errors to a text file according to the error reporting level assigned to the error_reporting directive in the php.ini configuration file, or that you set for an individual script with the the error_reporting() function. The php.ini configuration file includes several parameters for handling error logging, including the log_errors and error_log directives. The log_errors directive determines whether PHP logs errors to a file and is assigned a default value of "Off." The error_log directive identifies the text file where PHP will log errors. You can assign either a path and filename or syslog to the error_log directive. A value of syslog on UNIX/Linux systems specifies that PHP should use the syslog protocol to forward the message to the system log file. On Windows systems, a value of syslog forwards messages to the Event Log service.

Next, you modify your php.ini configuration file so errors are logged to a text file.

To modify your php.ini configuration file so errors are logged to a text file:

1. Create a directory named logs in your PHP installation directory. By default, the PHP installation directory is /usr/local/php5 on UNIX/Linux platforms and C:\PHP on Windows systems.

2. Open your **php.ini** configuration file in your text editor. For UNIX/Linux systems, you should have installed this file in the /usr/local/lib directory. On Windows systems, this file is installed automatically in your main Windows directory, which is usually C:\WINDOWS or C:\WINNT.

3. In the php.ini file, locate the log_errors directive. If the directive is assigned a value of "Off," change it to "On," so the statement reads as follows:

   ```
   log_errors = On
   ```

4. In the php.ini file, locate the display_errors directive. If the directive is assigned a value of "On," change it to "Off," so the statement reads as follows:

   ```
   display_errors = Off
   ```

5. Locate the error_log directive in the php.ini file and remove the semicolon from the beginning of the statement. Assign to the error_log directive the name of the directory you created in Step 1 and a filename of errors.log. If you installed PHP in the default installation directory of /usr/local/php5 on UNIX/Linux systems, the statement should read as follows:

   ```
   error_log = /usr/local/php5/logs/error.log
   ```

   If you installed PHP in the default installation directory of C:\PHP on Windows platforms systems, the statement should read as follows:

   ```
   error_log = C:\\PHP\\logs\\error.log
   ```

When assigning a directory in the php.ini configuration file on Windows platforms, you must escape the backward slashes in a directory (as shown in the preceding example) or use forward slashes.

6. Save the **php.ini** file and close it in your text editor.
7. Return to the **MovingEstimatorWithBugs.php** script in your text editor, and introduce a bug in the script by removing the underscore from the `require_once()` function in the first script section. The modified statement should appear as follows:

   ```
   requireonce("EstimatorClassWithBugs.php");
   ```
8. Save the **MovingEstimatorWithBugs.php** script, and then return to your Web browser and reload the Web page. The page should open as a blank page, but without any error messages. Leave the **MovingEstimatorWithBugs.php** script open in your Web browser.
9. Use your text editor to open the **error.log** file from the logs directory in your PHP installation directory. You should see the error entered on the first line of the file.
10. Close the **error.log** file in your text editor, and then return to the **MovingEstimatorWithBugs.php** script in your text editor and fix the bug you just introduced by adding the missing underscore to the **`require_once()`** function.
11. Save the **MovingEstimatorWithBugs.php** script.

Implementing Custom Error Handling

Recall from Chapter 9 when you studied MySQL error messages that although standard error messages generated by programming languages such as PHP are very helpful to programmers, they tend to scare users, who might think that they somehow caused the error. Errors can and will occur, but you should never let your users think that they did something wrong. Instead of allowing PHP to handle all the details of generating and logging errors, many programmers prefer to write their own error-handling code. Not only does this allow programmers to write more user-friendly messages, but it also gives them greater control over any errors that occur in their scripts. PHP includes several functions that allow you to write your own error-handling code.

Writing Custom Error-Handling Functions

You can take custom error handling a step further and define your own function to handle any errors raised in a PHP script. You use the `set_error_handler()` function to specify a custom function to handle errors. You pass to the `set_error_handler()` function a single text string argument containing the name of the custom function, but without the function's parentheses. The following statement sets a function named `processErrors()` as the custom error-handling function:

```
set_error_handler("processErrors");
```

You can define a custom error-handling function with five parameters. The first parameter contains the error reporting level and the second parameter contains the error message. Both the first and second parameters are required. The remaining three parameters are optional. The third parameter stores the filename that raised the error, the fourth parameter contains the line number in the file that raised the error, and the fifth parameter contains an array of the variables that existed when the error was raised. Custom error-handling functions can only handle the following types of error reporting levels:

- E_WARNING
- E_NOTICE
- E_USER_ERROR
- E_USER_WARNING
- E_USER_NOTICE

All other types of error reporting levels are handled by PHP's built-in error-handling functionality according to the values set in your php.ini configuration file or with the `error_reporting()` function. Keep in mind that when you use the `set_error_handler()` function to specify a custom function to handle errors, none of PHP's default error-handling functionality executes for the preceding types of error reporting levels, even if you have the `display_errors` and `log_errors` directive in your php.ini configuration file set to "On." Any error reporting levels you might have set with either the `error_reporting` directive or the `error_reporting()` function are also ignored for the preceding types of error reporting levels.

To print the error message to the screen, you must include `echo()` statements in the custom error-handling function, as demonstrated in the following example. The `switch` statement checks the value of the `$ErrLevel` parameter and then uses `echo()` statements to print the type of error message. Additional `echo()` statements then print the error message, filename, and line number. Notice that the last statement in the function is an `exit()` statement. Because PHP's built-in error-handling functionality is bypassed when you call a custom error-handling function, you call an `exit()` or `die()` statement to manually halt the script for any errors that will prevent your script from executing properly. Figure 12-9 shows the output after a user enters nonnumeric values.

```
set_error_handler("processErrors");
function processErrors($ErrLevel, $ErrMessage, $File, $LineNum) {
      switch ($ErrLevel) {
      case E_WARNING:
        $Message = "<p><strong>Warning</strong>: $ErrMessage<br />";
        break;
```

```
            case E_NOTICE:
              $Message = "<p><strong>Notice</strong>: $ErrMessage<br />";
              break;
            case E_USER_ERROR:
              $Message = "<p><strong>Error</strong>: $ErrMessage<br />";
              break;
            case E_USER_WARNING:
              $Message = "<p><strong>Warning</strong>: $ErrMessage<br />";
              break;
            case E_USER_NOTICE:
                $Message = "<p><strong>Notice</strong>: $ErrMessage<br />";
              break;
            }
            echo $Message;
             exit();
}
```

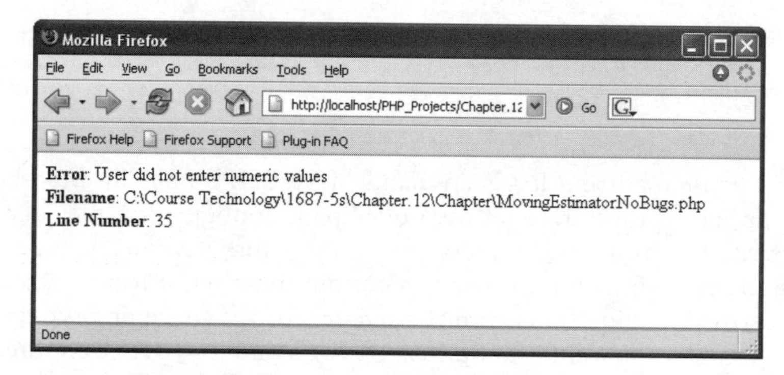

Figure 12-9 Moving Estimator page after entering nonnumeric values

To log an error with a custom error-handling function, you call the `error_log()` function. The easiest way to use the `error_log()` function is to pass it a string containing the error message you want to log. By default, the `error_log()` function logs an error message to the location specified by the `error_log` directive in the php.ini configuration file.

The following code demonstrates how to use an `error_log()` function in the `processErrors()` custom error-handling function. The code builds a variable named `$Log` that contains the same text as the `$Message` variable, but without the HTML tags. The last statement passes the `$Log` variable to the `error_log()` function.

```
$Log = strip_tags($Message);
$Message .= "<strong>Filename</strong>: $File<br />";
$Message .= "<strong>Line Number</strong>: $LineNum</p>";
$Log .=  " in $File on line $LineNum";
echo $Message;
error_log($Log);
exit();
```

To reset a script so it uses PHP's default error-handling functionality instead of a custom function, call the `restore_error_handler()` function. The `restore_error_handler()` function does not accept any arguments, so you can simply call it with the following statement:

```
restore_error_handler();
```

Next, you add a custom error-handling function to the MovingEstimatorWithBugs.php script.

To add a custom error-handling function to the MovingEstimatorWithBugs.php script:

1. Return to the **MovingEstimatorWithBugs.php** script in your text editor.
2. Replace the `error_reporting()` statement in the first script section with the following `set_error_handler()` function, which specifies a custom error-handling function named `handleErrors()`, which you create in the next step:

   ```
   set_error_handler("handleErrors");
   ```

3. Add the following error-handling function after the `set_error_handler()` statement:

   ```
   function handleErrors($ErrLevel, $ErrMessage, $File, $LineNum) {
          switch ($ErrLevel) {
          case E_WARNING:
            $Message = "<p><strong>Warning</strong>: $ErrMessage<br />";
            break;
          case E_NOTICE:
            $Message = "<p><strong>Notice</strong>: $ErrMessage<br />";
            break;
          case E_USER_ERROR:
            $Message = "<p><strong>Error</strong>: $ErrMessage<br />";
            break;
          case E_USER_WARNING:
            $Message = "<p><strong>Warning</strong>: $ErrMessage<br />";
            break;
          case E_USER_NOTICE:
            $Message = "<p><strong>Notice</strong>: $ErrMessage<br />";
            break;
          }
           $Log = strip_tags($Message);
           $Message .= "<strong>Filename</strong>: $File<br / >";
           $Message .= "<strong>Line Number</strong>: $LineNum</p>";
           $Log .= " in $File on line $LineNum";
           echo $Message;
           error_log($Log);
           exit();
   }
   ```

12

4. Save the **MovingEstimatorWithBugs.php** script, and then return to your Web browser and reload the Web page. You should see a notice message displayed about the use of the undefined constant "distance." Remember that this notice is caused by the references in the `MovingEstimator` class constructor function to the `$_GET` autoglobal variables, which are missing quotations around the variable names within the array brackets.
5. Use your text editor to open the **error.log** file from the logs directory in your PHP installation directory. You should see the notice message entered on the last line of the file.
6. Close the **error.log** file in your text editor.
7. Return to the **EstimatorClassWithBugs.php** script in your text editor and add quotations around the variable names in `$_GET` autoglobal references in the constructor function. The modified constructor function should appear as follows:

```
function __construct() {
     if (isset($_GET['distance']))
          $this->MileageCost = $_GET['distance'];
     if (isset($_GET['weight']))
          $this->LaborCost = $_GET['weight'];
     if (isset($_GET['flights']))
          $this->FlightsCost = $_GET['flights'];
     if (isset($_GET['appliances']))
          $this->AppliancesCost = $_GET['appliances'];
     if (isset($_GET['pianos']))
          $this->PianosCost = $_GET['pianos'];
}
```

8. Save the **EstimatorClassWithBugs.php** script, and then return to your Web browser and reload the Web page. The page should open without any error messages. Leave the **MovingEstimatorWithBugs.php** script open in your Web browser.

Raising Errors with the `trigger_error()` Function

You use the `trigger_error()` function to generate an error in your scripts. This is useful when you want to include error-handling capabilities in your code that execute when something prevents your program from functioning as expected. For example, if a user enters the wrong type of data in a form field that is submitted to a PHP script, you can use the `trigger_error()` function to generate an error.

The `trigger_error()` function accepts two arguments. You pass a custom error message as the first argument and either the `E_USER_ERROR`, `E_USER_WARNING`, or `E_USER_NOTICE` error reporting levels as the second argument. Calling the `trigger_error()` function executes PHP's built-in error-handling functionality. How PHP reports the error depends on the values assigned to the display and log directives in your php.ini file configuration and whether the current script executes an `error_reporting()` function to set the error reporting level.

The following code includes two `trigger_error()` functions to demonstrate how to raise a custom error in a script that calculates body mass index. One `trigger_error()` function executes if the `$_GET['height']` or `$_GET['weight']` variables do not contain values and another `trigger_error()` function executes if the `$_GET['height']` or `$_GET['weight']` variables do not contain numeric values. Figure 12-10 displays the error message that generates if the variables do not contain numeric values using PHP's built-in error-handling functionality.

```
if (isset($_GET['height']) && isset($_GET['weight'])) {
     if (!is_numeric($_GET['weight'])
               || !is_numeric($_GET['height'])) {
               trigger_error("User did not enter numeric values",
                    E_USER_ERROR);
               exit();
     }
}
else
     trigger_error("User did not enter values", E_USER_ERROR);
$BodyMass = $_GET['weight'] / ($_GET['height']
     * $_GET['height']) * 703;
printf("<p>Your body mass index is %d.</p>", $BodyMass);
```

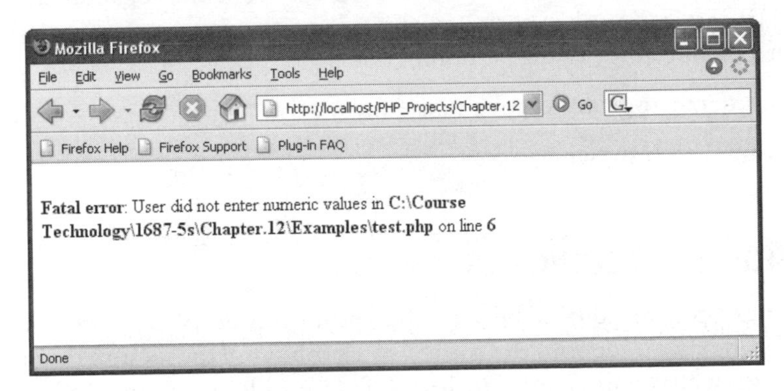

Figure 12-10 Error generated by the `trigger_error()` function

Next, you add a `trigger_error()` function to the MovingEstimatorWithBugs.php script that triggers an error if the user does not enter numeric values in the form fields.

To add a `trigger_error()` function to the MovingEstimatorWithBugs.php script:

1. Return to the **MovingEstimatorWithBugs.php** script in your text editor and add the following `if` statements above the `require_once()` statement in the first script section. The first `if` statement checks whether the `$_GET` autoglobal variables exist. If they do not exist, it means that this is the first time the user has loaded the script. If they do exist, it means that the user has entered values and clicked the Calculate button. The nested `if` statement checks if the variables contain numeric values and calls the `trigger_error()` function if one of them doesn't.

```
if (isset($_GET['distance']) && isset($_GET['weight'])
      && isset($_GET['flights']) && isset($_GET['appliances'])
      && isset($_GET['pianos'])) {
      if (!is_numeric($_GET['distance'])
            || !is_numeric($_GET['weight'])
            || !is_numeric($_GET['flights'])
            || !is_numeric($_GET['appliances'])
            || !is_numeric($_GET['pianos'])) {
            trigger_error("User did not enter numeric values",
                  E_USER_ERROR);
            exit();
      }
}
```

2. Save the **MovingEstimatorWithBugs.php** script, and then return to your Web browser.
3. Enter some nonnumeric values in the form fields and click the **Calculate** button.
4. Use your text editor to open the **error.log** file from the logs directory in your PHP installation directory. You should see the error message stating that the user did not enter numeric numbers.
5. Close the **error.log** file in your text editor.
6. Close your Web browser window.

USING BASIC DEBUGGING TECHIQUES

Although error messages are valuable because they point out problems with your scripts, they cannot always help you identify the source of a problem. This section discusses basic debugging techniques that you can use to help locate problems in your PHP scripts.

Examining Your Code

Although you might be using an HTML editor or an integrated development environment to develop your PHP scripts, chances are that you are probably just using a plain old text editor such as Notepad. An **integrated development environment**, or **IDE**, is a software application that you can use to develop other software applications. The Zend Studio is a popular commercial IDE for PHP development. The problem with basic text editors is that they usually display text in black and white, unlike HTML editors and IDEs, which often use colors to identify different types of code. This ability to identify different types of code elements quickly by their color is a valuable debugging technique. Programmers working in a basic text editor can approximate the color code feature of IDEs by using the `highlight_file()` function, which prints a color highlighted version of a file to a Web browser. The `highlight_file()` function prints everything contained in the specified file, including HTML elements and text. The function applies colors to text strings, comments, and keywords in a script as well as applies colors to the page text, background color, and HTML elements of the Web page.

You can also use the `highlight_string()` function to print a color highlighted version of a text string to a Web browser.

By default, the `highlight_file()` function prints each of these elements with the following colors:

- Code: blue
- Strings: red
- Comments: orange
- Keywords: green
- Page text (default color): black
- Background color: white
- HTML elements: black

You can change the default highlighting colors by modifying the following directives in the php.ini configuration file:

- highlight.string = #DD0000
- highlight.comment = #FF9900
- highlight.keyword = #007700
- highlight.default = #0000BB
- highlight.bg = #FFFFFF
- highlight.html = #000000

By default, the preceding directives are commented out with semicolons. Be sure to remove the semicolons if you want to change the default highlighting colors for a specific type of element. The colors assigned to the preceding directives are in hexadecimal format, although you can use standard color names such as blue or red. You can find a list of browser-safe colors and their hex values, along with a utility that converts RGB values to and from hex values, at *http://www.w3.org/MarkUp/Guide/Style*.

You pass to the `highlight_file()` function a text string containing the name of the file you want to view. For example, the following statement passes the name of the body mass index script, BodyMassIndex.php, to the `highlight_file()` function. Although the colors are not visible in this book, Figure 12-11 shows how the `highlight_file()` function prints the contents of the script to a Web browser.

```
highlight_file("BodyMassIndex.php");
```

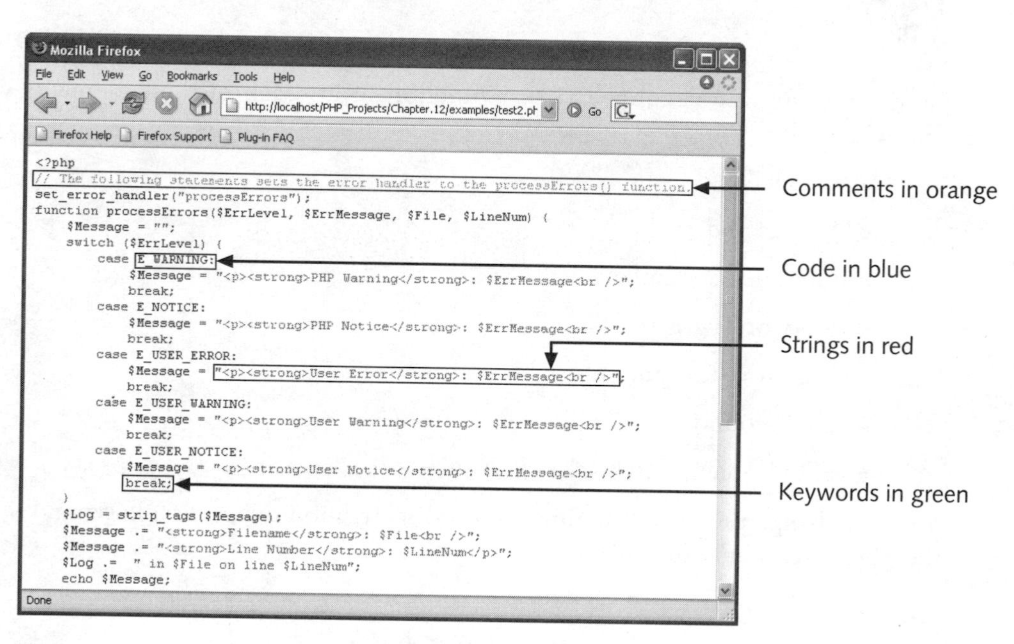

Figure 12-11 Output of a script with the `highlight_file()` function

In Chapter 3, you learned about the `print_r()`, `var_export()`, and `var_dump()` functions, which you can use to print or return information about variables and arrays. These functions are also very useful for quickly examining the contents of variables and arrays in your scripts to locate bugs.

Next, you create a script that uses the `highlight_file()` function to display a color-coded version of the `MovingEstimator` class.

To create a script that uses the `highlight_file()` function to display a color-coded version of the `MovingEstimator` class:

1. Create a new document in your text editor and add a script section to the document, which includes a `highlight_file()` statement that prints a color-coded version of the EstimatorClassWithBugs.php script. Because you are only using this document for testing purposes, you do not need to include a `<!DOCTYPE>` declaration, `<html>` element, or header and body sections.

```
<?php
highlight_file("EstimatorClassWithBugs.php");
?>
```

2. Save the script as **ShowHighlightedFile.php** in the Chapter directory for Chapter 12, and then close it in your text editor.

3. Open the **ShowHighlightedFile.php** script in your Web browser by entering the following URL: **http://localhost/PHP_Projects/Chapter.12/Chapter/ShowHighlightedFile.php**. Figure 12-12 shows the output. Although it's difficult to make out in the figure, the color coding makes it easier to debug code by helping you quickly identify keywords and strings in a PHP script.

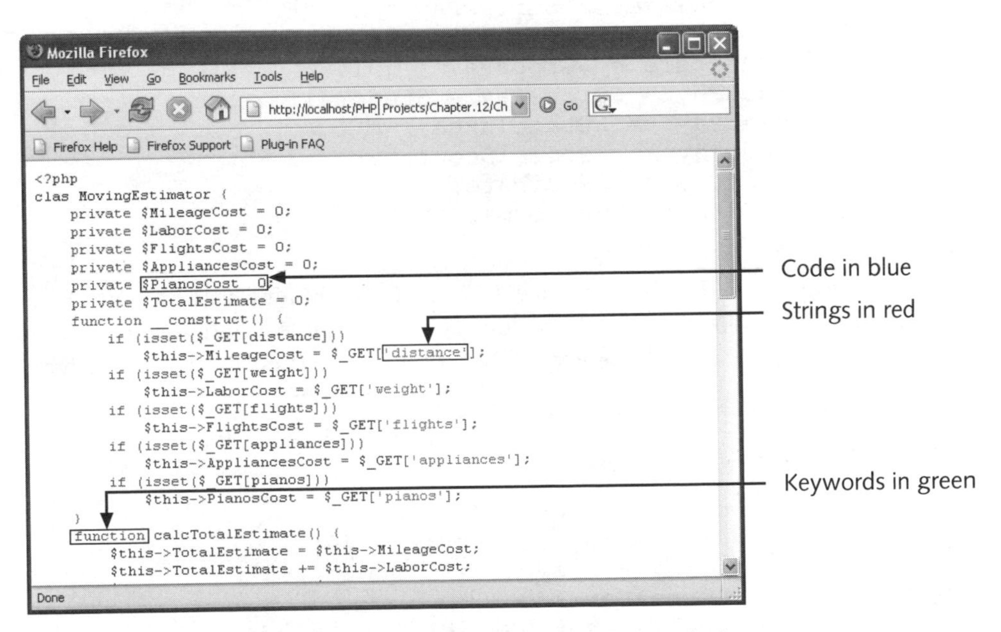

Figure 12-12 Output of the `MovingEstimator` class with the `highlight_file()` function

4. Close your Web browser window.

Tracing Errors with echo() Statements

When you are unable to locate a bug in your program by using error messages or examining your code, or if you suspect a logic error (which would not generate an error message), you must trace your code. **Tracing** is the examination of individual statements in an executing program. The echo() statement provides one of the most useful ways to trace PHP code. You place an echo() method at different points in your program and use it to display the contents of a variable, an array, or the value returned from a function. An echo() statement is especially useful when you want to trace a bug in your program by analyzing a list of values. Using this technique, you can monitor values as they change during program execution.

For example, examine the following function, which calculates weekly net pay, rounded to the nearest integer. The program is syntactically correct and does not generate an error message. However, the function is not returning the correct result, which should be 485. Instead, the function is returning a value of 5169107.

```
function calculatePay() {
     $PayRate = 15;
     $NumHours = 40;
     $GrossPay = $PayRate * $NumHours;
     $FederalTaxes = $GrossPay * .06794;
     $StateTaxes = $GrossPay * .0476;
     $SocialSecurity = $GrossPay * .062;
     $Medicare = $GrossPay * .0145;
     $NetPay = $GrossPay - $FederalTaxes;
     $NetPay *= $StateTaxes;
     $NetPay *= $SocialSecurity;
     $NetPay *= $Medicare;
     return number_format($NetPay, 2);
}
```

To trace the problem, you can place an echo() statement at the point in the program where you think the error might be located. For example, the first thing you might want to check in the calculatePay() function is whether the $GrossPay variable is being calculated correctly. To check whether the program calculates $GrossPay correctly, place an echo() statement in the function following the calculation of the $GrossPay variable as follows:

```
function calculatePay() {
     $PayRate = 15; $NumHours = 40;
     $GrossPay = $PayRate * $NumHours;
echo "<p>$GrossPay</p>";
     $FederalTaxes = $GrossPay * .06794;
     $StateTaxes = $GrossPay * .0476;
     $SocialSecurity = $GrossPay * .062;
     $Medicare = $GrossPay * .0145;
     $NetPay = $GrossPay - $FederalTaxes;
```

```
        $NetPay *= $StateTaxes;
        $NetPay *= $SocialSecurity;
        $NetPay *= $Medicare;
        return number_format($NetPay, 2);
}
```

Place any echo() statements used to trace program execution at a different level of indentation than other statements to clearly distinguish them from the actual program.

Because the `$GrossPay` variable contained the correct value (600), you would move the `echo()` statement to check the value of the `$NetPay` variable. You then continue with this technique until you discover the error. If you did, you would find that the `calculatePay()` function does not perform properly because the lines that add the `$StateTaxes`, `$SocialSecurity`, and `$Medicare` variables to the `$NetPay` variable are incorrect; they use the multiplication assignment operator (`*=`) instead of the subtraction assignment operator (`-=`).

An alternative to using a single `echo()` statement is to place multiple `echo()` statements throughout your code to check values as the code executes. For example, you could trace the `calculatePay()` function by using multiple `echo()` statements, as follows:

```
function calculatePay() {
     $PayRate = 15; $NumHours = 40;
     $GrossPay = $PayRate * $NumHours;
echo "<p>$GrossPay</p>";
     $FederalTaxes = $GrossPay * .06794;
     $StateTaxes = $GrossPay * .0476;
     $SocialSecurity = $GrossPay * .062;
     $Medicare = $GrossPay * .0145;
     $NetPay = $GrossPay - $FederalTaxes;
echo "<p>$NetPay</p>";
     $NetPay *= $StateTaxes;
echo "<p>$NetPay</p>";
     $NetPay *= $SocialSecurity;
echo "<p>$NetPay</p>";
     $NetPay *= $Medicare;
echo "<p>$NetPay</p>";
     return number_format($NetPay, 2);
}
```

Next, you use `echo()` statements to locate a bug in the Moving Estimator script.

To use `echo()` statements to locate a bug in the Moving Estimator script:

1. Open the **MovingEstimatorWithBugs.php** script in your Web browser by entering the following URL: **http://localhost/PHP_Projects/Chapter.12/Chapter/MovingEstimatorWithBugs.php**.

2. Click the **Appliances** text box, type **3**, and click the **Calculate** key. The estimated moving cost should be $75.00. Instead, it displays -$22.00.

Do not enter values into any of the other text boxes—the program still contains many bugs.

3. To trace the problem, return to the **EstimatorClassWithBugs.php** script in your text editor and locate the `calcAppliancesCost()` function. Add two `echo()` functions to the `calcAppliancesCost()` function, as follows. The first `echo()` function checks the value of the `$Appliances` variable before the calculation, and the second `echo()` function checks its value after the calculation.

```
function calcAppliancesCost() {
echo "<p>$this->AppliancesCost</p>";
     $this->AppliancesCost -= 25;
echo "<p>$this->AppliancesCost</p>";
     $this->calcTotalEstimate();
}
```

4. Save the **EstimatorClassWithBugs.php** script in your text editor, and then return to your Web browser and click the **Calculate** button. The first `echo()` statement you added correctly displays 3, which is the number you typed into the text box. However, the second `echo()` statement displays a value of -22 instead of the correct cost for moving three appliances (75). This tells you that there is something wrong with the statement preceding the second `echo()` statement.

5. Return to the **EstimatorClassWithBugs.php** script in your text editor and examine the statement above the second `echo()` statement. Note that instead of a compound multiplication operator, the statement includes a compound subtraction operator.

6. Replace the compound subtraction operator with a compound multiplication operator as follows:

```
$this->AppliancesCost *= 25;
```

7. Remove the two `echo()` statements from the `calcAppliancesCost()` function.

8. Save the **EstimatorClassWithBugs.php** script in your text editor, and then return to your Web browser and click the **Calculate** button. The estimated moving cost should correctly change to $75.

9. Close your Web browser window.

The key to using multiple `echo()` statements to trace program values is using them selectively at key points throughout a program. For example, suppose you were debugging a large accounting program with multiple functions. You could place an `echo()` statement at key positions within the program, such as wherever a function returns a value or a variable is assigned new data. In this way, you could get the general sense of what portion of the program contains the bug. After you discover the approximate location of the bug, for instance in a particular function, you can then concentrate your debugging efforts on that one function.

When using `echo()` statements to trace bugs, it is helpful to use a **driver program**, which is a simplified, temporary program that is used for testing functions and other code. A driver program is simply a PHP program that contains only the code you are testing. Driver programs do not have to be elaborate; they can be as simple as a single function you are testing. This technique allows you to isolate and test an individual function without having to worry about Web page elements, event handlers, global variables, and other code that form your program's functionality as a whole. A testing technique that is essentially the opposite of driver programs is the use of stub functions. **Stub functions** are empty functions that serve as placeholders (or "stubs") for a program's actual functions. Typically, a stub function returns a hard-coded value that represents the result of the actual function. Using stub functions allows you to check for errors in your program from the ground up. You start by swapping stub functions for the actual function definition. Each time you add the actual function definition, you rebuild and test the program. You repeat the process for each function in your program. This technique allows you to isolate and correct bugs within functions, or to correct bugs that occur as a result of how an individual function operates within your program as a whole.

Next, you use `echo()` statements to help locate bugs in the Moving Estimator script's `calcTotalEstimate()` function. The `calcTotalEstimate()` function should calculate the total of the `$MileageCost`, `$LaborCost`, `$FlightsCost`, `$AppliancesCost`, and `$PianosCost` variables. However, you need to be sure that the calculations are being performed properly before you can confidently include the function in the Moving Estimator program. The `calcTotalEstimate()` function is a very simple function, but it serves the purpose of demonstrating how to use a driver program to debug a function.

12

To use `echo()` statements in a driver program to locate bugs in the Moving Estimator script's `calcTotalEstimate()` function:

1. Create a new document in your text editor and add a script section to the document, which includes a `require_once()` statement to give the script access to the `MovingEstimator` class. Because you are only using this document for testing purposes, you do not need to include a `<!DOCTYPE>` declaration, `<html>` element, or header and body sections.

```
<?php
require_once("EstimatorClassWithBugs.php");
?>
```

2. Add the following statements to the end of the script section. These statements define the `$_GET` autoglobal variables that the `MovingEstimator` class uses to calculate the estimated moving cost, and assigns each variable a value of 100. For debugging purposes, this is easier and quicker than

developing a separate Web page to submit the necessary form variables that the `MovingEstimator` class requires.

```
$_GET['distance'] = 100;
$_GET['weight'] = 100;
$_GET['flights'] = 100;
$_GET['appliances'] = 100;
$_GET['pianos'] = 100;
```

3. Add the following statements to the end of the script section. The first statement instantiates a new `MovingEstimator` class object named `$EstimateTest` and the second statement calls the `calcTotalEstimate()` method.

```
$EstimateTest = new MovingEstimator();
$EstimateTest->calcTotalEstimate();
```

4. Save the script as **MovingEstimatorTest.php** in the Chapter directory for Chapter 12, and then close it in your text editor.
5. Return to the **EstimatorClassWithBugs.php** script in your text editor.
6. The `calcTotalEstimate()` function in the `MovingEstimator` class builds the `$TotalEstimate` variable by combining the values of the five other variables. Therefore, if each of the other variables contains a value of 100, the `$TotalEstimate` variable should be assigned a total value of 500. To test how the calculations perform under these conditions, add `echo()` statements to the `calcTotalEstimate()` function, as follows:

```
function calcTotalEstimate() {
     $this->TotalEstimate = $this->MileageCost;
echo "<p>Total estimate after adding mileage cost:
     $this->TotalEstimate</p>";
     $this->TotalEstimate += $this->LaborCost;
echo "<p>Total estimate after adding labor cost:
     $this->TotalEstimate</p>";
     $this->TotalEstimate = $this->FlightsCost;
echo "<p>Total estimate after adding flights cost:
     $this->TotalEstimate</p>";
     $this->TotalEstimate = $this->AppliancesCost;
echo "<p>Total estimate after adding appliances cost:
     $this->TotalEstimate</p>";
     $this->TotalEstimate += $this->PianosCost;
echo "<p>Total estimate after adding pianos cost:
     $this->TotalEstimate</p>";
}
```

7. Save the **EstimatorClassWithBugs.php** script.
8. Open the **MovingEstimatorTest.php** page in your Web browser by entering the following URL: **http://localhost/PHP_Projects/Chapter.12/Chapter/MovingEstimatorTest.php**. Your Web browser should resemble Figure 12-13. You can see from the output statements that the `calcTotalEstimate()` function did not assign a final value of 500 to the

`$TotalEstimate` variable. Instead, it assigned a value of 200 to the `$TotalEstimate` variable. Looking back over the individual statements that printed the value of the `$TotalEstimate` variable each time it was assigned a new value, you can see that the `$FlightsCost` and `$AppliancesCost` values were not added to the value of the `$TotalEstimate` variable, but instead replaced its value. As you probably already noticed, the two statements that assign these values to the `$TotalEstimate` variable used the assignment operator (=) instead of the compound addition assignment operator (+=). Although this is a very simple example, it does demonstrate how output statements can help you analyze a variable's changing values.

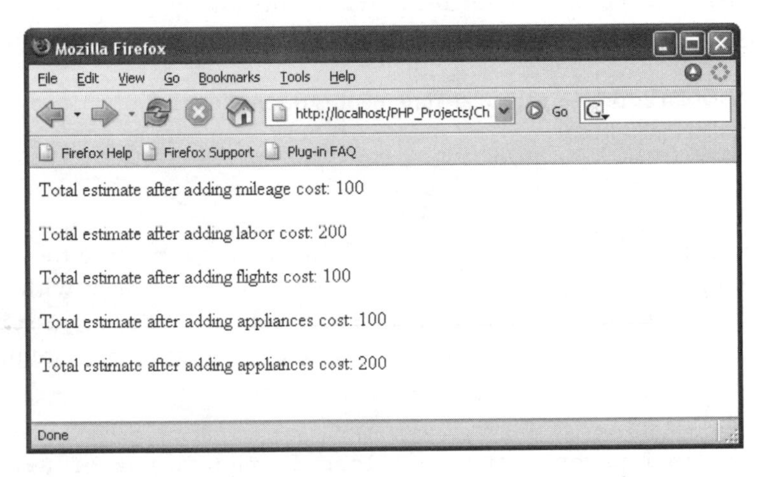

Figure 12-13 Output of the MovingEstimatorTest.php script

12

9. Close the Web browser window that displays the **MovingEstimatorTest.php** script.
10. Return to the **EstimatorClassWithBugs.php** script in your text editor. Remove the `echo()` statements from the `calcTotalEstimate()` function and modify the statements that assign the `$FlightsCost` and `$AppliancesCost` values to the `$TotalEstimate` variable using the compound addition assignment operator (+=) instead of the assignment operator (=), as follows:

```
function calcTotalEstimate() {
     $this->TotalEstimate = $this->MileageCost;
     $this->TotalEstimate += $this->LaborCost;
     $this->TotalEstimate += $this->FlightsCost;
     $this->TotalEstimate += $this->AppliancesCost;
     $this->TotalEstimate += $this->PianosCost;
}
```

11. Save the **EstimatorClassWithBugs.php** script, but do not try to use the program yet because it still contains some bugs.

Using Comments to Locate Bugs

Another method of locating bugs in a PHP program is to transform lines that you think might be causing problems into comments. In other words, you can "comment out" problematic lines. This technique helps you isolate the statement that is causing the error. In some cases, you can choose to comment out individual lines that might be causing the error, or you can choose to comment out all lines except the lines that you know work. When you first receive an error message, start by commenting out only the statement specified by the line number in the error message. Save the script, and then open it again in your Web browser to see if you receive another error. If you receive additional error messages, comment out those statements as well. After you eliminate the error messages, examine the commented out statements for the cause of the bug.

The cause of an error in a particular statement is often the result of an error in a preceding line of code.

The last five statements in the following code are commented out because they generate error messages stating that `$YearlyIntrest` is not defined. The problem with the code is that the `$YearlyInterest` variable is incorrectly spelled as `$YearlyIntrest` in several of the statements. Commenting out the lines isolates the problem statements.

```
$Amount = 100000;
$Percentage = .08;
printf("<p>The interest rate or a loan in the amount of $%.2f
     is %s%%.<br />", $Amount, $Percentage * 100);
$YearlyInterest = $Amount * $Percentage;
// printf("The amount of interest for one year is $%.2f.<br />",
     $YearlyIntrest);
// $MonthlyInterest = $YearlyIntrest / 12;
// printf("The amount of interest for one month is $%.2f.<br />",
     $MonthlyInterest);
// $DailyInterest = $YearlyIntrest / 365;
// printf("The amount of interest for one day is $%.2f.</p>",
     $DailyInterest);
```

Although the error in the preceding code might seem somewhat simple, it is typical of the types of errors you will encounter. Often, you will see the error right away and not need to comment out code or use any other tracing technique. However, when you have been staring at the same code for long periods of time, simple spelling errors, such as `$YearlyIntrest`, are not always easy to spot. Commenting out the lines you know are giving you trouble is a good technique for isolating and correcting even the simplest types of bugs.

Combining Debugging Techniques

When searching for errors, it's often helpful to combine debugging techniques. For example, the following code uses comments combined with `echo()` statements to trace errors in the `calculatePay()` function. Suppose that the `$GrossPay = $PayRate * $NumHours;` statement is the last statement in the function that operates correctly. Therefore, all of the lines following that statement are commented out. You would then use an echo() statement to check the value of each statement, removing comments from each statement in a sequential order, checking and correcting syntax as you go.

```
function calculatePay() {
     $PayRate = 15; $NumHours = 40;
     $GrossPay = $PayRate * $NumHours;
echo "<p>$GrossPay</p>";
//   $FederalTaxes = $GrossPay * .06794;
//   $StateTaxes = $GrossPay * .0476;
//   $SocialSecurity = $GrossPay * .062;
//   $Medicare = $GrossPay * .0145;
//   $NetPay = $GrossPay - $FederalTaxes;
//   $NetPay *= $StateTaxes;
//   $NetPay *= $SocialSecurity;
//   $NetPay *= $Medicare;
//   return number_format($NetPay, 2);
}
```

Next, you use comments to locate bugs in the Moving Estimator script.

To use comments to locate bugs in the Moving Estimator script:

1. Open the **MovingEstimatorWithBugs.php** script in your Web browser by entering the following URL: **http://localhost/PHP_Projects/Chapter.12/Chapter/MovingEstimatorWithBugs.php**.
2. Enter the following data for each of the moving cost calculations and click the **Calculate** button:

   ```
   Distance in Miles: 400
   Weight in Pounds: 900
   No. of Flights: 2
   No. of Appliances: 0
   No. of Pianos: 0
   ```

3. After you click the Calculate button, you should see an incorrect estimated cost of $3135.00 instead of a correct value of $735.00. To locate the code that is causing this problem, you start by adding comments to the `$Estimate` object's method calls.
4. Return to the **MovingEstimatorWithBugs.php** script in your text editor and add comments to the method call statements at the end of the last script

section, except the first statement, which calls the `calcMileageCost()` function. The script section should appear as follows:

```
<?php
$Estimate->calcMileageCost();
// $Estimate->calcLaborCost();
// $Estimate->calcFlightsCost();
// $Estimate->calcAppliancesCost();
// $Estimate->calcPianosCost();
   $NewEstimate =
printf("<p><strong>Estimated moving cost: $%.2f.</strong></p>",
     $NewEstimate);
?>
```

5. Save the **MovingEstimatorWithBugs.php** script, and then return to your Web browser and click the **Calculate** button. The correct value of $500.00 appears as the estimated moving cost. Therefore, the `calcMileageCost()` function is not the problem.
6. Return to the **MovingEstimatorWithBugs.php** script in your text editor and remove the comment from the **`$Estimate->calcLaborCost();`** statement.
7. Save the **MovingEstimatorWithBugs.php** script, and then return to your Web browser and click the **Calculate** button. At 15 cents a pound, the total cost of 900 pounds is $135. Adding 135 to 500 (the Distance in miles amount) results in an estimated moving cost of $635.00, which is the cost you should see displayed. Therefore, the program is functioning correctly so far.
8. Return to the **MovingEstimatorWithBugs.php** script, and remove the comment from the **`$Estimate->calcFlightsCost();`** statement.
9. Save the **MovingEstimatorWithBugs.php** script, and then return to your Web browser and click the **Calculate** button. At $50 per flight, a value of 2 should only increase the moving estimate by 100, for a total of $735.00. However, the estimated moving cost is $3135.00. The program functioned correctly until it tried to call the `calcFlightsCost()` function.
10. Remove the remainder of the comments from the statements in the last script section.
11. Save the **MovingEstimatorWithBugs.php** script and close it in your text editor.
12. Return to the **EstimatorClassWithBugs.php** script in your text editor and scroll to the `calcFlightsCost()` function. Note that the function includes an unnecessary statement, `$this->FlightsCost = 50;`, which causes the

calculation error. Do not think this is a trivial example. As you develop your own applications, you will often find yourself adding and deleting statements that can introduce simple, hard-to-detect bugs in your programs.

13. Delete the **`$this->FlightsCost = 50;`** statement from the `calcFlightsCost()` function.
14. Save the **EstimatorClassWithBugs.php** script, and then return to your Web browser and click the **Calculate** button. The correct value of $735.00 should appear as the estimated moving cost. Do not enter any numbers for the other calculations because the program still contains some errors.

Analyzing Logic

At times, errors in PHP code stem from logic problems that are difficult to spot using tracing techniques. When you suspect that your code contains logic errors, you must analyze each statement on a case-by-case basis. For example, the following code contains a logic flaw that prevents it from functioning correctly:

```
if (!isset($_GET['firstName']))
     echo "<p>You must enter your first name!</p>";
     exit();
echo "<p>Welcome to my Web site, " . $_GET['firstName'] . "!";
```

If you were to execute the preceding code, you would never see the last `echo()` statement, which welcomes the user to the Web site, even if a value were assigned to the `$_GET['firstName']` variable. If you examine the `if` statement more closely, you will see that the `if` statement ends after it prints the `echo()` statement. The `exit()` statement following the variable declaration is not part of the `if` structure, because the `if` statement does not include a set of braces to enclose the lines it executes when the conditional evaluation returns true. For this reason, the `exit()` statement always executes, even when the user correctly assigns a value to the `$_GET['firstName']` variable. For the code to execute properly, the `if` statement must include braces as follows:

```
if (!isset($_GET['firstName'])) {
     echo "<p>You must enter your first name!</p>";
     exit();
}
echo "<p>Welcome to my Web site, " . $_GET['firstName'] . "!";
```

The following `for` statement shows another example of an easily overlooked logic error:

```
for ($Count = 1; $Count < 6; ++$Count);
      echo "$Count<br />";
```

The preceding code should print the numbers 1 through 5 to the screen. However, the line `for ($Count = 1; $Count < 6; ++$Count);` contains an ending semicolon, which marks the end of the `for` loop. The loop executes five times and changes the value of `count` to 6, but does nothing else because there are no statements before its ending semicolon. The line `echo "$Count<br />";` is a separate statement that executes only once, printing the number 6 to the screen. The code is syntactically correct, but does not function as you anticipated. As you can see from these examples, it is easy to overlook very minor logic errors in your code.

Next, you fix the one last logic error in the Moving Estimator script that prevents it from functioning correctly.

To fix the last logic error in the Moving Estimator script:

1. Open the **MovingEstimatorWithBugs.php** page in your Web browser by entering the following URL: **http://localhost/PHP_Projects/Chapter.12/Chapter/MovingEstimatorWithBugs.php**.
2. Enter the following data for each of the moving cost calculations and click the **Calculate** button:
   ```
   Distance in Miles: 1000
   Weight in Pounds: 500
   No. of Flights: 2
   No. of Appliances: 3
   No. of Pianos: 2
   ```
3. After you click the Calculate button, the Moving Estimator displays an estimate of $1507.00, which isn't correct. (The value should be $1570.00.) Because you have already corrected the Distance in Miles, Weight in Pounds, and Flights calculations earlier in this chapter, you will start by examining the Appliances calculation. First, enter zeros in the **Distance in miles**, **Weight in pounds**, **Flights of stairs**, and **Pianos** text boxes, but type **3** in the **Appliances** text box and click the **Calculate** button. A correct value of $75.00 appears for the estimated moving cost. Therefore, the problem does not appear to be related to the appliances cost calculation.
4. Next, you examine the two values required by the piano calculation. Enter zeros in the **Distance in miles**, **Weight in pounds**, **Flights of stairs**, and **Appliances** text boxes, but type **2** in the Pianos text box and click the **Calculate** button. The correct value of $70.00 should appear. Instead, a value of $7.00 appears in the Command window. If you are observant, you have probably already noticed that the calculation multiplies the `pianos` variable by 3.5 instead of 35.
5. Return to the **EstimatorClassWithBugs.php** script in your text editor and modify the incorrect statement in the `calcPianosCost()` function so the `pianos` variable is multiplied by 35 instead of 3.5, as follows:
   ```
   $this->PianosCost *= 35;
   ```
6. Save the **EstimatorClassWithBugs.php** script, close it in your text editor, and then return to your Web browser and click the **Calculate** button. The

program should now function correctly, calculating a moving estimate of $70.00.

7. Close your Web browser window and text editor.

Chapter Summary

- Logic refers to the order in which various parts of a program run, or execute.
- Any error in a program that causes it to function incorrectly, whether because of incorrect syntax or flaws in logic, is called a bug. The term debugging refers to the act of tracing and resolving errors in a program.
- Syntax or parse errors occur when the scripting engine fails to recognize code.
- Run-time errors occur when the PHP scripting engine encounters a problem while a program is executing.
- Logic errors are flaws in a program's design that prevent the program from running as you anticipate.
- Parse error messages occur when a PHP script contains a syntax error that prevents your script from running.
- Fatal error messages are raised when a script contains a run-time error that prevents it from executing.
- Warning messages are raised for run-time errors that do not prevent a script from executing.
- Notice messages are raised for potential run-time errors that do not prevent a script from executing.
- The php.ini configuration file contains two directives, `display_errors` and `display_startup_errors`, that determine whether error messages print to a Web browser. Although displaying error messages is useful when you develop PHP scripts, the PHP Group strongly recommends that you turn this feature off for scripts that run in production environments and instead save any errors in a log file.
- The `error_reporting` directive in the php.ini configuration file determines which types of error messages PHP should generate, although it does not stop the errors from occurring.
- The `log_errors` directive determines whether PHP logs errors to a file and is assigned a default value of "Off." The `error_log` directive identifies the text file where PHP will log errors.
- You use the `set_error_handler()` function to specify a custom function to handle errors.
- The `trigger_error()` allows you to generate an error in your scripts.

- The `highlight_file()` function prints a color highlighted version of a file to a Web browser.
- Tracing is the examination of individual statements in an executing program. The `echo()` statement provides one of the most useful ways to trace PHP code.
- When using `echo()` statements to trace bugs, it is helpful to use a driver program, which is a simplified, temporary program that is used for testing functions and other code. Stub functions are empty functions that serve as placeholders (or "stubs") for a program's actual functions.
- Another method of locating bugs in a PHP program is to transform lines that you think might be causing problems into comments.

Review Questions

1. If the PHP scripting engine encounters a problem while a program is executing, that problem is called a(n) ______________ error.
   a. application
   b. logic
   c. run-time
   d. syntax
2. PHP error messages help you find logic errors in your programs. True or False?
3. ______________ errors are problems in the design of a program that prevent it from running as you anticipate.
   a. Application
   b. Logic
   c. Run-time
   d. Syntax
4. ______________ errors occur when you enter code that the scripting engine does not recognize.
   a. Application
   b. Logic
   c. Run-time
   d. Syntax
5. Which of the following types of error messages occur when a script contains a run-time error that prevents it from executing?
   a. parse error messages
   b. fatal error messages

c. warning messages

d. notice messages

6. Error messages point to the exact location in a script that is causing the error. True or False?

7. Which of the following statements causes a syntax error?

a. `echo "<p>Hello World</p>";`

b. `print("<p>Hello World</p>")`

c. `Return true;`

d. `$Clients = array();`

8. Which of the following functions causes a run-time error?

a.
```
function calcMarginPercent() {
        $GrossProfit = 100;
        $NetProfit = 100;
        $Margin = $GrossProfit - $NetProfit;
        $MarginPercent = $Margin / $GrossProfit;
        }
```

b.
```
function calcMarginPercent() {
        $GrossProfit = 200;
        $NetProfit = 100;
        $Margin = $GrossProfit - $NetProfit;
        $MarginPercent = $Margin / $GrossProfit;
        }
```

c.
```
function calcMarginPercent() {
        $GrossProfit = 200;
        $NetProfit = 100;
        $Margin = $GrossProfit - $NetProfit;
        $MarginPercent = $Margin / $GrossProfit;
        }
```

d.
```
function calcMarginPercent() {
        $GrossProfit = 0;
        $NetProfit = 100;
        $Margin = $GrossProfit - $NetProfit;
        $MarginPercent = $Margin / $GrossProfit;
        }
```

9. Which of the following `if` statements is logically incorrect?

a.
```
if ($Count < 5)
        echo "<p>$Count</p>";
```

b.
```
if ($Count =< 5)
        echo "<p>$Count</p>";
```

c.
```
if ($Count = 5);
        echo "<p>$Count</p>";
```

d.
```
if ($Count = 5) {
       echo "<p>$Count</p>";
}
```

10. Explain why the PHP Group strongly recommends that you turn off the display of errors for scripts that run in production environments.
11. Which of the following error reporting levels report run-time errors? (Choose all that apply.)

    a. `E_ERROR`

    b. `E_WARNING`

    c. `E_PARSE`

    d. `E_NOTICE`
12. To which of the following directives do you assign the path and name of the file where PHP will log errors?

    a. `log_errors`

    b. `error_log`

    c. `logging`

    d. `log_location`
13. Which of the following statements correctly specifies a custom error-handling function named `logProblems()`?

    a. `logProblems = set_error_handler();`

    b. `set_error_handler = logProblems();`

    c. `set_error_handler("logProblems");`

    d. `set_error_handler(logProblems());`
14. When you assign a custom function to handle errors, PHP's default error-handling functionality is completely bypassed for all types of error reporting levels. True or False?
15. Which of the following functions logs an error message to the location specified by the `error_log` directive in the php.ini configuration file?

    a. `error_log()`

    b. `log_error()`

    c. `log()`

    d. `error()`
16. Which of the following error reporting levels can you pass as the second argument of the `trigger_error()` function? (Choose all that apply.)

    a. `E_ALL`

    b. `E_USER_ERROR`

c. `E_USER_WARNING`

d. `E_USER_NOTICE`

17. Which of the following functions allow you to print a color highlighted version of a file to a Web browser?

a. `color_file()`

b. `file_color()`

c. `highlight_file()`

d. `file_highlight()`

18. ________________ refers to the examination of individual statements in an executing program.

a. Trailing

b. Tracing

c. Tracking

d. Commenting

19. Explain how to use a driver program.

20. Which of the following code structures prints the text "Hello World" five times?

a.
```
for ($Count = 1; $Count < 6; ++$Count);
      echo "<p>Hello World</p>";
      echo "<p>Hello World</p>";
      echo "<p>Hello World</p>";
      echo "<p>Hello World</p>";
      echo "<p>Hello World</p>";
```

b.
```
for ($Count = 0; $Count < 6; ++$Count)
      echo "<p>Hello World</p>";
```

c.
```
for ($Count = 0; $Count < 6; ++$Count) {
      echo "<p>Hello World</p>";
}
```

d.
```
for ($Count = 0; $Count < 6; ++$Count);
      echo "<p>Hello World</p>";
```


Hands-On Projects

Hands-On Project 12-1

1. Create a new document in your text editor, and type the `<!DOCTYPE>` declaration, `<html>` element, document head, and `<body>` element. Use the strict DTD and "Project 12-1" as the content of the `<title>` element.

2. Add the following script section to the document body:

```
<?php
?>
```

3. Add the following statements to the script section:

```
echo "<p>This is a text string.</p>;
echo "<p>This is another text string.</p>';
echo "<p>This should be a "quoted" text string.</p>";
```

4. Save the document as **Project12-01.php** in your Projects directory for Chapter 12, and then open it in your Web browser by entering the following URL: **http://localhost/PHP_Projects/Chapter.12/Projects/Project12-01.php**. You should receive an error message. Fix the errors in the statements you added in Step 4.
5. Close your Web browser window.

Hands-On Project 12-2

1. Create a new document in your text editor, and type the `<!DOCTYPE>` declaration, `<html>` element, document head, and `<body>` element. Use the strict DTD and "Project 12-2" as the content of the `<title>` element.
2. Add the following script section to the document body:

```
<?php
?>
```

3. Add the following statements to the script section:

```
$StockShares == 100;
$StockValue == 22.75;
echo "<p>Current stock value: ";
echo StockShares * StockValue . ".</p>";
```

4. Save the document as **Project12-02.php** in your Projects directory for Chapter 12, and then open it in your Web browser by entering the following URL: **http://localhost/PHP_Projects/Chapter.12/Projects/Project12-02.php**. You should receive an error message. Fix the errors in the statements you added in Step 3.
5. Close your Web browser window.

Hands-On Project 12-3

1. Create a new document in your text editor, and type the `<!DOCTYPE>` declaration, `<html>` element, document head, and `<body>` element. Use the strict DTD and "Project 12-3" as the content of the `<title>` element.

2. Add the following script section to the document body:

```
<?php
?>
```

3. Add the following statements to the script section:

```
$Count = 1;
while ($Count <= 10) {
     echo "<p>The number is $Count</p>";
}
```

4. Save the document as **Project12-03.php** in your Projects directory for Chapter 12, and then open it in your Web browser by entering the following URL: **http://localhost/PHP_Projects/Chapter.12/Projects/Project12-03.php**. The script continuously displays "The number is 1". You can stop the script by clicking your Web browser's Stop button. Fix the errors in the statements you added in Step 3 so the code displays the `$Count` variable 10 times.
5. Close your Web browser window.

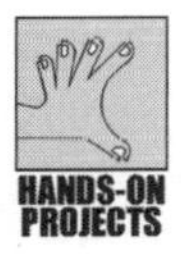

Hands-On Project 12-4

1. Create a new document in your text editor, and type the `<!DOCTYPE>` declaration, `<html>` element, document head, and `<body>` element. Use the strict DTD and "Project 12-4" as the content of the `<title>` element.
2. Add the following script section to the document body:

```
<?php
?>
```

3. Add the following statements to the script section:

```
$Mortgage = 120000;
$Interest = .08;
printf("<p>At an interest rate of $Interest, the first year's int
erest on a mortgage of $%.2s is $%.2s.", $Mortgage, $Interest);
```

4. Save the document as **Project12-04.php** in your Projects directory for Chapter 12, and then open it in your Web browser by entering the following URL: **http://localhost/PHP_Projects/Chapter.12/Projects/Project12-04.php**. At an interest rate of 8%, the first year's interest on a mortgage of $120000 is $9600. However, the script is printing "At an interest rate of 0.08, the first year's interest on a mortgage of $12 is $0.". Fix the errors in the document.
5. Close your Web browser window.

Hands-On Project 12-5

1. Create a new document in your text editor, and type the `<!DOCTYPE>` declaration, `<html>` element, document head, and `<body>` element. Use the strict DTD and "Project 12-5" as the content of the `<title>` element.

2. Add the following script section to the document body:

```
<?php
?>
```

3. Add the following statements to the script section:

```
for($Count = 1; $Count <=5; ++$Count) {
     if ($Count == 3)
          break;
     echo "<p>$Count</p>";
}
```

4. Save the document as **Project12-05.php** in your Projects directory for Chapter 12, and then open it in your Web browser by entering the following URL: **http://localhost/PHP_Projects/Chapter.12/Projects/Project12-05.php**. The code you typed should print the values 1, 2, 4, and 5 to the screen. Instead, the code prints only 1 and 2 to the screen. Fix the errors.
5. Close your Web browser window.

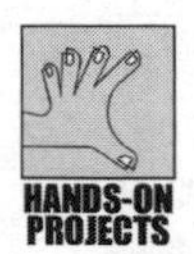

Hands-On Project 12-6

1. Create a new document in your text editor, and type the `<!DOCTYPE>` declaration, `<html>` element, document head, and `<body>` element. Use the strict DTD and "Project 12-6" as the content of the `<title>` element.
2. Add the following script section to the document body:

```
<?php
?>
```

3. Add the following statements to the script section:

```
function average_numbers($a $b $c) {
     $sum_of_numbers = $a + $b + $c;
     $return = $sum_of_numbers / 3;
     return return;
}
$retValue = average_numbers(3, 4, 5);
echo "<p>$retValue);
```

4. Save the document as **Project12-06.php** in your Projects directory for Chapter 12, and then open it in your Web browser by entering the following URL: **http://localhost/PHP_Projects/Chapter.12/Projects/Project12-06.php**. The PHP code should print a value of "4". Instead it generates a parse error. If the `display_errors` directive in your php.ini configuration file is assigned a value of "On", the parse error displays in your Web browser. Check your error log if the `display_errors` directive in your php.ini configuration file is assigned a value of "Off". Fix the errors in the statements you added in Step 3.
5. Close your Web browser window.

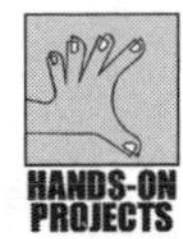

Hands-On Project 12-7

1. Create a new document in your text editor, and type the `<!DOCTYPE>` declaration, `<html>` element, document head, and `<body>` element. Use the strict DTD and "Project 12-7" as the content of the `<title>` element.
2. Add the following script section to the document body:

```
<?php
?>
```

3. Add the following statements to the script section:

```
$DisplayAlert = false;
if ($DisplayAlert = true) {
     $ConditionState = "<p>Condition is true.</p>";
     echo $ConditionState;
}
else if ($DisplayAlert = false) {
     $ConditionState = "<p>Condition is false.</p>";
     echo $ConditionState;
}
else {
     $ConditionState = "<p>No condition.</p>";
     echo $ConditionState;
}
```

4. Save the document as **Project12-07.php** in your Projects directory for Chapter 12, and then open it in your Web browser by entering the following URL: **http://localhost/PHP_Projects/Chapter.12/Projects/Project12-07.php**. The code you typed should print "Condition is false." to the screen. However, the code prints "Condition is true." to the screen. Locate and correct the error.
5. Close your Web browser window.

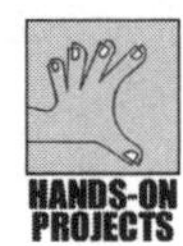

Hands-On Project 12-8

1. Create a new document in your text editor, and type the `<!DOCTYPE>` declaration, `<html>` element, document head, and `<body>` element. Use the strict DTD and "Project 12-8" as the content of the `<title>` element.
2. Add the following script section to the document body:

```
<?php
?>
```

3. Add the following statements to the script section:

```
$DaysOfWeek = Array();
$DaysOfWeek[] = "Monday";
$DaysOfWeek[] = "Tuesday";
$DaysOfWeek[] = "Wednesday";
$DaysOfWeek[] = "Thursday";
```

```
$DaysOfWeek[] = "Friday";
$DaysOfWeek[] = "Saturday";
$DaysOfWeek[] = "Sunday";
$Count = 1;
do {
     echo "<p>$DaysOfWeek[$Count]</p>";
     ++$Count;
} while ($Count <= 7);
```

4. Save the document as **Project12-08.php** in your Projects directory for Chapter 12, and then open it in your Web browser by entering the following URL: **http://localhost/PHP_Projects/Chapter.12/Projects/Project12-08.php**. The code you entered should print the days of the week. Instead, only Tuesday through Sunday print, and a warning notice about an undefined offset prints after Sunday. Locate and correct the error.
5. Close your Web browser window.

Case Projects

Case Project 12-1

The Cases directory for Chapter 12 on your Data Disk contains copies of some of the programs you created earlier in this book. However, all of the programs contain errors. Use any of the debugging skills you have learned in this chapter to correct the errors. You can review earlier chapters to see how the program should function—but do *not* copy or review the correct syntax. Use these exercises as an opportunity to test and improve your debugging skills. The chapter number in which you created each program is appended to the name of the document. Before you fix each document, remove the _Chapter0*x* portion of the filename and save the document. The documents you must correct are:

- SingleFamilyHome_Chapter03.php
- ExplorersQuiz_Chapter04.php & ScoreQuiz_Chapter04.php
- LeapYear_Chapter04.php & LeapYear_Chapter04.html
- PassengerTrain_Chapter05.php
- HitCounter_Chapter06.php
- WinningNumbers_Chapter07.php
- GuestBook_Chapter09.html, SignGuestBook_Chapter09.php, ShowGuestBook_Chapter09.php
- LastVisit_Chapter10.php

Case Project 12-2

One of the most important aspects of creating a good program is the design and analysis phase of the project. Conducting a good design and analysis phase is critical to minimizing bugs in your program. Search the Internet or your local library for information on this topic. Explain how you think you should handle the design and analysis phase of a software project.

Case Project 12-3

Equally important to minimizing bugs during software development is the testing phase. Search the Internet or your local library for information on software testing. Then design a plan for thoroughly testing your PHP programs before deploying them on the Web.

Case Project 12-4

Many advanced programming languages, including PHP 5, include a feature known as exception handling, which allows programs to handle errors as they occur in the execution of a program. Search the PHP documentation and the Internet for information on exception-handling topics, and explain how you would use exception handling in your projects.

WORKING WITH REGULAR EXPRESSIONS

UNDERSTANDING REGULAR EXPRESSIONS

One of the more complex methods of working with strings involves the use of **regular expressions**, which are patterns that are used for matching and manipulating strings according to specified rules. With scripting languages such as PHP, regular expressions are most commonly used for validating submitted form data. For example, you can use a regular expression to ensure that a user enters a date in a specific format, such as *mm/dd/yyyy* or a telephone number in the format (###) ###-####.

Most scripting languages support some form of regular expressions. PHP supports two types of regular expressions: POSIX Extended and Perl Compatible Regular Expressions (PCRE). POSIX Extended regular expressions are a little easier to use than PCRE. On the other hand, PCRE is more powerful than POSIX Extended regular expressions. PHP includes different sets of functions for each type of regular expressions. Although POSIX Extended regular expressions are not as powerful as PCRE, they are easier to learn and a great way to get started with regular expressions. After you master POSIX Extended regular expressions, you should be able to adapt your skills to PCRE with minimal effort.

Table A-1 POSIX Extended regular expression functions

Function	Description
`ereg("pattern", string[, array])`	Performs a case-sensitive search for a matching pattern
`ereg_replace("pattern", replacement_string, string)`	Performs a case-sensitive replacement of a matching pattern
`eregi("pattern", string[, array])`	Performs a case-insensitive search for a matching pattern
`eregi_replace("pattern", replacement_string, string)`	Performs a case-insensitive replacement of a matching pattern
`split("pattern", string[, max_elements])`	Returns from an input string an array of strings that are separated by a specified case-sensitive matching pattern
`spliti("pattern", string[, max_elements])`	Returns from an input string an array of strings that are separated by a specified case-insensitive matching pattern
`sql_regcase(string)`	Returns a case-insensitive regular expression pattern from a specified string

The two most commonly used POSIX Extended regular expression functions are the `ereg()` and `eregi()` functions. The only difference between these two functions is that the `ereg()` function performs a case-sensitive match, whereas the `eregi()` function performs a case-insensitive match. You pass to each function a regular expression pattern as the first argument and a string containing the text you want to search as the second argument. Both functions return either an integer representing the length of the string if a specified pattern is matched or a value of false if it's not. The following code demonstrates how to determine whether the `$String` variable contains the text "course technology," with lowercase letters. Because the code uses the case-sensitive `ereg()` function, the `if` statement prints "No match" because the value in the `$String` variable includes capitalized initials.

```
$String = "Course Technology";
if (ereg("course technology", $String))
     echo "<p>Match found</p>";
else
     echo "<p>No match</p>";
```

In comparison, the following code prints "Match found" because it uses the case-insensitive `eregi()` function:

```
$String = "Course Technology";
if (eregi("course technology", $String))
     echo "<p>Match found</p>";
else
     echo "<p>No match</p>";
```

The preceding examples simply demonstrate how to use the `ereg()` and `eregi()` functions. There is no point in using regular expression functions with the preceding examples because you can more easily determine whether the two strings match by using the comparison operator (==) or a string comparison function. The real power of regular expressions comes from the patterns you write.

Writing Regular Expression Patterns

The hardest part of working with regular expressions is writing the patterns and rules that are used for matching and manipulating strings. As an example of a common, albeit complicated, regular expression, consider the following code:

```
if (!eregi("^[_a-z0-9-]+(\.[_a-z0-9-]+)*@[a-z0-9-]+(\.[a-
z0-9-]+)*(\.[a-z]{2,3})$", $_GET['email']))
exit("<p>You must enter a valid e-mail address! Click your
browser's Back button to return to the previous
page.</p>");
```

The preceding code uses the case-insensitive `eregi()` function to determine whether the `$_GET['email']` variable is a valid e-mail address. If the `eregi()` function returns a value of false, an `exit()` statement halts the execution of the script. As you can see, the logic is straightforward: If the e-mail address doesn't match the regular expression, the script exits. The complex part of the code is the pattern passed as the first argument to the `eregi()` function.

NOTE

You can find many types of prewritten regular expressions on the Regular Expression Library Web page at *http://www.regexlib.com/*.

Regular expression patterns consist of literal characters and **metacharacters**, which are special characters that define the pattern matching rules in a regular expression. Table A-2 lists the metacharacters that you can use with POSIX Extended regular expressions.

Table A-2 POSIX Extended regular expression metacharacters

Metacharacter	Description
.	Matches any single character
\	Identifies the next character as a literal value
^	Matches characters at the beginning of a string
$	Matches characters at the end of a string
( )	Specifies required characters to include in a pattern match
[ ]	Specifies alternate characters allowed in a pattern match
[^]	Specifies characters to exclude in a pattern match
-	Identifies a possible range of characters to match
|	Specifies alternate sets of characters to include in a pattern match

MATCHING ANY CHARACTER

You use a period (`.`) to match any single character in a pattern. A period in a regular expression pattern really specifies that the pattern must contain a value where the period is located. For example, the following code specifies that the `$ZIP` variable must contain five characters. Because the variable only contains three characters, the `ereg()` function returns a value of false.

```
$ZIP = "015";
ereg(".....", $ZIP); // returns false
```

In comparison, the following `ereg()` function returns a value of true because the `$ZIP` variable contains five characters:

```
$ZIP = "01562";
ereg(".....", $ZIP); // returns true
```

Because the period only specifies that a character must be included in the designated location within the pattern, you can also include additional characters within the pattern. The following `ereg()` function returns a value of true because the `$ZIP` variable contains the required five characters along with the ZIP+4 characters.

```
$ZIP = "01562-2607";
ereg(".....", $ZIP); // returns true;
```

Matching Characters at the Beginning or End of a String

The ^ metacharacter matches characters at the beginning of a string, and the $ metacharacter matches characters at the end of a string. A pattern that matches the beginning or end of a line is called an **anchor**. To specify an anchor at the beginning of a line, the pattern must begin with the ^ metacharacter. The following example specifies that the `$URL` variable begin with `http`. Because the variable does begin with `"http"`, the `eregi()` function returns true.

```
$URL = "http://www.dongosselin.com";
eregi("^http", $URL); // returns true;
```

All literal characters following the ^ metacharacter in a pattern compose the anchor. This means that the following example returns false because the `$URL` variable does not begin with `"https"` (only `"http"` without the `s`), as is specified by the anchor in the pattern:

```
$URL = "http://www.dongosselin.com";
eregi("^https", $URL); // returns false;
```

To specify an anchor at the end of a line, the pattern must end with the `$` metacharacter. The following demonstrates how to specify that a URL end with `com`:

```
$Identifier = "http://www.dongosselin.com";
eregi("com$", $Identifier); // returns true
```

The preceding code returns true because the URL assigned to the `$Identifier` variable ends with `com`. However, the following code returns false because the URL assigned to the `$Identifier` variable does not end with `gov`:

```
$Identifier = "http://www.dongosselin.com";
eregi("gov$", $Identifier); // returns false;
```

Matching Special Characters

To match any metacharacters as literal values in a regular expression, escape the character with a backslash. For example, a period (`.`) metacharacter matches any single character in a pattern. If you want to ensure that a string contains an actual period and not any character, you need to escape it with a backslash. The domain identifier in the following code is appended to the domain name with a comma instead of a period. However, the regular expression returns true because the period in the expression is not escaped.

```
$Identifier = "http://www.dongosselin,com";
echo eregi(".com$", $Identifier); // returns true
```

To correct the problem, you must escape the periods as follows:

```
$Identifier = "http://www.dongosselin,com";
echo eregi("\.com$", $Identifier); // returns false
```

Escaping a dollar sign requires a little more work. To escape a dollar sign, you must use either single quotes to enclose the regular expression pattern or use double quotes and place three backslashes before the dollar sign. The following code demonstrates how to use both techniques:

```
$Currency="$123.45";
echo eregi('^\$', $Currency); // returns true
echo eregi("^\\\$", $Currency); // returns true
```

SPECIFYING QUANTITY

Metacharacters that specify the quantity of a match are called **quantifiers**. Table A-3 lists the quantifiers that you can use with POSIX Extended regular expressions.

Table A-3 POSIX Extended regular expression quantifiers

Quantifier	Description
?	Specifies that the preceding character is optional
+	Specifies that one or more of the preceding characters must match
*	Specifies that zero or more of the preceding characters can match
`{n}`	Specifies the preceding character repeat exactly *n* times
`{n,}`	Specifies the preceding character repeat at least *n* times
`{,n}`	Specifies the preceding character repeat up to *n* times
`{n1, n2}`	Specifies the preceding character repeat at least *n1* times but no more than *n2* times

The question mark quantifier specifies that the preceding character in the pattern is optional. The following code demonstrates how to use the question mark quantifier to specify that the protocol assigned to the beginning of the `$URL` variable can be either `http` or `https:`.

```
$URL = "http://www.dongosselin.com";
eregi("^https?", $URL); // returns false;
```

The addition quantifier (+) specifies that one or more of the preceding characters match, whereas the asterisk quantifier (*) specifies that zero or more of the preceding characters match. As a simple example, the following code demonstrates how to ensure that a variable containing a query string contains at least one equal sign:

```
$QueryString = "name=don";
eregi("=+", $QueryString); // returns true;
```

Similarly, because a query string might consist of multiple name=value pairs separated by ampersands (`&`), the following code demonstrates how to check whether the `$QueryString` variable contains zero or more ampersands:

```
$QueryString = "name=don";

eregi("&*", $QueryString); // returns true;
```

The `{ }` quantifiers allow you to specify the number of times that a character must repeat more precisely. The following code shows a simple example of how to use the `{ }` quantifiers to ensure that a zip code consists of at least five characters:

```
ereg("ZIP: .{5}$", " ZIP: 01562"); // returns true
```

NOTE

You can validate a zip code much more efficiently with character classes, which are covered later in this appendix.

The preceding code uses the period metacharacter and the `{ }` quantifiers to ensure that the `$Zip` variable contains a minimum of five characters. The following code specifies that the `$Zip` variable must consist of at least five characters but a maximum of ten characters, in case the zip code contains the dash and four additional numbers that are found in a ZIP+4 number:

```
ereg("(ZIP: .{5,10})$", "ZIP: 01562-2607"); // returns true
```

Specifying Subexpressions

As you learned earlier, regular expression patterns can include literal values; any strings you validate against a regular expression must contain exact matches for the literal values contained in the pattern. You can also use parentheses metacharacters, `( )`, to specify the characters required in a pattern match. Characters contained in a set of parentheses within a regular expression are referred to as a **subexpression** or **subpattern**. Subexpressions allow you to determine the format and quantities of the enclosed characters as a group. As an example, consider the following pattern, which defines a regular expression for a telephone number:

```
"^(1-)?(\(.{3}\) )?(.{3})(\-.{4})$"
```

Notice that the preceding pattern includes the ^ and $ metacharacters to anchor both the beginning and end of the pattern. This ensures that a string exactly matches the pattern in a regular expression.

The first and second groups in the preceding pattern include the ? quantifier. This allows a string to optionally include a 1 and the area code. If the string does include these groups, they must be in the exact format of 1-*nnn*, including the space following the area code. Similarly, the telephone number itself includes two groups that require the number to be in the format of "555-1212." Because the 1 and area code are optional, all of the following statements return a value of true:

```
ereg("^(1 )?(\(.{3}\) )?(.{3})(\-.{4})$", "555-1234");
ereg("^(1 )?(\(.{3}\) )?(.{3})(\-.{4})$", "(707) 555-1234");
ereg("^(1 )?(\(.{3}\) )?(.{3})(\-.{4})$", "1 (707) 555-1234");
```

Defining Character Classes

You use **character classes** in regular expressions to treat multiple characters as a single item. You create a character class by enclosing the characters that make up the class with bracket ([ ]) metacharacters. Any characters included in a character class represent alternate characters that are allowed in a pattern match. As an example of a simple character class, consider the word "analyze," which the British spell as "analyse." Both of the following statements return true because the character class allows either spelling of the word:

```
eregi("analy[sz]e", "analyse"); // returns true
eregi("analy[sz]e", "analyze"); // returns true
```

In comparison, the following regular expression returns false because "analyce" is not an accepted spelling of the word:

```
eregi("analy[sz]e", "analyce"); // returns false
```

You use a hyphen metacharacter (-) to specify a range of values in a character class. You can include alphabetical or numerical ranges. You specify all lowercase letters as `[a-z]` and all uppercase letters as `[A-Z]`. The following statements demonstrate how to ensure that only the values A, B, C, D, or F are assigned to the `$LetterGrade` variable. The character class in the regular expression specifies a range of A-D or the character "F" as valid values in the variable. Because the variable is assigned a value of `"B"`, the `ereg()` function returns true.

```
$LetterGrade = "B";
echo ereg("[A-DF]", $LetterGrade); // returns true
```

A

In comparison, the **ereg()** function returns false because **E** is not a valid value in the character class:

```
$LetterGrade = "E";
echo ereg("[A-DF]", $LetterGrade); // returns true
```

To specify optional characters to exclude in a pattern match, include the ^ metacharacter immediately before the characters in a character class. The following examples demonstrate how to exclude the letters **E** and **G-Z** from an acceptable pattern in the **$LetterGrade** variable. The first **ereg()** function returns a value of true because the letter **A** is not excluded from the pattern match, whereas the second **ereg()** function returns a value of false because the letter **E** is excluded from the pattern match.

```
$LetterGrade = "A";
echo ereg("[^EG-Z]", $LetterGrade); // returns true
$LetterGrade = "E";
echo ereg("[^EG-Z]", $LetterGrade); // returns false
```

The following statements demonstrate how to include or exclude numeric characters from a pattern match. The first statement returns true because it allows any numeric character, whereas the second statement returns false because it excludes any numeric character.

```
echo ereg("[0-9]", "5"); // returns true
echo ereg("^[0-9]", "5"); // returns false
```

Note that you can combine ranges in a character class. The first statement demonstrates how to include all alphanumeric characters and the second statement demonstrates how to exclude all lowercase and uppercase letters:

```
echo ereg("[0-9a-zA-Z]", "7"); // returns true
echo ereg("[^a-zA-Z]", "Q"); // returns false
```

The following statement demonstrates how to use character classes to create a phone number regular expression pattern.

```
ereg("^(1 )?(\([0-9]{3}\) )?([1-9]{3})(\-[1-9]{4})$",
"1 (707) 555-1234"); // returns true
```

As a more complex example of a character class, examine the following e-mail validation regular expression you saw earlier in this appendix. At this point, you should recognize how the regular expression pattern is constructed. The statement uses the **eregi()** function, so letter case is ignored. The anchor at the beginning of the pattern specifies that the first part of the e-mail address must include one or more of the characters A-Z (upper- or lowercase), 0-9, or an underscore (_) or hyphen (-). The second portion of the pattern specifies that the e-mail address can optionally include a dot separator, as in "don.gosselin." The pattern also requires the @ character. Following the literal @ character, the regular expression uses patterns that are similar to the patterns in the name portion of the e-mail address to specify the required structure of the domain name. The last portion of the pattern specifies that the domain identifier must consist of at least two, but not more than three alphabetic characters.

```
eregi("^[_a-z0-9-]+(\.[_a-z0-9-]+)*@[a-z0-9-]+(\.[a-z0-9-
]+)*(\.[a-z]{2,3})$", $_GET['email']);
```

POSIX Extended regular expressions include special expressions that you can use in character classes to represent different types of data. For example, the `[:alnum:]` expression can be used instead of the "0-9a-zA-Z" pattern to allow any alphanumeric characters in a character class. Table A-4 lists the POSIX Extended character class expressions.

Table A-4 POSIX Extended character class expressions

Expression	Description
[:alnum:]	Alphanumeric characters
[:alpha:]	Alphabetic character
[:blank:]	Tabs and spaces
[:cntrl:]	Control characters
[:digit:]	Numeric characters
[:graph:]	Printable characters with the exception of spaces
[:lower:]	Lowercase letters
[:print:]	All printable characters
[:punct:]	Punctuation characters
[:space:]	White space characters
[:upper:]	Uppercase letters
[:xdigit:]	Hexadecimal digits

The following statements demonstrate how to include and exclude numeric characters from a pattern match using the `"[:digit:]"` class expression:

```
ereg("[[:digit:]]", "5"); // returns true
ereg("[[:digit:]]", "A"); // returns false
```

TIP

Be sure to include the brackets that make up each class expression within the character class brackets.

The following statements show some additional examples of the class expressions. The first statement shows how to use the `[:alnum:]` expression to include all alphanumeric characters and the second statement demonstrates how to use the [:alpha:] and [:alpha:] expressions to include all lowercase and uppercase letters:

```
echo ereg([[:alnum:]]), "7"); // returns true
echo ereg([[:alpha:]], "Q"); // returns false
```

As a more complex example, the following statement demonstrates how to compose the e-mail validation regular expression with class expressions:

```
eregi("^[_[:alnum:]-]+(\.[_[:alnum:]-]+)*@[[:alnum:]-
]+(\.[[:alnum:]-]+)*(\.[[:alpha:]]{2,3})$", $_GET['email']));
```

Matching Multiple Pattern Choices

To allow a string to contain an alternate set of substrings, you separate the strings in a regular expression pattern with the | metacharacter. This is essentially the same as using the Or operator (||) to perform multiple evaluations in a conditional expression. For example, to allow a string to contain either "vegetarian" or "vegan," you include the pattern `vegetarian | vegan`.

The following code demonstrates how to check whether a domain identifier at the end of a string contains a required value of either .com, .org, or .net. The first statement returns a value of false because the URL contains a domain identifier of `.gov`, whereas the second statement returns a value of true because the domain identifier contains a valid value of `.com`.

```
echo eregi("\.(com|org|net)$",
     "http://www.dongosselin.gov"); // returns false
echo eregi("\.(com|org|net)$",
     "http://www.dongosselin.com"); // returns true
```

APPENDIX B

FORMATTING STRINGS

USING THE printf() AND sprintf() FUNCTIONS

PHP includes the `printf()` and `sprintf()` functions, which format text strings for output. The `printf()` function formats a text string and prints it, similar to the `print()` and `echo()` statements, whereas the `sprintf()` function formats a string and returns the formatted value so you can assign it to a variable.

Both functions accept as a first argument a **format control string**, which contains instructions for formatting text strings. You surround the format control string with single or double quotations, the same as other types of strings. Each function also accepts additional arguments containing the text strings to be formatted by the format control string. Within the format control string, you include a conversion specification for each of the strings you want to format, along with any other text that you want to output with the formatted strings. A **conversion specification** begins with a percent symbol (`%`) and specifies the formatting you want to apply to a string. You must include a conversion specification for each string argument that is passed to the `printf()` or `sprintf()` function. For example, the following code contains a `printf()` function with two conversion specifications in the format control string, one for the `$FirstName` variable and one for the `$SecondName` variable:

```
$FirstName = "Gosselin";
$SecondName = "Gauselin";
printf("<p>The name %s is also spelled %s.</p>",
     $FirstName, $SecondName);
```

Notice that each conversion specification consists of a percent symbol followed by the letter `s`. The letter following the percent symbol in a conversion specification is a **type specifier**, which determines the display format of each text argument that is passed to the `printf()` or `sprintf()` function. A type specifier of `s` simply displays the text argument as a standard string. You study additional type specifiers next.

SPECIFYING TYPES

Table B-1 lists the type specifiers you can use with the `printf()` and `sprintf()` functions.

Table B-1 PHP type specifiers

Type Specifier	Description
b	Displays a text argument as a binary integer
c	Converts the text argument to an integer; the ASCII character that the integer represents displays
d	Displays the argument as a decimal integer
u	Treats the argument as an unsigned integer that is displayed as a decimal number
f	Displays the argument as a floating-point number
o	Displays the argument as an octal integer
s	Displays the argument as a string
x	Displays the argument as a lowercase hexadecimal integer
X	Displays the argument as an uppercase hexadecimal integer

The following code demonstrates how to use each of the type specifiers listed in Table B-1. Figure B-1 shows the output.

```
$Value = 163;
print("<p>");
printf("Binary integer: %b<br />", $Value);
printf("ASCII character: %c<br />", $Value);
printf("Decimal integer: %d<br />", $Value);
printf("Unsigned decimal integer: %u<br />", $Value);
printf("Floating-point number: %f<br />", $Value);
printf("Octal integer: %o<br />", $Value);
printf("String: %s<br />", $Value);
printf("Lowercase hexadecimal integer: %x<br />", $Value);
printf("Uppercase hexadecimal integer: %X<br />", $Value);
print("</p>");
```

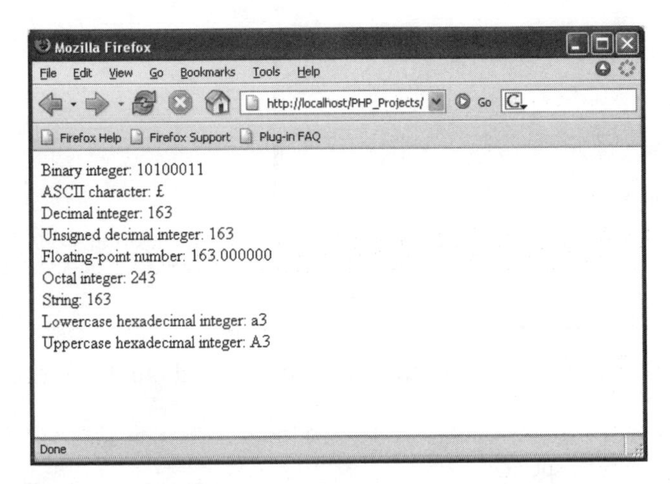

Figure B-1 Output of `printf ()` statements with various type specifiers

DETERMINING DECIMAL NUMBER PRECISION

A common use of the string formatting functions is to format numbers to print with a specified number of decimal places. For example, it's often necessary to format numbers as currency, with two decimal places. However, a variable containing the currency value you want to print might be an integer that does not contain decimal places or it might be a floating-point number that has more than two decimal places. By default, the `f` type specifier formats numbers with six decimal places. To specify a different number of decimal places, add a period and an integer representing the number of decimal places you want between the percent symbol and the `f` type specifier in a conversion specification. In the following code, a value of 99.5 is assigned to the `$RetailPrice` variable. The value in the `$RetailPrice` variable is then decreased by 10%, resulting in a value of 90.4545454545, which is assigned to the `$DiscountPrice` variable. The value is then formatted to two decimal places with the `printf()` statement. Figure B-2 shows the output.

```
$RetailPrice = 99.5;
$DiscountPrice = 99.5 / 1.1;
printf("<p>The retail price after a 10%% discount is
$%.2f.</p>",
     $DiscountPrice);
```

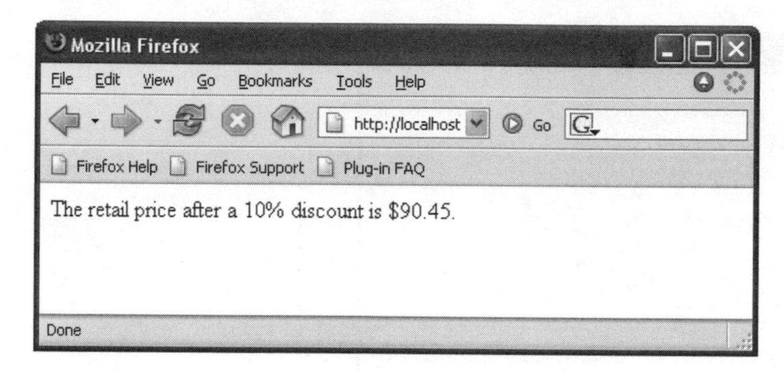

Figure B-2 Output of `printf ()` statement that specifies decimal number precision

You can only use a period and number of decimals in a conversion specification that uses the `f` type specifier.

Use two percent signs (`%%`) to include a percent symbol as a character in a format control string.

Specifying Padding

In addition to specifying the number of decimals that appear to the right of a decimal point, you can also specify the number of characters that a string should consist of. For example, you might have a variable that counts the number of visitors to your Web site. Instead of just displaying the number of visitors, you might want to format it so it displays the number of visitors out of a million by padding the beginning of the number with zeros. To pad the beginning of a string with zeros, include a 0 and an integer representing the number of characters that the number should consist of between the percent symbol and type specifier in a conversion specification. For example, the conversion specification in the `printf()` statement in the following code specifies that the number should consist of seven characters. Because the `$Visitors` variable only contains four characters, the beginning of the number is padded with three extra 0s, as shown in Figure B-3.

```
$Visitors = 5767;
printf("<p>You are visitor number %07d.</p>", $Visitors);
```

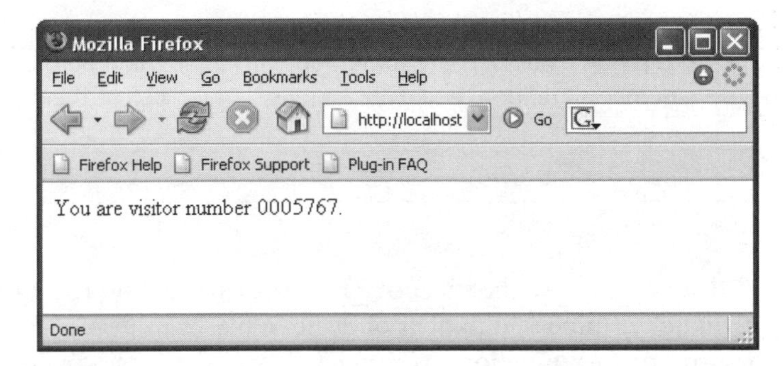

Figure B-3 Output of `printf ()` statement that includes padding

Padding takes into account the number of characters in a string, not the number of digits in an integer. This includes the decimal point and decimal places. For example, the number 345.10 consists of six characters. If you pad the formatting string with zeros and specify that the formatting string should contain eight characters, the number will be formatted to 00345.10.

You can specify that a string should be padded with spaces instead of a 0 by using a space instead of the 0 or by excluding the 0 in a conversion specification. However, most Web browsers automatically replace multiple spaces on a Web page with a single space, unless you use the `<pre>` element. If you want to pad a number with any character other than a 0 or a space, you must precede it with a single quotation mark (`'`). For example, the following code pads a string with asterisks (`*`) instead of spaces or zeros. Figure B-4 shows the output.

```
$Payment = 1410.23;
printf("<p>Pay the amount of $%'*9.2f.</p>", $Payment);
```

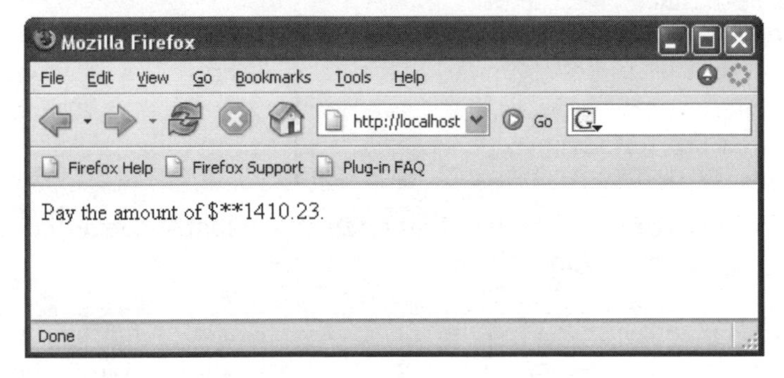

Figure B-4 Output of `printf ()` statement that pads a string with pound symbols

If you add a plus sign (+) immediately following the percent symbol in a conversion specification, positive numbers are formatted with a plus sign before them and negative numbers are formatted with a minus sign (–) before them.

FORMATTING NUMBERS

Recall from Chapter 3 that you can use the `number_format()` function to add commas that separate thousands and determine the number of decimal places to display. Even if you use the `printf()` or `sprintf()` functions, you need to use the `number_format()` function if you want to add commas to separate thousands in a number. However, you should understand that the `number_format()` function also converts numeric variables to strings. For this reason, you must use the `s` type specifier in a conversion specification that refers to a numeric variable that has been converted to a string with the `number_format()` function. For example, the following code uses the `number_format()` function to add comma separators and two decimal places to the `$Payment` variable. Because the `number_format()` function converts the `$Payment` variable to a string, the `printf()` statement uses the `s` type specifier in the conversion specification. Figure B-5 shows the output.

```
$Payment = 1410;
$Payment = number_format($Payment, 2);
printf("<p>Pay the amount of $%s.</p>", $Payment);
```

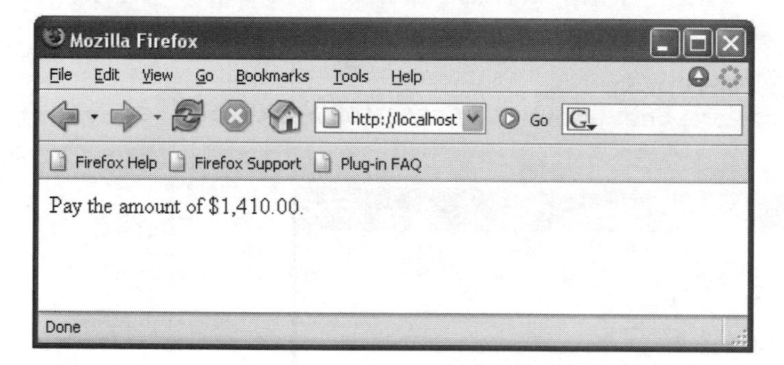

Figure B-5 Output of `printf ()` statement that refers to a variable converted with the `number_format ()` function

With UNIX/Linux systems, you can use the `money_format()` function to format a number as currency. However, this book does not use the `money_format()` function because it is not compatible with Windows platforms.

Formatting Alignment

By default, strings are formatted with right alignment. However, if you add a hyphen (-) immediately following the percent symbol in a conversion specification, a string is formatted with left alignment. For example, each of the `printf()` statements in the following code contain two conversion specifications: one for the description of a travel expense and one for the amount of a travel expense. The first conversion specification for the travel expense descriptions contain a hyphen (-) immediately following the percent symbol, which aligns the travel expense descriptions to the left. However, the second conversion specification for the amounts does not contain hyphens, so they are right aligned by default. Figure B-6 shows the output.

```
<p><strong>Expense Report</strong></p>
<pre>
<?php
$Travel = number_format(465.43, 2);
$Accomodations = number_format(276.2, 2);
$Meals = number_format(97.34, 2);
print("Description                  Amount<br />");
print("***********************************<br />");
printf("%-15s%20s<br />", "Travel", $Travel);
printf("%-15s%20s<br />", "Accommodations",
$Accommodations);
printf("%-15s%20s<br />", "Meals", $Meals);
?>
</pre>
```

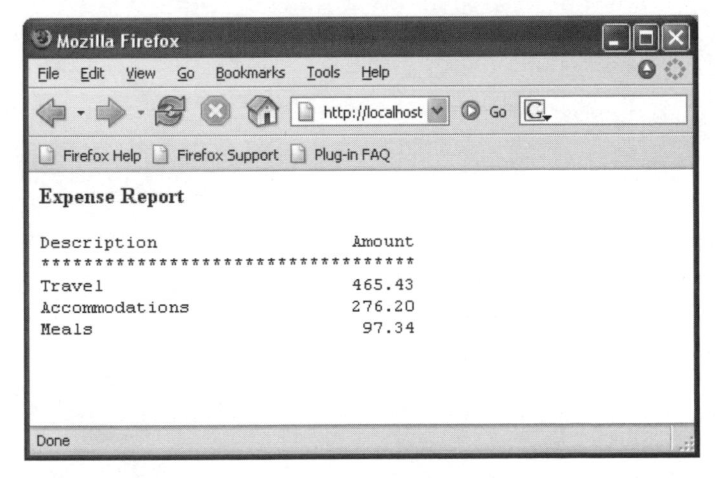

Figure B-6 Output of `printf()` statement with left and right alignment

Notice that the PHP script section in the preceding example is contained within a `<pre>` element. This element is necessary to instruct the Web browser to print the multiple spaces in the script.

APPENDIX

C

PROCESSING XML

THE BASICS OF XML

Extensible Markup Language, or **XML**, is a text-based format for defining and transmitting data between applications. The main benefit of XML is that it allows different applications running on different platforms to read and correctly interpret data that conforms to XML's rules. Like HTML, XML is based on SGML. Version 1.0 of XML achieved recommendation status by the W3C in 1998 and was still current at the time of this writing. Although XML is a markup language like HTML, it is not a replacement for HTML. However, HTML's successor, XHTML, is a combination of both HTML and XML. By itself, XML is primarily a way of defining and organizing data and does not include any of the display capabilities of HTML. The important thing to understand about XML is that it is now the de facto standard for defining and transmitting data across different applications and platforms, including the Internet. In your career as a PHP programmer, you will undoubtedly be called on to use PHP to process an XML document in some way. For this reason, you need a solid understanding of what XML is and how to work with it in PHP scripts.

In XML, you refer to a tag pair and the data it contains as an **element**. All elements must have an opening tag and a closing tag. The data contained within an element's opening and closing tags is referred to as its **content**. One concept that can be difficult to grasp is that XML does not specify any elements or attributes. Instead, you define your own elements and attributes to describe the data in your document. The following code is an example of an XML document that defines several elements that describe the data associated with an automobile:

```
<auto>
     <make manufacturer="GM">Chevrolet</make>
     <model>Corvette</model>
     <year>1967</year>
     <color>Red</color>
</auto>
```

The preceding code is the most basic form of an XML document. For your XML documents to be properly structured, they must also include an XML declaration and adhere to XML's syntax rules. You study these requirements in the next few sections.

THE XML DECLARATION

XML documents should begin with an **XML declaration**, which specifies the version of XML being used. You are not actually required to include an XML declaration because currently only one version of XML exists, version 1.0. However, it's good practice to always include the XML declaration because XML will almost certainly evolve into other versions that will contain features not found in version 1.0. Specifying the version with the XML declaration will help ensure that whatever application is parsing an XML document will know which version to use (assuming that newer versions will be released).

You can use the following three properties with the XML declaration: version, standalone, and encoding. All of the properties are optional, but you should at least include the version property, which designates the XML version number (currently "1.0"). The following statement is an XML declaration that only includes the version property:

```
<?xml version="1.0"?>
```

The XML declaration is not actually a tag, but a processing instruction, which is a special statement that passes information to the application that is processing the XML document. You can easily recognize processing instructions because they begin with `<?` and end with `?>`.

The encoding property of the XML declaration designates the language used by the XML document. Although English is the primary language used on the Web, it is certainly not the only one. To be a considerate resident of the international world of the Web, use the encoding property of the XML declaration to designate the character set for your XML document. English and many western European languages use the iso-8859-1 character set. Therefore, you should use the following XML declaration in your documents:

```
<?xml version="1.0" encoding="iso-8859-1"?>
```

The `standalone="yes"` attribute indicates that the document does not require a DTD to be rendered correctly. Unlike HTML, XML documents do not require a DTD to be rendered correctly. Because XML does not include predefined elements, it does not need a DTD to define them. However, some XML documents might benefit from a DTD, especially if multiple XML documents share the same elements. If your XML document requires a DTD, you assign the standalone property a value of "no." However, if you are certain that your XML document will not require a DTD, you assign the standalone property a value of "yes." For instance, you use the following XML declaration for any XML documents that do not require a DTD:

```
<?xml version="1.0" encoding="iso-8859-1"
standalone="yes"?>
```

PARSING XML DOCUMENTS

When you open an HTML document that is not written properly, such as a document that does not include the closing `</html>` tag, the browser simply ignores the error and renders the page anyway. In contrast, XML documents must adhere to strict rules. The most important of these rules is that all elements must be closed. When a document adheres to XML's syntax rules, it is said to be **well formed**. You study XML's rules for writing well-formed documents in the next section.

The W3C actually uses the term *well formedness*. Because this sounds strange grammatically, this book uses the term *well formed*.

You use a program called a **parser** to check whether an XML document is well formed. There are two types of parsers: non-validating and validating. A non-validating parser simply checks whether an XML document is well formed. A validating parser checks whether an XML document is well formed and also whether it conforms to an associated DTD. Firefox, Internet Explorer, and other browsers have the capability to act as non-validating parsers. A non-validating parser simply checks whether a document is well formed, and if it is, displays its XML elements and data. For instance, if you open the automobile XML document in Firefox and the document is well formed, Firefox correctly parses and displays the document, as shown in Figure C-1.

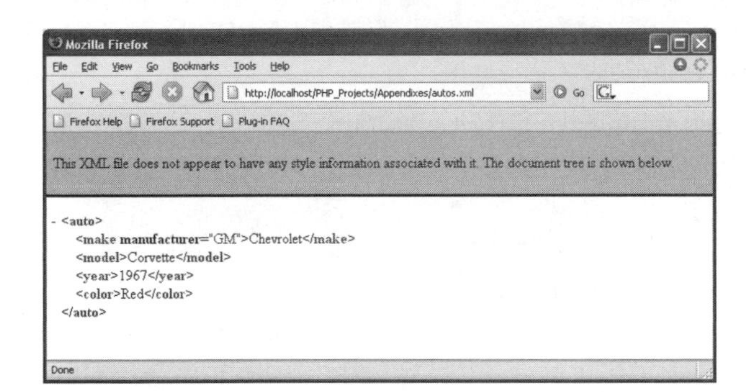

Figure C-1 Well-formed XML document in Firefox

The message at the top of the Web page in Figure C-1 indicates that the XML file does not contain any style information. To create formatted Web pages using XML, you must use **Extensible Stylesheet Language (XSL)**, which is a style sheet language for XML. Think of XSL as being roughly equal to the Cascading Style Sheets (CSS) you use with XHTML documents, although XSL is much more complex than CSS. For information on how to use XSL, refer to *XHTML* by Don Gosselin (the author of this book), published by Thomson Course Technology.

If an XML document is not well formed, the parser displays the error. For example, if the automobile XML document is missing the closing `</auto>` tag, it is not well formed. In this case, a Web browser points to the error, as shown in Figure C-2.

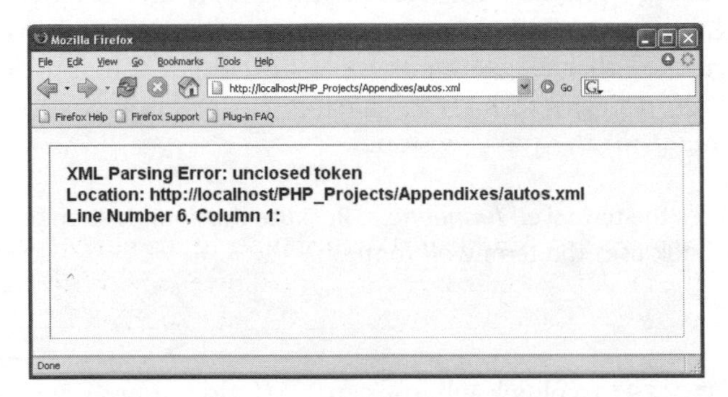

Figure C-2 XML document that is not well formed in Firefox

WRITING WELL-FORMED DOCUMENTS

One reason XML documents need to be well formed is to allow different applications to read the document's data easily. Most applications expect XML data to be structured according to specific rules, which allows the application to read data quickly without having to decipher the data structure.

In this section, you study the rules for writing well-formed XML documents. The most important of these rules are as follows:

- All XML documents must have a root element.
- XML is case sensitive.
- All XML elements must have closing tags.
- XML elements must be properly nested.
- Attribute values must appear within quotation marks.
- Empty elements must be closed.

Next, you study each of these rules.

All XML Documents Must Have a Root Element

A **root element** contains all the other elements in a document. The `<html>...</html>` element is the root element for HTML documents, although most Web browsers do not require a document to include it. On the other hand, XML documents require a root element that you define yourself. For instance, the root element for the XML automobile data document is the `<auto>` element. If you do not include a root element, the

XML document is not well formed. For instance, the following version of the XML document containing the automobile data is not well formed because it is missing the <auto> root element:

```
<?xml version="1.0" encoding="iso-8859-1"
     standalone="yes"?>
<make>Chevrolet</make><model>Corvette</model>
<year>1967</year><color>Red</color>
```


XML Is Case Sensitive

Unlike HTML tags, XML tags are case sensitive. For instance, in an HTML document it makes no difference whether the bold tag is uppercase or lowercase. Both of the following HTML statements will be rendered properly in a Web browser:

```
<B>This line is bold.</B>
<b>This line is also bold.</b>
```

You can even mix and match the cases tags in an HTML document, as in the following statements:

```
<B>This line is bold.</b>
<b>This line is also bold.</B>
```

With XML, however, you cannot mix the case of elements. For instance, if you have an opening tag named <color> that is all lowercase, you must also use lowercase letters for the closing tag, as follows:

```
<color>Red</color>
```

If you use a different case for an opening and closing tag, they are treated as completely separate tags, resulting in a document that is not well formed. The following statement, for instance, is incorrect because the case of the closing tag does not match the case of the opening tag:

```
<color>Red</COLOR>
```

All XML Elements Must Have Closing Tags

As mentioned earlier, most Web browsers don't care if the code in an HTML document is not properly structured and closing tags are missing. One common example is the paragraph element (<p>). The <p> element should be used to mark a block of text as a single paragraph by enclosing the text within a <p>...<p> tag pair, as follows:

```
<p>Sacramento is the capital of California.</p>
```

Many Web authors, however, do not follow this convention and simply place a <p> tag at the end of a block of text to create a new paragraph as follows:

```
Sacramento is the capital of California.<p>
```

One reason it is possible to omit closing tags is that Web browsers usually treat HTML documents as text that contains formatting elements. XML, however, is designed to organize data, not display it. As a result, instead of documents consisting of text that contains elements, as is the case with HTML, XML documents consist of elements that contain text. All elements must have a closing tag or the document will not be well formed. For instance, in the automobile data XML document you saw earlier, each element has a corresponding closing tag. The following version of the document is illegal because there are no corresponding closing tags for the `<make>`, `<model>`, `<year>`, and `<color>` elements:

```
<?xml version="1.0" encoding="iso-8859-1"
     standalone="yes"?>
<auto>
     <make>Chevrolet<model>Corvette
     <year>1967<color>Red
</auto>
```

You might have noticed that the XML declaration does not include a closing tag. This is because the XML declaration is not actually part of the document; it only declares the document as an XML document. For this reason, it does not require a closing tag.

XML Elements Must Be Properly Nested

Nesting refers to how elements are placed inside of other elements. For example, in the following code, the `<i>` element is nested within the `<b>` element, while the `<b>` element is nested within the `<p>` element:

```
<p><b><i>This paragraph is bold and italicized.
</i></b></p>
```

In an HTML document, it makes no difference how the elements are nested. Examine the following HTML statement, which applies bold and italic to the text within a paragraph:

```
<p><b><i>This paragraph is bold and italicized.</b></p></i>
```

In the preceding code, the opening `<i>` element is nested within the `<b>` element, which, in turn, is nested within the `<p>` element. However, notice that the closing `</i>` element is outside of the closing `</p>` element. This `<i>` element is the innermost element. In XML, each innermost element must be closed before another element is closed. In the preceding statement, however, the `<b>` and `<p>` elements are closed before the `<i>` element is closed. Although the order in which elements are closed makes no difference in HTML, in XML, to be correct the statement must be written as follows:

```
<p><b><i>This paragraph is bold and italicized.</i></b></p>
```

As another example, consider the following version of the automobile data XML document. The code is not well formed because the <make> and <model> elements are not properly nested.

```
<?xml version="1.0" encoding="iso-8859-1"
     standalone="yes"?>
<auto>
     <make>Chevrolet
          <model>Corvette</make>
     </model>
     <year>1967</year><color>Red</color>
</auto>
```

For the preceding XML code to be well formed, the <model> element must close before the <make> element, as follows:

```
<?xml version="1.0" encoding="iso-8859-1"
     standalone="yes"?>
<auto>
     <make>Chevrolet
          <model>Corevette</model>
      </make>
     <year>1967</year><color>Red</color>
</auto>
```

Attribute Values Must Appear Within Quotation Marks

The value assigned to an attribute in an HTML document can be either contained in quotation marks or assigned directly to the attribute, provided there are no spaces in the value being assigned. For example, recall that a common HTML attribute is the src attribute of the image element (<img>). You assign to the src attribute the name of an image file that you want to display in your document. The following code shows two <img> elements. Even though the first element includes quotation marks around the value assigned to the src attribute whereas the second element does not, both statements will function correctly.

```
<img src="dog.gif">Image of a dog</img>
<img src=cat.gif>Image of a cat</img>
```

With XML, you must place quotation marks around the values assigned to an attribute. An example is the company attribute of the <manufacturer> element you saw earlier in the automobile data XML document. You must include quotation marks around the value assigned to the company attribute using a statement similar to <manufacturer company="General Motors">. Omitting the quotation marks in the statement <manufacturer company=General Motors> results in a document that is not well formed.

CAUTION

You also cannot include an empty attribute in an element, meaning that you must assign a value to an attribute or exclude the attribute from the element. For instance, the statement, `<manufacturer company />`, is incorrect because no value is being assigned to the `company` attribute.

Empty Elements Must Be Closed

A number of elements in HTML do not have corresponding ending tags, including the `<hr>` element, which inserts a horizontal rule into the document, and the `<br>` element, which inserts a line break. Elements that do not require an ending tag are called **empty elements**. They are called empty elements because you cannot use them as a tag pair to enclose text or other elements. You can create an empty element in an XML document by adding a single slash (/) before the tag's closing bracket to close the element. Most often, you use an empty element for an element that does not require content, such as an image. For instance, in the XML document of automobile data, you can create a `<photo>` element with a single attribute that stores the name of an image file. This image file contains a photograph of the automobile. An example of the `<photo>` empty element is shown in the following XML code:

```
<?xml version="1.0" standalone="yes"?>
<auto>
     <photo image_name="corvette.jpg"/>
     <make>Chevrolet</make><model>Corvette</model>
     <year>1967</year><color>Red</color>
</auto>
```

TIP

Remember that the primary purpose of XML is to define and organize data. An empty image element like the one shown in the XML automobile document only provides the name of the associated image file—it does not display it. However, you can display an image from an XML document if you use XSL.

GENERATING XML WITH PHP

PHP includes numerous functions for working with XML in your scripts, including Dynamic Object Model functions. The **Dynamic Object Model**, or **DOM**, is a standard for representing structured documents, such as Web pages and XML documents, in an object-oriented model. Each element on a Web page or an XML page is represented in the DOM by its own object, which you can access programmatically in PHP with various DOM functions. However, DOM functions are most useful for generating complex XML documents. To use PHP to generate most types of XML documents, you only need to use arrays to organize the XML and output statements to send the XML to a Web browser.

To generate XML with PHP, you first need to use the `header()` function to specify the document's content type as "text/xml." You also need to use an `echo()` statement to send the XML declaration to the Web browser. The following statements use the `header()` function to specify the document's content type as "text/xml" and an `echo()` statement to send the XML declaration to the Web browser:

C

```
header("Content-Type: text/xml");
echo "<?xml version='1.0' encoding='iso-8859-1'
standalone='yes'?>";
```

The following statements use a multidimensional array named `$Autos[]` to store the contents of three `<auto>` elements:

```
$Autos = array(
     array('make'=>'Chevrolet',
           'manufacturer'=>'GM',
           'model'=>'Corvette',
           'year'=>'1967',
           'color'=>'Red'),
     array('make'=>'Ford',
           'manufacturer'=>'Ford Motor Company',
           'model'=>'Mustang',
           'year'=>'1969',
           'color'=>'Blue'),
     array('make'=>'Plymouth',
           'manufacturer'=>'Chrysler Corporation',
           'model'=>'Barracuda',
           'year'=>'1972',
           'color'=>'Green')
           );
```

The following statements then use `echo()` statements and a `foreach` statement to output the contents of the `$Autos[]` array in XML format. Figure C-3 shows the output in a Web browser.

```
echo "<autos>";
foreach ($Autos as $Auto) {
      echo "<auto>";
      echo "<make manufacturer=\"{$Auto['manufacturer']}\">
            {$Auto['make']}</make>";
      echo "<model>{$Auto['model']}</model>";
      echo "<year>{$Auto['year']}</year>";
      echo "<color>{$Auto['color']}</color>";
      echo "</auto>";
}
echo "</autos>";
```

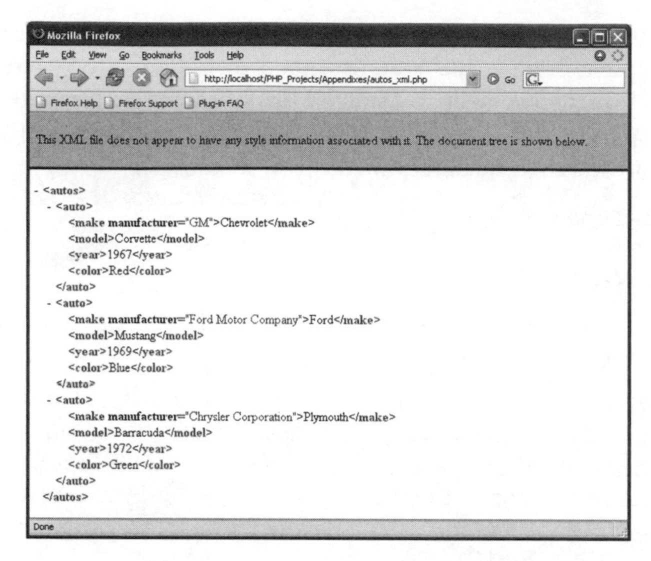

Figure C-3 XML document generated with PHP

You can use similar code to generate XML from database records. In Chapters 8 and 9, you worked with a MySQL database named `guitars` that contained a table named `inventory` with the following records and structure:

```
+----------+------------------------+---------+----------+
| make     | model                  | price   | quantity |
+----------+------------------------+---------+----------+
| Martin   | D15 Spruce and Rosewood| 1370.00 |        2 |
| Washburn | D30s                   |  799.99 |        5 |
| Washburn | D100                   |  329.90 |       10 |
| Martin   | D15 Limited Edition    | 1138.00 |        1 |
| Fender   | DG11                   |  285.70 |        8 |
| Martin   | DX1 Dreadnought        |  699.00 |        9 |
| Fender   | DG7                    |  228.55 |       14 |
| Taylor   | Baby Taylor Mahogany   |  348.00 |        7 |
| Taylor   | 210 Dreadnought        |  998.00 |        6 |
| Washburn | D10s                   |  349.99 |       18 |
+----------+------------------------+---------+----------+
10 rows in set (0.00 sec)
```

Suppose you want to generate an XML document for the preceding table that consists of the following structure:

```
<guitars>
     <guitar>
          <make>Martin</make>
          <model>D15 Spruce and Rosewood</model>
          <price>1370.00</price>
          <quantity>2</quantity>
     </guitar>
</guitars>
```

The following script demonstrates how to generate the preceding XML from the database records. The first statement uses the `header()` function to specify the document's content type as "text/xml" and the second statement sends the XML declaration to the Web browser. Database statements then retrieve all the records from the inventory table in the guitars database. Instead of a `foreach` statement, the following code uses a `do...while` statement and the `mysqli_fetch_assoc()` function to print the database records in XML format. Figure C-4 shows the output.

```
header("Content-Type: text/xml");
echo "<?xml version='1.0' encoding='iso-8859-1'
standalone='yes'?>";
$DBConnect = @mysqli_connect("localhost", 'root', 'paris')
      Or die("<p>Unable to connect to the database server.</p>"
      . "<p>Error code " . mysqli_connect_errno()
      . ": " . mysqli_connect_error()) . "</p>";
@mysqli_select_db($DBConnect, "guitars")
      Or die("<p>Unable to select the database.</p>"
      . "<p>Error code " . mysqli_errno($DBConnect)
      . ": " . mysqli_error($DBConnect)) . "</p>";
$SQLstring = "SELECT * FROM inventory";
$QueryResult = @mysqli_query($DBConnect, $SQLstring)
      Or die("<p>Unable to execute the query.</p>"
      . "<p>Error code " . mysqli_errno($DBConnect)
      . ": " . mysqli_error($DBConnect)) . "</p>";
echo "<guitars>";
$Row = mysqli_fetch_assoc($QueryResult);
do {
      echo "<guitar>";
      echo "<make>{$Row['make']}</make>";
      echo "<model>{$Row['model']}</model>";
      echo "<price>{$Row['price']}</price>";
      echo "<quantity>{$Row['quantity']}</quantity>";
      echo "</guitar>";
      $Row = mysqli_fetch_assoc($QueryResult);
} while ($Row);
echo "</guitars>";
mysqli_free_result($QueryResult);
mysqli_close($DBConnect);
```

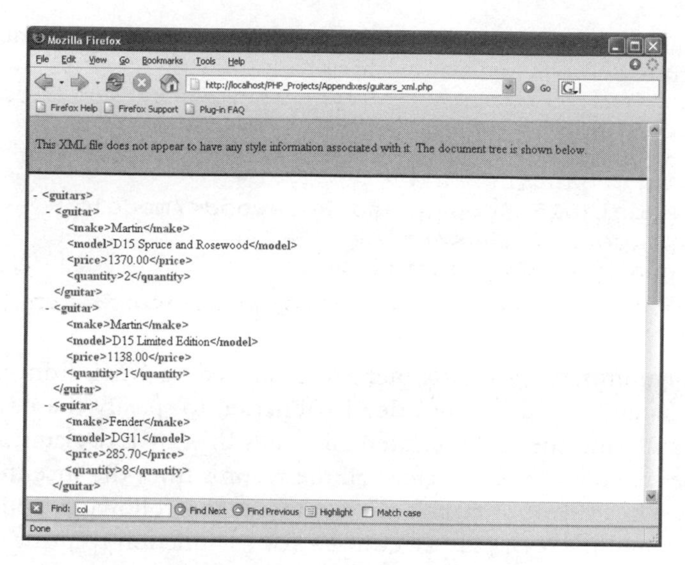

Figure C-4 XML document generated with PHP from a database

Parsing XML with SimpleXML Functions

PHP also contains numerous functions for parsing XML. PHP 5 introduces SimpleXML functions, which make it much easier to parse XML with PHP by converting XML documents to objects. You use the SimpleXML functions if you need to use an XML document's values in a PHP script. For example, you might want to take an XML document and create a table that displays the document's element and attribute values. The SimpleXML functions discussed in this section are `simplexml_load_string()` and `simplexml_load_file()`.

For complex XML parsing, refer to the XML parser functions in the PHP manual.

The `simplexml_load_string()` function creates an object out of the XML contained in a text string. More specifically, the `simplexml_load_string()` function assigns an XML document's element and attribute values to properties of the same name in the new object. You then access each property using member selection notation (->). The following code uses the `simplexml_load_string()` function to create an object from a string containing some simple weather forecast data for Albuquerque, New Mexico. Notice that the `echo()` statements refer to each XML element as an object of the `$Forecast` object. Figure C-5 shows the output.

```
$Forecast = simplexml_load_string("<forecast><city>
Albuquerque</city><high_temp>58</high_temp><low_temp>39
</low_temp><conditions>mostly cloudy</conditions> </forecast>");
echo "<h1>Weather Forecast</strong></h1>";
echo "<p><strong>City</strong>: {$Forecast->city}<br />";
echo "<strong>High temperature</strong>:
      {$Forecast->high_temp}<br />";
echo "<strong>Low temperature</strong>:
      {$Forecast->low_temp}<br />";
echo "<strong>Conditions</strong>: {$Forecast->conditions}</p>";
```


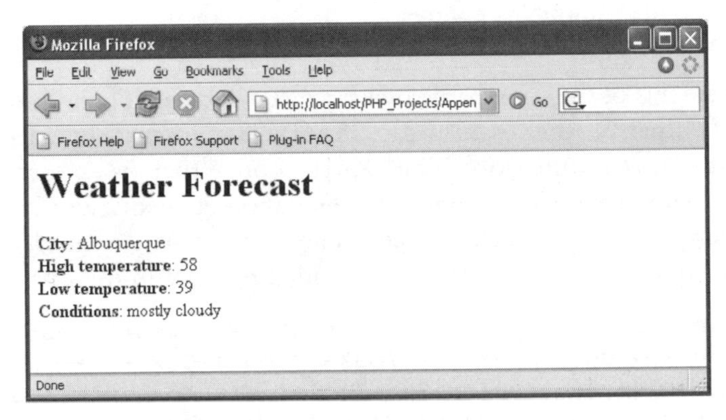

Figure C-5 Output of properties from an object created with the `simplexml_load_string()` function

The `simplexml_load_string()` function does not create a property for the root element in the object it creates. Instead, it only creates properties for each of the elements contained within the root element.

To refer to any nested elements, you append additional member selection notation operators along with the corresponding property name to the object. Also, element attributes are stored as keys in associative arrays of the corresponding element property in the object. For example, the following code contains a modified version of the forecast data. In this version, the `<city>`, `<high_temp>`, `<low_temp>`, and `<conditions>` elements are nested within a `<state>` element. The `<state>` element also includes a name attribute containing the name of the state. Notice that the `echo()` statements include additional member selection notation operators to append the `city`, `high_temp`, `low_temp`, and `conditions` properties to the `state` property. Also notice that the code refers to the state name as a key in the associative `state[]` array.

```
$Forecast = simplexml_load_string("<forecast><state name='New
Mexico'><city>Albuquerque</city><high_temp>58</high_temp><low_tem
p>39</low_temp><conditions>mostly
cloudy</conditions></state></forecast>");
echo "<h1>Weather Forecast</strong></h1>";
echo "<p><strong>City</strong>: {$Forecast->state->city}<br />";
echo "<strong>State</strong>: {$Forecast->state['name']}<br />";
echo "<strong>High temperature</strong>:
      {$Forecast->state->high_temp}<br />";
echo "<strong>Low temperature</strong>:
      {$Forecast->state->low_temp}<br />";
echo "<strong>Conditions</strong>:
      {$Forecast->state->conditions}</p>";
```

You refer to multiple elements of the same name by using array indexes. The following code demonstrates how to parse the `<autos>` XML document by using the `simplexml_load_string()` function. The XML code that is passed to the `simplexml_load_string()` function contains three `<auto>` elements, which creates an `auto[]` array as a property of the `$AutosXML` object. The `echo()` statements demonstrate how to access the model of each car by referring to its index number in the `auto[]` array.

```
$AutosXML = simplexml_load_string("<autos><test>test</test><auto>
<make manufacturer='GM'>Chevrolet</make><model>Corvette
</model><year>1967</year><color>Red</color></auto><auto><make
manufacturer='Ford Motor Company'>Ford</make><model>Mustang
</model><year>1969</year><color>Blue</color></auto><auto><make
manufacturer='Chrysler Corporation'>Plymouth</make>
<model>Barracuda</model><year>1972</year><color>Green</color>
</auto></autos>");
echo "<p>First car: {$AutosXML->auto[0]->model}<br />";
echo "Second car: {$AutosXML->auto[1]->model}<br />";
echo "Third car: {$AutosXML->auto[2]->model}</p>";
```

The following statements demonstrate how to use a `foreach` statement to build a table using the XML values stored in the `$AutosXML` created with the `simplexml_load_string()` function:

```
echo "<table width='100%' border='1'>";
echo "<tr><th>Make</th><th>Model</th><th>Year</th><th>
      Color</th></tr>";
$Count = 0;
foreach ($AutosXML->auto as $Auto) {
      echo "<tr><td>{$AutosXML->auto[$Count]->make}</td>";
      echo "<td>{$AutosXML->auto[$Count]->model}</td>";
      echo "<td align='right'>
            {$AutosXML->auto[$Count]->year}</td>";
      echo "<td align='right'>
            {$AutosXML->auto[$Count]->color}</td></tr>";
      ++$Count;
}
```

The simplexml_load_file() function performs exactly as the simplexml_load_string() function. The only difference between the two functions is the simplexml_load_file() function creates an object from a text file instead of from a text string, as does the simplexml_load_string() function. The following statement demonstrates how to create the $Forecast object from a text file named forecast_data.xml:

```
$Forecast = simplexml_load_file("forecast_data.xml");
```

APPENDIX

D

SECURE CODING WITH PHP

UNDERSTANDING PHP SECURITY ISSUES

Viruses, worms, data theft by hackers, and other types of security threats are now a fact of life when it comes to Web-based applications. If you put an application into a production environment without considering security issues, you are just asking for trouble. To combat security violations, you need to consider both Web server security issues and secure coding issues. Web server security involves the use of technologies such as firewalls, which use combinations of software and hardware to prevent access to private networks connected to the Internet. One very important technology is the Secure Sockets Layer (SSL) protocol, which encrypts data and transfers it across a secure connection. Although Web server security issues are critical, they belong in books on Apache, Internet Information Services, and other types of Web servers. Be sure to research security issues for your Web server and operating system before activating a production Web site.

To provide even stronger software security, many technology companies, including Microsoft and Oracle, now require their developers and other technical staff to adhere to secure coding practices and principles. **Secure coding**, or **defensive coding**, refers to the writing of code in such a way that it minimizes any intentional or accidental security issues. Secure coding has become a major goal for many information technology companies, primarily due to the exorbitant cost of fixing security flaws in commercial software. According to one study, it is 100 times more expensive to fix security flaws in released software than it is to apply secure coding techniques during the development phase. The National Institute of Standards & Technology estimates that $60 billion a year is spent identifying and correcting software errors. In addition, politicians have recently shown a great deal of interest in regulating software security. Tom Ridge, Secretary of the U.S. Department of Homeland Security, recently said, "A few lines of code can wreak more havoc than a bomb." Intense government scrutiny gives information technology companies strong incentive to voluntarily improve the security of software products before state and federal governments pass legislation that requires security certification of commercial software.

Basically, all code is insecure unless proven otherwise. Unfortunately, there is no magic formula for writing secure code, although there are various techniques that you can use to minimize security threats in your programs. You have already studied many of the basic secure coding issues throughout this book. This appendix reviews some of the secure coding techniques you have already studied.

For more information on PHP security, visit the PHP Security Consortium Web site at *http://phpsec.org/*. The PHP Security Consortium (PHPSC) is an international group of PHP experts dedicated to promoting secure programming practices within the PHP community.

DISABLING THE `register_globals` DIRECTIVE

Before PHP version 4.2.0, client, server, and environment information were automatically available as global variables that you could access directly in your scripts. For example, instead of using `$_SERVER["SERVER_SOFTWARE"]` to obtain information about your server software, you could simply use `$SERVER_SOFTWARE`. Similarly, a field named "email" in a submitted form could be accessed with `$email` instead of `$_GET["email"]`. However, making all client, server, and environment information automatically available as variables in a script exposes security issues that an unscrupulous hacker can take advantage of. You can still use the old global variables by changing the value assigned to the `register_globals` directive in your php.ini configuration file to "on." However, for your code to be secure, the PHP Group strongly recommends that you leave the `register_globals` directive turned off and instead use autoglobal arrays, such as `$_GET` and `$_POST`, to access client, server, and environment information in your scripts.

VALIDATING SUBMITTED FORM DATA

In Chapter 5, you learned how to validate data that is submitted to your scripts. Recall that JavaScript is often used with forms to validate or process form data before the data is submitted to a server-side script. For example, customers may use an online order form to order merchandise from your Web site. When a customer clicks the form's Submit button, you can use JavaScript to ensure that the customer has entered important information, such as his name, shipping address, and so on. The problem with using JavaScript to validate form data is that you cannot always ensure that the data submitted to your PHP script was submitted from the Web page containing the JavaScript validation code. Every self-respecting hacker knows how to bypass JavaScript validation code in an HTML form by appending a query string directly to the URL of the PHP script that processes the form. Because JavaScript validation code can be bypassed in this way, you should always include PHP code to validate any submitted data. If your PHP script lacks such code, you cannot be sure that all of the necessary data was submitted (such as a shipping address for an online order) nor can you tell if an unscrupulous hacker is attempting to submit malicious data that might cause problems in your script or on your Web site. Also recall that the `POST` method sends form data as a transmission separate from the URL specified by the `action` attribute. However, don't think that you can force users to submit form data from a Web page by specifying the `POST` method. Anyone who has a strong understanding of HTTP headers can construct a separate transmission containing the form data required by your script.

To ensure that your script receives the proper data, always use the `isset()` function and `empty()` function to determine if form variables contain values. The `isset()` function determines whether a variable has been declared and initialized (or "set"), whereas the `empty()` function determines whether a variable is empty. You pass to both functions the name of the variable you want to check. If a submitted form value must be numeric data, you should use an `is_numeric()` function to test the variable. This ensures that hackers do not try and break your code by sending alphabetic values to scripts that expect numeric values.

Using Sessions to Validate User Identities

Always use sessions to validate user identities. This is especially important for commercial sites that include shopping cart mechanisms. Because sessions store state information on a Web server, they are much safer to use—provided you properly secure your Web server. Because the randomly generated alphanumeric string that composes a session ID is extremely difficult to guess, it is unlikely that a hacker can use this value to impersonate a user. If a hacker does obtain another user's session ID, she can use the ID to steal sensitive data, such as credit card information.

Even with sessions, there is a chance that a hacker can obtain a user's session ID. For a detailed discussion of session security issues, refer to the PHP Security Consortium's PHP Security Guide at *http://phpsec.org/projects/guide/*.

Storing Code in External Files

Chapter 11 discusses how to store classes in external files. However, external files are not limited to classes; you can use them to store any type of code. Storing code in external files helps to secure your scripts by hiding the code from hackers. This also helps to protect your code from other programmers who might steal your scripts and claim them as their own.

In general, you should use the `include()` and `include_once()` functions for HTML code that will not prevent a script from running if the external file is not available. For PHP code that is required for your script to execute, you should use the `require()` or `require_once()` functions, which halt the processing of the Web page if the external file is not available.

You can use any file extension you want for include files, although many programmers use an extension of .inc for HTML and other types of information that do not need to be processed by the Web server. Although you can use the .inc extension for external files containing PHP scripts, you should avoid doing so unless your Web server is configured to process .inc files as PHP scripts. If your Web server is not configured to process .inc files as PHP scripts, anyone can view the contents of the file simply by entering the full URL in a Web browser. This creates a potential security risk, especially if the external file contains proprietary code or sensitive information such as passwords. Because most Web servers process the contents of a PHP script and only return HTML to the client, your safest bet is to always use an extension of .php for external files that contain PHP code.

Accessing Databases Through a Proxy User

In Chapter 8, you learned that for security purposes, you should create an account that requires a password for each user who needs to access your database. For most Web sites, it's impossible to predict how many visitors might need to use a Web application to access a database. Therefore, instead of creating a separate database account for each visitor, you only need to create a single account that a PHP script uses to access the database for a user by proxy. The term proxy refers to someone or something that acts or performs a request for another person. In general, you should create a separate account for each Web application that needs to access a database. You then use PHP code, similar to the following, to access the database for the user by proxy.

```
DBConnect = @new mysqli("localhost", "proxy_user", "password");
  if (mysqli_connect_errno())
    die("<p>Unable to connect to the database server.</p>"
      . "<p>Error code " . mysqli_connect_errno()
      . ": " . mysqli_connect_error()) . "</p>";
```

Handling Magic Quotes

Because the data a user submits to a PHP script might also contain single or double quotes, you should also use escape sequences for any user data your script receives, especially before you write it to a data source, such as a text file or database. PHP includes a feature called magic quotes, which automatically adds a backslash (\) to any single quote ('), double quote ("), or NULL character contained in data that a user submits to a PHP script.

By default, the `magic_quotes_gpc` directive is the only magic quote directive that is enabled in your php.ini configuration file when you first install PHP. Magic quotes are very unpopular with programmers because it's so easy to forget that they are enabled in a php.ini configuration file. Rather than relying on magic quotes to escape text strings, you should disable magic quotes in your php.ini configuration file and instead manually escape the strings with the `addslashes()` function. The `addslashes()` function accepts a single argument representing the text string you want to escape and returns a string containing the escaped string. If you want to display an escaped text string that contains escape characters, you can use the `stripslashes()` function to remove the slashes that were added with the `addslashes()` function.

REPORTING ERRORS

The php.ini configuration file contains two directives, `display_errors` and `display_startup_errors`, that determine whether error messages print to a Web browser. The `display_errors` directive prints script error messages, whereas the `display_startup_errors` directive displays errors that occur when PHP first starts. By default, the `display_errors` directive is assigned a value of "On" and the `display_startup_errors` directive is assigned a value of "Off." Although displaying error messages is useful when you develop PHP scripts, the PHP Group strongly recommends that you turn this feature off for scripts that run in production environments and instead save any errors in a log file. The reason for this is because hackers can use any displayed error messages to identify potential weaknesses in your Web site. The PHP Group also recommends that you only turn the `display_startup_errors` directive on when debugging a script. See Chapter 12 for detailed information on how to work with error messages.

Index

B

C

E

F

J

K

L

N

S